Developments and Trends in Intelligent Technologies and Smart Systems

Vijayan Sugumaran
Oakland University, USA

A volume in the Advances in Computational
Intelligence and Robotics (ACIR) Book Series

Published in the United States of America by
    IGI Global
    Engineering Science Reference (an imprint of IGI Global)
    701 E. Chocolate Avenue
    Hershey PA, USA 17033
    Tel: 717-533-8845
    Fax: 717-533-8661
    E-mail: cust@igi-global.com
    Web site: http://www.igi-global.com

                    Library of Congress Cataloging-in-Publication Data

Names: Sugumaran, Vijayan, 1960- editor.
Title: Developments and trends in intelligent technologies and smart systems
    / Vijayan Sugumaran, editor.
Description: Hershey, PA : Engineering Science Reference, [2018] | Includes
    bibliographical references.
Identifiers: LCCN 2017020847| ISBN 9781522536864 (hardcover) | ISBN
    9781522536871 (ebook)
Subjects: LCSH: Systems engineering. | Self-organizing systems.
Classification: LCC TA168 .D496 2018 | DDC 620/.0042--dc23 LC record available at https://lccn.loc.gov/2017020847

This book is published in the IGI Global book series Advances in Computational Intelligence and Robotics (ACIR) (ISSN: 2327-0411; eISSN: 2327-042X)

British Cataloguing in Publication Data
A Cataloguing in Publication record for this book is available from the British Library.

For electronic access to this publication, please contact: eresources@igi-global.com.

Advances in Computational Intelligence and Robotics (ACIR) Book Series

Ivan Giannoccaro
University of Salento, Italy

ISSN:2327-0411
EISSN:2327-042X

MISSION

While intelligence is traditionally a term applied to humans and human cognition, technology has progressed in such a way to allow for the development of intelligent systems able to simulate many human traits. With this new era of simulated and artificial intelligence, much research is needed in order to continue to advance the field and also to evaluate the ethical and societal concerns of the existence of artificial life and machine learning.

The **Advances in Computational Intelligence and Robotics (ACIR) Book Series** encourages scholarly discourse on all topics pertaining to evolutionary computing, artificial life, computational intelligence, machine learning, and robotics. ACIR presents the latest research being conducted on diverse topics in intelligence technologies with the goal of advancing knowledge and applications in this rapidly evolving field.

COVERAGE

- Brain Simulation
- Heuristics
- Intelligent control
- Pattern Recognition
- Cyborgs
- Neural Networks
- Synthetic Emotions
- Evolutionary computing
- Agent technologies
- Automated Reasoning

IGI Global is currently accepting manuscripts for publication within this series. To submit a proposal for a volume in this series, please contact our Acquisition Editors at Acquisitions@igi-global.com or visit: http://www.igi-global.com/publish/.

Titles in this Series

For a list of additional titles in this series, please visit: www.igi-global.com/book-series

Handbook of Research on Applied Cybernetics and Systems Science
Snehanshu Saha (PESIT South Campus, India) Abhyuday Mandal (University of Georgia, USA) Anand Narasim-hamurthy (BITS Hyderabad, India) Sarasvathi V (PESIT- Bangalore South Campus, India) and Shivappa Sangam (UGC, India)
Information Science Reference • copyright 2017 • 463pp • H/C (ISBN: 9781522524984) • US $245.00 (our price)

Handbook of Research on Machine Learning Innovations and Trends
Aboul Ella Hassanien (Cairo University, Egypt) and Tarek Gaber (Suez Canal University, Egypt)
Information Science Reference • copyright 2017 • 1093pp • H/C (ISBN: 9781522522294) • US $465.00 (our price)

Handbook of Research on Soft Computing and Nature-Inspired Algorithms
Shishir K. Shandilya (Bansal Institute of Research and Technology, India) Smita Shandilya (Sagar Institute of Research Technology and Science, India) Kusum Deep (Indian Institute of Technology Roorkee, India) and Atulya K. Nagar (Liverpool Hope University, UK)
Information Science Reference • copyright 2017 • 627pp • H/C (ISBN: 9781522521280) • US $280.00 (our price)

Membrane Computing for Distributed Control of Robotic Swarms Emerging Research and Opportunities
Andrei George Florea (Politehnica University of Bucharest, Romania) and Cătălin Buiu (Politehnica University of Bucharest, Romania)
Information Science Reference • copyright 2017 • 119pp • H/C (ISBN: 9781522522805) • US $160.00 (our price)

Recent Developments in Intelligent Nature-Inspired Computing
Srikanta Patnaik (SOA University, India)
Information Science Reference • copyright 2017 • 264pp • H/C (ISBN: 9781522523222) • US $185.00 (our price)

Ubiquitous Machine Learning and Its Applications
Pradeep Kumar (Maulana Azad National Urdu University, India) and Arvind Tiwari (DIT University, India)
Information Science Reference • copyright 2017 • 259pp • H/C (ISBN: 9781522525455) • US $185.00 (our price)

Advanced Image Processing Techniques and Applications
N. Suresh Kumar (VIT University, India) Arun Kumar Sangaiah (VIT University, India) M. Arun (VIT University, India) and S. Anand (VIT University, India)
Information Science Reference • copyright 2017 • 439pp • H/C (ISBN: 9781522520535) • US $290.00 (our price)

701 East Chocolate Avenue, Hershey, PA 17033, USA
Tel: 717-533-8845 x100 • Fax: 717-533-8661
E-Mail: cust@igi-global.com • www.igi-global.com

Table of Contents

Section 1
Semantic Technologies and Agent-Based Systems

Jon Atle Gulla, Norwegian University of Science and Technology, Norway
Özlem Özgöbek, Norwegian University of Science and Technology, Norway
Xiaomeng Su, Norwegian University of Science and Technology, Norway

Ghassan Beydoun, University of Technology Sydney, Australia
Alexey Voinov, University of Twente, The Netherlands
Vijayan Sugumaran, Oakland University, USA

Kalaivani Anbarasan, Saveetha School of Engineering, India
Chitrakala S., Anna University, India

Subramaniyaswamy Vairavasundaram, SASTRA University, India
Logesh R., SASTRA University, India

Moamin A Mahmoud, Universiti Tenaga Nasional, Malaysia
Mohd Sharifuddin Ahmad, Universiti Tenaga Nasional, Malaysia

Section 2
Application of Computational Techniques

Section 3
Web-Based Smart Systems

Detailed Table of Contents

Section 1
Semantic Technologies and Agent-Based Systems

Chapter 1

> Jon Atle Gulla, Norwegian University of Science and Technology, Norway
> Özlem Özgöbek, Norwegian University of Science and Technology, Norway
> Xiaomeng Su, Norwegian University of Science and Technology, Norway

Research on mobile news recommendation has become popular over the last few years, though the news domain is challenging and there are still few advanced commercial systems with success. This paper presents the exploratory news recommender system under development in the SmartMedia program. In exploratory news recommendation the reader can compose his own recommendation strategies on the fly and use deep semantic content analysis to extract prominent entities and navigate between relevant content at a semantic level. The readers are more likely to read a larger share of the relevant recommended articles, as there is no need to browse long tedious lists of articles or post explicit queries. The assumption is that more active and exploring readers will make implicit feedback more complete and more consistent with the readers' real interests. Tests shows a 5.14% improvement of accuracy when our collaborative filtering component is enriched with implicit feedback that combines correlations between explicit ratings with the reading times of articles viewed by readers.

Chapter 2

> Ghassan Beydoun, University of Technology Sydney, Australia
> Alexey Voinov, University of Twente, The Netherlands
> Vijayan Sugumaran, Oakland University, USA

Predictions for Service Oriented Architectures (SOA) to deliver transformational results to the role and capabilities of IT for businesses have fallen short. Unforeseen challenges have often emerged in SOA adoption. They fall into two categories: technical issues stemming from service components reuse difficulties and organizational issues stemming from inadequate support or understanding of what is required from the executive management in an organization to facilitate the technical rollout. This paper first explores and analyses the hindrances to the full exploitation of SOA. It then proposes an alternative service delivery approach that is based on even a higher degree of loose coupling than SOA. The approach promotes knowledge services and agent-based support for integration and identification of services. To support the arguments, this chapter sketches as a proof of concept the operationalization of such a service delivery system in disaster management.

Chapter 3

The content based image retrieval system retrieves relevant images based on image features. The lack of performance in the content based image retrieval system is due to the semantic gap. Image annotation is a solution to bridge the semantic gap between low-level content features and high-level semantic concepts Image annotation is defined as tagging images with a single or multiple keywords based on low-level image features. The major issue in building an effective annotation framework is the integration of both low level visual features and high-level textual information into an annotation model. This chapter focus on new statistical-based image annotation model towards semantic based image retrieval system. A multi-label image annotation with multi-level tagging system is introduced to annotate image regions with class labels and extract color, location and topological tags of segmented image regions. The proposed method produced encouraging results and the experimental results outperformed state-of-the-art methods

Chapter 4

The rapid growth of web technologies had created a huge amount of information that is available as web resources on Internet. Authors develop an automatic topic ontology construction process for better topic classification and present a corpus based novel approach to enrich the set of categories in the ODP by automatically identifying concepts and their associated semantic relationships based on external knowledge from Wikipedia and WordNet. The topic ontology construction process relies on concept acquisition and semantic relation extraction. Initially, a topic mapping algorithm is developed to acquire the concepts from Wikipedia based on semantic relations. A semantic similarity clustering algorithm is used to compute similarity to group the set of similar concepts. The semantic relation extraction algorithm derives associated semantic relations between the set of extracted topics from the lexical patterns in WordNet. The performance of the proposed topic ontology is evaluated for the classification of web documents and obtained results depict the improved performance over ODP.

Chapter 5

Norms and normative multi-agent systems have become the subjects of interest for many researchers. Such interest is caused by the need for agents to exploit the norms in enhancing their performance in a community. In open agent systems, an agent is not usually and explicitly given the norms of the host agents. Thus, when it is not able to adapt the communities' norms, it is totally deprived of accessing resources and services from the host. Such circumstance severely affects its performance resulting in failure to achieve its goal. While several studies have addressed this issue, their detection mechanisms are restricted to the use of sanctions by third party enforcement. Consequently, this study attempts to overcome this deficiency by proposing a technique that enables an agent to detect the host's potential norms via self-enforcement and update its norms even in the absence of sanctions from a third-party. The technique is called the Potential Norms Detection Technique (PNDT).

Section 2
Application of Computational Techniques

Chapter 6

 C. Sweetlin Hemalatha, VIT University, India
 V. Vaidehi, VIT University, India

Rapid advancement in Wireless Sensor Network (WSN) technology facilitates remote health care solutions without hindering the mobility of a person using Wearable Wireless Body Area Network (WWBAN). Activity recognition, fall detection and finding abnormalities in vital parameters play a major role in pervasive health care for making accurate decision on health status of a person. This chapter presents the proposed two pattern mining algorithms based on associative classification and fuzzy associative classification which models the association between the attributes that characterize the activity or health condition and handles the uncertainty in data respectively for an accurate decision making. The algorithms mine the data from WWBAN to detect abnormal health status of the person and thus facilitate remote health care. The experimental results on the proposed algorithms show that they work par with the popular traditional algorithms and predicts the activity class, fall or health status in less time compared to existing traditional classifiers.

Chapter 7

 Parvathavarthini S., Kongu Engineering College, India
 Karthikeyani Visalakshi N., NKR Government Arts College for Women, India
 Shanthi S., Kongu Engineering College, India
 Lakshmi K., Kongu Engineering College, India

Data clustering is an unsupervised technique that segregates data into multiple groups based on the features of the dataset. Soft clustering techniques allow an object to belong to various clusters with different membership values. However, there are some impediments in deciding whether or not an object belongs to a cluster. To solve these issues, an intuitionistic fuzzy set introduces a new parameter called hesitancy factor that contributes to the lack of domain knowledge. Unfortunately, selecting the initial centroids in a random manner by any clustering algorithm delays the convergence and restrains from getting a global solution to the problem. To come across these barriers, this work presents a novel clustering algorithm that utilizes crow search optimization to select the optimal initial seeds for the Intuitionistic fuzzy clustering algorithm. Experimental analysis is carried out on several benchmark datasets and artificial datasets. The results demonstrate that the proposed method provides optimal results in terms of objective function and error rate.

Chapter 8

Defense at boundary is nowadays well equipped with perimeter protection, cameras, fence sensors, radars etc. However, in battlefield there is more feasibility of entering of a non-native human and unknowing stamping of the explosives placed in the various paths by the native soldiers. There exists no alert system in the battlefield for the soldiers to identify the intruder or the explosives in the field. Therefore, there is a need for an automated intelligent intrusion detection system for battlefield monitoring. This chapter proposes an intelligent radial basis function neural network (RBFNN) technique for intrusion detection and explosive identification. The proposed intelligent RBFNN implements some intellectual components in the algorithm to make the neural network think before learning the training samples. Involvement of intellectual components makes the learning process simple, effective and efficient. The proposed technique helps to reduce false alarm and encourages timely detection thereby providing extensive support for the native soldiers and save the life of the mankind.

Chapter 9

One of the techniques that have been used in the literature to enhance the dependability of distributed applications is the detection of distributed predicates techniques (also referred to as runtime verification). These techniques are used to verify that a given run of a distributed application satisfies certain properties (specified as predicates). Due to the existence of multiple processes running concurrently, the detection of a distributed predicate can incur significant overhead. Several researchers have worked on the development of techniques to reduce the cost of detecting distributed predicates. However, most of the techniques presented in the literature work efficiently for specific classes of predicates, like conjunctive predicates. This chapter presents a technique based on genetic algorithms to efficiently detect distributed predicates under the possibly modality. Several experiments have been conducted to demonstrate the effectiveness of the proposed technique.

Chapter 10

Data mining techniques are useful to discover the interesting knowledge from the large amount of data objects. Clustering is one of the data mining techniques for knowledge discovery and it is the unsupervised learning method and it analyses the data objects without knowing class labels. The k-prototype is the most widely-used partitional clustering algorithm for clustering the data objects with mixed numeric and categorical type of data. This algorithm provides the local optimum solution due to its selection of initial prototypes randomly. Recently, there are number of optimization algorithms are introduced to obtain the global optimum solution. The Crow Search algorithm is one the recently developed population based meta-heuristic optimization algorithm. This algorithm is based on the intelligent behavior of the crows. In this paper, k-prototype clustering algorithm is integrated with the Crow Search optimization algorithm to produce the global optimum solution.

Section 3
Web-Based Smart Systems

Chapter 11

Christoph Peters, University of St. Gallen, Switzerland & University of Kassel, Germany
Axel Korthaus, Swinburne University of Technology, Australia
Thomas Kohlborn, Sanofi, Australia

The future cities of our societies need to integrate their citizens into a value-co-creation process in order to transform to smart cities with an increased quality of life for their citizens. Therefore, administrations need to radically improve the delivery of public services, providing them citizen- and user-centric. In this context, online portals represent a cost effective front-end to deliver services and engage customers and new organizational approaches as back-ends which decouple the service interface from the departmental structures emerged. The research presented in this book chapter makes two main contributions: Firstly, the findings of a usability study comparing the online presences of the Queensland Government, the UK Government and the South Australian Government are reported and discussed. Secondly, the findings are reflected in regard to a broader "Transformational Government" approach and current smart city research and developments. Service bundling and modularization are suggested as innovative solutions to further improve online service delivery.

Chapter 12

Fouad Omran Elgahwash, University of Wollongong, Australia

Self-service banking technology (SSBT) allow customers to perform services on their own without direct assistance from staff. This study focuses on factors affecting the value of adopting self-Service banking technology (SSBT) among customers. It is believed that the successful usage of self-service banking technology will be increasingly advantageous for all (banks & customers). This chapter's purpose is an extension to the technology acceptance model (TAM) and views customer responses to technology as an integrated part of SSBT. The sample used for this study was selected from users of banks in both Libya and Australia, with a total size of 141 respondents. Reliability and validity of the data collection instrument was tested using Cronbach Alpha. Descriptive and regression tests for data analysis were used. The domains in which subjects were tested were "ease of use of SSBT", "Usefulness of SSBT", "Quality of SSBT", "privacy of information" and "Trust of SSBT".

Chapter 13

Simon Polovina, Sheffield Hallam University, UK
Hans-Jurgen Scheruhn, Hochschule Harz, Germany
Mark von Rosing, Global University Alliance, Denmark

The development of meta-models in Enterprise Modelling, Enterprise Engineering, and Enterprise Architecture enables an enterprise to add value and meet its obligations to its stakeholders. This value is however undermined by the complexity in the meta-models which have become difficult to visualise thus deterring the human-driven process. These experiences have driven the development of layers and levels in the modular meta-model. Conceptual Structures (CS), described as "Information Processing in Mind and Machine", align the way computers work with how humans think. Using the Enterprise Information Meta-model Architecture (EIMA) as an exemplar, two forms of CS known as Conceptual Graphs (CGs) and Formal Concept Analysis (FCA) are brought together through the CGtoFCA algorithm, thereby mathematically evaluating the effectiveness of the layers and levels in these meta-models. The work reveals the useful contribution that this approach brings in actualising the modularising of complex meta-models in enterprise systems using conceptual structures.

The central hypothesis of Internet of Things is the term "connectivity". The IoT devices are connected to the Internet through a wide variety of communication technologies. This chapter explains the various technologies involved in IoT connectivity. The diversity in communication raises the query of which one to choose for the proposed application. The key objective of the application needs to be defined very clearly. The application features such as the power requirement, data size, storage, security and battery life highly influence the decision of selecting one or more communication technology. Near Field Communication is a good choice for short-range communication, whereas Wi-Fi can be opted for a larger range of coverage. Though Bluetooth is required for higher data rate, it is power hungry, but ZigBee is suitable for low power devices. There involves always the tradeoff between the technologies and the requirements. This chapter emphasizes that the goal of the application required to be more precise to decide the winner of the IoT connectivity technology that suits for it.

Preface

INTRODUCTION

In today's informatics age, there is a vast amount of information, from biomedical and genetic reports to environmental and lifestyle information, often stored as text or in different databases that are rarely communicating with each other and are often difficult to mine. Unfortunately, this severely limits our ability to fuse information from multiple sources and identify large-scale patterns that affect human health. Currently, there is a huge body of biomedical text and their rapid growth makes it impossible for researchers to address the information manually. The Research, Condition, and Disease Categorization (RCDC) project gets data from 7 databases (all containing well over 4 terabytes of content) that gets routed, processed, grouped, validated and ultimately used for regular reports and on-demand queries. It follows a pattern matching approach for categorization of diseases. This project by NIH allows research information in medical records to be explored proactively on homogeneous data. Other projects on clinical and medical mining focus on gene manipulation, EHR interpretation, personalized medicine recommendation based on EHR of individuals, Drug recommendation based on linked open data. To summarize the happening in the healthcare domain, all the systems focused on homogeneous data and suggested diagnostic and prescriptive medicine. The underlying interaction between the various data that is available, their side effects and disease propagations has not been researched on.

Evidence-based medicine (EBM) is becoming common in today's healthcare delivery. EBM requires an integrated system where the clinician can gain access to not only the best practices and evidence in assessing the benefits and risks of a treatment, but also the patient information that might be scattered across the healthcare organization. Clinical data integration is the need of the hour, which has been accomplished with very limited success. Designing an integrative system would provide consolidated information mined and correlated using heterogeneous medical data to help healthcare professionals in making effective decisions and improve healthcare delivery.

Extracting evidence and integrating appropriate patient data is a major research challenge. While hospitals are investing heavily in infrastructure where disparate systems can be seamlessly connected to facilitate data integration, no gold standard exists. One system is the METEOR system developed at Houston Methodist Hospital. This system attempts to integrate data from internal and external sources into an enterprise clinical and research data warehouse. However, this solution is specific to the hospital and is not scalable or easily transferable to other healthcare organizations. A new generation of interoperable system architecture has to be designed to create generic, flexible and scalable systems with open architecture which have the potential to secure a large market share.

Limited amount of work in linking medical data mined from the web with medical databases and medical Linked Open Data has been carried out. Lifestyle recommendations from social media has also been implemented. Fundamental work on text mining and NLP processing of domain oriented scientific Literature mining has been undertaken. However, information fusion from heterogeneous sources for Discovering Diagnostic and Predictive Measures, Disease Progression Models and investigating correlations between conditions and monitor changes over time is still in the idea stage. Current strategies to mine genetic information employ an integrated approach of genetics, biomedical data, and text mining to identify risk probabilities of developing diseases and predicting responses to cures for diseases with a clear single-gene association.

INTERACTIVE BIOMEDICAL SYSTEM

Other work on healthcare have dealt with one source of data that is terabytes in size. Integrating all sources of medical data like EHR, literature mining, gene mining is new and has never been tried upon. Here we carry out information fusion from heterogeneous sources for Discovering Diagnostic and Predictive Measures, Disease Progression Models and investigating correlations between conditions and monitor changes over time. Current strategies to mine genetic information employ an integrated approach of genetics, biomedical data, and text mining to identify risk probabilities of developing diseases and predicting responses to cures. While powerful for the analysis of mendelian diseases, this approach is still limited when dealing with complex diseases which are the result of the interaction of multiple factors, genetic and environmental. The focus on a single disease at a time is preventing our ability to identify commonalities among diseases that might be triggered by similar genetic or environmental backgrounds. To address both the above issues, a new interactive system is needed that will allow medical practitioners and researchers to explore factors that are shared by multiple conditions.

Such an interactive system should aim to capitalize on machine learning oriented integrated information fusion mining to provide up-to-date clinical decision support for diagnosis of diseases, and Lifestyle Recommendations. The system should be accessible through a web-interface and should use a combination of genetic/biomedical literature, census data (e.g., socioeconomic status, geographical region), and social media data. The goal should be to provide a flexible interface to show current diagnostic measures and investigate correlations between conditions and monitor changes over time (longitudinal studies). The focus should be on diseases such as cancer, diabetes and cardio-vascular diseases and on drug resistance and host infection strategies in pathogens.

To address the above-mentioned issues, a novel biomedical interactive system should be developed which is accessible through a web-interface. It should be based on machine learning methodology and use a combination of data about humans and human-pathogens from genetic/biomedical literature, census data (e.g., socioeconomic status, geographical region), gene related databases with gene functions, EHR data and social media data. The goal should be to provide a flexible interface to carry out information fusion of diagnostic terms and relations using heterogeneous data and investigate correlations between conditions and monitor changes over time (longitudinal studies) using heterogeneous data. The system could focus on a limited number of disease categories: systemic diseases (cancer, diabetes and cardio-vascular diseases) and infectious diseases (focusing on the pathogenicity and drug resistance of human pathogens). I designing such a system, emphasis should be placed on information fusion of the following: a) literature mining of diagnostic terms and relations and lifestyle issues and correlating with Gene context data and Linked Open Data by deriving patterns from genes associated with diseases, their intensity, and predicting gene interactions for new diseases; b) personalized database for medical researchers interested in testing significant correlations between multiple diseases and environmental factors; and c) identify gene functions that are most commonly related to changes in pathogenicity, due to mutations that increase or decrease infection rates or mutations involved in the emergence of drug resistance with Apicomplexa as a model system.

IMPLEMENTATION AND COMMERCIALIZATION

The new system should integrate information from a number of heterogeneous data sources. Integrating structured and unstructured data is a non-trivial task and the system should employ state of the art in machine learning, big data management and analytics, natural language processing and semantic technologies. This will enable easy access to the right information at the right time on demand and can make the clinical as well as managerial decision-making process quite effective. Such a new system would have tremendous appeal and garner considerable market share since every healthcare organization is attempting to become more efficient in terms of day to day operations as well as improve the quality of care provided. The market for an integrated system is wide open and thus, the new system has the potential to capture a big market share.

It can easily be seen that the ability to build a personalized database will be a valuable tool for medical researchers interested in testing significant correlations between multiple diseases and environmental factors. Doctors could use it also an aid to visualize consolidate report of patients in a multi-perspective view and as a tool to observe and monitor interaction of the disease-causing genes and their possible side effects to offer preventive care for their patients. It could act as a quick reference for junior doctor trainees during their internship. Limited access could be given to patients to understand the cause and effect of their diseases and their intensity.

In order to commercialize the new system described above, the "Strategic Alliances" approach to commercialization can be adopted. This strategy requires forming partnerships with customers for the purpose of R&D, marketing, testing, licensing, etc. Since Pharmacists and Medical representatives, Doctors and Hospitals/Patients are potential users of the system, a core group of these stakeholders can be identified and form a strategic partnership with them. The user requirements for the web-based applications can be elicited from these partners. Based on the requirements, working prototypes can be developed through agile software development and eventually turned into a production system. The stakeholders identified can also be used for eventually testing the applications. The need and the use of the web applications will be emphasized to patients to get their medical records in the initial stages. This could serve as an entry point for getting acquainted with a group of doctors/specialists and hospitals. In this manner some hospitals, doctors and patients can become aware of the system. These Doctors in turn could contact pharmaceutical companies who could use medical representatives to advertise this system in addition to advertising a particular brand of medicine.

ORGANIZATION OF THE BOOK

This book is organized into three sections. The first section discusses semantic technologies and agent based systems as well as their application in recommender systems, multi-label image annotation, knowledge services, and topic ontology construction. The second section discusses application of computational intelligence techniques in various domains such as healthcare, cluster analysis, intrusion detection, and distributed predicate detection. The third section discusses web-based smart systems in different areas such as public service delivery, self-service banking, enterprise systems and internet of things. A brief description of each of the chapters is provided below.

Section 1: Semantic Technologies and Agent-Based Systems

The first chapter of the book is titled "Exploratory News Recommendation," contributed by Jon Atle Gulla, Özlem Özgöbek, and Xiaomeng Su. This chapter presents an exploratory news recommender system under development in the SmartMedia program. In exploratory news recommendats the reader can compose his own recommendation strategies on the fly and use deep semantic content analysis to extract prominent entities and navigate between relevant content at a semantic level. The readers are more likely to read a larger share of the relevant recommended articles, as there is no need to browse long tedious lists of articles or post explicit queries. The assumption is that more active and exploring readers will make implicit feedback more complete and more consistent with the readers' real interests. Tests show a 5.14% improvement of accuracy when our collaborative filtering component is enriched with implicit feedback that combines correlations between explicit ratings with the reading times of articles viewed by readers.

The second chapter is titled "Beyond Service-Oriented Architectures: Knowledge Services?" written by Ghassan Beydoun, Alexey Voinov, and Vijayan Sugumaran. In this chapter, the authors point out that unforeseen challenges have often emerged in Service Oriented Architecture (SOA) adoption. They fall into two categories: technical issues stemming from service components reuse difficulties and organizational issues stemming from inadequate support or understanding of what is required from the executive management in an organization to facilitate the technical rollout. This chapter first explores and analyses the hindrances to the full exploitation of SOA. It then proposes an alternative service delivery approach that is based on even a higher degree of loose coupling than SOA. The approach promotes knowledge services and agent-based support for integration and identification of services. To support the arguments, this chapter sketches as a proof of concept the operationalization of such a service delivery system in disaster management.

The third chapter is titled "A Multi-Label Image Annotation With Multi-Level Tagging System," contributed by Kalaivani Anbarasan, and Chitrakala S. The authors contend that the lack of performance in the content based image retrieval system is due to the semantic gap. Image annotation is a solution to bridge the semantic gap between low-level content features and high-level semantic concepts Image annotation is defined as tagging images with a single or multiple keywords based on low-level image features. The major issue in building an effective annotation framework is the integration of both low level visual features and high-level textual information into an annotation model. This chapter focus on new statistical-based image annotation model towards semantic based image retrieval system. A multi-label image annotation with multi-level tagging system is introduced to annotate image regions with class labels and extract color, location and topological tagsof segmented image regions. The proposed method produced encouraging results and the experimental results outperformed state-of-the-art methods.

Subramaniyaswamy Vairavasundaram and Logesh R. have contributed the fourth chapter titled "Applying Semantic Relations for Automatic Topic Ontology Construction." The authors develop an automatic topic ontology construction process for better topic classification and present a corpus based novel approach to enrich the set of categories in the ODP by automatically identifying concepts and their associated semantic relationships based on external knowledge from Wikipedia and WordNet. The topic ontology construction process relies on concept acquisition and semantic relation extraction. Initially, a topic mapping algorithm is developed to acquire the concepts from Wikipedia based on semantic relations. A semantic similarity clustering algorithm is used to compute similarity to group the set of similar concepts. The semantic relation extraction algorithm derives associated semantic relations between the set of extracted topics from the lexical patterns in WordNet. The performance of the proposed topic ontology is evaluated for the classification of web documents and obtained results depict the improved performance over ODP.

The fifth chapter titled "Norms-Adaptable Agents for Open Multi-Agent Systems," is written by Moamin A Mahmoud and Mohd Sharifuddin Ahmad. This chapter shows that norms and normative multi-agent systems have become the subjects of interest for many researchers. Such interest is caused by the need for agents to exploit the norms in enhancing their performance in a community. In open agent systems, an agent is not usually and explicitly given the norms of the host agents. Thus, when it is not able to adapt the communities' norms, it is totally deprived of accessing resources and services from the host. Such circumstance severely affects its performance resulting in failure to achieve its goal. While several studies have addressed this issue, their detection mechanisms are restricted to the use of sanctions by third party enforcement. Consequently, this chapter attempts to overcome this deficiency by proposing a technique that enables an agent to detect the host's potential norms via self-enforcement and update its norms even in the absence of sanctions from a third-party. The technique is called the Potential Norms Detection Technique (PNDT).

Section 2: Application of Computational Techniques

The sixth chapter is contributed by C. Sweetlin Hemalatha and V Vaidehi and titled "A Pattern-Mining Approach for Wearable Sensor-Based Remote Health Care." The authors assert that rapid advancement in Wireless Sensor Network (WSN) technology facilitates remote health care solutions without hindering the mobility of a person using Wearable Wireless Body Area Network (WWBAN). Activity recognition, fall detection and finding abnormalities in vital parameters play a major role in pervasive health care for making accurate decision on health status of a person. This chapter presents the proposed two pattern mining algorithms based on associative classification and fuzzy associative classification which models the association between the attributes that characterize the activity or health condition and handles the uncertainty in data respectively for an accurate decision making. The algorithms mine the data from WWBAN to detect abnormal health status of the person and thus facilitate remote health care. The experimental results on the proposed algorithms show that they work par with the popular traditional algorithms and predicts the activity class, fall or health status in less time compared to existing traditional classifiers.

Parvathavarthini S., Karthikeyani Visalakshi N., S. Shanthi, and Lakshmi K. present the seventh chapter titled "Crow-Search-Based Intuitionistic Fuzzy C-Means Clustering Algorithm." This chapter points out that data clustering is an unsupervised technique that segregates data into multiple groups based on the features of the dataset. Soft clustering techniques allow an object to belong to various clusters with different membership values. However, there are some impediments in deciding whether or not an object belongs to a cluster. To solve these issues, an intuitionistic fuzzy set introduces a new parameter called hesitancy factor that contributes to the lack of domain knowledge. Unfortunately, selecting the initial centroids in a random manner by any clustering algorithm delays the convergence and restrains from getting a global solution to the problem. To come across these barriers, this work presents a novel clustering algorithm that utilizes crow search optimization to select the optimal initial seeds for the Intuitionistic fuzzy clustering algorithm. Experimental analysis is carried out on several benchmark datasets and artificial datasets. The results demonstrate that the proposed method provides optimal results in terms of objective function and error rate.

The eighth chapter is titled "Intelligent Radial Basis Function Neural Network for Intrusion Detection in Battle Field," written by Kirupa Ganapathy. This chapter begins by highlighting that defense at boundary is nowadays well equipped with perimeter protection, cameras, fence sensors, radars etc. However, in a battlefield there is more feasibility of entering of a non-native human and unknowing stamping of the explosives placed in the various paths by the native soldiers. There exists no alert system in the battlefield for the soldiers to identify the intruder or the explosives in the field. Therefore, there is a need for an automated intelligent intrusion detection system for battlefield monitoring. This chapter proposes an intelligent radial basis function neural network (RBFNN) technique for intrusion detection and explosive identification. The proposed intelligent RBFNN implements some intellectual components in the algorithm to make the neural network think before learning the training samples. Involvement of intellectual components makes the learning process simple, effective and efficient. The proposed technique helps to reduce false alarm and encourages timely detection thereby providing extensive support for the native soldiers and save the life of the mankind.

Eslam Al Maghayreh has contributed the ninth chapter titled "A Genetic-Algorithms-Based Technique for Detecting Distributed Predicates." This chapter posits that one way to enhance the dependability of distributed applications is the detection of distributed predicates techniques (also referred to as runtime verification). Several techniques are used to verify that a given run of a distributed application satisfies certain properties (specified as predicates). Due to the existence of multiple processes running concurrently, the detection of a distributed predicate can incur significant overhead. Several researchers have worked on the development of techniques to reduce the cost of detecting distributed predicates. However, most of the techniques presented in the literature work efficiently for specific classes of predicates, like conjunctive predicates. This chapter presents a technique based on genetic algorithms to efficiently detect distributed predicates under the possibly modality. Several experiments have been conducted to demonstrate the effectiveness of the proposed technique.

The tenth chapter is titled "Clustering Mixed Datasets Using K-Prototype Algorithm Based on Crow-Search Optimization," written by Lakshmi K, Karthikeyani Visalakshi N, Shanthi S, and Parvathavarthini S. They point out that clustering is one of the data mining techniques for knowledge discovery and it is the unsupervised learning method and it analyses the data objects without knowing class labels. The k-prototype is the most widely used partitional clustering algorithm for clustering the data objects with mixed numeric and categorical type of data. This algorithm provides the local optimum solution due to its selection of initial prototypes randomly. Recently, there are a number of optimization algorithms introduced to obtain the global optimum solution. The Crow Search algorithm is one such population based meta-heuristic optimization algorithm. This algorithm is based on the intelligent behavior of the crows. In this chapter, k-prototype clustering algorithm is integrated with the Crow Search optimization algorithm to produce the global optimum solution.

Section 3: Web-Based Smart Systems

The eleventh chapter is titled "Smart City Portals for Public Service Delivery: Insights from a Comparative Study," contributed by Christoph Peters, Axel Korthaus, and Thomas Kohlborn. The authors argue that the future cities of our societies need to integrate their citizens into a value-co-creation process in order to transform to smart cities with an increased quality of life for their citizens. Therefore, administrations need to radically improve the delivery of public services, providing them citizen- and user-centric. In this context, online portals represent a cost effective front-end to deliver services and engage customers and new organizational approaches as back-ends which decouple the service interface from the departmental structures emerged. The research presented in this book chapter makes two main contributions: Firstly, the findings of a usability study comparing the online presences of the Queensland Government, the UK Government and the South Australian Government are reported and discussed. Secondly, the findings are reflected in regard to a broader "Transformational Government" approach and current smart city research and developments. Service bundling and modularization are suggested as innovative solutions to further improve online service delivery.

Fouad Omran Elgahwash presents the twelfth chapter titled "A Quantitative Study of Factors Affecting Value of Adopting Self-Service Banking Technology (SSBT) Among Customers in Developing and Developed Countries." This chapter focuses on the factors affecting the value of adopting self-Service banking technology (SSBT) among customers. It is believed that the successful usage of self-service banking technology will be increasingly advantageous for all (banks & customers). This chapter's purpose is an extension to the technology acceptance model (TAM) and views customer responses to technology as an integrated part of SSBT. The sample used for this study was selected from users of banks in both Libya and Australia, with a total size of 141 respondents. Reliability and validity of the data collection instrument was tested using Cronbach Alpha. Descriptive and regression tests for data analysis were used. The domains in which subjects were tested were "ease of use of SSBT", "Usefulness of SSBT", "Quality of SSBT", "privacy of information" and "Trust of SSBT".

The thirteenth chapter is contributed by Simon Polovina, Hans-Jurgen Scheruhn, and Mark von Rosing titled "Modularizing the Complex Meta-Models in Enterprise Systems Using Conceptual Structures." The authors indicate that the development of meta-models in Enterprise Modelling, Enterprise Engineering, and Enterprise Architecture enables an enterprise to add value and meet its obligations to its stakeholders. This value is however undermined by the complexity in the meta-models which have become difficult to visualize thus deterring the human-driven process. These experiences have driven the development of layers and levels in the modular meta-model. Conceptual Structures (CS), described as "Information Processing in Mind and Machine", align the way computers work with how humans think. Using the Enterprise Information Meta-model Architecture (EIMA) as an exemplar, two forms of CS known as Conceptual Graphs (CGs) and Formal Concept Analysis (FCA) are brought together through the CGtoFCA algorithm, thereby mathematically evaluating the effectiveness of the layers and levels in these meta-models. The work reveals the useful contribution that this approach brings in actualizing the modularizing of complex meta-models in enterprise systems using conceptual structures.

The fourteenth chapter is titled "Communication Trends in Internet of Things," written by Bharathi N Gopalsamy. This chapter submits that the central hypothesis of Internet of Things is the term "connectivity". The IoT devices are connected to the Internet through a wide variety of communication technologies. This chapter explains the various technologies involved in IoT connectivity. The diversity in communication raises the query of which one to choose for the proposed application. The key objective of the application needs to be defined very clearly. The application features such as the power requirement, data size, storage, security and battery life highly influence the decision of selecting one or more communication technology. Near Field Communication is a good choice for short-range communication, whereas Wi-Fi can be opted for a larger range of coverage. Though Bluetooth is required for higher data rate, it is power hungry, but ZigBee is suitable for low power devices. There involves always the tradeoff between the technologies and the requirements. This chapter emphasizes that the goal of the application required to be more precise to decide the winner of the IoT connectivity technology that suits it.

Vijayan Sugumaran
Oakland University, USA

Acknowledgment

Dr. Sugumaran's research has been partially supported by a 2017 School of Business Administration Spring/Summer Fellowship, at Oakland University, Rochester, Michigan, USA.

Vijayan Sugumaran
Oakland University, USA

Section 1
Semantic Technologies and Agent-Based Systems

Chapter 1
Exploratory News Recommendation

Jon Atle Gulla
Norwegian University of Science and Technology, Norway

Özlem Özgöbek
Norwegian University of Science and Technology, Norway

Xiaomeng Su
Norwegian University of Science and Technology, Norway

ABSTRACT

Research on mobile news recommendation has become popular over the last few years, though the news domain is challenging and there are still few advanced commercial systems with success. This paper presents the exploratory news recommender system under development in the SmartMedia program. In exploratory news recommendation the reader can compose his own recommendation strategies on the fly and use deep semantic content analysis to extract prominent entities and navigate between relevant content at a semantic level. The readers are more likely to read a larger share of the relevant recommended articles, as there is no need to browse long tedious lists of articles or post explicit queries. The assumption is that more active and exploring readers will make implicit feedback more complete and more consistent with the readers' real interests. Tests shows a 5.14% improvement of accuracy when our collaborative filtering component is enriched with implicit feedback that combines correlations between explicit ratings with the reading times of articles viewed by readers.

INTRODUCTION

In spite of recent successes of news recommender systems from for example Washington Post and New York Times (Nieman Journalism Lab, 2015; Washington Post, 2015), there are fundamental challenges in news recommendation that render many traditional recommendation strategies and algorithms unsuitable. Whereas most recommender systems or personalization software deal with structured and stable data, like in Amazon and Netflix, unstructured textual news articles are short-lived, overlapping and hard

DOI: 10.4018/978-1-5225-3686-4.ch001

to analyze or relate to user interests. Das et al. (2017) list item churn and scalability as major concerns in their Google News service. In Özgöbek et al. (2014) the news-specific challenges also include data sparsity, recency, implicit feedback, unstructured content and serendipity, among others.

In mobile news recommendation there are additional limitations with respect to user interaction modes and screen sizes that further complicate the usability of the systems and ultimately the learning of high-quality user profiles. Whereas users of recommender systems in general only reluctantly provide explicit feedback (Thurman, 2011), it seems even more difficult to encourage mobile users to submit ratings that can help the system improve its recommendations. Also, only a small portion of the recommended list can be shown at the same time on a mobile device, which potentially prevents the readers from actually seeing and evaluating the news articles presented to her. However, since mobile news recommender systems have access to the readers' immediate geospatial context and are directly available as news are unfolding, the systems may introduce locational and time-dependent recommendation features that go beyond what is feasible in desktop solutions.

This paper discusses the experiences with a mobile news recommender system that is under development in the SmartMedia program at NTNU in Norway. Central in this program is the development of recommendation approaches that take advantage of readers' mobile availability while alleviating the problems of small screens and awkward input options. The intention is to develop a full context-aware and personalized news experience on the basis of deeper semantic analyses of news content and its relation to external sources. Linked data is employed to extract and disambiguate news entities that enable us to localize news, build and maintain semantic user profiles and follow trends and sentiments of news entities like people, organizations, and products.

The contribution of the paper is two-fold: Firstly, it introduces and explains a new concept in news recommendation, *exploratory news recommendation*, that allows readers actively to take charge of the recommendation process rather than providing feedback on system-generated lists only. This focus on exploration encourages users to reflect on their interests and be more conscious about what makes an article interesting and worth reading. Secondly, it shows how implicit feedback from reading times can be exploited to enhance system accuracy as readers get more active and leave more meaningful traces than just click-through logs.

The rest of the paper is structured as follows: Section 2 introduces the SmartMedia program for mobile news recommendation, in which the concept of exploratory recommender systems in introduced. Important related work – including the issue of implicit and explicit feedback – is discussed in Section 3. Whereas Section 4 shows how the news app is designed to support exploratory recommendations, the entity-based linking of articles for further drill-down is demonstrated in Section 5. An evaluation confirming the quality and value of implicit feedback in such recommender systems is explained in Section 6, followed by conclusions in Section 7.

BACKGROUND

The SmartMedia program at NTNU in Trondheim was established in 2012 as part of a collaboration with Norwegian telecom and media industry. With an emphasis on news recommendation and semantics, the program is investigating new and semantically deeper approaches for building real-world large-scale news recommender systems and analysis tools for data-driven journalism. The projects in SmartMedia are partly funded by industry, but have also received substantial support from Innovation Norway[1] and the Research Council of Norway[2].

Exploratory news recommendation is a specialization of news recommendation that is characterized by user-driven rather than system-driven processes, transparent rather than concealed recommendation strategies, and semantic rather than statistical exploration of recommended news stories. The idea is that both the system and the user need to be actively engaged to make an information seeking session successful. Exploratory recommender systems give users more initiative and control than traditional recommender systems and offer more system support than traditional search systems.

In exploratory news recommendation users take an active role in retrieving and navigating among relevant news articles. The iterative exploratory process is comprised of the following two user activities:

- Real-time composition and configuration of recommendation strategies.
- Iterative exploration of recommended news articles using semantic links between articles and decomposition of articles into meaningful semantic units.

The first activity above requires that hybrid recommendation strategies be split up in sub-strategies that are compositional, comprehensible to users and configurable in real-time. The second activity means that articles need to be broken down to meaning-bearing units like entities or concepts that semantically describe article content and are meaningful to users. Users do not provide any explicit feedback like article ratings or browse long and partly irrelevant lists of recommended articles, as this would undermine the sense of utilizing the system as a resource instead of being treated as a resource by the system.

The effect of exploratory news recommendation is that recommendations reflect a more fine-grained model of the user and her reading preferences. Moreover, less interaction is needed to select and view the desired articles among the set of recommended articles, and users are viewing more articles to get access to navigational links from within the article. A full-fledged exploratory mobile news recommender system is currently under development and evaluation (Tavakolifard et al., 2013; Su et al., 2016).

As seen from the architecture in Figure 1, the recommender system has a backend system that forms a news stream processing pipeline from raw and noisy news items to clean, semantically enriched, clustered and indexed stories. The system is sourcing news articles from Really Simple Syndication (RSS) feeds from all major Norwegian news content providers and a selection of English ones. Apache Storm is used to distribute the workload throughout the pipeline.

The RSS entries normally contain a title, a lead text, one or more URLs, and possibly information about geospatial properties and images. Geospatial properties are typically found in GeoRSS feeds for road messages and traffic warnings. For later processing of the news items we also include the contents of the full articles to which the URLs are pointing.

After removing ads and html tags from the news documents in the tokenizer, we have a stream of news items that are annotated with the correct language by the language identification component. A language-dependent Part-Of-Speech (POS) tagger and Named Entity Recognition component extract noun phrases that are collected as entity candidates for the news. Identified entity candidates need to be disambiguated before we can use them semantically in news recommendation. This means that the identified entities need to be linked to the correct structured entries in the Wikidata[3], Geonames[4], and the Norwegian Land Registry and Cadastre [5] knowledge bases.

Figure 1. Architecture of SmartMedia mobile news recommender system

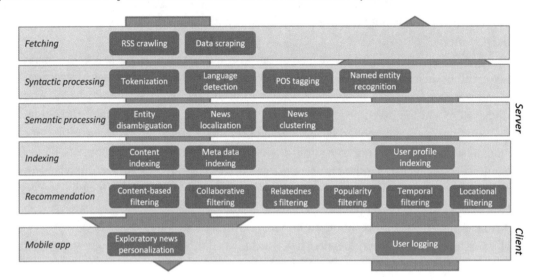

Wikidata is a community-driven repository of structured data about entities from all over the world. Most entities are associated with one or more types like *people, places*, and *books*, and they may have additional properties like *"date of birth"* for a person or latitude and longitude for a location. Even though the entities in Wikidata are well documented with both Wikipedia-based textual descriptions and entity relations, we have found it useful to use open data from Geonames and the Norwegian Land Registry and Cadastre to associate more data with geographical entities. Random forest models and a pre-annotated dataset from Dunietz and Gillick (2014) and the New York Times corpus (Sandhaus, 2008) are used to train the entity disambiguation component (Ingvaldsen & Gulla, 2015).

The SmartMedia mobile news recommender has adopted a hybrid recommendation approach. With content-based filtering we are computing similarities between tf.idf-based article vectors and user profiles (Gulla et al., 2013; Gulla et al., 2014), and preparing ranked lists of articles similar to user profiles. Our collaborative filtering component makes use of singular value decomposition (SVD) that decomposes the user-article matrix into two matrices $u \times l$ *and* $i \times l$, where u denotes the number of users, i denotes the number of articles and l denotes the number of latent factors chosen for the factorization (Monsen & Romstad, 2014). Implementationally, this is done with Mahout's SVD recommender with stochastic gradient descent factorization using 10 latent factors. In addition to content-based filtering and collaborative filtering, there are components for recommending similar news (relatedness filtering), popular news (popularity filtering), news from reader's current location (locational filtering) and news of particularly recent events (temporal filtering).

ElasticSearch is used to index news articles and their meta data. The user profiles are stored in MongoDB, while the updating of these profiles from logging user behavior is done with an Apache Hadoop batch job. The mobile news app is implemented with HTML5 and integrates personalized news features and user logging in a gesture-driven user interface.

RELATED WORK

News recommender systems cover a wide range of techniques and often combine both content-based filtering and collaborative filtering. Unlike popular sites like Netflix and Amazon there are no explicit transactions in news recommender systems that can serve as definite indications of interests or satisfaction. Some recommender systems use explicit ratings like a star scale or like/dislike buttons, but users are usually reluctant to provide explicit feedback on their interests in news articles (Thurman, 2011).

An alternative to explicit feedback is to use implicit feedback like browsing histories, search patterns, mouse movements, page viewing times, click behavior or actions for sharing articles. These user acts tend to say something about the users' attitude towards a news item, but the analysis of such acts is complex. Even though explicit feedback suffers from substantial noise, it is still considered more reliable than implicit feedback for most recommendation tasks (Amatriain et al., 2009). According to Hu et al. (2008) implicit feedback is problematic due to lack of negative feedback, noise, user confidence and missing evaluation methods. Research shows, however, that careful use of implicit feedback can be useful both when replacing and supplementing explicit scores from users. Parra and Amatriain (2011) used implicit feedback as a supplement to their explicit rating for a music recommender system and achieved a 6.5% improvement of accuracy.

Morita and Shinoda (1994) observed that there is a correlation between time spent reading a news article and the explicit rating given by the user. In the analysis of their Netnews article recommender system they collected user preferences in terms of time spent per article, the length of the article and the readability of the article. Their experiment showed that reading time was the most interesting type of implicit feedback, and they managed to get precision and recall values of 70% and 30% by assuming that users find articles interesting if they spend more than 20 seconds reading them. Our work draws heavily on this research and also assumes article reading times to be crucial for predicting user interests and preferences.

Daily Learner is a news recommender system that makes use of user click logs as implicit feedback to their content-based recommender engine (Billsus & Pazzani, 2000). A user click on the headline of an article is assumed to express a basic interest in the article and is represented as a score of 0.8. As the user is viewing more pages of the article, the score is increased until it reaches 1.0 if all pages have been viewed. Skipped articles are assumed to be uninteresting to the user and are given negative scores.

A click distribution approach is also adopted in Google News (Liu et al., 2010). For every month they generate a click distribution vector for the user that contains the user's normalized clicks on each news category. The hypothesis is that these category weights give a fair estimate of the user's overall interest in a specific news category, and this overall interest may change from one month to another. The actual interest at a particular point of time is calculated by combining user's overall interest with a measure of important breaking news. Implemented as part of a content-based filtering component in Google News, their approach was tested with about 10,000 users on live traffic at Google News and led to a 30% increase of click-through rates of the recommended news section. However, their feedback is rather coarse-grained, as for example any click on any sports event will be interpreted as an interest in any other sports event of any other sports.

None of these approaches have addressed the particular challenges of mobile platforms and suffer from some fundamental weaknesses when large amounts of data have to be inspected by users. Research from Internet search engines like AllTheWeb.com (Gulla et al., 2003) indicates that users only view about five Web documents per query. They spend 70% of the their time viewing only the top ten results, and over 50% of the users do not access results beyond the first page (Spink & Jansen, 2004). In mobile recommender systems this pattern is even more pronounced, as fewer articles can be shown together on the result page and more labor is needed to browse through the list of recommended articles. Implicit feedback based on click through rates is error-prone because users do not take the trouble to click on more than a few articles in a long list of recommendations, and a particular click does not necessarily mean that the user is interested and will read the article.

Our approach for turning news readers into active news explorers is not found directly in other mobile news recommender systems, though some of the same ideas are used in several recommender systems in other domains. Active learning is successfully incorporated into a mobile shopping recommender system, in which user critiques on displayed recommendations are iteratively collected until a satisfactory understanding of user preferences is reached (Lamche et al., 2014). The idea is that these critique cycles will lead to very precise user models and shorter and more accurate list of recommendations, though the approach necessitates systematic and consistent explicit feedback from users. Also, research on recommender systems from three shopping sites suggests that users appreciate exploratory browsing, as it increases the flow of the information seeking session and ultimately the users' satisfaction (Bauernfeind & Zins, 2006).

It is important in mobile exploratory recommender systems to reduce the dependency on large screens by replacing long result lists with semantically connected items. Similar to the entities of our recommender system, Fossati et al. (2012) identify and enrich news entities with semantic linked data from Freebase. In their *hybrid entity-oriented recommender system* they link articles together by means of linked data entities and use these links to suggest related articles to users. As opposed to our system, where entity-linking is used to navigate within a list of recommended articles, their system uses entity links as a recommendation strategy by itself. A slightly different approach is the facets implemented in the news recommender system by Ilievski & Roy (2013). Every article is annotated with a list of hand-crafted hierarchical facets that are subsequently used to model users' interests and preferences. In the result list, recommended articles may be clustered according to these facets to support some high-level drill-down facilities.

USER-COMPOSED RECOMMENDATION STRATEGIES

The SmartMedia mobile news app allows a reader to describe her desired recommendation strategies with reference to how user preferences, time and location should be used to rank news articles. Specifying weights for different recommendation sub-strategies seems too complex for users, but they can decide if a particular sub-strategy should be taken into account or not. And a user may also enter an imaginary context, for example entering a time and location different from the users' current coordinates or using some stereotypical user profile, to retrieve information that cannot be recommended by traditional recommender systems.

Consider the screen shots shown in Figure 2. Initially, the reader is presented a list of recommended articles. These are organized vertically, as seen in Figure 2(a), and the reader can scroll down to find the desired content. Each article is presented with a title, a summary text from the RSS feed and a suitable picture.

At the bottom of the screen in Figure 2(a) there are three non-transparent buttons that the user may use in real-time to compose a hybrid recommendation strategy that fits her contextual preferences. The

Figure 2. (a) Initial list of news stories recommended to a particular reader (b) Configuring the location-based recommendation strategy (c) Deselecting two recommendation strategies

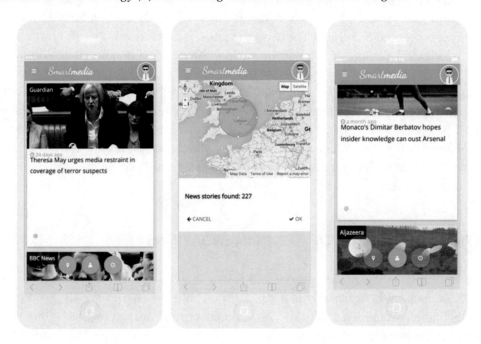

button to the left denotes *location*, the one in the middle stands for *user*, and the one to the right is *time*. Each of them may be active or disabled, and when they are active, there are various ways of configuring the sub-strategy to pursue different goals. Table 1 lists the options available for each button and the corresponding effects on the recommendations generated.

For example, setting the location to Sochi and the date to February 2014 while keeping your own profile, you will be presented personalized news from the Winter Olympics in Sochi.

Table 1. Composing hybrid recommendation strategies

UI button	Configuration	Recommendation Strategy
Location	Active: • Current GPS location • Other location	Locational filtering: Recommendations filtered and ranked according to indicated location
	Disabled	Location not a factor in recommendations
User	Active: • Own profile • Stereotypical profile	Collaborative filtering and content-based filtering: Recommendations filtered and ranked according to own user profile or some chosen static profile
	Disabled	Popularity filtering
Time	Active: • Current date & time • Other date & time	Temporal filtering: Recommendations filtered and ranked according to indicated time
	Disabled	Freshness or time not a factor in recommendations

The default configuration is that all sub-strategies (buttons) are active, where the location is the reader's current GPS location, the time is the current time, and the profile is the system's learned profile of the current reader. Figure 2(b) shows how the user may click the location button to set a different location than her current GPS position. The chosen location is London, and the circle around the capital indicates to what extent events close to London should also be taken into account. With this location, there are 227 articles recommended by the system to the user, and all of these should somehow be related to London and its immediate surroundings. In Figure 2(c) the location and the time buttons have been turned transparent to indicate that these strategies are disabled. This means that recommendations generated by the system now is solely based on the user profile and do not take into account the location of the news or its freshness. The icon in the upper right corner reveals that the reader is in fact not using his own user profile, but has decided to adopt a stereotypical profile built from monitoring the behavior of user clusters.

SEMANTIC EXPLORATION OF RECOMMENDATIONS

An average Norwegian news article is about 220 words and contains 1.6 location names, 2.3 person names and 2.3 organization names (Gulla et al., 2014). These 6-7 entities are all potential themes of the article, though its overall topic may also be some conceptual matters that are rather identified by particular nominal phrases or more complex grammatical structures in the text. We cannot know for sure what the user find intriguing in a particular article, as there is no obvious unambiguous correspondence between article and topic. It is likely, however, that the topic is captured by one or more of the extracted entities or nominal phrases of the article. To provide facilities for retrieving other relevant news on the basis of the current article, it seems reasonable to use the meaning-bearing disambiguated entities as entry points for further exploration of the result set.

The news app is organized around only four views that addresses aggregated versus individual views and article versus entity views, as seen in Figure 3. The aggregated news article view lists all the recommended articles consistent with the recommendation strategy chosen. Clicking on a particular news article opens a new view, the individual article view, that provides the full text of the chosen article together with some meta data. From both these article views, it is possible to swipe right to view extracted disambiguated entities for the chosen article(s). Information about individual entities – like their popularity or sentiment over time – is presented when the entity is chosen. The user may swipe back to the original list of articles, but may also narrow the list of recommended articles by selecting one or more entities and swiping right again to include only those articles from the result set that contain the ticked entities. Repetitive selection of entities in this way help us single out the most relevant articles to read without ever entering a search term or following some hierarchical menu structure.

Figure 4 illustrates how the mobile app is using extracted entities to help the user drill down to her most relevant articles. Originally, the user is looking at an article about the treatment of terrorist suspects in the UK. The extracted disambiguated entities, enriched with semantic information from Wikidata, are *Islamic State of Iraq and the Levant, Nia Griffith, Yvette Cooper, Syria, Theresa May* and *Sky News*. Any combination of these entities may define the user's interest in the article. As the user is primarily interested in the story because of Theresa May, she selects her in the entity view and swipes right to retrieve all articles about Theresa May within her list of recommended articles. Here she views another article involving Theresa May, but the topic here has nothing to do with terrorist suspects. The user now

Figure 3. Readers use gestures to switch between article and entity view of recommended news

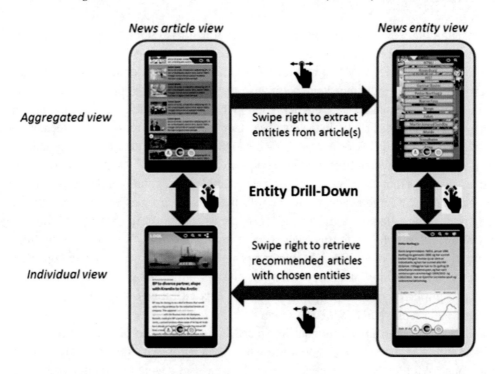

Figure 4. A reader using the entity view to retrieve other relevant news articles in an iterative way

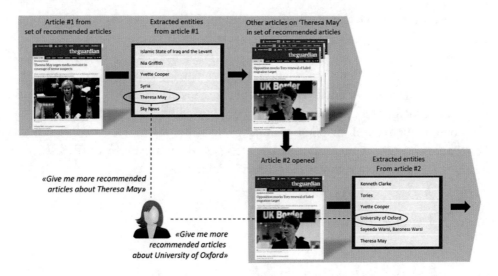

decides to follow another thread related to the last article, selecting the entity *University of Oxford* from the article's list of entities to retrieve recommended articles that are associated with this UK university.

With this approach the user can quickly inspect semantically related articles that are spread across a large set of recommended news articles. The identified entities may also trigger new associations that lend themselves for relevant serendipitous news retrieval.

EVALUATION

The effect of applying exploratory concepts in news recommender systems is hard to measure in controlled experiments. The recommendation strategies do not necessarily change in exploratory systems, but the nature of interaction between system and man is fundamentally altered and the ranked list of recommended articles is not the only important factor any more. Central to the approach is the fact that users do not provide explicit feedback, but are encouraged to view relevant articles and use them actively to find shortcuts to other interested articles in the result set. Consequently, the feasibility of the approach rests on the quality of implicit feedback generated, how it can be mapped onto explicit scores, and the accuracy of the recommendations when these mapped scores are incorporated into the recommendation engine.

Initial tests suggest that users' viewing patterns resemble those found for desktop solutions, in which users can easily browse large result sets to identify the relevant articles and have a number of options for finding interesting follow-up articles. The YOW[6] news data set from Carnegie Mellon University fit this description and was chosen for the evaluation of implicit feedback's value in predicting user scores for collaborative filtering in our SmartMedia app. The YOW data set was collected during a four week time period in 2005, contains 24 users, 5,921 news articles and a total of 10010 rows with several types of explicit and implicit feedback (Zhang, 2005). The explicit ratings range from -1 to 5, of which -1 indicates a missing rating and 5 is the top score.

The collaborative filtering component in SmartMedia makes use of Mahout's singular value decomposition and is kept stable throughout the whole evaluation with mapping implicit feedback into representations useful to the component. The evaluation itself, which is documented in Monsen and Romstad (2014), consists of the following five steps:

- Define a baseline, in which only the explicit scores in YOW are used to generate recommendations with our standard collaborative filtering component.
- Implement mappings from reading times (*TimeOnPage* in YOW) to explicit ratings (*User_like* in YOW) using the techniques correlation, time threshold, naive Bayes, K-Nearest Neighbor, Support Vector Machine, Artificial Neural Network, Clustering, and Multiple Linear Regression. Pairs of TimeOnPage and User_like scores are used to calibrate the mapping.
- For all configurations of all mapping techniques, pass the matrix extended with mapped scores to the recommendation engine and calculate the Root Mean Square Error (RMSE) of the recommendations given by the recommender. RMSE is defined as

$$RMSE = \sqrt{\frac{1}{n}\sum_{i=1}^{n}\left(p_i - r_i\right)^2}$$

where n is the number of predictions, p_i is the predicted score and r_i is the actual score. 10-fold validation with hold-out set is used, and the RMSE is calculated doing 5,000 iterations of each configuration and then returning the mean value

The first observation is that reading times are highly correlated with explicit ratings. As shown in Figure 5(a), longer reading times normally imply higher explicit scores. On average users spend about 63,000 ms (63 seconds) to read articles that were given the score 5, though there were five star articles that were read in less than 30 seconds and others that took more than 120 seconds to view. It seems

Figure 5. (a) Relationship between explicit ratings and reading time (b) Methods for mapping implicit feedback to explicit ratings

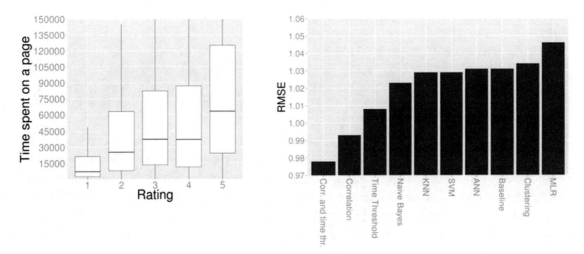

reasonable to assume that people spend more time reading articles that they find interesting. It is worth noting that the range of reading times is longer the more interesting an article is deemed to be. The figure also reveals that the mapping from reading time to explicit rating is not trivial, as a reading time of for example 50,000 ms (50 seconds) can be associated with scores from 2 to 5 in the data set.

In the evaluation we tested a wide range of configurations for each mapping technique and computed an RMSE score for every configuration of every technique. The best RMSE score for each technique is shown in Figure 5(b), which also includes the RMSE score of 1.031 for the baseline estimate with only explicit ratings. As seen from the figure, the best RMSE score is achieved when a correlation measure is combined with a reading time threshold.

The correlation coefficient is a measure of the linear relationship between two variables. The calculated values span from -1 to 1, where -1 represents perfect negative fit and 1 perfect positive fit. The correlation p between two pairs of data is calculated as follows:

$$p = \frac{n\Sigma xy - \left(\Sigma x\right)\left(\Sigma y\right)}{\sqrt{n\left(\Sigma x^2\right) - \left(\Sigma x\right)^2}\sqrt{n\left(\Sigma y^2\right) - \left(\Sigma y\right)^2}}$$

where n is the number of pairs of data. We use the correlation coefficient to find other ratings of an article that correlate sufficiently with the missing one. If we can find at least three other ratings that correlate at least 30% with the missing one, the system generates a pseudo rating for the unrated article by doing a nearest neighbor search with one neighbor.

The reading time threshold method simply assumes that an article is found interesting if the user spends a certain time reading it. Previous research from Parra and Amatriain (2011) and Morita & Shinoda (1994) support this assumption, though the exact reading time threshold can vary somewhat from one application to another. After experimentation with various configurations, the best results were achieved when the correlation and time thresholds were combined as follows:

```
1 Given an article a with a missing rating r for user u.
2 If a has 3 or more ratings & ratings have more than 30% correlation
3 Rating r is set to rating of closest neighbor
4 Else
5 If TimeOnPage for u's reading of a is larger than 25s
6 Rating r set to 4
7 Else
No rating allocated
```

The RMSE score with the configuration above was 0.978. It seems a bit arbitrary to assume that 25 seconds is the borderline between uninteresting and interesting articles, but all computations with different time thresholds, different correlation limits and different prediction methods indicate that a 5 second change of time threshold in either direction leads to at least a 0,2% increase of the RMSE score.

The method above yielded a healthy 5.14% improvement over the baseline estimate. In sum, the evaluation shows that reading times are clearly correlated with users' explicit feedback on her interest in a particular article. Given that some explicit ratings are available for initial calibration and there are not many other ratings to compare with, reading times is an excellent approach for mapping implicit feedback to explicit scores and generating news recommendations. When many correlated ratings are available, however, it seems better to use these correlated ratings to estimate an explicit score. More details about the evaluation experiment itself can be found in Monsen and Romstad (2014). For the exploratory news recommendation concept the evaluation indicates that time spent reading news articles is normally sufficient for inferring user interests in the news domain.

DISCUSSIONS AND CONCLUSION

The experiences with our exploratory news recommendation concept and news app are promising. The active user role seems easy to accept, as it is well supported by specially designed user interface features. No explicit feedback is deemed necessary, and users can concentrate their effort on deciding how recommendations should be generated or how the result set should be traversed.

There is no reason to believe that users prefer the same recommendation strategies in all situations and for all purposes. A user may be interested in other news on a slow weekend than on a busy day at work. Her preferences may be different if she is on the train for a holiday or just on her way to work. This is difficult to deal with in normal recommender systems that build one user profile that should capture all the interests and preferences of the user. Allowing the user to modify and compose her own recommendation strategy, she can easily adapt the strategy to her current situation, and the effect is easier and faster access to relevant news. There is a similar effect from breaking down articles into ranked lists of included news entities that are subsequently used to access other interested news that relate to the same entities and may not be easily found in the long list of recommended articles presented initially. In exploratory search, these entities may help readers narrow down the long list of recommended articles by gradually formulating the set of entities discussed in the desired news articles.

Moreover, reading and checking news articles' content and entities is encouraged, since this allows the user to follow entities to other relevant news stories and inspect news-related information about the entities themselves. In this way reading articles is part of the exploration process that ensures a more consistent and reliable correlation between reading patterns and user interests than what is common for mobile news applications. As discussed above, the increased quality of implicit feedback makes it possible – after some initial calibration of reading times and rating scores – to achieve satisfactory accuracy with reading times as the only feedback to the recommendation engine.

It is so far unclear how the different recommendation sub-strategies should be weighted when combined into a hybrid strategy by a user. The weighting system may need to change from one person to another, and maybe even adapt to the person's current context. We are experimenting with different ways of integrating the sub-strategies, though more work is needed to fully understand how the sub-strategies affect each other. As part of this work we are also investigating news sentiment analysis and its relevance in news recommendation (Liu et al., 2016).

Another issue is the use of stereotypical user profiles in SmartMedia. Analyzing click through logs from media companies, we are able to cluster users together on the basis of their news viewing patterns. Some of these clusters represent easily identifiable user stereotypes, like *sports person* or *technology nerd*, that can be represented as user profiles available to all users of the recommender system. If the user has no history, it may be beneficial to adopt a suitable stereotypical user profile initiate the recommender engine. In the future we will investigate several methods for identifying good user clusters and keeping them updated over time.

Ultimately, we like to analyze news at the level of affected entities. Extracting and disambiguating news entities with linked data is important to understand how news articles are linked together. Initial tests show that semantic disambiguation of location names has had a significant effect on the accuracy of the system. Deep semantic analysis of article entities and their relationship will be addressed further in the years to come, and we expect more semantically motivated features to be added into our mobile news recommender system in the future.

REFERENCES

Amatriain, X., Pujol, J. M., & Oliver, N. (2009) I like it... i like it not: Evaluating user ratings noise in recommender systems. In User Modeling, Adaptation, and Personalization (pp. 247–258). Springer.

Bauernfeind, U., & Zins, A. H. (2006). The Perception of Exploratory Browsing and Trust with Recommender Websites. *Information Technology & Tourism, 8*(2), 121–136. doi:10.3727/109830506778001456

Billsus, D., & Pazzani, M. J. (2000). User Modeling for Adaptive News Access. *User Modeling and User-Adapted Interaction, 10*(2/3), 147–180. doi:10.1023/A:1026501525781

Das, A., Datar, M., Rajaram, S., & Garg, A. (2007). Google News Personalization: Scalable Online Collaborative Filtering. In *Proceedings of the 16th international conference on World Wide Web (WWW'07)* (pp. 271-280). ACM. doi:10.1145/1242572.1242610

Dunietz, J., & Gillick, D. (2014). A New Entity Salience Task with Millions of Training Examples. *Proceedings of the 14th Conference of the European Chapter of the Association for Computational Linguistics*, Gothenburg, Sweden. (Vol. 2, pp. 205–209). doi:10.3115/v1/E14-4040

Fossati, M., Giuliano, C., & Tummarello, G. (2012). Semantic Network-driven News Recommender Systems: a Celebrity Gossip Use Case. In *Proceedings of CEUR Workshop* (pp. 25-36).

Gulla, J. A., Auran, P. G., & Risvik, K. M. (2003). *Linguistics in large-scale web search. In Natural Language Processing and Information Systems.* Springer.

Gulla, J. A., Fidjestøl, A. D., Su, X., & Castejon, H. (2014). Implicit User Profiling in News Recommender Systems. In *Proceedings of the 10th International Conference on Web Information Systems and Technologies (WEBIST'14)* (pp. 185-192).

Gulla, J. A., Ingvaldsen, J. E., Fidjestøl, A. D., Nilsen, J. E., Haugen, K. R., & Su, X. (2013). Learning User Profiles in Mobile News Recommendation. *Journal of Print and Media Technology Research, 2,* 183–194.

Hu, Y., Koren, Y., & Volinsky, C. (2008). Collaborative filtering for implicit feedback datasets. In *Proceedings of the Eighth IEEE International Conference on Data Mining ICDM'08* (pp. 263–272). IEEE. doi:10.1109/ICDM.2008.22

Ilievski, I., & Roy, S. (2013). Personalized news recommendation based on implicit feedback. In *Proceedings of the 2013 International News Recommender Systems Workshop and Challenge (NRS'13)* (pp. 10-15). ACM. doi:10.1145/2516641.2516644

Ingvaldsen, J. E., & Gulla, J. A. (2015). Taming News Streams with Linked Data. In *Proceedings of the IEEE 9th International Conference on Research Challenges in Information Science,* Athens.

Lamche, B., Trottmann, U., & Wörndl, W. (2014). Active learning strategies for exploratory mobile recommender systems. In *Proceedings of the 4th Workshop on Context-Awareness in Retrieval and Recommendation (CARR'14)* (pp. 10-17). ACM. doi:10.1145/2601301.2601304

Liu, J., Dolan, P., & Pedersen, E. R. (2010). Personalized News Recommendation Based on Click Behavior. In *Proceedings of the 15th International Conference on Intelligent User Interfaces (IUI'10)* (pp. 31-40). doi:10.1145/1719970.1719976

Liu, P., Gulla, J. A., & Zhang, L. (2016). Dynamic Topic-Based Sentiment Analysis of Large-Scale Online News. In *Proceedings of the 17th International Conference on Web Information Systems Engineering (WISE)* (Part 2, pp. 3-18). doi:10.1007/978-3-319-48743-4_1

Monsen, D. E., & Romstad, P. H. (2014). *Collaborative Filtering in the News Domain with Explicit and Implicit Feedback* [MSc thesis]. Norwegian University of Science and Technology, Trondheim.

Morita, M., & Shinoda, Y. (1994). Information filtering based on user behavior analysis and best match text retrieval. In *Proceedings of the 17th annual international ACM SIGIR conference on Research and development in information retrieval* (pp. 272–281). Springer-Verlag. doi:10.1007/978-1-4471-2099-5_28

Nieman Journalism Lab. (2015). *New York Times improves its recommendations engine.* Retrieved March 28, 2015, from http://www.niemanlab.org/2013/08/new-york-times-improves-its-recommendations-engine/

Özgöbek, Ö., Gulla, J. A., & Erdur, R. C. (2014). A Survey on Challenges and Methods in News Recommendation. In *Proceedings of the 10th International Conference on Web Information Systems and Technologies (WEBIST'14)* (pp. 278-285).

Parra, D., & Amatriain, X. (2011). Walk the talk: Analyzing the relation between implicit and explicit feedback for preference elicitation. In *Proceedings of the 19th International Conference on User Modeling, Adaption, and Personalization (UMAP'11)* (pp. 255–268). Springer-Verlag. doi:10.1007/978-3-642-22362-4_22

Post, W. (2015). Personalized news launches on washingtonpost.com. *Washington Post*. Retrieved March 28, 2015, from http://www.washingtonpost.com/community-relations/personalized-news-launches-on-washingtonpostcom/2012/02/24/gIQAxjsXXR_story.html

Sandhaus, E. (2008). *The New York Times Annotated Corpus Overview*. The New York Times Company, Research and Development. New York.

Spink, A., & Jansen, B.J. (2004). A Study of Web Search Trends. *Webololy, 1*(2).

Su, X., Özgöbek, Ö., Gulla, J. A., Ingvaldsen, J. E., & Fidjestøl, A. D. (2016). Interactive mobile news recommender system: A preliminary study of usability factors. In *Proceedings of the 11th International Workshop on Semantic and Social Media Adaptation and Personalization (SMAP)* (pp. 71-76). doi:10.1109/SMAP.2016.7753387

Tavakolifard, M., Gulla, J. A., Almeroth, K. C., Ingvaldesn, J. E., Nygreen, G., & Berg, E. (2013). Tailored news in the palm of your hand: a multi-perspective transparent approach to news recommendation. In *Proceedings of the 22nd international conference on World Wide Web companion* (pp. 305–308). doi:10.1145/2487788.2487930

Thurman, N. (2011). *Making 'the daily me': Technology, economics and habit in the mainstream assimilation of personalized news. In Journalism: Theory* (pp. 395–415). Practice & Criticism.

Zhang, Y. (2005). Bayesian graphical models for adaptive filtering. *SIGIR Forum, 39*, 57. doi:10.1145/1113343.1113358

ENDNOTES

[1] http://www.innovasjonnorge.no/

[2] http://www.forskningsradet.no/

[3] https://www.wikidata.org

[4] www.geonames.org

[5] www.statkart.no

[6] The full name of the data set is YOW User Study Data: Implicit and Explicit Feedback for News Recommendation and is found at http://users.soe.ucse.edu/~yiz/papers/data/YOWStudy.

Chapter 2
Beyond Service–Oriented Architectures:
Knowledge Services?

Ghassan Beydoun
University of Technology Sydney, Australia

Alexey Voinov
University of Twente, The Netherlands

Vijayan Sugumaran
Oakland University, USA

ABSTRACT

Predictions for Service Oriented Architectures (SOA) to deliver transformational results to the role and capabilities of IT for businesses have fallen short. Unforeseen challenges have often emerged in SOA adoption. They fall into two categories: technical issues stemming from service components reuse difficulties and organizational issues stemming from inadequate support or understanding of what is required from the executive management in an organization to facilitate the technical rollout. This paper first explores and analyses the hindrances to the full exploitation of SOA. It then proposes an alternative service delivery approach that is based on even a higher degree of loose coupling than SOA. The approach promotes knowledge services and agent-based support for integration and identification of services. To support the arguments, this chapter sketches as a proof of concept the operationalization of such a service delivery system in disaster management.

INTRODUCTION

Service Oriented Architecture (SOA) promotes loose coupling between components to enable faster and more flexible reconfiguration of business processes and provides a means of organizing system resources in an open and flexible way. It promises to avail systems that can easily adjust to changes in business requirements. From an enterprise management perspective, the successful delivery of such systems

DOI: 10.4018/978-1-5225-3686-4.ch002

translates into responsive business processes that can adjust to varying customer service requirements (Demirkan, Kauffman, Vayghan et al., 2008; Erl., 2008). Expected responsiveness and adjustment is based on leveraging the knowledge of relationships between various services and mixing and matching groups of services to satisfy new business requirements. The ability to easily integrate services can increase flexibility and agility not only in systems development but also in business process management. For instance, if an airline company decides to offer a new seating arrangement to create *"a kids free zone"* in their Airbus 380, the airline should be able to do this without having to worry about the software system that manages their ticketing orders. An SOA enterprise system would ensure that the service, which manages orders of this new type of seating, is easy to introduce. It would be composed of services similar to existing services but replacing one or two small service software components.

Attraction to SOA comes with the expectation that energies from software development and acquisition will be shifted to other core business activities, and at the same time deliver better alignment with business requirements (Demirkan, Kauffman, Vayghan et al., 2008). However, predictions for SOA have fallen short (Gartner, 2008). They did not deliver the anticipated transformational results to the role and capabilities of IT for businesses. Recently too, there has been a rapid expansion of publicly available data, mobile apps, web services, and rapid prototyping tools. This creates the potential for new customized services on demand. In this new context, the paper examines the obstacles encountered and argues for a new generation of service delivery systems which can provide effective use of this dispersed, continually and rapidly growing knowledge, and at the same time resolve the obstacles that hindered the take up of SOA.

The adoption of SOA presents two types of challenges: technical ones stemming from service components' reuse difficulties and organizational challenges stemming from inadequate support or understanding of what is required from the executive management (in an organization) to facilitate the technical rollout. The hindrances to the full exploitation of SOA were explored in a special issue of IJIIT in 2013 (Beydoun, Xu, & Sugumaran, 2013). This chapter reviews those hindrances with the further emergence of Web 2.0 services and calls for an alternative approach that harnesses domain knowledge and intelligent systems to deliver more effective service delivery systems.

SOA ADOPTION HINDRANCES

Service-oriented software engineering, with all its promised improvements to business process enablement, in practice has been hard to realize. The transition from requirements to design and implementation is typically fraught with problems. In a service oriented environment, this is further complicated as business requirements are normally developed independently from the services themselves. Services are typically developed by different groups and/or at different organizations from those doing service composition. It is unrealistic to expect that the business requirement models can predict the exact behavior of services required. Indeed, the first barrier to effective SOA adoption is whether customers of the organization are sufficiently understood by the organization to enable packaging of the services in a reusable form. Assuming that this understanding is in place, adequate communication between service component providers and service component users is a must (Elgahwash & Freeman, 2013). This will lead to the development of more relevant service components and evolving them over time. Innovative software development approaches are required to accommodate this continued relationship between service providers and service consumers. A cultural change is required within an organization to create a new level of understanding between consumers and providers of IT services. This is the second barrier to SOA adoption and indeed for some organizations, there is no simple solution to resolve this. It may simply be that the organization is not ready for SOA. This is an issue that is developed in (Abdul-Manan & Hyland, 2013) where a framework to assess the readiness of the company is proposed and validated.

It is very difficult to identify most suitable business services from the various providers and to specify how such a collection of services should be combined and integrated seamlessly. A related challenge is that existing service components do not provide a clear and comprehensive definition of the business process semantics, and therefore many existing services are often isolated and opaque to information system developers. Current software techniques and tools do not alleviate this and place too much burden on developers attempting to reuse existing services. This burden leads developers to opt out of reuse in favor of creating new software components. The result is that, despite its appeal to enable a high degree of flexibility in business process management, many information system developers have been reluctant to adopt SOA because of the high cost of customized service-composition solutions.

It is important to reduce the cost of the composition, service selection and customization efforts. Promising ideas towards this are closing the representation gap of services and the business requirements in order to enhance interoperability of services and enabling better development tools. Services need to be shared between teams of developers and across multiple organizations connected easily. 'Group think' however can hinder this process. This issue is discussed in (Coyle et al., 2013). Intelligent use of the web can also play a significant role in better exploitation of services at both the technical and business level. This is the focus of many researchers in this area, developing Web 2.0 technologies, particularly mash-up applications (Yu, Benatallah, Casati et al., 2008). This enables a single enterprise to use the Web to offer value-added customer services via connection to various services or applications from other public or commercial organizations. Business analysis and early requirements analysis phases need to compensate and be improved. This is an argument promoted by the semantic Web services researchers (Shi, 2008). The semantic richness required to be interwoven within and between services to support the automatic composition is significantly lacking. A key obstacle is the lack of semantic support for agents to evaluate various services and couple them appropriately (Yu, Zhang & Lin, 2007; Lin, Panahi, Zhang et al., 2009). Theories and tools to undertake requirements specification and analysis targeting dynamic environments (changing in response to business needs) are still lacking (Yau, Nong, Sarjoughian et al., 2009). To ensure the success of selection and composition of services, powerful tools that can bridge the gap between business customers and software developers are required. As noted in Coyle et al. (2013), the absence of such tools can lead to human factors hindering the collaboration.

Whilst much effort has gone into enabling adaptive behavior, few have dealt with how to ensure correctness of software before, during and after adaptation. Addressing these concerns has only recently started to receive attention in requirements engineering research. Existing efforts so far recognize that requirements engineering for such systems is not limited to the initial steps of the system development process, but is likely to continue in some form over the entire life cycle of the system. In this issue, (Al-wadain et al., 2013) develops that effort further, by providing a framework to assess the impact of SOA.

Information system developers and individual end users of web services can create integrated solutions by combining distributed services over the Internet. However, there are several issues that such integrators face. For example, some of the integration solution requirements that web services would have to address are: (1) efficiency - to scale on an industrial basis, web service execution must be very efficient; (2) expressiveness - B2B interactions in supply chain scenarios are complex, requiring an expressive set of supported integration concepts; (3) security - interactions within as well as across enterprises must be secured to prevent security attacks of all types, and non-repudiation must be provided for reliable record keeping; (4) reliability - remote and distributed communication must be reliable, and messages must be sent exactly once to ensure dependable interactions; and (5) manageability - inter-enterprise communication changes frequently, requiring easily manageable technology. These requirements pose a high demand on a technology that addresses their implementation (Bose & Sugumaran, 2006).

A service provider needs to consider many aspects of Quality of Service (QoS). Some web services adopt a best-effort QoS policy, which offers no guarantee that requests for services will be accepted (they could just be dropped in case of overload), and no guarantees on response time, throughput, or availability are provided (Bose & Sugumaran, 2006). While this type of policy may be acceptable in some cases, it is totally unacceptable in others, especially when a web service becomes an important part of an application composed of various web services. In these cases, web service providers may want longer-term relationships with users of their services. These relationships generate Service Level Agreements (SLAs), legally binding contracts that establish bounds on various QoS metrics.

Thus, from the consumers' point of view, several hindrances to SOA adoption exist. They include: (1) lack of efficient service provider processes such as metering, accounting, and billing; (2) lack of semantic consistency in business processes; and (3) a lack of workflow management mechanisms to orchestrate a group of specialized web services in support of a single business process. The QoS measure is also observed by web service users. Typically, these users are not human beings but programs that send requests for services to web service providers. QoS issues in web services have to be evaluated from the perspectives of both the providers of web services as well as the users of these services. To support web service management, factors that must be addressed include: WS monitoring, alert and notifications, alarm and traps handling, web services instrumentation at the application level, and web services interoperability with network management protocols. The standards organizations, therefore, are challenged to guide the development of several different standards in order to ease the web services adoption process. SOA cost advantages can be lost by difficulties in reusing existing service software components. An effective service selection platform responsive to changes in a business context is needed. An alternative that is based on intelligent agents that can work with appropriately represented services is proposed. The proposal is not only underpinned by the availability of agents but also appropriately created service interfaces. The proposal is described in the next section.

KNOWLEDGE SERVICES AS AN ALTERNATIVE TO SOA

Reuse problems are very evident where knowledge sharing is required between many organisations and under tight deadlines and pressing conditions of communication, collaboration and coordination (Farber et al., 2015). This is a lesson that has been often learnt again and again in attempts to resolve knowledge reuse to support composition of software components (e.g., Singh, Chopra, Desai, 2009). Identifying the best service component to reuse is difficult, let alone integrating without substantial modification (Erl, 2008). Existing approaches to automating component identification and composition produced very limited practical success. They also exacerbated the gap between the abstractions used to represent the software services and the description of operational services (Ermolayev, Keberle, Plaksin et al., 2004).

Services rich with knowledge tailored the context of request can offer critical support to many complex and knowledge intensive processes. We call such services knowledge services. Their support may be advisory as in say DM, informative as in say for online patient systems, or even encapsulated with a software component to facilitate reuse by a software developer. In other words, the content of services changes as the domain of the operational process changes. However, we observe that through the lens of appropriate abstractions and layering, retrieval systems that identify and deliver various types of knowledge services are doing tasks with the same structure, but with different knowledge content. That is, it is possible to decouple the coordination process in reusing knowledge from various sources from the actual content of the knowledge sources. It is possible to target this coordination process for reuse to streamline the development of knowledge services delivery in various domains.

It is well recognized that past efforts and experiences can be a rich source of guidance and plan formulation in many complex human endeavors and engineering activities e.g. software development, buildings design, environmental planning etc. In disaster management (DM), "lessons learnt" is also an important part of the culture, however the particular risks and the dynamic nature of situations often hinder accurate recording and sharing of past experiences effectively. Indeed, post-mortems of disaster responses often highlight that sufficient knowledge was present but knowledge transfer was insufficient (Bray, 2007). This knowledge coding designed for reuse is, however, difficult to reuse with a sufficient level of contextualizing and integrating with specific domain features of a given disaster. We propose to facilitate such knowledge reuse by first properly delineating knowledge workflow from the domain features, while offering extensive support to integrate both. This will enable reuse and the creation of context driven knowledge services in a cost-effective manner. Creating this approach requires:

1. Understanding of the nature of domain specific knowledge reuse for communication, collaboration and coordination.
2. Modeling techniques for improved representation of operational process requirements and adaptation of knowledge services to effectively underpin these requirements.
3. New methods to rapidly create more effective knowledge services.
4. Improved interfaces to communicate knowledge services to users and translate user requirements into new knowledge services or means to adapt existing knowledge services to changing requirements.

Unlike larger knowledge engineering efforts, which aim to produce a domain independent knowledge base, e.g. IBM's Watson computer system (IBM, 2014), this approach focuses on the reuse of domain specific knowledge. The approach proposed and the concomitant reuse processes are themselves transferrable across different domains and this does not require a constantly growing knowledge base. Previous efforts to produce domain independence were predicated on storing huge amounts of knowledge, which can be prohibitively expensive. A key requirement for the proposed approach is to ensure that reusable components provide a knowledge-based interface that enables a cost-effective integration and adjustment process during reuse. The delivery of knowledge services requires an agile approach using reusable models at design time to enable runtime adjustment and delivery of knowledge services. The knowledge services and the reusable components are tightly coupled as one reusable entity. This idea is not new. Reuse is actually very prominent in software engineering, for example many existing component libraries have good interfaces to index appropriate reusable code e.g. (Biffl et al., 2008; Decker et al., 2005). However, the approach described here is new in freeing users from identifying and integrating a complete set of components, and instead, enabling semi-automatic identification and integration using appropriately represented requirements. A tailored knowledge model provides the response to a knowledge service request.

Leveraging knowledge of relationships between various parts of operational processes, mixing and matching them as needs arise, requires a service delivery system. This delivery system will require a still higher level of loose coupling than a 'service oriented' system (Bieberstein, Bose, Walker et al., 2005). Intelligent agents can query service repositories. Agents themselves are software components capable of autonomous action. They can support the discovery, integration and delivery of knowledge services. As earlier indicated, reuse problems typically arise because reusable components are often developed by different groups and/or different organizations from those reusing and integrating them. Knowledge in the repositories needs enhancement with meta knowledge on how the various knowledge services can interlink. This meta knowledge can provide adequate definitions for both the identification of the process targeted and for the integration and reuse of the knowledge services. In other words, the cost of knowledge customization can be greatly reduced and informed by structural meta knowledge from the repository and by the context queries. The sources of services and how to integrate them can be decided iteratively and incrementally using repositories that are systematically enriched to target reuse.

Many organizations are considering the use of knowledge services for their information systems. In Disaster Management for example, such efforts are supported by government agencies at all three levels of government in Australia. For instance, Emergency Management Australia (EMA) (under the Federal Attorney General's Department) is promoting two modern requirements for managing emergencies described as "all hazard approach" and "all agencies approach". The first recognizes the strong overlap between knowledge requirements of various types of disasters (e.g. evacuation policies are common to bushfires and floods). The second recognizes the frequent need for many agencies to be involved in any one disaster. At the state government level, the State Emergency Services of New South Wales just completed a web portal to educate the public about flood risks in their local areas and to also share flood management plans between different local governments (www.floodsafe.com.au). Other state governments across Australia are also involved in similar efforts. Whilst there is this clear recognition for the need to integrate and share knowledge from different organizations, most efforts (be it in DM or in other sectors) are facing unexpected high integration and maintenance cost. With the support of the Web, the approach can semi-automate the reuse of knowledge components and to streamline the development of new and on-demand knowledge services. The operationalization of this is sketched in the next section with a disaster management domain used to illustrate the key ideas of the approach.

OPERATIONALIZATION OF KNOWLEDGE SERVICES AS AN ALTERNATIVE TO SOA

We target domain specific knowledge services supported by domain knowledge models that can be changed and reassembled in an agile manner. We propose a new development approach of knowledge services delivery systems. In disaster management, an area of significance, the idea can be illustrated using the following scenario:

Tracy is a State Emergency Service (SES) regional commander in New South Wales. She has been given the goal of developing a plan for monitoring and coordinating the evacuation locally in the town of Wagga Wagga as the Murrumbidgee River rises dangerously. At her disposal, are these sources of knowledge: 1. SES Flood Intelligence Cards (FICs), which highlight the impact on properties and people of rising water (gauge levels) at different river locations (which roads are cut, which houses are flooded etc.). The cards also highlight the likelihood of the gauge levels being reached (according to historical data). 2. Flood Emergency Plans drafted by local governments along the river. 3. Situational Reports (SitReps), prepared daily for SES headquarters (HQ) by her predecessor during a previous flood. Tracy must also prepare SitReps during the lead-up and response to the coming flood, on a regular basis. 4. Weather reports estimating water inflow in the river. Using state-of-the-art approaches document management systems, Tracy would sift through the documentation for these services and attempt to make best prediction where the highest evacuation priority is. For instance, the weather reports can be used to predict water flow speed and inflow into the river, the soil data can be used to predict run off rates, while the SitRep show a timeline of events during the previous flood, as reported to her superiors. These in turn combined with FICs historical data, and the resources described in the council plans, can point to the best course of action to evacuate most affected areas first. In this manner, currently hidden but critical relationships between water levels, rainfall, population distribution and resource constraints will be uncovered.

Ensuring that links between all above sources of knowledge are used in Tracy's knowledge analysis is difficult. Identifying many of the links requires the input from external stakeholders (Local Police, Local SES, Local Governments, and possibly potential victims). Our proposal is to integrate domain knowledge into the full cycle of service request-identification-delivery so that Tracy's tasks would consist of three simple steps: (1) specify the requirements in a lightweight and high-level domain language in conjunction with her stakeholders if required; (2) transform these domain models into knowledge requirements using intuitive tools; (3) match the requirements against combinations of existing knowledge services to provide new candidate services. The semantics required to deliver the services need to be available at both, the consumer end to provide sufficient input, and the producer end to give sufficient solutions. By using abstract domain models to explore the implicit interconnectedness between knowledge repositories, knowledge services can be tailored to the consumer of the service. In flood management for example, various Flood Intelligence repositories, local government flood plans, past SitReps and Bureau of Meteorology (BOM) reports will be accessed as one single integrated repository. All knowledge required will be availed to incident controllers when they request the knowledge services (e.g. for plans update or for generating SitReps for SES HQ). Generally, in any DM context, a knowledge service request will depend on the context (requirement) of the incident controller. By describing the requirements appropriately and using semiformal structures, appropriate knowledge components will be identified and reused. There is often a level of standardization available and this will be exploited. For example, in NSW, flood management plans follow a particular template and its use is legislatively mandated (Inan & Beydoun, 2016).

In particular wrapping models and knowledge elements (data, scenarios, etc.) as web services can make them more easily available for reuse and integration with stakeholder mental models (Voinov et al., 2016; Belete et al., 2017). There are developed techniques, which identify and retrieve relevant knowledge to reuse (in the form of ontologies) on the basis of input requirements (Beydoun, Low et al., 2014). In the generic context of knowledge service delivery, the components are simply a set of existing domain models (or ontologies) that can be used. New components or knowledge services can be created by integrating various smaller components using an appropriate domain language. In DM, this can be an existing DM metamodel (DMM) presented in (Othman, Beydoun, & Sugumaran, 2014). The integration of services will be supported by a semiautomatic agent-based process to identify and adjust the selected knowledge components. The decision on which components to reuse will be based on a domain knowledge repository to give a "bird's eye view" of the domain and a dynamic process that relies on data and knowledge exchanges between different repositories. The semi-automated process will be enacted with an intelligent agent-based software tool with access to the large overview of the domain (e.g. the DM metamodel) and dispersed repositories of semantically enriched components.

Towards the successful delivery of knowledge services, each group of knowledge service users will own one or more local repositories of knowledge components (shown in Figure 1 as the sequence of repositories i, j, l, m). The interface between the collective of repositories and the users (i.e. incident controllers in DM, developers in a software development setting, etc.) will consist of a distributed agent-based intelligence across various inter-networked usage sites (shown as the outer circle in Figure 1). This will provide an intelligent interface capable of processing the requirements provided by knowledge service users as input and producing the actual integrated knowledge services as output. The intelligent reuse environment will be adaptive and will consist of a collection of collaborative software agents (implemented as a Multi-Agent System (MAS)) (see Figure 1). Appropriately represented requirements will be used to query the DM plans repository constructed using DMM as a representational foundation. If that does not fulfill the request, external repositories are used. Agents collaborate to respond to the query. The repositories are continuously updated in the process

The first step is to convert DM plans into an intermediate representation that enables easier transfer into shared DMM-based repositories. We identified a set of agent oriented analysis templates to use for the basis for this representation. These agent models are analysis and partial behavioral models. They do not need to be fully detailed as say would be required to build a simulation. Formulating an initial version of the conversion process into the DMM-based repository has been completed in collaboration

Figure 1. Multi-Agent System (MAS) for providing knowledge services for disaster management

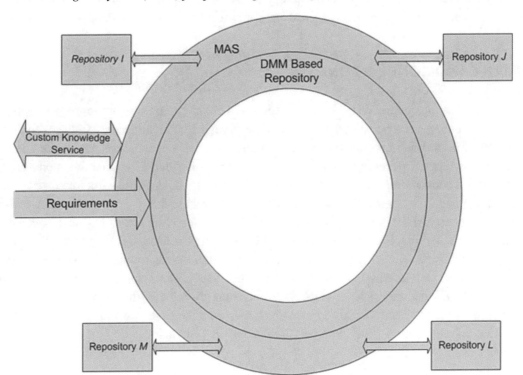

with NSW State Emergency in (Inan, Beydoun, Opper, 2015; Inan, Beydoun, Opper, 2016). In DM, the software agents providing the knowledge services environment (see Figure 1) will process knowledge service requests and provide automatic identification and merging of knowledge delivery components using their semantics.

It is critical to provide adequate semantic support for the software agents to evaluate the knowledge components and to couple them appropriately. Fulfilling a knowledge request involves three phases: The first phase represents the request appropriately as early requirement models. Building on (Miller et al., 2014), early phase requirements can be elicited and modeled using the agent-oriented paradigm. The second phase uses the early requirements models to facilitate the identification of relevant knowledge from existing DM repositories. An ontology-based approach as outlined in (Beydoun, Low et al., 2014) can be deployed. In the third phase, a richer representation of requirement models is produced to enable a software agent to seek out appropriate knowledge components from repositories controlled by other peer agents. During this third phase, when requirements models are submitted to a local agent, the agent extracts an appropriate retrieval ontology to enable it to seek out suitable knowledge components to reuse and integrate. It first uses the retrieval ontology to check its local repository of components. If this is not sufficient, the agent then tries to locate missing knowledge components by communicating with other agents. Throughout, the local repositories maintain a history of responses and requests obtained from other agents and this updated as the agent interacts with others and receives further input from the knowledge users. An agent thus maintains a record of what knowledge components other agents know about as they may be deemed potential candidates to cooperate with in the future (Beydoun, Low, Tran et al., 2011; Xu et al., 2011). Every agent will be guided by a generic reuse procedure. This may describe, for example, appropriate processes for zooming in and out during the search for an appropriate knowledge component. As agents respond to more queries, both their searching processes and their repositories are enhanced. Detecting an incomplete knowledge component is also important. As repositories grow larger, agents will become more effective at successfully responding to knowledge services requests.

SUMMARY AND CONCLUSION

With the rapid development of Web 2.0 technologies and cloud computing, appropriately represented, knowledge components can be shared across multiple organizations connected via the Web. This can lead to better exploitation of knowledge services at both the technical and the business process level. The approach proposed in this paper relies on a knowledge sharing distributed system relying on a collection of intelligent and cooperating software agents that will automate much of the work to create knowledge services on demand. The approach exploits the concept of agency. Interests of users making a knowledge service request will be form the basis on an interactive search process. The search process will also exploit semantic technologies to describe requirements and knowledge components. This can build on recent work on using agent-oriented modeling to elicit requirements for complex systems (Beydoun, Low et al., 2014; Lopez-Lorca et al., 2016; Miller et al., 2014). The resultant reuse environment can also enable service requesters (such as Tracey) to focus on articulating their requirements and ensuring their proper alignment with existing processes rather than the time-consuming task of component identification and integration – an outcome that has not yet been achieved by existing research (Yau, Nong, Sarjoughian et al., 2009).

Existing efforts so far recognize that requirements engineering for intelligent service delivery systems requires a deep effort to collaborate and is not limited to the initial steps of the system development process, but is likely to continue in some form over the entire life cycle of the system (Kumar and Stylianou, 2014). Little work has been done to provide support covering the whole life cycle from requirements to maintenance. The paper proposes a roadmap for customizing knowledge services on demand. The breakthrough will be the effective combination of the innovative semantic mediation techniques, an intelligent reuse environment and an appropriate reuse model to achieve runtime interoperability between knowledge components.

REFERENCES

Abdul-Manan, M., & Hyland, P. (2013). A framework for assessing ESOA Implementation Readiness. *International Journal of Intelligent Information Technologies, 9*(2), 21–37. doi:10.4018/jiit.2013040103

Alwadain, A., Fielt, E., Korthaus, A., & Rosemann, M. (2013). A Comparative Analysis of the Integration of SOA Elements in Widely-Used Enterprise Architecture Frameworks. *International Journal of Intelligent Information Technologies, 9*(2), 54–70. doi:10.4018/jiit.2013040105

Belete, G. F., Voinov, A., & Laniak, G. F. (2017). An overview of the model integration process: From pre-integration assessment to testing. *Environmental Modelling & Software, 87,* 49–63. Retrieved from http://linkinghub.elsevier.com/retrieve/pii/S1364815216308805 doi:10.1016/j.envsoft.2016.10.013

Beydoun, G., Low, G., García-Sánchez, F., Valencia-Garcia, R., & Bejar, R. M. (2014). Identification of Ontologies to Support Information Systems Development. *Information Systems Journal, 46*(November), 45–60. doi:10.1016/j.is.2014.05.002

Beydoun, G., Low, G., Tran, N., & Bogg, P. (2011). Development of a Peer-to-Peer Information Sharing System Using Ontologies. *Expert Systems with Applications, 38*(8), 9352–9364. doi:10.1016/j.eswa.2011.01.104

Beydoun, G., Xu, D., & Sugumaran, V. (2013). Service Oriented Architectures (SOA) Adoption Challenges *International Journal of Intelligent Information Technologies, 9*(2), 1–6. doi:10.4018/jiit.2013040101

Bieberstein, N., Bose, S., Walker, L., & Lynch, A. (2005). Impact of service-oriented architecture on enterprise systems, organisational structures, and individuals. *IBM Systems Journal, 44*(4), 691–708. doi:10.1147/sj.444.0691

Biffl, S., Mordinyi, R., & Moser, T. (2008), Ontology-supported quality assurance for component-based systems configuration. In *Proceedings of the 6th International Workshop on Software Quality*, Leipzig, Germany. ACM. doi:10.1145/1370099.1370113

Bose, R., & Sugumaran, V. (2006). Challenges for Deploying Web Services-Based E-Business Systems in SMEs. *International Journal of E-Business Research, 2*(1), 1–18. doi:10.4018/jebr.2006010101

Bray, D. (2007). *Knowledge Ecosystems: A Theoretical Lens for Organizations Confronting Hyperturbulent Environments. In T. McMaster, D. Wastell, E. Ferneley, and J. DeGross (Eds.), Organizational Dynamics of Technology-based Innovation.* doi:10.1007/978-0-387-72804-9_31

Chen, Z., Liu, Z., Ravn, A. P., Stolz, V., & Naijun, Z. (2009). Refinement and verification in component-based model-driven design. *Science of Computer Programming, 74*(4), 168–196.

Global CCCM Cluster. (2016). The Mend Evacuation Guide, Planning Mass Evacuations in Natural Disasters. Retrieved 1/2017 from http://www.globalcccmcluster.org/system/files/publications/MEND_download.pdf

Coyle, S., Conboy, K., & Acton, T. (2013). Group Process Losses in Agile Software Development Decision Making. *International Journal of Intelligent Information Technologies, 9*(2), 38–53. doi:10.4018/jiit.2013040104

Decker, B., Ras, E., Reck, J., & Klein, B. (2005), Self-organized Reuse of Software Engineering Knowledge supported by Semantic Wikis. In *Proceedings of the Workshop on Semantic Web Enabled Software Engineering*, Galway, Ireland.

Demirkan, H., Kauffman, R., Vayghan, J., Fill, H.-G., Karagiannis, D., & Maglio, P. P. (2008). Service-oriented technology and management. *Journal of Electronic Commerce and Applications, 7*(4), 356–376. doi:10.1016/j.elerap.2008.07.002

Elgahwash, F., & Freeman, M. (2013). Self-Service Technology Banking Preferences: Comparing Libyans Behaviour in Developing and Developed Countries. *International Journal of Intelligent Information Technologies, 9*(2), 7–20. doi:10.4018/jiit.2013040102

Erl, T. (2008). *SOA: Principles of Service Design*. Prentice Hall.

Ermolayev, V., Keberle, N., Plaksin, S., Kononenko, O., & Terziyan, V. (2004). Towards a Framework for Agent-Enabled Semantic Web Service Composition. *International Journal of Web Services Research, 1*(3), 64–87. doi:10.4018/jwsr.2004070104

Farber, J., Myers, T., Trevathan, J., Atkinson, I., & Andersen, T. (2015). Riskr: A web 2.0 platform to monitor and share disaster information. *Int. J. of Grid and Utility Computing, 6*(2), 98–112. doi:10.1504/IJGUC.2015.068825

Gartner. (2008). *27 Technologies in the 2008 Hype Cycle for Emerging Technologies* (Press Releases).

IBM. (n. d.). The Watson Ecosystem. Retrieved January 2016 from http://www-03.ibm.com/innovation/us/watson/

Inan, D., Beydoun, G., & Opper, S. (2015). Towards knowledge sharing in disaster management: An agent oriented knowledge analysis framework. In *Proceedings of the 26th Australasian Conference on Information Systems*, Adelaide, Australia.

Inan, D., Beydoun, G., & Opper, S. (2016). Customising Agent Based Analysis Towards Analysis of Disaster Management Knowledge. In *Proceedings of the 27th Australasian Conference on Information Systems*, Wollongong, Australia.

Kumar, R. L., & Stylianou, A. C. (2014). A process model for analysing and managing flexibility in information systems. *European Journal of Information Systems, 23*(2), 151–184. doi:10.1057/ejis.2012.53

Lopez-Lorca, A., Beydoun, G., Valencia-Garcia, R., & Martinez-Bejar, R. (2015). Supporting agent oriented requirement analysis with ontologies. *International Journal of Human-Computer Studies, 87*, 20–37. doi:10.1016/j.ijhcs.2015.10.007

Miller, T., Lu, B., Sterling, L., Beydoun, G., & Tavetar, K. (2014). Requirements engineering using the agent paradigm: A case study of an aircraft turnaround simulator. *IEEE Transactions on Software Engineering, 40*(10), pp1007–pp1024. doi:10.1109/TSE.2014.2339827

Othman, S., Beydoun, G., & Sugumaran, V. (2014). Development and validation of a Disaster Management Metamodel. *Information Processing & Management, 50*(2), 235–271. doi:10.1016/j.ipm.2013.11.001

Shi, X. (2008). The Challenge of Semantic Web Services. *IEEE Transactions on Intelligent Systems, 23*(2), 5–5. doi:10.1109/MIS.2008.36

Singh, M.P., Chopra, A.K., & Desai, N. (2009, November). Commitment-Based SOA. *IEEE Computer.*

Verma, K., Sivashanmugam, K., Sheth, A., Patil, A., Oundhakar, S., & Miller, J. (2005). METEOR-S WSDI: A scalable infrastructure of registries for semantic publication and discovery of Web services. *Journal of Information Technology Management, 6*(1), 17–39. doi:10.1007/s10799-004-7773-4

Voinov, A., Kolagani, N., McCall, M. K., Glynn, P. D., Kragt, M. E., Ostermann, F. O., & Ramu, P. et al. (2016). Modelling with stakeholders - Next generation. *Environmental Modelling & Software, 77*, 196–220. doi:10.1016/j.envsoft.2015.11.016

Xu, D., Wijesooriya, C., Wang, Y., & Beydoun, G. (2011). Outbound logistics exception monitoring: A multi-perspective ontologies' approach with intelligent agents. *Expert Systems with Applications, 38*(11), 13604–13611.

Yau, S. S., Ye, N., Sarjoughian, H. S., Huang, D., Roontiva, A., Baydogan, M., & Muqsith, M. A. (2009). Toward Development of Adaptive Service-Based Software Systems. *IEEE Transactions on Services Computing, 2*(3), 247-260.

Yu, J., Benatallah, B., Casati, F., & Daniel, F. (2008). Understanding Mashup Development. *Internet Computing, 12*(5), 44–52. doi:10.1109/MIC.2008.114

Yu, T., Zhang, Y., & Lin, K.J. (2007). Efficient Algorithms for Web Services Selection with End-to-end QoS Constraints. *ACM Transactions on the Web, 1*(1).

Chapter 3
A Multi-Label Image Annotation With Multi-Level Tagging System

Kalaivani Anbarasan
Saveetha School of Engineering, India

Chitrakala S.
Anna University, India

ABSTRACT

The content based image retrieval system retrieves relevant images based on image features. The lack of performance in the content based image retrieval system is due to the semantic gap. Image annotation is a solution to bridge the semantic gap between low-level content features and high-level semantic concepts Image annotation is defined as tagging images with a single or multiple keywords based on low-level image features. The major issue in building an effective annotation framework is the integration of both low level visual features and high-level textual information into an annotation model. This chapter focus on new statistical-based image annotation model towards semantic based image retrieval system. A multi-label image annotation with multi-level tagging system is introduced to annotate image regions with class labels and extract color, location and topological tags of segmented image regions. The proposed method produced encouraging results and the experimental results outperformed state-of-the-art methods

INTRODUCTION

Performance is still a long way off from satisfying human expectations in existing image retrieval systems built on high-level semantic representation, owing to the well-known semantic gap. Image descriptions based on semantics can focus on bridging the gap by annotating image objects or events depicted in scenes. The purpose of semantic image description is to retrieve images using a query-by-concept and not a query-by-keyword match or a query-by-low-level feature.

DOI: 10.4018/978-1-5225-3686-4.ch003

The lack of performance in the content based image retrieval system is due to the semantic gap. Image annotation, defined as tagging images with a single or multiple keywords based on low-level image features, is a solution to the issue of the semantic gap. The three types of image annotation approaches are manual, automatic and semi-automatic. Manual image annotation has users annotate images manually. Automatic image annotation annotates images based on low-level image features. Semi-automatic image annotation annotates images automatically with user feedback. The proposed chapter focus on Automatic Image Annotation, Related Work on Multi-Label Image Annotation, Proposed System with its module description, Algorithm of the proposed work. The paper is extended with the results and discussed of the proposed algorithm with the bench mark algorithms and finally the paper is concluded with future extension.

AUTOMATIC IMAGE ANNOTATION

Input images are automatically annotated into a set of pre-defined concepts representing objects or regions and are most suitable for image understanding. The automatic image annotation system accepts images as inputs and the system automatically annotates them without human intervention. Much research (Chih-Fong Tsai, 2012; Fu Hao, 2012; Pandya & Shah, 2014; Siddiqui et al., 2015) has progressed in the area of automatic image annotation based on a single / multiple concepts for a whole image or region of interest.

The process of describing image contents comprises region choosing, feature extraction and feature quantization. Region choosing can be done with any of these methods: fixed partition, segmentation and region saliency. Features are extracted from image regions and the pixel value of each region condensed into feature values. Features can be global or local, depending on the image region as a whole or a segmented image region. Image features extracted can be general or domain-specific. Feature quantization maps feature values of continuous spaces transformed into discrete spaces, and the entire process is shown in Figure 1.

The three types of semantics-based image annotation are manual, automatic and semi-automatic. Manual and semi-automatic annotation involves manual intervention whereas automatic annotation annotates images automatically without human involvement. Automatic image annotation involves attaching image semantics to the test image based on the trained annotation model. Semantic image description is better option, owing to the following reasons.

- Computational cost is reduced due to semantic similarity rather than visual similarity.
- Image retrieval is based on semantic matching, rather than visual matching, for a user input query image.
- A semantic description is better for image understanding than a visual feature image description.

Figure 1.Semantics based image description model

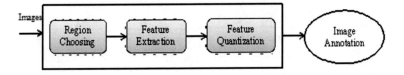

Image annotation is a solution to bridge the semantic gap between low-level content features and high-level semantic concepts (Yang et al., 2011; Yildrim, 2013; Jisha, 2013). The purpose of annotation is to assign relevant keywords to an image to improve image retrieval accuracy, reducing irrelevant images in image retrieval systems.

MULTI-LABEL IMAGE ANNOTATION APPROACHES

Automatically annotating images with multiple concepts is treated as a multi-class classification problem. Multi-label image annotation approaches are classified into statistical and machine learning approaches. Statistical approaches are further classified into parametric and non-parametric approaches, based on the way in which conditional probabilities are used. Machine learning approaches are used to assign semantic labels to images automatically through a supervised or unsupervised classifier. The classification of multi-label image annotation approaches is shown in Figure 2.

RELATED WORK

The statistical method is popularly used in the literature for automatic multi-label image annotation, and is further classified into parametric and non-parametric approaches (Cai et al., 2014; Yavlinsky et al., 2005; Raja et al., 2012), based on the way conditional probabilities are used. Various models that have originated include the co-occurrence model (Mori et al., 1999), machine translation model (Duygulu et al., 2002), cross-media relevance model (Jeon et al., 2003; Moran & Lavrenko, 2011; Sun et al., 2012; Deljooi & Moghaddam, 2012), continuous space relevance model (Lavrenko et al., 2003), multiple Bernoulli relevance model (Feng et al., 2004), and dual cross-media relevance model (Jing Liu et al. 2007). The Gaussian mixture model (Li & Wang, 2007; Carneiro et al., 2007; Wang et al., 2009; Yang et al., 2009) and its variations are proposed by researchers under the non-parametric statistical approach. Issues with the statistical parametric model comprise:

Figure 2. Classification of multi-label image annotation approaches

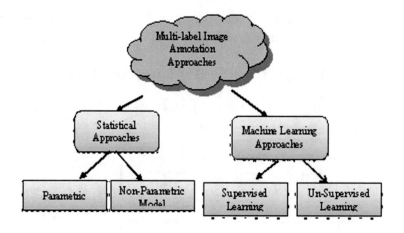

- Training set dependency
- Scalability
- Semantic gap
- Annotation performance

Issues with non-parametric models are that:

- The assumed feature distribution may be incorrect
- No correlation exists between concepts

Machine learning approaches are used to assign semantic labels to images automatically through a supervised or unsupervised classifier. Supervised machine learning classifiers are support vector machines, artificial neural networks, rule-based and decision tree classifiers. Unsupervised machine learning classifiers are clustering classifiers based on the Gaussian mixture model and its variants.

Automatic image annotation based on the supervised SVM classifier (Li & Sun, 2008; Lu, 2009; Li et al., 2010; Mao et al., 2013; Reshma et al., 2014; Chu et al., 2014) leads to class imbalance problems which degrade the quality of the classifier. The accuracy of the neural network classifier (Frate et al., 2007; Huang et al., 2013; Dabhi & Prajapati, 2014; Bahrami & Abadeh, 2014; Chu et al., 2014; Savita et al., 2013) depends on the number of neurons and hidden layers, neuron activation function, training time and lack of transparency. The decision tree classifier (Wan, 2011; Patil & Kolhe, 2014) is simple to understand yet unsuitable for high-dimensional feature vectors. The major issues to be addressed in the use of unsupervised clustering classifiers (Nasierding et al., 2009; He et al., 2010, Daniela Stan & Ishwar K Sethi et al. 2001; Raja 2012) are high performance and that they are scaled to work towards concept-based image retrieval.

It is observed from the literature that:

- The major issue is building an effective annotation framework. The integration of both low-level visual information and high-level textual information into an annotation model is a challenge.
- In most image retrieval systems, annotation and ranking are done simultaneously. Both can be done offline to improve image retrieval accuracy.
- The question of how to use an efficient similarity measure based on image conceptual semantic representation between images is still open.

All the variations mentioned above in automatic image annotation demand the development of new methods to address the said issues. With this in view, a new statistical-based automatic image annotation algorithm is proposed. An automatic Multi-Label Image Annotation with Color and Spatial Tags (MLIA-CSTAG) system introduced to annotate image regions with class labels and extract color, location and topological tags of segmented image regions. Since the images are annotated with multiple-level tagging, it helps retrieve relevant images based on image semantics, along with color, spatial location and topological tags.

AN AUTOMATIC MULTI-LABEL IMAGE ANNOTATION WITH COLOR AND SPATIAL TAG GENERATION (MLIA-CSTAG) SYSTEM

The automatic image annotation technique is used to reduce the semantic gap by assigning semantic labels to images automatically based on image features, in turn helping retrieve relevant images based on image semantics. This thesis has been motivated to derive color and spatial image property tags, along with image semantics, for better understanding of images. A statistical model-based automatic image annotation methodology is proposed to annotate images with multiple labels, along with color and spatial tags.

During offline processing, training database images are segmented automatically into several regions. Optimal visual features are extracted to build a visual feature space for every segmented region. Image region signatures are formed from the feature vector by clustering similar image regions and calculating the cluster centroid. The annotation model is built, based on the maximum probability of the non-parametric earth mover's distance kernel density estimator of the training image signatures. During online processing, when a user inputs a query image, the test image is initially segmented into multiple regions. A visual feature space is constructed from optimal features extracted from segmented regions. Regional automatic image annotation is done by annotating the test image region with the closest word in the semantic space.

Color tags are assigned to segmented image regions, based on the color naming system of 10 basic colors, to produce 93 semantic color names. The color naming system is based on a normalized mean HSV where H is quantized into 10 bins, S into 4 bins and V into 4 bins. Color semantics tags are assigned to segmented objects or regions based on the normalized H value for the base color, along with S and V values to produce color adjectives.

Spatial tags are generated based on the location tag which establishes an object's position, while the topological tag identifies the relationship of the object to regions in the image. Image sizes are partitioned into 3* 3 blocks and the centroid of each block calculated. The location tag of the object is identified, based on the maximum centroid. Topological relationship tags are generated to identify the spatial relationship of image objects with image regions based on fuzzy membership values. So, for a given image, multi-label image annotation is done with color and spatial tag generation.

MLIA-CSTAG SYSTEM DESCRIPTION

In this section, the processing of the proposed MLIA-CSTAG methodology is presented. The aim of the chapter is to build an automatic image annotation system which is able to annotate images with multiple labels and also annotate segmented image regions with color, location and topological tags.

The MLIA-CSTAG method follows the automatic image annotation approach and comprises the following processes: multi-label image annotation, color tag generation and spatial tag generation. The multi-label image annotation process is used to assign class labels to segmented regions based on the proposed statistical annotation model. The color tag generation process assigns color semantics to segmented image regions. Spatial tag generation identifies the object's location and spatial relationship between image objects and image regions. The process involves the assignment of spatial semantics such as location tags and topological tags to segmented image regions.

During offline processing, training database images are segmented automatically into several regions. Optimal visual features are extracted to build a visual feature space for every segmented region. Image region signatures are formed from the feature vector by clustering similar image regions and calculating the cluster centroid. The annotation model is built, based on the maximum probability of the non-parametric earth mover's distance kernel density estimator of the training image signatures. During online processing, when a user inputs a query image, the test image is initially segmented into multiple regions. A visual feature space is constructed from optimal features extracted from segmented regions. Regional automatic image annotation is done by annotating the test image region with the closest word in the semantic space.

The block diagram of the proposed methodology for multi-label image annotation is shown in Figure 3. The preprocessing technique of segmenting the color image into multiple regions, as well as extracting optimal features from the segmented regions, is done in the previous phase. Features from the extracted image regions are used to form region signatures.

The preprocessing technique segments the color image into multiple regions and optimal features are extracted. Features from the extracted image regions are used to form region signatures to build the statistical annotation model.

Image Signatures Formation

An image signature is a representation of clustered data defined as $s = \{(c_1, m_1), \ldots, (c_d, m_d)\}$, where c_i is the cluster centroid for cluster i and m_i the mass (number of points) belonging to that particular cluster. Given two such signatures, the earth mover's distance (EMD) is defined as the minimum amount of work required to transform one signature into another. Yossi Rubner et al. (1998) reported that using the EMD on images outperforms traditional distance measures applied to high-dimensional feature spaces.

Given a set of images $I = \{i_1, I_2, \ldots i_n\}$ in the training set, all images in I are segmented into a collection of image regions $R = \{r_1, r_2, \ldots r_n\}$. If $W = \{w_1, w_2, \ldots w_n\}$ is the set of words associated with all images in the training set and D the distinct feature vector extracted from the region, the image regions are represented by a set of feature vectors given by Equation (1).

$$Ri = dij \ , \ i \ \left(1, 2, ..n\right); j \ \left(1, 2, \ldots m\right) \tag{1}$$

Figure 3. MLLA-CSTAG system architecture

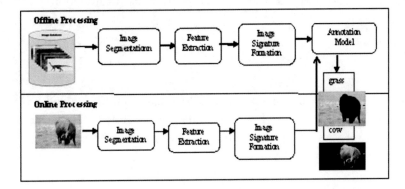

All image regions are thereafter grouped in a K class where those with the same label are clustered into the same category. For all image regions in the kth category, the cluster median centroid is computed and denoted as C_{km} which represents the kth category cluster centroid of m feature descriptors.

Image Annotation Model

Automatic image annotation is a recent alternative to querying a database of natural images based on image content specified by keywords or natural language. This facility helps the user search large collections of image repositories. The image annotation model assigns a word, based on Bayes' theorem, to image regions. The probability of assigning a word 'w' to an image region is given by Equation (2).

$$p\left(w|x\right) = \frac{\left(f\left(x|w\right)p\left(w\right)\right)}{f\left(x\right)} \tag{2}$$

where f(x) is the probability density of image x and f (x|w) is defined as the density of x conditional upon the assignment of annotation word 'w'. To build the annotation model, a sample T_w of training images with each label w is collected and formed as a training set. The densities f (x|w) will be modeled based on image representation. The two major image representations used are vectors and signatures of image features. The choice of representation is based on density, separable for different annotation classes. Density can be estimated, based on parametric or nonparametric forms. The former is based on prior knowledge, whereas the latter makes no prior assumptions about density.

The simplest empirical nonparametric estimator of a distribution function is the kernel smoothing function proposed by Parzen (1962) is used to improve the efficiency of finite samples. If x is a feature vector of real-value image features, the kernel estimate is given by Equation (3).

$$fw\left(x\right) = \frac{1}{nC}\sum_{i=1}^{n}k\left[\frac{\left(x - xw\right)}{h}\right] \tag{3}$$

Friedman et al. (1984) pointed out that kernel smoothing may be less effective in high-dimensional spaces due to problems with the curse of dimensionality. Consequently, image signatures under the earth mover's distance (EMD) measure are considered better reported by researchers (Yossi Rubner, 1988), and find applications in image retrieval. The EMD for kernel density estimation is given by Equation (4).

$$KE\left(s, si; h\right) = \frac{1}{h}e^{-\left(d\left(s,si\right)/h\right)} \tag{4}$$

where d(s, s$^{(i)}$) is the EMD between signatures s and s$^{(i)}$ and h the kernel bandwidth. The Bayesian model is reframed, based on kernel estimates. The probability density function, based on image signature, is specified in Equation (5) to assign the probabilities of a word w to a test image for transferring a word 'w' to the image region.

$$f\left(s \mid w\right) = \frac{1}{\left|Tw\right|} \sum_{s \in Tw} KE\left(s, si; h\right) \tag{5}$$

The prior probability p(w) of the word w is given by Equation (6)

$$p\left(w\right) = \frac{\left|Tw\right|}{\sum_{w} \left|Tw\right|} \tag{6}$$

where $|T_w|$ is the size of the training sample for the word w.

Tags provided by users can be grouped into content-related and context-related tags. However, content-related tags specify what appears in the image but lack information on how and where they appear. So then, property tags are used to restrict tags from the basic level to the subordinate level. Images indexed by property tags support refined and precise queries. Different tags assigned to segmented image regions include color, location and topological ones.

Color Tag Generation

The semantic-based image retrieval system can be developed by adding color names to segmented image regions. Although millions of colors can be defined in a computer system, those that can be named by users are limited. A color naming model (Krishnan et al., 2007; Li et al., 2007) relates numerical color spaces with the semantic color names used in natural language. Ying Liu et al. (2005) proposed a color naming method which maps the HSV color space into 93 semantic color names. By defining a color name for each segmented region. The system relates low-level HSV color features into high-level semantics by defining a color name for the segmented region. The color semantics can be later used by the SBIR system to retrieve images based on color semantics, alongside image semantics.

The color naming system initially segments an image into homogenous regions and a semantic color name is defined, using the system. After segmentation, each region is described by the average HSV value as the color feature of the region, following which the average HSV value is converted into a semantic color name.

The color naming procedure is as follows. Segmented image regions are converted into HSV color space. First, hue, saturation and value are normalized in the range [0-1]. The hue value is usually quantized into a small set of about 10 base colors such as violet, purple, red, orange, yellow, green, aqua, aquamarine, blue and magenta (Conway, 1992). Saturation and value are quantized into 4 bins respectively as adjectives, signifying the saturation and luminance of the color, and describe the color naming model as shown in Table 1. Asterisks in the table indicate special cases of gray, white and black. A dash indicates that there is no modifying adjective. Thus, we obtain a set of 10*3*3+3=93 semantic color names obtained by combining base color names with their adjectives.

Location Tag Generation

The key issue in semantic content extraction is the representation of semantic content. Researchers have studied semantic content representation from different perspectives and a simple representation is no more

Table 1. Color naming model

S.Nos.	Normalized HSV Value	Base Color Name	H adjectives	V adjectives
1.	0-0.1	orange	*	*
2.	0.1-0.2	yellow	pale	dark
3.	0.2-0.3	green		
4.	0.3-0.4	aqua		-
5.	0.4-0.5	aquamarine		
6.	0.5-0.6	Blue	-	
7.	0.6-0.7	Violet		
8.	0.7-0.8	Purple		
9.	0.8-0.9	magenta	pure	bright
10.	0.9-1.0	red		

(Source: Ying Liu et al. 2005)

than relating an image with low-level features. The effective use of spatial relations can achieve reliable image recognition. Spatial tags generated for the segmented regions are location and topological tags.

A location tag tells where the target object appears in the image. Location descriptors are assigned to the image objects. Each segmented image region is partitioned into 3-by-3 equal grids, and each grid corresponds to one location tag, as shown in Table 2, and nine location tags are specified. The location tag for the image objects is assigned according to the grid in which the centroid of its corresponding image region falls.

Topological Tag Generation

Topological spatial relations (Hollink et al., 2004, Muda et al., 2009, Shivakumar, 2013) depict relationships between image objects and image regions. For an image I, there can be an object as well as a region instance, represented by a minimum bounding rectangle R with an upper left-hand corner point represented with Pul, in which the length and width of region are stored. The area inside R_i is represented by R_i^α, where the edges of Ri are represented by R_i^β.

Topological relation types specified by Yakup Yildrim et al. (2013) are inside, partially inside, touches and disjoint. Membership values of the topological relationship are calculated by using Equation (6.7).

$$\mu top\left(Ri, Rk\right) = \frac{\left(Ri\alpha \,\hat{}\, Rk\alpha\right)}{Rk\alpha} \qquad (7)$$

Table 2. Image grid for location tag

top-left	above	top-right
left	center	right
bottom-left	Below	bottom-right

where $\mu_{top}(R_i,R_k)$ represents the topological relationship between image objects and image regions. The criteria on which the topological relationships exist are listed in Table 3.

MLIA-CSTAG Algorithm

The motivation for the algorithm is to assign class labels to the segmented image regions. This thesis aims to design an automatic multi-label image annotation algorithm, thereby improving image understanding and helping users retrieve images based on image semantics.

The pseudo code for automatic multi-label image annotation is shown in Table 4 and the notation explanation is listed below.

RS_{trim} : Regions signatures for training images

RS_{tsim} : Regions signatures for test images

IA_{im} : Class label assignment to segmented image regions

NHSV : Normalized HSV color component

$CT_{im:}$ Color Tag to segmented image regions

Table 3. Criteria for the generation of topological tags

Topological Tag	Criteria
inside	$\mu top\left(Ri, Rk\right) = 1$
partially inside	$0 < \mu top\left(Ri, Rk\right) < 1$
disjoint	$\mu_{top}(R_i,R_k) = 0 \wedge (R_i^{\beta} \wedge R_k^{\beta}) = 0$
touches	$\mu_{top}(R_i,R_k) = 0 \wedge (R_i^{\beta} \wedge R_k^{\beta}) <> 0$

Table 4. Pseudo code for automatic image annotation using the MLIA-CSTAG

MLIA-CSTAG(Q,R,F)
Input
Q- Query Image, R – Segmented Image Regions
F - Feature Vector of optimal color, texture and shape features
Output
Multi Label Image Annotation - A'
```
1:  RS_trim = F(c1:m1); : : : ; (cd:md)        // RS - Region Signature
2:  RS_tsim=F(c;m)             // Region Signature for test image
```
3: $f(s|w) = \frac{1}{|Tw|}\sum_{s \in Tw} KE(s, si; h)$
```
4:  CT_im= max(NHSV_m) // Image Color Tag Generation
5:  LT_im= max(C_m)        //  Image Location Tag Generation
6:  TT_im= MVr,o         //  Region and object spatial relationship
7:  MLIA_im = IA_im + CT_im + LT_im + TT_im
8:  return (MLIA_im)
```

C_m : Centroid of image block 3*3

LT_{im} : Location Tag to segmented image regions

MVr,o : Spatial relationship membership value of image regions and image objects

TT_{im} : Topological Tag to segmented image regions

$MLIA_{im}$: Multi-Label Image Annotation

This MLIA-CSTAG algorithm has been tested over 300 images which have been gathered from the sites of several research group such as Microsoft Research Cambridge Object Recognition, NUS-Wide Image Data Set and Corel Image Data Sets. The detailed description of the image data sets used as a training set for building the annotation model are listed in Table 5 and the test set to evaluate the model are listed in Table 6.

RESULTS AND DISCUSSION

The annotation model is built on the training set and region signatures are formed for each category of image class labels. The system has been tested on varied sets of segmented images with multiple regions,

Table 5. Training set image description

Attributes	Features
Total Number of Images Trained	300
Image Category	Set 1: 27 (cowgrass) Set 2: 58 (goatgrass) Set 3: 90 (horsegrass) Set 4: 33 (birdgrass) Set 5: 65 (birdsky) Set 6: 18 (cowgrasssky) Set 7: 9 (goatgrasssky)
Image Type	JPEG
Image Dimension	varying

Table 6. Test set image description

Attributes	Features
Total Number of Images Tested	70
Image Category	Set 1: 15 (cowgrass) Set 2: 11 (goatgrass) Set 3: 11 (horsegrass) Set 4: 9 (birdgrass) Set 5: 11 (birdsky) Set 6: 7 (cowgrasssky) Set 7: 6 (goatgrasssky)
Image Type	JPEG
Image Dimension	varying

multiple objects, shadow objects and occluded objects. A graphical user interface for the automatic multi-label image annotation system is shown in Figure 4.

Sample images annotated by the proposed system are shown in Table 7.

The semantic-based image retrieval system can be developed by adding color names to the segmented image regions. The color naming system initially segments the image into homogenous regions. For each region, a semantic color name is defined and a GUI screen for generating color tags is shown in Figure 5.

Location tag assigned to the image object appear in the segmented image. Location tags for image objects are assigned according to the image grid in which the centroid of its corresponding image region falls.

Figure 4. A GUI screen for automatic multi-label image annotation

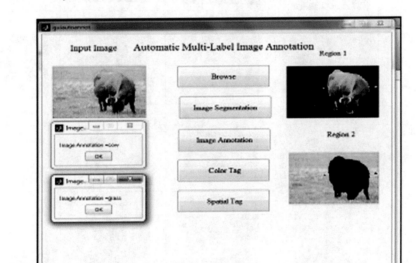

Figure 5. A GUI screen to generate color tag

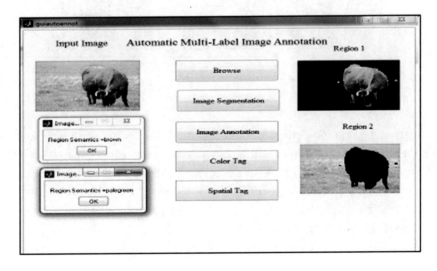

Table 7. Sample images with image semantics

S.Nos.	Input Images	Segmented region 1 semantics	Segmented region 2 semantics	Segmented region 3 semantics
1.		bird	grass	-
2.		bird	sky	-
3.		cow	sky	grass
4.		goat	grass	-
5.		goat	grass	sky
6.		goat	grass	-

The topological spatial relation depicts the relationship between image objects and image regions. For an image I, there can be an object as well as a region instance, represented by a minimum bounding rectangle R with an upper left-hand corner point represented by pul, wherein the length and width of region are stored. The diverse topological relations are inside, partially inside, touches and disjoint, generated based on membership values. A GUI screen for the generation of spatial tags, such as location and topological tags, is shown in Figure 6.

Figure 6. A GUI screen to generate spatial tags

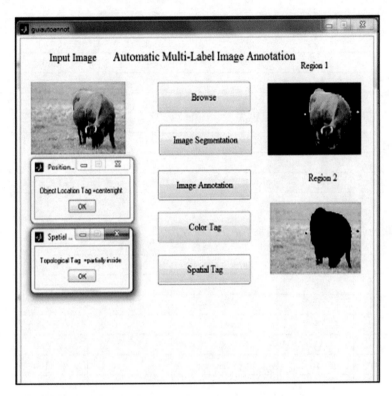

Samples of 70 test images are tested with the proposed algorithm to generate image semantics, and the test image results listed in Table 8. The performance measure of correctly classified instances (CCI) for the test image chosen constitutes 87% and incorrectly classified instance (ICCI) 13%.

Test images are tested in the proposed algorithm for the generation of color, location and topological tags from the segmented regions, and the results given in Tables 9 – 11.

The proposed method generates image descriptions based on image semantics, image color, image object location and the spatial relationship between image objects and image regions. A comparative

Table 8. Test images accuracy measures for image annotation

Images Group	Total Images	Correct Label	In-correct Label	CCI (%)	ICCI (%)
cowgrass	15	13	2	86.67	13.33
goatgrass	11	8	3	72.72	27.27
birdgrass	9	9	-	100	-
birdsky	11	8	3	72.72	27.27
horsegrass	11	10	1	90.90	9.09
cowgrasssky	7	7	-	100	-
goatgrasssky	6	6	-	100	-
Total	70	61	9	87.14	12.86

Table 9. Test images accuracy measures for color tag generation

Images Group	Total Images	Correct Label	In-correct Label	CCI (%)	ICCI (%)
cowgrass	13	11	2	84.62	15.38
goatgrass	8	8	-	100	-
birdgrass	9	7	2	77.78	28.57
birdsky	8	8	-	100	-
horsegrass	10	9	1	90	10
cowgrasssky	7	4	3	57.14	42.86
goatgrasssky	6	5	1	83.33	16.67
Total	61	52	9	85.25	14.75

Table 10. Test images accuracy measures for location tag

Images Group	Total Images	Correct Label	In-correct Label	CCI (%)	ICCI (%)
cowgrass	13	13	-	100	-
goatgrass	8	8	-	100	-
birdgrass	9	9	-	100	-
birdsky	8	8	-	100	-
horsegrass	10	10	-	100	-
cowgrasssky	7	7	-	100	-
goatgrasssky	6	5	1	83.33	16.67
Total	61	60	1	98.36	1.64

Table 11. Test images accuracy measures for topological tag

Images Group	Total Images	Correct Label	In-correct Label	CCI (%)	ICCI (%)
cowgrass	13	10	3	76.92	23.07
goatgrass	8	7	1	87.5	12.5
birdgrass	9	8	1	88.89	22.22
birdsky	8	7	1	87.5	12.5
horsegrass	10	8	2	80	20
cowgrasssky	7	5	2	71.43	28.57
goatgrasssky	6	5	1	83.33	16.7
Total	61	50	11	81.97	18.03

performance analysis of image semantic descriptions generated by the proposed method is shown in Figure 7. The proposed method works better for test images to generate image semantics, color tags, location tags and topological tags from the segmented image regions. The location tag performs better when compared with other image semantic generation methods. The topological tag turns in a diminished performance

Figure 7. Comparison of accuracy measures of MLLA-CSTAG algorithm

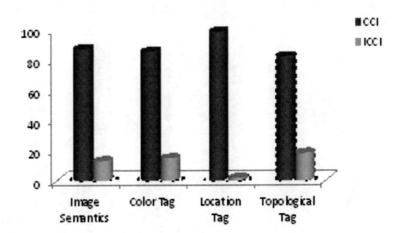

as a result of the minimum bounding rectangle not being formed for the entire image region, coupled with the fact that the wrong semantics often produce disjoint relations through the objects in the region.

The proposed algorithm for image annotation is compared with four benchmark learning algorithms, such as the J48, Function Tree, Simple Logistics and JRip (Witten & Frank, 2000) to evaluate the accuracy of the selected subset features. F-score measure and root mean square error are calculated for all datasets and their values listed in Table 12. These measures are estimated using the ten-fold cross-validation method.

A comparative performance analysis of the proposed method with other benchmark learning algorithms is depicted in Figure 8. The proposed method outperforms the others with better accuracy and reduced error measures.

CONCLUSION

In this chapter, a statistical-based automatic multi-label image annotation algorithm is proposed along with color, location and topological tags. The proposed method produced encouraging results and the

Table 12. Comparison of performance measures for MLIA-CSTAG and other methods

Classifiers	Measures			
	Precision	Recall	F-Score	RMSE
Proposed -MLIA	89.2	93.4	91.24	0.18
J48	74.6	74.5	74.5	0.28
Function Tree	81.6	82.3	81.9	0.21
Simple Logistics	81.7	82.8	82.1	0.20
JRip	70.1	73	71	0.27
IB1	75.6	75.5	75.5	0.29

Figure 8. Bar chart for performance measures comparison of MLLA-CSTAG and other methods

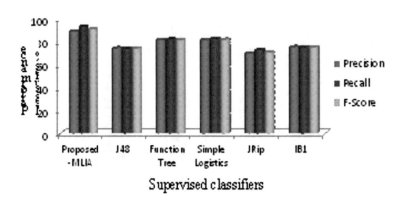

experimental results outperformed state-of-the-art methods. The results indicated that our methodology has the efficiency to annotate segmented image regions correctly and also generates color and spatial tags. The major benefits addressed by the proposed MLIA-CSTAG algorithm works for multiple types of segmented images with multiple objects, multiple regions, occluded objects and shadow objects. The use of semantic labeling helps to reduce semantic gap. Annotated images with color and spatial tags are useful to index image databases based on image semantics. Image repositories occupy minimal memory and retrieval speed is improved with reduced computation.

REFERENCES

Patil, M. P., & Kolhe, S. R. (2014). Automatic Image Annotation Using Decision Trees And Rough Sets. *International Journal of Computer Science and Applications*, *11*(2), 38–49.

Bahrami, S., & Saniee Abadeh, S. (2014). Automatic Image Annotation Using an Evolutionary Algorithm. In *Proceedings of the 7th International Symposium on Telecommunications* (pp. 320-325). doi:10.1109/ISTEL.2014.7000722

Cai, Y. Y., Mu, Z. C., Ren, Y. F., & Xu, G. Q. (2014). A Hybrid Hierarchical Framework for Automatic Image Annotation. In *Proceedings of the IEEE International Conference on Machine Learning and Cybernetics*, Lanzhou (pp. 30-36).

Carneiro, G., Chan, A. B., Moreno, P. J., & Vasconcelos, N. (2007). Supervised Learning of Semantic Classes for Image Annotation and Retrieval. *IEEE Transactions on Pattern Analysis and Machine Intelligence*, *29*(3), 394–410. doi:10.1109/TPAMI.2007.61 PMID:17224611

Chu, G., Niu, K., & Tian, B. (2014). Automatic Image Annotation Combining SVMS and KNN Algorithm. In *Proceedings of the IEEE 3rd International Conference on Cloud Computing and Intelligent Systems* (pp. 13-17).

Dabhi, A., & Prajapati, B. (2014). A neural network model for automatic image annotation refinement. *Journal Of Emerging Technologies And Innovative Research, 1*(6), 561-564.

Witten, I. H., Frank, E., Hall, M. A., & Pal, C. J. (2000). *Data Mining, Practical Machine Learning Tools and Techniques* (2nd ed.). Morgan Kaufmann Publisher.

Deljooi, H., & Amir, M. E. M. (2012). Automatic Image Annotation via the Statistical Semantic Model Based on the Relationship between the Regions. In *Proceedings of the 16th CSI International Symposium on Artificial Intelligence and Signal Processing* (pp. 101-106).

Duygulu, P., Barnard, K., Freitas, J., & Forsyth, D. (2002). Object Recognition as Machine Translation Learning a Lexicon for a fixed image vocabulary. In *Proceedings of the 7th European Conference on Computer Vision* (pp. 97-112). doi:10.1007/3-540-47979-1_7

Feng, S., Mammatha, R., & Lavrenko, V. (2004). Multiple Bernoulli Relevance Model for Image and Video Annotation. In *Proceedings of the IEEE Computer Society Conference on Computer Vision and Pattern Recognition* (pp. 1002-1009). doi:10.1109/CVPR.2004.1315274

Frate, F. D., Pacific, F., Schiavon, G., & Solimini, C. (2007). Use of neural networks for automatic classification from high resolution images. *IEEE Transactions on Geoscience and Remote Sensing, 45*(4), 800–809. doi:10.1109/TGRS.2007.892009

Hao, F. (2012), Semantic image understanding: from pixel to word [PhD thesis]. *University of Nottingham.*

He, D., Zheng, Y., Pan, S., & Tang, J. (2010). Ensemble of multiple descriptors for automatic image annotation. In *Proceedings of the IEEE 3rd International Congress on Image and Signal Processing* (pp. 1642-1646).

Huang, Y., Wang, W., Wang, L., & Tan, T. (2013). Multi-Task Deep Neural Network for Multi-Label Learning. In *Proceedings of the 20th IEEE International Conference On Image Processing* (pp. 2897-2900). doi:10.1109/ICIP.2013.6738596

Lavrenko, V., Mammatha, R., & Jeon, J. (2003). A Model for Learning the Semantics of Pictures. In *Proceedings of the Conference on Advance in Neural Information Processing Systems.*

Li, W., & Sun, M. (2008). Multi-model Multi-Label Semantic Indexing of Images using Un-Labeled Data. In *Proceedings of the International Conference on Advanced Language Processing and Web Information Technology* (pp. 204-209).

Li, R., Zhang, Y., Lu, Z., Lu, J., & Tian, Y. (2010). Technique of Image Retrieval based on Multi-label Image Annotation. In *Proceedings of the Second International Conference on Multimedia and Information Technology.* doi:10.1109/MMIT.2010.34

Liu, J., & Wang, B. (2007). Dual Cross-Media Relevance Model for Image Annotation. In *Proceedings of the 15th ACM international conference on Multimedia* (pp. 605-612).

Lu, H., Zheng, Y., Xue, X., & Zhang, Y. (2009). Content and Context-Based Multi-Label Image Annotation. In *Proceedings of the IEEE Computer Society Conference on Computer Vision and Pattern Recognition* (pp. 61-68).

Mao, Q. (2013). Objective-Guided Image Annotation. *IEEE Transactions on Image Processing*, *22*(4), 1585–1597. doi:10.1109/TIP.2012.2233490 PMID:23247859

Moran, S., & Lavrenko, V. (2011). Optimal Tag Sets for Automatic Image Annotation. *BMVC*, *2011*, 1–11.

Mori, Y., Takahashi, R., & Oka, R. (1999). Image-to-word Transformation Based on Dividing and Vector Quantizing Images with words. In *Proceedings of the First International Workshop on Multimedia Intelligent Storage and Retrieval Management.*

Nasierding, G., & Tsoumakas, G. & Abbas Z Kouzani (2009). Clustering Based Multi-Label Classification for Image Annotation and Retrieval. In *Proceedings of the IEEE International Conference on Systems, Man and Cybernetics* (pp. 4514-4519). doi:10.1109/ICSMC.2009.5346902

Pandya, D., & Shah, B. (2014). Comparative Study on Automatic Image Annotation. *International Journal of Emerging Technology and Advanced Engineering.*, *4*(3), 216–222.

Raja, R., Roomi, S. M. M., & Kalaiyarasi, D. (2012). Semantic Modeling of Natural scenes by Local Binary Pattern. In *Proceedings of the IEEE international conference on Machine Vision and Image Processing* (pp. 169-172).

Savita, P., Patel, D., & Sinhal, A. (2013). A Neural Network Approach to Improve the Efficiency of Image Annotation. *International Journal of Engineering Research & Technology*, *2*(1), 1–5.

Siddiqui, A., Mishra, N., & Verma, J. S. (2015). A Survey on Automatic Image Annotation and Retrieval. *International Journal of Computers and Applications*, *118*(20), 27–32. doi:10.5120/20863-3575

Stan, D. & Ishwar K Sethi (2001). Mapping low-level image features to semantic concepts. In *Proceedings of the Conference on Storage and Retrieval for Media Databases* (pp. 172-179).

Sun, Z. (2012). Image Annotation Based on Semantic Clustering and Relevance Feedback. In *Proceedings of the 8th International Conference on Intelligent Information Hiding and Multimedia Signal Processing* (pp. 391-394). doi:10.1109/IIH-MSP.2012.101

Tsai, C.-F. (2012). Bag-of-Words Representation in Image Annotation: A Review. *Artificial Intelligence.*

Wan, S. (2011). Image Annotation using the Simple Decision Tree. In *Proceedings of the IEEE International Conference on Management on e-Commerce and e-Government* (pp. 141-146).

Wang, C., Yan, S., Zhang, L., & Zhang, H.-J. (2009). Multi-Label Sparse Coding for Automatic Image Annotation. In *Proceedings of the IEEE International Conference on Computer Vision and Pattern Recognition* (pp. 1643-1650).

Yang, F., Shi, F., & Wang, J. (2009). An Improved GMM Based Method Or Supervised Semantic Image Annotation. In *Proceedings of the IEEE International Conference On Intelligent Computing And Intelligent Systems.*

Yang, K., Hua, X.-S., Wang, M., & Zhang, H.-J. (2011). Tag Tagging: Towards More Descriptive Keywords of Image Content. *IEEE Transactions on Multimedia*, *13*(4), 662–673. doi:10.1109/TMM.2011.2147777

Yavlinsky, A., Schoeld, E., & Ruger, S. (2005). Automated Image Annotation Using Global Features and Robust Nonparametric Density Estimation. *Chapter Image and Video Retrieval. Lecture Notes in Computer Science, 3568*, 50–517. doi:10.1007/11526346_54

Yildirim, Y., Yazici, A., & Yilmaz, T. (2013). Automatic Semantic Content Extraction in Videos Using a Fuzzy Ontology and Rule-Based Model. *IEEE Transactions on Knowledge and Data Engineering, 25*(1), 47-61.

Chapter 4
Applying Semantic Relations for Automatic Topic Ontology Construction

Subramaniyaswamy Vairavasundaram
SASTRA University, India

Logesh R.
SASTRA University, India

ABSTRACT

The rapid growth of web technologies had created a huge amount of information that is available as web resources on Internet. Authors develop an automatic topic ontology construction process for better topic classification and present a corpus based novel approach to enrich the set of categories in the ODP by automatically identifying concepts and their associated semantic relationships based on external knowledge from Wikipedia and WordNet. The topic ontology construction process relies on concept acquisition and semantic relation extraction. Initially, a topic mapping algorithm is developed to acquire the concepts from Wikipedia based on semantic relations. A semantic similarity clustering algorithm is used to compute similarity to group the set of similar concepts. The semantic relation extraction algorithm derives associated semantic relations between the set of extracted topics from the lexical patterns in WordNet. The performance of the proposed topic ontology is evaluated for the classification of web documents and obtained results depict the improved performance over ODP.

INTRODUCTION

The unbridled growth of World Wide Web (WWW) has made a huge amount of information and resources available over the Internet. This rapid growth of information has resulted in searching for information on the web a challenging task (Sridevi & Nagaveni, 2011). In order to access web resources, a large number of standard web mining algorithms and information retrieval techniques have been developed based on simple keyword based matching. Yet, in a large corpus of documents, the users are unable to retrieve the desired information because these techniques do not consider semantic concepts in the

DOI: 10.4018/978-1-5225-3686-4.ch004

web contents (Fortuna, Grobelnik, & Mladenic, 2005). To overcome this challenge, a semantic web is evolved with ontologies to describe the conceptual relationship between entities in a specific domain. Ontologies are simply defined as the taxonomy of the hierarchy of concepts. It is mainly constructed to provide the knowledgeable representation that can describe the web resources using intelligent techniques for human understanding and machine processing (David & Antonio, 2004). In ontology, concepts in a specific domain are formulated using a proper encoding mechanism that can support efficient information retrieval and reduced information load due to the large corpus of documents (Nicola, 1998). An Ontology creation methodology for domain experts should be efficient and easy to learn (Nikolai, 2011). Ontology represents a set of concepts and the relationships among them for a particular domain (Jongwoo & Veda, 2011).

Topic ontology is defined as a hierarchy of a set of topics that are interconnected using semantic relations (Xujuan, Yuefeng, Yue & Raymond, 2006). It is denoted as a graph in which each node represents the specific topic that forms a topic hierarchy. Further, a group of relevant topics is related to the specific concept in the topic ontology by maintaining a hierarchical semantic relationship among the concepts in topics. The construction process of topic ontology involves extracting keywords using standard text mining and information retrieval techniques. The construction is purely based on semantic relevance of the keywords. However, the keyword based construction approach is not efficient as it is not possible to construct ontology from the large corpus of web documents (Ana, Rocio, Carlos & Filippo, 2010).

Due to the shortcomings of keyword based construction, we propose the Open Directory Project (ODP), a multilingual open content directory of World Wide Web links (Dengya & Heinz, 2009). The ODP works on the principle of listing out the set of categories related to a specific concept. We propose a hyperlink based approach, wherein ontology is constructed through exploring and discovering the semantic concepts related to the categories associated in ODP. The main advantage of this approach is to allow the user to extend the categories according to their perspective to construct topic ontology. This approach merely requires the users to have a basic knowledge of the topic that they are searching to enrich the existing ontology. Hence, we deploy knowledge-based web resources, such as Wikipedia and WordNet to obtain the background semantic knowledge about the categories in the ODP.

Wikipedia, most commonly used as online encyclopedia by the Internet users, is a multilingual online encyclopedia which contains articles and categories that are related to a particular concept. In Wikipedia, each web page defines a set of topics related to the specific concept and is more formally organized in hierarchical fashion according to the general knowledge. In addition, unambiguity between similar words is removed by providing web pages according to the different word sense. Wikipedia uses a straightforward approach for searching; usually a set of keywords associated with each web page can be used to construct topic ontology. Constructing topic ontology based on keywords alone has limitations as keywords are just an arrangement of a set of relevant topics related to the specific concept and does not render any semantic relation among the set of concepts (Huan, Xing, Liang-Tien & Ah-Hwee, 2010).

WordNet is a lexical reference system that consists of a set of related usual language terms within the same lexical concepts. Each word possesses one or more synonyms depending upon the parts of speech, such as nouns, verbs, adjectives and adverbs. A collection of words that represent the same sense is known as synset and is organized hierarchically (Vaclav, Pavel & Jaroslav, 2005). A set of related terms in synset possess Hyponym/Hypernym (subclass/superclass, represented as is–a relation) and Meronym/Holonym (part-whole relationships) which is used to facilitate the efficient construction of topic ontology. Figure 1 shows the partial hierarchical structure of the tag "Java" based on the relations of WordNet.

Figure 1. Partial hierarchical structure of the tag "Java" based on the relations of WordNet

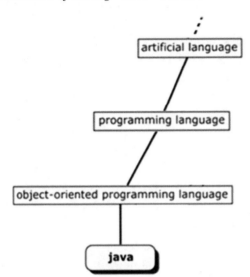

Ontology is defined as the knowledgeable representation of semantic concepts and their corresponding relationships. The ontology construction utilizes manual and semi-automatic approach. Ontologies constructed using semi-automatic approach has superior quality but expensive, time consuming and hard to maintain constructed ontology. On the other hand, automated approach can construct ontology automatically from the unstructured text without the intervention of the user. Yet, the automatic approach also has severe limitations in the form of noise, inconsistency, and missing information of concepts and their relationships. Such limitations call for a high quality and efficient topic ontology construction, which still remains to be an open research problem.

The aforementioned limitations are addressed by constructing ontologies automatically by extracting the concepts from the knowledge-specific hierarchically-structured semantic Wikipedia. Semantic relation between the extracted concepts has been determined from the lexical patterns occurring between the synsets using WordNet. Finally, the extracted concepts and their semantic relationships are hierarchically organized in the form of ontology.

This chapter describes the construction, implementation and evaluation of automatic topic ontology from text corpus, such as Wikipedia and WordNet. The major contributions are summarized below:

- Precise and dynamic construction of topic ontology through extracted knowledge.
- Extraction of relevant information for construction of topic ontology using Wiki-parser. Extraction of synset for the categories from the WordNet. Further, lexical relation, such as Meronym/Holonym and Hyponym/Hypernym has been predicted between the terms in synset.
- Designing of topic mapping algorithm to extract the set of topics to construct topic ontology. The conceptual mapping was performed between the set of relevant categories extracted from Wikipedia and the appropriate extracted set of synset from WordNet.
- Proposition of semantic similarity clustering algorithm to determine a set of topics which has a high semantic similarity between the related terms in Wikipedia and the frequent attributes in WordNet.

- Derivation of Semantic Relation Extraction algorithm to understand the semantic relation between the set of extracted topics based on the lexical patterns from WordNet.

The chapter is organized as follows. First, we analyze the basic concepts and related work of the topic ontology construction process. In section 3 we present an overview of automatic topic ontology construction and portray the Topic Mapping (TM), Semantic Similarity Clustering (SSC) and Semantic Relation Extraction (SRE) algorithms for the construction of topic ontology. In section 4 we describe the utilization of ODP for the topic ontology construction using Protégé tool. Then in section 5 we illustrate the classification of topics using SVM and present the experimental results to reveal the difference between ODP based categorization and topic ontology based categorization. Finally, section 6 draws the conclusions and presents the current trends and future research directions.

RELATED WORK

A considerable amount of research has been done on information retrieval through searching, navigating, and organizing the Internet information (Baeza-Yates & Ribeiro-Neto 1999). Ontologies are used as computational artifacts that encode knowledge of the domain in a machine processable form to ensure that it is available for information systems. Research has shown that there exists a problem to extend the existing ontology, WordNet using Web documents (Agirre et al., 2000); learn taxonomic, e.g., "is-a" relation (Cimiano, et al. 2004) and non-taxonomic, e.g., "has-part" relations (Maedche & Staab, 2004); utilize clustering for semi-automatic construction of ontologies from parsed text corpora (Reinberger & Spyns, 2004); and extract semantic relations from text based on collocations (Heyer, et al. 20004) and semantic graphs from text for learning summaries (Leskovec, 2004). Jung, Yoo, and Chung (2016) have made a suggestion to use associative context mining methodology to discover the ontology driven knowledge. Associative context mining method exploits potential new knowledge by association rule mining in the ontology-driven context modelling. The reasoning of the potential relationship between the external, internal and service context information is achieved with the Apriori mining algorithm. The hidden knowledge of the relationships and context information is discovered and applied to the semantic reasoning engine (SRE). The SRE supplements reasoning rule to analyze association between the subordinate layers of external and internal ontology.

As previously mentioned, the purpose of this chapter is to construct and implement automatic topic ontology to improve the existing ontology. Several authors have tried to use automatic ontology construction in the past. The methodology for automatically building ontologies proposed by Alani, et al. (2003) applied information extraction tools on online web pages and then combined the obtained information with ontology and the WordNet lexicon to populate a knowledgebase. However, when duplicate information was found, it resulted in redundant explanations. Ding and Foo (2002) proposed a solution for differentiating sentences that refer to the same concept through "differentiate them via the co-occurrence frequency," by considering how often the same sentence appears in the text. This research work uses a process that has similarities in the extraction of knowledge step since we need to extract terms and relations or associations in a text corpus.

Valencia (2002) used statistical treatment of biological literature for automatic construction of ontologies. However, the drawback of this method is that it uses ontologies built by group concepts that have similar information and functions in the literature.

Kawtrakul, Suktarachan, and Imsombut (2004) used a methodology for ontology construction through three main steps: 1) extraction of terms based on text corpus, 2) extraction of relational information using dictionary-based and 3) translation of thesaurus terms to ontology terms. This methodology has relatively high reliability, i.e., 87% accuracy for the system and the remaining 13% error was due to extraction terms errors.

The approach of reusing existing knowledge to construct ontologies automatically was suggested by Kong, Hwang, and Kim (2006). The main objective of this approach was to improve the reliability of automatically generated ontologies. Nevertheless, in this approach, automatic collection of the knowledge from the domain expert was not used. In order to generate ontologies from existing ontologies, an ontology search engine was used by Alani (2006) to find various ontologies of the same specific domain and then the fragments of those ontologies were combined to construct a more complete ontology. Though this approach had many advantages, e.g., reusing well-structured ontologies that have already been checked by domain experts, yet it was inefficient in building ontologies for a new domain, especially when only few ontologies were available through search engines or when the available ontologies could not be relied upon due to lack of domain experts.

To extract information about a specific domain, documents related to that domain are collected from the WWW and sifted through to extract the required information of that domain (Eneko, Olatz, David & Eduard, 2001). Consequently, WordNet, an English language lexical dictionary, was utilized to extract the synset for that domain (Miller et al., 1990). WordNet was used to derive the semantic relation between the extracted keywords. This type of ontology enrichment is an automatic process that improves the set of concepts of existing ontology using the extracted semantic relation between the topics of the documents resulting in efficient construction of topic ontology. The ontology enrichment is based on the core concept that assigns weights to the topics according to the number of similar words available in the specific concepts in WordNet.

In another approach using Wikipedia, information was extracted from Wikipedia articles where a group of related concepts were organized in the form of hierarchical categories to construct the topic ontology. In this approach, Persian Wikipedia (Mojgan et al., 2009) was used to gather the set of pages related to the specific domain and then Wikipedia parser was deployed to extract the title, keywords and existing links. The metadata repository maintained the extracted information which was used to construct the topic ontology. Among the extracted metadata, titles in each page were considered as the topic of the ontology and then associated links between the pages were used to derive the semantic relation between the topics in the ontology. A concept hierarchy between the set of topics were formed according to the weights of the links. Depending upon the information on the page, weights were assigned to the associated links (Subramaniyaswamy, Vijayakumar & Indragandhi, 2013).

The most relevant category plays an important role to form the strong semantic relation between the set of topics. Strong semantic relations were computed through two measures, a number of links between the categories and connectivity ratio (Sergey, Tereza, Wolfgang & Xuan, 2006). The extracted relationships were maintained in the database which was used to emphasize the meaningful semantic relation between the relevant categories and then irrelevant categories were ignored. From the extracted semantic relation, knowledge was acquired about the content of Wikipedia page that lead to the construction of topic ontology. Finally, OWL on the web was used to visualize the constructed topic ontology.

In semi-automatic approach, data mining algorithms, such as i) Centroid Vectors and ii) Support Vector Machine (SVM) were used. Among the two, centroid vector technique extracted keywords associated with the topic from a large collection of documents. SVM binary then classified the documents based on the computed cosine similarity measure between the extracted keywords (Blaz, Dunja & Marko, 2006). After detecting the semantic similarity between topics, k-means semantic clustering approach grouped the documents with high semantic similarity. The major drawbacks of this approach are i) insufficient data mining algorithms, ii) does not provide any support to identify the semantic relation between a set of concepts in the document though useful to discover the topics in the large corpus of documents and iii) requires user interaction to construct topic ontology, whereas system gives only suggestion by providing documents related to the specified topic. The manual construction of ontologies does not satisfy the rapidly growing demands of new applications and achieving dynamic ontology based on the demands cannot be attained with the human knowledge alone [Balachandran & Ranathunga 2016]. Ontology learning mechanism is recognized as a best solution for automatic or semi-automatic ontology building process. A new procedure to extract the terms to identify the concepts in ontology learning is proposed (Balachandran & Ranathunga 2016). The proposed ontology learning mechanism utilizes the statistical calculations and linguistic analysis to extract domain-specific terms to overcome existing limitations. The biasness is reduced by using the single contrastive corpus.

In order to improve the quality of existing ontology, Ontology Design Patterns (ODP) provides the precise design principles to enrich the overall structure of ontology using extracted semantic background knowledge. It is a language independent approach and also implemented through OWL ontologies. The retrieval and reuse phase in the enrichment process is improved through various approaches such as pattern ranking, concept coverage, relation coverage and utility measure. Though ontologies are widely used in many complex domains, still they are not efficient enough to address the uncertainty issues during the representation of the knowledge (Jamoussi & Hamadou, 2017). The authors have presented a probabilistic ontology construction methodology to address the uncertainties of OWL ontology with respect to relations. The proposed Prob-Ont utilizes Bayesian Network to represent uncertainties in the semantic web for the case study on scientific documentation system.

Ontologies serve as better tools in the classification of texts for the enhanced construction regulated documents (Zhou & El-Gohary, 2015). The authors had presented a multi-label text classification method to help the construction of Automated Compliance Checking procedure. They have also developed a domain specific ontology to represent the hierarchy of topics along with the associated relationships. They have utilized unsupervised deep learning technique to learn the similarities between each topic and each clause for the classification of clauses into topics with respect to the similarity thresholds. As the limitations of their work, the performance purely depends on the quality of the ontologies utilized and the classification is validated on the six topics which is very small number to establish the quality of the proposed work. The acquisition of the user's personal information from their local repository has become very complex and challenging task (Bashar, Li, and Gao, 2016). Personalized ontology has been adopted in many rapidly growing user applications to obtain the information needs of the users. To overcome the time-consuming processes of semi-automatic or manual ontology construction, an automatically learning model for personalized ontology construction is proposed. The presented automatic ontology construction method labels the topics with concepts and topic models were discovered from the location information repository of the user. The proposed TLPO (Topic-Model Labelling based Personalised Ontology) integrates the local information repository of the user with the standard ontology as a single conceptual model to learn user needs for improved information organization.

Wimmer, Yoon, and Rada, (2012, 2014) presented a system called ALIGN to demonstrate the usage of tools that are freely available to build and serve ontology alignment. The ontologies were built with the help of Protégé tool and used JENA (JAVA package) and SPARQL queries to access ontologies of drug-drug interaction problem. The developed ontologies are generic enough to be deployed on the other domains for the decision-support problems. Zhao, Ren and Wan (2015) had explored a semantic description approach based on primitive structure to benefit description of ontological relation in a concrete and precise manner. They have also introduced a procedure to extract words using a multi-label learning model and correlated label propagation.

In the recent times, the tagging activity has become a potential source of knowledge of the user's personal preferences, interests and other characteristic features. In our existing work, we have presented a detailed overview on tag recommendation approaches and through utilizing the spreading activation algorithm and studied the role of topic ontology in the tag recommendation systems (Vairavasundaram, Varadharajan, Vairavasundaram & Ravi, 2015). The constructed topic ontology has enhanced the keyword extraction process from the existing blogs and makes better prediction for the recommendation of tags. We have also proposed a Correlation-based Feature Selection–Hybrid Genetic Algorithm and classifier HGA-SVM (support vector machine) for the enhanced tag recommendation. The ontology based tag recommendation requires the further enhancement with the semantic annotation for better personalized tag recommendations.

TOPIC ONTOLOGY CONSTRUCTION USING SEMANTIC RELATIONS

The most relevant hierarchy of topics related to the concept and the associated semantic relation between the concepts must be derived to construct topic ontology (Sabrina, Rosni & Tang, 2001). In our corpus based approach, the required concepts and the semantic relationship are acquired through connecting the two external knowledge base called as Wikipedia and WordNet. The categories in Wikipedia are rich and consist of high quality topic contents that are available generously. On the other hand, WordNet can establish the semantic relation between the extracted relevant categories using ontologically well-defined taxonomy of synsets. The lexical relationship extracted from the WordNet is used to derive the semantic relationship between the set of related Wikipedia topical categories. The complete structure of this approach has been depicted in Figure 2.

Thus, this approach relies on two criteria: i) concept acquisition and ii) semantic relation extraction. In concept acquisition, topic mapping algorithm acquires the relevant topics from the Wikipedia categories and synsets of WordNet. The semantics similarity clustering algorithm computes the semantic similarity score to identify semantically similar concepts. In the second criteria, semantic relation extraction algorithm extracts the semantic relationship between the extracted topics using the lexical patterns between the synsets of WordNet. Finally, Jena API constructs the topic ontology using the set of concepts and their associated relationship and represented in the form of OWL.

This chapter takes cognizance of the first criteria to take one step forward to enrich the set of categories in existing small ontology, such as ODP. As discussed earlier, ODP can be relied to provide precise design principles to enhance the overall structure of ontology by applying background knowledge. The enrichment is achieved through linking the available web resources, such as Wikipedia and WordNet with near-perfect accuracy. Hence, the relevant categories of WordNet lexical system and Wikipedia are combined to obtain the background semantic knowledge. Further, it is possible extract a set of catego-

Figure 2. Automatic topic ontology construction

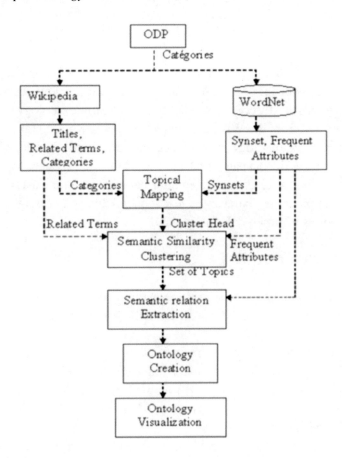

ries from the Wikipedia web pages that renders more useful information about the concepts in specific domain. The main objective of this chapter is to derive semantic relation to the WordNet, which is used to enrich the automatic construction of topic ontology using a set of highly interlinked topic categories extracted from Wikipedia pages (Marko & Dunja, 2005).

Open Directory Project

ODP is a small existing ontology composed of a set of categories related to the specific concept. The main concept for automatic topic ontology construction in the form of knowledgeable representation is through enriching the set of categories in ODP. In order to enrich the categories with a set of conceptually related topics, external background knowledge about the categories is needed. The set of conceptually related topics for the category is acquired from web resources, such as Wikipedia and WordNet. Our approach is mainly intended to describe the process of how to enrich the set of categories in existing ontology (ODP) using the semantic concepts (topics) and their corresponding semantic relation extracted from the external knowledge web resources.

Wikipedia Parsing

In Wikipedia, a large number of documents related to the specific concept are organized in the form of a graph where a group of related pages are linked together. The topic ontology for a specific concept is developed through extracting the relevant categories in the corresponding Wikipedia page. Each Wikipedia page is explicitly associated with one or more relevant categories. It can provide meaningful information by describing the set of topics mostly covered by that concept. So topic ontology is constructed using the relevant categories extracted from the Wikipedia page (Minghua, Kotaro, Takahiro & Shojiro, 2008). Efficient construction of topic ontology is facilitated by the recently developed Wiki-parser, which preprocesses the content of Wikipedia pages that can extract the title, articles, keywords, text, links and relevant categories from Wikipedia. The extracted information is maintained as a text file in a metadata warehouse. The metadata processor extracts the text sequentially, and it assigns a unique code to the extracted relevant categories (Carmen & Desislava, 2011).

Synset Extraction From WordNet

In this approach, WordNet can derive the semantic relation between the extracted relevant categories from Wikipedia. There are five steps to extract the semantic relation from WordNet:

- First, identify the conceptual category from the available extracted relevant categories using Noun Group parser that can parse the category name linguistically.
- Extract the Synset for the selected category from the lexical dictionary called WordNet.
- Determine the lexical relation such as Hyponym/Hypernym and Meronym/ Holonym from the synset for the selected category.
- Derive the semantic relation such as "is a", "part of" and "related to' for the list of word pairs according to the determined lexical relation from synset.
- Record the lexical and syntactic context using regular expression in large data base (Hearst, 1998).

Existing Ontologies

Building ontologies is more of art than of science where no one methodology is available to develop in the form required (Mizoguchi 2003; Grubic and Fan 2010). In order to construct high quality ontologies, it is essential for the developers to focus on choosing and following a methodology where a series of steps, activities, and guidelines, such as knowledge acquisition, purpose articulation, formalization and evaluation, to ensure that this information are organized in systematic manner. The ontologies vary from each other having specific characteristics and some ontologies may be better than the other under certain circumstances (Lee, 2006; Fernandez-Lopez et al., 1997; Holsapple & Joshi, 2002). Therefore, it is better to build ontologies by reusing existing methods and applying them appropriately instead of building from the scratch (Pinto & Martins, 2001).

Several ontology methods are available which has typical characteristics that are used in different scenarios. When there is a clear understanding of the requirement, ontologies such as TOVE (Gruninger & Fox, 1995), Ontology based KM System Methodology (Stabb et al., 2001), and Enterprise Ontology (Uschold & King, 1995) were used. In instances were requirements were not clearly understood, iteration approach was used in ontologies like Methontology (Fernandez-Lopez et al., 1997), Ontology Development 101 (Noy & McGuinness, 2001), Collaborative Design Approach (Holsapple and Joshi 2002) and Diligent (Pinto et al., 2009). Collaborative approaches were used in the past to modify ontologies based on usage and feedback (Holsapple & Joshi, 2002; Pinto et al., 2009). Two or more methodologies were combined together to structure an ontology (Uschold, 1996; Brusa et al., 2008). Lee, on the other hand, was more focused on using scenarios to develop different activities. Figure 3 shows simple ontology hierarchy.

Leung, et al. (2012) have analyzed in detail the development of ontologies based on reuse. They point out that Methontology uses the process of reusing existing ontologies. Yet even in such a methodology, only inspect meta-ontologies steps and search for appropriate terms have been used, which does give sufficient insight. Most of these approaches use a semi-automatic ontology; therefore, this study focuses on automatic ontology to overcome the challenges.

Topic Mapping Algorithm

XML/SGML derived standards for information and knowledge structuring and description have become popular in the recent past (Noy et al., 2001). These standards share a common goal of simplifying information structuring, accessing and processing by adding structured metadata to information resources. A Topic Map is structure of information that can be used as descriptive metadata for arbitrary data wherein document annotation becomes the most common application (Böhm, 2002). Creation of Topic Maps and their practical applications require extensive understanding of the knowledge engineering as the domains will have to be intellectually analyzed before defining the resource delineation. We propose a topic mapping map (FM) algorithm, which has significant advantages for knowledge discovery applications due to its low running time and hierarchical clustering capability compared with similar algorithms. This algorithm links two available open web resources, such as Wikipedia and WordNet, to construct topic ontology with near perfect accuracy (Minghua, Kotaro, Takahiro & Shojiro, 2008). In Wikipedia, relevant categories are arranged hierarchically in the form of a directed cyclic graph. On the other hand, WordNet has the capability to present the well-defined taxonomy of synsets. Based on

Figure 3. Simple ontology hierarchy

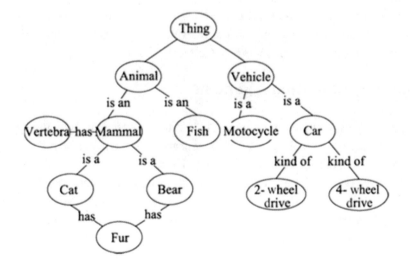

these two criteria, we have developed a new topic mapping algorithm to perform mapping between these two web resources. This mapping is used to extract a set of relevant topics to construct topic ontology.

An example of the pseudo code of topic mapping algorithm is as follows:

```
Input: Categories in ODP: C[k] = {C1, C2... Cp};
Synset S[i] = {S1, S2... Sn};
Relevant categories: R C[j] = {RC1, RC2 ... RCm};
Output: Topics {T1, T2... Tv}
Algorithm:
Pre = C[k];
Synset = S[i];
Post = S[j];
for (int i=0; j<n; i++) {
for (int j=0; j<m; j++) {
for (int k=0; j<m; k++) {
If (S[i] = = "C[k]") {
T = C[k];
Return T; // return topic
}
else (S[i] = = "RC[j]") {
T = S[i];
Return T; //return topic
}
}  }  }
```

The function of the topic mapping algorithm:

- The above algorithm takes two inputs, such as relevant categories from Wikipedia and synset from WordNet.
- Output of this algorithm is a set of topics to construct topic ontology.
- Similarity between extracted relevant categories and terms in WordNet is determined through topical mapping. Terms that match with the relevant categories are supposed to return topics to construct topic ontology (Fabian, Gjergji & Gerhard, 2007).

Semantic Similarity Clustering Algorithm

Many clustering techniques are studied in the past by authors. Clustering is an unsupervised classification technique (Koontz, et al., 2001; Frigui & Krishnapuram, 1999) where several approaches, like graph theoretic approach and K-means algorithm, (Selim & Ismail, 1984) have been studied. The quality of graph theoretic approach result is based on the quality of the estimation technique for the density gradient (Koontz, et al., 1995). K-means is an iterative hill-climbing algorithm that suffers the sub-optimization limitation and depends on the choice of initial clustering distribution. Further, these clustering algorithms mainly use vector space model (VSM) to represent text, for example, each unique word in vocabulary represents one dimension in vector space. Therefore, these algorithms become insufficient when bag of words representation is adopted because it uses matches produced by keywords. Further, one concept can be portrayed using many different terms (Zhang et al., 2008). Experiments conducted by Al-Mubaid and Nguyen HA (2006) using cluster-based approach for semantic similarity in the biomedical domain confirmed the efficiency of this method with similarity measure giving the best overall results of correlation with human ratings.

Semantic clustering algorithm is an efficient algorithm used to identify the semantically similar topics between related terms from Wikipedia and frequent attributes from WordNet. It is determined from the semantic similarity number of lexical patterns available for that topic in WordNet. The semantic similarity between the topics is computed depending upon the number of lexical patterns applicable between the corresponding topics. As suggested by Danushka, Yutaka and Mitsuru (2009), if two topics have high semantic similarity score, it means that so many lexical patterns are applicable between them. Semantic similarity score for each topic is determined and topic pairs, which have high similarity score with a large number of lexical pattern relationships, are clustered. The proposed algorithm scales linearly depending upon the number of lexical patterns are extracted between the two topics.

An example of algorithm for semantic similarity clustering is as follows:

```
Input: Lexical Pattern LP [i] ={ Hyponym, Hypernym,  Meronym, Holonym}
Semantic relation= { 'is a', 'part of, 'related to'}
Topic  T[k]= {T1,T2,T3,T4…Tm}
Output: Semantic Cluster SC;
Algorithm:
Arrange (LP)
SC ← { }
for pattern LPi Є LP do
SC ← null
for cluster SCj Є SC do
for (int k=1; k<m; k++)
max = SSS (T, T[k])
if (max < φ)
Return T =  T[k]  //forms semantic relation
else
Return T ≠T[k]  // discards Topic
End if;
End for;
```

The algorithm performs the following different tasks:

- Takes three inputs such as related terms, frequent attributes and Wordnet.
- Automatically extracts the lexical patterns for the topic which can make semantic relation to the superclass topic.
- Computes semantic similarity score for each topic pairs (related terms and frequent terms) according to the number of extracted lexical pattern relationships.
- Clusters the topic with a high semantic similarity score into the superclass topic. The semantic similarity score for all topics is computed with its corresponding superclass topic and clusters

the topics that have high semantic similarity score. The Semantic Similarity Score (SSS) for the two topics (T1&T2) in taxonomy is determined as the logarithmic value of the ratio between the weight of the subclass topic and superclass topic.

$$SSS = \log \frac{w(T2)}{w(T1) + w(T2)}$$

Here, $w(T1)$ is the weight of the superclass topic. $w(T2)$ is the weight of the sub-class topic.

If the value of SSS is less than the threshold, the topic forms the semantic relation with the superclass topic. Otherwise, superclass discards that topic from its hierarchy along with other topics in the ontology.

An experiment was conducted using our proposed Semantic Similarity Clustering Method for a bag of words. The semantic similarity clustering method was used to automatically identify if two topic segments are paraphrases of each other. In the proposed work, Microsoft paraphrase corpus consisting of 4,076 training and 1,725 test pairs were used to determine the number of correctly identified paraphrase pairs in the corpus using the semantic similarity clustering measure.

Eleven different similarity thresholds ranging from 0 to 1 with interval 0.1 have been used. For example, when the similarity threshold 0.6 using a test data set was used, the proposed method predicted 1369 correct pairs, while in the 1725 manually annotated pairs, 1022 pairs were found to be correct. The results depicted in Table 1 shows that this method achieves a high performance coefficient with the average human similarity ratings.

Semantic Relation Extraction Algorithm

After extracting the set of topics to construct topic ontology, we have determined the semantic relation between the extracted topics to construct the taxonomy of concepts from the ontological point of view. For this purpose, lexical patterns between topics are extracted from WordNet. There is a possibility for

Table 1. Efficiency of semantic similarity clustering method

Topics	Bag of Words (Sub-Topic Pairs)	Human Similarity (Mean)	Semantic Similarity Clustering Method
Cricket	Bat, ball	0.11	0.16
Personal	Stories, Hobbies	0.11	0.17
Humor	Jokes, laugh	0.15	0.22
Marketing	Products, services	0.11	0.16
Video games	Car race, bounce ball	0.14	0.27
Thoughts	Ideas, own stories	0.05	0.19
Sales	Products, services	0.09	0.31
Sketching	Sketch, water mark	0.02	0.13
Shuttle cock	Cock, bat	0.17	0.28
Workshops	Bike, Car	0.16	0.23
Schools, colleges	Subjects, technical	0.28	0.29

the same word pairs to possess different lexical relationship depending upon the contexts in which two topics co-occurred as word pairs. Therefore, lexical patterns between the topics are extracted only for the retrieved contexts which are used to represent the semantic relation between two topics. It should be noted that same semantic relation can be expressed through one or more lexical pattern. Here, the semantic relation, such as "is a" "part of" and "related to" for the extracted topics, is determined according to the lexical patterns named as Hyponym/Hypernym and Meronym/Holonym in WordNet.

In the proposed approach, the task is to obtain a score between 0 and 1 inclusively that will indicate the similarity between two topics T1 and T2 at semantic levels. The main idea is to find, for each word in the first topic, a matching that is most similar to the sub-topic. The weight of the topic is based on rating of the similarity of meaning of the topic pairs on a scale of 0.0 (minimum similarity) to 1.0 (maximum similarity).

An example of algorithm for semantic relation extraction is as follows:

```
Input: Lexical Pattern = {Hyponym, Hypernym, Meronym, Holonym}
Output: Semantic relation = {'is a', 'part of', 'related to'}
Algorithm:
if (Lexical Pattern = = Hyponym)
{
Semantic relation = "is a";
}
else if (Lexical Pattern = = Hypernym)
{
Semantic relation = "is a";
}
else if (Lexical Pattern = = Meronym)
{
Semantic relation = "related to";
}
else if (Lexical Pattern = = Holonym)
{
Semantic relation = "part of";
}
```

The proposed method determines the similarity of two topics that has semantic and syntactic information (in terms of common-word order). The main advantage of this system is that it uses less time and is less complex than other systems because of the use of the corpus-based measure, while integrating both corpus-based and WordNet-based measures.

Since our method adds string similarity measure on short strings, the search was very fast, which is yet another difference from other methods. Moreover, our method can be used with or without supervision.

We have also tested our proposed semantic text similarity method by setting common-word order similarity factor, $wf \in [0, 0.5)$ to observe the effects of common-word order similarity on both data sets for determining short text similarity.

This method can be improved by conducting a follow up study using a topic directory, such as Dmoz (where about 590,000 categories are available) to collect category descriptions. Our proposed can be used to compute semantic similarity for pairs of category descriptions. This approach would allow evaluation of a large number of pairs of topic descriptions as well as estimation of the expected similarity scores from the positions of the nodes in the topic ontologies available in Dmoz. Figure 4 depicts the complete architecture of proposed system for automatic topic ontology generation.

EXPERIMENTAL EVALUATION

The main process for construction ontology process along with the algorithms has been described in the preceding sections. In this section, the organization of the components with the algorithmic techniques to construct topic ontology has been provided. The Protégé tool is deployed in the construction has been used to visualize the built topic ontology in OWL representation.

Figure 4. System architecture of automatic topic ontology generation

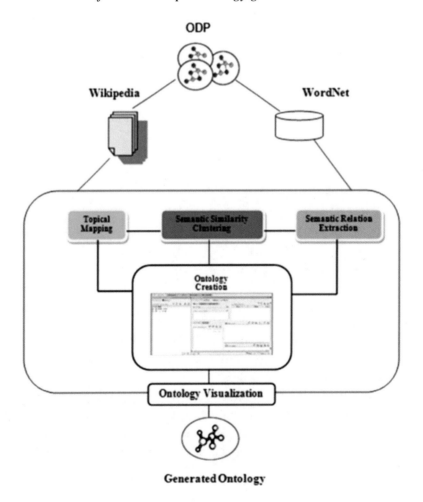

Ontology Creation

In order to publish and share the information available on the WWW, topic ontology is constructed through enriching the set of categories in existing small ontology called as Open Directory Project (ODP). It is enriched through extracting the N-list of concepts from the knowledge base Wikipedia and WordNet. Jena API provides a set of methods to construct ontology using the set of extracted concepts related to the categories in ODP. The constructed ontology is represented in the form of semantic markup language OWL. Protégé 2.0 is an ontology visualizing and editing tool that can visualize the constructed ontology with final hierarchy of classes and subclasses. It is used to perform a set of formal tests to evaluate the completeness and correctness of constructed topic ontology in terms of consistency and redundancy. Figure 5 shows an ontology example developed on Protégé tool.

Prototype Implementation

In order to evaluate the performance of our proposed topic ontology construction methodology, a suitable prototype is required to implement the proposed algorithm portrayed previously. The following tools were used in this study:

- **Html Parser 1.4:** A powerful HTML parser that allows parsing of the required information from the Wikipedia.

Figure 5. An ontology example developed on Protégé tool

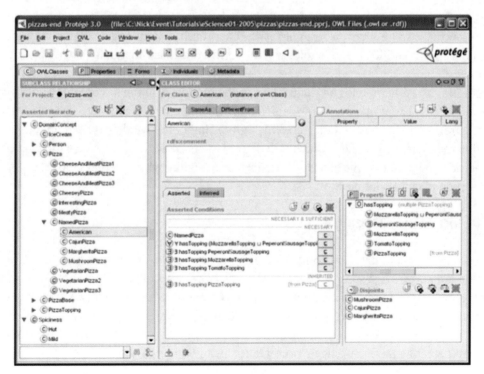

- **Jena API 2.6.4:** A Java API framework that provides classes and interfaces to create and manage ontologies for the Semantic Web. Ontology models are created through the Jena Model Factory (Jena, 2003).
- **OWL API 1.2:** One of the most important libraries that provide the methods and functions to construct and manage the ontologies in OWL.
- **Protégé 2.0:** An ontology visualization and edition tool with the ezOWL plug-in that can create a visual representation of OWL ontology.

Open Directory Project (ODP)

ODP is the largest and the most comprehensive human-edited web directory that offers a flat categorization of a specific set of categories. It consists of nearly 4.59 million submitted web sites, 82,929 editors and 590,000 categories. In addition, the entries of ODP are increasing continuously due to the explosive growth of web applications. Each of the categories in ODP contains related topics, a list of sub-categories, a list of web pages related to the category and description for each of the category. Examples of the categories are arts, science, society, business, entertainment, education, weather, travel, research, enterprise, etc.

Automatic Topic Ontology Construction Using Protégé Tool

Protégé is a free, open source ontology editor tool and is also considered as a knowledge acquisition system to construct topic ontology. Protégé tool uses two methodologies, frame-based and OWL-based approach, to model ontology. In our study, OWL methodology was used to construct topic ontology automatically without any user interface. The Protégé tool strongly relies on two design goals: i) Ontology visualization to visualize the constructed ontology in the form of knowledge representation (ontology) and ii) Concept Class Hierarchy, a straight-forward approach that automatically creates and displays the set of concepts or entities in the ontology in the form of the class hierarchy having parent and child relationships.

Figure 6 illustrates the ontology visualization of the proposed automatic ontology construction using the Protégé tool. The Protégé window depicted in the Figure 6 is divided into two regions: ontology visualization region and concept-class hierarchy region. Half of the window is used up for the ontology visualization region (the right side), which is dedicated to visualize the constructed topic ontology. The left side of the window shows the concept-class hierarchy region, which displays the set of topics in the form of parent and child relationships.

Constructed Topic Ontology

The proposed system automatically constructs the topic ontology using the set of conceptually related topics for the categories in the specific concept. Figure 7 shows an example of topic ontology construction for the category "Bank" in the existing ontology ODP. Our system automatically extracts the conceptually related terms for the category "Bank" from knowledge-based web resources, such as Wikipedia and WordNet. Thus, we show that the automatically constructed ontology is efficient to cover a set of topics in addition to depicting the knowledge representation using Jena API and Protégé tool.

Figure 6. Visualization of proposed topic ontology construction

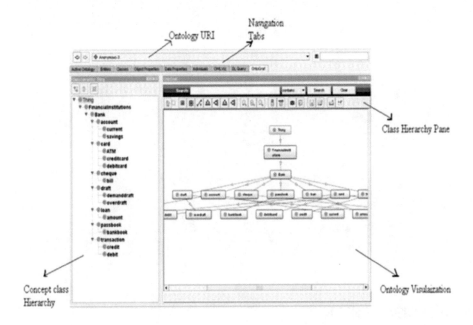

Figure 7. Topic ontology for the banking concept in ODP directory

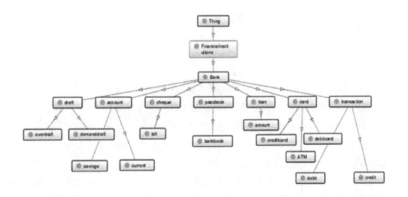

The proposed ontology construction approach is highly automatic and also eliminates the user interaction completely. The main goals of this work were to develop and implement an automatic methodology for topic ontology construction using highly specific topic concepts and their corresponding semantic relations. The optimal number of highly specific topics have been suggested and extracted through this approach. It provides support to annotate the web documents in the form of topic ontology with high quality of semantic topics and different kinds of semantic relations. Figure 8 shows the topic ontology for the category "Card" in ODP directory (Subramaniyaswamy & Pandian, 2012).

Figure 8. Zoom into topic ontology for the category "card" in ODP directory

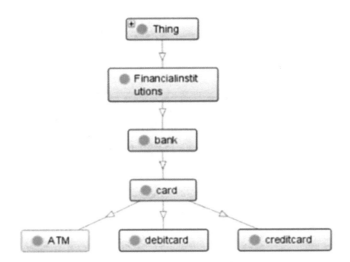

RESULTS AND DISCUSSION

This section presents the detailed experimental results for classification accuracy of web documents based on the constructed topic ontology. Characteristics and description of the data sets used for performing experiments are also summarized in this section.

Support Vector Machine

In order to investigate the performance of the topic ontology based categorization with respect to already existing ODP based categorization, Support Vector Machine (SVM) was used. SVM is the most popular supervised machine learning algorithm used to classify the web documents into two categories, i.e., relevant or non-relevant (Thorsten, 1998). Our past studies have demonstrated that SVM is more effective and competent for task classification (Subramaniyaswamy & Chenthur, 2012a). We have also proved in the past that SVM as one of the most powerful supervised learning algorithm for classification of web documents (Subramaniyaswamy & Chenthur, 2012b). In the present study, the algorithm takes input from the web documents which are represented in the form of vectors and also deals with each document as a multi-dimensional feature gap. It categorizes the documents based on the two inputs:

Web snippets S = {s1, s2, s3, ..., sn}, where n number of items are extracted from the web pages that are returned as results from the web search engines.

Topic Document Set T = {t1, t2, t3, ..., tm} consist of m number of topics in topic ontology.

Categorized Results

Table 2 depicts the categorized results for topic ontology based categorization. SVM performs efficient categorization, where each category is occupied by more relevant set of topics related to the specific concept.

Table 2. Categorized results for topic ontology

Topics	Categorized results
Ecommerce	1. Online Banking ▶ Fund Transfer ▶ Bill Payment ▶ Investment loan 2. Online shopping ▶ Logistics ▶ Product delivery ▶ Shopping cart
Financial Services	1. Banking ▶ Account ▶ Loan ▶ Card 2. Insurance ▶ Health Insurance ▶ Property Insurance ▶ Life Insurance
Commercial Enterprise	1. Management ▶ Human Resource ▶ Marketing ▶ Information 2. Manufacturing ▶ Textile Industry ▶ Chemical Industry ▶ Construction

Classification Accuracy

In order to examine the classification accuracy, experiments were carried out by collecting web snippet data set from the web documents and training set from the set of topics in constructed topic ontology. Based on the web snippets in test data, corresponding set of topics were collected from the topic ontology. SVM classifier is trained with the training set that aids to categorize the web documents according to the test set of web snippets.

Figure 9 shows classification accuracy between ODP and topic ontology based categorization using SVM classifier. The results demonstrate that accuracy of classification was highest when there was less number of web documents for both Topic ontology and ODP. In comparison to ODP, Topic ontology had significantly higher percentage of classification of accuracy. The performance of both the methods decreased with increasing number of web documents. Yet, the trend of Topic ontology based categorization was significantly higher than ODP.

The results demonstrate that topic ontology based categorization produces more accurate classification than existing ODP based categorization. The superior performance of our constructed topic ontology is due to the enrichment of topic ontology with more relevant set of topics. Further, conceptual semantic relation is associated with it. Consequently, topic ontology can classify web documents at a high classification accuracy of 92%. On the contrary, ODP based categorization achieves significantly lower classification accuracy than topic ontology. ODP yields category document set that only exposes the predefined categories related to the concepts arranged in knowledge hierarchy, which explains the lower performance.

Figure 9. Classification accuracy between ODP and topic ontology

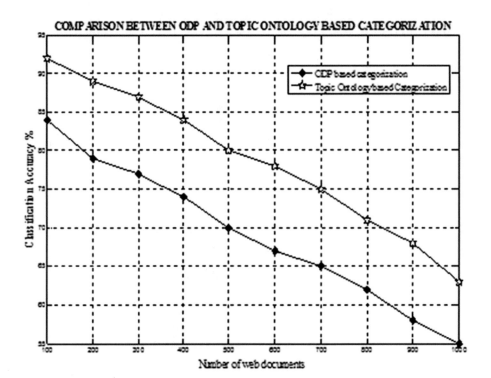

Performance Evaluation

Performance of the constructed topic ontology is measured based on standard metrics, such as precision, recall and F-measure. Therefore, experiments were conducted to evaluate the variation in the number of ODP concepts matched against the extracted terms with respect to the chosen string metric (Table 3). The prototype system used precision and the recall of the similarity metrics.

Precision

In Information Retrieval (IR), precision is the portion of retrieved instances that are relevant and a measure of the proportion of selected items that the system got right.

$$Precision = \frac{| Correctly\_Matched\_Concepts |}{| Total\_Number\_of\_Matched\_Concepts |}$$

Recall

In IR, recall is the portion of relevant instances that are retrieved and a measure of the proportion of the target items that the system selected.

Table 3. String similarity metrics comparison

String Similarity Metrics	Concepts in ODP	Matched Concepts	Effective Number of Concepts Matched	Precision (%)	Recall (%)
TFIDF	29	15	7	46.66	51.72
Jaro Winkler	29	29	14	48.27	100.00
Jaro Winkler TFIDF	29	17	13	76.47	58.62
Jaccard	29	3	3	100.00	10.34
Level2Jaro	29	29	17	58.62	100.00
Level2Jaro Winkler	29	29	17	58.62	100.00

$$Recall = \frac{| Correctly\_Matched\_Concepts |}{| Total\_Number\_of\_Concepts\_that\_should\_be\_Matched |}$$

F-Measure

F-measure combines recall and precision into one measure with equal weights and is defined as,

$$F - Measure = \frac{2 * Precision * Recall}{Precision + Recall}$$

Performance Evaluation

For the experimental evaluation, we used

- A corpus containing a collection of 15 texts from the software development literature available at the Wikipedia, an online encyclopedia. From this corpus a set of 450 terms and 19 associations were extracted by using the semantic similarity extraction algorithms.
- A pattern catalogue composed of two ontology design patterns, which had 29 concepts and 28 associations.
- A reference list of 98 matches, created from the text corpus and the ODP concepts to find the correct matches. This reference list included the exact matches, in addition to the terms that are not exact matches but have the same meaning as the concepts in the ODPs.

Figure 10- 12 illustrate the number of concepts matched, precision and recall value obtained using the algorithms. In the case of matching the number of concepts, it was found that the matched concepts were near perfect in the three of the concepts used. About 50% of the concepts demonstrated effective matching (Figure 10). In the case of precision measure, Jaccard had the highest precision Overall, the precision ranged from 45-60%, with maximum at 100% for Jaccard (Figure 11). At the same time, recall measures showed variation of 45% to 100%. Jaccard value touched as low as 10% (Figure 12).

A comparison of the string metrics for the string similarity metrics, number of matches, precision and recall demonstrated that precision was the highest for Jaccard (100%), followed by Jaro Winkler (78%),

Figure 10. Number of concepts matched with the string similarity metrics

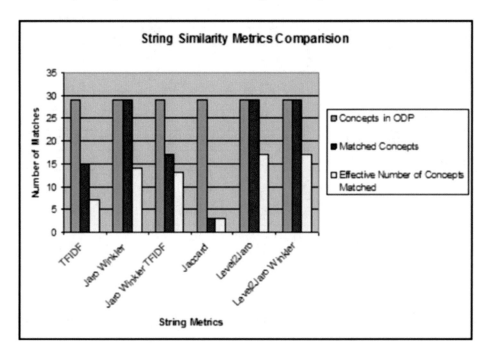

Figure 11. Precision value for similarity metrics

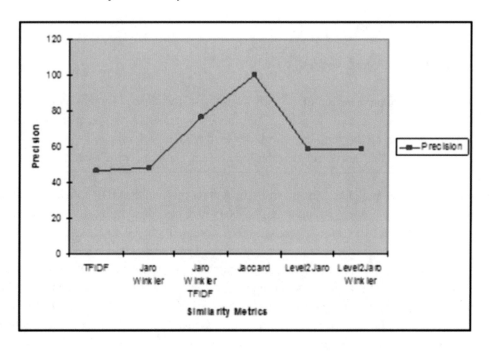

Figure 12. Recall value for similarity metrics

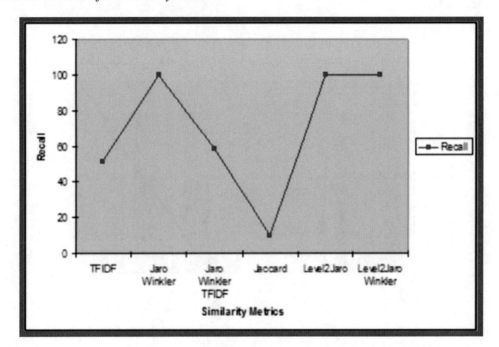

while others were in the range of 45% to 60%. Recall was the best at 100% for Jaro Winkler, Level2Jaro and Level2Jaro Winkler. On the contrary, Jaccard had the least recall (10%). Except for Jaccard, all others had F-measure values between 45% and 70% indicating that a combination of precision and recall could produce better results (Figure 13).

According to the different precision, recall and F-Measure values obtained by the algorithms, we can deduce that the reliability of the concepts and associations generated by the ontology is closely linked to the string similarity metric used for the terms and concept matching process. As a result, the choice of a string similarity metric with a high precision value will imply the construction of a topic ontology having few ODP concepts.

CONCLUSION AND FUTURE WORK

In this chapter, we have presented a novel approach for automatic construction of topic ontologies, which completely eliminates the user intervention. The proposed approach is based on concept acquisition and semantic relation extraction. The implementation of topic ontology construction with highly specific topic concepts and their corresponding semantic relations are the main contributions of this chapter. This approach was capable of suggesting and extracting optimal number of high quality topics. Further, it provided support to annotate the web documents in the form of topic ontology with high quality of semantic topics and different kinds of semantic relations. In order to support the topic ontology construction process, a software prototype was created and implemented. Using the developed prototype software, novel topic mapping algorithm was developed to acquire the concepts related to the category

Figure 13. Comparison of different string similarity metrics

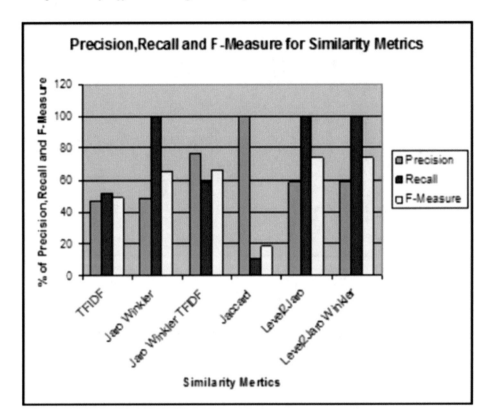

in ODP. The semantic similarity clustering algorithm was proposed to group the identified concepts and to determine the semantic distance between the concepts. In the semantic relation extraction algorithm, the semantic relation between the identified concepts was derived from the lexical relations of WordNet. The Jena API framework was used to hierarchically organize the identified concepts and their semantic relationship with topic ontology. The Protégé tool was effectively utilized to visualize the constructed topic ontology. The experimental results demonstrate the improved performance of the constructed topic ontology over ODP in terms of classification accuracy. In future, automatic topic ontology construction can be used in the enhancement of tag recommendation process. The constructed ontologies can help the tag recommender systems to make better prediction for the future tagging decisions.

REFERENCES

Agirre, E., Ansa, O., Martinez, D., & Hovy, E. 2001. Enriching WordNet Concepts with Topic Signatures. In *Proceedings of the NAACL workshop on WordNet and other lexical resources: Applications, Extensions and Customizations.*

Alani, H. (2006). Ontology Construction from Online Ontologies. In *Proceedings of 15th World Wide Web Conference*, Edinburgh, Scotland.

Alani, H., Kim, S., Millard, D. E., Weal, M. J., Lewis, P. H., Hall, W., & Shadbolt, N. R. 2003. Automatic Extraction of Knowledge from Web Documents. In *Proceedings of 2nd International Semantic Web Conference - Workshop on Human Language Technology for the Semantic Web and Web Services*, Sanibel Island, Florida.

Al-Mubaid, H., & Nguyen, H. A. (2006). A cluster-based approach for semantic similarity in the biomedical domain. In *Proceedings of the 28th Annual International Conference of the IEEE* (pp. 2713-2717). doi:10.1109/IEMBS.2006.259235

Baeza-Yates, R., & Ribeiro-Neto, N. 1999. Modern information retrieval. ACM Press.

Balachandran, K., & Ranathunga, S. (2016). Domain-Specific Term Extraction for Concept Identification in Ontology Construction. In *Proceedings of the 2016 IEEE/WIC/ACM International Conference on Web Intelligence* (pp. 34-41). IEEE Computer Society.

Bashar, M. A., Li, Y., & Gao, Y. (2016, October). A Framework for Automatic Personalised Ontology Learning. In *Proceedings of the 2016 IEEE/WIC/ACM International Conference on Web Intelligence* (pp. 105-112). IEEE. doi:10.1109/WI.2016.0025

Blaschke, C., & Valencia, A. (2002). Automatic Ontology Construction from the Literature. In *Proceedings of Genome Informatics Ser Workshop Genome Informatics* (Vol. 13, pp. 201–213).

Fortuna, B., Mladenič, D., & Grobelnik, M. (2006). Semi-automatic construction of topic ontologies. In *Semantics, Web and Mining* (pp. 121-131).

Blomqvist, E. (2006). OntoCase - Automatic ontology enrichment based on ontology design patterns. In *The Semantic Web, LNCS* (Vol. *5823*, pp. 65–80). doi:10.1007/978-3-642-04930-9_5

Böhm, K., Heyer, G., Quasthoff, U., & Wolff, C. (2002). Topic Map Generation Using Text Mining. *Journal of Universal Computer Science*, *8*(6), 623–633.

Brusa, G., Caliusco, M. & Chiotti, O. (2008). Towards ontological engineering: a process for building domain ontology from scratch in public administration. *Journal of knowledge engineering*, 2(5), 484-503.

Klaussner, C., & Zhekova, D. (2011). Pattern-Based Ontology Construction from Selected Wikipedia Pages. In *Proceedings of the Student Research Workshop associated with The 8th International Conference on Recent Advances in Natural Language Processing* (pp. 103-108).

Chernov, S., Iofciu, T., Nejdl, W., & Zhou, X. (2006). Extracting Semantic Relationships between Wikipedia Categories. In *Proceedings of the first International Workshop on Semantic Wikis*.

Chengzhi, Z., & Wei, S. (2008). Self-adaptive GA, quantitative semantic similarity measures and ontology-based text clustering. In *Proceedings of the 2008 IEEE International Conference on Natural Language Processing and Knowledge Engineering (NLP-KE08)*, Beijing, China (pp. 95-102).

Dahlem, N. (2011). OntoClippy: A User-Friendly Ontology Design and Creation Methodology. *International Journal of Intelligent Information Technologies*, *7*(1), 15–32. doi:10.4018/jiit.2011010102

Bollegala, D., Matsuo, Y., & Ishizuka, M. (2009). Measuring the Similarity between Implicit Semantic Relations from the Web. In *Proceedings of the 18th International Conference on World Wide Web* (pp. 651-660). doi:10.1145/1526709.1526797

David, S., & Antonio, M. (2004). Creating Ontologies from Web documents. In Recent Advances in Artificial Intelligence Research and Development (pp. 11-18). IOS Press.

Ding, Y., & Foo, S. (2002). Ontology research and development, Part 1 – A review of ontology generation. *Journal of Information Science, 28*(2), 123–136.

Farhoodi, M., Mahmoudi, M., Mohammad, A., Bidoki, Z., Yari, A. & Azadnia, M. (2009). Query Expansion Using Persian Ontology Derived from Wikipedia. *International journal of World Applied Sciences, 7*(4), 410-417.

Fernandez-Lopez, M., Gomez-Perez, A., & Juristo, N. (1997). Methontology: From ontological art towards ontological science. In *Proceedings of the Spring Symposium on ontology engineering of AAAI* (pp. 37-40).

Fortuna, B., Grobelnik, M., & Mladenic, D. (2005). Visualization of text document corpus. *Proceedings of the International Journal on Informatica, 29*(4), 497–502.

Frigui, H., & Krishnapuram, R. (1999). A Robust Competitive Clustering Algorithm with Application in Computer Vision. *IEEE Transactions on Pattern Analysis and Machine Intelligence, 21*(1), 450–465. doi:10.1109/34.765656

Ganapathy, G., & Sagayaraj, S. (2011). To Generate the Ontology from Java Source Code OWL Creation. *International Journal of Advanced Computer Science and Applications, 2*(2), 111–116. doi:10.14569/IJACSA.2011.020218

Grobelnik, M., & Mladenic, D. (2005). Simple classification into large topic ontology of Web documents. In *Proceeding of the 27th International Conference on Information Technology Interfaces* (pp. 188-193). doi:10.1109/ITI.2005.1491120

Grubic, T., & Fan, I. (2000). Supply chain ontology: Review, analysis and synthesis. *Computers in Industry, 61*(8), 776–786. doi:10.1016/j.compind.2010.05.006

Gruninger, M., & Fox, M. (1995). The role of competency questions in enterprise engineering. In *Proceedings of the IFIP WG5.7 Workshop on Benchmarking. Theory and Practice,* Troadhein, Norway. doi:10.1007/978-0-387-34847-6_3

Hearst, M. A. (1998). Automated Discovery of WordNet Relations. In C. Fellbaum (Ed.), *WordNet: An Electronic Lexical Database* (pp. 132–152). MIT Press.

Hlel, E., Jamoussi, S., & Hamadou, A. B. (2017). A New Method for Building Probabilistic Ontology (Prob-Ont). *International Journal of Information Technology and Web Engineering, 12*(2), 1–25. doi:10.4018/IJITWE.2017040101

Holsapple, C., & Joshi, K. (2002). A Collaborative approach to ontology design. *Communications of the ACM, 45*(2), 42–47. doi:10.1145/503124.503147

Jena. (2003). Jena – A Semantic Web Framework for Java. Retrieved from http://jena.sourceforge.ne t/ documentation.pdf

Joachims, T. (1998). Text Categorization with Support Vector Machines: Learning with Many Relevant Feature. In *Proceedings of the 10th European Conference on Machine Learning* (pp. 137-142). doi:10.1007/BFb0026683

Jung, H., Yoo, H., & Chung, K. (2016). Associative context mining for ontology-driven hidden knowledge discovery. *Cluster Computing*, *19*(4), 2261–2271. doi:10.1007/s10586-016-0672-8

Kawtrakul, A., Suktarachan, M., & Imsombut, A. (2004). Automatic Thai Ontology construction and Maintenance System. In *Proceedings of OntoLex Workshop on LREC*, Lisbon, Portugal.

Kong, H., Hwang, M., & Kim, P. (2006). Design of the Automatic Ontology Building System about the Specific Domain Knowledge. In *Proceedings of 8th International Conference on Advanced Communication Technology ICACT '06*. doi:10.1109/ICACT.2006.206235

Kim, J., & Storey, V. C. (2011). Construction of Domain Ontologies: Sourcing the World Wide Web. *International Journal of Intelligent Information Technologies*, *7*(2), 1–24. doi:10.4018/jiit.2011040101

Koontz, W. L. G., Narendra, P. M., & Fukunaga, K. (1975). A Branch and Bound Clustering Algorithm. *IEEE Transactions on Computers*, *C-24*(9), 908–915. doi:10.1109/T-C.1975.224336

Koontz, W. L. G., Narendra, P. M., & Fucunaga, K. (1975). A Graph Theoretic Approach to Nonparametric Cluster Analysis. *IEEE Transactions on Computers*, *C-25*(9), 936–944. doi:10.1109/TC.1976.1674719

Lee, J. (2006). The roles of scenario use in ontology development. *Knowledge and Process Management*, *13*(4), 270–284. doi:10.1002/kpm.264

Leung, N. K. Y., Kang, S. H., Lau, S. K., & Fan, J. (2009). *Ontology matching techniques: a 3- Tier classification framework. International Journal of the computer, the Internet and Management. 17* (pp. 22.1–22.7). SPI.

Leung, N. K., Lau, S. K., & Tsang, N. (2012). An ontology development methodology to integrate existing ontologies in an ontology development process. *Communications of the ICISA: An International Journal*, *13*(2), 31-61.

Maguitman, A. G., Cecchini, R. L., Lorenzetti, C. M., & Menczer, F. (2010). Using Topic Ontologies and Semantic Similarity Data to Evaluate Topical Search. In *Proceedings of 36th Latin American Informatics Conference*.

Miller, G. A., Beckwith, R., Fellbaum, C. D., Gross, D., & Miller, K. (1990). WordNet: An online lexical database. *Int. J. Lexicograph*, *3*(4), 235–244. doi:10.1093/ijl/3.4.235

Mizoguchi, R. (2003). Tutorial on ontology engineering: Introduction to ontology engineering (Part 1). *New Generation Computing*, *21*(4), 362–383. doi:10.1007/BF03037311

Nicola, G. (1998). Formal Ontology and Information Systems. In *Proceedings of the IEEE/WIC/ACM International Conference on Formal Ontology in Information Systems FOIS'98* (pp. 3-15).

Noy, N. & McGuinness, D. (2001). Ontology development 101: A guide to creating your first ontology. Stanford knowledge systems laboratory, California.

Noy, N. F., Sintek, M., Decker, St., Crubézy, M., Fergerson, R. W., & Musen, M. (2001). Creating Semantic Web Contents with Protégé-2000. *IEEE Intelligent Systems, 16*(2), 60–71. doi:10.1109/5254.920601

Pei, M., Nakayama, K., Hara, T., & Nishio, S. (2008). Constructing a Global Ontology by Concept Mapping Using Wikipedia Thesaurus. In *Proceedings of the 22nd International Conference on Advanced Information Networking and Applications Workshops* (pp. 1205-1210). doi:10.1109/WAINA.2008.117

Pinto, H., & Martin, J. 2001. A Methodology for ontology integration. In *Proceedings of the 1st International conference on knowledge capture*, British Columbia (pp. 131-138).

Selim, S.Z., & Ismail,, M.A. (1984). K-means-type Algorithm: Generalized Convergence Theorem andCharacterization of Local Optimality. *IEEE Transactions on Pattern Analysis and Machine Intelligence, 6*(1), 81–87.

Snasel, V., Moravec, P., & Pokorny, J. (2005). WordNet ontology based model for web retrieval. In *Proceedings of the International Workshop on Challenges in Web Information Retrieval and Integration* (pp. 220-225). doi:10.1109/WIRI.2005.38

Sridevi, U. K., & Nagaveni, N. (2011). An Ontology Based Model for Document Clustering. *International Journal of Intelligent Information Technologies, 7*(3), 54–69. doi:10.4018/jiit.2011070105

Stabb, R., Benjamins, V. & Fensel, D. (1998). Knowledge engineering: Principles and Methods. *Data and Knowledge engineering, 25*, 161-197.

Subramaniyaswamy, V., & Chenthur Pandian, S. (2012). Effective Tag Recommendation System Based on Topic Ontology using Wikipedia and WordNet. *International Journal of Intelligent Systems, John Wiley and Sons Ltd Periodicals, 27*(12), 1034–1048. doi:10.1002/int.21560

Subramaniyaswamy, V., & Chenthur Pandian, S. (2012a). An improved Approach for Topic Ontology based Categorization of Blogs using Support Vector Machine. *J. Comput. Sci., 8*(2), 251–258. doi:10.3844/jcssp.2012.251.258

Subramaniyaswamy, V., & Chenthur Pandian, S. (2012b). A Complete Survey of Duplicate Record Detection using Data Mining Techniques. *Inform. Technol. J., 11*(8), 941–945. doi:10.3923/itj.2012.941.945

Subramaniyaswamy, V., Vijayakumar, V., & Indragandhi, V. (2013). A Review of Ontology based Tag Recommendation Approaches. *International Journal of Intelligent Systems, 28*(11), 1054–1071. doi:10.1002/int.21616

Suchanek, F. M., Kasneci, G., & Weikum, G. (2007). YAGO: A Core of Semantic Knowledge Unifying WordNet and Wikipedia. In *Proceedings of the 16th International conference on World Wide Web.* doi:10.1145/1242572.1242667

Tiun, S., Abdullah, R., & Kong, T. E. (2001). Automatic Topic Identification Using Ontology Hierarchy. In *Proceedings of the Second International Conference on Computational Linguistics and Intelligent Text Processing* (pp. 444-453). doi:10.1007/3-540-44686-9_43

Uschold, M., & King, M. (1995). Towards a methodology for building ontologies. In *Proceedings of workshop on basic ontological issues in knowledge sharing (International joint conference on artificial intelligence)*, Montreal, Canada.

Uschold, M. (1996). Building ontologies: Towards a unified methodology. In *Proceedings of expert systems (Annual conference of the British computer society specialist group on expert systems)*, Cambridge, UK.

Vairavasundaram, S., Varadharajan, V., Vairavasundaram, I., & Ravi, L. (2015). Data mining-based tag recommendation system: An overview. *Wiley Interdisciplinary Reviews: Data Mining and Knowledge Discovery*, *5*(3), 87–112.

Wang, H., Jiang, X., Chia, L.-T., & Tan, A.-H. (2010). Wikipedia2Onto – Building Concept Ontology Automatically, Experimenting with Web Image Retrieval. *Informatica Slovenia*, *34*(3), 297–306.

Wimmer, H., Yoon, V., & Rada, R. (2012). Applying Semantic Web Technologies to Ontology Alignment. *International Journal of Intelligent Information Technologies*, *8*(1), 1–9. doi:10.4018/jiit.2012010101

Wimmer, H., Yoon, V., & Rada, R. (2014). Strategies and Methods for Ontology Alignment. *Recent Advances in Intelligent Technologies and Information Systems*, *1*.

Xujuan, Z., Li, Y., Xu, Y., & Raymond, L. (2006). Relevance assessment of topic ontology. In *Proceedings of the 4th International Conference on Active Media Technology*.

Zhao, L., Ren, H., & Wan, J. (2015). Automatic ontology construction based on clustering nucleus. *Wuhan University Journal of Natural Sciences*, *20*(2), 129–133. doi:10.1007/s11859-015-1070-4

Zhou, P., & El-Gohary, N. (2015). Ontology-based multilabel text classification of construction regulatory documents. *Journal of Computing in Civil Engineering*, *30*(4), 04015058. doi:10.1061/(ASCE)CP.1943-5487.0000530

Zhu, D., & Dreher, H. (2009). Discovering Semantic Aspects of Socially Constructed Knowledge Hierarchy to Boost the Relevance of Web Searching. *International Journal of Universal Computer Science*, *15*(8), 1685–1710.

Chapter 5
Norms–Adaptable Agents for Open Multi–Agent Systems

Moamin A Mahmoud
Universiti Tenaga Nasional, Malaysia

Mohd Sharifuddin Ahmad
Universiti Tenaga Nasional, Malaysia

ABSTRACT

Norms and normative multi-agent systems have become the subjects of interest for many researchers. Such interest is caused by the need for agents to exploit the norms in enhancing their performance in a community. In open agent systems, an agent is not usually and explicitly given the norms of the host agents. Thus, when it is not able to adapt the communities' norms, it is totally deprived of accessing resources and services from the host. Such circumstance severely affects its performance resulting in failure to achieve its goal. While several studies have addressed this issue, their detection mechanisms are restricted to the use of sanctions by third party enforcement. Consequently, this study attempts to overcome this deficiency by proposing a technique that enables an agent to detect the host's potential norms via self-enforcement and update its norms even in the absence of sanctions from a third-party. The technique is called the Potential Norms Detection Technique (PNDT).

INTRODUCTION

The concepts of norms and normative systems are used to determine the behaviors of agents within a community and are commonly accepted as efficient means to normalize their behaviors (Alberti et al., 2011). Norms represent desirable behaviors for a population of a natural or artificial community and they are generally understood as rules indicating actions they are expected to perform that are either obligatory, prohibitive or permissive based on a specific set of facts. Coleman (1998) defines two main categories of norms: conventions and essential norms. Correspondingly, Villatoro (2011) grounded the difference between conventions and essential norms. Conventions are natural norms that emerge without any enforcement. Conventions solve coordination problems when there is no conflict between an individual and the collective interests, such as everyone conforms to a desired behavior. Conventions

DOI: 10.4018/978-1-5225-3686-4.ch005

fix one norm amongst a set of norms which is always efficient as long as each one in the community employs the same norm i.e. greetings, driving side of the road (Villatoro, 2011). Essential Norms solve or ease collective action problems when there is a conflict between an individual and the collective interests (Villatoro et al., 2010). For example, "the norm not to pollute urban streets is essential in that it requires individuals to transport their trash, rather than dispose of it on the spot, an act that benefits everyone" (Piskorski et al., 2011).

Intelligent software agents have been widely used in distributed artificial intelligence and due to their autonomous, self-interested, rational abilities (Mahmoud et al., 2016c, 2016d, 2016e; Jassim et al., 2016), and social abilities (Subramainan et al., 2016a, 2016b; Mahmoud et al., 2013), agents are well-suited for automated negotiation on behalf of humans (Kexing, 2011).

In agent communities, norms are used to regulate agents' behaviors but agents may decide not to comply with the norms if this benefits them (Mahmoud et al., 2016a, 2016b). Consequently, norms enforcement is designed to offset these benefits and thus the motives for not complying with the norms (Perreau de Pinninck et al., 2010). To perform the enforcement, it requires a process that is able to detect the activity of the norms and their probable violations and handle this violation (Vázquez-Salceda et al., 2004). According to Perreau de Pinninck et al. (2010), norms enforcement can be achieved through a controller via stopping forbidden actions or applying reward and penalty on agents. However, the literature presented two types of enforcements, which are self-enforcement and third-party enforcement. Self-enforcement is also called as internally-directed enforcement (Hollander & Wu, 2011). It occurs when an agent punishes itself for violating a norm, which could happen when an agent has internalized the norm and is influenced by some forms of emotion or awareness. In self-enforcement, the violator performs its own penalty and this is often because its actions are not coordinated with the actions of other agents. In other words, there is no third-party involved in its actions to apply punishment (Posner & Rasmusen, 1999).

The literature referred to third-party enforcement type as externally-directed enforcement (Hollander & Wu, 2011). A third-party enforcement agent has the ability and authority to implement sanctions (reward or penalty) (Grossi et al., 2010; Mahmoud et al., 2014). It occurs when an agent observes another agent violating a norm (Flentge et al., 2001; Galan & Izquierdo, 2005) or during norm spreading when an agent does not adopt the norms of others. While norms and normative systems have been the subject of intense investigation (Castelfranchi et al., 1998; Broersen et al., 2001; Sadri et al., 2006), norms detection is quite a recent research issue, in which an agent attempts to decipher the normative protocol of a group of local agents. A search on the related work in norms detection shows a few results (Andrighetto et al., 20010; Savarimuthu et al., 2010; Centeno & Billhardt, 2012).

Norms detection is a process of updating an agent's norms based on discovering a society's potential norms through some detection mechanism, which rely on observing or interacting with other agents to infer the potential norms. According to (Hollander & Wu, 2011; Boella et al. 2008), when researchers attempt to build a normative multi-agent system, norms detection is one of main challenges faced by the designer. The literature provides other terms for norms detection such as norms recognition, norms adaptation (Hollander & Wu, 2011) and norms identification (Savarimuthu, 2010).

Norms detection is inspired by the process of norms learning and norms cognition (Hollander & Wu, 2011; Savarimuthu, 2010). Several studies have been made by researchers on norms learning based on mechanisms of imitation (Epstein, 2001; Andrighetto et al., 2010); social learning (Sen & Airiau, 2007; Bosse et al., 2009); case-based reasoning (Campos et al., 2010); and data mining (Symeonidis &

Mitkas, 2005; Savarimuthu et al., 2010). Others have worked on norms cognition (Andrighetto et al., 2007; Savarimuthu et al., 2010).

In this work, we propose a detection technique based on data mining and cognitive approach and the technique works based on self-enforcement that detects the norms in both situations, when reward and penalty events are absent or available. The self-enforcement model is based on imitation mechanism by (Epstein, 2001).

In open systems, agents are not conferred with the community's norms in offline mode. Instead, the agent must be able to identify the norms by using some detection algorithm. While we concur with the authors in this definition, we propose that an open community also refers to the agent's free and unrestricted movement from one community to another to achieve its goal. In such situation, when the agent visits a new community and it does not have any knowledge about the community's norms, it should be equipped with algorithms for detecting the norms.

Several recent studies addressed norms detection in open agents' communities but their detection mechanisms are restricted to the availability of sanction by third party enforcement (Savarimuthu et al., 2010). Consequently, this study attempts to overcome this deficiency by proposing a technique that enables an agent's self-enforcement ability to update its norms even in the absence of sanctions from a third-party. Our review of the literature suggests that researchers have not discussed norms detection in the absence of third-party enforcement. This is the most critical problem in public domains in which agent is not able to adapt to the norms. A BDI agent's (based on belief, desire, and intention) belief changes based on observing sanctions by an authorized third-party. But if sanctions are absent, the agent's belief cannot and does not change. Consequently, agents are not motivated to detect the norms, which could produce chaotic situations. To avoid such situations, such norms detection is critically important.

This work attempts to resolve the problem by enabling an agent to detect the host's potential norms via a technique called the Potential Norms Detection Technique (PNDT). PNDT enables an agent to be self-enforcing to update its norms even in the absence of sanctions from a third-party. However, the proposed technique is also applicable in domains that apply sanctions but does not make use of this property. In addition, detecting potential norms by PNDT avoids the agent from becoming deviant or undesirable in a community.

The PNDT consists of five components: agent's belief base; observation process; Potential Norms Mining Algorithm (PNMA) to detect the potential norms and identify the normative protocol; verification process, which verifies the detected potential norms; and updating process, which updates the agent's belief base with new normative protocol. This study assumes that an agent is able to reason on the surrounding events. It exploits the resources of the host system and uses the PNMA algorithm to implement data formatting, filtering, and extracting to identify the potential norms and subsequently, the normative protocol.

Savarimuthu et al. (2010b) defined the normative protocol as "the order of occurrence of events or protocols that are related to a set of norms". For example, arrive, order, eat, pay, tip and depart in that order is the normative protocol for dining in a restaurant. This work, however, defines a normative protocol as a set of computationally executable norms that are applied to some multi-agent communities.

The idea of this study is inspired from the need to resolve potential norms conflict between two people of different culture. For example, consider an English expatriate who is requested to work with his/her counterparts in Japan. He/She would find it difficult to practice the norms of the Japanese people if he/she does not attempt to discover the norms of the Japanese people. A serious problem could occur if norms conflict causes misunderstanding in communication, interactions, and coordination resulting in poor work performance or complete failure.

The objectives of this chapter are (i) to detect the potential norms of a domain that are not monitored by enforcing agents via rewards and penalties, (ii) to develop a self-enforcing agent, (iii) to identify the normative protocol, which avoids agents from becoming deviant or undesirable, and (iv) to develop a verification process that validates the detected norms. Our contribution in this chapter is four-fold. Firstly, we analyze the literature on norms learning and exploit the approaches that help in building a self-enforcing agent. Secondly, we develop a norms detection technique taking into account the absence of rewards and penalties. Thirdly, we develop a norm mining algorithm that extracts norms from a set of events. Fourthly, we build a virtual environment with number of variables to test the efficiency of the PNDT technique.

BACKGROUND

Norms detection attempts to discover the normative behavior of agents by 'observing' the agents in actions. In agent or robot communities, it is a very complicated problem for agents or robots to adapt the norms from different domains because doing so is costly and requires huge memory. Even if such feat is attempted, the problem will not be resolved due to the dynamic nature of norms, when new norms appear or are updated and others disappear (Boella et al., 2009). Failure to detect or discover a society's norms could subject the agent to probable sanction or penalty if it violates the norms. On the other hand, succeeding in discovering the norms earns the agent with rewards or at least avoids the penalty. If a visitor agent is equipped with mechanisms to detect a system's norms, then it becomes more flexible and is able to adapt itself to changes in the environment or its goals (Boella et al., 2009). Several studies have addressed the issue of norms detection. As we mentioned earlier, norms detection is inspired by norm learning and cognitive approach. The following research are either based on norm learning mechanisms which are imitation, social learning, case-based reasoning, data mining, or based on the cognitive approach. Norm learning is the ability of learning from others and it is an active technique to complement and support the learning of individuals. In particular, norm learning presents the basis for culture where norms spread within a society and pass down from one generation to another (Dautenhahn et al., 2003). The literature suggests four mechanisms of norm learning.

Epstein (2001) proposed an imitation model based on adopting the behavior of a majority of population. The phenomenon of imitation has been described as "When in Rome, do as the Romans do". This model is based on the local environment state and the amount of thinking of agent regarding its behavior. An agent thinks less when it conforms to its surrounding neighbors, but it thinks more otherwise. The mechanism of the model is an agent checks the conformity of norms with its surrounding neighbors within a personal vision radius. If it conforms, it keeps the norms and thinks less about them. If it does not conform, then the agent thinks more and changes the norms according to the majority of population. The proposed technique in this chapter (PNDT) exploits such mechanism to motivate an agent to be self-enforcing. Lòpez y Lòpez (2003) justified the need of learning mechanisms in normative systems because agents make decisions not only on their motivations and own goals, but also by observing the normative behavior of other agents. The author proposed three strategies to influence agents to comply with a norm of related actions of other agents. The strategies are simple imitation, reasoned imitation, and reciprocation. Andrighetto et al. (2010) presented a comparative study between two models of learning that are validated by simulations, which are imitation-based and recognition-based learning. The simulation study attempted to compare the normative agent's behavior provided with (i) a norm recognition module, which they called Norm Recognizers (NRs), and (ii) a social conformity population model, called Social Conformers (SCs), whose behavior is specified by imitation rule.

Social learning in agent society means that each agent learns from repeated interactions with other agents in a society (Sen & Airiau, 2007). The individual's behavior is largely influenced by the interaction with others, through social learning (Bosse et al., 2009). Sen and Airiau (2007) proposed a social learning theory, in which every agent in the community learns simultaneously from repeated interactions with randomly selected neighbors. The key to success of this method depends on how an agent learns from other agents within the social network. Bosse et al. (2009) presented a dynamic agent-based approach to simulate and formally analyze the process of social learning of agents' behaviors. The general mechanism is based on behavior changes by influence of peers. The approach involves the influence of three types of agent groups which are peers, parents, and school. Campos et al. (2010) used Case-based Reasoning (CBR) as a learning technique to decide how to adapt domain-level norms that depends on current system status. CBR learning is based on heuristics that tries to align the amount of serving/ receiving capacity, and this heuristic is used by the CBR to suggest a solution when no similar cases are found.

Few studies in norm detection emerged from data mining applications. Data mining entails scouring through data records in databases to identify significant patterns that are useful for a decision-making process (Kotsiantis & Kanellopoulos, 2006). Among the data mining tasks such as classification or clustering, association rule mining is one particular task that extracts desirable information structures like correlations, frequent patterns, associations or casual between sets of items in transaction databases or other stores of data (Kotsiantis & Kanellopoulos, 2006; Ogunde et al., 2011). Association rule mining is widely used in many different fields like telecommunication network, marketing, risk management, inventory control and others (Kotsiantis & Kanellopoulos, 2006). The association rule mining algorithm discovers association rules from a given database such that the rule satisfies a predefined value of support and confidence. The aim of using support and confidence thresholds is to ignore those rules that are not desirable, because the database is huge and users care about those frequently occurring patterns only (Symeonidis & Mitkas, 2006).

Symeonidis et al. (2005) presented an agent-oriented algorithm that deals with agent actions, which is called K-profile. K-profile is mainly used to predict an agent's behaviors by exploiting data mining techniques to extract the knowledge from historical data and express the actions of agents within the multi-agent systems. Savarimuthu et al. (2010a) develop algorithms to identify obligation norms is called Obligation Norm Identification (ONI). The algorithm is designed based on data mining, specifically on the association rule mining approach. In recent research on norm detection, a new approach has been suggested by Andrighetto et al. (2007), which is norm cognition or cognitive approach.

Andrighetto et al. (2007) proposed a norm innovation theory in coping with specific types of complex entities such as a social system called the EMIL architecture. Two-way dynamics are categorized by the theories which are emergent processes consisting of emergence from interaction among individual agents and emergent effects: emergence of entities (norms) at the aggregate level into the agents' minds. Savarimuthu et al. (2010) emphasized on the importance of the cognitive approach and presented a cognitive model, in which agents are located in a domain where other agents entering the domain may not be aware of the protocol associated with domain's norms. An agent located in the domain is able to observe other agents' actions and is able to extract a society's norms from these actions based on the ability of recognizing negative and positive signals (e.g. reward and penalty) events by using a filtering algorithm. The agent, after identifying the normative protocol of the society, updates its personal belief base by adding or removing norms.

INTRODUCTION TO POTENTIAL NORMS DETECTION TECHNIQUE (PNDT)

This section defines the terms relating to the development of PNDT and presents the full semantics of PNDT. These definitions are important to form the underlying theories of the potential norms detection process.

Definitions

Definition 1: A Domain[1], D, is the set of activities of a group of agents engaged in some particular work. Agents in a domain are often performing tasks and communicating between each other to share knowledge.

Definition 2: A Host Agent, α_h, is agent that resides and belongs to the same domain.

Definition 3: A Visitor Agent, α_v, is agent that resides in the domain but does not belong to the domain.

Definition 4: A nearby agent, α_c, is the agent that is located within the observation limit of other agents.

Definition 5: Norm[2], N, is a type of social rules that regulate an agent's behavior.

Definition 6: A Normative Protocol, P_N, is a set of executable norms that are applied to some multi-agent communities. For example, a normative protocol for an elevator domain is *arrive, wait, enter, excuse, depart.*

Definition 7: A Convention, C, is a type of norm that is expected to be used by every agent in the domain.

Definition 8: The Potential Norms, N_P, are the norms that are enacted by a majority of population.

Definition 9: The Weak Norms, N_w, are the norms that are enacted by a minority of population.

Definition 10: The Candidate Norms, N_C, are the norms that are either potential or weak norms prior to detection.

Definition 11: The Norm's Strength, S_N, refers to the degree of enactment of a specific norm by a population in a domain.

Definition 12: The Threshold, T, is the limit of the norm's strength that delineate whether a norm is potential or weak.

Definition 13: An Event, E, it is an action performed by an agent, e.g., order a meal.

Definition 14: An Episode, EP, is the sequence of events, which is performed by an agent, e.g., in the elevator domain, one possible episode is wait, enter, excuse, depart.

Definition 15: A Segment, EP_S, is a subset of an episode, e.g., in the elevator domain, if the episode is wait, enter, excuse, depart, then (enter, excuse) is a segment of the episode.

Definition 16: A History, H_{EP}, is a set of episodes in the record base.

FULL ABBREVIATION OF PNDT

This work focuses on developing a technique based on self-enforcement that enables an agent to detect a domain's norms. To do so, an agent needs some belief motivation to detect and adapt a domain's norms. We exploit the imitation mechanism by Epstein (2001) that is based on the local environment and an agent's behavior. In this mechanism, the agent's belief is triggered by its conformity to the norms of its surrounding neighbors. If it conforms, it enacts the norms. If it does not conform, then it attempts to detect the new norms.

We modify this mechanism by letting the agent to decide on launching the Potential Norms Detection Technique (PNDT). We assume that the agent belief is triggered by the benefit of imitating the majority, thus when the agent's norms do not conform to its surrounded nearby agents' norms, its belief is motivated to start detecting. We represent our cases as follows:

- If an agent in its local domain, conforms to the norms of nearby agents then it is not motivated to launch the PNDT.
- If an agent in its local domain does not conform to other nearby agents' norms, then it is motivated to launch the PNDT.
- If an agent is in a new domain then it is motivated to launch the PNDT.

From these cases, we notice that two reasons motivate the agent to update its norms which are the norms' conformity with its nearby agents and if it is in a new domain.

In this technique, the agent collects events and classifies those events into two different types, which are conventions and candidate norms. Conventions are norms that are expected to be adopted by every agent in the society, i.e., the agents adopt all conventions. According to Young (2008) and Villatoro (2011), conventions are intersections of all agents' events, i.e. the intersection set of events represents conventions.

The candidate norms can be either potential or weak, but the agent adopts the validated potential norms only. Candidate norms are extracted from events by filtering those events from conventions. Briefly, the PNDT algorithm is developed based on two theories which are, imitation theory by Epstein (2001) to motivate an agent belief and association rule mining and data sets to extract the potential norms. To develop the PNDT technique, the following points are assumed:

- An agent that does not conform its norms with the nearby agents triggers its thoughts about conforming to the norms.
- Agents in a domain are able to observe the actions of each other within the observation limit.

THE PNDT TECHNIQUE

In this technique, the detection process is based on the precondition, post-condition and agent's belief. When an agent observes that its norms do not conform to the surrounding nearby agents, it leads the agent to update its norms, which is considered as a precondition. Subsequently, its belief about its current norms is changed. The agent then launches the potential norms detection technique (PNDT) to detect the domain's norms.

The PNDT framework is built with five main components. The first component is the agent's Belief Base, which consists of the External Belief, represented by the Record Base and Internal Belief, represented by the Norms Model Base. The Record Base is the storage of all observed events and the Norms Model Base is a repository of all normative protocols for various domains.

The second component is the observation process, in which the agent collects data by observing other agents' interaction patterns and records those interactions in the Record Base. The third component is the Potential Norms Mining Algorithm (PNMA). Following the observation process, the agent launches the PNMA algorithm to work on the data in the Record Base. The PNMA algorithm extracts the candidate norms and identifies the potential norms and normative protocol.

The fourth component is verification process, which verifies the detected potential norms. The last component is updating process, which updates the agent Belief Base by adding new normative protocols to the Norms Model Base, or amending the existing ones in the Model Base by adding or removing events. Figure 1 shows the PNDT framework.

Based on Figure 1, an agent (1) observes the domain's events, (2) adds those events to its Record Base (External Belief), (3) mines the Record Base by using the PNMA algorithm, (4) detects the candidate potential norms, and (5) identifies the normative protocol, (6) verifies the detected potential norms, and (7) updates its Norms Model Base with the new normative protocol or amending the existing ones (Internal Belief).

THE PNDT PROCESS

The PNDT starts its process when necessary. However, an agent's external belief estimates this necessity based on its observation. Briefly, the process starts when a change in an agent's external belief occurred

Figure 1. The PNDT framework

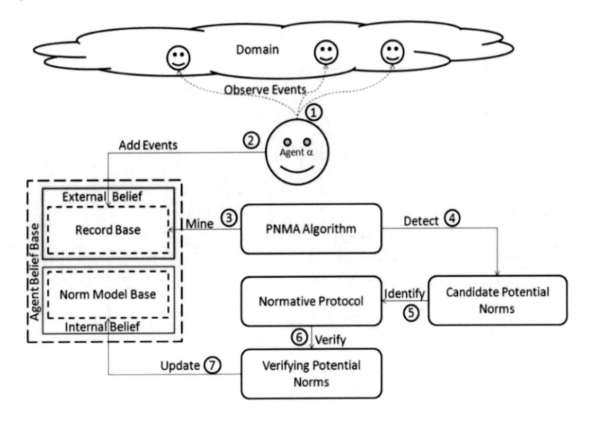

and it then collects episodes for PNDT's analysis. The PNDT uses the PNMA algorithms to mine those episodes and identifies the potential norms. Subsequently, the verifying process verifies the identified norms. Finally, the updating process updates the internal belief of the agent. As shown in Figure 2, the process flow starts when the agent, α, observes that its norms do not conform to its neighbors, then α uses PNDT technique.

The PNDT technique starts with observing the domain, collecting events and adding them to the record base. The PNMA algorithm mines the record base to discover new norms. The next step is verifying those norms and updating the norm model base.

AGENT'S BELIEF BASE

The agent's belief base entails external belief, B_X, and internal belief, B_I. The external belief is manifested by the Record Base and the internal belief is represented by the Norms Model Base.

Definition 17: An agent belief, B, is a component that represents an agent's view about a specific behavior[3] in the domain.

Definition 18: An internal belief, B_I, represents an agent's own belief about a specific behavior.

Definition 19: An external belief, B_X, represents an agent's belief about what others belief towards a specific behavior.

Figure 2. The PNDT process flow

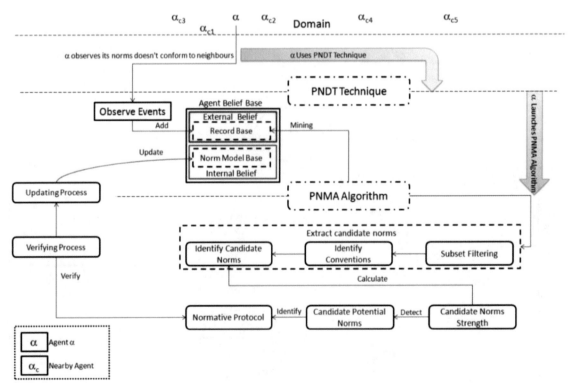

Definition 20: A Record Base, R, contains the records of all observed events and represents the history log of all observed events. When an agent observes that its norms do not conform to other nearby agents, it collects the relevant event's data and adds them to its Record Base.

Definition 21: The Norms Model Base, NB, is the storage for all detected normative protocols.

An agent uses the identified normative protocol to exercise the norms for the target domain, pending assimilation with the local agent's community. The agent stores the identified normative protocol by using the classification model to structure the protocol's data.

The norm model base represents the internal belief of an agent about its norms. Any update in the model base updates the agent's internal belief.

THE OBSERVATION PROCESS

An agent begins the observation process, P_{OB}, when it needs to update its norms. Observing event depends on the availability of other nearby agents. In the following elevator example we represent the activities agents, $\alpha_1 - \alpha_{13}$, as follows:

enter (α_1); agent 1 enter elevator
excuse (α_2); agent 2 excuse
depart (α_2); agent 2 depart elevator
litter (α_1); agent 1 litter in elevator
arrive (α_3); agent 3 arrive elevator
enter (α_3); agent 3 enter elevator

After observing those events, it represents each event as individual episode for each agent $\alpha_1 - \alpha_{13}$. The episodes are represented in the form of tuple of events as follows:

(α_1) = (enter, litter)
(α_2) = (excuse, depart)
(α_3) = (arrive, enter)

In data collection, the agent does not collect all the data in the domain, but only the relevant data. Similar observation process had been used by Savarimuthu et al. (2010)

POTENTIAL NORMS MINING ALGORITHM (PNMA)

The objectives of the Potential Norms Mining Algorithm (PNMA) are to extract the potential candidate norms and the subsequent normative protocol. To illustrate the novelty of the PNDT and validate the PNMA algorithm, we present an example of the elevator scenario in identifying and recognizing the potential norms and normative protocol. In this scenario, we assume an agent, α, moved from its local domain D_X to new domain D_Y. In the new domain, there is an elevator and α has the knowledge of the normative protocol from the previous domain D_X which is arrive; wait; enter; depart.

Since the agent is in a new domain, it is motivated to launch the PNDT to detect the new domain's norms and the normative protocol. We assume a set of norms that are commonly practiced in the elevator scenario, which are arrive; wait; enter; litter; excuse; depart. We suppose the following episodes are observed by the agent and stored in its Record Base to detect the domain's norms. Those episodes are collected from agent α_1 to α_{13}:

$(\alpha_{\lambda 1})$ = (enter, excuse, depart)
$(\alpha_{\lambda 2})$ = (arrive, wait, enter, excuse)
$(\alpha_{\lambda 3})$ = (wait, enter, litter, excuse)
$(\alpha_{\lambda 4})$ = (arrive, wait, enter, excuse, depart)
$(\alpha_{\lambda 5})$ = (arrive, wait, enter, depart)
$(\alpha_{\lambda 6})$ = (enter, depart)
$(\alpha_{\lambda 7})$ = (wait, enter, excuse)
$(\alpha_{\lambda 8})$ = (arrive, wait, enter, litter, excuse, depart)
$(\alpha_{\lambda 9})$ = (wait, enter, litter)
$(\alpha_{\lambda 10})$ = (arrive, wait, enter, excuse, depart)
$(\alpha_{\lambda 11})$ = (arrive, wait, enter)
$(\alpha_{\lambda 12})$ = (wait, enter, depart)
$(\alpha_{\lambda 13})$ = (excuse, depart)

The PNMA consists of three steps to achieve its objectives, which are:

Step 1: Extract the candidate norms from the Record Base by applying:
Subset Filtering (F-episodes): This is applied on all episodes (A-episodes) in the Record Base by removing the subset episodes (S-episodes) which have the same sequence of events as a bigger set.

From the Venn diagram shown in Figure 3, we can recognize two sets: the first set is Q = {a, b, c, d} and the second set is P = {b, c}. We can also recognize that the second set, P, is a subset of first set, Q, i.e. P ⊂ Q. If the set is true then the subset is true: "It is always the case that two compound statements

Figure 3. Venn diagram

are equivalent if and only if they have the same truth sets" (Kemeny et al., 1998). Therefore, we remove all events, which are subset of a bigger set or subset of itself, if they have the same sequence of the bigger set. In the above example, we remove the set P = {b, c}.

Mathematically, we can represent the subset filtering as follows:

$$Filter\left(agentX,setB\right) \Leftrightarrow \left(\left(A \cap B = B\right) \to B \subseteq A\right)$$

$$Filter\left(agentX,setA\right) \Leftrightarrow \left(\left(A \cap B = A\right) \to A \subseteq B\right)$$

F-episodes can be identified by getting the set-theoretic complement between A-episodes and S-episodes:

$$\text{F} - \text{episode}\left(\text{R}\right) = \text{A} - \text{episodes}\left(\text{R}\right) \setminus \text{S} - \text{episodes}\left(\text{R}\right) \tag{1}$$

Accordingly, subset filtering or filtered episodes (F-episodes) equals all episodes excluding subset episodes. Applying subset filtering from Eq. 1 on the episodes of the elevator example, Table 1 shows the complete results of the subset filtering operation.

Identify Conventions (C): Conventions can be identified from (F-episodes) by getting the intersection set of F-episodes. If Fe is a filtered episode, then,

$$\text{F} - \text{episodes} = F_{e1}, F_{e2}, \ldots, F_{e\kappa} \quad C = F_{e1} \cap F_{e2} \cap \ldots \cap F_{e\kappa} \Rightarrow C = \bigcap_{w=1}^{k} Fe_{\kappa} \tag{2}$$

The above formula means that conventions equal the intersections of filtered episodes sets. Identifying conventions based on Eq. 2 on the elevator example, gives the following F-episodes:

Table 1. Subset filtering operation

A-episodes	\	S-episodes	=	F-episodes
(enter, excuse, depart)		(enter, excuse, depart)		(arrive, wait, enter, excuse, depart)
(arrive, wait, enter, excuse)		(arrive, wait, enter, excuse)		(arrive, wait, enter, depart)
(wait, enter, litter, excuse)		(wait, enter, litter, excuse)		(arrive, wait, enter, litter, excuse, depart)
(arrive, wait, enter, excuse, depart)		(enter, depart)		(arrive, wait, enter, excuse, depart)
(arrive, wait, enter, depart)		(wait, enter, excuse)		
(enter, depart)		(wait, enter, litter)		
(wait, enter, excuse)		(arrive, wait, enter)		
(arrive, wait, enter, litter, excuse, depart)		(wait, enter, depart)		
(wait, enter, litter)		(excuse, depart)		
(arrive, wait, enter, excuse, depart)				
(arrive, wait, enter)				
(wait, enter, depart)				
(excuse, depart)				

F_{e1} = (arrive, wait, enter, excuse, depart)
F_{e2} = (arrive, wait, enter, depart)
F_{e3} = (arrive, wait, enter, litter, excuse, depart)
F_{e4} = (arrive, wait, enter, excuse, depart)

Then,

$$\Gamma = F_{e1} \cap F_{e2} \cap F_{e3} \cap F_{e4} \Rightarrow \Gamma = \left(\text{arrive, wait, enter, depart}\right)$$

Identify the Candidate Norms (Nc): Nc can be identified from F-episodes and conventions by getting the union of F-episodes sets, (U-F-episode). We then find the set-theoretic complement between U-F-episodes and conventions, C.

$$U - F - episode = F_{e1} \cup F_{e2} \cup ... \cup F_{e\kappa} \Rightarrow U - F - episode = \bigcup_{w=1}^{k} Fe_{\kappa} \qquad (3)$$

$$\aleph c = \left(U - F - episode\right) \setminus \left(C\right) \qquad (4)$$

This means that candidate norms equal the union of all filtered episodes sets excluding the conventions. Identifying the candidate norms based on Eq. 3 on the elevator example gives the following results:

$$U - F - episode = F_{e1} \cup F_{e2} \cup F_{e3} \cup F_{e4}$$

$$U - F - episodes = \left(\text{arrive, wait, enter, litter, excuse, depart}\right)$$

From above,

$$C = \left(\text{arrive, wait, enter, depart}\right)$$

The result from Eq. 4:

$$Nc = \left(\text{arrive, wait, enter, litter, excuse, depart}\right) \setminus \left(\text{arrive, wait, enter, depart}\right) \Rightarrow$$

$$Nc = \left(\text{litter, excuse}\right)$$

Step 2: Identify Candidate Potential Norms, N_p, and Weak Norms, N_w.

From the candidate norms we can identify the Potential Norms by association rule mining, which is based on frequently occurring patterns. We calculate each norm's strength, π, and compare it with a threshold, T. If η_c is a candidate norm,

$$Nc = \eta_{c1}, \eta_{c2}, \ldots, \eta_{c\kappa}$$

$$\pi\left(\eta_{c\kappa}\right) = \text{Number of episodes which include } \eta_{c\kappa} \text{ in } \Re / \text{Total episodes number in } \Re \tag{5}$$

$$\text{If } \pi\left(\eta_{c\kappa}\right) \geq T \Rightarrow \eta_c \in Np$$

$$\text{Otherwise } \pi\left(\eta_{c\kappa}\right) < T \Rightarrow \eta_{c\kappa} \in Nw \tag{6}$$

From the above, we observe that potential norms are the candidate norms that have the norm strength that is greater than the threshold, otherwise they are weak norms. The norm's strength is calculated by dividing the occurrence of candidate norms in the Record Base by the total number of all episodes in the Record Base. An agent, as an autonomous entity, determines the threshold value based on its experience, which is specified between 0 and 1. If X is the maximum value of T, Y is the decreasing rate, X_N is the new value of X and X_O is the old value of X, then,

$$\left(X_N = X_O - Y\right) \rightarrow \text{decreasing T} \tag{7}$$

In the elevator example we assume the threshold, T, of the candidate potential norms as 0.5. Identifying the candidate Potential and Weak Norms based on Eq. 5 and 6 on the elevator example gives the following results:

$$N_C = \left(\text{litter, excuse}\right)$$

$$\text{litter} \Rightarrow S_N\left(\text{litter}\right) = 3 / 13 = 0.23$$

$$\text{excuse} \Rightarrow S_N\left(\text{excuse}\right) = 8 / 13 = 0.61$$

$$\text{If } \pi\left(n_{c\kappa}\right) \geq 0.5 \Rightarrow n_{c\kappa} \in Np$$

$$\text{Otherwise } \pi\left(\eta_{c\kappa}\right) \leq 0.5 \Rightarrow \eta_{c\kappa} \in Nw$$

$$S_N \left(\text{litter} \right) = 0.23 \leq 0.5 \Rightarrow \text{litter} \in Nw$$

$$S_N \left(\text{excuse} \right) = 0.61 \geq 0.5 \Rightarrow \text{excuse} \in Np$$

Consequently,

$$Np = \left(\text{excuse} \right)$$

$$Nw = \left(\text{litter} \right)$$

Step 3: Identify the normative protocol (P_N). The agent identifies P_N by finding the set-theoretic complement between U-F- episode and Nw.

$$P_N = \left(\text{U} - \text{F} - \text{episodes} \right) \setminus \left(\text{Nw} \right) \tag{8}$$

This means the normative protocol equals the union of filtered episodes excluding the weak norms. Identifying the Normative Protocol based on Eq. 8 on the elevator example gives the following results:

$$U - F - episodes = \left(\text{arrive, wait, enter, litter, excuse, depart} \right)$$

$$N_w = \left(\text{litter} \right)$$

Thus

$$P_N = \left(\text{arrive, wait, enter, litter, excuse, depart} \right) \setminus \left(\text{litter} \right) \Rightarrow$$

$$P_N = \left(\text{arrive, wait, enter, excuse, depart} \right)$$

THE VERIFICATION PROCESS

The verification process, V_p, is necessary to ensure that the detected potential norms are valid as norms that are practiced in the agent society. When the norms have been extracted and identified, the agent starts the verification process on each norm. The agent verifies by querying any trusted nearby agents about the validity of detected norms. However, in this work we assume that the nearby agents are trusted and one nearby agent is enough for validation. There are three possible answers that can be given by the nearby agent, which are:

- **Confirm:** A nearby agent confirms the validity of the potential norms.
- **Refute:** A nearby agent refutes the validity of the potential norm.
- **No Information:** A nearby agent does not have information about the validity of the potential norms.

In the elevator example, we assume that there is a trusted nearby agent and that it knows those norms. The agent can use any form of agent communication language (ACL) to communicate with the nearby agents. We assume here that the agent uses the Foundation for Intelligent Physical Agents (FIPA) ACL (FIPA ACL, 2002). The agent requests from the nearby agent to inform it if it has the knowledge about the validity of Np.

The agent can use the performatives *request* and *inform-if* to ask the nearby agent and the nearby agent can reply by using the performative *inform* as shown below (FIPA KIF, 2002).

If α is an agent, α_c is a nearby agent, and *excuse* is a valid norm, then, agent α request from agent, α_c, to inform it about the validity of norm *excuse*:

```
(
request
: sender        α
: receiver       αc
: content         (inform-if
: sender        α
: receiver       αc
: Content        norm (?excuse)
: reply-with:        confirm; refute; no_info
)
Agent αc  informs Agent α about the validity of norm excuse
(
inform
: sender        αck
: receiver       αk
: content        norm (?excuse) ← (confirm)
: in-reply-to       confirm; refute; no_info
)
```

THE UPDATING PROCESS

The updating process, U_P, updates the Norms Model Base within the agent's belief base. The updating process is quite straight-forward, in which the agent simply updates the normative protocols at appropriate locations in the Norms Model Base. In the elevator example, the agent updates its belief by adding the identified normative protocol in the proper location in Norms Model Base as follows: The initial normative protocol is (arrive, wait, enter, depart). The updated normative protocol is (arrive, wait, enter, excuse, depart).

TESTING AND RESULTS

This section presents a simulation study to validate the proposed techniques of norms detection using the PNDT. The simulation is presented as a scenario of agents in an elevator domain to detect the potential norms by exploiting the Potential Norms Detection Technique (PNDT). We create a virtual environment of a typical elevator scenario to conduct the experiments. The simulator gives a flexibility to test various domains. However, one important characteristics of a domain which is highly suitable for our simulation is that it should entail a crowd of agents suitable for observation by other nearby visitor agents. The elevator domain exhibits such crowded characteristics. Furthermore, it demonstrates the two types of norms (Potential and Weak). Similar scenarios have been used for norms detection in the literature by Savarimuthu (2011) which are restaurant and park scenarios.

The simulation entails two experiments, each experiment comprises a number of tests. The first experiment presents how visitor agents exploits the PNDT technique to adopt new norms. While the second experiment shows the effect of the environmental settings on the detections' success rate. The environmental settings are stipulated by several variables that include cycle time, observation limit of visitor agent, domain size, and population density of host agents. The tests are conducted based on the five elements that are proposed by Harrison et al. (2007) which are, initial settings that are fixed in each test; time constraint which represents the cycle time in this test; output determination, which is represented by figures; repetitions in each test, which is represented by the number of runs; and variations that are represented by fixing all variables except one to test its effect.

The variables are classified into three categories and each variable is set an arbitrary value of Low, Medium or High for testing. According to Mahmoud et al. (2013) such values are adequate to show the effects of the variables and their combinations. However, this test is inspired by their experiments.

- The first category of variables belongs to the Task Condition category, which is the Cycle Time. It is the time given for one cycle of events.
- The second category of variables belongs to the Agent Ability category, which is the Observation Limit of Visitor agents. It is the extent to which a visitor agent is able to observe the actions of Host agents.
- The third category belongs to the Observed Domain category. The pertinent variables are:
  - Grid (Domain) Size, which is defined by a grid size of M by N cells.
  - Population Density of agents in a domain, which is the spread of Host agents occupying the grid.

In this simulation, each variable is assigned a measurement unit as follows:

- **Cycle Time:** It is defined as the time given to a number of event cycle for the domain. For example, in the elevator domain, the event cycle could be wait, enter, excuse, depart. Each host agent enacts these events. A visitor agent observes and learns those events in a number of cycles, which could be one or more cycles.
- **Grid Size:** The domain is simulated as a two-dimensional grid and the grid size represents the domain size.
- **Observation Limit of a Visitor Agent:** Each visitor agent has a limit of observation to monitor the host agents' behaviors. This study assumes that the visitor agents in the grid are able to observe

the surrounding host agents within the observation threshold limit. The unit of measuring the limit is a cell of the grid in the North, South, East and West direction, i.e., a visitor agent is able to observe the host agents located one cell besides it.

- **Population Density of Host Agents:** This is the number of Host Agents in the grid. If there are many agents, then the density is considered high.

Table 2 explains and clarifies each variable with regard to its symbol and its values for Low, Medium, and High.

The simulation model is built based on the above environmental variables and their values. The following defines the supplementary entities to complete the simulator:

- **Agent Types**: There are two types of agent in the PNDT scenario, which are: host agents, α_λ; and visitor agents, α_v.
- **The Domain Norms (Elevator Scenario):** This defines the norms of the elevator domain and assigns each norm type.
  - Enacted Norms (Normative Protocol, P_N): *wait, enter, litter, excuse, depart.*
  - Conventions (Γ) : *wait, enter, depart*
  - Potential norm ($\aleph_P$) : *excuse*
  - Weak norm ($\aleph_w$) : *litter*

THE SIMULATION AND RESULTS OF THE POTENTIAL NORMS DETECTION TECHNIQUE (PNDT)

In this simulation, we conduct two experiments: the first experiment tests when the visitor agents are equipped with the PNDT, and the second experiment conducts numerous tests on the effect of environmental settings on the success of norm detection by PNDT.

Calculating the Mean Value: For each test, the percentage mean of the test results is calculated after a number of runs, using this formula: If A_{vD} is the number of visitor agents that have successfully detected the norms, then,

$$Mean = \left(\frac{\text{Number of } A_{vD} \text{ in all runs}}{\text{Number of } A_v} \div \text{Number of runs} \right) \times 100 \qquad (9)$$

Table 2. Variables units and settings

Variables	Low	Medium	High
(O_L)	1 Cell	2 Cells	3 Cells
(G_S)	5*5	10*10	20*20
(C_N)	2 Cycles	3 Cycles	4 Cycles
$(A_{\lambda S})$	5 Agents	10 Agents	20 Agents

Initial Normative Protocol Generator: The generator is constrained with rules based on the agent's type:

- ○ **Host Agents**: Their knowledge about the domain's norms are generated as follows:
  - ▪ Conventions; all host agents know these norms and strictly comply with them.
  - ▪ The Potential norms; a majority of host agents comply with this type of norms.
  - ▪ The Weak Norm; a minority of host agents perform this type of norms.
- ○ **Visitor Agents**: They have a minimum knowledge about the domain's norms and are generated as follows:
  - ▪ Conventions, all visitor agents have knowledge about this type of norms and strictly comply with them.
  - ▪ The Potential norms, all visitor agents do not have any knowledge about this type of norms.
  - ▪ The Weak Norms, all visitor agents do not have any knowledge about this type of norms.

Experiment 1: The visitor agents are equipped with the PNDT technique. Figure 4 reveal some results as follows:

1. Grid size, G_S, is inversely proportional with norms detection. If G_S increases, the detection of norms decreases and vice versa.

Figure 4. Rate of Norms Detection among Variables G_S (Low, 5*5 grid: 36%), $A_{\lambda S}$ (High, 20 agents: 32%), C_N (High, 4 cycles: 36%), O_L (High, 3 cells: 22%)

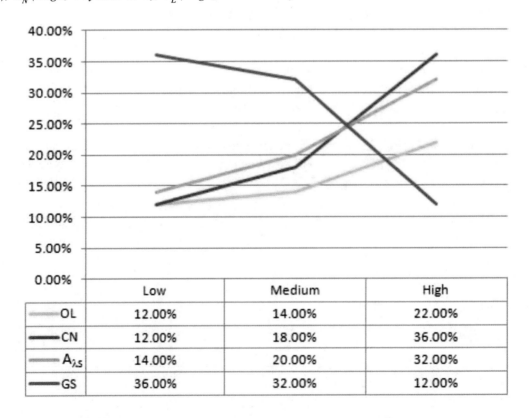

	Low	Medium	High
OL	12.00%	14.00%	22.00%
CN	12.00%	18.00%	36.00%
$A_{\lambda S}$	14.00%	20.00%	32.00%
GS	36.00%	32.00%	12.00%

2. Population density of domain agents, $A_{\lambda S}$; Cycle time, C_N; Observation Limit, O_L; are directly proportional to norms detection. If one of these factors increases, the detection of norms increases and vice versa.

3. Population density of domain agents, $A_{\lambda S}$, Cycle time, C_N, and Grid size, G_S, have strong positive effect (32%, 36%, 36% respectively) on norms detection.

4. Observation Limit, O_L, has the minimum positive effect (22%) on norms detection.

5. The results show that a variable of strong positive effect is not enough to bring the visitor agents to an acceptable level of performance. They should be provided with more than one variable of strong positive effect. The next section analyses the effect of such environments.

- **Test No. 7**: This test measures the effect of Grid Size, G_S, and the Cycle Time, C_N, on norms detection. The results are shown in Table 3.

Settings

A_v: 10 agents

$A_{\lambda S}$: 5 agents Low

C_N: X cycles Test (Medium, 3, High, $\hspace{6cm}$ 4)

G_S: N * M Test (Low, 5*5, Medium, 10*10)

O_L: 1 cell Low

Figure 5 shows the effect of Grid Size, G_S, and the Cycle Time, C_N, on norms detection. The rate increases from 52% when G_S and C_N are Medium (10*10 grid, 3 cycles) to 60% when G_S is Medium (10*10 grid) and C_N is High (,4 cycles) but decreases to 50% when G_S is Low (5*5 grid) and C_N is Medium (3 cycles) . The best result is 72% when G_S is Low (5*5 grid) and C_N is High (4 cycles).

- **Test No. 8**: This test measures the effect of Grid Size, G_S; Cycle Time, C_N; and Population Density of Host Agents, $A_{\lambda S}$, on norms detection. The results are shown in Table 4.

Table 3. The effect of the Grid Size (G_S) and the Cycle Time, C_N, on norms detection

Tests	Run 1	Run 2	Run 3	Run 4	Run 5	Mean
M*N= 10*10 – Medium (M), X =3 Cycles – Medium (M)	5	5	6	4	6	52.0%
M*N= 10*10 – Medium (M), X =4 Cycles – High (H)	7	5	5	6	7	60.0%
M*N= 5*5 – Low (L), X =3 Cycles – Medium	4	4	4	7	6	50.0%
M*N=5*5 – Low (L), X =4 Cycles – High (H)	7	8	6	7	8	72.0%

Figure 5. Grid Size and Cycle Time Test (G_S & C_N Medium, 10*10 grid, 3 cycles): 52%, (G_S Medium, 10*10 grid & C_N High, 4 cycles): 60%, (G_S Low, 5*5 grid, & C_N Medium, 3 cycles): 50%, (G_S Low, 5*5 grid & C_N High, 4 cycles): 72%

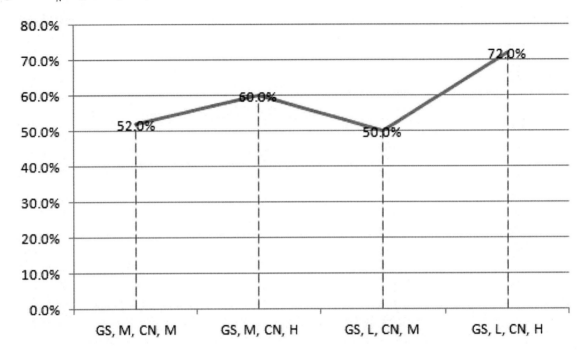

Table 4. The effect of Grid size, G_S; Cycle time, C_N; and population density of host agents, $A_{\lambda S}$, on norms detection

Tests	Run 1	Run 2	Run 3	Run 4	Run 5	Mean
M*N=10*10 – Medium (M), X =3 Cycles – Medium (M), Y = 10 Agents – Medium (M)	8	6	7	6	7	70.0%
M*N=5*5– Low (L), X =4 Cycles – High (H), Y = 20 Agents – High (H)	9	9	8	9	8	86.0%

Settings

A_V: 10 agents
$A_{\lambda S}$: Y agents Test (Medium, 10, High, 20)
C_N: X cycles Test (Medium, 3, High, 4)
G_S: N * M Test (Low, 5*5, Medium, 10*10)
O_L: 1 cell Low, 3

The above results show the effect of Grid Size, G_S, Cycle Time, C_N, and Population Density of Host agents, $A_{\lambda S}$, on norms detection. The rate increases from 70% when G_S, $A_{\lambda S}$, and C_N are Medium (10*10 grids, 10 agents, 3 cycles) to 86% when G_S is Low (5*5), and $A_{\lambda S}$ and C_N are High (20 agents, 4 cycles). However, the results are still not optimal.

In the following test, we set the four variables in strong positive effect G_S (Low), C_N (High), $A_{\lambda S}$ (High) and O_L (High). The results are shown in Table 5.

Figure 6 shows the effect of Grid Size, G_S; Cycle Time, C_N; Population Density of Host agents, $A_{\lambda S}$; and Observation Limit, O_L on norms detection. The rate increases from 70% when G_S, $A_{\lambda S}$, and C_N are Medium to 86% when G_S is Low, $A_{\lambda S}$ and C_N are High, and reaches 96% when G_S is Low, and $A_{\lambda S}$, C_N, and O_L are High.

CONCLUSION AND FUTURE WORK

This chapter presents the potential norm detection technique (PNDT) as a new tool to identify the potential norms from a domain. It could provide a suitable solution for software agents and robot community to adapt to the various environments and learn new behaviors which lead to improve capabilities.

Table 5. The effect on norms detection when the four variables are in strong positive effect, G_S (Low, 5*5), C_N (High, 4 cycles), $A_{\lambda S}$ (High, 20 agents) and O_L (High, 4 cells)

Tests	Run 1	Run 2	Run 3	Run 4	Run 5	Mean
G_S =5*5 – Low (L), C_N =4 Cycles – High (H), $A_{\lambda S}$ = 20 Agents – High (H), O_L = 3 Cells – High (H)	9	10	10	9	10	96.0%

Figure 6. Grid size, cycle time, observation limit and population density test (G_S & C_N & $A_{\lambda S}$) medium (10*10 grids, 10 agents, 3 cycles): 70%, (G_S low, 5*5 & C_N high, 4 cycles & $A_{\lambda S}$ High, 20 agents): 86%, (G_S Low, 5*5 & C_N high, 4 cycles & $A_{\lambda S}$ high, 20 agents, O_L high, 3 cells): 96%

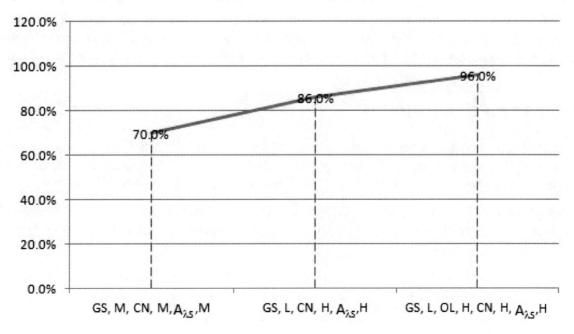

We demonstrate our work in potential norm detection technique via the potential norm mining algorithm. The Potential Norm Mining Algorithm entails the processes of data formatting, filtering and extracting the different types of norms and normative protocols. The preliminary results show that the PNDT succeed in detecting the potential norms in general. It overcomes the problem of having a third-party to enforce the norms and impose sanctions to change agent's belief.

In the validation simulation of the PNDT, we create a virtual elevator scenario and conduct several experiments which shows that (i) when agents are equipped with the PNDT technique, a high proportion of agents succeeds in detecting the domain's potential norms, (ii) the environmental variables setting (Grid Size, Cycle Time, Observation Limit, and Population Density) affect the success of detection and when all variables are in strong positive effect, they offer optimal environment for detection.

We believe that agents can exploit the PNDT to adapt norms in many domains such as in public areas (Park, Mall, Restaurant, Café, etc.); in working areas (University, Companies, etc.); private area (home); and games. But to avoid long discussion and analysis of different domains with more less similar results, we only tested the elevator scenario. The detection technique (PNDT) is not affected by the type of a simulated domain, but is influenced by the environment inputs to achieve detection. For example, a domain size influences the success of detection regardless if the domain is elevator, restaurant, or company. Consequently, we focused on the environmental setting to show various results.

While the results of our work in norms detection show considerable success with regard to the research objectives, there are also some limitations and deficiencies in this work. However, these deficiencies do not compromise the significance of this research. The PNDT is based on association rule mining, which ignores low frequency norms occurrence. Thus, agents that exploit PNDT are unable to adapt the useful norms, which are enacted by a minority.

For our future work, we shall study the issue of norm's benefit awareness. In this study and other similar studies in the literature, agents are not aware of the benefits of enacted norm. In this work, an agent's belief is triggered by its norms conformity with the majority. Thus, if it does not conform, it launches the PNDT to detect the norms. However, we exploit beliefs to use imitation for detection although beliefs can be exploited to use benefit awareness for detection too. Beliefs that are based on imitation is only triggered to adapt the majority norms, while when they are based on benefit awareness, they trigger agents' beliefs to adapt the norms of minority or majority of agents based on the expected benefits.

REFERENCES

Alberti, M., Gomes, A. S., Goncalves, R., Leite, J., & Slota, M. (2011). Normative Systems Represented as Hybrid Knowledge Bases. In *Proceedings of the 12th International Conference on Computational Logic in Multi-agent Systems CLIMA'11* (pp. 330-346). doi:10.1007/978-3-642-22359-4_23

Andrighetto, G., Campenni, M., Cecconi, F., & Conte, R. (2010). The complex loop of norm emergence: A simulation model. In S.-H. Chen, C. Cioffi-Revilla, N. Gilbert(Eds.), *Agent-Based Social Systems* (Vol. 7, pp. 19–35). Springer.

Andrighetto, G., Conte, R., Turrini, P., & Paolucci, M. (2007). Emergence in the Loop: Simulating the two way dynamics of Norm Innovation. In *Normative Multi-agent Systems*.

Boella, G., Pigozzi, G., & Torre, L. V. D. (2009). Normative Framework for Normative System Change. In *Proceedings of the 8th International Conference on Autonomous Agents and Multi-agent Systems, AAMAS'09* (pp. 169-176).

Boella, G., Torre, L. V. D., & Verhagen, H. (2008). Ten Challenges for Normative Multi-agent Systems. In R. Bordini et al. (Eds.), *Dagstuhl Seminar Proceedings*. Dagstuhl: SchlossDagstuhl - Leibniz-Zentrumfuer Informatik.

Bosse, T., Gerritsen, C., & Klein, M. C. A. (2009). Agent-Based Simulation of Social Learning in Criminology. In *Proc. of the Int. Conf. on Agents and AI, ICAART'09* (pp. 5-13).

Broersen, J., Dastani, M., & Torre, L. V. D. (2001). Resolving Conflicts Between Beliefs, Obligations, Intentions, and Desires. Symbolic and Quantitative Approaches to Reasoning with Uncertainty. In *Proceedings of the 6th European Conference, ECSQARU*, Toulouse, France (pp. 568-579). Springer.

Campos, J., López-Sánchez, M., & Esteva, M. (2010). A Case-based Reasoning Approach for Norm Adaptation. In *Proceedings of the 5th International Conference on Hybrid Artificial Intelligence Systems (HAIS'10)*, Spain (pp. 168-176). Springer. doi:10.1007/978-3-642-13803-4_21

Castelfranchi, C., Conte, R., & Paolucci, M. (1998). Normative Reputation and the Cost of Compliance. *Journal of Artificial Societies and Social Simulation, 1*(3), 3.

Centeno, R., & Billhardt, H. (2012). Auto-adaptation of Open MAS through On-line Modifications of the Environment. *Proceedings of the 10th international conference on Advanced Agent Technology AAMAS'11* (pp. 426-427).

Coleman, J. (1998). *Foundations of social theory*. Cambridge Harvard University Press.

Dautenhahn, K., Nehaniv, C. L., & Alissandrakis, A. (2003). Learning by Experience from Others—Social Learning and Imitation in Animals and Robots. In R. Kühn, R.Menzel, W. Menzelet al. (Eds.), Adaptivity and Learning: An Interdisciplinary Debate (pp. 217–421). Springer Verlag.

Epstein, J. (2001). Learning to be thoughtless: Social norms and individual computation. *Computational Economics, 18*(1), 9–24. doi:10.1023/A:1013810410243

Flentge, F., Polani, D., & Uthmann, T. (2001). Modelling the Emergence of Possession Norms using Memes. *Journal of Artificial Societies and Social Simulation, 4*(4), 3.

Galan, J. M., & Izquierdo, L. R. (2005). Appearances Can Be Deceiving: Lessons Learned Re-Implementing Axelrod's Evolutionary Approach to Norms. *Journal of Artificial Societies and Social Simulation, 8*(3), 2.

Grossi, D., Gabbay, D., & van der Torre, L. (2010). The Norm Implementation Problem in Normative Multi-Agent Systems. In Specification and verification of multi-agent systems (pp. 195–224). Springer.

Harrison, J. R., Lin, Z., Carroll, G. R., & Carley, K. M. (2007). Simulation modeling in organizational and management research. *Academy of Management Review, 32*(4), 1229–1245. doi:10.5465/AMR.2007.26586485

Hollander, C., & Wu, A. (2011). The Current State of Normative Agent-Based Systems. *Journal of Artificial Societies and Social Simulation, 14*(2), 6. doi:10.18564/jasss.1750

Jassim, O. A., Mahmoud, M. A., & Ahmad, M. S. (2015). A Multi-agent Framework for Research Supervision Management. In *Proceedings of the 12th International Conference on Distributed Computing and Artificial Intelligence* (pp. 129-136). Springer International Publishing. doi:10.1007/978-3-319-19638-1_15

Kemeny, J.G., Snell, J.L., Thompson, G.L., & Doyle, P. (1998). *Finite Mathematics, Mathematics at Dartmouth*. Retrieved from http://www.math.dartmouth.edu/~doyle/docs/finite/finite.pdf

Kexing, L. A survey of agent based automated negotiation. In *Proceedings of the 2011 International Conference on Network Computing and Information Security (NCIS)* (V*ol. 2*, pp. 24–27). IEEE. doi:10.1109/NCIS.2011.103

Kotsiantis, S., & Kanellopoulos, D. (2006). Association Rules Mining: A Recent Overview. *International Transactions on Computer Science and Engineering, 32*(1), 71–82.

Mahmoud, M. A., & Ahmad, M. S. (2015c, August). A self-adaptive customer-oriented framework for intelligent strategic marketing: A multi-agent system approach to website development for learning institutions. In *Proceedings of the 2015 International Symposium on Agents, Multi-Agent Systems and Robotics (ISAMSR)* (pp. 1-5). IEEE. doi:10.1109/ISAMSR.2015.7379121

Mahmoud, M. A., & Ahmad, M. S. (2016d, August). A prototype for context identification of scientific papers via agent-based text mining. In *Proceedings of the 2016 2nd International Symposium on Agent, Multi-Agent Systems and Robotics (ISAMSR)* (pp. 40-44). IEEE.

Mahmoud, M. A., Ahmad, M. S., Ahmad, A., Mustapha, A., Yusoff, M. Z. M., & Hamid, N. H. A. (2013). Optimal environmental simulation settings to observe exceptional events in social agent societies. *Journal of Artificial Intelligence, 6*(3), 191. doi:10.3923/jai.2013.191.209

Mahmoud, M. A., Ahmad, M. S., Ahmad, A., Yusoff, M. Z. M., Mustapha, A., & Hamid, N. H. A. (2013, May). Obligation and Prohibition Norms Mining Algorithm for Normative Multi-agent Systems. In KES-AMSTA (pp. 115-124).

Mahmoud, M. A., Ahmad, M. S., & Yusoff, M. Z. M. (2016a). Development and implementation of a technique for norms-adaptable agents in open multi-agent communities. *Journal of Systems Science and Complexity, 29*(6), 1519–1537. doi:10.1007/s11424-016-5036-1

Mahmoud, M. A., Ahmad, M. S., & Yusoff, M. Z. M. (2016b, March). A Norm Assimilation Approach for Multi-agent Systems in Heterogeneous Communities. In *Proceedings of the Asian Conference on Intelligent Information and Database Systems* (pp. 354-363). Springer Berlin Heidelberg. doi:10.1007/978-3-662-49381-6_34

Mahmoud, M. A., Ahmad, M. S., & Yusoff, M. Z. M. (2016e). A Conceptual Automated Negotiation Model for Decision Making in the Construction Domain. In *Proceedings of the 13th International Conference on Distributed Computing and Artificial Intelligence* (pp. 13-21). Springer International Publishing. doi:10.1007/978-3-319-40162-1_2

Mahmoud, M. A., Ahmad, M. S., Yusoff, M. Z. M., & Mustapha, A. (2014, December). Norms assimilation in heterogeneous agent community. In *Proceedings of the International Conference on Principles and Practice of Multi-Agent Systems*. Springer International Publishing.

Ogunde, A., Follorunso, O., Sodiiya, A., Oguntuase, J., & Ogunlleye, G. (2011). Improved cost models for agent-based association rule mining in distributed database. *SeriaInformatica.*, *9*(1), 231–250.

Perreau De Pinninck, A., Sierra, C., & Schorlemmer, M. (2010). A multiagent network for peer norm enforcement. *Autonomous Agents and Multi-Agent Systems*, *21*(3), 397–424. doi:10.1007/s10458-009-9107-8

Piskorski M.J. & Gorbatai A. (2011). Testing Coleman's Social-Norm Enforcement Mechanism: Evidence from Wikipedia. *HBS Working*, *11*(055).

Posner, R., & Rasmusen, E. (1999). Creating and enforcing norms, with special reference to sanctions. *International Review of Law and Economics*, *19*(3), 369–382. doi:10.1016/S0144-8188(99)00013-7

Sadri, F., Stathis, K., & Toni, F. (2006). Normative KGP agents. *Computational & Mathematical Organization Theory*, *12*(2), 101–126. doi:10.1007/s10588-006-9539-5

Savarimuthu, B. T. R., Cranefield, S., Purvis, M., & Purvis, M. (2010). Norm Identification in Multi-agent Societies (Discussion Paper). University of Otago.

Sen, S., & Airiau, S. (2007). Emergence of norms through social learning. *Proceedings of IJCAI '07* (pp. 1507–1512).

Subramainan, L., Mahmoud, M. A., Ahmad, M. S., & Yusoff, M. Z. M. (2016a). An Emotion-based Model for Improving Students' Engagement using Agent-based Social Simulator. *International Journal on Advanced Science, Engineering and Information Technology*, *6*(6).

Subramainan, L., Mahmoud, M. A., Ahmad, M. S., & Yusoff, M. Z. M. (2016b, August). A conceptual emotion-based model to improve students' engagement in a classroom using agent-based social simulation. In *Proceedings of the 2016 4th International Conference on User Science and Engineering (i-USEr)* (pp. 149-154). IEEE. doi:10.1109/IUSER.2016.7857951

Symeonidis, A., & Mitkas, P. (2005). A Methodology for Predicting Agent Behavior by the Use of Data Mining Techniques. In Autonomous Intelligent Systems: Agents and Data Mining, LNCS (Vol. 3505, pp. 161–174). Springer. doi:10.1007/11492870_13

Symeonidis, A. L., & Mitkas, P. A. (2006). Agent Intelligence Through Data Mining. In *Proceedings of the 17th European Conference on Machine Learning and the 10th European Conference on Principles and Practice of Knowledge Discovery in Databases*.

Villatoro, D. (2011). Self-organization in decentralized agent societies through social norms. In *Proceedings of the 10th International Conference on Autonomous Agents and Multiagent Systems AAMAS '11* (pp. 1373-1374).

Villatoro, D., Sen, S., & Sabater-Mir, J. (2010). Of social norms and sanctioning: A game theoretical overview. *International Journal of Agent Technologies and Systems*, *2*(1), 1–15. doi:10.4018/jats.2010120101

Young, H. P. (2008). Social Norms. In S. N. Durlauf & L. E. Blume (Eds.), *The New Palgrave Dictionary of Economics*. New York: Palgrave Macmillan. doi:10.1057/978-1-349-95121-5_2338-1

ENDNOTES

[1]   This study considers the term domain and environment as similar.

[2]   There is no unified definition for norm but in this work, we adopt this definition.

[3]   In this study, the agent belief only concerns with the behaviors of other agents.

Section 2
Application of Computational Techniques

Chapter 6
A Pattern-Mining Approach for Wearable Sensor-Based Remote Health Care

C. Sweetlin Hemalatha
VIT University, India

V. Vaidehi
VIT University, India

ABSTRACT

Rapid advancement in Wireless Sensor Network (WSN) technology facilitates remote health care solutions without hindering the mobility of a person using Wearable Wireless Body Area Network (WWBAN). Activity recognition, fall detection and finding abnormalities in vital parameters play a major role in pervasive health care for making accurate decision on health status of a person. This chapter presents the proposed two pattern mining algorithms based on associative classification and fuzzy associative classification which models the association between the attributes that characterize the activity or health condition and handles the uncertainty in data respectively for an accurate decision making. The algorithms mine the data from WWBAN to detect abnormal health status of the person and thus facilitate remote health care. The experimental results on the proposed algorithms show that they work par with the popular traditional algorithms and predicts the activity class, fall or health status in less time compared to existing traditional classifiers.

INTRODUCTION

Remote Patient Monitoring (RPM) facilitates monitoring of people in their respective locations (e.g. in home) and analyses the trends in physical and vital parameters, thus enabling early detection of occurrence of abnormal events. Recent advancement in Wireless Sensor Network (WSN) has led to the development of Wearable Wireless Body Area Network (WWBAN) which comprises of small miniaturized non-invasive and minimally invasive devices that can sense, process and communicate (Tripathi et

DOI: 10.4018/978-1-5225-3686-4.ch006

al., 2011). Wearable sensors provide mobility freedom by allowing people to do their daily life activities while being monitored. This technology decreases the cost and increases the quality of health care services by enabling continuous monitoring and timely alert generation during emergency.

Human activity monitoring enables detection of serious health risks such as sudden falls of elderly people who are home alone or people with chronic disease in near real time. This requires continuous monitoring of human movements and classifying normal low-level activities from abnormal event like fall. Wearable motion sensors such as accelerometers, gyroscopes etc. have been widely used to track movements.

Monitoring of vital signs such as heart rate, respiration rate, blood pressure and blood oxygen saturation enables detection of life threatening emergencies such as heart attacks in near real time. These parameters are good indicators of health status. For example, high blood pressure is an important indicator of heart attack. Hence, there is a need for continuous monitoring of vital parameters and analysing the data for tracking the health status.

Besides wireless sensing technologies, data stream analysis play a vital role in emergency incident detection such as fall and health abnormality. Mining sensor data streams pose great challenges in data mining as large amount of data are generated continuously with high speed in real time. Mining sensor data stream possesses different characteristics compared to traditional database model (Agrawal et. Al., 1993) such as (1) Each data element should be examined only once. (2) Though data gets generated continuously, memory usage for mining data streams is limited. (3) Each data element should be processed faster. (4) The outputs generated by online classifier algorithms should be instantly available when user requested.

Most of the existing fall detection methods are based on classifiers constructed using traditional methods such as decision trees, Bayesian Networks (Li, 2008) Neural Networks (Chen et al., 2010), Support Vector Machine (Kaiquan et al., 2011), K-Nearest Neighbour (Wang et al., 2015) etc. These classifiers may miss to cover certain hidden and interesting patterns in the data and thus suffer high false positives rates.

This chapter presents the proposed classifier for recognizing low-level activities and detecting human fall based on mining frequent patterns in tri-axial accelerometer and physiological sensor data streams. The proposed approach addresses the problem of mining sensor streams using time-sensitive sliding window based pattern mining algorithm. A classifier model is built based on Associative Classification (AC) (Liu et al., 1998) that mines frequent bit patterns and extracts rules for recognizing human activities like sitting/standing, lying and walking with an ultimate aim to detect human fall events. In order to handle the uncertainty in the data, another classifier model is proposed which is based on Fuzzy Associative Classification (FAC) (Mangalapalli & Pudi, 2011) that integrates the accelerometer data and physiological data for mining patterns to determine the health status of a person.

The chapter presents the following contributions.

- A pattern mining based human activity recognition and fall detection algorithm that encodes the features extracted from tri-axial accelerometer data to either 0 or 1 bit and mines the frequent bit patterns to discover rules for recognizing normal activity classes such as sitting/standing, lying and walking. The most significant bit of frequent bit pattern is set to 1 when fall is detected and 0 otherwise. Thus, fall is clearly distinguished from lying posture.

- A fuzzy pattern mining based fall detection and human health status detection algorithm that encodes the extended features extracted from tri-axial accelerometer data and vital parameters from physiological data to fuzzy values and mine the fuzzy association rules for detecting fall and health status.

BACKGROUND

Most of the existing works on human activity recognition (Krekovic et al., 2012) were based on computer-vision techniques that employ video cameras for collecting video sequences in order to recognize human actions and to detect fall. The major drawback of such systems is that they work well in the predefined illumination and lighting conditions but fail to give the same recognition accuracy in different home environments. Also, this method affects one's privacy as most people do not want them to be monitored continuously.

In pervasive computing, researchers are showing interest in using sensors that can recognize human movements directly. There exists significant research works on sensor based human activity recognition with an objective of detecting falls. Noury et al., (2007) presented a survey of systems, algorithms and sensors for early diagnosis of fall conditions occurring in elderly persons automatically. Chen et al., (2012) presented a survey on sensor based activity recognition in which the authors have discussed the distinctions of vision based and sensor based activity recognition and highlighted the strength and weakness of different approaches. A scalable, distributed software framework (Ali et al., 2008) for discovering routine patterns based on activity data collected from ear-worn activity recognition sensor. The authors have proposed a data structure called routine tree to describe routine behavior patterns. Accelerometry is a low-cost, reliable, and practical method for monitoring human movements in order to analyze gait patterns, physical activities and falls. Most of the works have extensively used one or more accelerometers for detecting falls. Other devices such as gyroscopes and tilt sensors are also used along with accelerometer for deciding fall. Doukas et al., (2011) have used motion, sound and visual sensors for human activity interpretation and emergency detection. Bianchi et al., (2010) have used barometric pressure sensors with accelerometer for detecting fall events. The location where the accelerometer sensor is placed plays a major role in activity recognition. Wang et al., (2016) have presented a comparative study on the use of accelerometer and gyroscope in smart phones for human activity recognition.

Analysis of human fall from standing or walking shows that maximum peak value is sensed along the axis of accelerometer only during fall and hence peak threshold forms the essential feature to distinguish normal activities like standing and walking from fall. Bourke et al., (2007) have proposed threshold based fall detecting algorithm for detecting forward falls, backward falls and lateral falls left and right using single tri-axial accelerometer placed at the trunk. Data analysis was done using MATLAB to determine the peak threshold for different kinds of fall events. Yang et al., (2010) have embedded Naive Bayes algorithm in Sun SPOT wireless sensors to implement a wearable real-time system to detect forward, backward, leftward and rightward falls using peak threshold. Li et al., (2009) have proposed popular features such as mean, energy, frequency-domain entropy, and correlation of acceleration data for recognizing human activities. Time-domain features such as mean, standard deviation, energy, correlation between axes, etc were used by Chen et al., (2008) to construct online classifier for recognizing human activities using tri-axial accelerometer. Jiang and Yin (2015) obtained an activity image by assembling the signal sequences of accelerometers and gyroscopes and employed Deep Convolution Neural Network (DCNN) to extract the optimal features automatically from the activity image. Wang et al. (2016) proposed accelerometer based activity recognition which uses ensemble empirical mode decomposition based features and game theory based feature selection methods to reduce the computational complexity and increase the recognition accuracy. The authors have verified the performance of the proposed methods using K-Nearest Neighbours and Support Vector Machine classifiers.

A hierarchical Neural Network based scheme for detecting static, transition and dynamic states to which a human physical activity belongs, was proposed by Khan et al., (2010) in which a single tri-axial accelerometer was placed on the person's chest and have shown that auto regression coefficients augmented with signal magnitude area and tilt angle improve average classification accuracy. Nazabal et al., (2016) proposed new Bayesian models to combine the output of the multiple inertial sensors and modeled the dynamic nature of human activities as a first-order homogeneous Markov chain. Acceleration and vital signs based activity recognition in mobile phone was proposed by Lara et al., (2012) in which the authors have used statistical, structural and transient features and analyzed the effect of vital parameters such as heart rate, respiration rate, skin temperature, ECG amplitude and acceleration along x, y and z axis in determining the human activities using the state of art classification algorithms such as Naive Bayes, Bayesian network, Decision tree, Back propagation Neural network, Additive Logistic Regression and Bagging. They showed that Additive Logistic Regression outperforms other classification algorithms. Guo et al. (2016) proposed multimodal activity recognition based on heart rate and acceleration with an ensemble of Neural network classifiers. Ha and Choi (2016) presented Convolution Neural Networks (CNN) for multi-modal data in order to model both modality specific characteristics and common characteristic across modalities.

Physiological sensors such as Electrocardiogram (ECG), pulse oximeter, body temperature, respiration rate and blood pressure are used to detect the presence of Chronic Obstructive Pulmonary Disease (COPD) using Decision Tree, Random Forest, Naïve Bayes (Bellos et al. 2010) and SVM classifier (Bellos et al. 2012). Thakker et al. (2011) detected abnormal pulse using Piezoresistive Pressure sensor and SVM classifier. Electroencephalograph (EEG) and ECG sensors are used to detect seizure arrhythmia modeled using SVM classifier (Lee et al., 2012). Vu et al. (2010) employed Artificial Neural Network (ANN) to detect Heart Rate Variability (HRV) using heart rate sensor. However, all the aforementioned learning methods create a model based on all features without considering the interesting patterns that decide the class.

Though several motion sensors are employed for human activity and fall detection, accelerometers are more suitable for long-term monitoring of human body motion (Mathie et al., 2004). The placement of accelerometer plays a major role in deciding the accuracy of the activity classification. For monitoring the whole-body movement, accelerometer is placed on the sternum (Najafi et al., 2003), waist (Sekine et al., 2000; Karantonis et al., 2006; Yang et al., 2009) and ankle and waist (Wang et al., 2016). The proposed method employs a single chest worn tri-axial accelerometer for monitoring the body acceleration.

Mohammad and AlModarresi (2009) presented a Fuzzy Inference System (FIS) for recognizing human activities such as moving forward, jumping, going upstairs and going downstairs. A unified fuzzy framework for recognizing human hand motion is proposed by Ju and Liu (2011).

In contrast to the state of art classifiers, very few works exist on pattern mining based human activity recognition. A hierarchical activity recognition model was proposed by Li et al., (2009) for generating personalization activity recognition rules using frequent pattern mining. Gu et al., (2011) presented a classification algorithm for recognizing interleaved activities from sequential activities by mining emerging patterns.

This chapter presents a pattern mining approach for recognizing low level human activity and detecting fall. The proposed approach is different from the traditional methods as normal activity and fall are detected based on frequent bit pattern based classifier that maps the frequent values in sensor data streams to bit patterns and they are mined to extract rules which form the classifier model. This model is then extended by considering the vital parameters and their uncertainties are modeled using fuzzy associative classifier.

MAIN FOCUS OF THE CHAPTER[1]

Issues, Controversies, Problems

Existing human activity recognition systems have employed several sensors, extracted a variety of features from sensor signals and experimented different classifiers for recognition. Table 1 shows the sensors used, features extracted and data processing techniques employed for human activity recognition and fall detection.

Table 1. Sensors, features and data processing techniques used for human activity recognition and fall detection

Authors	Sensors	Features	Data processing techniques
Bianchi et al., 2010	Tri-axial Accelerometer Barometric Pressure sensor	Signal Vector Magnitude (SVM), Signal Magnitude Area (SMA) and tilt angle Differential pressure	Threshold based heuristic decision tree classifier
Ghasemzadeh et al., 2010	Seven motes (accelerometer & gyroscope)	Motion template (motion primitive labelled with unique symbol)	Edit distance
Khan et al., 2010	Single tri-axial Accelerometer	Auto Regression (AR) Coefficient, Signal Magnitude Area (SMA) and tilt angle	Hierarchical Neural Network
Doukas et al., 2011	Motion sensor	X, Y, Z acceleration values	Bayes net, Naive Bayes, Multilayer perceptron, SVM, Nearest Neighbour, Decision tree, Adaboost Severity estimation using semantic model
Wang et al., 2012	Three motes (Tri-axial Accelerometer) & two RFID	Gesture templates	K-medoids clustering & Template matching algorithm Hierarchical model- Emerging pattern mining for real time recognition
Jiang et al., 2015	Accelerometer and Gyroscopes	Automated feature extraction from activity image obtained from time series sensor signals	Deep Convolutional Neural Network
Wang et al., 2015	Accelerometer	Ensemble empirical mode decomposition based features	game theory based feature selection methods K-Nearest Neighbours and Support Vector Machine classifiers
Nazabal et al., 2016	Four Inertial sensors	152 features	Extended Independent Bayesian Classifier Combination

The activities of human beings are continuously monitored and analyzed for several reasons. One of the major motivating reasons is to detect fall of geriatric people who are home alone. Fall may occur due to external factors such as slippery floor, obstacles on the floor etc. Most of the falls generally happen as a consequence of normal Activities of Daily Living (ADL) due to a small loss of balance while standing or walking. Such falls can be detected by continuously monitoring the movement of body with help of motion sensor. Once the fall occurs, the subject lies on the floor for some seconds or hours or may try to recover. The body of the subject is in a free-fall, i.e., its acceleration is same as the gravitational acceleration just before the impact on the floor. Existing methods for activity recognition and fall detection may miss to cover interesting patterns that characterize normal activity or fall. Moreover, using several body sensors affects the mobility of the person. This chapter presents a research work that aims at recognizing normal activities and detecting human fall by a pattern mining based approach to discover the hidden knowledge using single sensor node. The proposed approach monitors body motion by using a tri-axial accelerometer which measures the body acceleration. Accelerometers are normally placed in the part of the body such as wrist, thigh, arm etc., whose movement is to be monitored and analyzed. In order to capture the whole-body movement, the accelerometer is worn on the chest.

However, motion sensor based human activity recognition can detect fall that occurs due to external factors and fail to detect fall that occurs due to internal factors such as abnormal heart rate, high blood pressure etc. in static posture (i.e., sitting, lying). Remote health care facilitates monitoring of people in their respective locations (e.g. in home) and analyses the trends in vital parameters, thus enabling early detection of occurrence of abnormal events. Table 2 shows the sensors used, the kind of abnormality detected and data processing techniques used detecting the abnormalities

Vital parameters are uncertain in nature as the ideal values of normal range of vital parameters may not be met by an individual but even then the individual may be normal. For instance, a person who has chronic heart disease may have a different range of vital parameter values as normal, deviating from the ideal range. This chapter also presents an extension of research work that detects the health abnormality by taking uncertainty of vital parameters into account and detect fall that occurs due to abnormal health status.

Table 2. Sensors used, kind of abnormality detected and data processing techniques for health abnormality detection

Authors	Sensors used	Kind of abnormality Detection	Data processing technique
Tanbeer et al., 2016	Body sensors	Chronic disease	Incremental tree based classifier
Hemalatha et al., 2015	Single node with heart rate and breathing rate sensors	Abnormal heart rate and breathing rate	Minimal infrequent pattern based outlier detection
Bellos et al., 2012	ECG, Pulse oximeter, body temperature, Respiration, Blood pressure	Chronic Obstructive Pulmonary Disease (COPD)	Support Vector Machine (SVM)
Lee et al., 2012	Electroencephalograph (EEG), Electrocardiogram (ECG)	Seizure, Arrhythmia	Support Vector Machine (SVM)
Thakker et al., 2011	Piezoresistive Pressure	Abnormal pulse	
Vu et al., 2010	Heart rate	Heart Rate Variability (HRV)	Artificial Neural Network (ANN)
Bellos et al., 2010	ECG, Pulse oximeter, body temperature, Respiration, Blood pressure	COPD	Decision Tree, Random Forest, Naïve Bayes

SOLUTIONS AND RECOMMENDATIONS

This section presents two proposed solutions for recognizing activities and detecting fall: (1) By analyzing only the motion patterns to detect fall due to external factors (2) By analyzing the motion patterns along with vital parameters to detect fall due to internal factors.

The overview of activity recognition and fall detection system is illustrated in Figure 1. BioHarness 3 (ref) sensor with chest strap manufactured by Zephyr shown in Figure 2 is used for data collection and depicts how the raw sensor data generated by the device on the chest reaches PC. The dimension and the weight of the device are 28x7 mm and 18 grams. The device includes a tri-axial accelerometer, heart rate, breathing rate and class II Bluetooth (BT) link from Bluetooth Radios. Hence it is unobtrusive, lightweight and harmless and can be worn by any person.

Table 3 shows the sampling rate of sensors in BioHarness 3 and the specification of vital parameters. The sampling frequency is 50 Hz and the range of sensor output is ±16g, where g stands for acceleration due to gravity. For every 400 ms, the device generates one acceleration data packet and each packet contains 20 acceleration data measured in all three dimensions. That is, it generates 50 samples per second.

In order to detect fall occurring due to external factors, only accelerometer signals are considered. When a subject performs activities, the corresponding acceleration along three axes reaches PC via Bluetooth. Figure 3 illustrates the sample graph plotted using tri-axial accelerometer data for normal actions like standing, walking, lying and abnormal event like fall.

Figure 1. Overview of activity recognition and fall detection system due to external factors

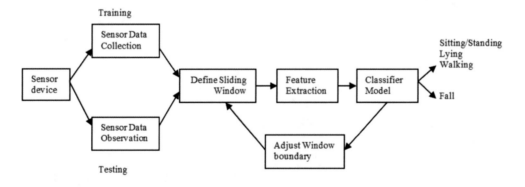

Figure 2. Sensing device and sensor data stream collection in PC

Table 3. Sampling rate and specification of vital parameters

Sensor	Sampling Rate	Description of Measuring Data	Normal Range for adults
Accelerometer	400ms/data	Acceleration along X, Y & Z axis	-
Heart rate	56ms/data	Frequency of cardiac cycle	60 – 100 beats/minute
Breathing rate	56ms/data	Respiration rate	16 – 20 breaths/minute

Figure 3. Acceleration signals for the activities standing, walking, lying and abnormal event like fall

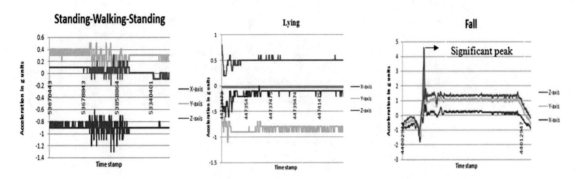

It is easy to visualize the pattern for dynamic activity like walking which is not there in static activity like standing and lying. Also, the data value along x-axis during standing is seen along y-axis during lying. During fall from walking or standing posture, the data values along all three axes exceed the data range of normal activities. A significant peak is perceived only during fall.

Fall occurring due to external factors are detected by analyzing the accelerometer data collected from different persons for different activities which constitute the training set. A sliding window of fixed length t_1 defines the size of data that is currently processed. The raw accelerometer sensor data cannot be processed for meaningful decision making. Hence, appropriate statistical features like mean, root mean square, standard deviation, peak acceleration, resultant acceleration, tilt angle, mean absolute deviation are extracted from each activity data set. An associative classifier based activity model named Frequent Bit Pattern based Associative Classification (FBPAC) is built which contains set of rules for determining each activity class and detecting fall that occurs while standing or walking. Figure 4 shows the block diagram of the proposed FBPAC method.

As fall event has maximum peak compared to other normal activities as shown in Figure 3, fall is determined by mining significant peak in the acceleration data and later part of fall data is same as that of lying activity data. The peak threshold is set as ±2g as no other normal activity has a peak greater than ±2g. Any value that exceeds peak threshold signals occurrence of significant peak. A separate field called significant bit is set, if significant peak is detected in the incoming data streams. This significant bit forms the most significant bit of frequent bit pattern which is 1 if fall is detected and 0 otherwise. Thus, fall which is often confused with lying activity can be distinguished from it by checking whether the significant bit is set or reset and hence true positive rate of fall is increased.

Frequent pattern mining requires discretized data for processing. But accelerometer data streams are continuous values and certain values along the axes are frequent. As each activity covers a range of

Figure 4. Block diagram of the proposed FBPAC method

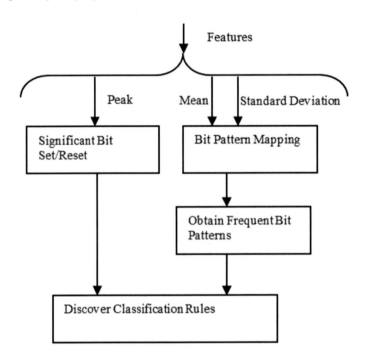

values for each feature, it is possible to map each feature to either bit 0 or 1. For example, the feature mean along x-axis has a value in the range -1.1 to -0.6 when a person is standing. Hence, the numerical value of feature mean in the specified range is mapped to 1 and any value falling outside that range is mapped to 0. The support of each feature to a class is determined by just counting the number of 1's along each feature.

The features whose support is greater than user specified minimum support are mapped to 1 and 0 otherwise and this gives Frequent Bit Pattern (FBP) for each activity class. For each activity, certain feature values occur frequently and hence minimum support threshold is set as 80% within an activity class.

Rule discovery is based on Associative Classification. A set of rules is discovered for fall and each activity class from frequent bit patterns for classifying abnormal and normal activities. A rule is of the form:

$X \Rightarrow C$, where X is a frequent featureset and C is a class label.

The antecedent part of the rule is obtained by considering only the features that crosses the minimum support threshold. The consequent part of the rule is one of the class labels. Also, those rules that satisfy the minimum confidence threshold of 90% constitute the classifier model. Associative Classification Rules (ACR) cover only maximum length frequently occurring features/patterns for all normal activities and fall. Hence only significant rules are considered in the proposed classifier model.

During testing phase, given an observation sequence from time $t = t_1$ to $t = t_n$, the proposed algorithm aims to assign correct activity class for the sensor data in the predefined window of length t_1.

The sensor data of length $t_1 + t_1$, forms the initial test instance from which the same statistical features are extracted and frequent patterns are mined. These frequent patterns are tested against the rule set constructed during training phase to determine the activity class corresponding to the test instance. A non-overlapping sliding window is chosen. So, the window is moved to its full length t_1 to obtain the next test instance and the same procedure is repeated to identify the activity class of the new test instance. The above processes are repeated until $t = t_n$.

The problem of activity recognition and fall detection is formulated as follows: Given a training data set that consists of series of Accelerometer Sensor Observations (ASO1, ASO2, …, ASOn) where 'n' is the number of observations and their associated activity labels (AL1, AL2, …, ALm) where 'm' is the number of activity class labels, the objective is to train a model that assigns correct activity label for each new observation. The proposed rule based classifier algorithm FBPAC is shown as sequence of steps as follows.

Frequent Bit Pattern Based Associative Classification Algorithm

Step 1: For each Sliding Window SW_size_t do

Step 2: $\quad$ Pattern$_t$ = " " // Initializing Pattern as empty string

Step 3: $\quad$ Rule$_t$ = " " // Initializing Rule as empty string

Step 4: $\quad$ for each block $blksize_i$ do

Step 5: $\quad\quad$ Extract peak, mean, and standard deviation to obtain Feature Vector FV_i

Step 6: $\quad\quad$ if Accelerometer Sensor Data Stream ADS in $blksize_i$ > peak threshold then

Step 7: $\quad\quad\quad$ Sigbit = 1 // set significant bit for $blksize_i$ for detecting fall

Step 8: $\quad\quad$ else

Step 9: $\quad\quad\quad$ Sigbit = 0 // reset significant bit for $blksize_i$ for "Not Fall" events

Step 10: $\quad\quad$ end if

Step 11: $\quad$ end for

Step 12: $\quad$ // Map the Feature Vector FV_i to Bit Pattern Vector BPV_i

Step 13: $\quad$ for each feature f_j do

Step 14: $\quad\quad$ if f_j >= $limit_{low}$ and f_j <= $limit_{high}$

Step 15: $\quad\quad\quad$ BPV_i^j = 1 // jth position in BPV_i is set

Step 16: $\quad\quad$ else

Step 17: $\quad\quad\quad$ BPV_i^j = 0 // jth position in BPV_i is reset

Step 18: $\quad\quad$ end if

Step 19: $\quad$ end for

Step 20: $\quad$ // Compute support for each feature using Bit Pattern Vector BPV_i

Step 21: $\quad$ for each mapped feature mf_j do

Step 22: $\quad\quad$ $support_{mf_j} = |BPV_i^j|$

Step 23: $\quad$ end for

Step 24: // Obtain Frequent Bit Pattern Vector $FBPV_i$ whose support > *minsupport*

Step 25: if $support_{mf_j}$ > *minsupport*

Step 26: $FBPV_i^j = 1$

Step 27: else

Step 28: $FBPV_i^j = 0$

Step 29: // Obtain the rule pattern whose support exceeds *minsupport* and confidence exceeds // *minconf*

Step 30: if $FBPV_i^j = 1$

Step 31: $Pattern_t = Pattern_t + j$

Step 32: end if

Step 33: $Rule_t = Rule_t + Sigbit_t + Pattern_t$

Step 34: end for

The algorithm takes Accelerometer Sensor Data Stream (ADS), Sliding Window size (SW_size in time units), block size (blksize), User specified minimum support threshold (minsupport) as input and discovers rules for detecting normal activities like sitting/standing, lying and walking and abnormal activity like fall. Once the feature vector FVi for each block is obtained, setting/resetting significant bit is decided by checking whether the incoming Accelerometer Sensor Data Stream ADS in any of the blocks within sliding window exceeds the peak threshold. Each feature vector FVi is mapped to either bit 1 or 0 depending on the range as evaluated for each activity to get Bit Pattern Vector BPVi. Support of each feature is calculated using count(BPVi). Frequent Bit Pattern Vector FBPVi is obtained by choosing the features whose support is greater than or equal to minsupport threshold. Only frequent patterns of maximum length are considered as rule of interest for recognizing activities. A classification rule is of the form X→C where X is a string containing significant bit followed by frequent bit pattern

Figure 5. Block diagram, of fuzzy frequent pattern based association classifier for fall and health abnormality detection

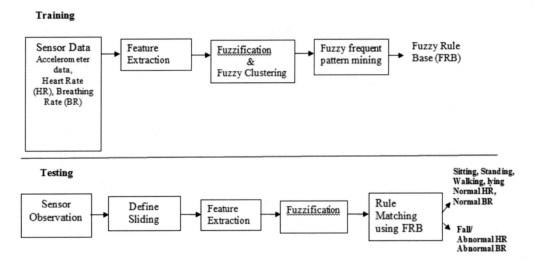

vector that represents feature set as determined using maximum length frequent pattern and C is one of the activity class labels.

In order to detect fall occurring due to internal factors, vital parameters such as heart rate and breathing rate are considered along with accelerometer signals. Fuzzy logic helps in modeling uncertainties. Hence, fuzzy logic is integrated into associative classification for handling the uncertainty nature of vital parameters. Figure 5 shows the block diagram of the proposed Fuzzy Associative Classifier (FAC) for detecting fall and health abnormality.

Besides extracting the aforementioned statistical features such as mean (m), standard deviation (sd), root mean square (rms), resultant acceleration (RA), peak acceleration (p), mean absolute deviation (mad) and tilt angle (TA) from acceleration along three axes, mean of heart rate (hr) and respiration rate (br) sensed from vital parameters are also extracted.

Fuzzification is a process of converting crisp data values into fuzzy values. In case of accelerometer data, acceleration feature value along x, y and z axis is mapped either to Low (L) or High (H) based on the range of values observed from the dataset collected from different subjects. In case of physiological sensors, mean and standard deviation feature values are mapped either to Low (L), Average (A) or High (H) based on normal ranges of vital parameters. Totally, it constitutes 40 features as shown in Table 4.

Fuzzy Associative Classifier employs fuzzy clustering for automatically grouping the incoming data followed by fuzzy frequent pattern mining. Fuzzy partitions are created for each numerical feature using the popular clustering algorithm Fuzzy C-Means Clustering (FCM) (Bezdek et al., 1984). FCM is a data-driven approach for creating fuzzy partitions and it is the fuzzy extension of the k-means algorithm. After partitioning, each feature has degree of membership in the associated fuzzy partitions resulting fuzzy version of the original numerical feature vector. This step eliminates any loss of information that arises due to sharp partition boundaries and prepares the dataset for performing Fuzzy Associative Classification

Fuzzy associative classification performs classification based on fuzzy rules constructed by training data set. The original dataset D containing the feature vector $x_i = \left\{ x_{i1}, x_{i2}, ..., x_{iq} \right\}$ with each feature

Table 4. Fuzzy clusters for features extracted

Feature No.		1	2	3	4
(Feature-Fuzzy class)		$(m_x\text{-}L)$	$(m_x\text{-}H)$	$(m_y\text{-}L)$	$(m_y\text{-}H)$
5	**6**	**7**	**8**	**9**	**10**
$(m_z\text{-}L)$	$(m_z\text{-}H)$	$(rms_x\text{-}L)$	$(rms_x\text{-}H)$	$(rms_y\text{-}L)$	$(rms_y\text{-}L)$
11	**12**	**13**	**14**	**15**	**16**
$(rms_z\text{-}L)$	$(rms_z\text{-}H)$	$(sd_x\text{-}L)$	$(sd_x\text{-}H)$	$(sd_y\text{-}L)$	$(sd_y\text{-}H)$
17	**18**	**19**	**20**	**21**	**22**
$(sd_z\text{-}L)$	$(sd_z\text{-}H)$	$(RA\text{-}L)$	$(RA\text{-}H)$	$(TA_1\text{-}L)$	$(TA_1\text{-}H)$
23	**24**	**25**	**26**	**27**	**28**
$(TA_2\text{-}L)$	$(TA_2\text{-}H)$	$(mad_x\text{-}L)$	$(mad_x\text{-}H)$	$(mad_y\text{-}L)$	$(mad_y\text{-}H)$
29	**30**	**31**	**32**	**33**	**34**
$(mad_z\text{-}L)$	$(mad_z\text{-}H)$	$(p_x\text{-}L)$	$(p_y\text{-}H)$	$(p_y\text{-}L)$	$(p_y\text{-}H)$
35	**36**	**37**	**38**	**39**	**40**
$(p_z\text{-}L)$	$(p_z\text{-}H)$	$(hr\text{-}L)$	$(hr\text{-}H)$	$(br\text{-}L)$	$(br\text{-}H$

x_{ik} is partitioned into f_k fuzzy sets and it is denoted as $F_{ik} = x_{ik}^1, x_{ik}^2, ..., x_{ik}^{f_k}$. Hence, the original dataset D is transformed into fuzzy dataset F. The fuzzy version of apriori algorithm is used to extract fuzzy frequent patterns. The patterns that cross the user defined minimum support min_support are said to be frequent and only those patterns are considered for in the next level. The T-norm "min" is used as conjunction operator. The proposed Fuzzy Frequent Pattern based Associative Classification (FFPAC) algorithm is shown as sequence of steps as follows:

Fuzzy Frequent Pattern Based Associative Classification Algorithm

```
Step 1: g=1
Step 2:  do
Step 3:   generate g-item set candidates
Step 4:   pattern= generate frequent_pattern_set using min-t-norm
Step 5:   if pattern < max_length_freq_pattern
Step 6:      max_length_freq_pattern=pattern
Step 7:   g=g+1
Step 8:  while pattern !=null
Step 9:  return max_length_freq_pattern
```

The algorithm takes as input the fuzzy clusters obtained using FCM and produces maximal length fuzzy frequent pattern as output. A maximal length fuzzy frequent pattern is considered as it covers most of the possible associated patterns in determining the output class.

Fuzzy classification rule contains fuzzy frequent item sets in the antecedent part and only a class label in the consequent part. A fuzzy rule $f \Rightarrow C$ is measured based on the support and confidence that are determined using Eq. 1 and Eq. 2 respectively.

$$support\left(f \Rightarrow C\right) = \sum_{\mathcal{F}[c] = C} \mu_f\left(\mathcal{F}\right) / |F| \qquad (1)$$

$$confidence\left(f \Rightarrow C\right) = \sum_{\mathcal{F}[c] = C} \mu_f\left(\mathcal{F}\right) / \sum_{\mathcal{F} \in F} \mu_f\left(\mathcal{F}\right) \qquad (2)$$

where $|F|$ denotes the number of records in F, f is the fuzzy set.

The rules thus obtained by mining fuzzy frequent patterns form the Fuzzy Rule Base (FRB). During testing phase, statistical features of the test data within the sliding window are extracted and fuzzification is done. The fuzzified features form the condition set which are then matched with the antecedent part of the rules in FRB to predict the activity, fall and health status based on the consequent part of the fuzzy rule.

The data set for the experiment was collected in a supervised manner at home. Data are collected for totally 3 normal activities such as sitting/standing, lying and walking and an abnormal event like fall as shown in Table 5.

Table 5. Activities recognized

Activities Recognized	Category
Sitting/standing	Not fall
Lying	
Walking	
Fall & recovered	**Fall**
Fall & lying	

Each activity is performed approximately for 1 minute and it is segmented into six 10 seconds data. The device generates 50 data/second. Therefore, totally 3000 data/activity is acquired. Accelerometer data is collected for both individual activity and activity sequence. A sample sequence of activities performed by a participant for normal activity category is sitting- standing- walking -sitting -lying. For fall, participants are asked to perform the sequence such as standing/walking -> fall backward, standing/ walking -> fall sidewise etc. The data set are manually annotated.

Ten healthy persons i.e., Seven females and three males with an average middle age of 32 and old age of 59 under female category and with an average middle age of 29 and old age of 65 under male category, participated in the experiment. Table 6 shows the physical characteristics of participants. Training data set constitute activity & fall data collected from 5 out of 10 persons and remaining 5 persons' data constitute the test data set. Approximately, 10 hours of activity data, i.e. 2 hours per person, are collected for conducting experiment.

A sliding window size of 10 seconds is chosen after experimenting with other time slice such as 6, 12, 16 and 20 seconds. The experiment shows that normal activities are recognized accurately for data manipulated for 10 seconds compared to other time slice. Figure 6 shows the recognition accuracy for data within sliding window of different time slice.

Table 7 shows the frequent bit pattern obtained for walking. The significant bit in the first column is 0 as walking is normal activity. The second column represents the column numbers and associated

Table 6. Physical characteristics of patients

Gender	Age	BMI	Average Age
Female	32	26	32 (Middle age)
	33	24.3	
	47	25.5	
	48	29.6	
	53	25.7	59 (Old age)
	60	23.5	
	65	23.9	
Male	23	21.9	29 (Middle age)
	35	25	
	63	21.3	63 (Old age)

Figure 6. Recognition accuracy within sliding window of different time slice

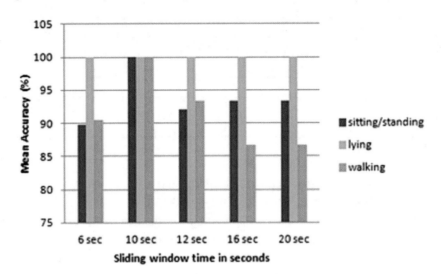

Table 7. Frequent bit pattern obtained for walking

Significant bit	Feature Column no. vs. Bit pattern					
0	0 (mean_x)	1 (mean_y)	2 (mean_z)	3 (standard deviation_x)	4 (standard deviation_y)	5 (standard deviation_z)
	1	0	0	1	1	1

features. The last row shows that the frequent bit pattern obtained for walking is 100111 and hence only the features mean_x, standarddeviation_x, standarddeviation_y and standarddeviation_z satisfy *minsupport* criteria.

Table 8 presents sample frequent bit pattern and rules discovered for each activity and fall during the experiments. The first column shows the set/reset part of significant bit in the bit pattern and it is 0 for normal activities and 1 for fall. The second column shows the frequent bit pattern which is obtained

Table 8. Sample bit patterns and rules discovered for normal activities and fall

Significant bit	Frequent bit pattern	Pattern Rules	Meaning
0	100000/100100	00->sitting/standing 030->sitting/standing	(mean_x,1)->sitting/standing {(mean_x,1), (standarddeviation_x,1)}-> sitting/standing
0	0100011	0541->lying	{(mean_y,1), (standarddeviation_x,1), (standarddeviation_y,1), (standarddeviation_z,1)}-> lying
0	100111	05430->walking	{(mean_x,1), (standarddeviation_x,1), (standarddeviation_y,1), (standarddeviation_z,1)}-> walking
1	100000	10-> fall but recovered	(mean_x,1}->fall but recovered
1	0100111	1541- >fall and lying	{(mean_y,1), (standarddeviation_x,1), (standarddeviation_y,1), (standarddeviation_z,1)}-> fall & lying

by considering only the features whose support exceeds minsupport threshold. Pattern rule in the next column specifies the significant bit value followed by column number of features in reverse order whose support exceeds minsupport threshold. The last column gives the meaning of pattern rules.

The proposed algorithm is evaluated under two experimental set up. The training data set used for experimental setup 1 is well distributed i.e., each 10 seconds, data pertains to either one of normal activity category such as sitting/standing, lying and walking or abnormal event like fall, whereas the testing data set used for experimental setup 2 is activity sequence of arbitrary time.

A set of 10 seconds accelerometer data collected from 5 different subjects are used for training and individual activity data of 10 seconds collected from the 5 other subjects are used for testing. Table 9 presents the recognition accuracy obtained for different subjects of which subjects 1-3 are elderly people and hence fall event is not attempted by them.

It is observed that 100% accuracy is achieved for all activities and for all subjects except for subject 2 because subject 2 is one among elderly people. The walking pattern is misclassified as sitting/standing due to slow walk with very less body acceleration. Since activity recognition rules are generated based on training data of 10 seconds sliding window, it is possible to achieve nearly 100% accuracy for test data collected over the same 10 seconds sliding window for different subjects.

Accelerometer data collected from 5 different subjects are used for training and activity sequence data collected from 5 other subjects are used for testing. Table 10 presents the recognition accuracy obtained for different subjects for different activity sequence.

Table 9. Activity sequence recognition results obtained for activity sequence

Subject/ Activity	Accuracy (%)					Mean Accuracy (%)
	Sitting/Standing	Lying	Walking	Fall & lying	Fall & recovered	
1	100	100	100	-	-	100
2	100	100	90	-	-	96.6
3	100	100	100	-	-	100
4	100	100	100	100	100	100
5	100	100	100	100	100	100
Mean Accuracy (%)	100	100	98	100	100	99.32

Table 10. Activity sequence recognition results obtained for activity sequence

Subject	Activity sequence	Average Accuracy (%)
1	Walking-sitting-lying-sitting-standing	100
2	Sitting-standing-walking-sitting-lying	80
3	Standing-walking-sitting-walking-fall&recovered	100
4	Sitting-standing-walking-sitting-lying	100
5	Standing-walking-sitting-standing-fall&lying	80
Overall average accuracy		92

The reason for misclassification is mainly due to non-overlapping sliding window. For example, in a sliding window, if only 60% of accelerometer data stream matches a pattern and remaining 40% matches one of other patterns, then the pattern will be misclassified as the minimum support threshold is 80%.

Hence, with the proposed approach, it is possible to achieve 99% overall accuracy for individual activity and 92% overall accuracy for random activity sequence. Also, the proposed method yielded reasonable accuracy when tested in real time.

Figure 7 and Figure 8 depict the mean classification accuracy and execution time in seconds respectively for traditional algorithms such as Naïve Bayes (NB), Bayesian Belief Network (BBN), Multi-layer perceptron (MLP), C4.5 Decision tree and the proposed algorithm FBPAC. Weka tool, a standard data mining tool is used for testing the performance of traditional classifiers. MLP is tested with learning rate of 0.3, momentum of 0.2, 500 epochs and 5 hidden neurons.

Figure 7. Comparison of FBPAC with traditional algorithms for classification accuracy

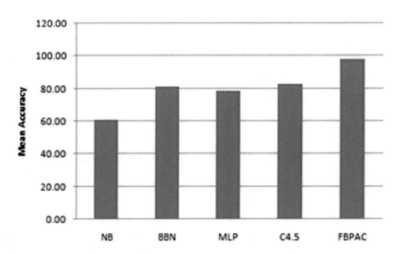

Figure 8. Comparison of FBPAC with traditional algorithms for execution time

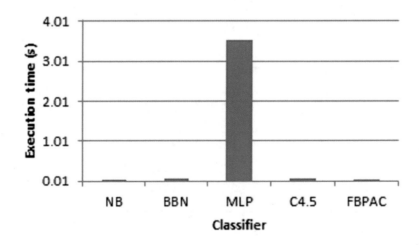

It is observed that FBPAC algorithm achieves competitive classification results within reasonable time as that of popular traditional approaches. High classification accuracy is achieved by the proposed algorithm because of considering the association between the feature patterns in deriving the classification rules for recognizing activities and detecting human fall.

Table 11 shows sample rules in FRB. Each numerical value in the Rule set corresponds to Feature No. presented in Table 4. For example rule [1 3 5 7 9] implies the pattern $m_x - L, m_y - L, m_z - L, rms_x - L, rms_y - L$.

Six-fold cross validation method is used for evaluating the proposed algorithm and it is shown that it is possible to achieve 92% classification accuracy. Table 12 shows the accuracy results for all activities using six-fold cross validation.

Figure 9 depicts the mean classification accuracy obtained for traditional algorithms such as Naïve Bayes (NB), Bayesian Belief Network (BBN), K-Nearest Neighbours (KNN), Multi-layer perceptron (MLP), C4.5 Decision tree (DT) and the proposed algorithm FFPAC. The performance of the proposed algorithm and the traditional algorithms is evaluated using Weka, a standard data mining tool. It is observed that FAC-HAR algorithm achieves competitive classification results compared to traditional approaches. It is possible to achieve good classification accuracy because of considering the association between the features in deriving the classification rules.

Table 11. Fuzzy rules obtained for normal activities, fall and health status

Activity/Health status	Rule Set	Rule Length
Stand	[1 3 5 9 11 13 20 21 23 25]	10
	[1 3 5 8 9 11 20 21 23 25]	10
	[1 3 5 8 9 11 13 20 21 23 25]	11
Sit	[1 3 5 11 13 20 23]	7
	[1 3 5 11 13 20 23 25]	8
	[1 5 11 13 20 23 25]	7
Lie	[2 4 10 13 19 25]	6
	[2 4 7 10 13 19 25]	7
	[2 4 7 10 19 22 25]	7
Walk	[1 3 5 9 11 16 20 21 23 28]	10
	[1 3 5 8 9 11 20 21 23 28]	10
	[1 3 5 8 9 11 20 21 23]	9
Forward Fall	[15 33 34]	3
Backward Fall	[15 33 34]	3
Abnormal	[1 3 5 9 11 13 20 21 23 25 33 34]	12
	[2 4 7 10 19 22 25 32 34]	9
	[1 3 5 8 9 11 20 21 23 32 34]	11
	[15 33 34]	3

Table 12. Average accuracy for normal activities and fall using six-fold cross validation

Activity/ Subject	Accuracy (%)						
	1	2	3	4	5	6	Mean (%)
Standing	100	100	100	100	100	100	100
Sitting	95	85	90	92	94	95	91.83
Lying	100	100	100	100	100	100	100
Walking	100	80	100	85	85	100	91.66
Fall	100	100	100	100	100	100	100
Total accuracy	99	93	98	95.4	95.8	99	96.7

Figure 9. Comparison of proposed FFPAC with traditional algorithms for classification accuracy

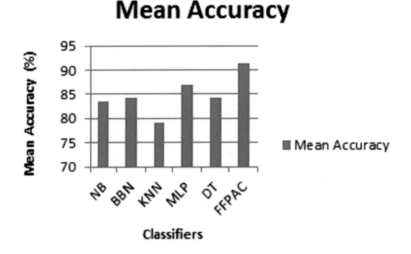

FUTURE RESEARCH DIRECTIONS

Recent research in human activity recognition shows increased interest in recognizing more complex activities and collaborative activities. Therefore, in future it is planned to leverage deep learning for complex activity recognition in streaming data with improved accuracy. The limitation of the proposed methods is that they work based on the classifier model constructed using generic data collected from a few subjects of varied age group. Hence, it also planned to refine the proposed algorithms to include personalized pattern mining model which would be adaptive to the changes in activity data and vital parameters of an individual.

CONCLUSION

Two pattern mining algorithms namely Frequent Bit Pattern based Associative Classification (FBPAC) algorithm and Fuzzy Frequent Pattern based Associative Classification (FFPAC) algorithm have been proposed in this chapter. The FBPAC algorithm is used for classifying normal activities and abnormal event like fall based on single tri-axial accelerometer data. It reduces the false positive rates for fall events which are normally confused with lying posture. Because of mapping the feature vector to bit patterns, calculating support of features for all the activities covered under the sliding window is eased and is done faster. The algorithm is evaluated by observing sensor data streams of arbitrary activity sequence performed by three subjects who have not participated in training phase. The highest overall mean accuracy for activity recognition is 92% for a sliding window size of 10 seconds. Thus, the FBPAC algorithm enables human activity recognition and fall detection which may occur due to extrinsic cause such as hitting on an obstacle, slippery floor etc., with only accelerometer data. The FFPAC algorithm recognizes both low level activities and detects fall and abnormal health status based on physiological sensor data such as heart rate, respiration rate along with tri-axial accelerometer data. Thus, it detects fall that occurs due to intrinsic factor like high or low heart rate and breathing rate. Both activity data and health data are uncertain and varies between people to people. Hence, determining a crisp boundary leads to misclassification error. The FFPAC algorithm handles uncertainty by providing a fuzzy boundary for deciding the activity, fall and health status and thus provides reasonable classification accuracy.

REFERENCES

Agrawal, R., Imielinski, T., & Swami, A. (1993). Mining association rules between sets of items in large databases. In *Proceedings of the ACM SIGMOD Conference on Management of Data*, Washington, D.C.(*Vol. 22,* pp. 207-216). doi:10.1145/170036.170072

Ali, R., ElHelw, M., Atallah, L., Lo, B., & Yang, G. Z. (2008). Pattern Mining for Routine Behaviour Discovery in Pervasive Healthcare Environments. In *Proceedings of the 5th International Conference on Information Technology and Application in Biomedicine*, Shenzhe (pp. 241-244). doi:10.1109/ITAB.2008.4570576

Bellos, C., Papadopoulos, A., Rosso, R., & Fotiadis, D. I. (2012). A Support Vector Machine Approach for Categorization of Patients Suffering from Chronic Diseases. In *Wireless Mobile Communication and Healthcare* (pp. 264–267). Springer Berlin Heidelberg. doi:10.1007/978-3-642-29734-2_36

Bellos, C. C., Papadopoulos, A., Rosso, R., & Fotiadis, D. I. (2010, November). Extraction and Analysis of features acquired by wearable sensors network. In *Proceedings of the 2010 10th IEEE International Conference on Information Technology and Applications in Biomedicine (ITAB)* (pp. 1-4). IEEE. doi:10.1109/ITAB.2010.5687761

Bezdek, J. C., Ehrlich, R., & Full, W. (1984). FCM: The fuzzy c-means clustering algorithm. *Computers & Geosciences*, *10*(2-3), 191–203. doi:10.1016/0098-3004(84)90020-7

Bianchi, F., Redmond, S. J., Narayanan, M. R., Cerutti, S., & Lovell, N. H. (2010). Barometric Pressure and Triaxial acclerometry based falls event detection. *IEEE Transactions on Neural Systems and Rehabilitation Engineering*, *18*(6), 619–627. doi:10.1109/TNSRE.2010.2070807 PMID:20805056

Bourke, A. K., OBrien, J. V., & Lyons, G. M. (2007). Evaluation of a threshold-based tri-axial accelerometer fall detection algorithm. *Gait & Posture*, *26*(2), 194–199. doi:10.1016/j.gaitpost.2006.09.012 PMID:17101272

Chen, F. L., & Li, F. L. (2010). Comparison of the Hybrid Credit Scoring Models Based on Various Classifiers. *International Journal of Intelligent Information Technologies*, *6*(3), 56–74. doi:10.4018/jiit.2010070104

Chen, L., Hoey, J., Nugent, C. D., Cook, D. J., & Yu, Z. (2012). Sensor-based activity recognition. *IEEE Transactions on Systems, Man and Cybernetics. Part C, Applications and Reviews*, *42*(6), 790–808. doi:10.1109/TSMCC.2012.2198883

Chen, Y. P., Yang, J. Y., Liou, S. N., Lee, G. Y., & Wang, J. S. (2008). Online classifier construction algorithm for human activity detection using a tri-axial Accelerometer. *Applied Mathematics and Computation*, *205*(2), 849–860. doi:10.1016/j.amc.2008.05.099

Doukas, C., & Maglogiannis, I. (2011). Emergency fall incidents detection in assisted living environments utlilizing motion, sound and visual perceptual components. *IEEE Transactions on Information Technology in Biomedicine*, *15*(2), 277–289. doi:10.1109/TITB.2010.2091140 PMID:21062686

Guo, H., Chen, L., Peng, L., & Chen, G. (2016, September). Wearable sensor based multimodal human activity recognition exploiting the diversity of classifier ensemble. In *Proceedings of the 2016 ACM International Joint Conference on Pervasive and Ubiquitous Computing* (pp. 1112-1123). ACM. doi:10.1145/2971648.2971708

Ha, S., & Choi, S. (2016, July). Convolutional neural networks for human activity recognition using multiple accelerometer and gyroscope sensors. In *Proceedings of the 2016 International Joint Conference on Neural Networks (IJCNN)* (pp. 381-388). IEEE. doi:10.1109/IJCNN.2016.7727224

Helmi, M., & AlModarresi, S. M. T. (2009). Human Activity Recognition Using a Fuzzy Inference System. In *Proceedings of IEEE International conference on fuzzy systems* (pp. 1897-1902). doi:10.1109/FUZZY.2009.5277329

Hemalatha, C. S., Vaidehi, V., & Lakshmi, R. (2015). Minimal infrequent pattern based approach for mining outliers in data streams. *Expert Systems with Applications*, *42*(4), 1998–2012. doi:10.1016/j.eswa.2014.09.053

Iváncsy, R., & Vajk, I. (2005). Automata Theory Approach for solving Frequent Pattern Discovery Problems. World Academy of Science, Engineering and technology.

Jiang, W., & Yin, Z. (2015, October). Human activity recognition using wearable sensors by deep convolutional neural networks. In *Proceedings of the 23rd ACM international conference on Multimedia* (pp. 1307-1310). ACM. doi:10.1145/2733373.2806333

Kaiquan, S. J., Wang, W., Ren, J., Jin, S. Y., Liu, L., & Liao, S. (2011). Classifying Consumer Comparison Opinions to Uncover Product Strengths and Weaknesses. *International Journal of Intelligent Information Technologies*, *7*(1), 1–14. doi:10.4018/jiit.2011010101

Karantonis, D. M., Narayanan, M. R., Mathie, M., Lovell, N. H., & Celler, B. G. (2006). Implementation of a real-time human movement classifier using a triaxial accelerometer for ambulatory monitoring. *IEEE Transactions on Information Technology in Biomedicine*, *10*(1), 156–167. doi:10.1109/TITB.2005.856864 PMID:16445260

Khan, A. M., Lee, Y. K., & Kim, T. S. (2010). A triaxial accelerometer based physical activity recognition via augmented signal features and a hierarchical recognizer. *IEEE Transactions on Information Technology in Biomedicine*, *14*(5), 1166–1172. doi:10.1109/TITB.2010.2051955 PMID:20529753

Lara, D. O., Perez, J. A., Labrador, A. M., & Posada, D. J. (2012). Centinela: A human activity recognition system based on acceleration and vital sign data. *Pervasive and Mobile Computing*, *8*(5), 717–729. doi:10.1016/j.pmcj.2011.06.004

Lee, K. H., Kung, S. Y., & Verma, N. (2012). Low-energy formulations of support vector machine kernel functions for biomedical sensor applications. *Journal of Signal Processing Systems for Signal, Image, and Video Technology*, *69*(3), 339–349. doi:10.1007/s11265-012-0672-8

Li, H. F., & Lee, S. Y. (2009). Mining frequent itemsets over data streams using efficient window sliding techniques. *Expert Systems with Applications*, *36*(2), 1466–1477. doi:10.1016/j.eswa.2007.11.061

Li, X. (2008). Inference Degradation of Active Information Fusion within Bayesian Network Models. *International Journal of Intelligent Information Technologies*, *4*(4), 1–17. doi:10.4018/jiit.2008100101

Liu, B., Hsu, W., & Ma, Y. (1998). Integrating classification and association rule mining. In *Proceedings of the 4th International Conference on Knowledge Discovery and Data Mining* (pp. 80-86).

Mangalampalli, A., & Pudi, V. (2011, March). Fuzzy Associative Rule-based Approach for Pattern Mining and Identification and Pattern-based Classification. In *Proceedings of the 20th international conference companion on World wide web* (pp. 379-384). ACM.

Mathie, M.J., Coster, A.C.F., Lovell, N.H., & Celler, B.G. (2004). Accelerometry: providing an integrated, practical method for long-term, ambulatory monitoring of human movement. Physiological measurement, 25(2).

Najafi, B., Aminian, K., Paraschi v-Ionescu, A., Loew, F., Büla, C. J., & Robert, P. (2003). Ambulatory system for human motion analysis using a kinematic sensor: Monitoring of daily physical activity in the elderly. *IEEE Transactions on Bio-Medical Engineering*, *50*(6), 711–723. doi:10.1109/TBME.2003.812189 PMID:12814238

Nazábal, A., García-Moreno, P., Artés-Rodríguez, A., & Ghahramani, Z. (2016). Human activity recognition by combining a small number of classifiers. *IEEE journal of biomedical and health informatics*, *20*(5), 1342-1351.

Noury, N., Fleury, A., Rumeau, P., Bourke, A. K., Laighin, G. O., Raille, V., & Lundy, J. E. (2007). Fall detection – principles and methods. In *Proceedings of the 29th Annual International Conference of the IEEE EMBS* (pp. 1663-1666).

Sekine, M., Tamura, T., Togawa, T., & Fukui, Y. (2000). Classification of waist-acceleration signals in a continuous walking record. *Medical Engineering & Physics*, *22*(4), 285–291. doi:10.1016/S1350-4533(00)00041-2 PMID:11018460

Tanbeer, S. K., Hassan, M. M., Almogren, A., Zuair, M., & Jeong, B. S. (2016). Scalable regular pattern mining in evolving body sensor data. *Future Generation Computer Systems*.

Thakker, B. (2011). Support Vector Machine.

Tripathi, A., Gupta, P., Trivedi, A., & Kala, R. (2011). Wireless Sensor Node Placement Using Hybrid Genetic Programming and Genetic Algorithms. *International Journal of Intelligent Information Technologies*, *7*(2), 63–83. doi:10.4018/jiit.2011040104

Vu, T. H. N., Park, N., Lee, Y. K., Lee, Y., Lee, J. Y., & Ryu, K. H. (2010). Online discovery of Heart Rate Variability patterns in mobile healthcare services. *Journal of Systems and Software*, *83*(10), 1930–1940. doi:10.1016/j.jss.2010.05.074

Wang, A., Chen, G., Yang, J., Zhao, S., & Chang, C. Y. (2016). A comparative study on human activity recognition using inertial sensors in a smartphone. *IEEE Sensors Journal*, *16*(11), 4566–4578. doi:10.1109/JSEN.2016.2545708

Wang, Z., Wu, D., Chen, J., Ghoneim, A., & Hossain, M. A. (2016). A triaxial accelerometer-based human activity recognition via EEMD-based features and game-theory-based feature selection. *IEEE Sensors Journal*, *16*(9), 3198–3207. doi:10.1109/JSEN.2016.2519679

Yang, C. C., & Hsu, Y. L. (2009). Development of a wearable motion detector for telemonitoring and real-time identification of physical activity. *Telemedicine Journal and e-Health*, *15*(1), 62–72. doi:10.1089/tmj.2008.0060 PMID:19199849

KEY TERMS AND DEFINITIONS

Activity Recognition: Detecting low level actions like sitting, standing, walking, lying, etc.

Associative Classification: A classifier model built based on association of features with the class label.

Fall Detection: Detecting human fall due to imbalance or due to unconscious state.

Fuzzy Associative Classification: A classifier model built based on association of fuzzy features with the class label.

Pattern Mining: Extracting hidden but interesting patterns from the data.

Remote Health Care: Providing health care services to individuals without physically being present in hospitals.

Wearable Wireless Body Area Network: A network of wireless sensing elements worn on human body.

Wireless Sensor Network: A network of sensing elements communicated in wireless manner.

Chapter 7
Crow-Search-Based Intuitionistic Fuzzy C-Means Clustering Algorithm

Parvathavarthini S.
Kongu Engineering College, India

Karthikeyani Visalakshi N.
NKR Government Arts College for Women, India

Shanthi S.
Kongu Engineering College, India

Lakshmi K.
Kongu Engineering College, India

ABSTRACT

Data clustering is an unsupervised technique that segregates data into multiple groups based on the features of the dataset. Soft clustering techniques allow an object to belong to various clusters with different membership values. However, there are some impediments in deciding whether or not an object belongs to a cluster. To solve these issues, an intuitionistic fuzzy set introduces a new parameter called hesitancy factor that contributes to the lack of domain knowledge. Unfortunately, selecting the initial centroids in a random manner by any clustering algorithm delays the convergence and restrains from getting a global solution to the problem. To come across these barriers, this work presents a novel clustering algorithm that utilizes crow search optimization to select the optimal initial seeds for the Intuitionistic fuzzy clustering algorithm. Experimental analysis is carried out on several benchmark datasets and artificial datasets. The results demonstrate that the proposed method provides optimal results in terms of objective function and error rate.

DOI: 10.4018/978-1-5225-3686-4.ch007

INTRODUCTION

Data Mining pertains to the task of discovering hidden knowledge from a huge volume of data. The role of data mining has become inevitable because of the large volumes of data available in various fields. The world has become a village connected by global data. Due to their voluminous nature, these data cannot be dealt with manually. It is tedious to analyze these data manually and also difficult to identify the patterns associated with them.

Data Mining recognizes the patterns that are available in data with the help of several techniques like Classification, Clustering, Association rule mining, Prediction, etc. Classification is a supervised technique that categorizes data as belonging to which class. Prediction tries to guess the relationship between the variables in data objects and Association rule mining correlates the behavior of data with the outcome of events. Data Mining finds its applications in various fields like Biomedical research, Behavioral and social sciences, Earth sciences, Market Analysis, web search, Decision Support Systems, Buying pattern prediction, etc.

Need for Clustering

Clustering is an exploratory and descriptive data analysis technique that divides objects into several homogeneous groups based on their traits. Due to the increase in large multidimensional datasets, the need for summarizing, analyzing the qualitative and quantitative aspects of data has become unavoidable. Objects with similar features are put into a single cluster. Clustering algorithms should show the same performance irrespective of the number of instances in the dataset. There may be different types of attributes in the dataset. Many real-world problems have several constraints to be satisfied while clustering data. Application areas of clustering include but are not limited to Medical image processing, Pattern recognition, Spatial database technology, Information retrieval, Computer vision, etc.

Types of Clustering Algorithms

Clustering algorithms can be categorized into partitional, hierarchical, density-based and grid-based methods. (Jain, Murty & Flynn, 1999) Partitional algorithms tend to find spherical clusters based on distance measures and generally use mean or medoid to represent cluster center. Hierarchical methods perform multiple levels of decomposition either in top-down or bottom-up fashion which is termed as divisive or agglomerative respectively. They are distance-based or density- and continuity based methods. Density-based algorithms continuously form a cluster until the density in the neighborhood exceeds some threshold and are good in finding arbitrarily shaped clusters. Grid-based methods use a multi-resolution grid structure and are very fast in nature.

Clustering algorithms can be classified into hard and soft based on the allotment of objects. A hard clustering algorithm like K-Means allows an object to be assigned to exactly one cluster. In case of soft clustering methods like Fuzzy C-Means (FCM), (Bezdek, Ehrlich & Full, 1984) an object is allocated to multiple clusters based on the membership value of the object to each of those clusters. The non-membership value is obtained by subtracting the membership value from one.

Fuzzy Set and Intuitionistic Fuzzy Set

Fuzzy sets are designed to manipulate data and information possessing non-statistical uncertainties. A Fuzzy set is represented (Zadeh, 1965) as follows

$$FS = \{< x, \mu_{FS}(x) > | \ x \in X\}$$ (1)

where μ_{FS}: $X \to [0, 1]$ and ν_{FS}: $X \to [0, 1]$ and $\nu_{FS}(x) = 1 - \mu_{FS}(x)$. Here μ_{FS} is the membership value and ν_{FS} is the non-membership value.

An Intuitionistic Fuzzy Set (Atanassov, 2003) can be symbolized as below

$$IFS = \{< x, \mu_{IF}(x), \nu_{IF}(x) > | \ x \in X\}$$ (2)

where μ_{IF}: $X \to [0, 1]$ and ν_{IF}: $X \to [0, 1]$ and $\pi_{IF}(x) = 1 - \mu_{IF}(x) - \nu_{IF}(x)$ such that $0 < \mu_{IF}(x) + \nu_{IF}(x) < 1$ where π_{IF} is the hesitancy value used to represent the uncertainty.

An IFS is generally a triplet which consists of the membership, non-membership and hesitation degree out of which at least two values should be known in order to calculate the third parameter.

Fuzzy C Means Clustering

FCM (Bezdek et al., 1984) is the most popular soft clustering algorithm. In fuzzy sets, the uncertainty in the dataset is preserved by representing the data as a combination of membership and non-membership values. Let $D = \{d_1, d_2 ..., d_n\}$ be the data set and D has to be partitioned into C clusters based on the features of the dataset. The data has to be fuzzified before proceeding with the execution of clustering algorithm.

A membership function $\mu_i(d_j)$ for the fuzzy representation is defined by

$$\mu_i(d_j) = \frac{d_{ij} - \min(d_j)}{\max(d_j) - \min(d_j)}$$ (3)

where $i = 1, 2, ..., n$ and $j = 1, 2, ... t$. Here n is the number of instances in the dataset and t is the number of attributes in each instance of the dataset. The initial task is to estimate the similarity between the data sets using any distance measure like Euclidean distance.

The belongingness of an object d_i to the cluster c_j is given by

$$U_{ij} = \frac{1}{\sum_{r=1}^{C} \left(\frac{dis(d_j^{'}, v_i)}{dis(d_j^{'}, v_r)} \right)^{\frac{2}{m-1}}}, 1 \leq i \leq C, 1 \leq j \leq n, m = 2$$ (4)

The objective function of FCM algorithm can be given as follows

$$J_m(x,y) = \sum_{i=1}^{c} \sum_{j=1}^{p} U_{ij}^m \parallel X_j^{'} - C_i \parallel, 1 \leq m \leq \infty \tag{5}$$

The centroids are updated using the following formula

$$V_j = \sum_{i=1}^{n} (u_{ij})^m x_i \Big/ \sum_{i=1}^{n} (u_{ij})^m, \forall j = 1, 2, ..., C \tag{6}$$

The centroids are updated and again the membership values are computed. The process is repeated until the consecutive iterations produce the same centroids or until the objective function is saturated. Finally, the defuzzification process is done by finding the cluster to which the object has a higher membership value. This will serve as the index of the cluster for that object.

The main drawback of FCM algorithm is that it doesn't allow the user to thrive for a global solution. To avoid this problem, optimization algorithms can be run first and the best outcome of these algorithms can be given as input to the FCM algorithm.

ISSUES IN FCM

FCM is a partitional clustering algorithm which initially puts all the objects in a single group and then data points are relocated between clusters in a flexible manner. At each iteration, the value of criterion function is reduced and when it is stabilized, the algorithm is said to be converged. There are several issues in clustering such as the structure of datasets is unknown, the clusters can be of arbitrary shapes and inability to deal with noisy or missing data. The FCM algorithm minimizes the intra-cluster distance well but it leads to local minimum results only.

Intuitionistic Fuzzy Clustering

Fuzzy clustering deals with uncertainty and fuzziness. Uncertainty arises because there is a hesitation in assigning membership value due to its imprecise nature and also it varies from person to person. To avoid such confusions, Atanassov (2003) introduced another higher order fuzzy set named the Intuitionistic fuzzy set.

Intuitionistic Fuzzy Set (IFS) is a special type of fuzzy set that provides one additional factor called hesitancy degree which means that it is unclear whether the object belongs to or not belongs to a cluster. It is an intermediate state between yes and no and hesitation indicates a state of 'may be'. Intuitionistic fuzzy clustering algorithms are proposed by several authors for clustering images (Ananthi, Balasubramaniam, & Lim, 2014; Bhargava et al., 2013; Chaira, 2011; Huang et al., 2015) and numeric data (Lin, 2014; Xu, & Wu, 2010). The vagueness in data can be well represented using this hesitancy degree.

Need for Optimization

All the clustering algorithms have a general practice of choosing the initial clusters randomly. However, this heavily influences the result of a clustering algorithm. This may lead to getting trapped in local minima. So, the strive for a global solution necessitates the hybridization of the clustering algorithm with some optimization techniques.

There are several swarm-based meta-heuristic algorithms available in literature. The list includes but is not limited to Particle Swarm optimization (Kennedy, Kennedy, Eberhart et al., 2001), Ant Colony Optimization (Dorigo, Maniezzo, & Colorni, 1996), Bee Colony optimization (Karaboga, 2005), Krill herd optimization (Gandomi, & Alavi, 2012), Artificial Fish swarm (Li, & Qian, 2003), Bat optimization (Yang, & Hossein Gandomi, 2012), Cuckoo search Optimization (Yang, & Deb, 2009), Black hole optimization (Hatamlou, 2013), etc. (Jose-Garcia, & Gomez-Flores, 2016). Crow search Optimization is a novel algorithm based on the behavior of crow. This paper combines Intuitionistic fuzzy clustering with crow search optimization so that global optimal solutions can be reached. The crow search algorithm is used to find the best initial seed for the Intuitionistic Fuzzy C-Means (IFCM) Algorithm. The focus of this paper is towards effective clustering of data with a faster convergence in the value of objective function.

Contributions in this Paper

In order to efficiently cluster large and real time datasets, our contributions include

- Developing a novel, hybrid, highly scalable clustering algorithm by combining crow search optimization (one of the recent swarm based techniques) with Intuitionistic Fuzzy C-Means clustering. No such work exists in the literature
- The application of Crow search optimization to clustering has not yet been discussed by any author.
- Combining the best features from Chaira (2011) and Xu (2010) method and thus relieving users from the burden of having domain knowledge and ability to deal with noisy data

This paper is organized as follows: Section 2 focuses on the preliminaries, Section 3 provides an overview of the related literature, Section 4 gives a glimpse of crow search algorithm, Section 5 explains the proposed methodology, Section 6 concentrates on experimental analysis and results, Section 7 gives the concluding remarks.

INTUITIONISTIC FUZZY C-MEANS CLUSTERING

The first and foremost task for IFCM algorithm (Chaira, 2011) is to convert crisp data into fuzzy data which in turn would be converted to Intuitionistic fuzzy data. This process involves the task of fixing the lambda value which is a value that varies for each dataset. Entropy is the amount of fuzziness present in any given dataset. The value of lambda is chosen as the one which maximizes the entropy value.

Yager-generating function can be used to create IFS. The crisp data is converted into fuzzy data using Equation (3). Then the fuzzy data is converted to Intuitionistic fuzzy data as follows:

$$\mu_i(d_j; \lambda) = 1 - (1 - \mu_i(d_j))^{\lambda} \tag{7}$$

$$\nu_i(d_j; \lambda) = 1 - (1 - \mu_i(d_j))^{\lambda(\lambda+1)} \text{ } where \text{ } \lambda \in [0,1] \tag{8}$$

The intuitionistic fuzzification converts the intermediate fuzzy dataset to intuitionistic fuzzy dataset. The hesitancy factor is calculated by summing up the membership and non-membership degrees and subtracting the sum from one.

The clustering procedure given by Xu, & Wu, (2010) is followed. The distance matrix is calculated based on the Intuitionistic fuzzy Euclidean distance. Then, the membership matrix is calculated. This membership value is used to calculate non-member-ship and hesitancy values. Using these values, the mass (weight) factor given to each attribute t is calculated. Using these mass values, the new centroids are calculated. The algorithm proceeds until either the objective function converges or there is no change in the centroids for the consecutive iterations.

The objective function of IFCM can be given as

$$J_m(x,y) = \sum_{i=1}^{c} \sum_{j=1}^{p} U_{ij}^m \parallel X_j' - C_i \parallel, 1 \le m \le \infty \tag{9}$$

RELATED WORKS

To overcome the drawbacks of clustering algorithms, lot of researchers have combined them with the optimization techniques. But still the combination of Intuitionistic fuzzy clustering with the optimization algorithms is at its infant stage. There is not much research works published in this area. But fuzzy clustering based optimization has grown to a great extent and several noteworthy references can be found in the literature.

Cuckoo search optimization based fuzzy clustering defines egg laying radius (Amiri & Mahmoudi, 2016) for the eggs being laid by cuckoo and the best habitat is chosen and then fuzzy rules are applied to get optimal solutions that reduce the error rate. Binu (2015) compared the performance of various optimization algorithms like Genetic Algorithm, PSO and Cuckoo search over seven newly designed objective functions. When experimenting with large scale data, PSO-based methods are found to be efficient. Cobos et al., (2014) clustered web document search results by introducing a description-centric algorithm that exploits balanced Bayesian information criterion as the fitness function and thus the number of centroids can be deliberated automatically in advance. In order to retain the merits of both FCM and fuzzy PSO, Izakian & Abraham, (2011) proposed a novel algorithm that found a global solution with reduced execution time. A set of satellite images related to agriculture are segmented using FCM by Parvathavarthini, Visalakshi, & MadhanMohan (2011).

Rajabioun (2011) proposed Cuckoo Optimization Algorithm (COA) with an extension to cuckoo search by adding a parameter called Egg Laying Radius (ELR). This determines the maximum range within which the egg has to be laid. The surviving birds immigrate to a new habit and setup their nests.

The performance of the algorithm is verified by using it against standard benchmark datasets. Cuckoo search algorithm (Yang, & Deb, 2009, 2010) imitates the breeding behavior of the bird cuckoo. The authors utilized Levy flight distribution using Mantegna's algorithm to obtain new solutions and the algorithm is demonstrated with standard and stochastic test functions. Certain percentage of eggs are identified by the host bird and abandoned. The best nest to lay eggs is found and the algorithm proved to be efficient in arriving at an optimal result. A novel hybridization of cuckoo search algorithm with IFCM (Parvathavarthini, Karthikeyani, Shanthi, & Mohan, 2017) is proposed and experiments show that the resulting clusters are efficient.

Kanade and Hall (2007) utilized ACO to cluster the objects and reformulated the cluster centers using FCM and Hard C-Means to determine the number of clusters in each dataset. The intelligent foraging behavior of honey bees is simulated (Karaboga & Ozturk, 2010) and this algorithm is used for clustering. Employee bees collect nectar and share position of food with onlooker bees. Position of food source indicates the solution and the amount of nectar indicates quality of solution. In the black hole algorithm (Hatamlou, 2013), a random population of stars is generated, the fitness is evaluated and the best candidate is selected to be the black hole. All the other candidates are moved towards the black hole by changing position in every iteration. If a star reaches a location with lower cost than black hole, then their locations are exchanged. The author explains how blackhole optimization can be used for clustering.

Krill herd optimization (Li, Yi, & Wang, 2015) is the idealization of herding of krill swarms in sea. The position of an individual krill is determined by three motions such as: movement induced by other krill individuals, foraging action, and random diffusion. The authors used the elitism strategy i.e. instead of updating the positions of all the krill individuals, certain best krill individuals are retained in memory, and then all the krill are updated by three motions. Finally, certain worst krill individuals in the new population are replaced by the memorized best ones in the last generation. The best individual forms the initial centroids for FCM algorithm.

Jose-Garcia, & Gomez-Flores (2016) reviewed the major nature-inspired meta-heuristic algorithms for finding the number of clusters in any dataset automatically. Also, the encoding schemes, cluster validity indices and proximity measures are discussed in this paper. Kumutha, & Palaniammal (2014) converted PSO into fuzzy PSO and finally transformed it into Intuitionistic fuzzy PSO and combined this IF-PSO with FCM to yield faster convergence and thus reduce the computational complexity of IFCM algorithm.

A novel method for IF clustering using a multi-objective criterion function is developed by Chaira (2011) to segment CT scan brain images. IFS representation is generated with Yager type IF generator, the objective function is modified and the cluster center updation is incorporated by considering the hesitancy factor also. Shanthi, & Bhaskaran, (2011) utilized this clustering to classify mammogram images and built decision tree for effective diagnosis. Visalakshi, Thangavel, & Parvathi (2010) utilized IFCM algorithm for clustering distributed datasets.

A new clustering algorithm which considered the car data set is built by Xu & Wu (2010) for clustering both IFS and Interval-valued IFS. This proved to be more efficient with numerical datasets. A novel IF approach for Tumor/ hemorrhage detection is proposed in (Chaira, & Anand, 2011) and the images are edge detected by forming an IF divergence matrix, thresholding and thinning it. A robust IFCM and kernel version of IFCM is presented (Kaur, Soni, & Gosain, 2011) with a new distance metric incorporating the distance variation of data-points within each cluster. Krishnamoorthy, Sadasivam, Rajalakshmi, Kowsalyaa, & Dhivya (2017) used PSO to hide sensitive privacy information available in clusters. Bhargava et al. (2013) hybridized rough set with IFS in order to describe a cluster by its centroid and its lower and upper approximations. The method introduces modified Rough FCM with the membership of IFCM. Shanthi, & Bhaskaran. (2013) processed a set of mammogram images to detect and classify breast cancer by finding the region of interest and separating the affected part.

An image is represented as several fuzzy sets with the membership functions for symbolizing the foreground and background and then converted to IFS (Ananthi et al., 2014). The gray scale images are segmented using IFS. The entropy is calculated to find the threshold. The value that minimizes the entropy is taken as the threshold for segmenting the image. An artificial bee colony algorithm is designed (Naser, & Alshattnawi, 2014) for effectively grouping the social networks by collecting people with common interests. Sumathi, Sendhilkumar, & Mahalakshmi (2015) ranked the web pages using weighted page rank algorithm and utilized PSO for clustering the web users. Tripathy, Basu, & Govel (2014) segmented images by defining a spatial function which represents the degree of likeliness a pixel will have to each cluster. This value reaches its maximum for a cluster when most of the neighborhood pixels belong to the same cluster.

An evolutionary kernel IFCM (Lin, 2014) is introduced by maximizing the good points in the kernel space. Genetic Algorithm is used for selecting the parameters involved in this algorithm. A population of chromosomes is initialized, the fitness function is evaluated, roulette wheel selection is applied to choose chromosomes for reproduction, cross over and mutation is performed to get the next generation until the number of epochs are reached. The membership function proposed by Chaira is modified by (Huang et al., 2015) using neighborhood pixel tuning. The membership value is determined using a similarity measurement that represents the difference between the intensity of a pixel and the cluster and has no effective resistance to noise. Balasubramaniam, & Ananthi (2016) segmented nutrition deficiency in incomplete crop images using IFCM. The missing pixels in the incomplete images are imputed using IFCM algorithm. The resulting membership matrix efficiently portrayed the deficiency region of the crop.

CROW SEARCH ALGORITHM

Crows are well-known for their unity and intelligence. They have some special characteristics like self-awareness, recognizing faces and memorizing food sources. Crow Search Algorithm (CrSA) is a new population-based metaheuristic algorithm that simulates the behavior of these intelligent birds in order to solve optimization problems (Askarzadeh, 2016).

Crows live in flocks and they observe other birds to know where they hide food. They are stealthy by nature and are cautious in hiding their caches from being identified by other birds with a probability. To do thievery, a crow always tries to follow another. Crows defend their caches from being pilfered by others. Based on these characteristics, the algorithm has the goal of finding a better food source or hiding place. The algorithm is so simple that it needs to handle two parameters: Awareness Probability (AP) and Flight Length (FL).

Let D be the problem dimension and N be the population size. The position of the crow i at time t is given as $X^{i,t} = [x_1^{i,t}, x_2^{i,t}, ..., x_d^{i,t}]$ where $i = 1, 2, ..., N$; $t = 1, 2, ...,$ itmax, and itmax is the number of iterations. The hiding position of crow A at time t is given by $m^{A,t}$.

Suppose crow B wants to visit its hiding place $m^{B,t}$, and if crow A chooses to follow crow B, this results in two possible states such as

1. Crow B is not aware of crow A following it and thus crow A reaches the hiding place of crow B.

2.   Crow B is conscious that it is being followed by crow A and thus changes its position to any random flight direction in the search space.

PROPOSED METHODOLOGY

The IFCM algorithm selects the initial seeds randomly and also it suffers from the problem of falling into local minima. Due to this, there is a delay in the convergence of the clustering algorithm. Instead of choosing random points, this work uses crow search optimization algorithm for selecting the best initial seeds for performing the IFCM clustering. The crow search algorithm uses very few parameters like flight length and awareness probability and thus has reduced complexity. Thus, the implementation of such simple and user-friendly metaheuristic algorithm leads to promising results.

Crow Search-Based Intuitionistic Fuzzy C-Means Algorithm (CrSA_IFCM)

The parameters like population or flock size N, number of clusters C, Maximum number of iterations itmax, flight length fl and awareness probability AP are initialized. The position of the crows denoted by pos is set by generating a random matrix of cluster centers and the data objects are encoded. Here the initial seed values are taken as the crows, the dataset is the search space, each position of the crow is a feasible solution, and the quality of a set of centroids is determined by the objective function. The encoding is done in such a way that the set of initial centroids are taken as the population. The optimal value for initial centroid is obtained as a result of running the crow search optimization algorithm.

The dataset is converted into fuzzy representation using Eq. (3). This in turn is converted into Intuitionistic fuzzy representation using Eq. (5) and (6). The lambda value for this conversion is fixed by a heuristic method and it varies for each dataset. The lambda value which maximizes the entropy is fixed for each dataset. The entropy value is found using the following formula

$$IFE = \frac{1}{N \times M} \sum_{i=0}^{N-1} \sum_{j=0}^{M-1} \frac{2\mu_i\left(d_j\right)\nu_i\left(d_j\right) + \pi_i^2\left(d_j\right)}{\pi_i^2\left(d_j\right) + \mu_i^2\left(d_j\right) + \nu_i^2\left(d_j\right)} \qquad (10)$$

Initially the crows do not have any experience. So their memory is initialized same as the initial position assuming that they have hidden the food at their initial position. For each crow, the distance measure is computed and the membership values of each object to various clusters are calculated as follows:

$$U_{ij} = \frac{1}{\sum_{r=1}^{C} \left(\frac{dis\left(d_j', v_i\right)}{dis\left(d_j', v_r\right)} \right)^{\frac{2}{m-1}}}, 1 \leq i \leq C, 1 \leq j \leq n, m = 2 \qquad (11)$$

The fitness of initial positions is calculated using the objective function in Eq. (7). Assume that the crow B wants to visit its hiding place, then any crow A is randomly chosen to follow it. There are two possibilities now: either the crow may be aware of its follower or it is unaware. If crow B is conscious that crow A is following, it chooses a random new position to fool crow A. If crow B is not aware of crow A following it and thus crow A reaches the hiding place of crow B, new position of B is computed using

$$x_{A,t+1} = x_{A,t+1} + r_A.fl^{A,t}.\left(m^{B,t} - x^{B,t}\right) \tag{12}$$

The feasibility of new position is then checked and position is updated only if it is feasible. Otherwise no change to the position is made. The fitness of new position of crows is evaluated again. If the quality of the new position is better than the earlier position, the memory of crows is updated using

$$m_{A,t+1} = x_{A,t+1} \tag{13}$$

Similarly, random followers are selected for all the crows and the search is continued until the maximum iteration (itmax) is reached for crow search algorithm. As an outcome of crow search algorithm, the best initial seeds are found that minimize the fitness function to a greater extent. Now, the IFCM algorithm is executed to find the membership function and the fitness value. In order to calculate the membership function, a mass value is assigned to each attribute initially.

Then, the mass values for each attribute are updated during every iteration using the following formula

$$ma_i\left(k+1\right) = \left\{\frac{u_{i1}(k)}{\sum_{j=1}^{n}u_{ij}(k)}, \frac{u_{i2}(k)}{\sum_{j=1}^{n}u_{ij}(k)}, ..., \frac{u_{in}(k)}{\sum_{j=1}^{n}u_{ij}(k)}\right\}, 1 \leq i \leq C \tag{14}$$

Finally, the centroids are updated as follows:

$$V_i = \left\{\left[d_s, \sum_{j=1}^{n}ma_j\mu_{Aj}\left(d_s\right), \sum_{j=1}^{n}ma_j\nu_{Aj}\left(d_s\right)\right], 1 \leq s \leq n\right\}, 1 \leq i \leq C \tag{15}$$

The IFCM algorithm is run till the maximum number of iterations is reached. The cluster index of the objects is found based on the highest membership value obtained. To obtain better results, the CrSA_IFCM algorithm is repeated for 100 runs and the results are found to be better than the existing methods.

Pseudocode for CrSA_IFCM

```
Create intuitionistic fuzzy representation of data
Initialize the population of N crows, C clusters and maximum iterations itmax
Assign initial values for flight length and awareness probability.
Initialize the position of crows randomly with NxD dimension search space
Initialize the memory of the crows equivalent to the position of crows.
While run < maxruns
```

```
while t < itmax
  for A = 1 : N
     Calculate membership matrix using Eq. (13)
     Calculate the fitness of each crow using Eq. (9)
     Randomly choose one of the crows to follow (for example B)
     If r_B >=AP^{B,t} calculate new position using Eq. (12)
     Else x^{A,t+1}= a random position of search space
    end if
  end for
  Check the feasibility of new positions
     If it is feasible, Evaluate the cost of new position of the crows and
     Update the memory
  if f(x^{A,t+1}) is better than f(m^{i,t}) update memory using Eq. (13)
  else m^{A,t+1}=m^{A,t}
  end if
end while
Find the best position of the crow that minimizes the fitness function
   while iter < maxiterations
   Calculate membership matrix using the best position obtained above
   Calculate mass values using Eq. (14)
   Update cluster centers using Eq. (15)
   end while
end while
```

Benefits of Proposed Algorithm

The prominent benefits yielded from the above methodology are

- Well-separated and compact clusters are obtained
- Global optimal solutions are achieved
- Good solutions are memorized and the best solutions found are used to find the better positions
- A non-greedy algorithm in which the crow moves to a new position if the generated solution is not better than its current position
- Novel hybridization is applied to reduce convergence time
- Efficient in terms of validity indices, accuracy and fitness function

IMPLEMENTATION

The algorithm is developed using MATLAB Programming. There are several algorithm-specific parameters for the IFCM algorithm. The first and foremost being the lambda value which is computed based on the entropy or amount of fuzziness in each dataset. The value that maximizes the entropy is fixed for lambda. The second parameter is the mass (weight) value that is allotted for each attribute of the dataset. This plays a dominant role since the centroids are updated by considering the mass values. Initially, the mass values are equally distributed for all the attributes that is mass of each attribute is set to 1/n where n is the number of attributes. Then they are updated as the IFCM algorithm is executed. The IFCM algorithm is run up to a maximum of 20 iterations. CrSA_IFCM algorithm is repeated for 100 runs.

With respect to the crow search algorithm, the parameters include the number of crows = 20, maximum iterations = 50, and the values for flight length = 2 and awareness probability = 0.1 are taken from (Askarzadeh, 2016). The experiment is repeated for 100 runs and the best, worst and average values are selected for analysis. A salient characteristic of this algorithm is that it is highly adaptable with less number of attributes.

In this section, the algorithm is tested over eleven different datasets which include both real and artificial datasets. Experiments are done in three aspects, first one in terms of error rate, second in terms of cluster validity indices and the other in terms of objective function. The classification accuracy is higher when compared to the other algorithms.

Performance Analysis on Real Datasets

Real datasets are taken from UCI data repository (Asuncion, & Newman, 2007). The algorithm is tested over six types of real data like iris, wine, seed, Contraceptive Method Choice (CMC), glass and vowel. The details of the datasets are given in Table 1. The vowel and glass datasets have large number of clusters and CMC and vowel datasets have large number of instances.

Error Rate

For each dataset, the classification error percentage is calculated. It is the percentage of wrongly classified objects in the test datasets. The error rate is computed by comparing the cluster indices obtained by the CrSA_IFCM algorithm with that of the cluster indices of the benchmark datasets.

The classification error percentage is computed using the following formula

$$ER = \frac{\text{No. of misclassified samples}}{\text{No. of instances in the dataset}} \times 100 \tag{16}$$

Table 1. Benchmark datasets taken for the experiment

Dataset	Number of clusters	Number of attributes	Number of Instances (size of each class)
Iris	3	4	150 (50,50,50)
Wine	3	13	178 (59,71,48)
Seed	3	8	210(70,70,70)
CMC	3	10	1473 (629,333,511)
Vowel	6	3	871 (72,89,172,151,207,180)
Glass	6	9	214 (70,17,76,13,9,29)

COMPARISON WITH STATE OF THE ART TECHNIQUES

The error rate of the proposed methodology is shown in Table 2 and is compared with the other optimization techniques like PSO, GSA, Blackhole, Cuckoo Optimization and Fuzzy cuckoo optimization algorithm. It is evident from the results that the proposed method shows a significant improvement in the error rate for the datasets iris and glass. In case of CMC and vowel datasets, there is slight decrease in the error rate. For wine and seed datasets, the CrSA_IFCM algorithm tends to have a minor increase in error rate.

Comparison With Xu Method Using the Car Dataset

To quantitatively evaluate the performance of the proposed method, the fitness values are calculated. For each run, the best criterion values are stored and finally the fitness function that produces a best partition by generating the minimum error rate is chosen. If many fitness values generate the same error rate, then the fitness function with the least standard deviation is chosen. Algorithms like PSO need four user-defined parameters such as inertia weight, upper bound for velocity, individual and social learning factors. But crow search achieves more accuracy only with the help of two user-defined parameters. From Table 3, it is known that the CrSA_IFCM produces a better result for the best, average and worst values of the objective function.

Xu, & Wu (2010) proposed the Intuitionistic Fuzzy C-Means Clustering algorithms for IFS and Interval valued-IFS. The experiment is conducted using the car dataset which contains the information of cars sold in the Guangzhou car market in Guangdong, China. Ten instances of data are taken and the result of the clustering algorithm is derived. These cars have six attributes such as Fuel economy, Aerod degree, Price, Comfort, Design and Safety and for the first iteration, a mass value is fixed for these attributes. The mass values for the six attributes are 0.15, 0.10, 0.30, 0.20, 0.15 and 0.10 respectively. The cars are to be classified into three categories. The results of proposed method are compared to Xu method in Table 4 and were found to have a closest match.

The instances R1, R6 which did not match with any specific cluster are grouped in the first cluster. Additionally, R5 which belongs to the second cluster is brought into the first cluster. R8 is moved into cluster 3 and it is found that all the items except the instance R5 are grouped as per Xu method. Thus, the accuracy is 90 percentage when compared to Xu IFCM.

Table 2. Comparison of error rate with COAC and FCOAC

Dataset	PSO	GSA	Blackhole	COAC	FCOAC	CrSA_IFCM
Iris	10.06	10.04	10.02	11.53	9.81	**6.67**
Wine	28.79	29.15	28.47	9.44	**6.18**	6.74
Seed	16.67	14.76	14.29	13.67	**10.13**	10.47
CMC	51.50	57.68	54.39	11.24	10.26	**10.18**
Vowel	42.39	42.26	41.65	14.11	12.13	**12.05**
Glass	41.20	41.39	36.51	35.21	33.35	**31.78**

Table 3. Comparison of objective function with COAC and FCOAC

Dataset	Objective function	COAC	FCOAC	CrSA_IFCM
Iris	Mincost	1.8429	1.7345	1.0670
	Avgcost	1.8869	1.6567	1.1132
	Maxcost	3.0229	2.4341	1.1643
Wine	Mincost	240.3569	238.4567	203.4671
	Avgcost	248.0417	231.0465	207.6163
	Maxcost	550.8276	548.6783	230.1835
Seed	Mincost	5.4613	5.1287	1.4312
	Avgcost	3.3368	3.1262	1.4623
	Maxcost	3.2680	3.0630	1.4763
CMC	Mincost	0.5681	0.4961	0.4159
	Avgcost	0.5787	0.3784	0.5003
	Maxcost	0.7676	0.6826	0.7026
Vowel	Mincost	558.3689	557.3098	529.3124
	Avgcost	582.4493	580.2345	571.3691
	Maxcost	715.8966	713.6643	708.9372
Glass	Mincost	50. 0535	49.1934	49.0137
	Avgcost	53.1587	51.9231	53.6831
	Maxcost	74.2647	68.2312	69.3928

Table 4. Comparison of car dataset result with Xu method

Cluster Id	IFCM Xu Method	CrSA_IFCM
1	R4, R9	R1, R4, R5, R6, R9
2	R5, R10	R10
3	R2, R3, R7	R2, R3, R7, R8
No significant membership of any cluster	R1, R6, R8	–

Also, the objective function value is minimized to a greater extent. The values of Partition Coefficient and Partition Entropy are 0.941 and 0.192 respectively. Also, the number of clusters is varied and in this case, the optimal values are achieved when there are three clusters.

Performance Analysis on Artificial Datasets

Artificial data from University of Eastern Finland site is tested to validate the performance of the algorithm with respect to various size, shapes and overlapping clusters. Four shape datasets given in Figure 1such as flame, jain, pathbased and compound datasets are considered for evaluation. All the data are two-dimensional which means that they contain two attributes. Jain and flame datasets have two clusters while pathbased and compound datasets have three and six clusters respectively. The class label associated with the datasets is provided so that error rate and validity measures are calculated. The number of instances present in the dataset is as follows: flame: 240, jain: 373, pathbased: 300 and compound: 399.

Validity Measures

Cluster evaluation can correlate the structures found in the data with the externally provided class information and are used to check whether data consists of non-random structures. If the number of clusters for a dataset is not known, cluster evaluation helps in fixing the ideal number of clusters and assists in ranking the alternative clustering arrangements with regard to their quality. Cluster validation is the predominant way of judging the performance of a clustering algorithm. There are three categories of validation indices such as internal indices, external indices and relative indices. In order to incorporate external validity measures, there is a need for apriori knowledge about data (Visalakshi, Parvathavarthini, & Thangavel, 2014). Internal validation measures are based on two essential factors: separation and compactness. Separation indicates the degree with which a cluster is well-separated from others and compactness shows the relative closeness among the objects in a cluster. Thus, it is essential to measure how far the objects in the dataset are clustered based on their intrinsic characteristics.

Four famous indices for measuring the cluster accuracy have been considered to evaluate benchmark datasets. Out of these, Rand Index, Adjusted Rand Index and F-Measure are the external indices and Partition entropy (Halkidi, Batistakis, & Vazirgiannis, 2002) is an internal measure. A greater value closer to one indicates good performance in F-Measure, Adjusted Rand index and Rand indices. Lesser value results in good clusters in case of Partition entropy. The performances of all the four datasets have been evaluated using these indices.

For the artificial datasets, the best error rate is achieved for the flame dataset. However, the results of the objective function values are presented as the fuzzy values which show some minute details and the fitness values are minimized as well. It can be seen that the error rate increases as the number of clusters increase. Even though Flame and Jain datasets have same number of clusters, there is substantial increase in the error rate since the number of instances in the Jain dataset is more than that of flame dataset. So, the error rate is directly proportional to the number of clusters and number of instances.

Rand Index

A true positive (TP) decision assigns two similar documents to the same cluster; a true negative (TN) decision assigns two dissimilar documents to different clusters. In general, two types of errors occur frequently. A false positive (FP) decision means that two objects with different features are assigned to the same cluster. A false negative (FN) decision assigns two objects with similar traits to different clusters. The Rand index (Rand, 1971) measures the percentage of decisions that are correct.

$$RI = \frac{TP + TN}{TP + FP + FN + TN} \tag{17}$$

Figure 1. Two dimensional artificial datasets with different shapes of clusters

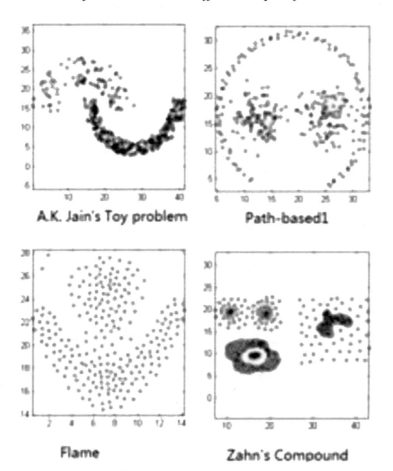

Table 5. Error rate for the artificial datasets

Dataset	Error rate	Objective Function Values			
		Best	Worst	Average	Std
Flame	12.9167	3.79	4.05	4.01	0.07
Jain	24.3968	10.45	11.07	10.87	0.12
Pathbased	25.3333	8.5628	8.9110	8.8505	0.1010
Compound	30.6015	2.2628	2.6333	2.5281	0.1142

F-Measure

The F-Measure (Van Rijsbergen, 1979) is an external index. It is the harmonic mean of the precision and recall coefficients. If the precision is high and recall value is low, this results in a low F-measure. If both precision and recall are low, a low F-measure is obtained. On the other hand, if both are high, a high F-measure value is obtained. F-Measure can be computed using the formula

$$F = \frac{2TP}{2TP + FP + TN} \tag{18}$$

Adjusted Rand Index

The peculiarity of Adjusted Rand Index (Hubert & Arabie, 1985) is that it is not sensible to the number of clusters. Thus, this measure can be used to compare two partitions with varying cluster numbers. The range of permissible values falls within -1 to +1. A value of 1 indicates a perfect partition similar to the apriori class label. Negative values signify the inability to discriminate the clusters and the values near zero show the random solution.

$$ARI = \sum_{i=1}^{C}\sum_{j=1}^{D}\binom{n_{ij}}{2}\binom{n}{2}^{-1}\sum_{i=1}^{C}\binom{n_i}{2}\sum_{j=1}^{D}\binom{n_j}{2} \Big/ \frac{1}{2}\left[\sum_{i=1}^{C}\binom{n_i}{2}+\sum_{j=1}^{D}\binom{n_j}{2}\right] - \binom{n}{2}^{-1}\sum_{i=1}^{C}\binom{n_i}{2}\sum_{j=1}^{D}\binom{n_j}{2} \tag{19}$$

Partition Entropy

Partition entropy (Dumitrescu, 1993) is an internal measure that involves only the membership values. The value ranges between 0 to number of clusters. The closer the value of PE to 0, the harder the clustering is. When the cluster structure is properly identified, partition entropy reaches its minimum value. It is calculated as follows

$$PE = -\frac{1}{N}\sum_{i=0}^{N-1}\sum_{j=0}^{M-1}\mu_{ij}\log_a\left(\mu_{ij}\right) \tag{20}$$

Where N is the number of instances in the dataset and k is the number of clusters

Tables 6 and 7 present the index values that play a prominent role in measuring the clustering accuracy. The highest value is for ARI is achieved by flame dataset and the least value is for Jain dataset. In case of Rand index, compound dataset scores the maximum.

The experiments in Table 8 show that the Iris dataset produces the significant value for best rand index value. The overall minimum value is obtained for the glass dataset which consists of spherical clusters. The least optimal value for partition entropy is achieved by the CMC dataset.

Table 6. Best, Mean and standard deviation values for Adjusted Rand Index and Rand Index

Dataset	ARI	ARI Mean	ARI Std	Rand	Rand Mean	Rand Std
Flame	0.5482	0.4651	0.0268	0.7741	0.7369	0.0134
Jain	0.2607	0.2317	0.0003	0.6301	0.6231	0.0004
Pathbased	0.3696	0.3613	0.0053	0.7031	0.7000	0.0021
Compound	0.5412	0.5380	0.0370	0.8342	0.8323	0.0113

Table 7. Best, Mean and standard deviation values for Partition entropy and F-Measure

Dataset	Partition entropy	PE Mean	PE std	F-Measure	FM Mean	FM std
Jain	0.4778	0.4376	0.0005	0.8035	0.7709	0.0008
Flame	0.2866	0.2671	0.0073	0.8733	0.8478	0.0098
Pathbased	0.5881	0.5211	0.0136	0.6378	0.6317	0.0060
Compound	0.5250	0.5212	0.0085	0.7099	0.6816	0.0203

Table 8. Validation Indices for Real datasets

Dataset	ARI	Rand Index	Partition entropy	F-Measure
Iris	0.8176	0.9195	0.4207	0.9333
Wine	0.8253	0.8042	0.3865	0.8093
Seed	0.8607	0.8576	0.2672	0.8729
CMC	0.7890	0.7947	0.1986	0.7543
Vowel	0.7234	0.8152	0.3150	0.7211
Glass	0.5246	0.6730	0.5234	0.5907

CONCLUSION

Optimization techniques have become the need of the hour because of their ability to explore and exploit the problem space in order to achieve a near optimal solution. Traditional algorithms are suffering from local minima solutions which necessitate a fast move towards hybridization. To mine useful information from data and grouping them into clusters with a weightage for the hesitation makes sense in the current scenario. This work provides an innovative clustering algorithm by combining Intuitionistic Fuzzy Clustering with crow search optimization. Investigations on data show that the proposed method combines the benefits of IFCM and Optimization techniques. Since crow search being a non-greedy algorithm, the range and variety of the solutions that are generated is increased.

REFERENCES

Amiri, E., & Mahmoudi, S. (2016). Efficient protocol for data clustering by fuzzy Cuckoo Optimization Algorithm. *Applied Soft Computing*, *41*, 15–21. doi:10.1016/j.asoc.2015.12.008

Ananthi, V. P., Balasubramaniam, P., & Lim, C. P. (2014). Segmentation of gray scale image based on intuitionistic fuzzy sets constructed from several membership functions. *Pattern Recognition*, *47*(12), 3870–3880. doi:10.1016/j.patcog.2014.07.003

Askarzadeh, A. (2016). A novel metaheuristic method for solving constrained engineering optimization problems: Crow search algorithm. *Computers & Structures*, *169*, 1–12. doi:10.1016/j.compstruc.2016.03.001

Asuncion, A., & Newman, D. (2007). UCI machine learning repository.

Atanassov, K. T. (2003, September). Intuitionistic fuzzy sets: past, present and future. In *Proceedings of the EUSFLAT Conf.* (pp. 12-19).

Balasubramaniam, P., & Ananthi, V. P. (2016). Segmentation of nutrient deficiency in incomplete crop images using intuitionistic fuzzy C-means clustering algorithm. *Nonlinear Dynamics, 83*(1-2), 849–866. doi:10.1007/s11071-015-2372-y

Bezdek, J. C., Ehrlich, R., & Full, W. (1984). FCM: The fuzzy c-means clustering algorithm. *Computers & Geosciences, 10*(2-3), 191–203. doi:10.1016/0098-3004(84)90020-7

Bhargava, R., Tripathy, B. K., Tripathy, A., Dhull, R., Verma, E., & Swarnalatha, P. (2013, August). Rough intuitionistic fuzzy c-means algorithm and a comparative analysis. In *Proceedings of the 6th ACM India Computing Convention* (p. 23). ACM. doi:10.1145/2522548.2523140

Binu, D. (2015). Cluster analysis using optimization algorithms with newly designed objective functions. *Expert Systems with Applications, 42*(14), 5848–5859. doi:10.1016/j.eswa.2015.03.031

Chaira, T. (2011). A novel intuitionistic fuzzy C means clustering algorithm and its application to medical images. *Applied Soft Computing, 11*(2), 1711–1717. doi:10.1016/j.asoc.2010.05.005

Chaira, T., & Anand, S. (2011). A novel intuitionistic fuzzy approach for tumour/hemorrhage detection in medical images.

Cobos, C., Muñoz-Collazos, H., Urbano-Muñoz, R., Mendoza, M., León, E., & Herrera-Viedma, E. (2014). Clustering of web search results based on the cuckoo search algorithm and balanced Bayesian information criterion. *Information Sciences, 281*, 248–264. doi:10.1016/j.ins.2014.05.047

Dorigo, M., Maniezzo, V., & Colorni, A. (1996). Ant system: Optimization by a colony of cooperating agents. *IEEE Transactions on Systems, Man, and Cybernetics. Part B, Cybernetics, 26*(1), 29–41. doi:10.1109/3477.484436 PMID:18263004

Dumitrescu, D. (1993). Fuzzy measures and the entropy of fuzzy partitions. *Journal of Mathematical Analysis and Applications, 176*(2), 359–373. doi:10.1006/jmaa.1993.1220

Gandomi, A. H., & Alavi, A. H. (2012). Krill herd: A new bio-inspired optimization algorithm. *Communications in Nonlinear Science and Numerical Simulation, 17*(12), 4831–4845. doi:10.1016/j.cnsns.2012.05.010

Halkidi, M., Batistakis, Y., & Vazirgiannis, M. (2002). Cluster validity methods: Part I. *SIGMOD Record, 31*(2), 40–45. doi:10.1145/565117.565124

Hatamlou, A. (2013). Black hole: A new heuristic optimization approach for data clustering. *Information Sciences, 222*, 175–184. doi:10.1016/j.ins.2012.08.023

Huang, C. W., Lin, K. P., Wu, M. C., Hung, K. C., Liu, G. S., & Jen, C. H. (2015). Intuitionistic fuzzy c-means clustering algorithm with neighborhood attraction in segmenting medical image. *Soft Computing, 19*(2), 459–470. doi:10.1007/s00500-014-1264-2

Hubert, L., & Arabie, P. (1985). Comparing partitions. *Journal of classification, 2*(1), 193-218.

Izakian, H., & Abraham, A. (2011). Fuzzy C-means and fuzzy swarm for fuzzy clustering problem. *Expert Systems with Applications, 38*(3), 1835–1838. doi:10.1016/j.eswa.2010.07.112

Jain, A. K., Murty, M. N., & Flynn, P. J. (1999). Data clustering: A review. [CSUR]. *ACM Computing Surveys, 31*(3), 264–323. doi:10.1145/331499.331504

Jose-Garcia, A., & Gomez-Flores, W. (2016). Automatic clustering using nature-inspired metaheuristics: A survey. *Applied Soft Computing, 41*, 192–213. doi:10.1016/j.asoc.2015.12.001

Kanade, P. M., & Hall, L. O. (2007). Fuzzy ants and clustering. *IEEE Transactions on Systems, Man, and Cybernetics. Part A, Systems and Humans, 37*(5), 758–769. doi:10.1109/TSMCA.2007.902655

Karaboga, D. (2005). *An idea based on honey bee swarm for numerical optimization* (Technical report-tr06). Erciyes University, Engineering Faculty, Computer Engineering Department.

Karaboga, D., & Ozturk, C. (2010). Fuzzy clustering with artificial bee colony algorithm. *Scientific Research and Essays, 5*(14), 1899–1902.

Kaur, P., Soni, A. K., & Gosain, A. (2011, November). Robust Intuitionistic Fuzzy C-means clustering for linearly and nonlinearly separable data. In *Proceedings of the 2011 International Conference on Image Information Processing (ICIIP)* (pp. 1-6). IEEE. doi:10.1109/ICIIP.2011.6108908

Kennedy, J. F., Kennedy, J., Eberhart, R. C., & Shi, Y. (2001). *Swarm intelligence*. Morgan Kaufmann.

Krishnamoorthy, S., Sadasivam, G. S., Rajalakshmi, M., Kowsalyaa, K., & Dhivya, M. (2017). Privacy Preserving Fuzzy Association Rule Mining in Data Clusters Using Particle Swarm Optimization. *International Journal of Intelligent Information Technologies, 13*(2), 1–20. doi:10.4018/IJIIT.2017040101

Kumutha, V., & Palaniammal, S. (2014). Improved Fuzzy Clustering Method Based On Intuitionistic Fuzzy Particle Swarm Optimization. *Journal of Theoretical & Applied Information Technology, 62*(1).

Li, X. L., & Qian, J. X. (2003). Studies on artificial fish swarm optimization algorithm based on decomposition and coordination techniques. *Journal of Circuits and Systems, 1*, 1–6.

Li, Z. Y., Yi, J. H., & Wang, G. G. (2015). A New Swarm Intelligence Approach for Clustering Based on Krill Herd with Elitism Strategy. *Algorithms, 8*(4), 951–964. doi:10.3390/a8040951

Lin, K. P. (2014). A novel evolutionary kernel intuitionistic fuzzy C-means clustering algorithm. *IEEE Transactions on Fuzzy Systems, 22*(5), 1074–1087. doi:10.1109/TFUZZ.2013.2280141

Naser, A. M. A., & Alshattnawi, S. (2014). An Artificial Bee Colony (ABC) Algorithm for Efficient Partitioning of Social Networks. *International Journal of Intelligent Information Technologies, 10*(4), 24–39. doi:10.4018/ijiit.2014100102

Parvathavarthini, S., Karthikeyani, N., Shanthi, S., & Mohan, J. M. (2017). Cuckoo-search based Intuitionistic Fuzzy Clustering Algorithm. *Asian Journal of Research in Social Sciences and Humanities, 7*(2), 289–299. doi:10.5958/2249-7315.2017.00091.0

Parvathavarthini, S., & Visalakshi, N. K. & MadhanMohan J, Identification of optimal clusters by Segmenting Satellite Images. In *Proceedings of ICNICT '11*.

Rajabioun, R. (2011). Cuckoo optimization algorithm. *Applied Soft Computing*, *11*(8), 5508–5518. doi:10.1016/j.asoc.2011.05.008

Rand, W. M. (1971). Objective criteria for the evaluation of clustering methods. *Journal of the American Statistical Association*, *66*(336), 846–850. doi:10.1080/01621459.1971.10482356

Shanthi, S., & Bhaskaran, V. M. (2011). Intuitionistic fuzzy C-means and decision tree approach for breast cancer detection and classification. *European Journal of Scientific Research*, *66*(3), 345–351.

Shanthi, S., & Bhaskaran, V. M. (2013). A novel approach for detecting and classifying breast cancer in mammogram images. *International Journal of Intelligent Information Technologies*, *9*(1), 21–39. doi:10.4018/jiit.2013010102

Sumathi, G., Sendhilkumar, S., & Mahalakshmi, G. S. (2015). Ranking Pages of Clustered Users using Weighted Page Rank Algorithm with User Access Period. *International Journal of Intelligent Information Technologies*, *11*(4), 16–36. doi:10.4018/IJIIT.2015100102

Tripathy, B. K., Basu, A., & Govel, S. (2014), December. Image segmentation using spatial intuitionistic fuzzy C means clustering. In *Proceedings of the 2014 IEEE International Conference on Computational Intelligence and Computing Research (ICCIC)* (pp. 1-5). IEEE.

Van Rijsbergen, C. J. (1979). *Information retrieval*. Dept. Of Computer Science, University Of Glasgow.

Visalakshi, N. K., Parvathavarthini, S., & Thangavel, K. (2014). An intuitionistic fuzzy approach to fuzzy clustering of numerical dataset. In Computational Intelligence, Cyber Security and Computational Models (pp. 79-87). Springer India.

Visalakshi, N. K., Thangavel, K., & Parvathi, R. (2010). An Intuitionistic fuzzy approach to distributed fuzzy clustering. *International Journal of Computer Theory and Engineering*, *2*(2), 295–302. doi:10.7763/IJCTE.2010.V2.155

Xu, Z., & Wu, J. (2010). Intuitionistic fuzzy C-means clustering algorithms. *Journal of Systems Engineering and Electronics*, *21*(4), 580–590. doi:10.3969/j.issn.1004-4132.2010.04.009

Yang, X. S., & Deb, S. (2009, December). Cuckoo search via Lévy flights. In *Proceedings of the World Congress on Nature & Biologically Inspired Computing NaBIC '09* (pp. 210-214). IEEE.

Yang, X. S., & Deb, S. (2010). Engineering optimisation by cuckoo search. *International Journal of Mathematical Modelling and Numerical Optimisation*, *1*(4), 330–343. doi:10.1504/IJMMNO.2010.035430

Yang, X. S., & Hossein Gandomi, A. (2012). Bat algorithm: A novel approach for global engineering optimization. *Engineering Computations*, *29*(5), 464–483. doi:10.1108/02644401211235834

Zadeh, L. A. (1965). Fuzzy sets. *Information and Control*, *8*(3), 338–353. doi:10.1016/S0019-9958(65)90241-X

KEY TERMS AND DEFINITIONS

Clustering: It is an unsupervised learning technique that groups the data objects without apriori knowledge of class labels.

Data Mining: It is one of the steps in Knowledge Discovery in Databases (KDD). It discovers interesting patterns or knowledge from huge volume of data.

Fuzzy Logic: Fuzzy logic can assign many real values between 0 and 1. There may be partial truth or different degrees of membership for a statement.

Optimization: It aims at finding the best among the feasible solutions to a problem based on either minimizing or maximizing the fitness function.

Chapter 8
Intelligent Radial Basis Function Neural Network for Intrusion Detection in Battle Field

Kirupa Ganapathy
Saveetha University, India

ABSTRACT

Defense at boundary is nowadays well equipped with perimeter protection, cameras, fence sensors, radars etc. However, in battlefield there is more feasibility of entering of a non-native human and unknowing stamping of the explosives placed in the various paths by the native soldiers. There exists no alert system in the battlefield for the soldiers to identify the intruder or the explosives in the field. Therefore, there is a need for an automated intelligent intrusion detection system for battlefield monitoring. This chapter proposes an intelligent radial basis function neural network (RBFNN) technique for intrusion detection and explosive identification. The proposed intelligent RBFNN implements some intellectual components in the algorithm to make the neural network think before learning the training samples. Involvement of intellectual components makes the learning process simple, effective and efficient. The proposed technique helps to reduce false alarm and encourages timely detection thereby providing extensive support for the native soldiers and save the life of the mankind.

INTRODUCTION

Automation does not involve human intervention. Automation of a system is feasible and successful as it involves the integration of wireless sensor network and information technology. Automation in real world applications involves machine learning algorithms.

Machine learning is a software tool that constructs algorithms which can learn data and make predictions on its own. These software tools substitute human intelligence for various applications such as speech recognition, pattern classification, face recognition, etc., there are different kinds of learning techniques applied for different real world problems. Machine learning that involve mathematics for derivative process of learning is termed as data mining algorithms. Similarly, machine learning that are derivative free and

DOI: 10.4018/978-1-5225-3686-4.ch008

the algorithms are inspired from human biology and nature are termed as soft computing techniques. The complexity in implementation of data mining approaches bends to implement soft computing learning algorithms. Most commonly, the learning techniques are classified as supervised, unsupervised, hebbian, reinforcement and competitive. Selection of above mentioned learning technique is entirely based on available data sample. Most of the real-world applications have patterns/samples that has input and output relationship. Therefore, supervised learning that has training samples with prior known input and output relationship is highly suitable for proposed intrusion detection system in battle field.

The most commonly used supervised learning algorithm is Artificial Neural Network (ANN) technique. ANN is inspired from the biological human nervous system. ANN is one of the learning algorithms in soft computing approach. Wide usage and suitability of soft computing approach for automation is due to its simplicity, adaptability, flexibility, and derivative free model. ANN supervised learning includes algorithms such as Back Propagation Neural Network (BPNN), Adaptive Neural Fuzzy Inference System (ANFIS) and Radial Basis Function Neural Network (RBFNN). Due to the complexity of the algorithm and complex network structure, the BPNN and ANFIS are not suitable for real time or dynamically changing applications.

Learning algorithms require complete training data set to build a model. In real world, the training data is nonlinear and non-stationary. Existing neural network model utilizes whole data set for processing, adjusts the network parameters, grows the network size without pruning and uses entire sample data for training. These approaches increase the complexity of the model, poor generalization, low learning accuracy and large model size. Compared to other neural networks, RBFNN is widely suitable for static and dynamic applications due to its flexibility, speed, accuracy (Han, H.-G., & Qiao, J.-F., 2012; Sajavičius, 2014; Várkonyi-Kóczy, 2016) and simple structure. Therefore, this chapter proposes a novel Radial Basis Function neural network for battlefield monitoring that includes higher level thinking components. The proposed Intelligent RBFNN uses intellectual components such as sample addition, sample deletion and neuron addition.

The remainder of this chapter is organized as follows. Section I presents the preliminaries of the Radial Basis Function Neural Network. Section II describes the recent developments carried out by various researchers on Radial Basis Function Networks. Section III discusses the proposed intellectual radial basis function neural network for intrusion detection in battle field. Section IV details the Intrusion detection in Battle field for alert generation using intelligent RBFNN- A case study. Section V gives the results and discussions. Section VI discusses the conclusion.

Preliminaries on RBFNN

The guiding principle of RBFNN is covers theorem which states that "A complex pattern-classification problem cast in high-dimensional space non-linearly is more likely to be linearly separable than in a low dimensional space." Figure 1 shows the traditional Radial Basis Function Neural Network.

A RBF Neural Network (Martel, J. M., & Platte, R. B.,2016) consists of mainly three layers along with a nonlinear radial basis functions. The layers are Input layer, Hidden layer and Output layer. The hidden layer performs nonlinear mapping from input space to higher dimensional space by using activation function in the network.

Due to the universal approximation capability of Gaussian function (J. Rashidiniaa et al,2016) it is highly preferred. The number of nodes in the hidden layer is highly dependent on the input patterns

Figure 1. Basic radial basis function neural network

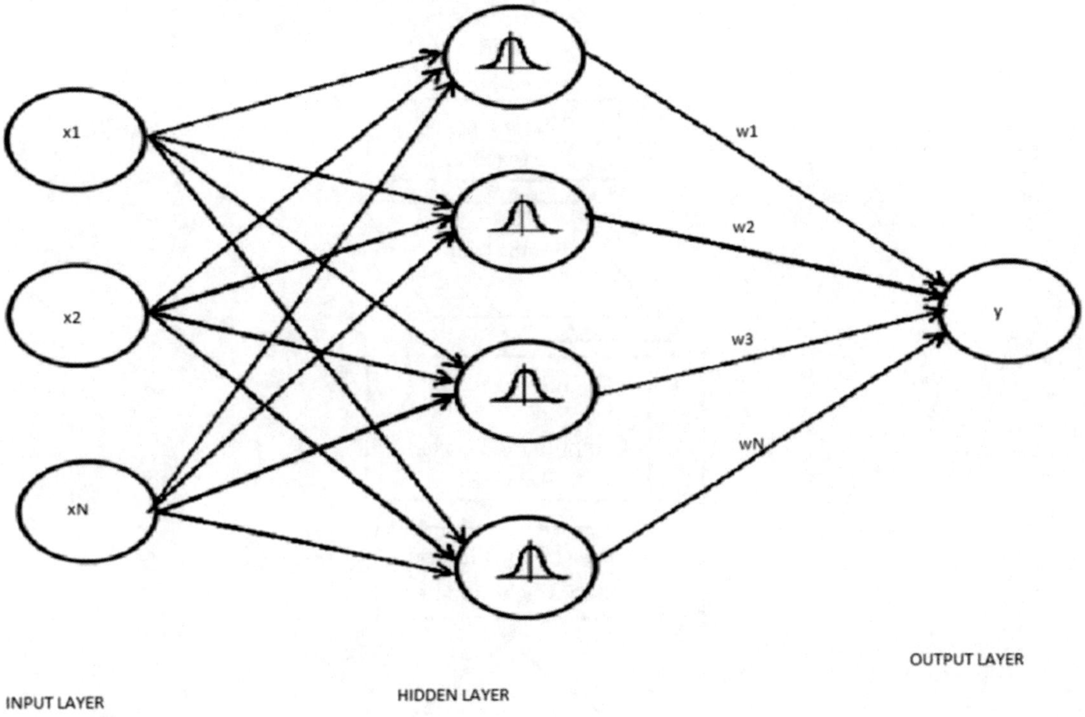

INPUT LAYER   HIDDEN LAYER   OUTPUT LAYER

provided. Each node in the hidden layer will have unique center value and spread value based on the input patterns. The working procedure of the RBF Neural network is given as flow chart in Figure 2. The RBF algorithm begins with initializing a neuron with the input data (x_i) and initializes random weights (w_{ij}). The centers of the RBF are chosen from the set of input vectors. The center calculation is normally based on the Euclidean distance as given in Equation 1.

$$a_j = \sqrt{\sum_{i=1}^{n} \left(x_i - w_{ij} \right)^2}$$

(1)

Where

a_j = Euclidean distance

x_i = input vector

w_{ij} = weight between input vector i and hidden neuron j

The Gaussian activation function holds the center value as given in Equation 2.

Figure 2. Flow chart of radial basis function neural network

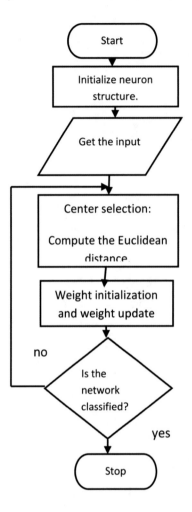

$$\phi_j = \exp\left(-\frac{\sum_{i=1}^{n}\left(x_i - \mu_j\right)^2}{2\sigma^2}\right) \tag{2}$$

Where

$$\sigma = \frac{{}^- d \max}{\sqrt{2n}} \tag{3}$$

n = number of basis functions

d_{max} = distance between input and neuron in the hidden layer

σ = width of the hidden neuron

μ_j = center of the basis function

The output of hidden neuron (ϕ_j) is computed and also it initializes weights between hidden layer and output layer to small random values as given in Equation 4.

$$y_j = \sum_{i=1}^{n} \phi_j w_{ij} \tag{4}$$

Where

y_j = output of the network

Number of output neurons (y_j) is estimated based on the number of classes to be classified. Iterations are repeated until a stopping criterion with reduced error is achieved. RBFNN is highly suitable for multi class classification problem. (Zhang et al., 2016)

Algorithm 1 for Traditional/Classic RBF

```
Start
The centers for RBF are chosen from the vectors of the input data set.
Initialize random weights (w_mn) where m = 1....M and n = 1....n
Each neuron in the hidden layer gets the input data from the input layer.
Calculate RBF.
The output of the hidden neuron is Y_m
Initialize random values to the weights from hidden layer to the output layer.
Output of the neural network is computed as Z_n
Calculate error value.
Update the weights w_n = w_0+Δw
Stop the iteration process if the criteria are met.
```

Classic RBF architecture has fixed number of neurons and neuron centers in the hidden layer are given a priori for training. Algorithm 1 gives the step by step procedure of traditional/classic RBF. Severity of this classic RBF is more in non-stationary system. Even when the samples are enormous, all the samples are learned by the fixed hidden neurons. (Chen, Gong, & Hong, 2013) This learning process leads to erroneous output where selection of centers is not based on the incoming pattern. As an extension of the classic RBF, few preliminary studies have selected RBF function hidden nodes equal to the number of training patterns.

This technique becomes worse and increases the architecture complexity by adding more hidden neurons in case of large data set or higher dimension. To improve the learning accuracy, excessive number of hidden nodes is reduced by proper centre selection. Similarly, the accuracy of the model is improved by adjusting the RBF parameters such as variances, weight (Regis, 2014), activation function selection and node topology.

Synaptic weighted connections are established between the hidden and output neurons. Initially, random weights are assigned to all connections. Weight value (He et al., 2016) is the amount of information contributed by the hidden neurons with respect to the output class. If the weight value is less or more it reflects its effect on the error. The error is dependent on weight; hence the weights are to be adjusted between 0 to 1 in order to reduce the misclassification error in every iteration. Few researchers in literature use different weight parameter estimation techniques for determining optimal weight.

Recently, there have been enormous works carried out in improving the architecture of the RBF network. Initially, growing of the RBF network is modeled but growing leads to large model size. Therefore, this paved way for the researchers in introducing pruning technique to remove the inactive hidden nodes. However, growing as well as pruning techniques have direct link to the efficiency of the system.

Pruning of the neurons may remove the information of the system which is need in future. To overcome the above issues, this research proposes a novel Radial Basis Function neural network for online modeling and dynamic learning that includes higher level thinking components. This component uses the knowledge gained from the previously learned sample while learning the new information.

The communication between the learned sample and learning sample strengthens the online learning strategy by allowing the network to think before learning. It is possible to design a strong classifier for any real-world problems by adding these higher-level components with the classic RBF parameters. Higher level learning focuses on nature of learning, goal of learning, context of learning, knowledge construction, strategic thinking and thinking about thinking. This research suggests a novel Intelligent RBFNN network for dynamic learning as a solution to handle real world problems.

Recent Works

Many research works have been performed in recent years to make the network more dynamic and best suitable for automation. There are various parameters in RBFNN that contributes to accuracy and speed of the classifier. The parameters or factors that determine the speed and accuracy of the RBFN are center value, hidden neurons, width and the weight between the hidden and the output layer. The overview of Radial Basis Function Neural Network classification is given in Figure 3.

Several techniques are applied to improve traditional RBFN learning mechanism in static and dynamic environments. To solve the issues, various static and dynamic RBFN methods have been experimented and tested. In recent years, investigation of RBFN in changing environment problems has become one of the most important issues for real time applications. Few techniques recently developed tries to improve the performance of RBF neural network and their issues are briefly discussed below.

Center Selection

K.Z. Mao (2002) proposes a radial basis function neural network for discriminate RBF centers. The centers are initially selected randomly and fisher ratio class separability orthogonal class transfer method is used to identify the center that provides large class separation. This algorithm was experimented for several benchmark data sets and compared with other algorithms such as SUM, CART, c4.5 and naive bayes algorithm. The accuracy of this algorithm was improved for the given sample data set. The com-

Figure 3. Overview of radial basis function neural network classification

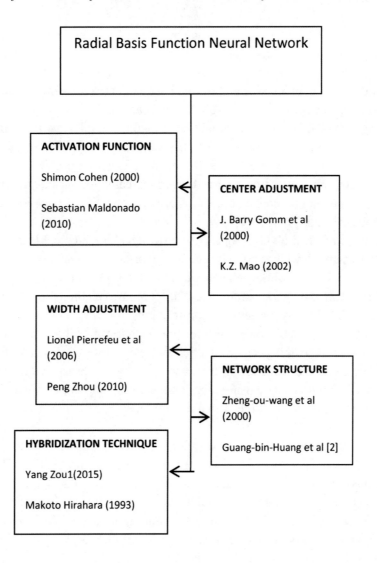

parison of performance is carried out using data mining technique. However, this work uses complex mathematical modeling for determining the centers.

J. Barry Gomm (2000) uses recursive orthogonal least square algorithm for selecting the hidden neuron centers. The optimal weights are achieved using orthogonal selection procedures. This work uses forward selection and backward selection process for center selection. This work has strong mathematical foundation. However too many selection procedures are followed thereby increasing the computational time. Also, this method achieves only acceptable accuracy.

Dianxaun Gong (2011) focuses on center selection of RBF. Various algorithm such as greedy, geometrical greedy, k-means clustering, arc length equi-partition for function selection and width selection were discussed in detail. Finally, this work concludes that the approximate center selection depends entirely on the activation function and interpolation of the activation function depends on the data set.

Network Structure

Guang-bin-Huang et al (2004) propose a new radial basis function neural network for growing and pruning of the hidden neurons, this sequence based learning algorithm uses piece wise linear approximation for the Gaussian function. When compared to the other similar algorithm this work proves to be better in terms of generalization, network size and training speed but no real-time application appears to be sequential. Therefore, this work may not be suitable for real world problems.

Zheng-ou-wang et al (2008) propose a radial basis function neural network for improving the classification. This work uses competitive learning based clustering technique for grouping the input samples. In order to minimize the hidden neurons in RBF network. Structure pruning is performed. Weight is updated using RLS algorithm as the number of cluster increases for various training and testing data. This work reduces the number of hidden neurons. Therefore, over fitting is avoided and high generalization performance is achieved.

S. Chen, Y. Wu, and B. L. Luk (1999) propose a two-level hierarchical learning method for radial basis function (RBF) network which employs regularized orthogonal least squares (ROLS) algorithm at lower level to construct RBF networks and genetic algorithm (GA) at the upper level to find the global optimum for width and regularization parameters. This combined method provides better computational efficiency than using GA directly for network construction.

Dajun Du et al developed a multi-output fast recursive algorithm (MFRA) for multi-output RBF networks construction where by making center selection and weight estimation in a well-defined regression. Center is defined based on the reduction in the trace of the error covariance matrix and also network weights are estimated simultaneously using a back-substitution approach, thus reduces computational complexity. The total number of multiplication/division operations is much less in number compared to that of OLS.

Gao Daqi and Yang Genxing (2002) propose an adaptive RBF neural network for pattern classification which defines structures and parameters of network based on sample distribution. These results in higher classification precision even in multiple distribution regions and irregular shapes for one class in case of multi-dimensional spaces. The input and the hidden layers in traditional feedforward RBF network are taken as a single-layered RBF and the hidden and output layers are considered as a two-layered LBF. This cascaded RBF-LBF network has lesser possibility to fall into local minima. However, the training time is higher and a small error in training samples causes bigger errors in classification.

Width Selection

Lionel Pierrefeu et al (2006) proposed a RBFNN for optimal width selection. This method is implemented for face recognition application. Existing literature implements k-means clustering method. This work does not form the cluster and the cluster head. From the database of images, the statistical properties are analyzed and the width is adjusted for every neuron. Based on the input parameter, the width is optimized. Similarly, Mark Orr (1998) proposed a RBFNN using Generalized cross validation (GCV) method to improve the computational efficiency, identification of global minima and width optimization. Instead of selecting one width this work goes for much number of iterations to find minimum and maximum huygen values. From the trails, global minimum is achieved. The point at which the global minima achieved is considered as width of the activation function.

Peng Zhou et al (2010) developed a RBFNN using orthogonal least square (OLS) algorithm and differential evolution (DE) algorithm for efficient training of the network. The number of neurons in the hidden layer is selected using OLS method.

These techniques discussed above are well suitable for various applications. To summarize, many researchers have tried to improve the classification accuracy and speed of the network in different ways by performing Centre adjustment, width selection, number of hidden neurons, optimization of the weights, strengthening of the hidden and output neuron connections, pruning, growing etc. These methods compromise either on accuracy or computation time. If accuracy is given higher priority, the network structure increases. Similarly, if computational time is considered then the accuracy of the classifier is compromised. Therefore, there is a need for an adaptive structure network for real world applications that balances accuracy and detection time. The proposed intelligent RBFN involves intellectual components to develop adaptive network structure (Gillebaart, T et al.,2016) and also provide intelligent learning process. Also, intelligent RBFNN avoids batch learning process and therefore highly suitable for any static and dynamic applications. The network structure of the proposed RBFNN adapts to any real time change of the dimensions too. Therefore, proposed RBFNN is suitable for high dimensional data classification or multiclass classification.

Intelligent Radial Basis Function Neural Network

Input neurons are selected based on the input patterns that are given to the network. As the network structure is dynamic there is only one hidden layer with any number of centers in the structure with a constant width for all the neurons. The network is initialized with random centers which are unique for each category of input samples and the output neurons are selected based on the target values.

The training sample k = (P, T) is the combination of the input pattern P and the corresponding target value T. A mapping is done from a lower dimensional input space into a higher dimensional space to detect the class of the non-linear input data pattern.

The input pattern can be binary or integer values, the number of neurons in the input layer is equal to the dimension of the input pattern. The output of the network is a linear combination of radial basis function of the inputs and neuron parameters.

$$G_k = \left(e^{\left(-Hi \right)} \right)^2 \tag{5}$$

$$Hi = a_j = \sqrt{\sum_{i=1}^{n} \left(x_i - w_{ij} \right)^2} \tag{6}$$

Where $i = 1....$ N

Where N represents the number of neurons in the hidden layer, X_i represents the input sample and H_i is the Gaussian activation function for i^{th} hidden neuron. X_{ik} and σ_i are the center and spread of the ith hidden neuron. The spread value of the Gaussian activation function is given by

$$\sigma_i = \varphi_j = \exp\left(-\frac{\sum_{i=1}^n \left(x_i - \mu_j\right)^2}{2\sigma^2}\right) \tag{7}$$

Where

N is the number of radial basis functions

D_m is the distance between the neurons in the input and the hidden layer

σ_i = width of the activation function.

The output equation from the output layer is given by H_j

$$Z_k = \sigma = \frac{d_{\max}}{\sqrt{2n}} \tag{8}$$

The connection between input layer and the hidden layer is hypothetical whereas the connection between hidden layer and the output layer is a weighted one. Initially the weights are initialized with some random values that are later updated to reduce the mean square error (MSE) value to 0. MSE value is highly dependent on the training sample hence it is an important factor to be considered and to be maintained as less as possible in order to reduce false outputs. The error equation is given by

$$MSE = y_i = \sum_{i=1}^n \varphi_j w_{ij} = \frac{1}{m} \sum_{a=1}^m \left(zk * -zk\right)^2 \tag{9}$$

Where

z_k^* = Predicted output

z_k = Obtained output

h_k = Gaussian activation function

W_{ik} = weight between i^{th} input and k^{th} hidden layer neuron.

Algorithm 2: Intelligent RBFNN

```
Start
Initialize the number of centers m→1
Get the training sample (P, T)
For each input (Calculate the euclidean distance between the training sample
and the center value) →R (P_i, cn)
```

```
If(R<=threshold)
Send sample to c_n
else
If(R>threshold)
Add a new hidden neuron
Else
  if (R==0)
Delete the sample
End if
End if
Calculate the output of hidden neuron→Y_k
Calculate the output of output neuron→z_j
Calculate the MSE
If(error>0)
w_n=w_0+Δw
End if
End for
If the stopping criteria is met
End the process
```

Algorithm 2 represents the procedure of the intelligent radial basis function neural network with neuron addition and sample deletion intelligent components. The intelligent components proposed in Intelligent RBFNN assure to reach the specified goal at a swift rate by using its previous knowledge obtained from already trained samples. The network uses its knowledge to analyze the incoming training sample and takes decision whether the sample centre exists in the network or not. The learning process involves in the following components:

Neuron/Sample Addition

The samples are a prior known for static applications. Therefore, the number of hidden neurons and its centre are fixed. However, to model real time applications it is difficult as the input patterns are not known a prior. Structure of the network varies as the pattern is learned by the network. Correspondingly, more number of neurons in the hidden layer may increase the complexity of the system. The proposed work introduces an intellectual component known as neuron addition.

This RBFNN structure initially learns the centre of the first sample and starts with one hidden neuron. When a new pattern arrives, the centre similarity is calculated between the first neuron center and the input pattern using the Euclidean distance. Thereby, if the distance between the pattern centers are high then the sample is learnt by adding new neuron to the structure. i.e. If the centre distance is higher than the threshold value(α_h) a new hidden neuron is added with a new center. The value of α_h is in the range of 0 to 1. The distance value is mapped to the range 0 to 1. If the calculated distance is towards 0, then no neuron is added. In case, closer to 1, new neuron is added.

The equation for Euclidean distance is given by

$$R_j = \sqrt{\sum_{i=1}^{n}\left(xi - xij\right)^2} \tag{10}$$

Where x_i is the training sample and x_{ij} is the center of the hidden neuron. Euclidean distance is real value of the distance between x_i and x_{ij}.

$$N_h = \arg\max R(x, H_j), j = 1....j \tag{11}$$

Where N_h represents the distance between the training sample and hidden neuron center. If N_h is greater than α_h, there is a need for adding a new hidden neuron as the training sample is not near to any of the existing centers.

If $N_{h>=}\alpha_h H_{new} = x$

If $N_{h<}\alpha_h$ add to the nearest center

Where H_{new} indicates new hidden center, which is added when the training sample is not in the range of existing hidden neurons center.

Deletion of Sample

Next intellectual component in the proposed RBFNN is sample deletion. The samples in the training set may appear to be similar to the samples that are already learnt by the network. Addition of this sample in the network or repeated learning of the similar sample increases the computation time while test data is given to the network.

Hence if any new pattern maps exactly to the center of the existing hidden neurons, that new sample is deleted before training. The threshold value for deletion of the training sample is determined a prior.

$$N_d = \arg\min R(x, H_j), j = 1....j \tag{12}$$

Where N_d represents the distance between training sample and hidden neuron center.

If the distance calculated is less than the threshold value then the training sample is already trained in the network. Therefore, the sample is deleted without training in the network. The performance of the algorithm is not affected as the structure has gained knowledge from the existing trained samples. This intellectual component of IRBFNN reduces the computational time and proportionally increases the performance of the system.

Intrusion Detection in Battle Field for Alert Generation Using Intelligent Rbfnn: A Case Study

As a case study, the proposed Intelligent RBFNN is applied to battle field monitoring application for intrusion detection and unknown explosive stamping by the native soldiers. Battle field monitoring system requires fast and accurate decision making system for alert generation as it involves the lives of mankind.

False alarm may lead to panic situation. Figure 4 shows the flow diagram of the proposed Intrusion detection system in Battle field monitoring. The proposed battle field monitoring involves identification of non-native soldier or intruder and explosives buried in the field to protect our native soldiers from the life or death situation. The battlefield monitoring involves the usage of RFID and wireless pressure sensors. Scenario of the battle field is considered to be as follows.

The proposed case study considers 3 random paths in the battlefield. The bombs/explosives are placed in every path. Figure 5 shows the random paths with buried explosives. Five explosives are buried in a path respectively.

Native soldier is given an RFID tag. Group of five RFID tag with a reader is considered. RFID gives the identity of the person. When the RFID reader senses the RFID tag at a distance it sends the signal with the identity. PR sensor is used to detect the presence of a person in a specified path. PR sensor sends digital representation 0 or 1 to the receiver. In case of any signal received from a RFID tag with binary 1 from PR sensor, then this indirectly indicates the presence of a person in that location. The location of the person or the native soldier is obtained from the Global Positioning System (GPS). Number of soldiers in the area is known a prior. Table 1 represents the sensor and the device used for identification of the native soldier in the battlefield.

Table 2 represents the three paths considered for implementation in the proposed work also random deployment of explosives in the paths. Intelligent RBFNN for this application involves ten-dimensional input data. Figure 6 shows the adaptive network structure of Intelligent RBFNN in battlefield monitoring.

Figure 4. Flow diagram of intrusion detection system using intelligent RBF for battle field monitoring

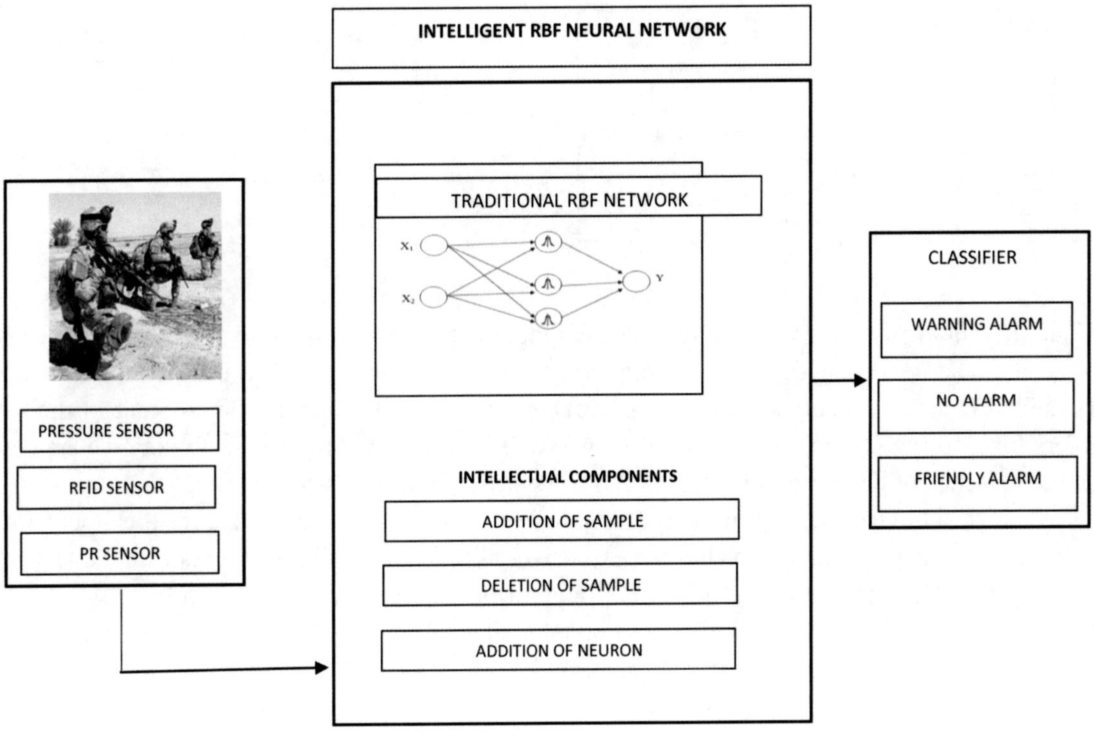

Figure 5. Random path in battlefield with explosives

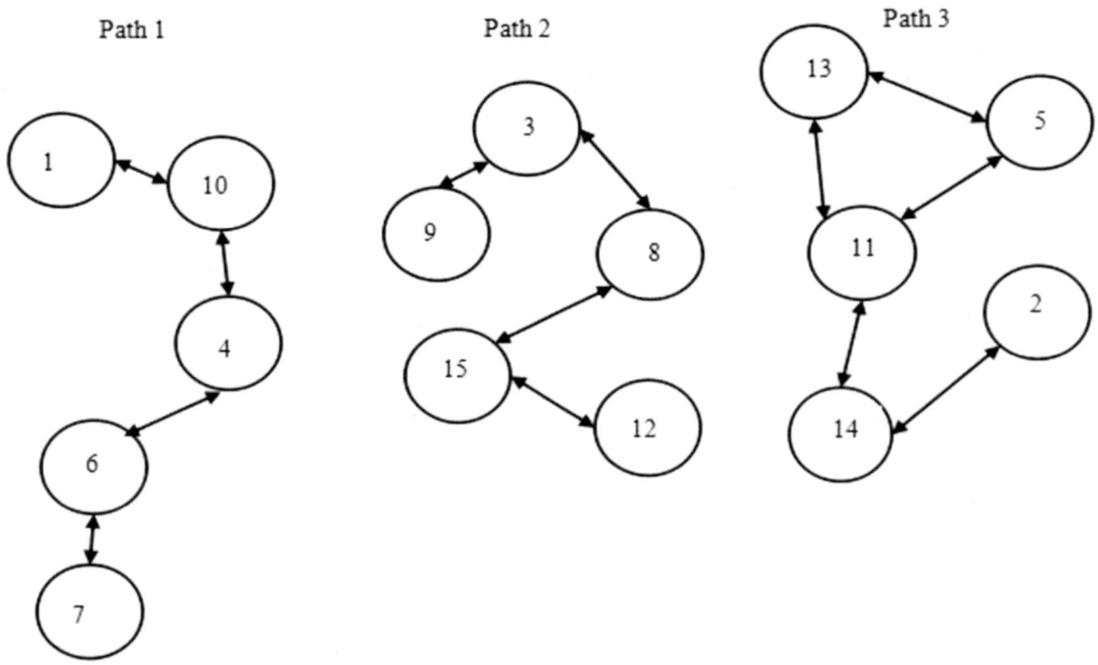

Path 1   Path 2   Path 3

Table 1. Sensor and sensor description

Sensor type	Purpose
PR sensor	To detect the presence of a person in the battle field.
RFID sensor	To get the unique ID allotted to an individual
GPS device	To locate the place of the person

Table 2. Paths and explosives in the battlefield

Path number	Explosives in various path
1	1,10,4,6,7
2	9,3,8,15,12
3	2,5,11,13,14

Sample training samples with ten-dimensional input data is given in Table 3. The pressure sensors are placed in the field along the paths to a distance away from the explosives. If the pressure is detected, then the RFID value is identified. In case of RFID is detected, this confirms the presence of the native soldiers for alert generation. Otherwise, if the pressure is sensed and the RFID do not give any value, then the presence of the person in that location is identified to be an intruder.

The center of hidden neuron is initially fixed randomly to some constant values as the input patterns considered are binary except path value and explosives as it is not possible to represent in binary value. Intelligent RBFNN applied for the battlefield monitoring application performs multi class classification. Three output neurons that classify the sample for alert generation. Intruder alert, friendly alert and warning (explosive) alert is classified from the samples. Table 4 represents the permutation sample alert generation data with respect to RFID.

Figure 6. Adaptive network structure of intelligent RBFNN in battlefield monitoring

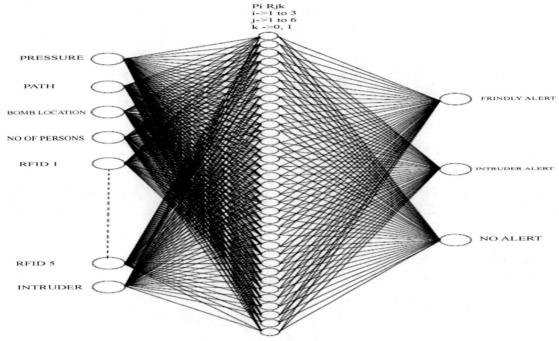

Table 3. Training sample set for input neurons of Intelligent RBFNN

Pressure	Path value	Location (Bomb Number)	Number of persons detected (Pressure Sensor)	RFID1	RFID2	RFID3	RFID4	RFID5	Intruder
0	1	10	3	1	0	0	1	0	1
1	1	7	4	1	0	1	1	1	0
1	3	5	2	0	1	1	0	0	1
1	2	9	5	1	1	0	1	1	1
1	1	9	5	1	1	0	1	1	0
0	3	11	3	1	1	1	0	0	0
1	3	2	2	1	0	1	0	0	0
1	2	8	4	1	0	1	1	0	1
1	3	14	3	0	1	0	1	1	0

For example: Considering sample 4 from the Table 4, it can be inferred that an intruder is identified among the native soldiers whose RFID are 1, 2, 4 and 5. RFID 3 is not detected as the soldier may be away from the path. But 5 persons are detected by the PR sensor. Therefore, the person whose RFID is not detected is the intruder or the non-native soldier. An alert is generated to RFID 1, 2, 4 and 5 for immediate attention. Similarly, considering sample 2 from the Table 4, no intruder is detected. Number of

Table 4. Sample alert generation pattern

Intruder alert to RFID 1	Intruder alert to RFID 2	Intruder alert to RFID 3	Intruder alert to RFID 4	Intruder alert to RFID 5	Friendly alert to RFID 1	Friendly alert to RFID 2	Friendly alert to RFID 3	Friendly alert to RFID 4	Friendly alert to RFID 5
0	0	0	0	0	0	0	0	0	0
0	0	0	0	0	1	0	1	1	1
0	0	0	0	0	0	0	0	0	0
1	1	0	1	1	0	0	0	0	0
0	0	0	0	0	0	0	0	0	0
0	0	0	0	0	0	0	0	0	0
0	0	0	0	0	1	0	1	0	0
1	0	1	1	0	0	0	0	0	0
0	0	0	0	0	0	1	0	1	1

persons identified from the PR sensor equals the number of RFID count. To comfort the native soldier, the number of other native soldiers near to them is also intimated by friendly alert generation. These samples with input and output relationship are trained in the intelligent RBFNN for automatic generation of alert without human intervention for protecting the lives of our native soldiers.

RESULTS AND DISCUSSION

Total number of samples obtained after permutation of the input with equal number of target data sets is 15,360. From the total number of samples, 70% of the sample is considered for training the neural network with equal number of target classes. Remaining samples are considered for testing and validation of the proposed network. Weights between the hidden neuron and the output neurons are initiated randomly. Iterations are carried out to update the weight and reduce the mean square error. If the mean square error is closer to 0, then the trained samples are learnt efficiently. If the mean square error is closer or equal to 1 then error is high and minimized by adjusting the weights. Table 5 represents the sample of mean square error value obtained from 36 hidden neurons after weight update in various iterations.

Each hidden neuron has learnt its center value and plotted in the activation function for the relevant samples. For the performance study, experiments are conducted for the Intelligent RBFNN classifier on datasets using the MATLAB programming language on a desktop PC with Intel Core 2 Duo, 2.6-GHz CPU and 3-GB RAM. For any new classification algorithm, it is essential to validate its performance. Figure 7 shows the error output for training, validation and test instances. Error histogram is plotted for 20 mean square error output obtained from the neural network. It is inferred from the histogram that the error decreases for increase in the number of instances. Also, the error obtained from the training data is closer / similar to the error value of the testing and validation data. Number of instances used for testing and validation is less compared to the training.

The accuracy of the classifier depends on fitting of the training output with the ideal classification line. From Figure 8 it is observed that, the classifier is 95% accurate as the training data gets fit with the ideal dotted line (function). Similarly, while observing the test data from Figure 9, the few outputs

Table 5. Sample - Mean square error calculation of intelligent RBFNN

Neuron number	MSE	Neuron number	MSE
1	0.0105469	19	0.0123242
2	0.0123242	20	0.0105469
3	0.0105469	21	0.0123242
4	0.0123242	22	0.0102148
5	0.0105469	23	0.0120312
6	0.0123242	24	0.0105469
7	0.0105469	25	0.0123242
8	0.0123242	26	0.0105469
9	0.0105469	27	0.0123242
10	0.0123242	28	0.0102148
11	0.0120312	29	0.0120312
12	0.0105469	30	0.0105469
13	0.0123242	31	0.0123242
14	0.0105469	32	0.0123242
15	0.0123242	33	0.0105469
16	0.0105469	34	0.0123242
17	0.0123242	35	0.0102148
18	0.0105469	36	0.0120312

Figure 7. Error histogram of intelligent RBFNN for training, testing and validation instances

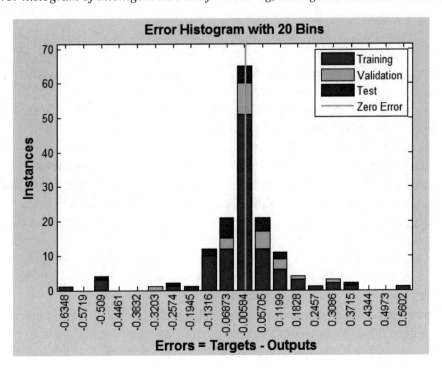

Figure 8. Accuracy of the intelligent RBFNN classifier in the training phase

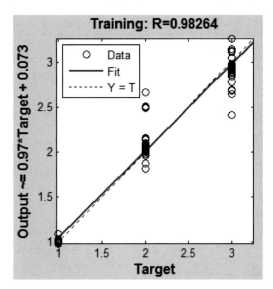

Figure 9. Accuracy of the intelligent RBFNN classifier in the testing phase

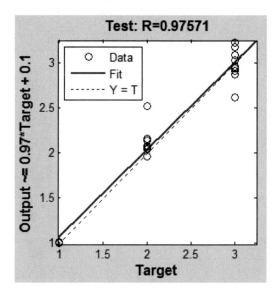

obtained from the test samples deviates from the exact target output. Therefore, the efficiency of the test data in intelligent RBFNN is observed to be 89%.

Mean square error determines the accuracy of the classifier. To adjust and update the weight for reduced error, iterations are performed over the sample data. This ensures the learning capacity of the algorithm. Figure 10 shows the graphical representation of mean square error determination for performance evaluation. It is observed that mean square error for testing and validation data appears to be 0.1544 at the 12th iteration. This is the near optimal value obtained for minimum error. After 12th iteration, the deviation of the output with respect to test data and training data appears to be high. Therefore, this 12th iteration appears to be the stopping criteria of the iteration for further classification. Figure 11 shows the case study output for friendly alarm class using intelligent RBFNN classifier.

Friendly alarm comforts the native soldier that there are few other native soldiers in the same path. Also, there is no intruder and no explosive detection. Figure 10 shows the case study output for no alarm if there exist no native soldiers in the prescribed path.

Next class in the intelligent RBFNN is intruder detection alert. A screenshot of the sample output obtained for intruder alert generation is shown in Figure 13. To safe guard the life of the native soldier, the most important alert generation is the intruder or non- native soldier detection. A sample screenshot of the alert generated for an intruder with RFID 2 native soldier in path 1 is detected.

The efficiency or the accuracy of the intelligent RBFNN algorithm by applying to the intruder detection battle field monitoring system is given in Table 6. Efficiency performance comparison of the traditional RBF and Intelligent RBFNN for battlefield monitoring is shown in Table 6. While Comparing the efficiency of the traditional RBFNN, the proposed Intelligent RBFNN is highly efficient of 13% in training, 21.58% in testing and 14.97% in validation data.

The traditional RBFNN learns any number of samples in the fixed number of hidden neurons. But, the proposed uses intelligent components to unlearn certain samples and adds neuron by checking the similarity or the distance between the sample centres. Therefore, deletion of sample and dynamic neuron

Figure 10. Mean square error comparison of Training, testing and validation data in intelligent RBFNN classifier

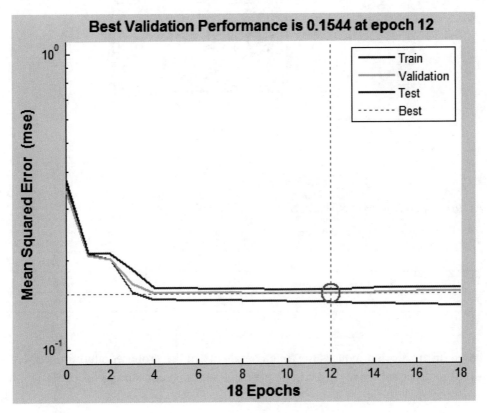

Figure 11. Screenshot on friendly alert generation in the battlefield

Figure 12. Screenshot on no alarm scenario in the battlefield

Figure 13. Screenshot on intruder alert generation in the battlefield

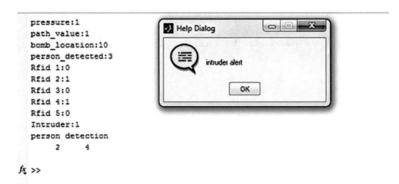

Table 6. Accuracy percentage of RBF and Intelligent RBFNN

Data	RBF	Intelligent RBFNN
Training data	78.46	**92.31**
Testing data	65.92	**87.5**
Validation data	75.43	**90.4**

addition based on application reduces the time complexity of the proposed algorithm. From the above given results, the proposed work proves to be efficient and time consuming for battlefield monitoring intruder detection application.

CONCLUSION

In this chapter, we presented a new RBF neural network classifier for multiclass classification of the data. New RBF includes intelligent learn and think components such as neuron addition and sample deletion for learning. This facilitates timely and accurate decision making. Most of the challenges such as fixed network structure, fixed center and randomized weight do not support the usage of existing RBFNN in dynamic applications. In most of the real-world application, the samples are not known a prior and not in sequence. Therefore, existing RBFNN are suitable for static environment.

The existing RBF either exist with fixed neurons or add hidden neurons continuously for every sample. This increases the computation time of the network. All real-world application resist time delay and recommend quick output generation. There is a need for an efficient network that think before learning the samples. Intelligent RBFNN is highly suitable for various dynamically changing applications. Since the samples are tested for its similarity with the learnt samples, the increase in the network structure is reduced. As a case study, the proposed Intelligent RBFNN is applied to an intrusion detection application for saving the life of the native soldiers. Intrusion detection helps to identify the non- native soldiers and the explosives buried in the battlefield. Unknowing stamping of the explosives by the native soldier and entry of Unknown Soldier in the battlefield may lead to chaos. To overcome these issues, the application identifies the intruder and the explosives using wireless sensors and generates alert for creating the comfort situation for the soldiers. On an average, the proposed work is 90% efficient for the battlefield application.

For future work, the addition of intelligent components along with the proposed may still increase the efficiency of the system for the real-world applications. Also, the proposed work has to be implemented in various other applications for its global acceptance in terms of efficiency and timely decision making.

REFERENCES

Chen, H., Gong, Y., & Hong, X. (2013). Online modelling with tunable RBF network. *IEEE Transactions on Neural networks and Learning Systems*, *43*(3), 935–947.

Chen, S. Wu, Y. & Luk, B.L. (1999, September). Combined genetic algorithm optimization and regularized orthogonal least squares learning for radial basis function networks. *IEEE Transactions on Neural Networks*, *10*(5).

Cohen, S., & Intrator, N. (2000, June). A hybrid projection based and radial basis function architecture. In *Proceedings of the First International Workshop on Multiple Classier Systems*, Sardingia.

Daqi, G., & Genxing, Y. (2002, May 12-17). Adaptive RBF neural networks for pattern classifications. In *Proceedings of the 2002 International Joint Conference on Neural Networks IJCNN '02*.

Gillebaart, T., Blom, D. S., van Zuijlen, A. H., & Bijl, H. (2016). Adaptive radial basis function mesh deformation using data reduction. *Journal of Computational Physics*, *321*, 997–1025. doi:10.1016/j.jcp.2016.05.036

Gomm, J. B., & Yu, D. L. (2000, March). Selecting Radial Basis Function Network Centers with Recursive Orthogonal Least Squares Training. *IEEE Transactions on Neural Networks*, *11*(2), 306–314. doi:10.1109/72.839002 PMID:18249762

Gong, D., Chang, J., & Wei, C. (2011, October). An Adaptive Method for Choosing Center Sets of RBF Interpolation. *Journal of Computers*, *6*(10), 2112–2119. doi:10.4304/jcp.6.10.2112-2119

Han, H.-G., & Qiao, J.-F. (2012). Adaptive computation algorithm for RBF neural network. *IEEE Transactions on Neural Networks and Learning Systems*, *23*(2), 342–347. doi:10.1109/TNNLS.2011.2178559 PMID:24808512

He, Y. L., Wang, X. Z., & Huang, J. Z. (2016). Fuzzy nonlinear regression analysis using a random weight network. *Information Sciences*, *364*, 222–240.

Hirahara, M., & Oka, N. (1993, October). A hybrid model composed of a multilayer perceptron and a radial basis function network. In *Proceedings of 1993 International Joint Conference on Neural Networks IJCNN '93*, Nagoya (Vol. 2, pp. 1353-1356).

Huang, , G. B., Saratchandran, P., & Sundararajan, N. (2004, December). An Efficient Sequential Learning Algorithm for Growing and Pruning RBF (GAP-RBF) Networks. *IEEE Transactions on Systems, Man, and Cybernetics. Part B, Cybernetics*, *34*(6), 2284–2292. doi:10.1109/TSMCB.2004.834428

Maldonado, S., & Weber, R. (2010). Feature Selection for Support Vector Regression via Kernel Penalization. In *Proceedings of the 2010 International Joint Conference on Neural Networks (IJCNN)*.

Mao, K. Z. (2002, September). RBF Neural Network Center Selection Based on Fisher Ratio Class Separability Measure. *IEEE Transactions on Neural Networks, 13*(5), 1211–1217. doi:10.1109/TNN.2002.1031953 PMID:18244518

Martel, J. M., & Platte, R. B. (2016). Stability of Radial Basis Function Methods for Convection Problems on the Circle and Sphere. *Journal of Scientific Computing*.

Orr, M. (1998). Optimizing the Widths of Radial Basis Functions Optimizing the Widths of Radial Basis Functions. In *Proceedings of the Fifth Brazilian Symposium on Neural Networks* (pp. 26-29). doi:10.1109/SBRN.1998.730989

Pierrefeu, L., Jay, J., & Barat, C. (2006). Auto-adjustable method for Gaussian width optimization on RBF neural network. Application to face authentication on a mono-chip system. In *Proceedings of the 32nd Annual Conference on IEEE Industrial Electronics IECON* (pp. 3481-3485). doi:10.1109/IECON.2006.347848

Rashidiniaa, J., Fasshauerb, G. E., & Khasi, M. (2016). A stable method for the evaluation of Gaussian radial basis function solutions of interpolation and collocation problems. Computers and Mathematics with Applications, 72, 178 -193.

Regis, R. G. (2014). Evolutionary programming for high-dimensional constrained expensive black-box optimization using radial basis functions. *IEEE Transactions on Evolutionary Computation, 18*(3), 326–347. doi:10.1109/TEVC.2013.2262111

Sajavičius, S. (2014). Radial basis function method for a multidimensional linear elliptic equation with nonlocal boundary conditions. *Computers & Mathematics with Applications (Oxford, England), 67*(7), 1407–1420. doi:10.1016/j.camwa.2014.01.014

Várkonyi-Kóczy, A. R., Tusor, B., & Bukor, J. (2016). Data classification based on fuzzy-RBF networks. In Advances in Intelligent Systems and Computing, AISC (Vol. 357, pp. 829-840). Springer Verlag. doi:10.1007/978-3-319-18416-6_65

Wang, Z. O., & Zhu, T. (2000). An efficient learning algorithm for improving generalization performance of radial basis function neural networks. *Neural Networks, 13*(4), 545–553.

Yun, Z., Quan, Z., Caixin, S., Shaolan, L., Yuming, L., & Yangvv, S. (2008, August). RBF Neural Network and ANFIS-Based Short-Term Load Forecasting Approach in Real-Time Price Environment. *IEEE Transactions on Power Systems, 23*(3), 853–858. doi:10.1109/TPWRS.2008.922249

Zhang, C., Wei, H., Xie, L., Shen, Y., & Zhang, K. (2016). Direct interval forecasting of wind speed using radial basis function neural networks in a multi-objective optimization framework. *Journal Neuro computing, 205*(C), 53-63.

Zhou, P., Li, D., Wu, H., & Chen, F. (2010). A Novel OLS Algorithm for Training RBF Neural Networks with Automatic Model Selection. In *Proceedings of the International Conference on Computer Application and System Modeling (ICCASM '10)*.

Zhou, P., Li, D., Wu, H., & Chen, F. (2010). A Novel OLS Algorithm for Training RBF Neural Networks with Automatic Model Selection. In *Proceedings of the International Conference on Computer Application and System Modeling (ICCASM '10)*.

Zou, Y., Lei, G., Shao, K., Guo, Y., Zhu, J., & Chen, X. (2015, March). Hybrid Approach of Radial Basis Function and Finite Element Method for Electromagnetic Problems. *IEEE Transactions on Magnetics, 51*(3), 1–4. doi:10.1109/TMAG.2014.2354371

Chapter 9
A Genetic–Algorithms–Based Technique for Detecting Distributed Predicates

Eslam Al Maghayreh
King Saud University, Saudi Arabia

ABSTRACT

One of the techniques that have been used in the literature to enhance the dependability of distributed applications is the detection of distributed predicates techniques (also referred to as runtime verification). These techniques are used to verify that a given run of a distributed application satisfies certain properties (specified as predicates). Due to the existence of multiple processes running concurrently, the detection of a distributed predicate can incur significant overhead. Several researchers have worked on the development of techniques to reduce the cost of detecting distributed predicates. However, most of the techniques presented in the literature work efficiently for specific classes of predicates, like conjunctive predicates. This chapter presents a technique based on genetic algorithms to efficiently detect distributed predicates under the possibly modality. Several experiments have been conducted to demonstrate the effectiveness of the proposed technique.

INTRODUCTION

Enhancing the dependability of distributed applications is a very difficult task. Many techniques were proposed and developed by several authors to help in improving the dependability of distributed applications. Distributed predicates detection techniques are one of the key techniques that have been developed and used by several researchers (Yingchareonthaworchai et al., 2017; Zhu et al., 2016; Shen and Kshemkalyani, 2014; Garg, 2002; Dumais & Li, 2002; Freiling & Jhumka, 2007; Chu & Brockmeyer, 2008; Garg & Waldecker, 1994; Garg & Waldecker, 1996). These techniques are used to verify that a specific run of a given distributed application satisfies certain properties. Figure 1 depicts the main components of a distributed predicates detection framework.

DOI: 10.4018/978-1-5225-3686-4.ch009

Model checking and theorem proving techniques can be used to verify that a particular model of a distributed application satisfies certain properties. However, for some distributed applications, especially those employed in safety critical environments, it is important to verify the correctness of a particular implementation rather than an abstract model of the application. This is one of the main strong sides of distributed predicates detection techniques (Garg, 2002; Al Maghayreh, 2010).

Algorithms for detecting distributed predicates have several applications, including the following:

- **Detection of Stable States in Distributed Systems:** Stable states are usually described by conditions that once become true they will not turn false anymore. For example, deadlock detection and loss of token in a token ring.
- **Testing and Debugging of Distributed Applications:** For example, to test a leader election program, we can monitor the system to detect the presence of multiple leaders.
- **Identifying Bottlenecks:** This involves locating positions during the execution of a distributed application when more than n processes are blocked simultaneously.
- **Symmetry in Communications:** For example, identifying when a producer starts generating items faster than what the corresponding consumer can receive and process.

Due to the concurrency in distributed applications, the detection of distributed predicates is a tedious time-consuming task. In order to reduce the time to solve this problem, several techniques have been proposed and developed in the literature (Yingchareonthawornchai et al., 2017; Zhu et al., 2016; Al Maghayreh, 2010; Garg, 2002; Chase & Garg, 1998). A brief review of these techniques will be presented in Section 4. However, most of these techniques work efficiently for certain classes of predicates only. It has been proved that the detection of the satisfaction of certain property (predicate) in a run of a distributed application is, in general, an NP-complete problem (Garg, 2002).

In this chapter, genetic algorithms based detection technique will be presented as a more powerful technique for detecting distributed predicates. This technique is efficient for detecting distributed predicates under the possibly modality (a predicate under the possibly modality is evaluated to true if it is true in at least one global state (Garg, 2002)). A genetic algorithm is a well-known artificial intelligent search technique that can be used effectively to solve problems with exponential size search space which is the case in distributed predicates detection. Later in this chapter, we will provide a brief introduction to genetic algorithms.

Figure 1. The main components of a distributed predicates detection framework

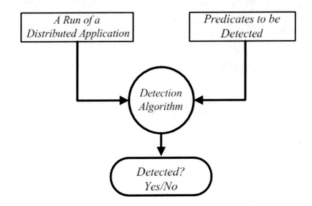

BACKGROUND AND MODEL

A distributed application consists of a set of *n* processes (P_1, P_2, ..., P_n) and a set of unidirectional channels. The result of executing a statement in a distributed program is called an event. The set of events resulting from the execution of a distributed application are related by the happened-before relation ($\rightarrow$) proposed by Lamport (1978).

Definition 1: A run of a distributed application (E, $\rightarrow$) is the set of events (E) executed by all of the processes in the application along with the happened-before relation ($\rightarrow$) among these events.

Figure 2 shows a simple run of a distributed application depicted using a space time diagram. The run involves two processes (space is depicted vertically and time is depicted horizontally). The transmission of a message is represented by a directed edge connecting the corresponding send and receive events. Two events e_i and e_j are related by the happened-before relation ($e_i \rightarrow e_j$) if there is a directed path in the space-time diagram from e_i to e_j. The happened-before relation ($\rightarrow$) is a partial order relation. Hence, two events may not be related by the happened-before relation, such events are called concurrent events. For example, events e_1 and e_5 are considered concurrent ($\neg (e_1 \rightarrow e_5)$ and $\neg (e_5 \rightarrow e_1)$).

A *consistent cut* of a run of a given distributed application is a subset of the events of that run such that if e_i is an event in this subset, then all of the events that happened-before e_i are also in this subset. The state of a given distributed program reached upon the execution of the events in a given consistent cut is called a *global state*. According to (Mattern, 1989), the set of global states of a given run endowed with set union and set intersection operations forms a distributive lattice (known as the state lattice). Based on the state lattice, we can verify whether a run of a given distributed program satisfies the necessary properties or not (runtime verification).

The state lattice corresponding to the run of Figure 2 is shown in Figure 3. Each global state has a label involving the most recent event executed by each process upon reaching this global state. For example, (e_3, e_7) is the state reached after executing event e_3 in P_1 and event e_7 in P_2. (-, -) is the initial state and (e_3, e_7) is the final state.

A distributed predicate is a predicate that involves variables of more than one process. The evaluation of such predicates requires the collection of information from all of the processes involved in the predicate. A predicate expressed using the variables of a single process is called local predicate. A predicate possibly:φ is true if φ is evaluate to true in at least one global state in the state lattice. A predicate definitely:φ is true if, for all paths from the initial global state to the final global state, φ is true in at least one global state along that path (Cooper & Marzullo, 1991; Jegou et al., 1995). In this chapter, we will consider predicates under the possibly modality.

Figure 2. A space-time diagram depicting a simple run of a distributed application

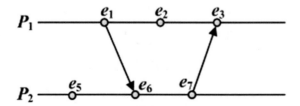

Figure 3. The state lattice corresponding to the run shown in Figure 2

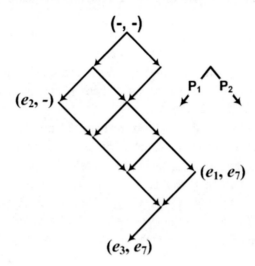

Detecting distributed predicates is not an easy task. This is due to the following properties of distributed applications (Garg, 2002):

1. The processes of a distributed application do not have a common clock. As a result, the events of any run of a given distributed application can only be partially ordered.
2. Processes in distributed applications communicate by sending and receiving messages. This means that evaluating a distributed predicate will incur significant message overhead to collect the information necessary for evaluation.
3. Processes in distributed applications are running concurrently, and hence the number of global states to be examined to detect a predicate will be exponential in number of processes.

Generally, detecting a distributed predicate in a given run of a distributed application is an NP-complete problem (Garg, 2002). In the next section, we will explore the techniques presented in the literature to check the satisfaction of a predicate in a run of a given distributed application.

RELATED WORKS

The main techniques introduced in the literature to detect the satisfaction of a distributed predicate in a given run of a distributed application are summarized below.

1. Detection based on the global snapshot algorithm proposed by Chandy and Lamport (Chandy & Lamport, 1985; Bouge´, 1987; Spezialetti & Kearns, 1986). According to this technique, the snapshot algorithm is used to capture a global state of the given run. The desired predicate is verified in the captured state, if it is true, then the predicate is detected and we are done, otherwise, another global state is captured and the same process is repeated again until we capture a global state that

satisfies the predicate. This technique works well for stable predicates (do not turn false once they become true).

2. Constructing the whole state lattice and verifying the predicate on each global state. This approach was proposed by Cooper and Marzullo (1991). It can be used to detect any predicate. However, it is an expensive approach due to the fact that the size of the state lattice that has to be constructed is exponential (m^n global states in the worst case, where n is the number of processes and m is the number of local states in each process).

3. Exploiting the structure of the predicate. According to this technique, a subset of the global states of a given run can be identified based on the structure of the predicate (i.e. conjunctive predicate) such that if the predicate is true, it should be true in one of the states in this subset. This technique is not as general as the second technique. However, it is considered the base of several efficient detection algorithms of some classes of predicates. In (Garg & Waldecker, 1994; Garg & Waldecker, 1996), the authors have presented an algorithm of complexity $O(n^2m)$ to detect *possibly*:φ and *definitely*: φ when φ is a conjunction of local predicates.

Several researchers have proposed techniques to reduce the cost of predicate detection. Computation slicing is a well-known technique introduced in (Chauhan et al., 2013; Li et al., 2004; Sen & Garg, 2003; Garg & Mittal, 2001; Mittal & Garg, 2001) as an abstraction technique to reduce the cost of analyzing execution traces of distributed programs. The slice of a computation derived with respect to a given predicate is a computation with the smallest number of global states that contains all global states of the original computation for which the predicate evaluates to true. Computation slicing eliminates the irrelevant global states of the original computation, and keep only the states that are relevant for the predicate to be detected. (Mittal & Garg, 2001) proved that a slice exists for all global predicates. However, computing the slice is, in general, an NP-complete problem. Efficient algorithms have been developed to compute slices for some classes of predicates.

A theorem on atomicity to reduce the cost of verifying distributed and parallel systems has been proposed by Lamport (1990). Based on this theorem, an atomic action can receive messages from other processes, followed by at most one externally visible event (for example, changing a variable relevant to some of the properties to be verified) before sending any message to any other process. According to this theorem, a distributed program can be abstracted to reduce the cost of its verification.

In (Al Maghayreh, 2011; Li et al., 2007a; Li et al., 2007b), the notion of atomic actions in message-passing distributed programs has been exploited in reducing the state space to be considered in runtime verification of message-passing distributed programs.

In this chapter, the authors have exploited genetic algorithms in developing a more general and efficient detection technique to detect distributed predicates under the possibly modality. In the following two sections, we will present a brief introduction to genetic algorithms and we will present the details of our proposed detection algorithm.

INTRODUCTION TO GENETIC ALGORITHMS

A Genetic Algorithm (GA) is a metaheuristic algorithm based on the principles of genetics and natural selection (Burke & Kendall, 2005). The algorithm is a population based search algorithm. Each member of the population is called a chromosome. Each chromosome encodes the decision variables of the problem under consideration and represents a possible solution for the problem. A mathematical model, called the objective function, is then used to evaluate the quality of the solutions. Genetic algorithms have been used widely to solve several problems (Feng & Wang, 2012; Pelusi, 2011; Tripathi et al., 2011; Thangamani & Thangaraj, 2011; Eastridge & Schmidt, 2008; Alba & Chicano, 2005; Montana et al., 1998; Wright, 1991). Genetic algorithms operate as follows:

1. Initialization: The initial population is generated randomly within the search space of the problem.
2. Evaluation: The fitness value of each candidate solution is evaluated after initializing the population and after generating the offspring.
3. Selection: Solutions with higher fitness value are selected to apply survival- of-the-fittest principle. There are several selection mechanisms proposed to be used with GAs such as roulette-wheel selection, stochastic universal selection, ranking selection and tournament selection (Ba¨ck, 1995; Baker, 1985).
4. Crossover: Two or more parent solutions (chromosomes) are used to generate new solutions (i.e., offspring). The generated offspring will not be identical to any of the parents. Several techniques are designed for applying crossover (Spears, 1997; Eiben, 1997; Syswerda, 1989).
5. Mutation: A solution is modified randomly according to a specific mechanism to generate a new solution. Different mutation techniques were proposed to generate better solutions and to explore the search space (Sastry & Goldberg, 2004).
6. Replacement: The generated offspring by selection, crossover, and mutation will replace the original population. Several replacement techniques were suggested in the literature (Thierens & Goldberg, 1994).
7. Repeat steps 2-6 until the stop criteria are met.

DETECTING DISTRIBUTED PREDICATES USING GENETIC ALGORITHMS

In this section, we will describe how we can develop a genetic algorithms based detection technique for detecting the predicate *Possibly:P* where P is a distributed predicate. We have shown earlier that there are some techniques that can efficiently detect *Possibly:P* for certain classes of predicates P, like conjunctive predicates. However, there is no efficient technique that can detect *Possibly:P* in general for any predicate P. This is due to exponential number of global states that need to be considered in detection (m^n global states in the worst case, where n is the number of processes and m is the number of local states in each process). Genetic algorithms can be used in this case to provide a powerful general solution in such a case where the search space size to be considered is exponential.

Detection algorithms can be online or offline. Online detection works during the execution of the application. As a result, the behavior of the application may change in unexpected manner. However, online detection avoids the need to keep very large trace files as it is the case in offline detection. In offline detection, the information necessary to detect a predicate are collected in a trace file, and later the trace is analyzed to decide whether the predicate has been satisfied during the execution or not. Consequently, offline detection does not have a strong impact on the behavior of the application. However, the size of the collected trace files is usually very large.

In this chapter, we will demonstrate the development of an offline detection technique. The use of genetic algorithms does not fit properly with the use of online detection approach due to the fact that genetic operators investigate global states in the whole search space randomly and do not investigate global states in the order in which they may appear at runtime.

Now we will give a detailed description of how we have exploited genetic algorithms in our solution. We will first describe the representation of a run of a distributed program that the genetic algorithm can manipulate. We will use our approach to develop an algorithm to detect the predicate *Possibly:P* where P is the predicate $x_1 + x_2 + \ldots + x_n = c$ where x_i is a variable of process P_i and c is a constant.

Each process will be instrumented to collect at runtime the necessary information about all of the local states that may affect the desired predicate along with their vector clock timestamps (The vector clock is a very well-known technique to assign timestamps to the events of a run of a given distributed program (Mattern, 1989; Fidge, 1988)). The collected information of a process P_i is stored in a trace file of the following form:

$Value_1$, $timestamp_1$
$Value_2$, $timestamp_2$
$Value_m$, $timestamp_m$

Where $Value_j$ is the value of variable x_i of process P_i in the local state number j. $Timestamp_j$ is the vector clock timestamp of local state j. Figure 4 (a) depicts a run of a distributed program. If we assume

Figure 4. An example to demonstrate the use of GAs in detecting distributed predicates

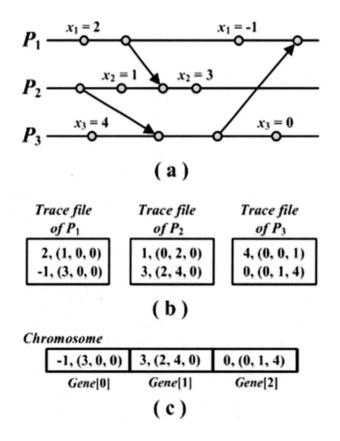

that we want to detect the predicate $x_1 + x_2 + x_3 = 2$, then the trace files of these processes will be as shown in Figure 4 (b). A trace file of a process involves all of the local states that may be part of a global state satisfying the desired predicate in the given run. The first local state of process P_1 is 2, (1, 0, 0). This means the value of variable x_1 (which is one of the variables involved in the predicate of interest) at this local state is 2 and the vector clock timestamp of this local state is (1, 0, 0).

We will have n trace files (one for each process). The size of each trace file is linear with respect to the number of events executed by the corresponding process. These files represent the input to the proposed detection algorithm. Additional information can be added to the contents of the trace files depending on the predicate to be detected. For example, if the desired predicate involves two or more variables of one or more processes, then the values of these variables has to be added to each local state in the trace files.

Now we will move to the details of the genetic algorithm itself starting with the representation of the population to be used. Each chromosome in the population represents a global state of the application. Consequently, each chromosome will have n local states (one from each process) such that all of the local states form a global state of the application.

For example, if we have the run shown in Figure 4 (a) and we want to detect the predicate $x_1 + x_2 + x_3 = 2$, then a chromosome in the population can have the form shown in Figure 4 (c) where Gene[i] is a local state of process P_{i+1} taken from its trace file. For example, the first gene of the chromosome shown in Figure 4 (c) is one of the local states of process P_1 as shown by its trace file depicted in Figure 4 (b).

Regarding the selection procedure we can use any selection procedure. We will use the standard single point crossover operation. The mutation operator will work as follows:

- It will randomly select a gene i from a given chromosome.
- It will replace the local state in this gene with another local state selected randomly from the trace file of process P_{i+1}.

Crossover and mutation operators may result in chromosomes that do not represent global states due to the fact that the cuts represented by the resulting chromosomes are not consistent. This problem can be solved by using a repair function to move the chromosome into a consistent global state or by reducing the fitness of such chromosomes. In our algorithm, we will use the second approach and we will assign the value of -1 as the fitness value for any chromosome that does not represent a global state.

The next step is to design the fitness function. This step is considered as the most important step in our detection algorithm. All of the above-mentioned steps of the detection algorithm will be identical for any predicate of interest. The only difference between two algorithms to detect two different predicates is in the design of the fitness function. This is considered as an advantage of using genetic algorithms in detections. If we want to develop a detection algorithm for another predicate, then the only thing that we have to do is to modify the fitness function. The remaining steps are identical.

The fitness function has to evaluate each chromosome (possible solution) and assign to it a value indicating whether the solution encoded by this chromosome is close to the optimal solution or not. The larger the value assigned to a chromosome the better the solution represented by the chromosome. In our algorithm, the value assigned by the fitness function to each chromosome will indicate whether the global state represented by the chromosome satisfies the predicate of interest or not, and if it does not satisfy the predicate, how close it is to the values that can satisfy the predicate.

Figure 5 shows the fitness function to be used in the algorithm to detect the predicate $(x_1 + x_2 + \ldots + x_n = c)$. The fitness function will first check whether the chromosome represents a global state or not (consistent cut) if the chromosome does not represent a global state then the fitness value assigned to it will be -1 indicating that this chromosome cannot represent a global state that satisfies the predicate. Otherwise, the fitness function will assign a value to the chromosome according to the following formula:

$$Fitness = \frac{1}{\left| x_1 + \ldots + x_n - c + 0.0000001 \right|}$$

For example, the fitness of the chromosome shown in Figure 4 (c) is $\dfrac{1}{\left| -1 + 3 + 0 - 2 + 0.0000001 \right|}$

The value 0.0000001 is used to avoid division by zero because if the chromosome satisfies the predicate then $x_1 + \cdots + x_n$ - c will be equal to zero. Consequently, when the chromosome satisfies the predicate its fitness value will be 10000000. This large value indicates that this chromosome represents a good solution. When the algorithm finds a global state that satisfies the predicate, it will terminate directly since we are looking for the predicates under the possibly modality.

Figure 5. The function used to evaluate the fitness of each chromosome in the population where the predicate to be detected is $(x_1 + x_2 + \cdots + x_n = c)$

```
public double evaluate(IChromosome globalState) {
        /* First the function make sure that the global state
        represented by the chromosome is consistent */
        if (isConsistent(globalState)){
                /* The function first evaluate the left side of the
                predicate.
                Function valueOfXi(i, globalState) returns
                the value of variable Xi of process Pi in one of
                its global states. */
                Integer sum = 0;
                for (int i = 1; i <= n; i++)
                    sum += valueOfXi(i, globalState);
                /* If the global state under consideration satisfies the
                predicate, then we are done and the algorithm will
                terminate. */
                if (sum == c) done = true;

                return 1.0/(Math.abs(sum - c) + 0.0000001);
        }
        /* if the chromosome represents an inconsistent cut then
        it cannot be considered as a global state
        and hence it will be assigned a very small fitness
        value. This will help in ignoring this chromosome in the
        selection process of the next generation*/
        else
                return -1;
}
```

If there is no global state satisfying the desired predicate in a given run, the algorithm will keep running for a very long time. To avoid such a situation, we can fix the maximum number of iterations the genetic algorithm can go through. The maximum number of iterations should be large enough depending on the number of processes and the length of the trace files

IMPLEMENTATION AND EXPERIMENTAL RESULTS

In this section, we will give more details about the implementation of the proposed detection algorithm, and we will present some experimental results.

We have used JGAP (Java Genetic Algorithms Package) (JGAP, 2012) to implement our algorithm. We assume that the algorithm to be developed wants to detect the predicate *Possibly: P* where P is the predicate $(x_1 + \cdots + x_n = c)$ where x_i, is a variable of process P_i and c is a constant. We assume that we have n processes. Figure 5 shows the fitness function used in our example. Other parts of the genetic algorithm can be implemented in a general manner and can be used in detecting any other predicate. The only thing that has to be modified to detect other predicates is the fitness function.

We have executed our algorithm on a computer with Intel Core 2 Duo CPU, 2.4GHz with 2GB of RAM. We have tested the algorithm on several runs of a distributed program involving 50, 75, 100, 125 and 150 processes where each process has executed 1000, 2000, and 3000 events in each run. The results are presented in Table 1. For example, given a run that involves 150 processes where each process has executed 3000 events, the algorithm was able to detect the predicate $x_1 + x_2 + \ldots + x_{150} = 100$ after 2769 iterations and the total time required to detect the predicate was 102156ms.

The other technique that can be exploited in detecting predicates under the possibly modality is to construct the entire state lattice of a run and to test all of its global states one by one until we find a global state where the predicate of interest is true (the second approach described in Section 4). According to this approach, we will explore $O(m^n)$ global states in the worst case where n is the number of processes and m is the number of local states in each process. Exploring such a large number of global states will require much more time compared with the genetic-based detection algorithm. For example, a run that involves only 15 processes where each process has executed 10 events will have (10^{15}) global states in the worst case. If we want to examine all the global states in this small run, and assuming that we can examine 10^9 global states per second, then we need around 277.7 hours to finish. Hence, the results presented in Table 1 shows that the detection algorithm based on genetic algorithms is much more efficient.

Another practical example is the use of distributed predicate detection in monitoring distributed applications. In this example, we will consider a simple multi-agent based e-commerce application where there are a number of seller agents and a number of buyer agents. Seller agents sell different products. The price of a product may change from time to time. When a buyer agent decides to buy certain product, he will send a call for proposal for all seller agents selling the desired product. After receiving the proposals from seller agents, the buyer agent will buy the product from the seller agent who has proposed the lowest price (Al Maghayreh et al., 2012).

Suppose that we need to monitor the price of product x to make sure that not all of the seller agents sell this product at a price greater than 20$. This problem is equivalent to the problem of detecting the following conjunctive predicate in a given run of the e-commerce application (Al Maghayreh et al., 2012).

$(Price_1 > 20) \wedge (Price_2 > 20) \wedge \cdots \wedge (Price_n > 20)$

Table 1. The results of several experiments on detecting the predicate $x_1 + ... + x_n = 100$

Number of Processes	Number of events executed by each process	Time spent to detect the predicate/ms	Number of Iterations
50	1000	172	13
	2000	187	13
	3000	203	15
75	1000	782	42
	2000	812	43
	3000	719	39
100	1000	2266	89
	2000	2938	115
	3000	2546	99
125	1000	11750	393
	2000	15922	534
	3000	9719	317
150	1000	49844	1368
	2000	116531	3163
	3000	102156	2769

Where *n* is the number of seller agents selling product *x*, and $Price_i$ is the price of product *x* offered by seller agent *i*.

To detect this predicate we can use the same genetic algorithm developed earlier except the fitness function. As we have mentioned earlier, the detection approach based on genetic algorithms is a general approached that can be easily tailored to detect any predicate by changing the fitness function only.

The above predicate consists of *n* terms $(Price_1 > 20)$, $(Price_2 > 20)$, . . ., $(Price_n > 20)$. Each term is a local predicate that belongs to one seller agent. Each chromosome in the population of the genetic algorithm will involve n genes. Each gene corresponds to one of the terms of the predicate. For a given chromosome, the value of Gene[i] is true if the corresponding term evaluates to true, otherwise it will be false. The predicate is evaluated to true in a given global state if and only if all of its terms are evaluated to true individually in the same global state. If the predicate is evaluated to false, then at least one of its terms is false, and hence one of the genes in the corresponding chromosome is false.

The fitness function has to assign to each chromosome a value that indicates whether the global state represented by this chromosome satisfied the above predicate or not, and if not, how close it is to a global state that satisfies the predicate. The fitness function that we have proposed is shown in Figure 6. If the global state represented by the chromosome considered by the evaluate function satisfies the predicate, then its fitness will be equal to the number of terms of the predicate. Otherwise, the *evaluate* function will assign to the chromosome a fitness value equal to the number of terms evaluated to true. The larger the fitness value the better the chromosome, and hence the global state represented by it is closer to a global state that satisfies the predicate.

For example, suppose we have a run of the above application with 10 seller agents, then the above predicate will involve 10 terms. A global state that satisfies the predicate will have a fitness value of

Figure 6. The function used to evaluate the fitness of each chromosome in the population where the predicate to be detected is (Price$_1$ > 20)∧(Price$_2$ > 20)∧· · ·∧(Price$_n$ > 20).

```
public double evaluate(IChromosome globalState) {
    /* First the function make sure that the global state
       represented by the chromosome is consistent */
    if (isConsistent(globalState)){
        /* The function first evaluate the left side of the
           predicate.
           Function  valueOfXi(i, globalState) returns
           the value of variable Xi of process Pi in one of
           its global states. */
        Integer sum = 0;
        for (int i = 1; i <= n; i++)
            if( valueOfXi(i, globalState) >= 20)
                  sum++;
        /* If the global state under consideration satisfies
           the predicate, then we are done and the algorithm will
           terminate. */
        if (sum == n) done = true;

        return sum;
    }
    /* if the chromosome represents an inconsistent cut then it
       cannot be considered as a global state
       and hence it will be assigned a very small fitness value.
       This will help in ignoring this chromosome in the
       selection process of the next generation*/
    else
        return -1;
}
```

10. If a global state does not satisfy the predicate, then it will have a fitness value less than 10 because at least one of the terms involved in the predicate is false. For example, if chromosome A has a fitness value of 7 then there are 3 terms evaluated to false in the global state represented by this chromosome. However, chromosome A is considered better than another chromosome B with fitness value of 4 since there are 6 terms evaluated to false in the global state represented by chromosome B.

We have executed the algorithm on a trace of a distributed application that involves 50, 75, 100, 125 and 150 agents where each agent has executed 1000, 2000, and 3000 events in each run. The results are summarized in Table 2. For example, given a run that involves 150 agents where each agent has executed 3000 events, the algorithm was able to detect the predicate (Price$_1$ > 20) ∧ (Price$_2$ > 20) ∧ · · · ∧ (Price$_{150}$ >20) after 1235 iterations and the total time required to detect the predicate was 47093ms.

CONCLUSION AND FUTURE WORK

Several techniques have been presented in the literature to detect the satisfaction of a distributed predicate in a run of a given distributed application. These techniques (also known as runtime verification techniques) are used to verify that a particular implementation of a given distributed system satisfies

Table 2. The results of several experiments on detecting the predicate (Price1 > 20) $\wedge$ (Price2 > 20) $\wedge$ $\cdots\wedge$(Pricen > 20)

Number of Agents	Number of events executed by each Agent	Time spent to detect the predicate/ms	Number of Iterations
50	1000	296	23
	2000	313	25
	3000	406	32
75	1000	1203	66
	2000	1031	55
	3000	1485	81
100	1000	1875	71
	2000	2156	85
	3000	2938	116
125	1000	9422	312
	2000	17719	593
	3000	13922	457
150	1000	52922	1355
	2000	44813	1199
	3000	47093	1235

certain properties. In this chapter, we have exploited genetic algorithms to design and implement an efficient distributed predicates detection technique. The proposed technique can be used to efficiently detect distributed predicates under the possibly modality. Several experiments have be conducted to demonstrate the effectiveness of the proposed technique.

One possible avenue for future work is to consider the use of other metaheuristic algorithms for the design and development of distributed predicate detection techniques, and to compare its performance with the performance of the proposed genetic algorithms based technique.

In genetic algorithms, there are many selection, crossover, and mutation operators. One other possible avenue for the continuation of this work is to consider the effect of different selection, crossover and mutation operators on the performance of the proposed algorithm.

REFERENCES

Al Maghayreh, E. (2010). *Simplifying Runtime Verification of Distributed Programs: Ameliorating the State Space Explosion Problem.* Secaucus, NJ, USA: VDM Verlag.

Al Maghayreh, E. (2011). Block-based atomicity to simplify the verification of distributed applications. In *Proceedings of the 24th Canadian Conference on Electrical and Computer Engineering (CCECE)* (pp. 887–891). doi:10.1109/CCECE.2011.6030585

Al Maghayreh, E., Samarah, S., Alkhateeb, F., Doush, I. A., Alsmadi, I., & Saifan, A. (2012). A framework for monitoring the execution of distributed multi-agent programs. *International Journal of Advanced Science and Technology, 38*(01), 53–66.

Alba, E., & Chicano, F. (2005). On the behavior of parallel genetic algorithms for optimal placement of antennae in telecommunications. *International Journal of Foundations of Computer Science, 16*(02), 343–359. doi:10.1142/S0129054105003029

Bäck, T. (1995). Generalized convergence models for tournament- and (mu,lambda)-selection. In *Proceedings of the 6th International Conference on Genetic Algorithms*, San Francisco, CA (pages 2–8). Morgan Kaufmann Publishers Inc.

Baker, J. E. (1985). Adaptive selection methods for genetic algorithms. In *Proceedings of the 1st International Conference on Genetic Algorithms*, Hillsdale, NJ (pp. 101–111). L. Erlbaum Associates Inc.

Bougé, L. (1987). Repeated snapshots in distributed systems with synchronous communications and their implementation in CSP. *Theoretical Computer Science, 49*(2-3), 145–169. doi:10.1016/0304-3975(87)90005-3

Burke, E. K., & Kendall, G. (2005). *Search Methodologies: Introductory Tutorials in Optimization and Decision Support Techniques*. Springer. doi:10.1007/0-387-28356-0

Chandy, K. M., & Lamport, L. (1985). Distributed snapshots: Determining global states of distributed systems. *ACM Transactions on Computer Systems, 3*(1), 63–75. doi:10.1145/214451.214456

Chase, C. M., & Garg, V. K. (1998). Detection of global predicates: Techniques and their limitations. *Distributed Computing, 11*(4), 191–201. doi:10.1007/s004460050049

Chauhan, H., Garg, V. K., Natarajan, A., & Mittal, N. (2013). A distributed abstraction algorithm for online predicate detection. In *Proceedings of the IEEE 32nd Symposium on Reliable Distributed Systems SRDS '13*, Braga, Portugal (pp. 101–110). doi:10.1109/SRDS.2013.19

Chu, C., & Brockmeyer, M. (2008). Predicate detection modality and semantics in three partially synchronous models. In *Proceedings of the Seventh IEEE/ACIS International Conference on Computer and Information Science* (pp. 444 –450). doi:10.1109/ICIS.2008.95

Cooper, R., & Marzullo, K. (1991). Consistent detection of global predicates. *SIGPLAN Not., 26*(12), 167–174. doi:10.1145/127695.122774

Dumais, G., & Li, H. (2002). Distributed predicate detection in series-parallel systems. *IEEE Transactions on Parallel and Distributed Systems, 13*(4), 373–387. doi:10.1109/71.995818

Eastridge, R., & Schmidt, C. (2008). Solving n-queens with a genetic algorithm and its usefulness in a computational intelligence course. *Journal of Computing Sciences in Colleges, 23*(4), 223–230.

Eiben, A. E. (1997). Multi-parent recombination. In Handbook of Evolutionary Computation (p. 3). IOP Publishing Ltd. and Oxford University Press.

Feng, S., & Wang, X. (2012). Research on fault diagnosis of mixed-signal circuits based on genetic algorithms. In *Proceedings of the International Conference on Computer Science and Electronics Engineering (ICCSEE)* (Vol. 3, pp. 12-15). doi:10.1109/ICCSEE.2012.60

Fidge, C. (1988). Timestamps in Message-Passing Systems that Preserve the Partial Ordering. In *Proceedings of the 11th Australian Computer Science Conference* (pp. 56–66).

Freiling, F. C., & Jhumka, A. (2007). Global predicate detection in distributed systems with small faults. In *Proceedings of the 9th international conference on Stabilization, safety, and security of distributed systems SSS'07* (pp. 296–310). Springer-Verlag. doi:10.1007/978-3-540-76627-8_23

Garg, V. K. (2002). *Elements of distributed computing*. New York, NY, USA: John Wiley & Sons, Inc.

Garg, V. K., & Mittal, N. (2001). On slicing a distributed computation. In *Proceedings of the The 21st International Conference on Distributed Computing Systems ICDCS '01* (p. 322).

Garg, V. K., & Waldecker, B. (1994). Detection of weak unstable predicates in distributed programs. *IEEE Transactions on Parallel and Distributed Systems, 5*(3), 299–307. doi:10.1109/71.277788

Garg, V. K., & Waldecker, B. (1996). Detection of strong unstable predicates in distributed programs. *IEEE Transactions on Parallel and Distributed Systems, 7*(12), 1323–1333. doi:10.1109/71.553309

Jegou, R., Medina, R., & Nourine, L. (1995). Linear space algorithm for on-line detection of global predicates. In *Proceedings of the International Workshop on Structures in Concurrency Theory (STRICT)*, Berlin (pp. 175–189). doi:10.1007/978-1-4471-3078-9_12

JGAP. (n. d.). Retrieved 19 April, 2017 from http://jgap.sourceforge.net/

Lamport, L. (1978). Time, clocks, and the ordering of events in a distributed system. *Communications of the ACM, 21*(7), 558–565. doi:10.1145/359545.359563

Lamport, L. (1990). A theorem on atomicity in distributed algorithms. *Distributed Computing, 4*(2), 59–68. doi:10.1007/BF01786631

Li, H. F., Al Maghayreh, E., & Goswami, D. (2007a). Detecting atomicity errors in message passing programs. In *Proceedings of the Eighth International Conference on Parallel and Distributed Computing, Applications and Technologies PDCAT '07* (pp. 193–200). IEEE Computer Society. doi:10.1109/PDCAT.2007.56

Li, H. F., Al Maghayreh, E., & Goswami, D. (2007b). Using atoms to simplify distributed programs checking. In *Proceedings of the Third IEEE International Symposium on Dependable, Autonomic and Secure Computing DASC '07* (pp. 75–83). doi:10.1109/DASC.2007.24

Li, H. F., Rilling, J., & Goswami, D. (2004). Granularity-driven dynamic predicate slicing algorithms for message passing systems. *Automated Software Engineering, 11*(1), 63–89. doi:10.1023/B:AUSE.0000008668.12782.6c

Mattern, F. (1989). Virtual Time and Global States of Distributed Systems. In *Proceedings of the International Workshop on Parallel and Distributed Algorithms,* Chateau de Bonas, France (pp. 215-226).

Mittal, N., & Garg, V. K. (2001). Computation slicing: Techniques and theory. In *Proceedings of the 15th International Conference on Distributed Computing DISC '01*, London, UK (pp. 78–92). Springer-Verlag.

Montana, D., Brinn, M., Moore, S., & Bidwell, G. (1998). *Genetic algorithms for complex, real-time scheduling. In Proceedings of the 1998 IEEE international conference on systems, Man, and Cybernetics* (pp. 2213–2218). IEEE.

Pelusi, D. (2011). Optimization of a fuzzy logic controller using genetic algorithms. In *Proceedings of the International Conference on Intelligent Human-Machine Systems and Cybernetics (IHMSC)* (Vol. 2, pp. 143 –146). doi:10.1109/IHMSC.2011.105

Rani, C., & Deepa, S. N. (2011). An Intelligent Operator for Genetic Fuzzy Rule Based System. *International Journal of Intelligent Information Technologies*, 7(3), 28–40. doi:10.4018/jiit.2011070103

Sastry, K., & Goldberg, D. (2004). Let's get ready to rumble: Crossover versus mutation head to head. In Genetic and Evolutionary Computation, LNCS (Vol. 3103, pp. 126–137). Springer.

Sen, A., & Garg, V. K. (2003). Detecting temporal logic predicates in distributed programs using computation slicing. In OPODIS (pp. 171–183).

Shen, M., & Kshemkalyani, A. D. (2014). Hierarchical detection of strong unstable conjunctive predicates in large-scale systems. *IEEE Transactions on Parallel and Distributed Systems*, 25(11), 2899–2908. doi:10.1109/TPDS.2013.306

Spears, W. M. (1997). Recombination parameters. In *The Handbook of Evolutionary Computation* (pp. 1–3). University Press. doi:10.1887/0750308958/b386c73

Spezialetti, M., & Kearns, P. (1986). Efficient distributed snapshots. In ICDCS (pp. 382–388).

Syswerda, G. (1989). Uniform crossover in genetic algorithms. In *Proceedings of the 3rd International Conference on Genetic Algorithms*, San Francisco, CA (pp. 2–9). Morgan Kaufmann Publishers Inc.

Thangamani, M., & Thangaraj, P. (2011). Effective fuzzy ontology based distributed document using non-dominated ranked genetic algorithm. *International Journal of Intelligent Information Technologies*, 7(4), 26–46. doi:10.4018/jiit.2011100102

Thierens, D., & Goldberg, D. E. (1994). Convergence models of genetic algorithm selection schemes. In *Proceedings of the International Conference on Evolutionary Computation. The Third Conference on Parallel Problem Solving from Nature: Parallel Problem Solving from Nature*, London, UK (pp. 119–129). doi:10.1007/3-540-58484-6_256

Tripathi, A., Gupta, P., Trivedi, A., & Kala, R. (2011). Wireless sensor node placement using hybrid genetic programming and genetic algorithms. *International Journal of Intelligent Information Technologies*, 7(2), 63–83. doi:10.4018/jiit.2011040104

VidyaBanu, R., & Nagaveni, N. (2012). Low Dimensional Data Privacy Preservation Using Multi-Layer Artificial Neural Network. *International Journal of Intelligent Information Technologies*, 8(3), 17–31. doi:10.4018/jiit.2012070102

Wright, A. H. (1991). Genetic algorithms for real parameter optimization. In *Foundations of Genetic Algorithms* (pp. 205–218). Morgan Kaufmann.

Yingchareonthawornchai, S., Valapil, V. T., Kulkarni, S., Torng, E., & Demirbas, M. (2017). Efficient algorithms for predicate detection using hybrid logical clocks. In *Proceedings of the 18th International Conference on Distributed Computing and Networking ICDCN '17*, New York, NY. ACM. doi:10.1145/3007748.3007780

Zhu, W., Cao, J., & Raynal, M. (2016). Predicate detection in asynchronous distributed systems: A probabilistic approach. *IEEE Transactions on Computers, 65*(1), 173–186. doi:10.1109/TC.2015.2409839

Chapter 10

Clustering Mixed Datasets Using K-Prototype Algorithm Based on Crow-Search Optimization

Lakshmi K.
Kongu Engineering College, India

Karthikeyani Visalakshi N.
NKR Government Arts College for Women, India

Shanthi S.
Kongu Engineering College, India

Parvathavarthini S.
Kongu Engineering College, India

ABSTRACT

Data mining techniques are useful to discover the interesting knowledge from the large amount of data objects. Clustering is one of the data mining techniques for knowledge discovery and it is the unsupervised learning method and it analyses the data objects without knowing class labels. The k-prototype is the most widely-used partitional clustering algorithm for clustering the data objects with mixed numeric and categorical type of data. This algorithm provides the local optimum solution due to its selection of initial prototypes randomly. Recently, there are number of optimization algorithms are introduced to obtain the global optimum solution. The Crow Search algorithm is one the recently developed population based meta-heuristic optimization algorithm. This algorithm is based on the intelligent behavior of the crows. In this paper, k-prototype clustering algorithm is integrated with the Crow Search optimization algorithm to produce the global optimum solution.

DOI: 10.4018/978-1-5225-3686-4.ch010

INTRODUCTION

Knowledge Discovery in Databases (KDD) is an automatic, exploratory analysis and modelling of large data repositories. It is the organized as the process of identifying valid, novel, useful, and understandable patterns from large and complex data sets. Data Mining is the heart of the KDD process, involving the large number of algorithms that explore the data, develop the model and discover previously unknown patterns.

Data clustering is the process of grouping the heterogeneous data objects into homogeneous clusters such that data objects within the cluster are similar with each other and dissimilar between the other clusters.

Clustering is used in variety of fields like data mining and knowledge discovery, market research, machine learning, biology, pattern recognition, weather prediction, etc. An early specific example of the use of cluster analysis in market research is given in (Green, Frank & Robinson, 1967). A large number of cities were used as test markets and the cluster analysis was used to classify the cities into a small number of groups on the basis of variables includes city size, newspaper circulation and per capita income. It shows that cities within a group is very similar to each other, choosing one city from each group was used for selecting the test markets.

Another example is, Littmann (2000) applies cluster analysis to the daily occurrences of several surface pressures for weather in the Mediterranean basin, and finds the groups that explain rainfall variance in the core Mediterranean regions. Liu and George (2005) use fuzzy k-means clustering to account for the spatiotemporal nature of weather data in the South-Central USA. Kerr and Churchill (2001) investigate the problem of clustering tools applied to gene expression data.

There are number of clustering algorithms are available for grouping the instances of the same type. The clustering algorithms are categorized into Partitional clustering algorithms, Hierarchical clustering algorithms, Density-Based clustering algorithms and Grid-Based clustering algorithms. Partitional clustering algorithms form the clusters by partition the data objects into groups. Hierarchical clustering algorithms form the clusters by the hierarchical decomposition of data objects.

The partitional clustering algorithms include k-means, k-modes, k-medoids and k-medians. The hierarchical clustering algorithms can be classified as single linkage and complete linkage, agglomerative algorithms. Density based clustering algorithms can be listed as DBSCAN, DENCLUE, OPTICS. The grid based clustering algorithms include GRIDCLUS, BANG and STING.

The k-means algorithm handles the large amount of data objects but it handles numeric type data objects. Huang introduced the two extensions of the k-means clustering algorithm. First extension is the k-modes clustering algorithm (Huang, 1997a) and second extension is the k-prototype clustering algorithm (Huang, 1997b). The k-modes algorithm efficiently handles the large amount of categorical data objects. The k-prototype algorithm efficiently handles the large amount of data objects with numeric and categorical types of data objects. This algorithm is the integration of k-means and k-modes clustering algorithms. For the mixed numeric and categorical datasets, the Euclidean distance is calculated for numeric data and the matching similarity measure is calculated for categorical data.

The k-prototype clustering algorithm selects the initial prototypes randomly from the data objects and it leads to the local optimum solution. To overcome this problem, optimization algorithm is integrated with k-prototype clustering algorithm.

Recently, there are number of optimization algorithms are introduced to obtain the global optimum solution. Some of the nature-inspired metaheuristic optimization algorithms are Genetic Algorithm (GA)

(Holland, 1975; Goldberg, 1989), Ant Colony Optimization (ACO) (Dorigo, 1992), Simulated Annealing (SA) (Brooks & Morgan, 1995), Particle Swarm Optimization (PSO) (Eberhart & Kennedy, 1995), Tabu Search (TS) (Glover & Laguna, 1997), Cat Swarm Optimization (CSO) (Chu, Tsai & Pan, 2006), Artificial Bee Colony (ABC) (Basturk & Karaboga, 2006), Cuckoo Search (CS) (Yang & Deb, 2009, 2010), Gravitational Search (GS) (Rashedi, Nezamabadi-Pour & Saryazdi, 2009), Firefly Algorithm (FA) (Yang, 2010), Bat Algorithm (BA) (Yang, 2010), Wolf Search Algorithm (WSA) (Tang, Fong, Yang & Deb, 2012), Krill Herd (KH) (Gandomi & Alavi, 2012).

Crow Search Algorithm (CSA) (Askarzadeh, 2016) is one of the metaheuristic population based optimization algorithms and it was introduced by Askarzadeh in 2016. This algorithm simulates the intelligent behavior of the crows. Crows are considered as one of the world's most intelligent birds. This algorithm is based on finding the hidden storage position of excess food of crows. Finding food source is hidden by another crow is not easy task because if a crow finds any one following it, the crows tries to fool the crow by moving to another position. This algorithm is very simple and easy to understand. Each optimization algorithm has controlling parameters to achieve the performance of the algorithms. Also, the number of controlling parameters for CSA algorithm is two namely awareness probability and flight length.

The reason behind this work is k-prototype algorithm produces the local optimum solution. Also, Huang (1997b) suggested the global optimization for the k-prototype algorithm. To overcome the k-prototype local optimum problem, this paper Crow Search optimization algorithm combined with the k-prototype clustering algorithm.

The organization of this paper is as follows: Section 2 describes the related researches in the literature. Section 3 describes the k-prototype clustering algorithm. Section 4 describes the Crow Search Algorithm. Section 5 describes the proposed algorithm. The experimental analysis is discussed in Section 6. Conclusion and future works are provided in Section 7.

RELATED WORK

Ant Colony Optimization approach for clustering problem is given in (Shelokar, Jayaraman & Kulkarni, 2004). Simulated Annealing algorithm approach for clustering algorithms is proposed in (Selim & Alsultan, 1991). Particle Swarm Optimization approach for clustering problem is given in (Chen & Ye, 2004). Tabu Search algorithm approach for clustering problem is proposed in (Al-Sultan, 1995). Artificial Bee Colony Optimization approach for clustering algorithms is given in (Zhang, Ouyang & Ning, 2010; Karaboga & Ozturk, 2011). Cat Swarm Optimization approach for clustering problem is given in (Santosa, & Ningrum, 2009).

Genetic Algorithm combined with k-means was proposed in (Krishna & Murty, 1999). Hybrid clustering algorithm based on k-means and ant colony algorithm was proposed in (Lu & Hu, 2013). Cluster analysis with k-means and Simulated Annealing was introduced in (Sun, Xu, Liang, Xie, & Yu, 1994). Particle Swarm Optimization based k-means clustering algorithm was proposed in (Van der Merwe & Engelbrecht, 2003; Ahmadyfard & Modares, 2008). Tabu Search based k-means was developed in (Liu, Liu, Wang & Chen, 2005). Artificial Bee Colony based k-means algorithm was proposed in (Armano & Farmani, 2014). Gravitational Search algorithm, combined with k-means was introduced in (Hatamlou, Abdullah & Nezamabadi-Pour, 2012). Firefly Algorithm is combined with k-means was proposed in (Hassanzadeh & Meybodi, 2012). Bat Algorithm is combined with k-means was proposed in (Komarasamy & Wahi, 2012). Wolf Search Algorithm, Cuckoo Search, Bat Algorithm, Firefly Algorithm and Ant Colony Optimization algorithms are integrated with k-means in introduced in (Tang, Fong, Yang & Deb, 2012).

Tabu search algorithm is combined with k-modes is introduced in (Ng & Wong, 2002). Genetic Algorithm is combined with k-modes is developed in (Gan, Yang & Wu, 2005). It finds the global optimum solution for the given categorical dataset and the crossover operator is replaced with k-modes operator. Fuzzy based k-modes algorithm is proposed in (Huang, & Ng, 1999). In hard clustering, each data object is assigned to single cluster. In fuzzy clustering, each object belongs to more than one cluster and the membership degree value is varying from one cluster to another. The fuzzy k-modes algorithm integrated with Genetic Algorithm for categorical data was proposed in (Gan, Wu & Yang, 2009). It treated the fuzzy k-modes algorithm as an optimization problem and Genetic Algorithm is used to obtain the global optimum solution.

Swarm-based k-modes algorithm is introduced in (Izakian, Abraham & Sná, 2009). A novel approach for combining Particle Swarm Optimization with k-modes is proposed in (Mei & Xiang-Jun, 2012). First, the categorical data are mapped to natural numbers, find the similarity between the data objects and initial centroids and finally update the mode by using the frequency based method.

The Particle Swarm Optimization algorithm integrated with k-modes clustering algorithm and this hybridized algorithm is applied to retrieve the three dimensional objects was proposed in (Zhao & Lu, 2013). Artificial Bee Colony based k-modes is developed in (Ji, Pang, Zheng, Wang & Ma, 2015). In this paper, one-step k-modes clustering algorithm procedure is executed and then integrate this procedure with the artificial bee colony approach.

Yin & Tan (2005) proposed the new way of clustering mixed numeric and categorical type of data objects. In this paper, proposed the improved k-prototype clustering algorithm. For clustering, first step is use the *CF**-tree to pre-cluster datasets. After the dense regions are stored in leaf nodes, then each dense region as a single point and use an improved k-prototype to cluster such dense regions.

Ahmad and Dey (2007) proposed the new cost function for clustering mixed numeric and categorical attributes. It provides the cost for both numeric and categorical attributes. It is computed from each attribute from the given data objects. But Huang provides the cost only for categorical attributes. Also apply a new distance method between two categorical attribute values. In this, the new distance is computed from the overall distribution of values in a single class and the overall distribution of values in the dataset.

The evolutionary k-prototypes (EKP) algorithm by (Zheng, Gong, Ma, Jiao & Wu, 2010) integrates the evolutionary framework with k-prototype algorithm. In this paper, proposed the Evolutionary based k-prototype algorithm for mixed numeric and categorical datasets. The cross over operator and mutation operator is applied separately for each kind of data. Also apply the simulated binary crossover operator for numerical and single point crossover for categorical data object in the dataset. Also apply the polynomial mutation for numerical data objects and uniform mutation for categorical data objects in the dataset. The tournament selection with elitism strategy is used for selecting the individuals for each generation.

Chatzis (2011) introduce an extension of the GG algorithm to allow for the effective handling of data with mixed numeric and categorical attributes. Traditionally, fuzzy clustering of such data is conducted by means of the fuzzy *k*-prototypes algorithm, which merely consists in the execution of the original FCM algorithm using a different dissimilarity functional, suitable for attributes with mixed numeric and categorical attributes.

Pham, Suarez-Alvarez, and Prostov (2011) developed the new clustering algorithm called RANKPRO that is combines the honey bee optimization algorithm with k-prototype clustering algorithm. The honey bee algorithm uses the random search method instead of using genetic algorithm operators like crossover and mutation. Also apply the normalization procedure to balance the sum of numeric and categorical attributes and avoid either type of attribute.

Ji, Pang, Zhou, Han and Wang (2012) proposed the fuzzy based k-prototype algorithm for clustering mixed numeric and categorical datasets. In this paper, fuzzy c-mean type clustering algorithm for mixed numeric and categorical attributes is presented. In this algorithm, combination of mean and fuzzy centroids to represent prototype for a cluster and apply the new mew measure based on co-occurrence of values to assess the dissimilarity between the data objects and prototypes of clusters.

Ji, Bai, Zhou, Ma & Wang (2013) proposed the improved k-prototype clustering algorithm for mixed numeric and categorical attributes is proposed. In this algorithm, introduce the distribution centroids to represent the prototypes of cluster with mixed attributes and propose the new measure to assess the dissimilarity between the data objects and prototypes of clusters. The new measure is based on the Huang strategy of evaluate the significance of the attributes in the dataset.

Wu Sen, Chen Hong, and Feng Xiaodong (2013) proposed a new dissimilarity measure for incomplete data set with mixed numeric and categorical attributes and a new approach to select k objects as the initial prototypes based on the nearest neighbors. The improved k-prototypes algorithm cluster incomplete data without need to impute the missing values, randomness in choosing initial prototypes.

Madhuri, Murty, Murthy, Reddy and Satapathy (2014) implemented algorithms which extend the k-means algorithm to categorical domains by using modified k-modes algorithm and domains with mixed categorical and numerical values by using k-prototypes algorithm k-prototypes algorithm which is implemented by integrating the Incremental k-means and the Modified k-modes partition clustering algorithms.

Ji et al., (2015) propose a novel cluster center initialization method for the k-prototypes algorithms to address this issue. In the proposed method, the centrality of data objects is introduced based on the concept of neighbor-set, and then both the centrality and distance are exploited together to determine initial cluster centers.

Prabha and Visalakshi (2015) proposed the particle swarm optimization based k-prototype algorithm. In this paper, binary particle swarm optimization is integrated with the k-prototype clustering algorithm to obtain the global optimum solutions.

Lakshmi, Visalakshi and Shanthi (2017) proposed the cuckoo search based k-prototype algorithm. In this work, cuckoo search optimization algorithm is integrated with the k-prototype clustering algorithm to obtain the global optimum solutions.

In (Arun & Kumar, 2017) applied the Artificial Bee Colony (ABC) optimization algorithm for on-line analytical query processing in data warehouse. The authors apply the ABC algorithm for OLAP to minimize the query response time. Also proposed the Artificial Bee Colony (ABC) based view selection algorithm.

Krishnamoorthy, Sadasivam, Rajalakshmi, Kowsalyaa and& Dhivya (2017) proposed Particle Swarm Optimization based system is to hide a group of interesting patterns which contains sensitive knowledge. This system also reduces the side effects like number of modifications.

Naser and Alshattnawi (2014) proposed the new way to group the social networks based on Artificial Bee Colony optimization algorithm, which is a swarm based meta-heuristic optimization algorithm. This approach aims to maximize the modularity, which is a measure that represents the quality of network partitioning.

K-PROTOTYPE ALGORITHM

The k-prototype algorithm (Huang, 1997b) is the partition based clustering algorithm that clustering the data objects with both the numeric and categorical and also efficiently handles the large amount of data objects.

Let $X = \{x_{11}, x_{12},...,x_{nm}\}$ be the data object with n number of instances with m attributes. Let k is the number clusters given by the user. The objective of k-prototype clustering algorithm is to divide the n number of data objects into k number of clusters and minimize the cost function defined in the following equation (1):

$$E\left(U,Q\right) = \sum_{l=1}^{k}\sum_{i=1}^{n} u_{il} dis\left(x_i, Q_l\right) \tag{1}$$

u_{il} the element of the partition matrix U_{nxk}; Q_l is the prototype of cluster l; x_i is the data object. The $dis(x_i,Q_l)$ is calculated using the following equation (2):

$$dis\left(x_i, Q_l\right) = \sum_{j=1}^{p}\left(x_{ij}^r - q_{lj}^r\right) + \alpha \sum_{j=p+1}^{m} \delta\left(x_{ij}^c - q_{lj}^c\right) \tag{2}$$

$\sum_{j=1}^{p}\left(x_{ij}^r - q_{lj}^r\right)$ is the Euclidean distance between the data objects and the prototype of cluster for numeric attributes. The Euclidean distance is calculated using the equation (3):

$$d_{num}(x, y) = \sqrt{\sum_{i=1}^{m}\left(x_i - y_i\right)^2} \tag{3}$$

$\sum_{j=p+1}^{m} \delta\left(x_{ij}^c - q_{lj}^c\right)$ is the matching dissimilarity measure between the data objects and the prototype of cluster for categorical attributes. The α specifies the weight for categorical attributes. The matching dissimilarity is evaluated using the equation (4):

$$d_{cat}(x, y) = \begin{cases} 0, & x_i = y_i \\ 1, & x_i \neq y_i \end{cases} \tag{4}$$

The k-prototype clustering algorithm is described as follows:

Step 1: Randomly select k initial prototypes as the initial cluster centres from the dataset X.
Step 2: For each data object in X, calculate the distance between the data object and the initial centroids using the equation (1)

Step 3: Assign the data objects to cluster whose data object have the minimum distance.

Step 4: After the initial assignment of data objects to clusters, update the initial prototype based on the newly assigned data objects using the equation (1).

Step 5: Repeat the step 4 until no changes in the clustership of data objects.

CROW SEARCH ALGORITHM

The Crow Search Algorithm (CSA) (Askarzadeh, 2016) mimics the intelligent and foraging behaviour of the crows. The crow follows the other crows to steal the food hidden by that crows. The principles of crow search algorithm are (i) They live in the form of groups (ii) remember the position of food hiding locations (iii) follow the each other for stealing food (iv) protect their food source. In CSA, diversification and intensification are controlled by the Awareness Probability (AP).

The number of crows i.e flock size is P with D attributes and the position of the crow is i at time in iteration in the search space is specified as $X_{i,iter}$, i = 1, 2, ..., N; iter = 1, 2, ..., itmax, itmax is the maximum number iterations. Each crow has a memory m to remember the position of the hiding place. At each iteration, the position of food hidden place for crow i is specified by $m_{i,iter}$ and it shows the best position obtained so far.

The CSA is described as follows:

Step 1: Initialize number of flocks P, maximum number of iterations itmax, flight length fl, awareness probability AP.

Step 2: Initialize the position of each crow randomly with PxD dimensional search space. Initialize the memory of the crows with the initial position of crows.

Step 3: Evaluate the position of the crows.

    a. While iter < maxiter

        i. for all crows

            1. Randomly choose any one of the crows to follow (for example μ)

            2. If crow μ does not know that crow ν is following it, new position of μ is obtained using the equation (5):

$$x^{i,iter+1} = x^{i,it} + r_i \times fl^{i,it} \times \left(m^{j,iter} - x^{i,it} \right) \tag{5}$$

            3. If crow μ does know that crow ν is following it, new position of μ is obtained by the randomly using the following equation (6):

$$x^{i,iter+1} = \text{a random position} \tag{6}$$

            4. The equations (5) and (6) is combined in the following equation (7):

$$\begin{cases} x^{i,it} + r_i \times fl^{i,it} \times \left(m^{j,iter} - x^{i,it} \right) & r_j \geq AP^{j,iter} \\ \text{a random position} & \text{otherwise} \end{cases} \tag{7}$$

5. Check the feasibility of the new position. If the new position of crow is feasible, its position is updated, otherwise the crow stays in the current position.
6. Evaluate the new position of the crows
7. Update the memory of the crows by using the equation (8):

$$\begin{cases} x^{i,it+1} & f\left(x^{i,it+1}\right) is\,better\,than\,f\left(m^{i,it}\right) \\ m^{i,iter} & otherwise \end{cases} \tag{8}$$

b. End of while

PROPOSED ALGORITHM

The k-prototype clustering algorithm is the combination of k-means and k-modes clustering algorithm. Both the k-means and k-modes clustering algorithms are efficiently handling large amount of numeric and categorical data respectively. The k-prototype algorithm also efficiently handling large amount of mixed numeric and categorical datasets. The main drawback of this algorithm is producing local optimum solutions. To obtain the global optimum solutions, k-prototype is combined with global optimization algorithms. The Crow Search algorithm is the population based metaheuristic optimization algorithm and it mimics the intelligent behaviour of the crows. In this proposed work, Crow Search Algorithm combined with k-prototypes algorithm to obtain the global optimum solution.

Algorithm Steps

Step 1: Input the datasets X with the N number data objects with D number of attributes, Number of clusters K, Flock size P, Maximum number of iterations maxiter, flight length fl, and awareness probability AP.

Step 2: Initialize the position of crows for P by generating the matrix with the random numbers with the size of P rows with KxD columns. The maximum range of random numbers is the total number of instances in the data objects.

Step 3: Encode the random numbers with the data objects. Each row specifies the K cluster center for clustering algorithm.

Step 4: Initialize the memory of the crows with the values of the initial position of the crows because initially crows hidden their foods in their initial positions.

Step 5: Evaluate the fitness of initial position of crows by using the equation (1).

Step 6: Initialize the fitness of memory of the crows with the fitness position of the crows.

Step 7: Update the position of crows:

    a. while iteration<=maxiter

        i. for all crows

            1. Choose any one of the crows to follow randomly (for example μ).

            2. If crow μ does not know that crow ν is following it, new position of μ is obtained using the equation (5).

            3. If crow μ does know that crow ν is following it, new position of μ is obtained by the randomly using the equation (6).

            4. Check the feasibility of the new position. If the new position of crow is feasible, its position is updated, otherwise the crow stays in the current position.

    b. End of while

Step 8: Evaluate the fitness of new position of crows by using the equation (1).

Step 9: Update the memory of the crows by using the equation (8).

Step 10: Finally, the best position G_{best} is obtained.

Step 11: Run the k-prototype algorithm with G_{best} as the prototype for clusters.

Step 12: Calculate the Euclidean distance for numeric data and matching similarity for categorical data from each data to G_{best} obtained from CSA.

Step 13: Repeat Step 12 until convergence criteria is met.

EXPERIMENTAL RESULTS

The algorithms are implemented using Matlab R2015a on Intel i5 2.30 GHz with 4GB RAM. The k-prototypes, PSOk-prototypes and CSAk-prototypes are executed 20 distinct runs. The algorithm specific parameters are specified in Table 1. The values for the Particle Swarm Optimization algorithm are suggested in (Van den Bergh, 2001). The values for the Crow Search algorithm are suggested in (Askarzadeh, 2016).

Table 1. Algorithm specific parameters

Criteria	k-prototype	PSOk-prototype	CSAk-prototype
Iterations	20	100	100
Particles	N/A	15	15
Parameters	$\alpha = 0.5$	w = 0.72 c1 = 1.49 c2 = 1.49	fl = 2 AP = 0.1

Datasets

The proposed CSAk-prototype clustering algorithm is tested with the benchmark mixed datasets such as Bupa, Credit Approval, Heart, Hepatitis, Post-Operative Patient and Zoo. These datasets are are obtained from the UCI machine learning repository (Asuncion & Newman, 2007). The details of these datasets are described in the Table 2. In this work, with the help of standard metrics such as FMeasure, Accuracy and Rand Index to assess the quality of the clustering results.

Measures

For all measures, use the four terms namely, TP, TN, FP and FN. TP means True Positive, it is the count of actual and predicted values are same. TN means True Negative and the actual and predicted values are different. A FP means False Positive, decision means that values with different features are assigned to the same cluster. A FN means False Negative, decision means that the values with similar traits to different clusters. N is the total number of objects.

The FMeasure (Van Rijsbergen, 1979) is an external index. It is the harmonic mean of the precision and recall coefficients. If the precision is high and recall value is low, this results in a low FMeasure. If both precision and recall are low, a low FMeasure is obtained. On the other hand, if both are high, a high FMeasure value is obtained. FMeasure can be computed using the formula (9):

$$FMeasure = 2 \times \frac{Precision \times Recall}{Precision + Recall} \tag{9}$$

Precision is calculated as the number of correct positive predictions divided by the total number of positive predictions. The best precision is 1, whereas the worst is 0. Precision is calculated as true positive divided by the sum of false positive and true positive. It is calculated using the equation (10):

$$Precision = \frac{TP}{TP + FP} \tag{10}$$

Table 2. Details of datasets

Dataset	No. of Instances	No. of Attributes	No. of Numeric Attributes	No. of Categorical Attributes	No. of Classes
Bupa	345	6	5	1	2
Credit Approval	690	15	6	9	2
Heart	270	13	6	7	2
Hepatitis	155	19	6	13	2
Post Operative Patient	90	8	1	7	3
Zoo	101	16	1	15	7

Recall is calculated as the number of correct positive predictions divided by the total number of positives. The best sensitivity is 1.0, whereas the worst is 0.0. It is calculated using the equation (11):

$$Recall = \frac{TP}{N} \tag{11}$$

Accuracy is calculated as the number of all correct predictions divided by the total number of the data objects. In case of accuracy, the value 1 indicates data object is clustered exactly same. Highest value of this measure indicates better performance. It is calculated using the equation (12):

$$Accuracy = \frac{TP + TN}{N} \tag{12}$$

Rand Index (Rand, 1971) is a measure of the similarity between true labels and predicted labels. It is calculated using the equation (13):

$$RandIndex = \frac{TP + TN}{TP + FP + TN + FN} \tag{13}$$

The Rand index has the value lies between 0 and 1, 0 indicating that the two data clusters do not agree on any pair of points and 1 indicating that the data clusters are exactly the same.

Results

The following Table 3 shows the best, worst, average and standard deviation of objective function values for the benchmark datasets.

For bupa, hepatitis and zoo datasets, the CSAk-prototype algorithm outperforms compared to k-prototype and PSOk-prototype algorithms. That is, best, worst, average and standard deviation values are better than k-prototype and PSOk-prototype algorithms.

For credit approval and Post-Operative Patient datasets, the CSAk-prototype algorithm outperforms compared to k-prototype and PSOk-prototype algorithms. The best, worst and average values are better than k-prototype and PSOk-prototype algorithms. But the standard deviation of k-prototype is better than PSOk-prototype and CSAk-prototype algorithms.

For heart dataset, the CSAk-prototype algorithm outperforms compared to k-prototype and PSOk-prototype algorithms. That is worst, average values and standard deviation are better than k-prototype and PSOk-prototype algorithms. But the best value of k-prototype is better than PSOk-prototype and CSAk-prototype algorithms.

The following Table 4 shows the FMeasure, Accuracy, and Rand Index scores for the benchmark datasets.

For Bupa dataset, k-prototype algorithm gives the best FMeasure compare with PSOk-prototypes and CSAk-prototypes algorithms. CSAk-prototype algorithm gives the best accuracy and rand index values compare with k-prototypes and PSOk-prototypes algorithms. For Credit Approval, CSAk-prototype

Table 3. Comparison of objective function values obtained from three algorithms

Dataset	Criteria	k-prototype	PSOk-prototype	CSAk-prototype
Bupa	Best	10485.9368	10463.1151	**9974.8872**
	Worst	14955.1969	11472.9706	**10944.1463**
	Average	10806.3294	10549.9688	**10518.6544**
	Std	1150.9185	265.6908	**184.7416**
Credit Approval	Best	544174.2443	538637.2660	**534710.9724**
	Worst	666640.7309	677683.5431	**657656.5320**
	Average	595637.6748	594218.9867	**592486.4524**
	Std	**23750.1241**	29164.7700	24935.0278
Heart	Best	**11025.7623**	11033.0958	11060.3928
	Worst	17158.3642	12732.6091	**11742.8632**
	Average	11488.5261	11176.5074	**11107. 2340**
	Std	1568.6460	431.1003	**175.8933**
Hepatitis	Best	9225.7405	9057.2432	**9050.6731**
	Worst	13914.3494	9994.0377	**9990.3276**
	Average	9887.5603	9708.6395	**9687.2750**
	Std	1119.6490	204.6099	**190.6814**
Post Operative Patient	Best	194.1308	118.0000	**116.0000**
	Worst	214.8000	212.8529	**200.0833**
	Average	197.1877	192.3803	**189.0477**
	Std	**6.5806**	27.4801	20.2992
Zoo	Best	131.5000	112.5000	**102.0000**
	Worst	252.2500	249.1818	**196.8548**
	Average	224.1747	185.2364	**170.7366**
	Std	29.0243	33.6960	**21.0479**

Table 4. Comparison of FMeasure, accuracy and RandIndex of three algorithms

Dataset	FMeasure			Accuracy			Rand Index		
	k-prototype	PSOk-prototype	CSAk-prototype	k-prototype	PSOk-prototype	CSAk-prototype	k-prototype	PSOk-prototype	CSAk-prototype
Bupa	**0.5568**	0.5551	0.5561	55.16	55.71	**55.87**	0.5040	0.5051	**0.5055**
Credit Approval	0.6358	0.6384	**0.6392**	66.84	67.03	**67.08**	0.5560	0.5573	**0.5576**
Heart	0.6018	0.6024	**0.6045**	60.09	60.12	**60.33**	0.5187	0.5188	**0.5196**
Hepatitis	**0.6465**	0.6460	0.6433	61.16	61.06	**60.74**	**0.5219**	0.5214	0.5214
Post Operative Patient	0.5129	**0.5445**	0.5223	45.52	**49.25**	46.32	0.4844	**0.4937**	0.4862
Zoo	0.6535	0.6809	**0.6899**	59.90	62.82	**64.51**	0.8221	0.8416	**0.8459**

algorithm gives the best FMeasure, accuracy and rand index compare with k-prototypes and CSAk-prototypes algorithms.

For Heart, CSAk-prototype algorithm gives the best FMeasure, accuracy and rand index values when compared with k-prototypes and CSAk-prototypes algorithms. For Hepatitis, k-prototype algorithm gives the best FMeasure compare with PSOk-prototypes and CSAk-prototypes algorithms. CSAk-prototype algorithm gives the best accuracy and rand index compare with k-prototypes and PSOk-prototypes algorithms. For Post Operative Patient, PSOk-prototype algorithm gives the best FMeasure, accuracy and rand index compare with k-prototypes and CSAk-prototypes algorithms. For Zoo, CSAk-prototype algorithm gives the best FMeasure, accuracy and rand index compare with values when compared with k-prototypes and PSOk-prototypes algorithms.

The Figures 1 to 3 show the overall performance of Accuracy, FMeasure and RandIndex of k-prototypes, PSOk-prototypes and CSAk-prototypes algorithms.

Comparison of CSA With PSO

All optimization algorithms have individual controlling parameters. But the number of parameters is varying from one to another algorithm. Parameter setting is the time-consuming task and lagging in setting the proper values for algorithms. In PSO, requires four parameters like maximum velocity, inertia weight, social learning factor and individual learning factor. In CSA, requires two parameters like flight length and awareness probability.

In PSO, have the complexity like need to initialize and check the boundaries of velocity. If the velocity is reached below minimum and it is set to the minimum velocity. If the velocity is reached beyond the upper maximum and it is set to the maximum velocity. In CSA, need to check the upper and lower bounds of newly obtained position of the crow. If the position is greater than lower bound and less than upper bound, it is set to the new position of the crow.

Figure 1. Comparison of accuracy values of three algorithms

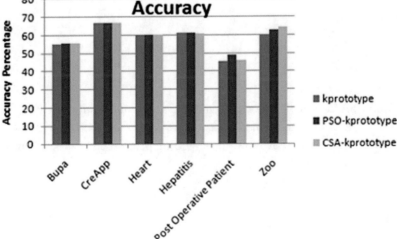

Figure 2. Comparison of FMeasure values of three algorithms

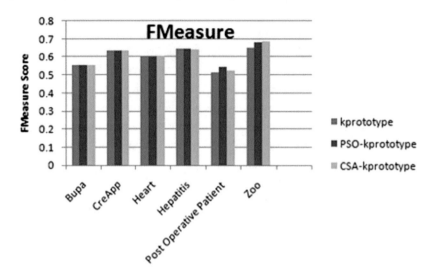

Figure 3. Comparison of RandIndex values of three algorithms

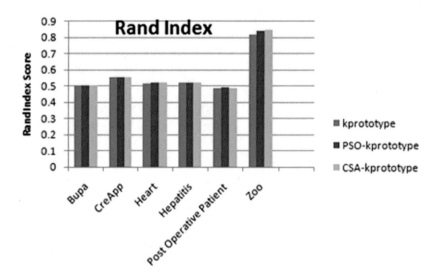

Both the PSO and CSA have the memories to maintain the good solutions. In PSO, each particle attracted towards the best positions maintained in its memory. In CSA, at each iteration, each crow selects randomly one of the flock crows to move towards its hiding place. The best positions found are directly used to find the better position.

CONCLUSION

This work is motivated by the problem of clustering large mixed datasets because most of the datasets are mixed numeric and categorical. Mixed datasets are ubiquitous in real world database. However, few efficient algorithms are available for clustering mixed numeric and categorical data objects. The k-prototype clustering algorithm is easy to implement and efficiently handling large numeric and categorical datasets. In this paper, incorporate the k-prototype clustering algorithm with Crow Search Optimization algorithm to obtain the global optimum solution. The efficiency of the proposed algorithm is experimented with six benchmark datasets and the results are compared with k-prototype and Particle Swarm Optimization with k-prototype algorithms. The experimental results show that the Crow Search algorithm with k-prototype is outperforms for Credit approval, heart and Zoo datasets than k-prototype and Particle Swarm Optimization with k-prototype algorithms. It also shows that the PSO with k-prototype is outperforms for Post Operative Patient than k-prototype and Crow Search algorithm with k-prototype algorithms. In future, extend this work with measure the clustering results with internal validity measures.

REFERENCES

Ahmad, A., & Dey, L. (2007). A k-mean clustering algorithm for mixed numeric and categorical data. *Data & Knowledge Engineering*, *63*(2), 503–527. doi:10.1016/j.datak.2007.03.016

Ahmadyfard, A., & Modares, H. (2008). Combining PSO and k-means to enhance data clustering. In *Proceedings of the International Symposium on Telecommunications IST '08* (pp. 688-691). IEEE. doi:10.1109/ISTEL.2008.4651388

Al-Sultan, K. S. (1995). A tabu search approach to the clustering problem. *Pattern Recognition*, *28*(9), 1443–1451. doi:10.1016/0031-3203(95)00022-R

Armano, G., & Farmani, M. R. (2014). Clustering analysis with combination of artificial bee colony algorithm and k-means technique. *International Journal of Computer Theory and Engineering*, *6*(2), 141–145. doi:10.7763/IJCTE.2014.V6.852

Arun, B., & Kumar, T. V. (2017). Materialized View Selection using Artificial Bee Colony Optimization. *International Journal of Intelligent Information Technologies*, *13*(1), 26–49. doi:10.4018/IJIIT.2017010102

Askarzadeh, A. (2016). A novel metaheuristic method for solving constrained engineering optimization problems: Crow search algorithm. *Computers & Structures*, *169*, 1–12. doi:10.1016/j.compstruc.2016.03.001

Asuncion, A., & Newman, D. (2007). UCI machine learning repository.

Basturk, B., & Karaboga, D. (2006). An artificial bee colony (abc) algorithm for numeric function optimization. In *Proceedings of the IEEE Swarm Intelligence Symposium 2006*, Indianapolis, Indiana, USA.

Brooks, S. P., & Morgan, B. J. (1995). Optimization using simulated annealing. *The Statistician*, *44*(2), 241–257. doi:10.2307/2348448

Chatzis, S. P. (2011). A fuzzy c-means-type algorithm for clustering of data with mixed numeric and categorical attributes employing a probabilistic dissimilarity functional. *Expert Systems with Applications*, *38*(7), 8684–8689. doi:10.1016/j.eswa.2011.01.074

Chen, C. Y., & Ye, F. (2004). Particle swarm optimization algorithm and its application to clustering analysis. In *Proceedings of the 2004 IEEE International Conference on Networking, Sensing and Control* (Vol. 2, pp. 789-794). IEEE.

Chu, S. C., Tsai, P. W., & Pan, J. S. (2006). Cat swarm optimization. In *Proceedings of the Pacific Rim International Conference on Artificial Intelligence* (pp. 854-858). Springer Berlin Heidelberg.

Dorigo, M. (1992). Optimization, learning and natural algorithms [Ph.D thesis]. Politecnico di Milano, Italy.

Eberhart, R. C., & Kennedy, J. (1995). A new optimizer using particle swarm theory. In *Proceedings of the sixth international symposium on micro machine and human science* (Vol. 1, pp. 39-43). doi:10.1109/MHS.1995.494215

Gan, G., Wu, J., & Yang, Z. (2009). A genetic fuzzy k-Modes algorithm for clustering categorical data. *Expert Systems with Applications, 36*(2), 1615–1620. doi:10.1016/j.eswa.2007.11.045

Gan, G., Yang, Z., & Wu, J. (2005). A genetic k-modes algorithm for clustering categorical data. In *Proceedings of the International Conference on Advanced Data Mining and Applications* (pp. 195-202). Springer Berlin Heidelberg. doi:10.1007/11527503_23

Gandomi, A. H., & Alavi, A. H. (2012). Krill herd: A new bio-inspired optimization algorithm. *Communications in Nonlinear Science and Numerical Simulation, 17*(12), 4831–4845. doi:10.1016/j.cnsns.2012.05.010

Glover, F., & Laguna, M. (1997). *Tabu search*. Boston: Kluwer Academic Publishers. doi:10.1007/978-1-4615-6089-0

Goldberg, D. (1989). *Genetic Algorithms in Search, Optimization and Machine Learning*. Addison-Wesley.

Green, P. E., Frank, R. E., & Robinson, P. J. (1967). Cluster analysis in test market selection. *Management Science, 13*(8), 387–400. doi:10.1287/mnsc.13.8.B387

Hassanzadeh, T., & Meybodi, M. R. (2012). A new hybrid approach for data clustering using firefly algorithm and K-means. In *Proceedings of the 2012 16th CSI International Symposium on Artificial Intelligence and Signal Processing (AISP)* (pp. 007-011). IEEE.

Hatamlou, A., Abdullah, S., & Nezamabadi-Pour, H. (2012). A combined approach for clustering based on K-means and gravitational search algorithms. *Swarm and Evolutionary Computation, 6*, 47–52. doi:10.1016/j.swevo.2012.02.003

Holland, J. (1975). *Adaption in Natural and Artificial Systems*. Ann Arbor, MI: University of Michigan Press.

Huang, Z. (1997a). A Fast Clustering Algorithm to Cluster Very Large Categorical Data Sets in Data Mining. In DMKD (p. 0).

Huang, Z. (1997b). Clustering large data sets with mixed numeric and categorical values. In *Proceedings of the 1st pacific-asia conference on knowledge discovery and data mining, (PAKDD)* (pp. 21-34).

Huang, Z., & Ng, M. K. (1999). A fuzzy k-modes algorithm for clustering categorical data. *IEEE Transactions on Fuzzy Systems, 7*(4), 446–452. doi:10.1109/91.784206

Izakian, H., Abraham, A., & Sná, V. (2009). Clustering categorical data using a swarm-based method. In *Proceedings of the World Congress on Nature & Biologically Inspired Computing NaBIC '09* (pp. 1720-1724). IEEE. doi:10.1109/NABIC.2009.5393623

Ji, J., Bai, T., Zhou, C., Ma, C., & Wang, Z. (2013). An improved k-prototypes clustering algorithm for mixed numeric and categorical data. *Neurocomputing, 120,* 590–596. doi:10.1016/j.neucom.2013.04.011

Ji, J., Pang, W., Zheng, Y., Wang, Z., & Ma, Z. (2015). A novel artificial bee colony based clustering algorithm for categorical data. *PLoS ONE, 10*(5), e0127125. doi:10.1371/journal.pone.0127125 PMID:25993469

Ji, J., Pang, W., Zheng, Y., Wang, Z., Ma, Z., & Zhang, L. (2015). A novel cluster center initialization method for the k-prototypes algorithms using centrality and distance. *Applied Mathematics & Information Sciences, 9*(6), 2933.

Ji, J., Pang, W., Zhou, C., Han, X., & Wang, Z. (2012). A fuzzy k-prototype clustering algorithm for mixed numeric and categorical data. *Knowledge-Based Systems, 30,* 129–135. doi:10.1016/j.knosys.2012.01.006

Karaboga, D., & Ozturk, C. (2011). A novel clustering approach: Artificial Bee Colony (ABC) algorithm. *Applied Soft Computing, 11*(1), 652–657. doi:10.1016/j.asoc.2009.12.025

Kerr, M. K., & Churchill, G. A. (2001). Bootstrapping cluster analysis: Assessing the reliability of conclusions from microarray experiments. *Proceedings of the National Academy of the USA, 98*(16), 8961–8965. doi:10.1073/pnas.161273698 PMID:11470909

Komarasamy, G., & Wahi, A. (2012). An optimized K-means clustering technique using bat algorithm. *European Journal of Scientific Research, 84*(2), 26–273.

Krishna, K., & Murty, M. N. (1999). Genetic K-means algorithm. *IEEE Transactions on Systems, Man, and Cybernetics. Part B, Cybernetics, 29*(3), 433–439. doi:10.1109/3477.764879 PMID:18252317

Krishnamoorthy, S., Sadasivam, G. S., Rajalakshmi, M., Kowsalyaa, K., & Dhivya, M. (2017). Privacy Preserving Fuzzy Association Rule Mining in Data Clusters Using Particle Swarm Optimization. *International Journal of Intelligent Information Technologies, 13*(2), 1–20. doi:10.4018/IJIIT.2017040101

Lakshmi, K., Visalakshi, N. K., & Shanthi, S. (2017). Cuckoo Search based K-Prototype Clustering Algorithm. *Asian Journal of Research in Social Sciences and Humanities, 7*(2), 300–309. doi:10.5958/2249-7315.2017.00092.2

Littmann, T. (2000). An empirical classification of weather types in the Mediterranean Basin and their interrelation with rainfall. *Theoretical and Applied Climatology, 66*(3-4), 161–171. doi:10.1007/s007040070022

Liu, S., & George, R. (2005). *Mining Weather Data using Fuzzy Cluster Analysis.* Berlin: Springer. doi:10.1007/3-540-26886-3_5

Liu, Y., Liu, Y., Wang, L., & Chen, K. (2005). A hybrid tabu search based clustering algorithm. In *Proceedings of the International Conference on Knowledge-Based and Intelligent Information and Engineering Systems* (pp. 186-192). Springer Berlin Heidelberg. doi:10.1007/11552451_25

Lu, J., & Hu, R. (2013). A new hybrid clustering algorithm based on K-means and ant colony algorithm. In *Proceedings of the 2nd International Conference on Computer Science and Electronics Engineering*. doi:10.2991/iccsee.2013.430

Madhuri, R., Murty, M. R., Murthy, J. V. R., Reddy, P. P., & Satapathy, S. C. (2014). Cluster Analysis on Different Data Sets Using K-Modes and K-Prototype Algorithms. In *ICT and Critical Infrastructure: Proceedings of the 48th Annual Convention of Computer Society of India-Vol II* (pp. 137-144). Springer International Publishing. doi:10.1007/978-3-319-03095-1_15

Mei, L., & Xiang-Jun, Z. (2012). A Novel PSO k-Modes Algorithm for Clustering Categorical Data. In Computer, Informatics, Cybernetics and Applications (pp. 1395-1402). Springer Netherlands. doi:10.1007/978-94-007-1839-5_150

Naser, A. M. A., & Alshattnawi, S. (2014). An Artificial Bee Colony (ABC) Algorithm for Efficient Partitioning of Social Networks. *International Journal of Intelligent Information Technologies*, *10*(4), 24–39. doi:10.4018/ijiit.2014100102

Ng, M. K., & Wong, J. C. (2002). Clustering categorical data sets using tabu search techniques. *Pattern Recognition*, *35*(12), 2783–2790. doi:10.1016/S0031-3203(02)00021-3

Pham, D. T., Suarez-Alvarez, M. M., & Prostov, Y. I. (2011). Random search with k-prototypes algorithm for clustering mixed datasets. In *Proceedings of the Royal Society of London A: mathematical, physical and engineering sciences* (Vol. 467, No. 2132, pp. 2387-2403). The Royal Society. doi:10.1098/rspa.2010.0594

Prabha, K. A., & Visalakshi, N. K. (2015). Particle Swarm Optimization based K-Prototype Clustering Algorithm. *Journal of Computer Engineering*, *1*(17), 56–62.

Rand, W. M. (1971). Objective criteria for the evaluation of clustering methods. *Journal of the American Statistical Association*, *66*(336), 846–850. doi:10.1080/01621459.1971.10482356

Rashedi, E., Nezamabadi-Pour, H., & Saryazdi, S. (2009). GSA: A gravitational search algorithm. *Information Sciences*, *179*(13), 2232–2248. doi:10.1016/j.ins.2009.03.004

Santosa, B., & Ningrum, M. K. (2009). Cat swarm optimization for clustering. In *Proceedings of the International Conference of Soft Computing and Pattern Recognition SOCPAR '09* (pp. 54-59). IEEE. doi:10.1109/SoCPaR.2009.23

Selim, S. Z., & Alsultan, K. (1991). A simulated annealing (SA) algorithm for the clustering problem. *Pattern Recognition*, *24*(10), 1003–1008. doi:10.1016/0031-3203(91)90097-O

Shelokar, P. S., Jayaraman, V. K., & Kulkarni, B. D. (2004). An ant colony approach for clustering. *Analytica Chimica Acta*, *509*(2), 187–195. doi:10.1016/j.aca.2003.12.032

Sun, L. X., Xu, F., Liang, Y. Z., Xie, Y. L., & Yu, R. Q. (1994). Cluster analysis by the K-means algorithm and simulated annealing. *Chemometrics and Intelligent Laboratory Systems, 25*(1), 51–60. doi:10.1016/0169-7439(94)00049-2

Tang, R., Fong, S., Yang, X. S., & Deb, S. (2012). Integrating nature-inspired optimization algorithms to K-means clustering. In *Proceedings of the 2012 Seventh International Conference on Digital Information Management (ICDIM)* (pp. 116-123). IEEE.

Tang, R., Fong, S., Yang, X. S., & Deb, S. (2012). Wolf search algorithm with ephemeral memory. In *Proceedings of the 2012 Seventh International Conference on Digital Information Management (ICDIM)* (pp. 165-172). IEEE. doi:10.1109/ICDIM.2012.6360147

Van Den Bergh, F. (2001). *An Analysis of Particle Swarm Optimizers*. PSO.

Van der Merwe, D. W., & Engelbrecht, A. P. (2003). Data clustering using particle swarm optimization. In Proceedings of the 2003 Congress on Evolutionary Computation CEC'03 (Vol. 1, pp. 215-220). IEEE. doi:10.1109/CEC.2003.1299577

Van Rijsbergen, C. J. (1979). Information retrieval. University Of Glasgow.

Wu Sen, C. H., Chen Hong, C. H., & Feng Xiaodong, F. X. (2013). Clustering algorithm for incomplete data sets with mixed numeric and categorical attributes. *International Journal of Database Theory and Application, 6*(5), 95–104. doi:10.14257/ijdta.2013.6.5.09

Yang, X. S. (2010). A new metaheuristic bat-inspired algorithm. In Nature inspired cooperative strategies for optimization (NICSO 2010) (pp. 65-74). Springer Berlin Heidelberg. doi:10.1007/978-3-642-12538-6_6

Yang, X. S. (2010). Firefly algorithm, Levy flights and global optimization. In *Research and development in intelligent systems XXVI* (pp. 209–218). Springer London. doi:10.1007/978-1-84882-983-1_15

Yang, X. S., & Deb, S. (2009). Cuckoo search via Lévy flights. In *Proceedings of the World Congress on Nature and Biologically Inspired Computing NaBIC '09* (pp. 210-214). IEEE.

Yang, X. S., & Deb, S. (2010). Engineering optimisation by cuckoo search. *International Journal of Mathematical Modelling and Numerical Optimisation, 1*(4), 330–343. doi:10.1504/IJMMNO.2010.035430

Yin, J., & Tan, Z. (2005). Clustering mixed type attributes in large dataset. In *Parallel and Distributed Processing and Applications* (pp. 655-661).

Zhang, C., Ouyang, D., & Ning, J. (2010). An artificial bee colony approach for clustering. *Expert Systems with Applications, 37*(7), 4761–4767. doi:10.1016/j.eswa.2009.11.003

Zhao, X., & Lu, M. (2013). 3D Object Retrieval Based on PSO-K-Modes Method. *JSW, 8*(4), 963–970. doi:10.4304/jsw.8.4.963-970

Zheng, Z., Gong, M., Ma, J., Jiao, L., & Wu, Q. (2010). Unsupervised evolutionary clustering algorithm for mixed type data. In *Proceedings of the 2010 IEEE Congress on Evolutionary Computation (CEC)* (pp. 1-8). IEEE. doi:10.1109/CEC.2010.5586136

KEY TERMS AND DEFINITIONS

Clustering: It is data mining technique to discover the hidden relationships between the data. It is the unsupervised learning technique and it groups the data objects without knowing class labels.

Data Mining: It is one of the steps in Knowledge Discovery in Databases (KDD). It discovers the interesting knowledge from large amount of data.

Optimization: These are the techniques to give the best possible solutions for the given objective problems. It minimizes the unfavorable solutions and maximizes the favorable solutions to the given problem.

Section 3
Web-Based Smart Systems

Chapter 11
Smart City Portals for Public Service Delivery:
Insights From a Comparative Study

Christoph Peters
University of St. Gallen, Switzerland & University of Kassel, Germany

Axel Korthaus
Swinburne University of Technology, Australia

Thomas Kohlborn
Sanofi, Australia

ABSTRACT

The future cities of our societies need to integrate their citizens into a value-co-creation process in order to transform to smart cities with an increased quality of life for their citizens. Therefore, administrations need to radically improve the delivery of public services, providing them citizen- and user-centric. In this context, online portals represent a cost effective front-end to deliver services and engage customers and new organizational approaches as back-ends which decouple the service interface from the departmental structures emerged. The research presented in this book chapter makes two main contributions: Firstly, the findings of a usability study comparing the online presences of the Queensland Government, the UK Government and the South Australian Government are reported and discussed. Secondly, the findings are reflected in regard to a broader "Transformational Government" approach and current smart city research and developments. Service bundling and modularization are suggested as innovative solutions to further improve online service delivery.

INTRODUCTION

Digital transformation changes the ways we communicate and how we navigate through our cities (Peters et al. 2016). Our todays and our future cities thereby can be regarded as service systems comprise constellations of resources (Kleinschmidt et al. 2016b) that needs to be designed properly in order to co-create the best results for the end customer (Kleinschmidt et al. 2016a), i.e. the citizen of our future cities.

DOI: 10.4018/978-1-5225-3686-4.ch011

In this context, governments are under continual pressure to improve the delivery of public services in an adequate citizen-friendly manner. Instead of focusing on a specific set of services for targeted customer segments, as is common for organisations in the private sector, the public sector has to deal with a large, heterogeneous portfolio of different services to be offered to all citizens (Wang, Bretschneider, & Gant, 2005). Although different groups of citizens will have different characteristics and demands, accessibility to government services and information has to be ensured (Gouscos, Laskaridis, Lioulias, Mentzas, & Georgiadis, 2002), while at the same time cost efficiency and effectiveness of the service delivery need to be maintained or achieved.

Information and Communication Technology (ICT) has been introduced to offer an increasing number of services electronically, in order to provide the citizens with an online access channel and to decrease the cost of service delivery. These activities can be subsumed under the term e-government, which aims to "...enable and improve the efficiency with which government services and information are provided to citizens, employees, businesses and government agencies..." (Carter & Belanger, 2004, p. 5 f.). With regard to communication channels for delivery of government services, the online channel has probably become the priority for governments, particularly due to its cost efficiency (Ebbers, Pieterson, & Noordman, 2008). Thus, governments have an inherent interest in the adoption of the online service delivery channel by their citizens. Consequently, content and structure of government portals need to focus on those varying needs and aim at the "customers'" (= citizens', residents' and businesses') satisfaction (Kubicek & Hagen, 2000). In light of these requirements, governments have to decide on a specific online service delivery model, which includes both structure and content.

Since the early days of e-government, jurisdictions from an internal managerial perspective have been focusing on standardisation, departmentalisation and operational cost-efficiency, which Ho (2002) has labelled as the traditional bureaucratic paradigm. Often, the way that public services offered to citizens were grouped together was determined by the internal structure of the specific government. Each department offered their services on separate web sites independently from the online offerings of other departments.

E-government has not always delivered all the benefits that were hoped for (Dada, 2006). A more holistic view of government reform strategies has been proposed under the term "Transformational Government", which is defined as "a managed process of ICT-enabled change in the public sector, which puts the needs of citizens and businesses at the heart of that process and which achieves significant and transformational impacts on the efficiency and effectiveness of government" (OASIS, 2012, p. 7). Proponents of the "Transformational Government" approach promote a new business model for governments that introduces "a new virtual business layer within government, focused round the needs of citizens and businesses (the "Franchise Marketplace"), which enables the existing silo-based structure of government to collaborate effectively in understanding and meeting user needs" (OASIS, 2012, p. 16). The "franchise" metaphor is used here to denote collaborative organisations for specific customer segments for government services (e.g. parents, motorists, disabled people), following the principle of "Build services around customer needs, not organisational structure" (OASIS, 2012, p. 13), which requires governments to re-think and re-design their service delivery on all levels of the organisation. At the front end, governments have started to investigate the use of one-stop online portals (OSPs) (Kohlborn, Weiss, Poeppelbuss, Korthaus, & Fielt, 2010) following the desire to further increase customer satisfaction and operational excellence. These portals commonly apply the 'single window concept', i.e. they offer a single point of access to electronic services and information provided by different public authorities or even private service providers (M. Wimmer & Tambouris, 2002).

While the ideas of 'one-stop portal' and 'franchise model' seem appealing, little is known about how governments are actually implementing them. This book chapter describes and critically examines the initiatives of one government organization, Smart Service Queensland (SSQ), in developing a one-stop portal via a usability study from 2009 and 2010 that has been previously published in an article of the International Journal of Intelligent Information Technologies (Kohlborn et al. 2013). The study can be positioned as practice-driven research (Zmud, 1998), where the research team collaborated with SSQ, as sponsor of the research, and a market research company (MR company), as external experts. In this book chapter we include the usability study and also position it within a more recent smart city perspective. The original study was, to the best of the authors' knowledge, the first study reporting in detail on a usability study as part of a market research approach for the development of a governmental one-stop portal. Moreover, based on the market research, the book chapter also provides insights into the relative strengths and weaknesses of the different one-stop portal approaches as used by Queensland Government, the UK Government and the South Australian Government. In addition, a critical reflection on the limitations of the usability study in the context of a broader "Transformational Government" approach is provided and service bundling is suggested as an innovative solution to further improve online service delivery. To position this practice-driven research within the broader academic literature, a structured literature review was conducted first to provide insight into the portal models as currently reported in academic papers. To add to the existing body of literature and to enhance the original publication of the study, we reflect on current smart city approaches and further developments of the transformational government approach in the discussion section.

The remainder of this book chapter is structured as follows. The next section introduces the practical context of this study. Thereafter, an overview of the current literature in this field is provided. In particular, a structured literature review has been conducted to identify related work focusing on assessing satisfaction with online portals. The following section is dedicated to presenting the objectives of the usability study, describing the particular setting of the market research approach and outlining the roles of both the company conducting the market research sessions and the university researchers acting in the role of critical observers. After outlining the used research method, we describe the sample selection process and its reasoning. Then, we provide a detailed description of the report created by the conductor of the market research sessions before we present our critical reflections as the sessions' observers. Additionally, we will discuss the development towards "Transformational Government" in some detail in the critical reflection section of this book chapter and reflect on the current developments in regard to the results of our study. The conclusions summarise the most important findings and highlight the contribution to the field.

PRACTICAL CONTEXT

Smart Service Queensland (SSQ) is an Australian state government agency that serves as the "front door" to the public by delivering all services offered by the Queensland Government to businesses and citizens. SSQ decided to advance the maturity of their online service delivery. This involved the identification of the benefits of alternative service delivery models as well as the corresponding implementation steps required. As a foundation, an investigation of the relative performance of the current online presence of the Queensland Government compared to the online presences of the United Kingdom (UK) Government, one of the leaders in e-government (Accenture, 2009; United Nations, 2008), and the South

Australian Government was commissioned. Both the UK Government and the South Australian Government have adopted the "franchise" approach. The aim of the investigation of the study described in this book chapter was to understand citizens' preferred model for interacting in the online channel and to identify the relative strengths and weaknesses of the existing websites. The market research (MR) was conducted by an expert service provider in the field, from now on referred to as MR company, and involved a representative sample of the Queensland public to assess all three websites.

Having collaborated with the Queensland Government in the context of the Smart Services CRC, the researchers were asked to accompany and contribute to this research commissioned by SSQ. The researchers' project work focuses on service portfolios in both the private and public sector, and, within this context, puts particular attention to service bundles and their strategic role within service portfolios. The researchers participated in the market research sessions as critical observers, which allowed gaining important and valuable insights feeding into the research agenda of the larger collaborative research initiative.

This book chapter will revisit the findings of the commissioned market research and reflect on the observations made in this study, which has previously been reported in Peters et al. (2011)[1]. In addition, we have extended our previous study by reflecting on the status-quo of research on assessing satisfaction of online portals in the relevant body of knowledge. The findings of the usability study produced by the MR company and the critical reflection contributed by the authors of this book chapter not only provide important insights for the governmental partner regarding current opinions and behaviours of a representative sample of its target users. Even if their generalizability is limited, they will also be of interest to all governments that are currently on the verge of considering the development of a one-stop portal as a part of their journey towards the next stage of e-government, i.e. transformational government, as currently drafted and proposed by the Organization for the Advancement of Structured Information Standards (OASIS). By positioning the study against the background of a comprehensive transformational government approach and discussing the potential benefits of service bundling, which matches the idea of creating customer franchises but remained largely unconsidered in the study, the book chapter also makes an academic contribution and extends the existing body of knowledge with regard to service bundling and service portfolios in the public sector.

LITERATURE REVIEW

Overview

In this section, we focus on evaluating online service delivery through governmental portals only and leave the discussion of the broader context of transformational government to the critical reflection section further below.

Mahdavi, Shepherd, & Benatallah (2004) characterise portals as Internet-based applications, which enable users to access information from different sources through a single interface. According to the Oxford English Dictionary (Anonymous, 1989), a portal is defined as: "…a web site or service that provides access to a number of sources of information and facilities, such as a directory of links to other web sites, search engines, email, online shopping, etc."

Utilising a portal has several advantages for the user (Lim et al., 2002). On the one hand, portals are supposed to offer information from different sources in a well-categorised manner, so that the user can relatively easily identify information that is of relevance to him/her. On the other hand, portals typically offer some sort of search capability that enables the user to query indexed resources. However, simply focusing on implementing some categorisation of information and search capabilities does not ensure the adoption of a portal by its intended target users. The quality of the portal has been put forward by some authors as the main reason why users return to a portal (Offutt, 2002).

In order to identify the status-quo of evaluating quality and satisfaction in the context of portals in the government domain, a structured literature review has been conducted.

Approach to Structured Literature Review

The literature review presented in this study draws from articles published in journals, as they typically publish mature, validated and peer-reviewed research findings. Rankings for journals within the domain of e-government do not yet exist. However, having identified this issue, Scholl (2009) profiled the e-government research community and identified core sources based on different criteria. These were included as sources for the literature review:

- Government Information Quarterly (GIQ).
- Electronic Government, an International Journal (EG).
- Transforming Government: People, Process and Policy (TGPPP).
- Information Polity: The International Journal of Government & Democracy in the Information Age (IP).
- International Journal of Electronic Government Research (IJEGR).
- Electronic Journal of e-Government (EJEG).
- Journal of Information Technology & Politics (JITP).

Additionally, the ProQuest and EBSCO databases have also been utilised for conducting the review.

Following the search strategy proposed by Leidner & Kayworth (2006), a systematic keyword search was executed and the references of an article and further work of the same author(s) were examined if the analysis of an article resulted in new insights. After brainstorming on potential keywords and related synonyms, it was decided to use the search phrase ((portal) AND (government* OR "public domain" OR "public sector" OR" public administration") AND (satisfaction OR quality)) to conduct the search in the title, abstract and keywords of the publications within the ProQuest and EBSCO databases, which resulted in 36 (three relevant) and 23 (three relevant) hits respectively.

The queries of the journals (except for IP, which was fully covered by ProQuest, and IJEGR, which was screened manually) were conducted using the search functionality provided on the respective journal's website with the search term "portal". In total, 53 results were received, but upon closer examination only eight publications turned out to be relevant for the objectives of the study. Based on these publications, different e-portal quality models for the public sector are listed and described in the following.

Analysis and Comparison

Table 1 provides a tabular overview of the identified portal models. The column 'Author (Year)' details the last names of the authors of the related publication and the year the model was published. The col-

Table 1. Portal models for the public sector

Author (Year)	Focus	Perspective	Construct of analysis	Dimensions	Conceptualisation	Validation
Sutherland, Wildemuth, Campbell, Haines (2005)	Nutrition portal	P	Quality	Content (accuracy, currency), usability (navigation, quality of links, aesthetics and affect)	T	N/A (A)
Choudrie, Ghinea, & Weerakkody (2004)	Web site diagnostic tools	P	Quality	Accessibility, quality, and privacy	N/A	N/A (A)
Tripathi, Gupta, & Bhattacharya (2011)	Portal in India	P	Integration	Process integration, data integration, communication integration	B	N/A
Henriksson, Frost, & Middleton (2007)	Website in Australia	P	Quality	Security/privacy, usability, content, services, citizen participation, features	B	N/A
Lai & Pires (2010)	Portal in Macao	C	Satisfaction and adoption	Information quality, perceived effectiveness, system quality, social influence	T	E

umn titled 'Focus' provides information with regard to the specific area or domain that has been used for assessing quality.

The 'Perspective' differentiates between the provider (P) and consumer (C) perspective on quality. The provider perspective typically is based on a content analysis of the respective unit of analysis (e.g. website). In particular, the unit of analysis is analysed with regard to the provided features and characteristics, such as the existence of 'contact information' as part of a website, for example. The consumer perspective typically is based on involving the consumer directly, to elicit the perception of quality via interviews, focus groups, or surveys. A consumer side analysis of the government website or portal requires the conceptualisation of different constructs that are considered to be related to the user's perception of quality and satisfaction, which is similar to the requirements for utilising content analysis. The main difference lies in the way to measure or operationalise the constructs. The focus of such studies is on the end users' perception of these constructs, so they require end user participation either in interviews or by answering various questions as part of a survey or questionnaire (Kaisara & Pather, 2011). Although each model contains a construct that represents 'quality', the model itself might focus on a different construct, e.g. behavioural intention.

Information about the 'Construct of analysis' is provided in the respective column. The target construct is typically represented or measured via multiple dimensions or factors, each in turn measured by multiple items that, however, are not depicted in the following table.

The column 'Dimensions of the quality construct' lists the labels of these dimensions that have been used by the respective authors to evaluate quality. The last two columns, 'Conceptualisation' and 'Validation', provide information about the approach that has been taken in developing and testing the model. The conceptualisation of the model can, to a large extent, be based on theoretical approaches (T), which encompasses the review of related literature or theories. Alternatively, it can be based on empirical approaches (E), which encompass the involvement of people to identify dimensions and items of relevance to quality. Additionally, both approaches may have been utilised in conceptualising the model (B). The validation can also be differentiated on the basis of these three approaches (B, T, and E), although the research methods might differ with regard to the conceptualisation. For the theoretical validation, for example, formal approaches might be used (T), whereas for empirical validation, questionnaires and surveys might be appropriate (E). Sometimes, no statistical validation is made, but an application of the evaluation instrument can be focussed on (N/A (A)).

The identified models typically employ a provider perspective and none of them is purely built on empirical research methods. 'Integration' has been proposed as a major aspect in evaluating a quality model for the public sector. Compared to 'satisfaction', the majority of models focus on 'quality'; however, it has been identified that both constructs are different but very closely related (Sureshchandar, Rajendran, & Anantharaman, 2002), which means that an increase in one is likely to correlate with an increase in the other. Only one of the identified models has been rigorously evaluated utilising empirical data. The conceptualisation of the instruments has either been done purely theoretically or has involved some kind of empirical analysis. None of the approaches is solely based on empirical data gained from focus groups, interviews, or Delphi Studies.

It is interesting to note that no models contain the same dimensions or focus on the same scope. Next to 'integration', 'privacy' and 'security' seem to be important, but these dimensions have not been mentioned by more than two publications. It seems that there is limited overlap in the dimensions uncovered by different studies, which also characterises the research domain around e-service quality (Hofacker, Goldsmith, Bridges, & Swilley, 2007, p. 18). Besides these dimensions ('system quality' also belongs to them) which mainly focus on functional and technical attributes, other important dimensions can be revealed from the found publications. 'Content' or 'information quality' clearly state the need for governments to be a trustworthy service provider delivering precise and up-to-date information. 'Usability' as well as 'perceived effectiveness' emphasise the ease-of-use which is expected when handling such services. 'Accessibility' and related aspects play – in contrast to non-governmental portals – a key role and represent a mandatory requirement for government portals as all citizens need to be supported. The dimension 'citizen participation' reflects a consequence of the citizens' every-day private online life, i.e. citizens might expect government portals to offer ways of participation they are familiar with due to experience with Web 2.0 environments. In sum, the found publications present a heterogeneous field of dimensions. Thus, future research should focus on properly conceptualising dimensions for portal quality and satisfaction in the e-government domain by theoretical as well as empirical approaches.

Overall, the search yielded only a limited number of results, which hints at either limited relevance in the domain or at a gap in the literature that should be addressed. Given that the idea of Transformational Government is emerging and OSPs start to play a major role in the online delivery of services, the latter scenario is more likely. The first manuscript on portal satisfaction/quality in the e-government domain was published in 2004, which underlines the infancy of this research domain.

Having discussed these results, we now have a closer look at the status quo of the three online portals of the examined jurisdictions and how the findings of our literature review are realized in the service delivery models.

OBJECTIVES AND METHODOLOGY OF USABILITY STUDY

Objectives of the Usability Study

Each department of the Queensland Government has its own (sub-) website and is responsible for delivering all relevant services within that online area. The (sub-) websites of the departments are linked within the Queensland Government's portal, which basically functions as a gateway. Contrarily, the UK one-stop portal aims at providing access to information and government services in one place based on presenting customer-oriented bundles of services to the customers. It is important to note that the boundaries of these bundles cannot be seen as the boundaries between the existing departments. They are much more flexible, taking into account that users digest provided government services differently. The bundle-approach is supposed to lead to a much more citizen-centric service provision when implemented adequately. In order to analyse the potential effect of cultural influences, the portal of South Australia has been included in the study. South Australia is currently implementing a one-stop portal for their online delivery of services. However, the portal cannot be considered as mature as its UK counterpart.

In this context, as mentioned earlier, the overall goal for SSQ was "to gather a holistic view of what customers think of the proposed franchise model of online government services and identify any problems with various models." The study's objective included, as mentioned earlier, to understand customers' preferred model for interacting with Queensland Government in the online channel, and to understand the relative strengths and weaknesses of existing websites and approaches for presenting government information online.

The market research sessions of the MR company were designed to address the following questions, among others:

- How do customers locate government information and what are paths commonly taken to find information?
- Do customers get confused when navigating between portal sites and agency sites and vice-versa and does this affect their user experience?
- What overall model do customers prefer based on their use of various government sites?
- Which overall model is more efficient for customers?

Questions that guided the critical reflection of the study by the authors of this book chapter were intended to provide further insight for addressing SSQ's overall goal stated above:

- Was the study comprehensive enough to establish superiority of a particular service delivery model?
- How can the study be positioned with regard to the larger goal of embarking on a transformational government reform strategy?
- Which role can service bundling play in a franchise-based service delivery model context to improve customer satisfaction?

Methodology of the Usability Study

From a methodology perspective, two aspects need to be clearly separated.

Firstly, the design of the market study will be described. It is important to note that this design was beyond the control of the researchers, as it was the responsibility of the MR company. The market research can be characterised as an observational usability study (Nielsen 1993) in an experimental setting. An observational approach provides several advantages and disadvantages. The main benefits are twofold. First, the reality aspect is prevalent, i.e. the study covers events in real time. Second, also the concept is captured. As disadvantages one can regard its time-consumptive characteristic and the threat that the study proceeds differently, because participants are feeling unfamiliar with being observed while performing the task. The latter disadvantage could be mitigated through the setting described below.

The observation was conducted in a permanent usability laboratory at the facilities of the contractor the Queensland Government had selected. As recommended by Nielsen (1993), the facilities comprised two main rooms: a test room and an observation room. The participant and a facilitator were sitting in the test room. From here, the participant's face and his/her screen were videotaped and the sound (the participant's oral expressions) was captured. Thus, the think aloud method could be applied. This method is designed to not only capture the final task completion, but also its process. In addition, it encourages the user to articulate whatever he/she does (Lewis & Rieman, 1993). The advantages of participants thinking aloud are various, e.g. one can anticipate and trace the source of problems much more easily (Rubin & Chisnell, 2008).

Two of the authors of this book chapter were sitting in the observation room, accompanied by delegates from our government partner. Within the observation room, the screen of the participant and the face of the participant were projected via a data projector. This was supported by a usability testing and market research software, which also reproduced the sound from the test room, i.e. the articulated thoughts and answers of the participant as well as the questions of the facilitator. This highly recommended setting allowed us to discuss user actions without disturbing the user when they occurred. As these sessions were also recorded, it is also possible to re-examine them. Each session was conducted within a 90 minute timeframe and with one participant only.

The participants were supposed to be a representative sample of the Queensland public. 44 market research sessions were conducted in both urban (61%) and rural areas (39%), with participants that have not participated in any web usability testing within the last 6 months. The number of male and female participants did not differ more than 20% overall. Also, other demographical requirements to ensure representativeness of the sample, such as age groups, educational and occupational background, household incomes and Internet usage confidence, were taken into account. As an integral prerequisite, participants had to have used a Queensland Government website in the past 6 months. The sample included business owners, indigenous Australians and people who have a visual or cognitive impairment. As incentive, all participants received 75AUD for the session.

The second aspect, from a methodology perspective, relates to the contribution made by the authors of this book chapter. The aim of the qualitative research was to provide a critical reflection of the study based on the researchers' involvement as session observers and to theorise by anchoring the observations in the broader literature on transformational government. The approach can be categorised as explorative research, as the problem has no clear definition yet and more insight is required. The objective of exploratory research is to gather preliminary information that will help define problems and suggest hypotheses. In the following, we will start by describing the findings from the market study in more detail.

FINDINGS FROM THE USABILITY STUDY

Based on the analysis of the data that was captured during the market research sessions, the MR company presented the following key findings in their report, which we will briefly summarise below:

Search Engine Optimization

In an attempt to answer the first study question, the pathways chosen by participants to find government information have been examined. The goal was to identify how website visitors use and navigate through government websites and to better understand the natural browsing habits of the participants. Therefore, participants were asked to recreate a service encounter that they had recently performed visiting the Queensland Government websites. Taking into account the findings of analysing the navigation paths of all participants, mostly four distinct first steps were taken to arrive at the relevant services, which are displayed in Table 2. Users either used the search engine 'Google' as a starting point or they tried to find information starting at the respective government's or department's website. However, most users were unaware of the governments' website address. Navigation paths comprised in "Others" in Table 1 are for example other search engines such as Microsoft's Bing. For all three websites, at least 80% of the users started their search for a service with the search engine Google.

The results clearly show that Google as the Internet's most favoured search engine plays the dominant role regarding pathways to government websites. Thus, the report concludes, search engine optimisation is critical, so that Queensland Government sites are ranked highly for key search terms. Thereby, explicit consideration should be placed on the fact that several users ignored sponsored links.

User Satisfaction

The next aspect examined was the preferred model for interacting with government online. Users were asked to complete a task on one of the three government websites which they already attempted on the Queensland Government website during the last six months. After completion of these so-called "real-life" tasks, the users were asked to rank the websites in order of personal preference. For the highest preference three points were given, two points for the second highest and one point, respectively, for the lowest preference. As a result, users were in favour of the websites of South Australia and Queensland with both 43 points versus 28 points for the UK Government sites. The preference for the Australian sites was explained with the higher level of familiarity due to two facts: the tasks were already performed at Queensland's Government websites before and the UK websites included linguistic particularities the Australian test users were not used to. Also, the consistent user experience layout of the Queensland

Table 2. Comparative overview of starting points for finding a service

	Queensland	**South Australia**	**United Kingdom**
Google	82%	80%	87%
Government homepage	6%	12%	9%
Department site	7%	3%	1%
Others	5%	5%	3%

websites featuring a prominent Queensland Government logo was perceived more trustworthy than the brandings of the UK government sites called DirectGov and Businesslink, which are perceived as "made-up" by the users. For government websites, users prefer the government to be mentioned explicitly.

In order to identify an overall preferred model, users were then asked to perform a number of prescribed tasks. After a participant completed all tasks for one website, they were asked to evaluate the website in five different categories on a scale between 0 (strongly disagree) and 10 (strongly agree). The rating criteria and results of this assessment were chosen by the MR company and are displayed in Table 3:

These results are described as minor differences between the regions in the report. Still, it is outlined that Queensland performed lowest on all levels of satisfaction.

After all tasks were performed, users were asked to rank the three websites in order of preference again. This was done to capture the difference in perceived usability before and after the execution of prescribed tasks. Interestingly, a "significant switch" of preference could be monitored and the websites of the UK (49% of votes as most preferred model) outperformed the websites of South Australia (23%) and Queensland (28%) clearly. Some users had difficulties to choose their preferred model. They liked the level of information on the websites based on the franchise service delivery model and "the way in which it was set out", but were more familiar with the Queensland websites based on the traditional approach. The report draws attention to the test environment this switch was achieved in and concludes that in the real world such a change of preference could take much more time as users do not perform as many tasks as in the testing scenario. The report also distinguishes between users from Brisbane and Rockhampton as well as between general users, business users and customer service advisors of the Queensland Government, but due to the limited space these aspects are left out of this book chapter. The report summarises by stating that "users are currently satisfied with the existing Queensland approach, but prefer franchise sites after frequent use" and in terms of satisfaction all three regions performed to a "relatively similar standard". As users were also asked to highlight 10 out of 50 adjectives after they had completed all tasks for one website, so-called word clouds could be created. In this context, the UK Government site's word cloud particularly highlights words such as understandable, convenient, usable, useful and detailed. The choice of adjectives was not as positive for the other two websites.

Efficiency and Ease-of-Use of the Websites

The comparison of the service delivery models in regard to efficiency is measured by a task completion rate. The completion rate was assessed by the session conductors after each task. The possible ratings were: 'Easy' (task is completed easily), 'Medium' (user took one or two attempts, and experienced some difficulty), 'Hard' (user took more than two attempts, and/or experienced a great deal of difficulty) and

Table 3. User satisfaction for each criterion for each region after all tasks for a website were completed

Criterion	Queensland (QLD)	South Australia (SA)	United Kingdom (UK)
Right level of detail	7.71	8.26	8.43
Reliability	8.45	8.79	8.55
Easy to complete	6.93	8.21	8.02
Clear and easy to understand	7.36	8.24	8.07
Visually appealing	6.85	7.38	7.20

'Fail' (user was not able to complete the task). Here, the UK sites had the lowest completion rates – despite the fact that they were the most preferred ones. Overall, the report states that "no single model appears to be more efficient and easier for users" and when looking at overall completion rates, all three regions were very close and there is no clear leader. As implications, it is noteworthy to consider the following factors which highly influence user satisfaction: visual design (including consistency), trustworthiness and credibility of the site, information design and previous experiences on these sites. The report concludes that "users must be able to complete their tasks with relative ease whichever model is chosen". However, it states that the franchise approach can be advantageous because of the "overall consistency of experience" that can be offered and the possibility to enable a consistent management of search engine optimisation across all areas of government responsibility.

Content of Websites

Users appreciate websites that provide relevant information in a format that supports readability and that is clear and concise. Therefore, the report states that "content is critical". In comparison over all provided services, a high-level consistency of quality content is what users are looking for. Delivery models which support the users by providing content of high quality and enable intuitive findability are going to outperform other models. The UK and the South Australia model delivered a consistent experience in terms of content at the right level of detail for their users, which was highly appreciated. The report also states that in order to control the content quality of the websites, the according group in charge needs to be "sufficiently resourced with appropriately skilled people".

Linking to Multiple Websites

The next objective was to investigate the users' awareness of pathways. While most users were at least peripherally aware, some users did not recognise when they were being taken to other websites, sometimes even when there were changes in the graphical layout of the websites. In the case of the Queensland Government websites they often did not notice, presumably due to the consistency of the layout which creates a consistent user experience. As an interesting finding, some users stated that they do not care about being taken from site to site – as long as they find the information they are searching for. A more critical factor for government sites are signs for credibility such as the domain-ending ".gov" in the address bar or specific government logos. Additionally, graphical guidance and orientation, e.g. through the use of so-called breadcrumbs (a navigation aid that shows the page's location in the website hierarchy in a compact manner) - as used in the websites of South Australia - were perceived helpful. Although users are unconcerned with being linked to multiple websites, the franchise sites were ranked higher overall than the Queensland site, because the users found that the websites based on the franchise model were "easy to use" and "everything they needed was just there".

Distribution of Content Between Websites

The superior role of the UK model was also supported by the users' comments that they liked "size and simplicity of the [UK] website". The report suspects that the preference for the UK website goes back to the size and simplicity of the website and the proportion of content that has been migrated to the franchise site – compared to content that is still available on the different government department websites. More specifically, the franchise service delivery model does not provide the full scope of government services on the portal itself. For certain services, the user has to visit specific agency websites for their consumption. The MR company assumed that only 10% of all UK government information is migrated to the portal site. Based on the MR company's experience, they suspect that the Pareto principle is applicable, which states that 80% of the users look for 20% of the content published on the website. Building on that statement, it is brought forward that only the most popular content should be centralised in a portal, but not more than 20%, and the long tail of the rest of the services should be kept on the departmental websites. The report assumes that there might be a "sweet spot" for the right proportion of content to be migrated. Whichever proportion is chosen, this should be closely and continuously monitored and adapted accordingly.

CRITICAL REFLECTION

Overview

In the following critical reflection, we will briefly revisit some of the findings of the report to offer additional considerations, particularly with regard to the potential role of service bundles in one-stop portals, an area that needs future research beyond the study presented in this book chapter in order to better evaluate the full potential of a franchised approach. Related to these considerations, we are going to discuss the role of the study in the context of a more comprehensive reform strategy towards transformative government. We also add current developments which have taken place since 2009 and take a smart city perspective.

User Preference Between Websites

With regard to the objective of understanding the relative strengths and weaknesses of the existing websites as perceived by users, the study has produced some interesting and important insights as summarised in the last section of this book chapter. However, no strong conclusions could be drawn. Although the report states that "Users are currently satisfied with the existing Queensland approach, but prefer franchise sites after frequent use", it also comes to the conclusion "that there are no significant differences in overall user satisfaction ratings between each model" and that no single model appears to be more efficient and easier for users.

Yet, revisiting the outcomes of the preference assessment, it appears to be important to direct attention towards the switch in user preferences. The participants were twice asked to rank the existing websites in order of preference. For the first time, they had to make the assessment after they finished the user-generated tasks, i.e. the ones they had already performed before. The second assessment occurred after the users had finished the prescribed tasks. Table 4 shows the preferred government websites of the participants at these two different stages.

With regard to the first assessment, one has to keep in mind that the users re-created a 'real-life' task which they had already executed at the Queensland Government website before (within the last six months). This characteristic most likely explains the high preference rate at this stage for Queensland's websites, particularly due to the users' familiarity with this task on the website. It is more surprising that the South Australian government websites could position themselves at the top of the ranking. The fact

Table 4. Preferred government websites before and after the prescribed tasks

	Queensland	South Australia	United Kingdom
Before the prescribed tasks	42%	47%	11%
After the prescribed tasks	28%	23%	49%

that the government website of the United Kingdom was hardly mentioned as a first choice is likely to correlate with the participants' familiarity with Australian government structures as also mentioned in the report. However, the change of preference in favour of the UK Government websites after the previously unknown prescribed tasks were performed was very strong and demands a closer look for explanation. The UK Government has the most comprehensive implementation of a franchised approach, whereas South Australia had only partially realised the approach when the study was done. Also, it should be noted again that after all tasks were performed, the current Queensland Government website was rated lowest (see Table 3), i.e. the satisfaction rates for franchise-based service delivery models outweighed the ratings for the traditional approach in each of the five categories user satisfaction were examined.

Measuring Satisfaction

The five criteria that were chosen to 'measure' satisfaction have not been applied in this form in past research efforts as presented in the literature review section. Typically, 'satisfaction' is measured by 3-4 reflective items along statements like 'I am satisfied with the presented portal' (Lai & Pires, 2010). 'Satisfaction' is then influenced by other constructs, such as 'System Quality', which, in turn, is measured by a number of items. At this level, statements, similar to the ones chosen by the MR company in this study, can be found. However, the statements typically relate to different constructs. For example, Lai & Pires (2010) relate 'clear design' and 'ease of use' (similar to 'Clear and easy to understand', in this study) to 'System Quality', whereas Sutherland et al. (2005) relate 'aesthetics and affect' (similar to 'visually appealing', in this study) to 'usability'. Thus, the items chosen by the MR company seem to relate to different facets or constructs that might (or might not) influence 'satisfaction'. The design of the statements does not allow drawing statistically valid conclusions in this regard. However, they provide first insights into facets that differ between the analysed portals, which might be sufficient, if statistical analysis is not a feasible option due to insufficient numbers of participants.

It is important to state that in the last decade the digital transformation of society and our daily lives has highly affected the typical technology use and the expectations of ICT-enabled offers. This should be considered in all new smart city initiatives and projects.

Utilisation of Service Bundles as Part of the Franchise Approach

On a more general level, one might challenge the study's ability to fully assess users' preferences for the different service delivery models. The underlying question is, how would online service delivery of a government that uses franchises in the backend differ from one that does not, and was the study suitable to capture that potential difference to the full extent? The report alludes to the potential benefits of the franchise approach by stating that the approach can be advantageous because of the "overall consistency of experience" that can be offered and the possibility to enable a consistent management of search engine optimisation across all areas of government responsibility. However, beyond that an important aspect would be that a franchised website is aimed at offering more citizen-centric service bundles (groupings of services) in the information architecture. For example, Kernaghan & Berardi (2001) distinguish three types of bundling, namely bundles based on life events, bundles based on demographics such as seniors or disabled people and bundles based on topics such as 'tourism' or 'health'. These service bundles can be mapped to the franchise organisations in the virtual business layer of the government, i.e., each service bundle represents an aggregated offering of the services the corresponding user franchise organisation is responsible for. The main benefit of such service bundles is that they group services together which are related to specific needs or customer segments and typically would be consumed together or at least, by being presented together as a group, fulfil an important information function with regard to the offered portfolio of services that are related to that specific need.

Due to testing that was mainly based on unrelated prescribed tasks, the study could not fully appreciate the potential benefits of customer segment-specific or need-specific service bundles (franchises). Although government websites are often not browsed through on a very regular and frequent basis (in contrast to news or social networking portals) but are visited having a dedicated purpose in mind, namely to access a specific government service, the "cross-selling" of government services (and possibly even external services) based on their offering in topical service bundles could potentially be a very positive influencing factor on user satisfaction in the longer term relationship with the government. This effect could not be tested based on the design of the current study.

An approach leveraging the idea of service bundles to the maximum will also potentially have an impact on navigability, intuitiveness, ease of use and overall user experience. The report focuses strongly on the initial navigation pathway that brings users to the government website that offers the service the user is looking for. It stresses the importance of the "Google" search engine and derives from this insight recommendations with regard to search engine optimisation. However, it does not investigate the potential benefits of improving navigability etc. within the domain of government websites, facilitated by the service bundle concept. The main scenario described in the report is the one in which the user arrives at the government website on the exact page of the specific service that was searched for. Still, it is desirable for the government to guarantee that users see more than only the service they searched for (cross-selling). By increasing customer awareness of the content offering over time cross-selling reduces customer effort and retains customers in the cost-effective online channel. Therefore, the government needs to provide other relevant links and related services as well as a straightforward navigation structure that does not confuse the customer. An approach based on service bundles can accomplish this requirement. Service bundles themselves can either consist of services with a high topic-originated relatedness or they might be useful in the environment of a specific life-event such as "getting married" (Wimmer, 2002). What is of utmost importance is that instead of a strict alignment of services with specific government departments, as it is common in the traditional approach, it is the understandability and intuition for the customer that counts and is put into practice using the service bundle approach. Departments keep changing their names, and the franchise approach with corresponding service bundles at the front end frees citizens from the need to have detailed knowledge about the machinery of government. As the MR report already points out, one of the "pros" of the UK Government franchised approach is that "users do not need to know which department looks after their specific enquiry – the information is arranged according to topic, rather than department." This development hints to a philosophical shift in government from agency-centric to customer-centric service delivery that service bundling exemplifies so well. Moving from department-structure to bundles is the first (and arguably largest) culture shift, and it paves the way for changing the focus to meeting customer needs and reducing customer effort.

In order to integrate a service bundling strategy, one has to consider design services which are both, highly efficient and customer-centric for the citizens of a smart city. In this regard, the modularization of services and corresponding systematic approaches (Peters 2015) should be considered.

Positioning This Study's Objective

From a bigger picture, it is important to note that the study discussed here is a usability study only. While it was conducted having the objective in mind to "gather a holistic view of what customers think of the proposed franchise model of online Government services", it has to be stated very clearly that a usability study alone cannot probe the core of the franchise approach as proposed, e.g., by the OASIS Transformational Government Framework (TGF) (OASIS, 2012). The reason for this lies in the much broader view that this proposed approach takes, as it "aims beyond purely technical aspects of better enabling e-government processes towards addressing the cultural and organisational barriers which have hindered public service benefits realisation." By encompassing "a new 'virtual' business layer within government which allows an integrated, government-wide, citizen-focused service to be presented to citizens across all channels, but at no extra cost and without having to restructure government to do so", it addresses not only the online channel of service delivery, but also all other channels such as call centres and over-the-counter services or other frontline public services in an integrated way. Thus, the online front-end is just one single element that might reflect changes based on the adoption of a franchise model, but most likely not the essential one.

The "Franchise Marketplace" as the virtual business infrastructure within which "Customer Franchises" collaborate with each other and other stakeholders to deliver user-centric, trusted and interoperable content and transactions to citizens and businesses lies at the conceptual heart of the Transformational Government approach.

According to OASIS (2012), the "Customer Franchises" as collaborative organisations created by the government serve purposes of "understanding the needs of a specific customer segment for government services (such as, for example, parents, motorists, disabled people, land and property); championing the needs of that segment within government; aggregating content and transactions for that segment across government and beyond; and delivering that content and services as part of the wider Franchise Marketplace" (OASIS, 2012).

Due to the holistic nature of the approach, the journey towards a Transformational Government reform involves much more than just restructuring the online channel or implementing a one-stop portal. The Transformational Government Framework has been specified by the OASIS Technical Committee and builds the basis for a first smart city standard (OASIS 2014). In 2010, it was still in its planning phase and included a series of policy documents necessary to implement the change, a value chain for citizen service transformation, a series of guiding principles, a business model for change, a best practice delivery roadmap and a checklist of critical success factors. Transformational Government is a far reaching organisational strategy to meet expectations "to deliver better and more services for less cost whilst maintaining high-level oversight and governance". As done for other domains (Peters et al. 2015), the study of business model patterns where the franchise approach is only one potential pattern for successful smart city implementations deems appropriate.

Comparative usability testing as in the case of the study discussed in this book chapter can only be one element to support decision making processes in governments that consider embarking on a government transformation process leveraging the franchise service delivery model in its entirety. However, it should be noted that usability testing can be a good way to measure an organisation's commitment to customer-centricity, which will be the key determining factor in the success of any service-delivery channel.

In regards to the franchise approach, it can be stated that further development needed to take place and has taken place, e.g. as the "British Smart Cities Specification" uses the OASIS "Transformational Government Framework" (OASIS 2014).

When thinking of smart cities and future cities we want to live in, recommendations such as "be obsessive about understanding your customers" or "build services around citizens, not organizational structures" (CSTransform 2010) are crucial. Also, interoperability of systems and solutions (CSTransform 2011) needs to be considered. Thereby, the further development of standards as already realized (OASIS 2014; The British Standards Institution 2014) are equally important than finding innovative ways to activate and incentivize citizens active involvement, e.g. as implemented with the European passport for active citizenship (European Economic and Social Committee 2015), for the citizen side. For the provider and government side, joint efforts and working groups and the collection and analysis of good practices and case studies as documented in (National League of Cities 2016) are worthwhile to consider and might be useful, especially in regards to not reinventing the wheel city-by-city. If decision makers of municipalities realize and embrace the fact that "new technologies can support more effective joint working, and new and more collaborative relationships with the citizen" (UK Department for Business Innovation and Skills 2014), we are getting closer to cities that really become smarter.

CONCLUSION

Smart cities have at least two highly important stakeholders in regards to service delivery: citizens and the government and community being responsible for the service delivery. In this context, the perspective of the city as a service system with citizens that are co-creators of services is important. Thereby, transformational government approaches have shown that they can potentially have a large impact on how government services are provided and used. While the potential benefits are appealing, it also comes with a substantial investment and risk. Therefore, gaining a deeper insight into the actual implementation and sharing lessons learned is paramount from an academic as well as from a practical perspective. This study looked in particular into the implementation of the 'one-stop portal' concept and followed a practice-driven approach based on the collaboration between Smart Service Queensland (SSQ), responsible for developing a governmental one-stop portal, and the researchers. This study of this book chapter is, as far as we know, the first reporting in detail on the development of a governmental one-stop portal, in particular a usability study based on a market research approach.

This book chapter presented and discussed the findings of a usability study commissioned by SSQ, which included a comparative assessment of three governmental web sites, of which two followed a franchise approach, by a representative sample of the Queensland public, and reflected on the observations made in that study. With regard to the objective of understanding the relative strengths and weaknesses of the existing websites as perceived by users, the study has produced some interesting and important insights. A critical reflection pointed out potential limitations of the study's design as it does not allow testing potential benefits of presenting service bundles (based on the organisational franchises in the background) to citizens and businesses. By prescribing individual tasks to be performed, the advantage of collocating services in bundles based on an analysis of citizen needs and expectations were not tested. Besides the limitations described in the critical reflections section, it has to be considered that implementation of the proposed service delivery model requires a high level of top management support. This is especially due to existing power structures within and between different government departments. Also, required implementation efforts might vary significantly depending on the complexity of the government structure, e.g. consider the United States federal government structures versus those of Hong Kong or Singapore as city states.

In terms of our practical contributions, the findings are of interest to all governments that are currently on the verge of considering the development of a one-stop portal as a part of their journey towards the next stage of becoming a smart city and trying to implement according standards. By positioning the study against the background of a comprehensive transformational government approach and discussing the potential benefits of service bundling, which maps to the idea of creating customer franchises but remained largely unconsidered in the study, the study presented in this book chapter also makes an academic contribution and extends the existing body of knowledge with regard to service bundling and service portfolios in the public sector. Extending the service bundling idea to modular service structures that are valuable for the provider and the citizen side are worth studying. Also, the perspective of service systems that consider the heterogeneity of citizens and stakeholders of our future smart cities, should be taken in interdisciplinary research approaches in order to arrive at citizen-centric solutions.

ACKNOWLEDGMENT

This research was carried out as part of the activities of, and funded by, the Smart Services Cooperative Research Centre (CRC) through the Australian Government's CRC Programme (Department of Innovation, Industry, Science and Research). The responsibility for the content of this publication lies with the authors. We would also like to thank Smart Services Queensland for giving us the opportunity to collaboratively conduct research in the area of online service delivery.

REFERENCES

Accenture. (2009). Leadership in Customer Service: Creating Shared Responsibility for Better Outcomes Retrieved 10.07.2010 from http://www.accenture.com/Global/Research_and_Insights/Institute_For_Public_Service_Value/2008LCSROutcomes.htm

Carter, L., & Belanger, F. (2004). Citizen adoption of electronic government initiatives. *Paper presented at the 37th Hawaii International Conference on System Sciences*, Big Island, HI, USA.

Choudrie, J., Ghinea, G., & Weerakkody, V. (2004). Evaluating global e-government sites: A view using web diagnostic tools. *Electronic Journal of E-Government, 2*(2), 105–114.

CSTransform. (2010). Citizen Service Transformation: A manifesto for change in the delivery of public services.

CSTransform. (2011): Interoperability A comparative analysis of 30 countries. London, UK.

Dada, D. (2006). The failure of e-government in developing countries: A literature review. *The Electronic Journal of Information Systems in Developing Countries, 26.*

Ebbers, W., Pieterson, W., & Noordman, H. (2008). Electronic government: Rethinking channel management strategies. *Government Information Quarterly, 25*(2), 181–201. doi:10.1016/j.giq.2006.11.003

European Economic and Social Committee. (2015): European passport to active citizenship. Retrieved May 15th, 2017 from http://www.eesc.europa.eu/?i=portal.en.publications.35346

Gouscos, D., Laskaridis, G., Lioulias, D., Mentzas, G., & Georgiadis, P. (2002). An Approach to Offering One-Stop e-Government Services — Available Technologies and Architectural Issues. In R. Traunmüller & K. Lenk (Eds.), Electronic Government (Vol. 2456, pp. 113-131). Springer.

Henriksson, A., Yi, Y., Frost, B., & Middleton, M. (2007). Evaluation instrument for e-government websites. *Electronic Government, an International Journal, 4*(2), 204-226.

Hofacker, C. F., Goldsmith, R. E., Bridges, E., & Swilley, E. (2007). E-services: a synthesis and research agenda. *E-Services: Opportunities and Threats - Journal of Value Chain Management, 1*(1/2), 13-44.

Kaisara, G., & Pather, S. (2011). The e-Government evaluation challenge: A South African Batho Pele-aligned service quality approach. *Government Information Quarterly, 28*(2), 211–221. doi:10.1016/j.giq.2010.07.008

Kleinschmidt, S., Burkhard, B., Hess, M., Peters, C., & Leimeister, J. M. (2016a): Towards Design Principles for Aligning Human-Centered Service Systems and Corresponding Business Models. In Proceedings of the ICIS '16. Retrieved from http://aisel.aisnet.org/icis2016/ISDesign/Presentations/13

Kleinschmidt, S., Peters, C., & Leimeister, J. M. (2016b): ICT-Enabled Service Innovation in Human-Centered Service Systems: A Systematic Literature Review. In Proceedings ICIS '16. Retrieved from http://aisel.aisnet.org/icis2016/Sustainability/Presentations/3

Kohlborn, T., Korthaus, A., Peters, C., & Fielt, E. (2013). A Comparative Study of Governmental One-Stop Portals for Public Service Delivery. *International Journal of Intelligent Information Technologies, 9*(3), 1–19. doi:10.4018/jiit.2013070101

Kohlborn, T., Weiss, S., Poeppelbuss, J., Korthaus, A., & Fielt, E. (2010). Online Service Delivery Models – An International Comparison in the Public Sector. *Paper presented at the 21st Australasian Conference on Information Systems*, Brisbane, Australia.

Kubicek, H., & Hagen, M. (2000). One stop government in Europe: an overview. In H. Kubicek & M. Hagen (Eds.), *One Stop Government in Europe. Results from 11 National Surveys* (Vol. 11, pp. 1–36). Bremen, Germany: University of Bremen.

Lai, C. S. K., & Pires, G. (2010). Testing of a Model Evaluating e-Government Portal Acceptance and Satisfaction. *Electronic Journal Information Systems Evaluation, 13*(1), 35–46.

Leidner, D., & Kayworth, T. (2006). A Review of Culture in Information Systems Research: Toward a Theory of Information Technology Culture Conflict. *Management Information Systems Quarterly, 30*(2), 357–399.

Lewis, C., & Rieman, J. (1993). Task-centered user interface design.

Lim, E. P., Goh, D. H. L., Liu, Z., Ng, W. K., Khoo, C. S. G., & Higgins, S. E. (2002). G-Portal: a map-based digital library for distributed geospatial and georeferenced resources. *Paper presented at the 2nd ACM/IEEE-CS Joint Conference on Digital Libraries.* doi:10.1145/544220.544307

Mahdavi, M., Shepherd, J., & Benatallah, B. (2004). A collaborative approach for caching dynamic data in portal applications. *Paper presented at the 15th Australasian Database Conference (ADC2004) Dunedin*, New Zealand.

National League of Cities. (2016): Trends in Smart City Development. Retrieved May 15th, 2017 from http://www.nlc.org/sites/default/files/2017-01/Trends%20in%20Smart%20City%20Development.pdf

Nielsen, J. (1993). *Usability engineering.* San Francisco, CA, USA: Morgan Kaufmann.

OASIS. (2012). Transformational Government Framework Primer Version 1.0 Retrieved 08.03.2012 from http://docs.oasis-open.org/tgf/TGF-Primer/v1.0/cn01/TGF-Primer-v1.0-cn01.pdf

OASIS. (2014): New British Smart Cities Specification Uses OASIS Transformational Government Framework. Retrieved May 15th, 2017 from https://www.oasis-open.org/news/pr/new-british-smart-cities-specification-uses-oasis-transformational-government-framework

Offutt, J. (2002). Quality attributes of web software applications. *IEEE Software*, *19*(2), 25–32. doi:10.1109/52.991329

Peters, C. (2015): Modularization of services [Dissertation]. Kassel University Press GmbH.

Peters, C., Blohm, I., & Leimeister, J. M. (2015). Anatomy of Successful Business Models for Complex Services: Insights from the Telemedicine Field. *Journal of Management Information Systems*, *32*(3), 75–104. doi:10.1080/07421222.2015.1095034

Peters, C., Kohlborn, T., Korthaus, A., Fielt, E., & Ramsden, A. (2011). Service Delivery in One-Stop Government Portals – Observations Based on a Market Research Study in Queensland. *Paper presented at the 22nd Australasian Conference on Information Systems (ACIS)*, Sydney.

Peters, C., Maglio, P., Badinelli, R., Harmon, R., Maull, R., Spohrer, J., … & Griffith, T. L. (2016). Emerging Digital Frontiers for Service Innovation. *Communications of the Association for Information Systems*, *39*(1). Retrieved from http://aisel.aisnet.org/cais/vol39/iss1/8

Rubin, J., & Chisnell, D. (2008). *Handbook of Usability Testing: How to plan, design and conduct effective tests* (2nd ed.). Indianapolis, IN, USA: Wiley India Pvt. Ltd.

Scholl, H. J. (2009). Profiling the EG Research Community and Its Core. In M. Wimmer, H. J. Scholl, M. Janssen, & R. Traunmüller (Eds.), *EGOV 2009, LNCS* (Vol. *5693*, pp. 1–12). Berlin, Heidelberg: Springer. doi:10.1007/978-3-642-03516-6_1

Sureshchandar, G., Rajendran, C., & Anantharaman, R. (2002). The relationship between service quality and customer satisfaction–a factor specific approach. *Journal of Services Marketing*, *16*(4), 363–379. doi:10.1108/08876040210433248

Sutherland, L. A., Wildemuth, B., Campbell, M. K., & Haines, P. S. (2005). Unraveling the web: An evaluation of the content quality, usability, and readability of nutrition web sites. *Journal of Nutrition Education and Behavior, 37*(6), 300–305. doi:10.1016/S1499-4046(06)60160-7 PMID:16242061

Tat Kei Ho, A. (2002). Reinventing Local Governments and the E Government Initiative. *Public Administration Review, 62*(4), 434–444. doi:10.1111/0033-3352.00197

The British Standards Institution (2014): The Role of Standards in Smart Cities.

The Oxford English Dictionary (2 ed.). (1989). portal (computing) Oxford University Press.

Tripathi, R. P., Gupta, M., & Bhattacharya, J. (2011). Identifying Factors of Integration for an Interoperable Government Portal: A Study in Indian Context. *International Journal of Electronic Government Research, 7*(1), 64–88. doi:10.4018/jegr.2011010105

UK Department for Business Innovation and Skills. (2014): Making cities smarter: Guide for city leaders.

United Nations. (2008). United Nations e-Government Survey 2008 - From e-Government to Connected Governance. Retrieved from http://unpan1.un.org/intradoc/groups/public/documents/UN/UNPAN028607.pdf

Wang, L., Bretschneider, S., & Gant, J. (2005). Evaluating Web-based e-government services with a citizen-centric approach. *Paper presented at the 38th Hawaii International Conference on System Sciences*, Hawaii, USA.

Wimmer, M., & Tambouris, E. (2002). Online one-stop government. *Paper presented at the IFIP 17th World Computer Congress-TC8 Stream on Information Systems: The e-Business Challenge*, Montréal, Québec, Canada. doi:10.1007/978-0-387-35604-4_9

Wimmer, M. A. (2002). Integrated service modelling for online one-stop Government. *Electronic Markets, 12*(3), 149–156. doi:10.1080/101967802320245910

ENDNOTES

[1]   SSQ has authorised the authors of this paper to report on the findings of the MR company's usability study for the purposes of this publication.

Chapter 12
A Quantitative Study of Factors Affecting Value of Adopting Self-Service Banking Technology (SSBT) Among Customers in Developing and Developed Countries

Fouad Omran Elgahwash
University of Wollongong, Australia

ABSTRACT

Self-service banking technology (SSBT) allow customers to perform services on their own without direct assistance from staff. This study focuses on factors affecting the value of adopting self-Service banking technology (SSBT) among customers. It is believed that the successful usage of self-service banking technology will be increasingly advantageous for all (banks & customers). This chapter's purpose is an extension to the technology acceptance model (TAM) and views customer responses to technology as an integrated part of SSBT. The sample used for this study was selected from users of banks in both Libya and Australia, with a total size of 141 respondents. Reliability and validity of the data collection instrument was tested using Cronbach Alpha. Descriptive and regression tests for data analysis were used. The domains in which subjects were tested were "ease of use of SSBT", "Usefulness of SSBT", "Quality of SSBT", "privacy of information" and "Trust of SSBT".

INTRODUCTION

Most banks throughout the world are moving closer to their customers and expending more effort in finding new ways to create value for themselves and transform their customer relationships. Customer support and service comprises the way that a product is delivered, explained, billed, installed, repaired, renewed – and redesigned (Galliers & Leidner, 2003).

DOI: 10.4018/978-1-5225-3686-4.ch012

SSBT is an essential element for increasing customer relationships because it can be used to improve customer service strategies in several ways. Individual services can be enhanced, with services and products transformed to meet new customer demands and SSBT tools being used to increase interaction with customers (Wells, Fuerst, & Choobineh, 1999). Interactions with SSBT will reflect directly on customers' decisions about banks. A study by Kardaras and Papathanassiou (2000) suggested that the Internet can provide businesses with a cheaper way to perform activities and to access customers' views and positions about products and services.

A study by Costello and Tuchen (1998) identified that information & communication technologies (ICTs) were used to facilitate communications in the Australian insurance sector as early as 1998; these ICTs included SSBT (self-service banking technologies) such as email, electronic mediums and the Internet. These tools have created the potential for change in banks' delivery of products for clients, and as a result SSTs creates market-wide accessibility to service face-to-face customers. A number of the tools used in SSBT (such as mobile phones, e-mail, Internet, audio and video conferencing) will together likely change the future of Libyan financial firms and clients. SSBT seeks to move processes towards individual customers (Leek, Turnbull, & Naude, 2003), and facilitate the provision of better products and services at lower prices. Thus, SSBT are significant at reducing costs and increasing flexibility.

Self- service has become an active strategic imperative to generate successful long-term customer relationships and effectively support customers. Indeed, customer support and service are becoming one of the most critical core business processes. The importance of customer support and service needs are driving SSTs knowledge and significances more than ever before, and facilitating much faster responses to resolving customer enquiries, so it refers to "Smarter and faster ways of creating, capturing, sharing, and accessing knowledge about complex products and services". (Blut, Wang, & Schoefer, 2016; Zeng, 2016).

Self-service systems are useful for banks to modularize and automate the repetitive fundamentals of services, focusing their resources and personnel on more personalised aspects of the bank-customer relationship, and thus providing more added-value to their consumers. On the other hand, SSBT systems give customers the feeling that they have a better control of the service choice and delivery. This is especially true for time-consuming services that require adaptive research of information and the selection of a best alternative among several available offers and solutions (Gurau, 2011).

The business press praises self-service channels for their great potential to increase bank productivity while reducing the costs of service delivery at the same time. The costs for a banking transaction, for instance, can be reduced from 1.15 U.S. dollars to only 2 cents by switching from an o-site to an online transaction (Scherer, Wünderlic, & Wangenheim, 2015).

A study by Mouelhi (2009) has determined that up to 56% of businesses in the banking sector commonly use Internet-based SSTs for online transactions. A study by Leek et al. (2003) noted that only 38% of banks used the Internet for purchase processes and only 10% of banks used the Internet for customer support services. It can be clearly seen that SSBT tools have the potential to provide beneficial applications for both customers and the Libyan banking sector in the near future.

Zeng (2016) identified that Self-service banking technologies (SSBT) are "technological interfaces that enable customers to produce a service independent of direct service employee involvement". For Example, SSBT includes automated teller machines (ATMs), Internet banking, M-banking, Money Transfer, airline check-in machines, automated hotel checkouts, package tracking systems, pay-at-the-pump terminals, self-ordering machines and so on.

Most institutions in the Libyan banking sector now have a network of computers and related devices to use SSBT, because the core functions of storage, processing and communication are facilitated through these devices. The following section provides details of the two main examples of SSBT that are currently being adopted by Libyan banks - mobile banking and Internet banking (Elgahwash & Freeman, 2013).

This chapter presents the recent advancements in the banking sector generally, with the adoption of comprehensive SSBT used to create improved customer relationships (Karim & Hamdan, 2010). A review of the potential benefits of SSBT to the customer, through mobile banking (m- banking) and electronic banking (e- banking), is then provided. Finally, a preliminary investigation of the SSBT that are used by Libyans in Libya compared to Australia is presented, highlighting the differences in use between the two countries. This study provides the starting point for identifying the types of services that future Libyan professionals could use on their return to Libya (Cleveland, 2016). In fact, this chapter is providing unique methods and results regarding self-service banking technology adoption within a specific developed and developing country.

BACKGROUND

Self-Service Banking Technology (SSBT) has become a requirement for banking worldwide and now plays a vital role in creating and supporting customer satisfaction (Al-Mabrouk & Soar, 2009). This SSBT revolution has the potential to improve the Libyan banking sector and establish a more customer-centric focus (Leek et al., 2003), creating benefits for banks and their customers in both ways "directly and indirectly". Overall success of the banking sector is fuelled by the electronic technologies revolution; so it has heavily influenced both formal communications and relationship processes (Al-Mabrouk & Soar, 2009). The use of Internet banking and M-banking within the Libyan banking sector has expanded rapidly in recent years as banks have recognized its ability to provide staff with faster access to detailed information with regard to customer enquiries (Zammuto & Laube, 2003).

Previous study by Liao, Palvia, and Liang (2009), has reported that software, the Internet, mobile phones, voice conversations and procedures related to SSBT create greater interactivity with customers. Furthermore, in many developing countries, such as Libya, the banking sector is looked upon as a significant component in the permanent structure of business because it plays a key role in selling products and services.

The introduction of SSBT in the banking sector in developing countries (Libya) has created increasing competition among banks, forcing them to further develop their use of technology to help them to stay competitive and serve their customers. SSBT is seen as an approach for banks to deliver better, faster and more effective service in all banking interactions with their customers, forming the basis of the banking sector's customer-centric operations (Ho & Mallick, 2006).

SSBT have found their way into all areas of business, banking services, education and governments. Internet banking, for example, allows customers to conduct their banking interactions when and where it is most suitable to them. As result, comprehensive access to banking-related services and facilities is now available to customers. This has also enabled reduction in errors and the potential to remove or automate daily routines, thereby saving time (Banerjee, 2009).

The banking sector in Libya has utilized Internet connections with customers since 1998 (Twati, 2008). The Internet has emerged as a new business tool for greater interaction with customers; it provides many methods for communication between customers and banks. The transformation delivered by the

Internet across the developed world has been evolutionary, and these gradual but significant changes have also been seen in the banking sector (Davison, Vogel, Harris, & Jones, 2000). As the banking sector, has become more competitive, many banks have realized the advantages offered by the Internet for establishing good customer relationships (Banerjee, 2009).

The Internet is increasingly being seen as the main channel to deliver banking services "24 / 7" i.e. 24 hours per day, 7 days per week. It enables customers to access accounts, transfer funds and buy products online (Mastoori, 2009). Previous study by Akel and Phillips (2001), found that the Internet transformed most businesses by integrating computers and networks, viewing it as a tool for economic purposes because it generates profits. Banks use the Internet to supply services based on the needs of customers. According to (Al-Sukkar, 2005), Internet banking allows customers the ability to interact with their bank on their own computer, serving as a new channel for customers to be in contact with banks that provides an alternative to the traditional physical branch network. Many customers are adopting this technology because it delivers greater control over their personal assets and access to financial services. It removes the traditional branch limitations by allowing customers to access their accounts 24/7 with reduced waiting time, regardless of a customer's geographic location. Internet banking delivers banking products and services directly to customers (Wamalwa, 2006), consequently delivering convenience, building trust, providing satisfaction and enhancing customer loyalty (Nasri & Charfeddine, 2012).

Through the use of Internet banking, banks provide another means for their customers to conduct business. Internet banking allows customers to access and perform financial transactions on their own bank accounts from any computers with an Internet connection (Al-Sukkar, 2005) Internet banking facilities typically include the use of the bank's web site for viewing an account, balance and transactions records, paying bills, statement delivery and opening an account. Internet banking has the potential to reduce the costs and inconvenience for customers wanting to switch between banks, while simultaneously enabling banks to offer low-cost, value-added financial services to their customers (Safeena, Date, & Kammani, 2011).

Mobile phones are another technology which has dramatically changed the daily lifestyles of individuals throughout the world. In only a few decades, mobile technologies have changed from simple voice transmitting and receiving devices to a total computing and communication solution that can accommodate voice, text, pictures, video, SMS and other types of multimedia. These features have transformed mobile phones from expensive functional tools to general-purpose accessories that are used by all people of all classes for a vast array of purposes (Alhinai, 2009). Currently, it is common for people to use mobile phones for accessing the Internet, watching movies, conducting shopping and making financial transactions (Cheah, Teo, Sim, & Tan, 2011).

Recent developments of mobile banking (M-Banking) present an opportunity for banks to retain their existing, technology-focused customer base by offering value-added, innovative services and to attract new customers (Donner & Tellez, 2008).

M-banking is a term that refers to performing balance checks, account transactions and payments via a mobile (Alhinai, 2009). Described M-banking as the use of data-enabled mobile handheld devices to perform activities such as communicating, obtaining information, and transacting, so that technologies have a direct or indirect monetary value through wireless connections to the internet or to banks' private networks M-banking is most often presented via SMS, mobile voice or the Internet, but it can also be used as a program downloaded onto a customer's phone. Numerous studies have concluded that m-banking has had a positive influence on the relationship processes between banks and customers (Cheah et al., 2011).

There are approximately sixteen banks in the Libyan banking sector (Libyan Central Bank, 2015). From an extensive literature review, no previous studies of the Libyan banking sector have been conducted that focus on the customers' perspectives. Thus, I was motivated to develop methods to be used for identifying and explaining the usefulness of Internet banking and m-banking services in Libyan banks. Hence, the data, analysis and conclusions of this present chapter make an important contribution to the understanding the adoption of SSBT and use of internet and mobile banking systems by banking customers in Libya.

Statement of the Problem

The motivation for this chapter stems from an increasing need for the evaluation of how the adoption of SSBT into the banking sector affects customer relationships in the developing world. There are banks wishing to integrate SSBT into their businesses processes to create customer relationships (Cavusoglu, 2003), in the developing world, and especially in Libya. Some Libyan banks continue to restrict their operations to traditional manual techniques, and actual SSBT has not been adopted across the majority of the banking sector in Libya.

Some banks are still dealing with customers in inefficient ways. In many institutions, only basic transactions (such as accounts balances or simple payroll systems) are available to customers. Currently, there is limited networking between many banks and their branches; customers are forced to wait in lines for manual cheque processing - this is the only way to access cash in their bank accounts (Twati, 2008). The Libyan banking sector has undergone little change in recent years – it has not embraced SSTs in the same way as the banking sector in other countries (Rose, 2007). As a result, rapid implementation of effective SSBT has now become essential to support service processes, automate many routine activities and provide the ability for Libya's banking sector to remain relevant and competitive. It can also act as a promotional tool, used to attract customers to a bank's website for self-service interactions. Self-service i.e. allowing customers to perform a process without intervention by any person (Vogel, 2005) has been identified as having a positive effect on customer satisfaction, trust and loyalty for banking (Hamed, Ball, Berger, & Cleary, 2008).

Therefore, some Libyan banks have adopted SSBT programs through the introduction of websites, but these websites do not actively connect with most customers. It can be concluded from previous research that SSBT offers opportunities for the Libyan banking sector to improve their business by enhancing access to customers and creating an improved customer experience.

The application of SSBT across the developed world has positively impacted on businesses by providing strategies for building and enhancing customer relationships and increasing the speed and flexibility of work (Zammuto & Laube, 2003). SSBT is playing an increasingly critical role in the design of relationship processes and implementation in the banking sector specifically. SSBT delivers the tools needed for growing long-term customer relationships and for integrating banking processes into customers' daily operations (Shaw, 2000).

The Libyan banking sector currently has recently had an increasing amount of competition from the local and international market. This can be attributed to the reason that traditional banks in Libya were not interested or do not have the customer service experience to allow transactions to be completed through electronic applications, that enhance relationships.

An understanding of how the use of SSBT in banks in developed nations, such as Australia, can be helpful for developing and maintaining customer expectations and driving a competitive advantage for

Libyan banks. The target of this chapter draws attention of these issues for banks by providing evidence showing that SSTs adoption can provide positive benefits for building and enhancing customers' relationships. It is believed that relationships can enhance the overall banking strategies and provide competitive advantages for Libyan banks in the long term. This chapter will address the following questions:

1. How does prior exposure to self-service Technologies banking in developed nations influence customers' expectations of and engagement with the Libyan banking sector?
2. Why are banking customers are still queuing in the bank when they can receive the same service via self-service banking technology?

LITERATURE REVIEW

Self-service technologies are the newest additions to many banks within the past two decades. These recent developments are becoming more customary as consumers and employees find themselves dependent on machines like ATMs and self-checkouts, refers to technology based self- service banking as "using automated banking services that customers access without interaction with bank teams".

The more recent self-service Banking technology research has been well grounded in theory drawn from customer decision making and choice models based on the SSBT process (Sindwani & Goel, 2016). The use of technology in the delivery of services holds great promise for future simplification of processes for both banks and customers in the area of self-service (Simon & Usunier, 2007).

Self-service Banking technologies are technological interfaces that facilitate customers conducting a service, independent of direct service employee involvement. The self-service concept is simple for customers, as it allows them to perform tasks that were once done for them by others (Salomann, Kolbe, & Brenner, 2006). Self-service technologies are ideal for banks because information processing is essential to their service delivery, and self-services are expected to reduce the need for face to face services in banks (Sannes, 2001).

Self-service technologies are often implemented with the expectation that customers want to use them and will happily explore them. However, many customers are hesitant to use a new self-service Banking technology, especially if it departs from the existing script of how the service is supposed to progress (Blut et al., 2016).

The information a customer needs to engage in self-service banking will depend on their knowledge and experience with banking self-service technologies. A successful relationship using self-service technology requires positive customer experiences; these may arise due to convenience, satisfaction and loyalty (Yu & Guo, 2008). Offering technology-based self-services, whether on- or off-site, can result in significant cost savings for banks as well (Simon & Usunier, 2007).

Salomann et al. (2006) has compared the following three self-service technologies: automated teller machines (ATMs), telephone banking and online banking. Their research provides evidence that a variety of different factors influence attitudes toward each of these technologies. Prior research has also suggested that customers benefit by new experiences of using SSBT in their banking transactions because they have a positive feeling about SSBT and they believe that SSBT allows them to use banks' services without direct contact with banks (Travica, 2008).

Self-service technologies in customer relationships are becoming increasingly important developments that have been enhanced by customers' increasing and diverse use of the technologies (Salomann et al., 2006). A study by Rajagopal and Rajagopal (2007) suggested that Technology-enabled self-service includes three main elements that positively influence acceptance and support the positive relationship process between customers and banks; these are trust, quality and time. Technology-based self-service has been divided into the three comprehensive categories of transactions, customer service and self-service. Transactions in self-service may include payments, loans and online trading services. Customer self-services may include functions such as online balance statements and the ability to change personal information (Sannes, 2001).

Self-service technologies play a large role in making it possible for customers to achieve service delivery themselves. Adoption requires customers to modify their behaviour (McPhail & Fogarty, 2004), as well as positive customer experiences using SSBT generally (Sannes, 2001). It is important for banks to discover and understand the ability and willingness of customers to use technologies before broadly implementing self-service options.

In order for self-service to be successfully integrated into banking operations, banks must integrate their self-service activities with traditional customer services to create balance across modern technology interfaces and high contact customer relationships (Salomann et al., 2006). In short, self-service banking technologies have customers co-producing a service with banks facilitating. Thus, it is important for providers of self-service banking technologies to understand how customers evaluate, so that banks can improve their performance towards customers (Vogel, 2005).

Self-service banking technologies can be considered as a replacement for at-branch transactions, yet there is the issue of complementary services, which may be difficult to implement effectively when interaction is spread across self-service and face-to-face channels or when customers engage entirely in self-service without a full understanding of other available options (Rajagopal & Rajagopal, 2007). Most banks offer self-service banking technology; however, the scale and scope differs. Banks are accepting that ICT technologies allow services to be delivered at low cost and to larger volumes of customers. For example, the Amtrak company introduced telephone self-service by means of the Interactive Voice Response system that allowed cost savings of $13 million (Salomann et al., 2006). Furthermore, the adoption of self-service has the potential to decrease the cost of processing and transmitting information. Sannes (2001) views self-service technologies in banking, such as m-banking, as being used to transfer money at point of sale and to exchange information

There have been rapid changes in the ways that customers deal with their banking institutions, with technical innovations leading to the adoption of technology-enabled banking (E-banking) and M-banking. These have become a common channel of choice for interactions between customers and their banking institution, compared with traditional face-to-face interactions. Self-Service Technologies (SSBT) have made it easier for customers to complete banking transactions and other related banking services as they provide increased availability of services, with customers being less dependent upon the opening hours and location of their bank (Zeng, 2016).The incentives for customers to use these new banking channels are expectations of increased productivity, decreased costs and increased added value. The ubiquitous nature of e-banking has created a shift in the relationship between customers and their banking institution.

This technological development has influenced the range of services and led to improved availability for increasingly larger client groups. Self-service has become one of the key concepts of technologies (Banerjee, 2009). Despite these advances in the developed world, the situation has been remarkably different in developing nations, as the core technologies have not previously been available to customers and face-to-face service has remained the norm.

The Libyan Case

In most developed countries, such as USA and Australia, technology is a central element in dealing with the challenges of modern banking, including lowering costs and enabling efficiency improvements. Certainly, most banks worldwide are highly successful at utilising SSBT to provide efficient banking services to their customers. Libya as developing country is in a unique position to realign its priorities for the use of technology throughout its banking system, with an acting Government being formed on December 2011, and most of the UN sanctions that had previously frozen Libya's foreign assets being lifted on December 16, 2011. These events have provided the Central Bank of Libya with the ability to support the exchange rate, increase economic stability and manage public expectations. It should be noted that the modernisation of the Libyan banking system is clearly identified in the Strategic Plan for the Central Bank of Libya (Central Libyan Bank, 2012).

In 1993, Libya created a new law allowing the establishment of private-sector banks. Rules allowing Libyan banks to seek foreign partnerships provided opportunities for greater foreign investment in the local banking sector. However, as with other sectors of the economy, the business environment created a disincentive for foreign banks due to regulations and the unpredictable nature of government policy. In 2006, the government of Libya introduced laws enabling greater financial liberalisation and introduced a flexible banking system, albeit, in a cautious fashion (Central Libyan Bank, 2012). with general recognition that development of the banking sector was essential for Libya's economic reform (Twati, 2008). It has been identified that the adoption and ongoing use of e-commerce by Libyan citizens has been constrained by three main challenges, one of which was Libya's banking system (Hunaiti, Mansour, & Al-Nawafleh, 2009). In 2008, most Libyan banks were still using manual systems of banking, and technology-enabled systems had not yet found their way to most banks (Twati, 2008).

Although banks in Libya have been able to differentiate themselves using a low -cost model, many banks have focused on achieving excellence through customer service. In contrast, the Commerce and Development Bank has benefited by serving their customers through adoption of SSBT technologies since their inception. Eighty three percent of the funding of Libyan banks comes from customer deposits. In the current and substantial modernisation program, underway across the Libyan banking system it is essential to upgrade available services, and deal with the use of non-cash payment instruments (credit and debit cards) as used in most other parts of the world.

According to the Central Bank of Libya Annual Reports (2012) most banks in Libya have adopted new SSBT. These SSBT include core banking systems with automated cheque processing, Visa, MasterCard and Automatic Teller Machines (ATMs). These SSBT programs were designed to introduce SSBT to customers. To allow Libya to keep pace with the rest of the world, the SWIFT system (used for transferring money worldwide) has been introduced in the last few years (Twati & Gammack, 2006).

Table 1. Population and Internet users statistics

Country	Population (2016 Est.)	Internet Users 31-Dec-2000	Internet Users 30-Jun-2016	Penetration (% Population)
Libya	6,541,948	10,000	2,800,000	42.8%
Australia	22,992,654	6,600,000	21,176,595	92.1%

Source: (Central Intelligence Agency CIA, 2016).

With an understanding of the change in banking polices within Libya, it is important to also consider the access that citizens have to utilize these SSBT. The number of Internet users in Libya was approximately 2,800,000 in 2016, with a population of approximately 6,541,948 in 2016 (Central Intelligence Agency CIA, 2016). In 2016, approximately 42.8% of the Libyan population had direct access to the Internet, which is a small percentage in comparison with a developed country such as Australia which had 92.1% of internet users in same year.

Kridan (2006) mentioned the popularity of Internet cafes within Libya which increases the level of Internet use significantly beyond that of direct (in-home) access. In 2010, there were 72,800 fixed broadband lines in the country, with overall Internet use increasing to 14% of the new Libyan generation by 2011 (The World Bank, 2012). As a result, some banks have considered this low level of adoption as a reason not to provide technology-enabled banking services via the Internet. However, telephone and mobile banking is a service that is starting to be used by banks, with estimates that approximately 10.9 million mobile phones are in service (The World Bank, 2012). Historically, Libyan banking has relied heavily on traditional face-to-face channels to provide banking services to customers; this is one of the many reasons why many banks suffer from an inefficient manual process of banking.

Libyan banks have understood that improving SSBT is an important factor for success, and that the cost to acquire a new customer is always higher than to maintain a loyal customer (Afsar, Rehman, Qureshi, & Shahjehan, 2010). It requires customers to accept and adapt to new SSBT, and depends on the interaction between customers and service providers (Thao & Swierczek, 2008).

Therefore, Libyan banks require information to inform the development of a realistic strategy to insert SSBT programs and applications into their business process, which in turn will lead to enhanced customer relationships. In a review of Libyan banks in 2011, only one bank had implemented both online and mobile banking for customer use (Commerce and Development Bank), and one bank was using SMS banking (Wahada Bank). Two other banks had banners on their websites advertising that online and mobile banking were 'coming soon'. This status is notably different to banking in developed counties (e.g. Australia), where all banks have forms of online and mobile banking.

Mobile Banking

Mobile banking (M-banking) is defined as 'a channel whereby the customer interacts with a bank via a mobile device, such as a mobile phone or a personal digital assistant'. The term m-banking refers to performing banking activities (such as viewing an account balance or performing an account transaction) via a mobile device. This is most often presented via SMS, mobile voice and mobile banking applications. M-banking provides an additional channel to reach customers. Services that can be provided through m-banking include viewing account balance; viewing account transaction history; viewing credit card information; viewing loan statements; monitoring of term deposits; processing of one to one payments; bill payment processing; domestic and international fund transfers; status of requests for credit, including mortgage approval, and insurance coverage; loyalty-related offer based services; and exchange of data messages and email, including complaint submission and tracking (Laukkanen & Pasanen, 2008).

Mobile banking is using a cellular phone or smart phone to access bank accounts and perform accounting functions. It also includes accessing other features of bank websites such as loan applications and interactive investment banking data to mention a few (Cleveland, 2016). Previous studies have identified that m-banking has had a positive influence on relationships and processes involving banks and customers. M-banking has significantly changed the way many customers access their bank account

(Pousttchi & Schurig, 2004). It has been strongly established as the most important distribution and communication channel for retail banking, its broad reach across the developing world has shown it to be one of the most significant technologies for customers (Donner & Tellez, 2008), and it provides an opportunity for banking institutions to introduce new services to customers (Amin, 2008).

However, in developing nations such as Libya, there has been little demand for m-banking services in the banking sector (Dewan, Low, Land, & Dewan, 2009). Libyan banks have traditionally delivered services through face-to-face interactions with customers at branch offices. Recent modernization of telecommunications has enabled new access methods for banking services. As stated previously, only two Libyan banks currently utilize mobile banking as part of their services, however, with the penetration of mobile phones in the country, this is one potential channel that could be used to increase customer loyalty. Notably, m-banking is the first communications technology to have more users in developing countries than in developed ones; e.g. more than 800 million mobile phones were sold in developing countries in 2003 (Ivatury & Pickens, 2006).

Internet Banking

Internet banking has been defined by Al-Fahim (2013) as "the service that allows consumers to perform banking transactions using a computer with an internet connection", likewise, electronic banking technologies refer to banking activities that involve use of electronic technology such as automatic teller machines, telephone banking and internet banking to do other services such as direct deposits, fund transfers, e-bill payment, and checking the current balance. Internet banking has offered an extra effective delivery channel for traditional banking products.

The changes facilitated by the Internet are evolutionary and have influenced the financial sector internationally (Davison et al., 2000). The adoption of Internet technology is occurring in developed and developing countries, and it has changed banking from traditional delivery channels to electronic delivery channels (Ahmed, Anjomshoaa, & Tjoa, 2007). In developed countries like the USA, Sweden and Australia, Internet technologies have been used by the banking industry for several years ago, (89%; 94.6%; 92.1% of users respectively), and banks have followed strategies to encourage their clients to employ e-banking. For example, a study by Evans and Sawyer (2009) in Australia reported that 37% of business services were delivered to the customer via the Internet in 2009, in comparison with 21% of business services during 2005.

Internet banking is one of most important forms of dealing online and building relationships with individual customers because it allows banks to provide services through the use of the Internet without traditional temporal and spatial borders (Xu, Shao, Lin, & Shi, 2009). Therefore, the Internet can serve as an interactive channel for direct communication and information exchange between clients and bankers. It helps customers to access accounts, transfer funds and buy products online (Mastoori, 2009). Eighty two percent of the clients who visited web sites preferred to interact with banks via the Internet because of the logic and predictability of the interactions, and 22% of customers believed they were likely to get the best service for the best price because of the Internet (Elalagg, 2003).

A study of Jordanian banks by Al-Sukkar (2005) has reported two main benefits of using the Internet; Firstly, bankers can deliver a great level of information about the bank's services showing full costs via the Internet in a short amount of time. Potential customers can use it to identify deals and then use self-service banking after they have made a decision about which product is suitable for their needs. Secondly, e-banking allows interaction between the bank's systems and clients, with a high degree of flexibility of communications and interaction. In fact, the Internet is an important element for banks to create relationships and attract new customers. Voice or e-mail responses are one of the most effective technologies for providing good opportunities for fast business and very high value for customers. Bank employees can use e-mail for personalised communication, or to communicate with all customers simultaneously.

VALUE IN THE CONTEXT OF TECHNOLOGY BASED SELF-SERVICE

Prior research provides sufficient evidence that customers are more likely to remain with their provider if they consider this behaviour beneficial (Kim, Jin, & Swinney, 2009), so it maintain a loyalty; which indicates a favourable attitude toward maintaining a long-term relationship with the provider, "results from cognitive perceptions about the current value of using the SSBT." Hence, to fully understand how technology-based self-service channels affect customers' retention by a service provider, we consider the value that customers can derive from both personal and self-service channels over the duration of their relationship with the provider.

According to basic concepts of economics and psychology, customers will only be willing to pay high prices or continue using service offers of a bank when they perceive value from their side. The concepts of value-in-use and value-in-context are essential pillars of the SSBT. In other words, value is created for the customer through a unique combination of the customer's and the provider's resources (e.g. customer's knowledge and skills to use a self-service banking technology). The customers are the ones who determine value by integrating the bank's SSTs offering into their own lives. Accordingly, different customers experience and, in consequence, will values the technology and the self -service offers differently. Scherer et al. (2015) insist that the term "value"-in context reflects the phenomenological perspective of value and requires that value is always co-created, contextually specific, and contingent on the integration of SSBT.

Customers should hence also be able to derive value from SSBT channels even when used for complex tasks. As Gurau (2011) noted, customers' unique skills and capabilities are especially important for value-creation in self-service settings. Once customers are confident in their own skills, they can easily deliver more complex service options by themselves. Indeed, (Schuster, Lisa, Proudfoot, Judy, & Drennan, 2015) have shown that novice customers' self-efficacy (i.e., their perception of their own ability to accomplish a task successfully) increases their perceptions of service performance and the overall value they derive from a technology-based self-service channel. This suggests that even when tasks are more complex, customers can derive value from self-service channels when confident in their own skills and abilities. Similarly, customers can derive value from a personal service even when used for a rather simple and repetitive task. Some customers, for instance, derive a high relational value from personal service encounters through the enjoyment of building up a relationship, while others derive a higher economic value from self-service encounters through increased customization and more control. The extent of such value creation, however, again strongly depends on the customers' unique characteristics. Marshall and Parulekar (2009) for instance, have demonstrated that customers from a highly collectivist cultural background can derive greater relational value through their participation in service production than their individualist counterparts. Self-service research also acknowledges that customers differ in their need for interaction with service personnel (Augustine, 2013). While some customers are known to simply enjoy "doing it by themselves" (i.e., using self-service channels), as it enables them to derive experiential benefits (Halstead & Richards, 2014), others enjoy human interaction as it enables them to create close social bonds with the provider. As suggested in media effectiveness research, Chan et al. also propose, but have not tested, that time or experience with a provider might also affect the co-creation of both economic and relational value (Scherer et al., 2015).

THEORETICAL FRAMEWORK

In this section, a new framework is developed for analysis of self-service banking technology based on the background theory discussed in the previous section. A review of prior studies in the economic literature has suggested a theoretical model based on an extension of the TAM model which relates it to the SSBT context. It is used to explain customer intentions to use SSBT in relation to Internet and M-Banking and to encompass the reliability and accuracy of the technology based self-services technology usage in banking sector.

This framework model is a model that depends on five items as shown diagrammatically here (Figure 1).

SSBT Trust

Trust is an important component for operational success in the banking sector. Trust is defined as the willingness to rely on an exchange partner in whom one has confidence. It is essential for customers to have confidence in using SSBT, particularly in the areas of reliability and integrity (Afsar et al., 2010). Trust is reflected by the collective beliefs held by a person, based on their customer perception about certain qualities of the bank. Customer trust is shown when customers accept delivery of a banking service; it reflects customer willingness to accept risk by putting themselves into a weak position (Ayo, Adewoye, & Oni, 2010).

Figure 1.

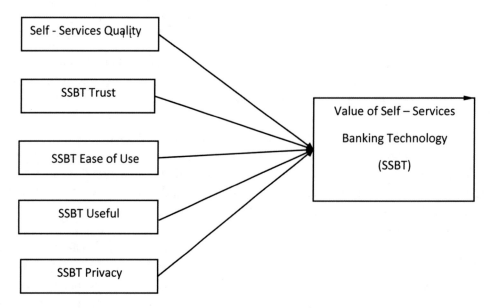

A trusting belief refers to users' perceptions of attributes of services providers, including the ability, integrity and benevolence of the providers. Indeed, when customers trust self-service banking technology there will be increased satisfaction and loyalty towards these banks as a result. The author maintains that trust can reduce feelings of risk in relation to the process of creating reciprocal relationships between customers and the bank. Consequently, when customers trust their self-service, they will continue using the chosen services and will recommend these services to others (Deng, Lu, Wei, & Zhang, 2010).

The banking sector values customer trust because it can provide greater stability in customer relationships, and hence can reduce stressful interactions for banks. It creates commitment, reduces the costs of negotiating agreements and lessens customers' fear of opportunistic behaviour by the service provider (Flavian, Guinaliu, & Gurrea, 2006). Trust is prioritized in relationship processes embedded in electronic banking channels, because customers must first trust the business before engaging in a banking relationship (Vatanasombut, Igbaria, Stylianou, & Rodgers, 2008).

SSBT and Service Quality

Service quality is an important element for banks in creating relationships with groups of customers. The issue of quality management within banking services has drawn considerable attention over the past few years. The move to managed service has increased demands for outcome-based accountability, cost containment and attention to customer-focused quality, in order to remain competitive in a rapidly changing environment (Al-Fawzan, 2005). Addressing the issue of service quality is critical for banks. Typical customer involvement and interaction with their bank is characterized by frequent contact that can occur as frequently as daily. Due to this frequency, service quality assumes considerable significance for the customer and for the bank (Spears, 2004).

Service quality is essential for banks to have competitive advantage in a competitive marketplace. Most of the banking sector is using technology for increasing customer expectations and their own benefits. With time, acceptance of mechanized banking services is increasing among customers. Measuring and managing service quality has become a key area of interest for practitioners, managers and researchers as service quality influences business performance and helps build competitive advantage and profitability (Sindwani & Goel, 2016).

Service quality is an important concept for both customers and providers in the banking sector, so customers usually look for high quality services. Service providers hope that quality services will enhance their image, sales and profitability (Dabholkar, 1996). Nowadays, service quality is a widely-used program in the banking industry. It can be defined in many different ways from the viewpoint of the customer. Service quality can be defined as economic activities that create value and positive benefits for customers at specific times and place as result of bringing about a desired change in, or on the behalf of, the recipient of the services (Sadek, Zainal, Taher, & Yahya, 2010). An alternative definition is that service quality is the difference between the dimensions in customers' perceived service and opportunity of service (Wei, 2009). If banks provide services of poor quality, they will not be able to perform their work effectively. Moreover, as products and customer services within the banking industry become more similar and substitutable, switching costs become lower and more affordable for customers (Vogel, 2005).

Service quality is a relative concept, linked on the one hand to the ability of the product to satisfy the requests of the customer. The increasing focus on quality has enhanced banks' ability to produce goods or provide services that are able to meet the needs of customers. Service quality is also linked to the ability to achieve the wishes of the customers in a form that corresponds with their expectations and achieves complete satisfaction with the product (Petridou, Spathis, Glaveli, & Liassides, 2007).

Customers often evaluate quality of service via groups of criteria. One common criterion is reliability, which means achievement in a manner that is what the customer wants. The second common criterion is the speed of response when the customer needs help. It refers to the access a customer has to their bank to receive the required service in a given (Spathis & Georgakopoulou, 2007). Customers are considered key for any business to survive; the ability of banks to deliver their products and services appropriately defines their success within the industry (Toelle, 2006).

Recently, Libyan banks have come to understand the importance of offering online services to their customers, to the point where such services are now an essential and inevitable convenience. Fortunately, online banking services do not represent merely an expense for banks. Thanks to such services, customers' satisfaction levels rise while retention costs drop. In addition, online transaction costs of SSBT are lower than all other channels combined (Mashat, Ritchie, Lovatt, & Pratten, 2005).

SSBT Ease of Use

The ease of use of the website is the most important factor that positively affect a continuing customer in using electronic banking services. "Ease of use" means that access to the system is easy and operating the system requires little effort (Mehmood, Shah, Azhar, & Rasheed, 2014). For SSBT it means customers' perception of access to the service and the ease and smoothness of making financial transactions is more favourable compared to the traditional methods. A study of AL-Hawary and Hussien (2017) defined SSBT ease of use as the ability of customers to try new innovation and benefit from its advantages more easily, in their study they found a statistically significant relationship between the ease of use of a particular system and customer satisfaction, which in turn affects their loyalty to the service (AL-Hawary & Hussien, 2017).

SSBT Usefulness

A study by (Mukthtar, 2015) addressed this dimension as the degree of belief by a customer that use of an electronic banking system will achieve their desired outcome. Self-service systems give additional responsibilities to the customer, who will "initiate, generate, and consume" the service by interacting directly with the banking system (Gurau, 2011; Sindwani & Goel, 2016). A study by Nippatlapalli (2013) defined SSBT Usefulness as the ability of the electronic system to improve banking transactions compared to the traditional method. It is the ability of the system to meet the needs and expectations of the customers, and its effectiveness in solving their requests with a goal to creating loyalty among customers of the bank.

Banks have the ability to reduce overall costs for both the customers and the Bank in comparison to traditional banking. Actually, all banks need to reduce costs as a result of the extended reach of commercial banks and rising competition and customer awareness about the cost of providing service around the world, and the time taken in getting service. Banks have become able to reduce costs, and reach larger numbers of customers without having to create new branches. From the viewpoint of the customers, a high degree of benefit is gained, but it is considered almost a free service not linked to a specific time or place, and reduces the costs of physically getting to the bank (AL-Hawary & Hussien, 2017).

SSBT Privacy

This is one of the most important factors that may affect both the customer and bank, which pushes the customer to either repeat the electronic banking services or complain and leave. The definition of SSBT privacy as customer confidence in the bank's ability to provide privacy of electronic services, that may affect their willingness to accomplish their transactions via the Internet, and involves providing security controls to protect data from either an internal or external attack. The Privacy measures of SSBT protect customers' financial and personal information from risks of fraud and espionage and generate a positive feeling for customers, so it is valuable to banks to protect the privacy of their information, and provide a high level of protection while letting service proceed smoothly (AL-Hawary & Hussien, 2017).

METHODOLOGY

This chapter explores the operations of the Libyan banking sector through quantitative data. Analysis of this data is used to provide a unique contribution to the literature on SSBT and customers' relationships with the Libyan banking sector, as investigated (Twati & Gammack, 2006). The author has adopted a survey questionnaire method to understand the relationships between SSBT use and banking customers' perceptions of their banks and the extent of increased SSBT offerings.

As this chapter focused on Libyans who are in a foreign country (Australia) and use SSBT in both Libya and Australia, it is important to consider the population of this sample. The present population of Libyans who are studying in Australia is 2,601 (753 in higher education & 1,848 in ELICOS) (Australian Education International, 2011).

The process used herein is a technique of sampling in which each possible respondent had the same probability of being selected from the overall target population. The sample was chosen from the Libyan community (students) who live in different cities in Australia. A cover letter in official language was sent explaining the importance of the study and requesting a response from the respondent. Although this sample may not be fully typical of the entire ex-Libyan population within Australia, previous studies in other countries have shown that professionals are more likely to engage in online activities (Ahmed et al., 2007). These participants were also chosen by the Government to come to Australia and study advanced degrees (typically masters degrees and above) as they were leaders in Libya and on their return, they should have greater input to benefit the country's economy.

Respondents were asked about their interactions with their bank in both Libya and Australia. Participants were asked to state whether a particular technology was available at their bank and, if it was, whether they used or did not use the technology. Participants were asked if they used the traditional method of going to a teller to complete their transactions and then were asked about a number of technologies. The technologies that were focused on were: Automatic Teller Machines (ATMs); telephone banking; Internet banking; and mobile banking. Descriptive analysis of the data was conducted using SPSS 18 (18 or 20??) and there were 141 responses that were suitable for analysis from the 384 surveys sent (approximately 36.7% valid response rate).

RESULTS

The data collected from the respondent was coded and entered in SSPS V20 for data analysis. The following section of this chapter present the results from the factor analysis, descriptive statistics and multiple Regression test of the participant demographics. This is followed by an analysis of the responses to technology use and banking technology use by participants in both Libya and Australia.

Reliability and Validity

Analysis of reliability is done as to quantify the level of reliability of the data. Its purpose is to help the reader evaluate whether the data collected are reliable or not reliable. Cronbach α's were computed as a measure for construct reliability (Suki, 2015).

Cronbach's alpha (α) refers to the scale's stability over a range of conditions. Cronbach's α is based on the average correlation of items in a test if the items are standardized, and lies in the range of 0 to 1. Reliability is used to measure the extent to which a group will yield the same score even when each item is removed (Selamat & Jaffar, 2011).

The survey instrument with 58 items was developed based on self-services technologies (SSBT) as independent variables with five aspects: (1) Ease of Use, (2) Usefulness, (3) Trust, (4) Privacy (5) Quality.

Reliability analysis is used herein in order to determine the data reliability for the Self services. All individual loadings were above the minimum of 0.5 recommended by Suki (2015); and Al-Hawary and Hussien (2017). A Cronbach α greater than 0.70 is generally considerate reliable. Thus, Cronbach α statistics can conclude that the measures used are reliable.

Validity is concerned with the extent to which the tools in a model measure what they are believed to measure, and only that; i.e. it refers to the degree to which a measure accurately represents what it is supposed to measure (Toelle, 2006). The purpose of assessing content validity is to ensure that the items developed in the previous steps reflect the content areas encompassed in the specific variables included (Rose, 2007).

Validity can be assessed in a number of ways, two of which are: content validity and statistical validity (including criterion-related validity and construct validity). This thesis evaluates whether the instrument used is statistically valid and whether the survey was designed sufficiently well to determine relationships between variables as discussed by Abu-Jaber (2007).

Table 2. Cronbach α; variance Eigenvalue communalities

Items	N of items	Cronbach (α)	Eigenvalue	Variance
Ease of Use	7	0.824	4.706	78.435
Useful	6	.897	4.242	84.844
Trust	9	.771	2.979	74.478
Quality	23	.806	3.327	83.182
Privacy	7	.835	4.276	85.514
SSBT	6	.871	4.671	82.642

Descriptive Analysis

Descriptive analysis of data is important for understanding the sample of participants and how they relate to the overall population. From the frequency distribution of the respondents (Table 3) it can be seen that there was a total of 141 respondents. Seventy four percent of the respondents were male and twenty six percent of respondents were female. Although this does not reflect the Libyan population (Central Intelligence Agency (CIA), 2012), so the figures may reflect the population that is being educated in developed country. In terms of age, 1.4% of the respondents were 24 years or less. The age group analysis shows that the majority of the respondents (52.8%) were in the age range of 25-34 years, and 37.7% were in the 35-44 years' range. Only 5.6% of the respondents exceed 45 years. In Libya, 62.7% of the population are 15-64 years old, and the median age of a Libyan is 24.5 years (Central Intelligence Agency (CIA), 2012). Hence, the sample respondents' average age is slightly above the national average. However, the sample age range reflects those people most likely to engage in e-banking and m-banking on their return to Libya. With respect to the level of education, respondents were primarily people with high education. Hence, although, this sample average age is slightly above the national average, as stated above studies in other countries have shown that professionals are more likely to engage in online activities (Ahmed et al., 2007; Donner & Tellez, 2008).

Table 4 shows a comparison of the use of self -service banking technologies by participants in both Libya and Australia. The results indicate that there is greater use of most technologies when participants were in Australia. All participants stated that they used the Internet and M-phones while in Australia. The only exception to higher technology usage in Australia was the traditional telephone, with a large

Table 3. Demographics for participants

Measure	Item	Frequency	Percentage %
Gender	Male	104	73.8
	Female	37	26.2
Total		141	100
Age	18 – 24	2	1.4
	25 – 34	74	52.5
	35 – 44	53	37.6
	45 – 54	8	5.7
Total		137	97.2
Missing		4	2.8
Education Level	High school	3	2.1
	High diploma	34	24.1
	Undergraduate	46	32.6
	Postgraduate	53	37.6
Total		136	96.5
Missing		5	3.5

Source: prepared by author

Table 4. SSBT device use in Libya and Australia

	Telephone		Mobile Phone		Computer		Internet	
	Libya	**Australia**	**Libya**	**Australia**	**Libya**	**Australia**	**Libya**	**Australia**
Use	89	55	119	133	113	136	119	139
Total	105	89	127	138	124	138	124	139
Missing	*36*	*52*	*14*	*3*	*17*	*3*	*17*	*2*

number of participants stating that they did not use that technology in Australia. The Computer and Internet usage differs greatly from the national average of Libya, where only 14% of the population currently use the Internet (The World Bank, 2012). This may be a reflection of the sample population; the fact that the participants are in Australia furthering their education indicates that this is not a normal cross-section of the overall Libyan population. This sample population that uses the Internet in both Libya and Australia have a greater chance for adopting SSBT as they are already using ICT technology in other areas of their life (e.g. education) and have observed its benefits.

With regards to Table 5 about the usage of self-service banking technologies in both Libya and Australia by participants. There is increased usage of technology-enabled banking services while participants are in Australia compared with how they conducted their banking in Libya. This identifies areas that Libyan banks should focus their attention on when reviewing the technologies that they are implementing. Previous research by Twati (2008) focused only on low level of SSBT adoption in Libya. These results are of interest as they show that a technology that is taken for granted in Australia, such as the ATM, is not available to a large majority of Libyans when they bank in Libya. The results also show that traditional face-to-face interactions with a bank teller (used by 106 participants in Libya compared with 75 participants in Australia) are used less by Libyans when other technology-enabled services are available.

According to Table 6 shows how customers have changed their use of the five-different means of conducting banking. A review of the relevant survey responses identified that, for surveys where data was missing, the participant either did not use that banking service or perceived that the banking service was not available to them. Therefore, 'Missing' responses are recorded as 'Don't' in Table 5. The "Don't: Don't" row indicates the participants who did not use the service when they were in Libya or in Australia. The "Don't: Do" row shows participants who did not use the service in Libya but have adopted the service in Australia. The "Do: Don't" row indicates the participants who used the service while they were in Libya but do not use it in Australia. The "Do: Do" row indicates the participants that use the service both in Libya and Australia. From Table 4, an increase in the adoption of SSTs while the par-

Table 5. Banking technologies used in Libya and Australia

	At a teller		ATM		Internet Banking		Mobile Banking	
	Libya	**Australia**	**Libya**	**Australia**	**Libya**	**Australia**	**Libya**	**Australia**
Don't Use	4	36	37	4	35	14	37	75
Use	106	75	19	136	6	118	13	46
Total	110	111	56	140	41	132	50	121
Missing	*31*	*30*	*85*	*1*	*100*	*9*	*91*	*20*

Table 6. SSBT changes between Libya and Australia

	At a teller	ATM	Phone Banking	Internet Banking	Mobile Banking
Don't:Don't	31	4	85	21	88
Don't:Do	4	118	44	114	40
Do:Don't	35	1	8	2	7
Do:Do	71	18	4	4	6

ticipants were in Australia can be seen. To analyse whether these results showed any significant changes in participant use of SSTs between Libya and Australia, a McNemar Chi-squared test was conducted.

Table 7 shows the results of the McNemar Chi-squared tests conducted on the data from below table the tests all show significant changes in participant use of the services. For the 'at the teller' service (a traditional face-to-face service), a significant decrease in the use of this service was shown by the result. This could be due to a number of factors, from language issues (English is not the participants' native language) to geographic boundaries. For the SSBT (ATM, phone banking, Internet banking and mobile banking), the significant difference occurred in the direction of increased adoption of the services. The increased level of adoption could be attributed to the increased availability of the banking SSBT to the participants, an increased level of general Internet access (as all the participants were in Australia under Student Visas, it would be expected by their educational institutions that they will use this technology), and/or that it was easier for participants to interact with SSBT compared to 'at the teller' due to language and geographic issues. Future research through participant interviews would inform an increased understanding of the reasons for these changes in service usage between the developed and developing country.

DISCUSSION

The results from this chapter present preliminary findings about the technology usage of Libyans before they left Libya (i.e. a developing country) to further their studies compared to during their studies in Australia (i.e. a developed country). The data from this study can contribute new knowledge to fill the gap in literature addressing technology adoption while a person is in a foreign county for an extended period of time. Further research is needed to understand this relationship between what a person does

Table 7. McNemar Chi-squared test on banking changes

	Chi-Squared	Df	P
At the teller	23.077	1	0.000*
ATM	113.076	1	0.000*
Phone Banking	23.558	1	0.000*
Internet Banking	106.216	1	0.000*
Mobile Banking	21.787	1	0.000*

* statistically significant as P<0.05

when living in a developing nation compared to how they interact when they are in a developed nation for an extended period of time, as well as their expectations upon returning to the developing nation.

Self-service banking technology in Libya is likely to become increasingly more important. Banks struggle to maximize competitive advantages and need to introduce self-service in order to remain competitive in expanding marketplace. Also, bank managers need to continually assess consumers' propensity to accept and use the new self-service technology that they offer. The unique contribution of this chapter for the developing Libyan banking sector is the rich data on customer beliefs about self-service technologies and their use, gathered through the dual use of surveys and interviews. Both the approach and findings of this study can guide future research investigating this phenomenon in other developing countries. The findings not only enhance the existing understanding of the influence of customers' relationships in banking, but also provide new knowledge in this field to fill the gap in the literature about the strategic alignment of Internet- and m- banking across the banking sector in developing countries.

One implication of these results is that Libyan banks need to highlight the benefits of SSBT applications to their customers, particularly those systems that are self-service and customer-facing. Benefits of these technologies that are important to customers are convenience and increased availability.

Libyan banks should be adopting existing technologies from the developed world to meet the challenges of speed, efficiency and changing customer needs; providing value added services to their customers. These techniques will let customers use self-service technologies and help customers to complete banking transactions. Internet- and m-banking assist customers to check balances, pay bills, transfer money and identify information on their accounts.

The main benefit for Libyan banks is the creation of competitive advantage through the adoption of SSBT for customer use. The major contribution of this study is that it provides significant evidence that SSBT plays a vital role in enhancing customer relationships in the Libyan banking sector. As a result, SSBT is forcing changes to banks' business processes and the way they operate. SSBT has the potential to offer benefits such as better management of customer relationships, and through this, creation of a competitive advantage.

LIMITATIONS

There are several limitations that are should be considered as potential future research opportunities and areas of future improvement when researching self-service technologies and their adoption in the developing world.

Actually, it is almost impossible for any single study to cover every aspect within the research field of SSTs and customer relationships. The author has been used a sampling of Libyan citizens who were studying in Australia and who were aged between 18 – 54, they were educated (currently completing undergraduate; master and doctoral degrees). However, the sample respondents are limited to customers in the SSTs field who were willing to be surveyed.

Although every effort was made to make this study as comprehensive as possible, certain limitations were present. The response rate was lower than was hoped for, and this is mainly attributed to difficulties in advertising the questionnaire. Due to the low response rate, the results are less statistically significant, and this may mean that some of the rejected hypotheses would have been accepted had the sample sizes been much larger, and significance levels thus higher.

RECOMMENDATIONS AND FUTURE RESEARCH

The following recommendations, both about findings and areas requiring further investigation, are made to the Libyan banking sector in particular, and to the banks of other developing countries that are seeking the adoption of SSTs in customer-facing systems to enhance bank interaction with customers:

Further study is needed to develop a comprehensive view of determinants that influence individuals' attitudes and decisions around SSTs adoption. This requires an understanding of how to best integrate the concepts of consumer relationships, banking, and SSBT applications. To achieve this, research must go beyond the theoretical and conceptual bases of SSBT, and join forces with other experts and researchers from related areas (such as consumer attitude and customer relationships management) to establish outcomes that are useful for practitioners.

Another interesting area for further research could be a detailed study on online banking usage, measuring online banking acceptance along with other possible factors derived from various sources of literature. Testing of acceptance in conjunction with innovation theories may yield interesting outcomes for customer relationships.

Future research could be conducted to better understand how banks can facilitate greater commitment of customers to effectively use new SSBT systems, particularly customer-focused knowledge of self-service technologies. One possible example is investigating the impact of involving end users in the decision-making process for adopting new SSBT in banks.

Further studies should examine other predictors of propensity to use technology. Finally, future research could examine models of the relationship between the SSBT and security, access, and competitive advantages when smart phones are used in using self-service banking technology.

CONCLUSION

This chapter has presented the results from the survey. Initially, respondents' demographics and technology usage were summarised. A multiple regression analysis was employed to identify whether SSBT was positively influenced by EOS, U, SQ, P, and T. Table 8 summarizes the results from this analysis.

Multiple linear regression models were used to investigate the effect of independent variables against dependent variable. The study results in Table 8 record an adjusted R squared of 0.340, indicating that joint contribution of ease of use of SSBT and facilitating condition explains 34% variation of Use of self service banking technology in Libya.

Table 8. Coefficient and significant of model items

Items	$R2$	Coefficient	Sig
E o U	0.340	0.088	0.005
U	0.340	0.561	0.000
T	0.339	0.330	0.050
Q	0.167	0.409	0.000
P	0.339	0.433	0.000
SSBT	0.339	0.260	0.000

The results from the multiple regression analysis support a number of the studies in this field. The analysis confirms that a customer's Trust in relation to self-service technologies in the banking sector is not significantly related to Customer self- services. However, when such self-service technologies are offered, customers' perceptions of Online Banking Quality are significantly related to their Customer Trust, and it is significantly related to their Customer Loyalty in using SSBT.

In practice, this means that if a Libyan bank chooses to employ self-service banking technologies for their customers, and these technologies are of an appropriate quality standard (such as the level provided by Australian banks and used by participants in this study), then customers are likely to use these technologies and this will ultimately increase Customer Loyalty. The usage rates of Australian banking self-service technologies, as provided by survey respondents, reflect that high-quality services are more likely to be adopted by customers, even when those customers do not have a positive attitude towards technology. Therefore, Internet- and m-banking have come to be considered highly effective banking services methods because they process many advantages that traditional banking channels cannot offer.

While the current chapter generally highlights the benefits of self-service channels, it mostly disregards prior findings on the merit of personal service channels for both customer and the bank. Scherer et al. (2015) notes that more and more service providers are actively "pushing" their customers toward self-service channels.

As shown in the section above, SSBT provides the potential for Libyan banks to attract new customers and create positive relationships through utilization of technology-enabled services, as these services are used by Libyans when they are in developed countries. This issue has previously been highlighted in the literature, where technology-enabled services were used to offer customers an enhanced range of services at very low cost, resulting in banks having the potential to provide advantages to their customers (Cracknell, 2004). However, the low level of SSBT infrastructure in developing countries like Libya is a barrier to develop these technology-enabled services and to allow customers to adopt them. One specific significant challenge is the lack of uniform e-payment systems; credit cards are not common in Libya because of SSBT infrastructure limitations, trust and security issues. As a result, many customers have not been able to fully profit from technologies and banks cannot develop better relationships with their customers (Thao & Swierczek, 2008; Twati, 2008)

This conclusion has important implications for Libyan banks' use of SSBT. They can be used to support Libyan banking staff to better understand the key SSBT channels on which they must focus in order to improve customer satisfaction and their services. Effective SSBT has become an absolute necessity to engage with customers. It can also improve banks' efficiency, usefulness, flexibility, cost saving, competitive advantage, data collection and management, and service quality of interactions with customers. SSBT has changed banks' business processes and method of operation internationally. These changes must be understood and responded to by Libyan banks if they are to compete in the rapidly progressing international financial sector.

Additional challenges faced by Libya, as a developing country, include: the level of customers' experience with SSBT which impacts on m-banking uptake and the need for provision of support services during the introduction of new banking channels(Khatri & Kurnia, 2011); the management of perceptions about the acceptability of new banking channels; the implementation of the technologies and related systems within banks to support the implementation of SSBT for customers; and the development of awareness and knowledge about how to derive maximum benefits from new banking channels.

REFERENCES

Abu-Jaber, M. (2007). *Readiness of the Palestinian banking sector in adopting the electronic banking system (exploratory study)*. Unpublished master's thesis, The Islamic University.

Afsar, B., Rehman, Z. U., Qureshi, J. Z., & Shahjehan, A. (2010). Determinants of customer loyalty in the bank sector: The case of Pakistan. *African Journal of Business Management, 4*(6), 1040–1047.

Ahmed, M., Anjomshoaa, A., & Tjoa, A. M. (2007). User data privacy in web services context using semantic desktop - semanticLife case study. *Paper presented at the 9th International Conference on Information Integration and Web-based Applications & Services (iiWAS '07)*, Jakarta, Indonesia.

Akel, M., & Phillips, R. (2001). The internet advantage: A process for integrating electronic commerce into economic development strategy. *The Journal of Economic Development Review, 17*(3), 13–20.

Al-Fahim, N. H. (2013). An Exploratory Study of Factors Affecting the Internet Banking Adoption: A Qualitative Study among Postgraduate Student. *Global Journal of Management and Business Research Finance, 13*(8), 11.

Al-Fawzan, M. A. (2005). Assessing service quality in a Saudi bank. *Journal of King Saud University Engineering and Science, 18*(1), 101–115.

AL-Hawary. S. I. S., & Hussien, A. J. A. (2017). The Impact of Electronic Banking Services on the Customers Loyalty of Commercial Banks in Jordan. *International Journal of Academic Research in Accounting, Finance and Management Sciences, 7*(1), 50 - 63.

Al-Mabrouk, K., & Soar, J. (2009). Delphi examination of emerging issues for successful information technology transfer in North Africa: A case of Libya. *African Journal of Business Management, 3*(3), 107–114.

Al-Sukkar, A. S. (2005). *The application of information systems in the Jordainan banking sector: A study of the acceptance of the Internet.* Unpublished doctoral dissertation, University of Wollongong.

Alhinai, Y. S. (2009). *The adoption of advanced mobile commerce services by individuals: investigating the impact of the interaction between the consumer and the mobile services provider.* Unpublished doctoral dissertation, University of Melbourne.

Amin, H. (2008). Factors affecting the intentions of customers in Malaysia to use mobile phone credit cards. *Management Research News Journal, 31*(7), 493–503. doi:10.1108/01409170810876062

Ayo, C., Adewoye, J., & Oni, A. (2010). The state of e-banking implementation in Nigeria: A post-Consolidation review. *Journal of Emerging Trends in Economics and Management Science, 1*(1), 37–45.

Banerjee, M. (2009). Internet banking: An interaction building channel for bank customer relationships. In Self-Service in the Internet Age (pp. 195 - 212). London Springer-Verlag. doi:10.1007/978-1-84800-207-4-10

Blut, M., Wang, C., & Schoefer, K. (2016). Factors Influencing the Acceptance of Self-Service Technologies: A Meta-Analysis. *Journal of Service Research, 19*(4), 396–416. doi:10.1177/1094670516662352

Cavusoglu, H. (2003). *The economics of information technology investments.* Unpublished doctoral dissertation, University of Texas at Dallas.

Central Intelligence Agency (CIA). (2016). *The World Factbook.* Retrieved from https://www.cia.gov/library/publications/the-world-factbook/geos/ly.html

Central Libyan Bank. (2012). *Central Libyan Bank Report.*

Cheah, C. M., Teo, J. J., Sim, K. H., & Tan, B. T. (2011). Factors affecting Malaysian mobile banking adoption: An empirical analysis. *International Journal of Network and Mobile Technologies., 2*(3), 12.

Cleveland, C. E. (2016). *A Study on How Mobile Banking Has Affected the Banking Industry: Has Mobile Banking Improved Bank Performance? (Master Degree).* University of Mississippi.

Costello, G. I., & Tuchen, J. H. (1998). A comparative study of business to consumer electronic commerce within the Australian insurance sector. *Journal of Information Technology, 13*(3), 153–167. doi:10.1080/026839698344800

Cracknell, D. (2004). Electronic banking for the poor - panacea, potential and pitfalls. *MicroSave, 15.*

Dabholkar, P. A. (1996). Consumer evaluations of new technology-based selfservice options: An investigation of alternative models of service quality. *International Journal of Research in Marketing, 13*(1), 29–51. doi:10.1016/0167-8116(95)00027-5

Davison, R., Vogel, M., Harris, A., & Jones, N. (2000). Technology Leapfrogging in Developing Countries - An Inevitable Luxury? *The Electronic Journal of Information Systems in Developing Countries, 1*(5), 1–10.

Deng, Z., Lu, K., Wei, J., & Zhang, J. (2010). Understanding customer satisfaction and loyalty: An empirical study of mobile instant messages in China. *International Journal of Information Management, 30*(4), 289–300. doi:10.1016/j.ijinfomgt.2009.10.001

Dewan, S. M., Low, G., Land, L., & Dewan, A. (2009). Consumer choice model of mobile banking. *Paper presented at the 20th Australasian Conference on Information Systems*, Melbourne, Australia.

Donner, J., & Tellez, C. A. (2008). Mobile banking and economic development: Linking adoption. *impact, and use. Asian Journal of Communication, 18*(4), 318–322. doi:10.1080/01292980802344190

Elalagg, B. (Ed.). (2003). *Marketing in internet era.* Oman: Jourden.

Elgahwash, F. O., & Freeman, M. B. (2013). Self-Service Technology Banking Preferences: Comparing Libyans Behaviour in Developing and Developed Countries. *International Journal of Intelligent Information Technologies, 9*(2), 7–20. doi:10.4018/jiit.2013040102

Evans, N., & Sawyer, J. (2009). Internet usage in small businesses in regional South Australia: Service learning opportunities for a local university. *Education in Rural Australia, 19*(1), 15–33.

Flavian, C., Guinaliu, M., & Gurrea, R. (2006). The role played by perceived usability, satisfaction and consumer trust on website loyalty. *Information & Management Journal, 43*(1), 1–14. doi:10.1016/j.im.2005.01.002

Galliers, R. D., & Leidner, D. E. (2003). *Strategic Information Management Challenges and strategies in managing information systems.*

Gurau, G. (2011). Online Self-Services: Investigating the Stages of Customer-SST Systems Interaction. In *Developing Technologies in E-Services, Self-Services, and Mobile Communication: New Concepts.* Hershey, PA: IGI Global. doi: Retrieved from www.igi-global.com/chapter/online-self-services/54958 ?camid=4v110.4018/978-1-60960-607-7.ch005

Halstead, D., & Richards, K. (2014). From high tech to high touch: Enhancing customer service experiences via improved self-service technologies. *Innovative Marketing Journal, 10*(4), 16.

Hamed, A., Ball, D., Berger, H., & Cleary, P. (2008). The three-quarter moon: A new model for e-commerce adoption. *The Journal of Communications of the IBIMA, 4*(11), 88–96.

Ho, S. J., & Mallick, S. K. (2006). The impact of information technology on the banking industry: Theory and Empirics. Retrieved from http://webspace.qmul.ac.uk/pmartins/mallick.pdf

Hunaiti, Z., Mansour, M., & Al-Nawafleh, A. (2009). Electronic commerce adoption barriers in small and medium-sized enterprises (SMEs) in developing countries: The case of Libya. *IBIMA Business Review Journal, 2*(5), 37–45.

Ivatury, G., & Pickens, M. (2006). *Mobile phone banking and low-income customers -evidence from South Africa: Consultative Group to Assist the Poor.*

Kardaras, D., & Papathanassiou, E. (2000). The development of B2C e-commerce in Greece: Current situation and future potential. *Journal of Internet Research, 10*(4), 284–299.

Karim, A. J., & Hamdan, A. M. (2010). The impact of information technology on improving banking performance matrix: jordanian banks as case study. *Paper presented at the European, Mediterranean & Middle Eastern Conference on Information Systems (EMCIS)*, Abu Dhabi, UAE, Ahlia University, Manama, Kingdom of Bahrain.

Khatri, A., & Kurnia, K. (2011). Mobile banking adoption: In Australian rural areas. *Paper presented at the Pacific Asia Conference on Information Systems (PACIS)*, Brisbane, Australia.

Kim, J., Jin, B., & Swinney, J. L. (2009). The role of etail quality, e-satisfaction and e-trust in online loyalty development process. *Journal of Retailing and Consumer Services, 16*(4), 239–247. doi:10.1016/j. jretconser.2008.11.019

Kridan, A. B. (2006). *A knowledge management implementation framework for the Libyan banking sector.* Unpublished doctoral dissertation, University of Salford.

Laukkanen, T., & Pasanen, M. (2008). Mobile banking innovators and early adopters: How they differ from other online users. *Journal of Financial Services Marketing, 13*(2), 86–94. doi:10.1057/palgrave. fsm.4760077

Leek, S., Turnbull, P. W., & Naude, P. (2003). How is information technology affecting business relationships? Results from a UK survey. *Industrial Marketing Management Journal, 32*(2), 119–126. doi:10.1016/S0019-8501(02)00226-2

Liao, C., Palvia, J., & Liang, C. (2009). Information technology adoption behavior life cycle: Toward a technology continuance theory (TCT). *International Journal of Information Management*, *29*(4), 309–320. doi:10.1016/j.ijinfomgt.2009.03.004

Libyan Central Bank. (2015). Libyan Central Bank.

Marshall, I., & Parulekar, A. (2009). *Research Study on The Revolution in Self-Service Channels in the Financial Services Sector*. Newcastle University and Business & Decision: Newcastle University and Business & Decision.

Mashat, A., Ritchie, B., Lovatt, C., & Pratten, J. (2005). *The Social Role of Accounting: Views and Perceptions of the Accounting Community in Libya towards Corporate Social Responsibility and Accountability*.

Mastoori, Y. (2009). *Reasons barring customers from using Internet banking In Iran: An integrated approach based on means - end chains and segmentation*. Unpublished master's thesis, Lulea University of Technology.

McPhail, J., & Fogarty, G. (2004). *Predicting senior consumers' acceptance and use of self-service banking technologies: Test of the extended technology acceptance model*. Australia, Dunedin, New Zealand: James Cook University.

Mehmood, N., Shah, F., Azhar, M., & Rasheed, A. (2014). The Factors Effecting E-banking Usage in Pakistan. *Journal of Management Information System and E-commerce*, *1*(1), 57–94.

Mouelhi, R. B. A. (2009). Impact of the adoption of information and communication technologies on firm efficiency in the Tunisian manufacturing sector. *Economic Modelling, 26*(5), 961-967. doi:http://www.sciencedirect.com/science/article/pii/S0264999309000480

Mukthtar, M. (2015). Perceptions of UK Based Customers toward Internet Banking in the United Kingdom. *Journal of Internet Banking and Commerce, 20*(1). Retrieved from http://www.arraydev.com/commerce/jibc/

Nasri, W., & Charfeddine, L. (2012). Factors affecting the adoption of Internet banking in Tunisia: An integration theory of acceptance model and theory of planned behavior. *The Journal of High Technology Management Research, 23*(1), 1–14. doi:10.1016/j.hitech.2012.03.001

Nippatlapalli, A. R. (2013). A Study On Customer Satisfaction Of Commercial Banks: Case Study On State Bank Of India. *IOSR Journal of Business and Management, 15*(1), 60 - 86. doi:www.iosrjournals.org

Petridou, E., Spathis, N., Glaveli, N., & Liassides, C. (2007). Bank service quality: Empirical evidence from Greek and Bulgarian retail customers. *International Journal of Quality & Reliability Management*, *24*(6), 568–585. doi:10.1108/02656710710757772

Pousttchi, K., & Schurig, M. (2004). Assessment of today's mobile banking applications from the view of customer requirements. *Paper presented at the 37th Hawaii International Conference on System Sciences (HICSS)*, Big Island, Hawaii. doi:10.1109/HICSS.2004.1265440

Rajagopal, & Rajagopal, A. (2007). *Emerging perspectives on self service technologies in retail banking*. Marketing Working Papers.

Rose, J. (2007). *Predicting mature consumers' attitudes towards use of self-service technologies in the financial services context.* Unpublished doctoral dissertation, University of Southern Queensland.

Sadek, D., Zainal, N., Taher, M., & Yahya, A. (2010). Service quality perceptions between Cooperative and Islamic Banks of Britain. *American Journal of Economics and Business Administration, 2*(1), 1–5. doi:10.3844/ajebasp.2010.1.5

Safeena, R., Date, H., & Kammani, A. (2011). Internet banking adoption in an emerging economy: Indian consumers' perspective. *International Arab Journal of E-Technology, 2*(1), 56–64.

Salomann, H., Kolbe, L., & Brenner, W. (2006). Self-services in customer relationships: Balancing high-tech and high-touch today and tomorrow. *E-Service Journal, 4*(2), 65–84. doi:10.2979/ESJ.2006.4.2.65

Sannes, R. (2001). Self-service banking: Value creation models and information exchange. *Journal of Informing Science Special Series on Information Exchange in Electronic Markets, 4*(3), 139–149.

Scherer, A., Wünderlic, N., & Von Wangenheim, F. (2015). The Value of Self-Service: Long-Term Effects of Technology based Self- Services usage on Customer Retention. *Journal of MIS Quarterly, 39*(1), 177-200.

Schuster, Lisa, Proudfoot, Judy, & Drennan. (2015). Understanding consumer loyalty to technology-based self-services with credence qualities. *Journal of Services Marketing, 29*(6/7), 522-532. Retrieved from http://eprints.qut.edu.au/88010/1/88010.pdf

Selamat, Z., & Jaffar, N. (2011). Information technology acceptance: From the perspective of Malaysian bankers. *International Journal of Business and Management, 6*(1), 207–217.

Shaw, D. M. (2000). *The role of information technology in the development of small firm market capabilities.* Unpublished doctoral dissertation, Kent State University.

Simon, F., & Usunier, J. C. (2007). Cognitive, demographic, and situational determinants of service customer preference for personnel-in-contact over selfservice technology. *International Journal of Research in Marketing, 24*(2), 163–173. doi:10.1016/j.ijresmar.2006.11.004

Sindwani, & Goel, M. (2016). The Relationship between Service Quality Dimensions, Customer Satisfaction and Loyalty in Technology based Self Service Banking. *International Journal of E-Services and Mobile Applications, 8*(2). doi:10.4018/IJESMA.2016040104

Spathis, C., & Georgakopoulou, E. (2007). The adoption of IFRS in South Eastern Europe: The case of Greece. *International Journal of Financial Services Management, 2*(1), 50–63. doi:10.1504/IJFSM.2007.011671

Spears, W. S. (2004). *The impact of bank consolidation on services quality.* Unpublished doctoral dissertation, Nova Southeastern University.

Suki, N. M. (2015). An Empirical Study of Factors Affecting the Internet Banking Adoption among Malaysian Consumers? *Journal of Internet Banking and Commerce.*

Thao, H. T. P., & Swierczek, F. W. (2008). Internet use, customer relationships and loyalty in the Vietnamese travel industry. *Asia Pacific Journal of Marketing and Logistics, 20*(2), 190–210. doi:10.1108/13555850810864551

The World Bank. (2012). *Annual Report* Retrieved from http://siteresources.worldbank.org/EXTAN-NREP2012/Resources/8784408-1346247445238/AnnualReport2012_En.pdf

Toelle, S. (2006). *The linkages among services quality attributes, customer value, customer satisfaction, and customer loyalty in Indonesian retail banking settings* [Doctoral Degree]. Nova Southeastern University.

Travica, B. (2008). Influence of information culture on adoption of a self-service system. *Journal of Information System, Information Technology and Organizations, 3.*

Twati, J.M. (2008). The influence of societal culture on the adoption of information systems: The case of Libya. *Communications of the IIMA Journal, 8*(1), 1-12. Retrieved from http://scholarworks.lib.csusb.edu/ciima/vol8/iss1/1/

Twati, J. M., & Gammack, J. G. (2006). The impact of organizational culture innovation on the adoption of IS/IT: The case of Libya. *Journal of Enterprise Information Management, 19*(2), 175-191.

Vatanasombut, B., Igbaria, M., Stylianou, A. C., & Rodgers, W. (2008). Information system continuance intention of web-based applications customers: The case of online banking. *Information and Management Journal, 45*(7), 419–428. doi:10.1016/j.im.2008.03.005

Vogel, M. A. (2005). *Leveraging information technology competencies and capabilities for a competitive advantage.* Unpublished doctoral dissertation, University of Maryland.

Wamalwa, T. (2006). *The impact of Internet banking on banks: A descriptive and evaluative case study of a large U.S. bank.* Unpublished doctoral dissertation, Capella University.

Wei, K. (2009). Service quality index: A study on Malaysian banks. *Journal of Contemporary Management Research, 5*(2), 109–124.

Wells, J. D., Fuerst, W. L., & Choobineh, J. (1999). Managing information technology (IT) for one-to-one customer interaction. *Information and Management Journal, 35*(1), 53–62. doi:10.1016/S0378-7206(98)00076-7

Xu, B., Shao, B., Lin, Z., & Shi, Y. (2009). Enterprise adoption of Internet banking in China. *Journal of Global Information Technology Management, 12*(3), 7–28. doi:10.1080/1097198X.2009.10856495

Yu, J., & Guo, C. (2008). An exploratory study of applying ubiquitous technology to retail banking. *Paper presented at the Allied Academies International Conference*, Tunica, USA.

Zammuto, R. F., & Laube, D. R. (2003). *Business-Driven Information Technology* (S. B. Books, Ed.).

Zeng, L. (2016). *Factors Influencing the Adoption of Self-Service Technologies* [Master Degree Master]. Norwegian School of Economics, Bergen.

Chapter 13
Modularising the Complex Meta-Models in Enterprise Systems Using Conceptual Structures

Simon Polovina
Sheffield Hallam University, UK

Hans-Jurgen Scheruhn
Hochschule Harz, Germany

Mark von Rosing
Global University Alliance, Denmark

ABSTRACT

The development of meta-models in Enterprise Modelling, Enterprise Engineering, and Enterprise Architecture enables an enterprise to add value and meet its obligations to its stakeholders. This value is however undermined by the complexity in the meta-models which have become difficult to visualise thus deterring the human-driven process. These experiences have driven the development of layers and levels in the modular meta-model. Conceptual Structures (CS), described as "Information Processing in Mind and Machine", align the way computers work with how humans think. Using the Enterprise Information Meta-model Architecture (EIMA) as an exemplar, two forms of CS known as Conceptual Graphs (CGs) and Formal Concept Analysis (FCA) are brought together through the CGtoFCA algorithm, thereby mathematically evaluating the effectiveness of the layers and levels in these meta-models. The work reveals the useful contribution that this approach brings in actualising the modularising of complex meta-models in enterprise systems using conceptual structures.

DOI: 10.4018/978-1-5225-3686-4.ch013

INTRODUCTION

The development of meta-models in Enterprise Modelling, Enterprise Engineering, and Enterprise Architecture provide insight into the complexity of bus ness organizations (Bork et al., 2015; von Rosing and von Scheel, 2016). These meta-models are extensible across whole industries, individual businesses, their sub-organisations (e.g. departments) and individual workplaces where the actual activity takes place. Thus, a business enterprise's myriad resources (e.g. physical assets, human resources and IT systems) can be aligned with its purpose and strategy ('vision and mission'). The meta-models thereby facilitate enterprises to develop a conceptual model that creates the right context. These meta-models thereby enable enterprises to add value and reduce unnecessary cost and risk in meeting its obligations to its stakeholders (e.g. shareholders, employees, regulatory bodies and the wider environment).

Computer science has over its history contributed to the expressibility in these meta-models through its advances in ontology and semantics; together they capture the objects and relations that describe the interplay and effects of business in a formal, computable model (Floyd, 1967; Gruber, 1995; Oberle, 2013; von Rosing and Laurier, 2015). Computer productivity is thus brought to bear on the creativity of human endeavour, which identifies and sustains enterprise opportunities. Enterprise Architecture and modelling tools are predicated on formally conceptualized meta-models, and this success is already evident (Mayall & Carter, 2015; Bork et al., 2015; von Rosing et al., 2015; von Rosing, 2016).

The meta-models themselves however have become large, unwieldy and error-prone. Whilst the size of these models does not initially present a computational hurdle and the software can reveal errors and gaps that surface to human modellers (e.g. enterprise architects) and end-users (e.g. business decision-makers), the readability of the original meta-models have become illegible thus unreviewable by the human modellers. This aspect is pertinent; given the models are instigated by humans they should be re-viewable by them.

To support this review, there needs to be a consistency of concepts and their relations in these meta-models. The objects, their subtypes, descriptions, semantic relations and how they are viewed that collectively make up the meta-models must be consistently interrelated including the level at which they relate and how they could or should interconnect. For example, enterprise strategy permeates across all the areas of an enterprise; it should not just be captured as a disjointed function. Added to these mistakes are the uneven levels of composition and decomposition of the objects and relations. Put simply, the objects are wrongly thrown together at arbitrary levels, in what apparently are obvious connections but emerge to be much more complex. The meta-model ends up undermining rather than elucidating the effectiveness of the enterprise.

LAYERS AND LEVELS IN ENTERPRISE META-MODELS

To rebalance human creativity with computational execution, meta-models have been broken down into components then coupled together by interfaces analogous to the software engineering principles found in object-oriented design. Like programming-in-the-large, this approach has enabled 'metamodelling-in-the-large' (Zivkovic and Karagiannis, 2015). In Enterprise Architecture, the meta-models have been modularised into layers and levels that collectively describe how a business works. A study describes the benefits of this approach (Bork, 2015). The outcome is a matrix structure that is superficially akin to the grid originally pictured by Zachman, the 'father of enterprise architecture' (Zachman, 1987; Sow& Zachman, 1992).

Unlike Zachman however, these layer-and-level components have associated meta-models that include the underlying ontology and semantics, even though Zachman's framework is referred to as the 'Enterprise Ontology' (Zachman, 2015; Malik, 2009). One well-known metamodel example is the Open Group Architecture Framework (TOGAF)'s Content Metamodel (Group, 2011). It articulates the ontology and semantics by formally identifying the relations between the entities (objects) in the meta model. Given that a meta-model is the model about the model, we can refer to these entities or objects as meta-objects.

Semantics are an aspect of semiotics, like syntax, which distinguishes valid from invalid symbol structures, and like pragmatics, which relates symbols to their meaning within a context e.g. the community in which they are shared (Cordeiro & Filipe, 2004). Organizations should thus be considered holistically according to views and models that are laid out in a principled way that capture the:

- Business Perspective: Such as the purpose and goal, competencies, processes, and services aspects;
- Information Perspective: Such as the application systems, as well as the data components;
- Technology Perspective: Such as the platform and infrastructure components.

From the research and analysis conducted by the Global University Alliance (GUA)[1]. The GUA has been developing these contexts and structures, the most common identified structures and context in organizations are represented in Figure 1.

Figure 1. The layered enterprise view

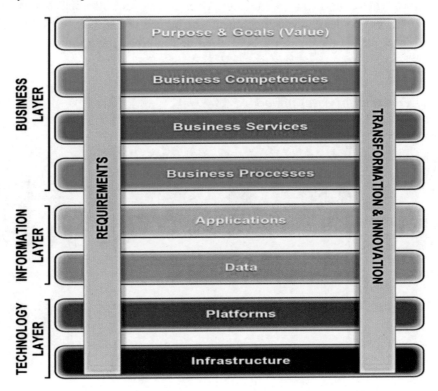

Relating Layers to Levels

Using layers enables the enterprise metamodel to be modularised so that it is human understandable. For example, a policy, act, regulation or even a strategy is a part of the business layer, while the application systems and data aspects is a part of the information systems layer. In Enterprise Architecture (as well as Enterprise Modelling and Enterprise Engineering) such layers need to relate to the levels represented within the organisation. Relating levels to layers creates a matrix structure as illustrated in Figure 2, where the overall enterprise layers i.e. business, information and technology are on top and the levels with the relevant views are represented on the left side.

Figure 2's Layered Enterprise way of working was developed by Zachman and the Global University Alliance (GUA), as mentioned earlier. and fathered the Business Ontology (von Rosing & Laurier, 2015). The practitioners' enterprise standard body LEADing Practice[2] has embodied this work as the Layered Enterprise Architecture Development (LEAD) (von Rosing & von Scheel, 2016).

THE EIMA

A thread within this work is the Enterprise Information Model (EIM), which demonstrates the above described modularized layout (Scheruhn et al., 2015; Polovina et al., 2016b). The EIM features an information-centric view that takes as its starting point the information concepts within the enterprise. It thus has a layer for value, one for competency, and others for service, process, IT applications and data respectively. Furthermore, these models occur at different levels in the enterprise, hence the layers-and-levels structure. Thus level 1 may be the enterprise itself, level 2 its departments, and level 3 the workplaces. Then last but not least, level 4 documents the other 3 layers. It governs the input and output data structures. These reflect the enterprise's external and internal environment that provides its op-

Figure 2. The layered enterprise way of working

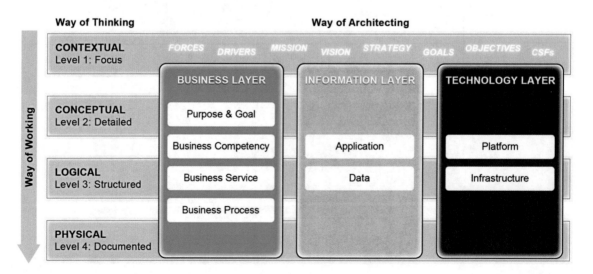

portunities and sets its constraints from level 1 downwards. As such, level 4 epitomizes the performance indicators of the other 3 layers that make up each layer.

Figure 3 outlines the layer-and-level structure as the resulting 6 x 4 matrix. The shading highlights that Value, Competency, Service and Process are a Business Layer. Application and Data are an Information Systems Layer shown in the earlier Figures 1 and 2. Table 1 explicates the layers and shows how that matrix is populated with the corresponding information concept specific meta-objects. They illustrate the meta-model matrix for the EIM i.e. the Enterprise Information *Meta*-model Architecture (EIMA).

The modularisation depicted in the matrix can equally be applied to other enterprise meta-models, including those that are orthogonal to it e.g. the a) business, informational, application and technology layers with the b) conceptual, logical and physical levels for each layer in the Essential meta-model (Mayall and Carter, 2015). The EIMA is applied to an SAP ERP (Enterprise Resource Planning) exemplar known as 'Global Bike Inc.' (GBI) that is used in SAP's University Alliances program[3]. The GBI exemplar incorporates the GUA and LEADing Practice's Layered Enterprise views, initiated by the earlier Figures 1 and 2. It continues previous academic work based on SAP as a case study, as a market-leadership and industrial-strength exemplar (Scheruhn et al., 2006; Scheruhn et al., 2013; Scheruhn et al., 2015; Zhao et al., 2014; Polovina et al., 2016a; Polovina et al., 2016b). The case study therefore serves as a further reminder of the enterprise layers-and-levels underlying rigor and practical application.

CONCEPTUAL STRUCTURES

There are undoubtedly many ways that the metamodels effectiveness could be evaluated. Whilst the comparative benefits of each approach are not evaluated here, amongst them is the disciple of Conceptual Structures (CS). In his seminal text, Sowa describes CS as "Information Processing in Mind and Machine" (Sowa, 1984). Enterprises essentially arise as acts of human creativity in identifying business opportunities or other organizational solutions to social needs (e.g. government bodies, charities, schools or universities to name a few). Formal depictions of the metamodels (and the models that they in turn represent) enable them to be computable. Software tools (among them Essential as mentioned earlier) bring the productivity of computers to bear, offering more expressive knowledge-bases leading to better decision-making. CS brings human creativity and computer productivity into the same mindset; CS thus offers an attractive proposition for capturing, interrelating and reasoning with enterprise meta-models within and across the layers and levels of the EIMA.

Figure 3. EIMA overview

Layer ➔ Level ⬇	Value	Competency	Service	Process	Application	Data
1						
2						
3						
4						

Table 1. Enterprise Information Meta-model Architecture (EIMA)

Level	Layer:					
	Business Layer Value	**Competency**	**Service**	**Process**	**Information Application**	**Systems Layer Data**
1	Vision, Mission	Business Function	Business Service	Business Process	Application Module	Enterprise Data Cluster
	Strategy, Goal	Organizational unit			Organizational unit	
2	Vision, Mission	Business Function	Business Service	Process Step	Application Function	
	Strategy, Goal	Organizational unit			Organizational unit	Department Data Cluster
3	Vision, Mission	Business Function	Business Service	Process Activity	Application Task	Workplace Data Entity
	Strategy, Goal				Transaction Code, System organizational Unit	
	Objective	Business Object		Event	Business Object	Dimension
					Data Entity Event	Data Entity
		Business Media/ Accounts		Data Object	Data Object (Media)	
		Business Roles	Service Roles	Process Role	Application Roles	
		Business Roles	Service Roles	Process Rules	Application Rules	
4	Performance Indicator	Business Compliance	Service Level Agreement (SLA)	Process Performance Indicator	IT Governance	Fact Table Customizing Data Table
						Master Data Table/View
						Transaction Data Table
		Revenue/ Cost Flow			System Measurements	Key Foreign Key
						Describing Attributes

To demonstrate CS, Sowa devised Conceptual Graphs (CGs) (Sowa, 1984; Polovina, 2007; Sowa, 2008). Essentially, CGs are a system of logic that express meaning in a form that is logically precise, humanly readable, and computationally tractable. CGs serve as an intermediate language for translating between computer-oriented formalisms and natural languages. CGs graphical representation serve as a readable, but formal design and specification language.

Although CGs provide a logical level of rigor, their constituent concepts and relations are essentially put together by hand according to the human's subjective interpretation of the real-world phenomena for it to be captured in a logical structure. A second form of CS known as Formal Concept Analysis (FCA) provides an objective mathematical interpretation of CGs' logical but subjective human interpretations (Ganter et al., 2005). FCA is brought to bear through the *CGtoFCA* algorithm (Andrews and Polovina, 2011). The outcome is then presented as a Formal Concept Lattice (FCL). A CG (Conceptual Graph) was produced for each layer. Each layer has a meaning its own right given their distinctive headings (i.e. Value, Competency, Service, Process, Application, and Data). Our intention was thereby to capture each layer as a modular 'semantic unit' in its own right.

The Business Layer

Value

The result for the Value Layer module is accordingly shown in Figure 4. It reveals how CGs follow an elementary concept→ relation concept structure that describes the ontology and semantics of the metamodel as explained earlier. Furthermore the figure shows how we can make use of CGs [Type-Label: Referent] components in each CGs concept. Its significance will be explained during the following discussion.

The Value CG depicts the each meta-object name (i.e. Vision, Mission, Strategy, Goal) as a CG type label. To instantiate it a particular meta-object, a unique identifier appears in the referent field. For example, v1V denotes that a meta-object that is Vision (v), Level 1 (1), and V (Value layer). Likewise, g3V for example describes Goal, Level 3, Value and so on. The [Enterprise: @enterprise] concept follows an alternative pattern where @enterprise is a CGs measure referent. The pointer to @enterprise follows that of previous work (Polovina et al., 2016a; Polovina et al., 2016b). The key significance of this concept is that all the activities that make up an enterprise ultimately point to the enterprise, even though Enterprise is absent in the table. The relations (e.g. (assigned_to)) also do not appear in the table; they are however in the EIM (Scheruhn et al., 2015). Essentially (assigned_to) refers to a horizontal relation usually in the same layer while (consists_of) is a vertical relation between the levels in the layers. (There is no associated layer or level for Enterprise as it reflects the ultimate culmination of all the layers and levels). The relation (measured-by) has its usual meaning.

Figure 5 shows the FCL (Formal Concept Lattice) ((Formal Concept Lattice) for the Value layer. It is the result of the *CGtoFCA* algorithm transforming the meta-object → relation → meta-object triples

Figure 4. Value, CGs

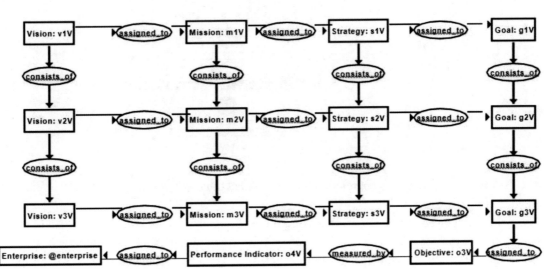

Figure 5. Value, FCL

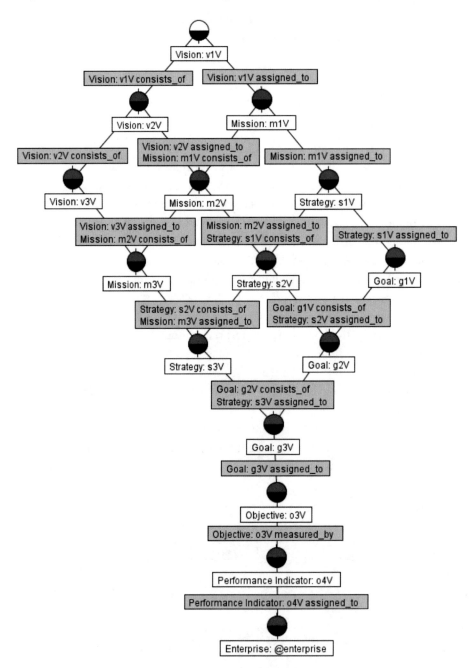

in the CG of Figure 4 to meta-object relation → meta-object binaries[4]. An example binary is Vision:v1V assigned to→Mission: m1V.

The neatly displayed lattice shows that [Enterprise: @enterprise] is bottommost. It is arguably a semantic unit, as the concept [Vision: v1V] passes transitively through the intermediate concepts and culminating in [Enterprise:@enterprise]. In FCA terminology a CGs concept (that we've mapped to a meta-object) is referred to as an FCA object and, in *CGtoFCA's* case, the meta-object relation is an FCA attribute. A concept in FCA – called a Formal Concept – is the result of when certain conditions are met in a formal *context*. Mathematically:

- A formal context is a triple K = (*G, M, I*), where *G* is a set of objects, *M* is a set of attributes, and *I GM* is a binary (true/false) relation that expresses which objects have which attributes.
- (*A, B*) is a formal concept precisely when:
  - Every object in *A* has every attribute in *B*,
  - For every object in *G* that is not in *A*, there is some attribute in B that the object does not have,
  - For every attribute in M that is not in *B*, there is some object in A that does not have that attribute.

To the uninitiated this may be confusing or a little too high-level; however, fuller explications of FCA with formal proofs and lucid worked examples can be found (Wolff, 1993; Ganter et al., 2005; Priss, 2006; Andrews et al., 2011)[5].

Competency

Figure 6 shows the CG for the Competency layer module. Some of the CG concepts in Figure 6 are shaded to highlight where they appear in the other layers. The shading scheme matches that shown by

Figure 6. Competency, GCs

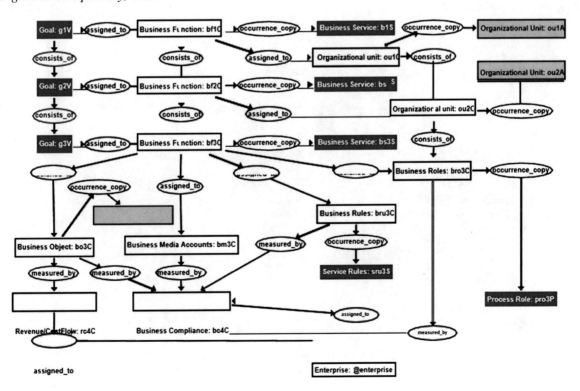

the earlier EIMA overview Figure 3. Again, the same mapping through *CGtoFCA* is applied and Figure 7 shows the resulting FCL. This time [Enterprise:@enterprise] is not bottommost.

An inspection of the CG reveals that there are concepts, such as [Business Service: b1S], [Service Rules: sru3S], [Process Role: pro3P] that have their identical concept in another business layer (e.g. S for Service, P for Process). Likewise [Business Object: bo3A], and [Organizational Unit: ou1A] in A the Application information layer do not transitively end up at [Enterprise: @enterprise] unlike the Value CG Figure 6 above. It is therefore harder to discern that this a semantic unit; it had dependencies with the other layers that will only be resolved when the CGs from those other relevant layers are joined with this layer. If, together, a transitive path to [Enterprise: @enterprise] is discovered they are (interdependent) semantic units.

While a simple inspection of the CG for this layer without the FCL reveals the incomplete transitivity, in the combined form this would be harder especially if the CGs for all the layers are joined. Note also the FCL, which is computer generated rather than hand-drawn, horizontally lays out the meta-objects according to their levels – unless they are all not transitive to [Enterprise: @enterprise], thereby offering another highlight. Compare Figure 7 with Figure 5 for example.

Service

Figure 8 shows the Service layer CG, which highlights similar findings to that of Competency. It exhibits the same [Type-Label: Referent] and (relation) pattern as illustrated by Value and Competency. So as a

Figure 7. Competency, FCL

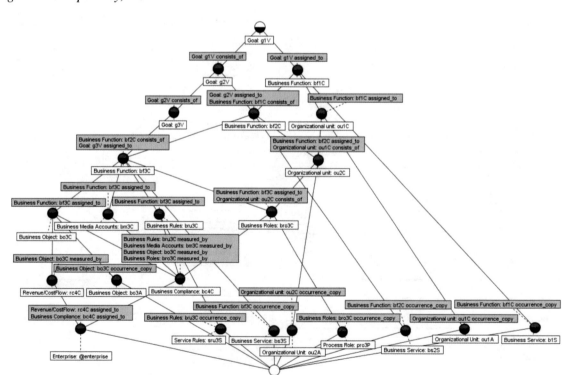

Figure 8. Service, CGs

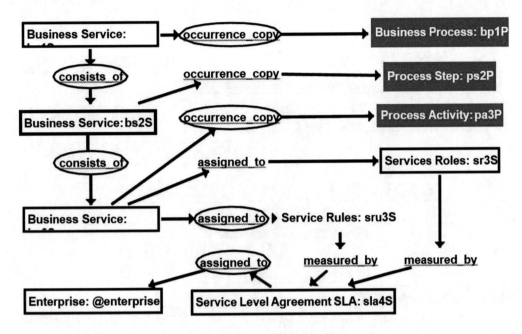

reminder, bs1S in [Business Service: bs1S] for example, describes bs for Business Service, 1 is Level 1, and S is Service. Certain concepts are also shaded to highlight their occurrence in another layer.

In this layer, there is an (occurrence_copy) relation too. This relation occurred in Competency too but we'll use Service to remark on it further. Essentially, this relation describes two concepts (meta-objects) that are synonymous, except they appear in different layers. For example, [Business Service: bs1S] (occurrence_copy) [Business Process: bp1P]. They are therefore not co-referent, and might be described as 'pseudo-synonym' meta-objects[6]. The FCL generated by *CGtoFCA* for the Service layer is shown by Figure 9. Put simply, Process needs Service to be a semantic unit, and vice versa. The same issue applies to Competency and its same dependencies with Service.

Figure 9's FCL evidences that [Enterprise: @enterprise] again is not bottommost. Looking at the reason that we already know from Competency but from another perspective, this is because of the meta-object relation attributes that are outside the *intent* of the level 4 key performance indicator (KPI) meta-object [Service Level Agreement (SLA): sla4s], which evaluates the Service layer. Intent here is an FCA term that reading upwards from a given Formal Concept towards the top of the lattice shows all the attributes that the concept has. Thus, [Enterprise: @enterprise] – given all the other concepts in the layer (as in Value) transitively arrive to it – has *all* the attributes in the lattice. Therefore, it is clearly shown that [Enterprise: @enterprise] captures all the features (attributes) that make up the given layer and nothing is left out. Unless they are out of its intent, as evident in Competency and Service.

Process

The Process layer is described by Figure 10 for the CG and Figure 11 for the FCL. [Enterprise: @enterprise] again is not bottommost. By now the behaviour of the transformation of the CG to FCL using CGtoFCA and the associated tools described earlier should be self-explanatory.

Figure 9. Service, FCL

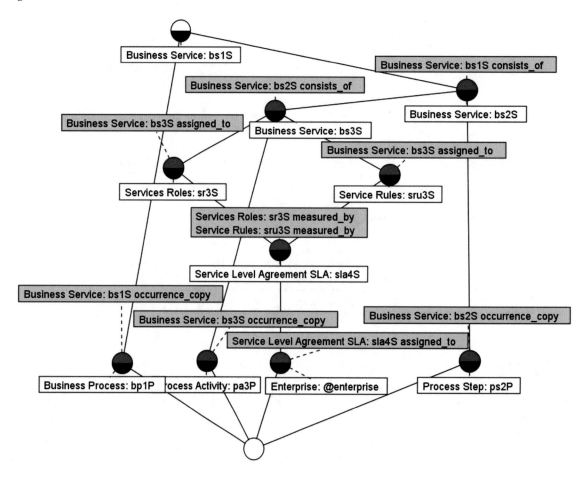

Figure 10. Process, CGs

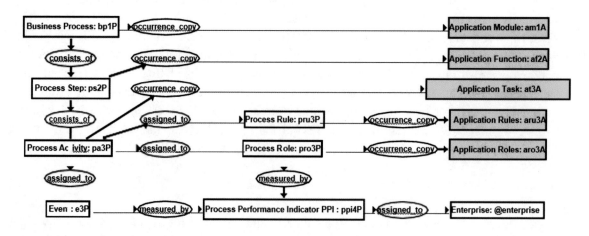

Figure 11. Process, FCL

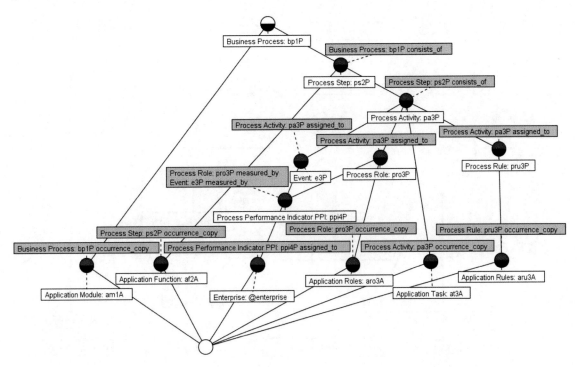

To aid our understanding however, we can consider FCA in more detail. In FCA, the bottommost concept is known as the *infimum* and the top most formal concept in a FCL is the *supremum*. In the Process layer the supremum is [Business Process: bp1P]. The FCA intent of a lattice through its attributes (e.g. Business Process: bp1P consists_of) has already been described; the *extent* is all the objects in the path of a given object down to the infimum. (The inverse of which is that the intent goes the other way up to the top of the lattice through the attributes to the supremum.) Thus, for example the extent of Process Activity: pa3P is Process Role: pro3P, Application Roles: aro3A, Application Task: at3A, Application Roles: aro3A, Process Rule: pru3P, Application Rules: aru3A, Event: e3P, Process Role: pro3P, Process Performance Indicator PPI: ppi4P, and Enterprise: @enterprise. Enterprise: @enterprise is *not* however in the extent of Application Roles: aro3A, Application Task: at3A, Application Roles: aro3A. In this layer as it stands these concepts (meta-objects) do not extend to the enterprise, when they ought to be given their expected impact on it!

The Information Systems Layer

Application

Figure 12 depicts the Application layer CG. Figure 13 evidences that [Enterprise: @enterprise]is not bottommost. That is because of the meta-object relation attributes that are outside the intent of the level 4 key performance indicator (KPI) meta-object [System Measurements: sm4A], which evaluates the Application layer. Also emerged in the middle of the lattice is another formal concept without its own

Figure 12. Application, CGs

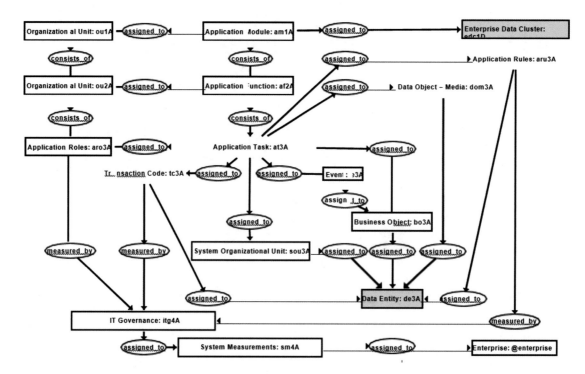

object. So far this has only occurred at the infimum, with Enterprise: @enterprise. We can follow the intent and extent from and to this concept for example, to:

- Get a sense of what name we might give this meta-object,
- Identify a structural issue in this layer, or
- Confirm that it's simply warranted, and left simply without a name.

It thus reveals a focus for further investigation.

Data

Figure 12 depicts the Application layer CG. Figure 13's FCL evidences that [Enterprise: @enterprise is bottommost i.e. at the infimum. Like Value, the extent of all the attributes from the topmost formal concept i.e. the supremum is [Enterprise: @enterprise] including from all the relevant KPIs (level 4 meta-objects) including [System Measurements: sm4A]. In this layer as it stands all its concepts (meta-objects) extend to the enterprise, demonstrating that they all impact on the enterprise as expected!

A MODULARISED, HOLISTIC META-MODEL

While most of the individual modules do not have [Enterprise: @enterprise] as their bottommost formal concept, modularising the EIMA makes them more readable by a human reviewer. Given they are (or

Figure 13. Application, FCL

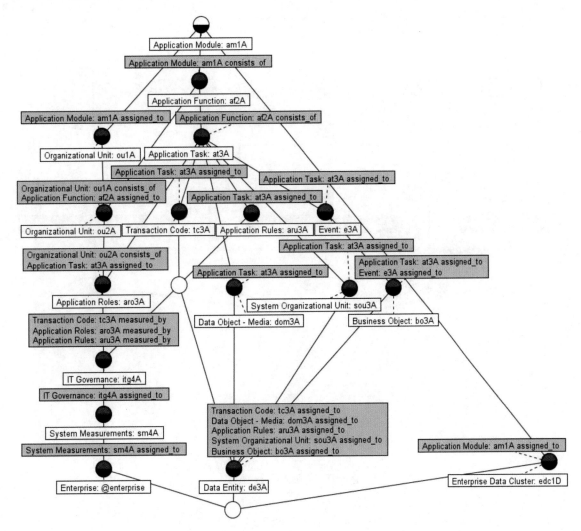

should be) semantic units also reinforces their need to be modular, rather than in one heterogeneous mass. However apart from Value and Data, the layers are not evidently semantic units without resolving their interdependencies with the other layers. Therefore, the next stage is to combine the modules according to their co-referent links thereby discovering that when so combined whether [Enterprise: @ enterprise] emerges to be bottommost or not. Through CGs join operation the co-referent links enable the CGs for each layer to be joined into one, large CG. When that joined CG is passed to *CGtoFCA*, the resulting FCA is shown by Figure 16.

The attributes and objects are not in this figure for convenience, but it shows (although not labelled for this reason) that [Enterprise: @enterprise] remains at the infimum (bottommost). That clarifies Competency, Service, Process and Application as se mantic units. Also noticeable are other formal concepts that do not have their own meta-objects in the lattice, and as before warranting further investigation as discussed above for the Application layer.

Figure 14. Data, CGs

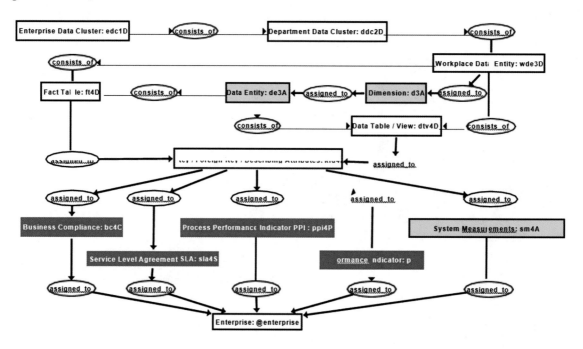

Figure 15. Data, FCL

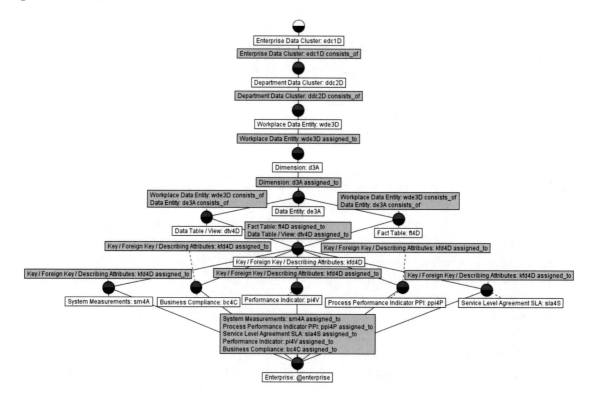

Figure 16. Combined EIMA, FCL   *Figure 17. Combined EIMA with disjoin, FCL*

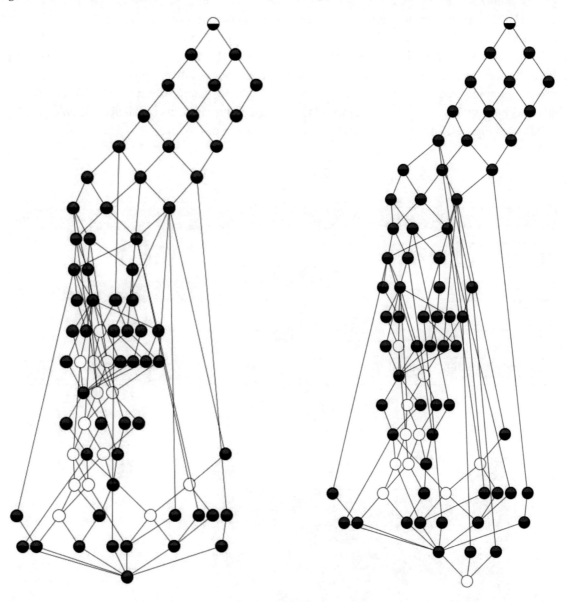

What's happens if a co-referent doesn't join? That might be because there is a disagreement between the human modelling team for one layer viewing a given concept as having a different meaning thus not harmonised across the whole meta-model. We can reflect this discord by simply giving it a different co-referent. For example [Organizational Unit: not-ou1A] in the Competency layer and [Organizational Unit: ou1A] in the Application layer have a different referent because the modellers for each respective layer do not (currently) agree they are the same meta-object even though they share the same name[7]. Also, in this example there is disagreement over [Organizational Unit: not-2A] in the Competency layer and [Organizational Unit: ou2A] in the Application layer. This latter example is compounded by a typo i.e. not-2A in the Application layer should be not-ou2A following the (mis)naming convention in this example?

In any event, a differing FCL results as Figure 17 demonstrates. Not surprisingly, [Enterprise: @ enterprise] is no longer at the infimum. As [Organizational Unit: ou1A] and [Organizational Unit: ou1A] no longer have semantic relations directed from them to a target concept, they are the other two formal concepts along with [Enterprise: @enterprise] directly above the infimum. Figure 18 shows an extract of the CGs involved and Figure 19 these three formal concepts and where they are situated in the FCL.

From a simple visual inspection Figure 17's shape has also altered from Figure 16 including the formal concepts without their own meta-objects, suggesting other impacts of the discord. We can in any event see how Figure 17's altered structure captures the nature of the discord i.e.:

Figure 18. Combined EIMA CGs Extract, FCL

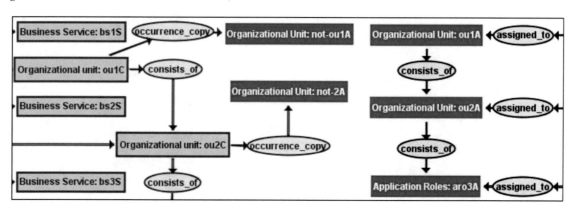

Figure 19.

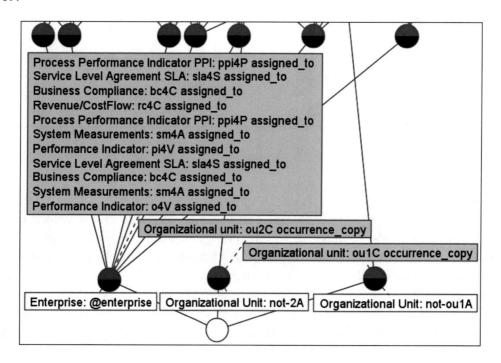

1. *Syntactic* (the typo),
2. *Semantic* (the different meanings of the same meta-object), and
3. *Pragmatic* (the process of sharing meaning that in this case hasn't been achieved yet).

Towards the beginning of this paper we pointed out that semantics are an aspect of semiotics, like syntax, which distinguishes valid from invalid symbol structures, and like pragmatics, which relates symbols to their meaning within a context e.g. the community in which they are shared (Cordeiro & Filipe, 2004). We also brought in Conceptual Structures, which Sowa describes as "Information Processing in Mind and Machine" (Sowa, 1984). FCA adds a mathematical dimension to logic, depicted by the CGs. The productivity of the computer through *CGtoFCA* augments the human creativity from which enterprises emerge. That contextual way of thinking as it traverses though the conceptual, logical and physical way of working is conceptually structured through the interplay between informal and formal concepts. Figure 20 depicts this added dimension to the earlier Figure 2.

Whilst focusing on EIMA for the purposes of our discussion, there is the potential for our approach to be applied as a general vehicle for harmonising meta-models (Henderson-Sellers, 2012). Formal concepts can pinpoint the disharmonies ranging from the simply syntactic cases, the meaning-driven semantic cases and – eventually – sharing meaning (pragmatcs) based on where the differences actually lie.

CONCLUSION

Using EIMA as the illustration, we have portrayed how the layers-and-levels meta-models of the GUA and other bodies adopting this approach can be enhanced by Formal Concepts. The use of CGs (Conceptual Graphs) and FCA (Formal Concept Analysis) through the *CGtoFCA* algorithm provide a rigorous unification of modularised meta-models. That included the validation of each layer (module) as semantic units where they have to have the necessary interdependencies with other layers (modules). In EIMA's case, through the co-referent links it revealed the cross-layer levelling of its information content specific meta-objects in its Business and Information Systems layers. As such it also revealed the syntax, semantics

Figure 20. The layered enterprise way of working, conceptually structured

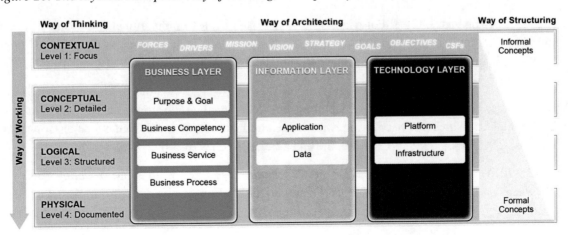

and pragmatics in the levels (Contextual, Conceptual, Logical and Physical) that in EIMA's case is the Enterprise, Department, Workplace, and Document (with its associated Key Performance Indicators).

The integration of a technical layer in the next version of EIMA will also apply the approach taken in this paper, so that it is better integrated at the outset. Moreover, EIMA will be rolled back into the overarching GUA meta-models. For historic and expediency reasons, there has been a little divergence of EIMA from GUA's (thus LEADing Practices') meta-models. Again, the approach described in this paper will ease that process, bringing together EIMA's valuable experience with SAP's GBI set of case studies with the developments that have since happened with GUA's meta-models. Naturally this harmonisation can extend into the meta-models of other standards or recommendations bodies such as the OMG, the Open Group, ISO, Web and others[8].

The findings of this paper may also outline mismatches in the "supporting work products" by offering support mechanisms from the highest contextual level to a system design. The resulting identification of any such gaps in the physical layer is beneficial to system builders so as to prevent running into unforeseen interoperability issues during implementation. In our vision, the mathematical interpretation through formal concepts that are enacted by the computer support the transition into the physical layer along with the informal concepts that characterise existing approaches. Essentially there a rich interaction between the computer and human modeller or designer in reconsidering their CG (Conceptual Graph) models from the FCL (Formal Concept Lattice). It thus acts as a supporting tool to the logical and other layers, and actualises the modularising of complex meta-models in enterprise systems using conceptual structures.

ACKNOWLEDGMENT

The authors would like to acknowledge the support of the Global University Alliance for this work, as well as access to the practitioner resources of LEADing Practice including its CEO Henrik von Scheel. Acknowledgements also to the SAP University Alliances program, particularly Stefan Weidner of the SAP University Competence Center & School of Computer Science, University of Magdeburg, Germany.

REFERENCES

Andrews, S., Orphanides, C., & Polovina, S. (2011). Visualising Computational Intelligence through Converting Data into Formal Concepts. In Next Generation Data Technologies for Collective Computational Intelligence (pp. 139–165). Springer Berlin Heidelberg, Berlin, Heidelberg. doi:10.1007/978-3-642-20344-2_6

Andrews, S., & Polovina, S. (2011). A Mapping from Conceptual Graphs to Formal Concept Analysis. In Conceptual Structures for Discovering Knowledge, the 19th International Conference on Conceptual Structures, LNCS (Vol. 6828, pp. 63–76). Springer. doi:10.1007/978-3-642-22688-5_5

Bork, D. (2015). *Development Method for the Conceptual Design of Multi-View Modeling Tools with an Emphasis on Consistency Requirements* [Doctoral Dissertation]. University of Bamberg, Germany.

Bork, D., Buchmann, R., & Karagiannis, D. (2015). Preserving multi-view consistency in diagrammatic knowledge representation. In *Proceedings of the International Conference on Knowledge Science, Engineering and Management* (pp. 177–182). Springer.

Cordeiro, J., & Filipe, J. (2004). The semiotic pentagram framework – a perspective on the use of semiotics within organisational semiotics. In *Proceedings of The 7th International Workshop on Organisational Semiotics*.

Floyd, R. W. (1967). Assigning Meanings to Programs. In *Mathematical Aspects of Computer Science* (Ch. 19, pp. 19–32). American Mathematical Society.

Ganter, B., Stumme, G., & Wille, R. (2005). Formal Concept Analysis: Foundations and Applications. Springer.

Group, T. O. (2011). 34. content metamodel. Retrieved from http://pubs.opengroup.org/architecture/togaf9-doc/arch/chap34.html

Gruber, T. R. (1995). Toward principles for the design of ontologies used for knowledge sharing? *International Journal of Human-Computer Studies*, *43*(5), 907–928.

Henderson-Sellers, B. (2012). Standards harmonization: Theory and practice. *Software & Systems Modeling*, *11*(2), 153–161. doi:10.1007/s10270-011-0213-0

Malik, N. (2009). Why the Zachman framework is not an ontology.

Mayall, A. and Carter, J. (2015). The essential project: Harnessing conceptual structures to expose organizational dynamics. *International Journal of Conceptual Structures and Smart Applications*, *3*(2), 1–11.

Oberle, D. (2013). *How ontologies benefit enterprise applications*. Semantic Web Journal.

Polovina, S. (2007). An introduction to conceptual graphs. In *Proceedings of the 15th International Conference on Conceptual Structures: Knowledge Architectures for Smart Applications ICCS '07*. Springer-Verlag.

Polovina, S., Scheruhn, H.-J., Weidner, S., & von Rosing, M. (2016a). Discovering the gaps in enterprise systems via conceptual graphs & formal concept analysis. In *Poster Proceedings, the 22nd International Conference on Conceptual Structures (ICCS)* (pp. 5–8).

Polovina, S., Scheruhn, H.-J., Weidner, S., & von Rosing, M. (2016b). Highlighting the gaps in enterprise systems models by interoperating CGS and FCA. In S. Andrews & S. Polovina (Eds.), *Proceedings of the Fifth Conceptual Structures Tools & Interoperability Workshop (CSTIW '16)* (pp. 46–54). CEUR-WS.

Priss, U. (2006). Formal concept analysis in information science. *Annual Review of Information Science & Technology*, *40*(1), 521–543. doi:10.1002/aris.1440400120

Scheruhn, H., Fallon, R., & Rosing, M. (2015). Information Modelling and Process Modelling. In The Complete Business Process Handbook (Vol. 1, pp. 511–550). Elsevier.

Scheruhn, H.-J., Ackermann, D., Braun, R., & Förster, U. (2013). Human-Computer Interaction. Users and Contexts of Use. In *Proceedings of the 15th International Conference, HCI International 2013* (pp. 446–455). Springer Berlin Heidelberg, Berlin, Heidelberg.

Scheruhn, H.-J., Rautenstrauch, C., Pegnetter, R., and Weidner, S. (2006). Strategische ausrichtung eines internationalen masterprogramms mit dem schwerpunkt integrationskompetenz am beispiel von mysap. *Die neue Hochschule DNH*.

Sowa, J. F. (1984). *Conceptual Structures- Information Processing in Mind and Machine*. Addison-Wesley.

Sowa, J. F. (2008). Conceptual Graphs. In Handbook of Knowledge Representation, Foundations of Artificial Intelligence (Vol. 3, pp. 213–237). Amsterdam: Elsevier.

Sowa, J. F., & Zachman, J. A. (1992). Extending and formalizing the framework for information systems architecture. *IBM Systems Journal, 31*(3), 590–616. doi:10.1147/sj.313.0590

von Rosing, M. (2016). What are artefacts & how can they be used. Retrieved from http://www.leading-practice.com/knowledge-center/recorded-webinars/what-are-artefacts-2/

von Rosing, M., & Laurier, W. (2015). An introduction to the business ontology. *International Journal of Conceptual Structures and Smart Applications, 3*(1), 20–41.

von Rosing, M., Urquhart, B., & Zachman, J.A. (2015). Using a business ontology for structuring artefacts: Example- northern health. *International Journal of Conceptual Structures and Smart Applications, 3*(1), 42–85.

von Rosing, M., & von Scheel, H. (2016). Using the business ontology to develop enterprise standards. *International Journal of Conceptual Structures and Smart Applications, 4*(1), 48–70.

Zivkovic, S., & Karagiannis, D. (2015). Towards metamodelling-in-the-large: Interface-based composition for modular metamodel development. In *International Conference on Enterprise, Business-Process and Information Systems Modeling* (pp. 413–428). Springer.

Wolff, K. E. (1993). A first course in Formal Concept Analysis. In Proceedings of StatSoft '93 (pp. 429–438). Gustav Fischer Verlag.

Zachman, J. A. (1987). A framework for information systems architecture. *IBM Systems Journal, 26*(3), 276–292. doi:10.1147/sj.263.0276

Zachman, J.A. (2015). John Zachman's concise definition of the Zachman Framework.

Zhao, F., Scheruhn, H.-J., & Rosing, M. (2014). Human-Computer Interaction. In *Applications and Services* (pp. 776–785). Cham: Springer International Publishing.

ENDNOTES

[1]   GUA (www.globaluniversityalliance.net) is a non-profit body consisting of over 450 universities, professors and researchers.

[2]   www.leadingpractice.com

[3]   http://uac.sap.com

[4]   The CGs are drawn in CharGer (http://charger.sourceforge.net/) as it has support for the ISO/IEC24707 CGIF (CG Interchange Format). At http://www.jfsowa.com/cg/cgdpansw.htm there is

more information on the standard. Concept Explorer (http://conexp.sourceforge.net/) was used to generate the FCL.

5   On this occasion https://en.wikipedia.org/wiki/Formal_concept_analysis is also a good starting point.

6   In passing it is worth remarking in the ARIS software (www.aris.com) that is used to model GBI, these occurrences are the same object, so in that sense the problem may appear to go away. But it doesn't as they are 'pseudo-synonyms', evidenced by them not being co-referent semantically.

7   To clarify, EIMA itself would not be 'broken' in this way; rather it would be some derivative of this or any other well-formed meta-model for a particular enterprise context.

8   www.omg.org, www.opengroup.org, www.iso.org, www.w3c.org

Chapter 14
Communication Trends in Internet of Things

Bharathi N. Gopalsamy
Saveetha University, India

ABSTRACT

The central hypothesis of Internet of Things is the term "connectivity". The IoT devices are connected to the Internet through a wide variety of communication technologies. This chapter explains the various technologies involved in IoT connectivity. The diversity in communication raises the query of which one to choose for the proposed application. The key objective of the application needs to be defined very clearly. The application features such as the power requirement, data size, storage, security and battery life highly influence the decision of selecting one or more communication technology. Near Field Communication is a good choice for short-range communication, whereas Wi-Fi can be opted for a larger range of coverage. Though Bluetooth is required for higher data rate, it is power hungry, but ZigBee is suitable for low power devices. There involves always the tradeoff between the technologies and the requirements. This chapter emphasizes that the goal of the application required to be more precise to decide the winner of the IoT connectivity technology that suits for it.

INTRODUCTION

The portrayal of Internet of things(IoT) becomes the Internet of Everything which includes public individuals, locations under monitoring, electronic gadgets, medical devices and the list is ever increasing. The notion of Internet of Things is conceived by Kevin Ashton who is one of the pioneer and executive director of the Auto-ID Center at MIT and the vision in a RFID journal in 1999 on IoT as "We need to empower computers with their own means of gathering information, so they can see, hear and smell the world for themselves, in all its random glory. RFID and sensor technology enable computers to observe, identify and understand the world without the limitations of human-entered data". The IoT has started to reside its foot prints in almost all domains (Selecting a Wireless Technology for New Industrial Internet of Things Products 2016). The IoT analytics has released the top ten IoT applications which are ranked based on people search and talk on Internet and social network. The list has its top ranker as smart home

DOI: 10.4018/978-1-5225-3686-4.ch014

followed by wearables, smart city, smart grids, industrial Internet, connected cars, connected health, smart retail, smart supply chain and smart farming. The two key concepts that forms the backbone of IoT are the smartness and connectivity. Although a device works in a more smarter way, it relies on the strength of the communication technology to reach the rest of the world.

The Internet of things emerges the communication between living things and inanimate to sight this world as completely connected ecosystem in which anyone can access anything from anywhere through any device at any time. The vision of RFID community on IoT as "The worldwide network of interconnected objects uniquely addressable based on standard communication protocols". The definition of IoT European Research Cluster is "The Internet of Things allows people and things to be connected anytime, anyplace, with anything and anyone, ideally using any path/network, and any service". The impression of the International Telecommunication Union on IoT is "From anytime, anyplace connectivity for anyone, we will now have connectivity for anything". Essentially any object which is monitored using sensor and controlled through Internet connectivity is a part of IoT. The communication technology roadmap as shown in Figure 1, eventually influences the IoT domain. It starts its journey with host to host communication and matured as communication between hosts and world wide web, communication includes mobile phones, communication using social network with people involvement and finally communication reaches IoT which connects everything in this world.

The successive sections are elucidating the communication technologies that are competing to reach the peak of IoT market. The following communication technologies such as ZigBee, Thread, Sigfox, LoRa, Weightless, Bluetooth, Zwave, Near Field Communication (NFC), Cellular and Wi-Fi are discussed with its architecture and capabilities to support IoT (The Complete List Of Wireless IoT Network Protocols,

Figure 1. Communication technology roadmap inclined to IoT

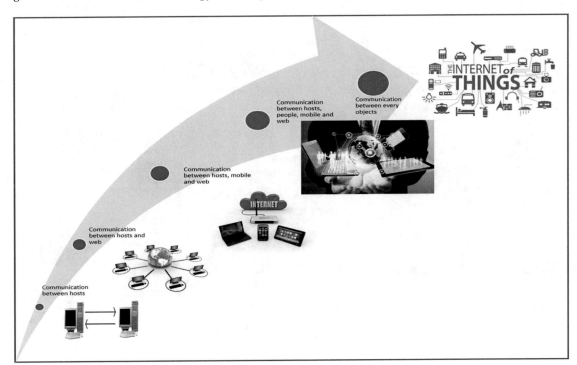

February 08, 2016).. Finally, the top ten IOT application domains that are shortlisted by google based on the search by people are listed with their supporting communication technologies and its decision factors.

ZigBee

ZigBee is an open standard protocol which is proposed primarily for smart homes. In particular, it is devised for sensor networks and its monitoring and control. It is based on the wireless personal area network(WPAN) standard IEEE 802.15.4. The low power, low data rate devices are the nodes in ZigBee WPAN which is operating at GSM band. The data rate supported is 250 kbps which is quite suitable for periodic sampling from the sensors and control signals to the controllers (Ata Elahi, Dec. 2009). ZigBee is simpler and requires less cost to deploy for control and monitoring applications which needs the coverage range from 10 to 100 meters. ZigBee defines different network configurations viz. router to end device and between routers for communication. Nodes in ZigBee network also capable of saving its battery power by operating in sleep mode if necessary (Tarun Agarwal,2015).

The ZigBee protocol stack layers are Physical layer, Mac layer, Network layer and Application support sub-layer. The Physical layer and Mac layer are defined by IEEE 802.15.4 standard. The Network and application layer are detailed by ZigBee-alliance specifications. The concern of physical layer is to accomplish modulation and demodulation on the data transmitted as well as received every time. It transfers data in ISM band with 250 kbps as maximum data rate. The MAC layer provides reliable communication by accessing the network with carrier sense multiple access with collision avoidance, achieves synchronization by transmitting beacon packets (Fouad, H.,2017). The four different types

Figure 2. ZigBee network for smart home

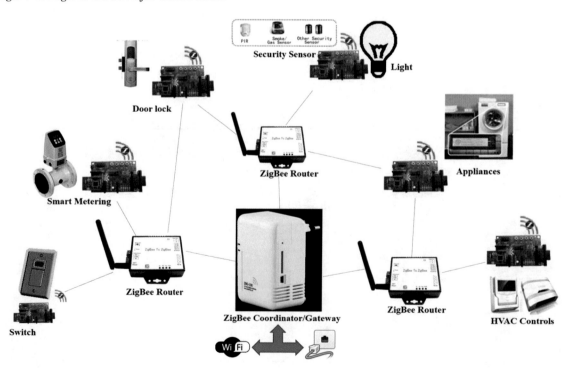

of frames in the MAC layer are Data, Acknowledgement, Beacon and MAC Command. The Network layer starts a ZigBee specification based network and governing the connection and disconnection of nodes. It also discovers each node's neighbors and eventually determines the route to any node in the network using Ad-hoc on-demand Distance Vector Routing protocol (AODV). The network topology supported are star, mesh and tree. The Application support sublayer provides a framework for application objects and ZigBee Device Object(ZDO). ZigBee alliance also specified the security services and ZDO management across the application support sublayer and network layer. The device security starts with 128 bit AES encryption key which is shared among devices in a PAN. With its features, ZigBee is most apposite protocol for Industrial and home automation, smart metering and smart grid monitoring as shown in Figure 2.

The nodes in ZigBee network are categorized into three types viz., ZigBee Coordinator (ZC), Zig-Bee Router (ZR) and ZigBee End Device (ZED). Each ZigBee network should have at least one ZC, which handles the data transmission and storage of required application information. The ZR nodes are responsible for enabling the communication among ZEDs and to or from ZC. The functionality of ZEDs is limited to communicate with parent ZR node. One or more ZED nodes can be attached with a ZR node and one ZED node can be attached with more than one ZR node depending upon the network topology used.

The characteristics of ZigBee are 40-250 Kbps data rate, with 20meters coverage area ISM band 2.4 GHz frequency. ZigBee is quite suitable for applications which are looking for short-range, less cost and supports more number of devices and low power consumption (Thread Vs. ZigBee, For IoT Engineers, March 2016). The main application area where ZigBee can be used are Industrial automation, Home automation, Smart grid and Smart metering. The limitation of ZigBee is that message transfer to the end device is not direct and only through ZigBee network coordinator/gateway. Multimedia file sharing and instant connectivity applications cannot choose as the bandwidth is limited in ZigBee.

Thread

The thread is an open standard protocol which highly satisfied the need to access the end devices in a network directly from cloud or vice versa using simple IP addressing. It is devised for home automation with IP oriented networks. The setting up of network such as joining and leaving the network and its maintenance are simple. Thread allows the range of devices connected are from tens to hundreds of devices. Additionally, spread spectrum technology helps to reduce the interference. The network is self-configurable by resolving the routing problem itself, when a node fails and hence it easily overcome the failure of individual devices (Application Development Fundamentals: Thread 2017). The no. of failures is very less since it can operate on AA batteries for quite a lot of years and all its data transfers are authorized and secured.

The thread network architecture consists of four types of devices namely border routers, routers, router-eligible end devices and sleepy end devices as shown in Figure 3. Border routers are responsible for establishing the connections with other type of adjacent networks such as wi-fi and Ethernet. They are also offering services like routing, to internal nodes in 802.15.4 network. More than one border routers are allowed, to handle failures. Routers are by the virtue of its name performs routing. They also provide services like joining authorization for new nodes and security services for internal network devices. Routers can be relieved from their duties and can become REEDS (Router Eligible End Devices) when the network is required to do so under certain circumstances to save the power (Naito, K. 2017). REEDS are

Figure 3. Thread architecture and protocol stack

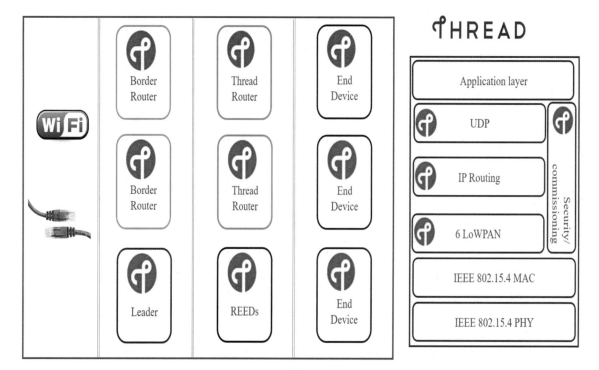

the nodes that are possessing the capability of the router and becomes router whenever necessary. They cannot provide security and join authorization services unless, it becomes the router. Sleepy end devices are actual leaf nodes that can interact only with its parent router. The end devices can go to sleep mode if it is not involved in any kind of data transfer. The network topology depends on the number of routers involved. If one router exists, the star topology is configured whereas mesh topology is automatically configured if more than one router exists (Thread Stack Fundamentals, 2015). The number of routers is limited to 32 and the allowed router addresses are 64 for reusing.

Each device in thread network are addressed based on IPv6 addressing. Every node possesses one or more ULA (Unique Local Address), GUA (Global Unicast Address) and multicast addresses. A 16-bit address is allocated for any device joining into thread network and it is used for locating that device in thread network. The higher order 6 bits represent the router with which it is associated and the lower order bits depicts its position under that router. The routing information are exchanged based on RIP (Routing Information Protocol) in terms of MLE (Mesh Link Establishment) messages to assure the connectivity and updated routes. MLE messages are used to convey identity and configuration of devices and to establish secure links with neighbors when the topology/physical environment changes. MLE advertisement packets are sent from each router to all other router periodically to update the routing table. The link cost of neighboring routers and path costs of other routers are updated in the routing table whenever a MLE advertisement packets are received at every router. Link cost and path cost are measured in terms of RSSI (Received Signal Strength Indicator). Multicasting of MLE messages in thread network is achieved by MPL (Multicast Protocol for Low power and Lossy networks. End devices and REEDS transfer messages, echo request, echo reply and error messages based on UDP (User Datagram Protocol) and ICMPv6 (Internet Control Message Protocol version 6).

6LoWPAN (IPv6 Over Low Power Wireless Personal Area Networks) is devised to handle the IPv6 packets from other networks to 802.15.4. The issues such as small payload, low power and low reliability in 802.15.4 standard are overcome by the 6LoWPAN adaptation layer between the IPv6 network layer and 802.15.4 link layer (Thread Usage of 6LoWPAN, 2015). 6LoWPAN adaptation layer bridges the gap between IPv6 and 802.15.4 by IPv6 packet encapsulation, fragmentation and reassembly, IPv6 header compression and 802.15.4 link layer packet forwarding (J. Olsson 2014).

The main distinguishing feature of thread network is that there is no single point of failure. The failures of routers and end nodes are dynamically detected and managed corrected immediately with backup nodes like REEDs. Thread uses simple IP addressing which makes it more convenient that ZigBee in transferring messages to end devices directly. The features of thread network are 250 Kbps data rate, 30 meters theoretically and works in 2.4 GHz frequency.

Weightless

Weightless is one of the open standard in wireless communication. It supports currently in 3 different flavors viz., Weightless-P, Weightless-W, Weightless-N. The name weightless indicates the light weight nature of the protocols and reduced data transmission overheads (Ian Poole). Weightless-P offers 2-way communication with slightly increased cost and supports high performance. The extensive feature support with television white space spectrum is focused in Weightless-W. Simple, low cost and 1 way communication are the features of weightless-N. Weightless-N works in Ultra Narrow Band (UNB) technology with DBPSK digital modulation and frequency hopping. It is proposed mainly for Low power wide area network (LPWAN) and more than one network can be overlapped spatially (A Comprehensive Look at Low Power, Wide Area Networks, 2016). Security is supported using 128 bit AES algorithm.

The specification of weightless explicates the access of base station and radio system involved. So, vendors are well equipped to supply weightless devices with very low cost and offers interoperability. The radio interface along with Phase Shift Keying (PSK), Quadrature Amplitude Modulation (QAM) and whitening makes the signal immune to interference. Besides, the use of time division duplex (TDD) supports the uplink as well as down link transmissions in single channel.

Weightless network architecture consists of (i) *Base station controller*: monitors and controls all the base stations and exchanges data between base stations (ii) *Base station*: the end device can communicate with the base station if it needs to report any contextual information. Base station sends the information to the database and in turn to client IT system. (iii) *End device:* weightless inexpensive end device can communicate only with its base station. The weightless communication is uplinked to base station, from the base station to network manager/ base station controller through Internet as depicted in Figure 4. The database provides the support to base station to identify its network end devices. The authorization and authentication is carried out between base station and each end devices to ensure secure transfer of data. The location register and broadcast register are maintained for detecting the last known location and storing the group membership and messages respectively. The white space database is maintained to keep track of the available spectrum in the given location. Billing process is mandatory for recording the transmissions and related activities of any end device. Operations and maintenance center is designated for overall functionality and control of the network. It manages the detection of errors and failures.

The significant factors that are contributed to the success of Weightless-N in contrast to its competing technologies are simpler, very low cost with longer battery life, coverage range is in terms of kilometers. Cost of the weightless device is very low, since it is open standard and more number of

Figure 4. Weightless information flow

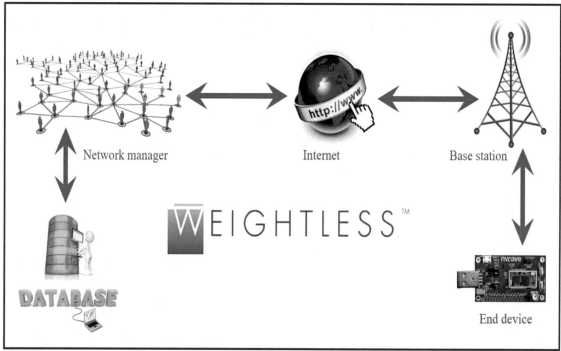

vendors are supporting weightless. The transmission power and time spent in active state contributes to power consumption. The 17dBm transmission power with optimal power amplification enables longer battery life. For any wireless network data throughput and network capacity is dependent on supporting packet length, transmission frequency and time and measure of interference. The network capacity of weightless-N is optimized for uplink oriented traffic with moderate payload in narrow band channels. The end device support is up to 780 in weightless-N based on UNB technology. Application areas in which Weightless M2M communication technology are widely employed are energy based communications, retails, consumer goods, healthcare, transportation and security.

Sigfox

Sigfox is based on binary phase shift keying technique in radio transmission. It encrypts the data by changing the phase of the carrier radio waves that are narrow chunks of spectrum. This concept highly reduces the noise at the receiver end. Sigfox communication consist of inexpensive end nodes with highly matured basestation to handle the network. The perspective of Sigfox from end devices is as an open standard whereas from basestation is as a service provider (Fernández-Garcia, 2017). Sigfox is completely for IoT applications without the need of deploying the infrastructure for each application separately. It earns by selling technology stack to network operators who deploy the network base stations. The end to end communication can be achieved using Sigfox from end objects to information storage such as cloud (Sethi, 2017). Sigfox communication is based on Ultra Narrow Band (UNB). The high sensitivity of UNB devices saves enormous resources in terms of hardware used. The Sigfox technology reduces the number of antennas when deploying the communication network (Pitì, 2017). Besides, the

Figure 5. Components of Sigfox network

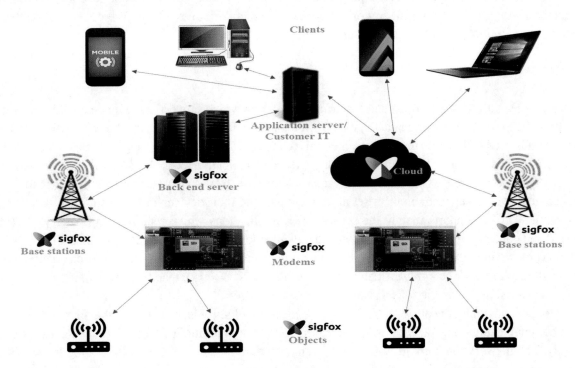

modem used for Sigfox communication is also less energy consuming device than its counterparts in other technologies. Hence the subscription to Sigfox network connection is cost effective when compared with competing technologies.

The basestation of Sigfox network manages a maximum of one million connected devices. However, it is scalable in nature by enhancing the density of base station (Sallouha, 2017). The density range of the basestation is about 3-10km in urban and 30-50km in rural areas. In the case of outdoor objects in line of sight, supports up to 1000km.

The devices in Sigfox technology communicates through Sigfox supporting modem by instructing to send and receive messages on demand as described in Figure 5. The Sigfox transceivers are responsible to pick the data from the modem and route to the Sigfox server where security parameters are validated. Finally, the data are sent to the application server.

The unique characteristics of Sigfox network are (i) Radio frequencies: ISM band is used for communication which is managed by national governments. The frequency may vary based on the nationality in which the Sigfox network is operating and it is governed by international regulation bodies. (ii) uplink and down link: Mono and bi directional data transfer is supported. Among them, mono data transfers consume very less power if bidirectional is rarely required. (iii) Reliable connectivity: redundancy exist in receiving messages at network server from more than one antennas and hence reliability is assured. (iv) Security and privacy: message interception is prevented by frequency hopping technique and false signals are not permitted with the use of anti-replay mechanism, (v) Standardization: worked in partnership with European Telecommunication Standards Institute (ETSI) for framing the standard of low throughput network.

The limitations of Sigfox are (i) There is no alternative way to establish Sigfox network other than directly working with Sigfox; (ii) Sigfox network deployment are in exclusive fashion, i.e., more than one network cannot be deployed in the same area.

LoRa

Long Range (LoRa) uses chirp spread spectrum modulation which supports long range communication by preserving the low power characteristics of frequency shift keying (FSK) modulation. chirp spread spectrum is used by LoRa as the first commercial technology to support long ranges (Petäjäjärvi, 2017). The LoRa is having higher link budget than any other communication technology and hence its coverage ranges from 50 square KMs to hundreds of square KMs. It is well known fact that a single technology is not sufficient to support complete set of applications and their devices in IOT and LoRa is not the exemption. LoRa supports mainly the sensor based applications which requires long battery life (in years) and transfers small chunks of data periodically over long range (LoRa applications). LoRaWAN is responsible for higher layers in the network protocol stack that describes the communication architecture and protocol. LoRaWAN highly influences the factors such as network capacity, battery lifetime, secured data transmission and quality of service.

Most of the communication technology, uses mesh topology which increases the size of network and communication range at the cost of increased complexity and limited battery life and network capacity. The network topology in LoRa is long range star architecture which supports long battery life and simple to manage (Mikhaylov, 2017). The battery life time reduction is mainly due to exchanging messages periodically for synchronization and handover mechanism. In the LoRaWAN the communication is asynchronous and transfers data when it is ready based on ALOHA protocol (Sinha, R. S.,2017). Almost 3 to 5 times energy saving is achieved in LoRaWAN based on its communication mechanism.

The communication capability of devices in LoRaWAN are identified based on how devices are receiving packets from gateway and hence devices are heterogenous in nature during communication (Zhang, 2017). The device classes are determined based on the compromise between latency in network communication downlink and battery lifetime. The devices are categorized into three classes viz., class A, class B and class C. class A handles bidirectional end devices. In this class, the end device has its rights to communicate with the server using uplink and immediately it receives messages in two short downlinks. Since downlink happens only after the uplink, the server cannot communicate with end device at any time and it needs to wait for next uplink initiated from end device. Class B supports bidirectional end devices with scheduled receive slots. Besides the random slots as in class A, this class offers additional scheduled receiving slots. The scheduled receive slots are initiated after receiving beacon packet from the gateway for synchronization. Class C manages bidirectional end devices with maximal receive slots. In this class, server can send packets almost at any time to this type of devices as the downlink/receiving window is opened always except during transmission.

The communication stages are explained in the Figure 6. A node in a LoRaWAN is not at all required to associate with a gateway, instead its data can be received by more than one gateway. The gateways are responsible for transferring the data which are received from end node to the network server. The integrity and validation of data takes place in the network server. Redundancy in received packets and acknowledgements for received data through the appropriate gateway, data rate adjustment, etc., are also handled by network server. The key benefit is the avoidance of handover when a node is moving. The network capacity needs to support long range star network which is accomplished with multi-modem

Figure 6. LoRa communication stages

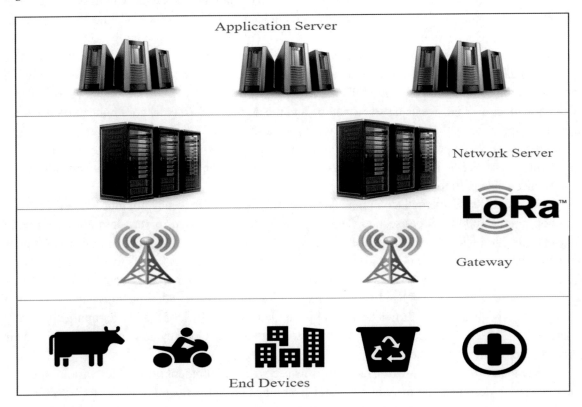

transceiver in the gateway. The key factors that influence the network capacity are support for concurrent channels, data rate, length of the payload and frequency of data transmission from a node.

The strength of LoRaWAN is that different spreading factors are used to receive the signals independent of each other. The date rate can also be tuned by modifying the spreading factor. This makes the gateway more efficient to receive more than one data at the same time through same channel using different data rates. The flexibility in data rate greatly increases the battery life by consuming less power and helps LoRaWAN to maintain the symmetric uplink and downlink along with enough downlink capacity. Due to these features, the scalability of network can be achieved nearly 6-8 times greater than the competing communication technologies. With these benefits LoRaWAN opens its door for wide variety of applications such as air pollution monitoring, Animal tracking, Agriculture processing, Liquid presence detection, elderly people fall detection, waste management etc.

Bluetooth

Bluetooth is a short-range communication protocol that substitutes for cable communications such as RS232. IEEE 802.15.1 standard denotes Bluetooth, but later Bluetooth standards are governed by Bluetooth Self Interest Group (SIG). Bluetooth technology gains its market by releasing hands free headsets for mobile phones. The use of Bluetooth is increased in PAN technology because of its 2MBps maximum data throughput.

The Bluetooth architecture consists of devices that can communicate without an infrastructure. The two link types that are associated with Bluetooth communication is Asynchronous Connectionless (ACL) and Synchronous Connection Oriented (SCO). As ACL is connectionless, it is mainly used for broadcast messages and handles data traffic with the data rate of 721 kbps. SCO is dedicated link type for voice traffic with data rate of 64 kbps. Bluetooth communication requires the set of devices exists within the network communication range is called Piconet (Kevin Townsend, 2014). Most of the devices in Bluetooth network communicates using star topology and the device initiating the communication becomes the master of the piconet. More than one piconet forms a scatternet. The frequency range of piconets in one scatternet is same but separated with different hop frequencies. Up to 8 devices are allowed in one piconet in a classical Bluetooth. Even though the number of nodes in a piconet is theoretically unlimited the optimized size is 10 to 20.

The interference in Bluetooth communication is resolved using frequency hopping spread spectrum with hop rate of 1600 hops per second. This hop rate is high compared to very less hops defined in competing technologies. The interference immunity is attained by allocating only a fraction (625µs) of frequency band for each channel. Besides, error correction mechanism also exists to avoid interference. The maximum number of hop carriers is 79, but countries like Japan, France and Spain have only 23 hop carriers because of narrow ISM band. The hop sequence and its phase decides the hop channel. The hop sequence and the phase are in turn determined by the identity and clock of the master unit respectively (Klasman, 2017). The slave devices are synchronized with master clock by adding an offset with their clock in case of any discrepancy.

The key factor for the success of Bluetooth is its user-friendly protocol profiles for various applications. A profile describes the mapping of specific application with Bluetooth (Ali, 2017). Based the profile, the communication messages and processes are chosen from the Bluetooth specification. The options and parameter ranges for each protocol is determined by the protocol profile as it is specified in Bluetooth protocol stack (Perez-Diaz de Cerio, 2017). Primarily, four all-purpose protocol profiles viz., General Access Profile (GAP), Service Discovery Application Profile (SDAP), Serial Port Profile (SPP) and Generic Object Exchange Profile (GOEP) are offered which become the base for other application specific protocol profiles. The GAP is responsible for establishment of connection between two Bluetooth devices after discovering each other. Among the plentiful services available across the Bluetooth link, SDAP discovers the services that are required to the application. SDAP is dependent on GAP to define the protocol and procedures to access the services. The data communication is achieved by SPP that emulates R232 control signals virtually with the support of GAP. Applications are exchanging information in terms of objects and it is governed by GOEP.

The recent specification released from Bluetooth SIG is Bluetooth smart/Bluetooth Low Energy (BLE) which is a boon for devices that demand for low power consumption and low data throughput. The devices that supports Bluetooth Smart can also withstand the power for multiple years. The BLE also presented proximity capabilities which paves the way for a new dimension of location based application services along with existing wide range of applications.

The main difference between BLE and classic Bluetooth is generic attribute (GATT) profile. GATT is depending on GAP for connection establishment. Later, data is transferred based on the Attribute Protocol which is based on lookup table with 16-bit ID for each entry. If a peripheral/slave device is connected to central/master device, then immediately it stops advertising its existence and other devices cannot feel its presence till it detaches.

Figure 7. Bluetooth communication framework

BLE has two types of devices namely Bluetooth Smart Ready and Bluetooth Smart. Bluetooth Smart Ready devices (dual mode) such as computers, tablets and mobile phones can act as masters. They are also intermediating between Bluetooth smart and Classic Bluetooth devices as shown in Figure 7. However, these devices cannot have any power consumption improvements like BLE devices. Bluetooth Smart devices (single mode) possess only BLE characteristics and hence cannot communicate directly with Classic Bluetooth devices which often requires high throughput.

The noteworthy feature of Bluetooth technology is its rich set of profiles that outline the communication mechanism for each application domain such as cordless telephony profile, intercom profile, headset profile, dial-up networking profile, fax profile, LAN access profile, object exchange profile, file transfer profile, synchronization profile, etc., Even though Bluetooth is originally proposed for the replacement of physical RS232 cable, it spreads its roots to almost all kind of applications and few most suitable applications are wearables, personal area networks, car automation, wireless I/O devices, etc.

Zwave

Zwave protocol stack has 3 layers viz., radio layer, network layer and application layer. Radio layer is responsible for mediating the signals between radio hardware and the network layer (Lin, 2017). It involves encoding, error correction, hardware access etc., Network layer describes the way how the control data is communicated between any two devices. The control data includes network topology, routing, addressing, service discovering etc. Application layer redirection of received messages to the intended application to achieve the task in that received device. The network layer is further divided into sub layers namely Media access layer, transport layer and routing layer. Media access layer controls the accessing of underlying hardware in the physical layer through wireless interface. The transport layer governs the communication of the messages by assuring the end- to- end error free transmission between any two wireless nodes. Routing layer is responsible for routing the messages to the destination node reliably in

Figure 8. Routing in Zwave network

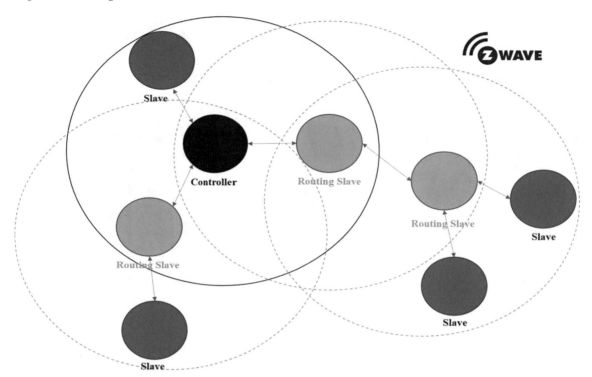

Zwave's mesh. Zwave mesh network is one of the reliable network in which every command send to a device is acknowledged from receiver for its arrival (Zwave Overview, 2016). The message transmission is tried for 3 times for its acknowledge (ACK) and announce the failure if ACK is not received.

Each node in the Zwave network possesses 2 identities for uniquely addressing it in the network (About Z-Wave Technology). Home ID is of length 32 bits and it is same for all nodes in one logical network. Node ID which is unique to each node in one logical network and it has 8 bits. Hence ideally the maximum of 256 nodes are allowed in one logical network. But reservation to special nodes leaves 232 node IDs for normal nodes (Why is Z-Wave the Preferred Choice for Smart Home IoT?, 2016). It is observed that nodes which are having same node ID should belong to different network and hence nodes in different logical network cannot able to communicate. Zwave supporting devices are of three types namely controllers, routing slaves and standard slaves as represented in Figure 8. Controllers which possess home ID in-built are responsible for including the slaves in the network and allocates home ID and node ID. Slaves that are controlled by the controllers receives their identity using inclusion process. Nodes regain the factory default IDs when they are detached from the network during exclusion process. Among the slave nodes routing slaves helps the controller in reaching the nodes that are located out of controller's coverage range.

In any wireless star network topology, the nodes that are located out of coverage area of a central controller, cannot be reached and hence lost connectivity with the network. This drawback is overcome in this network by forming mesh among the routing slaves dynamically and connectivity of lost node is regained to the controller at the cost of delay. Maximum of four routing slaves are permitted between the controller and the lost node. The controller initially try to send messages to all slaves directly and if any message loss occurs, it tries via routers. Three possible routes can be tried before it announces a failure in reaching any slave node. The different network configurations that are supported in Zwave are with single static (cannot move) controller, multiple controller along besides single primary controller and portable controller (remote control) as primary controller.

The key benefits of Zwave network is open standard, interoperable, whole home coverage, easy to get started and backward compatible. The competing technologies such as Wi-Fi suffers high power consumption, Bluetooth lacks in coverage range for home automation and industrial applications. Zwave provides the precise attributes that are really required for IoT such as less power consumption, low cost, decent coverage range, sufficient bandwidth. The interoperability support makes Zwave, one of the best for the enormous application of IoT.

NFC

Near-field communication (NFC) is based on RF communication and it is developed for very short range and supports half duplex. It is used in contactless payments using mobile phones such as google wallet (Talari, 2017). Though it is a subgroup of RFID Protocol, it is different from RFID in certain aspects. NFC Architecture is very simple in which devices are categorized into either initiator or target. Initiator which must be an active device commence the communication by generating the PF field to power the target. Target may be an active or passive device which responds to the initiator after receiving its initiation message. If target is passive, it consumes the required power for its operation from initiator device.

The NFC transmission and reception of messages are based on inductive coupling with only 4 to 10 cm distance between two devices (Coskun, 2013). The 3 different kinds of NFC devices are NFC mobile, NFC tag and NFC reader as depicted in Figure 9. They can operate under 3 different modes such as reader/writer mode, peer-to-peer mode and card emulation mode (Near Field Communication White Paper, ECMA International, 2005). In reader/writer mode the communication is between NFC mobile/NFC reader and NFC tag. In peer-to-peer mode the communication occurs between NFC mobile and NFC mobile. In card emulation mode, the communication happens between NFC mobile and NFC reader. The choice of operation mode also influences the data rates, modulation technique and coding schemes used in it (Rohde-Schwarz, 2016). The data rates supported are 106,212 and 424 kbps. Modulation techniques followed are Amplitude Shift Keying (ASK) under diverse modulation depth of 10 to 100% and load modulation. The coding schemes employed are Non-Return-to-zero level, Manchester encoding and modified miller coding on data.

NFC forum is non-proprietary association for NFC technology to encourage the development and usage of NFC communication. The major components of NFC that are standardized for NFC communication are NFC tag types, NFC Record Type Definitions (RTDs), Logical Link Control Protocol (LLCP). The tag types supported in reader/writer operation mode are Type 1,2,3 and 4. The NFC tag or passive RFID tag which is also known as NFC transponders are read by NFC mobile and retrieve data from the tag. Based on the data retrieved, proper action is carried out afterwards. NFC Data Exchange Format (NDEF) is used to transfer data between any two NFC devices in all operation modes. An NDEF message is divided into various records and each record carries one payload. Each record can be of variable length format and set of formats for each record type are predefined by NFC Forum.

In Peer to peer operation mode, the communication is framed as request-response model. The initiator NFC mobile can transfer and receive any kind of data to target NFC mobile. The NFCIP-1 protocol is approved as data link layer protocol for governing the segmentation and reassembly, data flow control

Figure 9. NFC devices and its usage

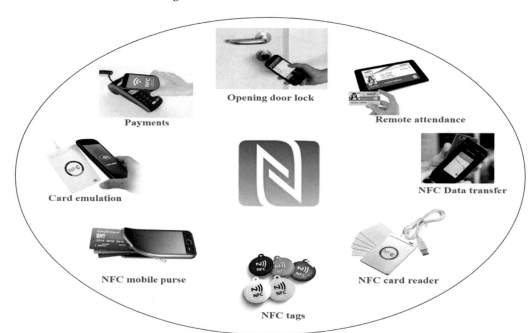

with go and wait, error control with ACK and NACK frames. Later, LLCP is released by NFC forum to improve the flow mechanisms of peer to peer operation mode. connectionless and connection-oriented transport; link activation, supervision and deactivation; asynchronous balanced communication, and protocol multiplexing are the major functionalities that are provided by LLCP.

Security plays a major role in card emulation mode. In this mode, NFC mobile behaves like smart card and NFC reader interacts with Secure Element (SE) in the NFC enables mobile phones. The NFC mobile has components such as NFC communication interface, SE and Host controller. The NFC communication interface comprises of NFC Contactless Front-end (NFC CLF), an NFC antenna and an NFC controller to govern NFC transactions. Host controller administrates all the activities and operation modes of NFC controller and SE through Host Controller Interface (HCI). The communication protocol practiced between NFC controller and SEs is either Single Wire Protocol (SWP) or NFC Wired Interface (NFC-WI).

NFC utilizes touching paradigm which is useful in sharing any kind of information by simply touching 2 NFC devices together (Solat, 2017). NFC mobiles are faster, secure and more comfortable for the people to handle either payments. RFID tags can be read using NFC mobiles to track objects in retails and industries. The applications that are currently employing NFC techniques are Mobile Payment, Ticketing & Loyalty Applications, Entertainment Applications, Smart Environment Applications, Work Force and Retail Management Applications, Educational Service Applications, etc.

Cellular Network

Cellular networks are well established network infrastructure extending further to provide the reliable and secure connectivity to IOT devices and applications. Single solution is not sufficient to support the enormous need of IoT applications. Cellular networks designed diverse solutions to fulfill the various requirements and heterogeneity of IoT applications. The set of 3rd Generation Partnership Project (3GPP) Release 13 solutions that are encompassing almost all the necessities of IoT are Extended Coverage GSM (EC-GSM), Long Term Evolution for Machines (LTE-M), Narrowband IoT (NB-IoT). The content-rich high performance IoT applications can go for LTE-M whereas cost and coverage focused IoT applications are quite fit with NB IoT. EC-GSM is reserved for IoT feature support in GSM networks. The advantageous factor of above 3 solutions is that building a well-equipped communication mechanism over already deep-rooted network. The data rate, coverage, battery life and module cost is depicted in figure 10. The architecture of cellular network is well known and this section focusses only on solutions contributing to IoT.

EC – GSM

EC-GSM is an IoT communication technology based on cellular networks that supports the GSM market worldwide. The existing GSM cellular network is improved to support massive need of IoT applications. The EC-GSM is resulted based on the improvement proposed on GSM and it is quite good in coverage of up to 20dB on 900MHz. The coverage support is extended by dynamically handling the repetitions and signal combining mechanism with several coverage classes. The practical steadiness is ensured between the performance and coverage. Since GSM is already established network, it is more appropriate to develop only the required support for IoT to realize EC-GSM.

LTE-M

LTE has reached nook and corner of the world because of its efficient coverage. The key features like Carrier aggregation, Multiple input multiple output (MIMO), Gigabit performance, etc. serves for the high performance of LTE. The successor of LTE is LTE-M which is mainly focusing the Machine type communication (MTC) along with extended discontinuous reception (eDRX) and power saving mode. The battery life is extended up to 10 years for devices in LTE-M network. The LTE – M data traffic is multiplexed over LTE carrier and all the existing feature of LTE is utilized.

NB-IoT

NB-IoT is proposed for ultra-low-end devices and IoT applications. It is an independent carrier of 200kHz and supports lean setup procedures with minimum of 200,000 subscribers. Scalability in NB-IoT is achieved by addition of multiple NB-IoT enables scalability of the network. The extended coverage NB-IoT is one of the attractive feature along with battery saving and eDRX for minimum 10 years. The unified nature NB-IoT with LTE enables better flexibility in positioning NB-IoT either in the guard band of LTE or in band with LTE using time sharing technique without disturbing LTE carrier. In the absence of LTE support, NB-IoT can be standalone carrier to serve basic functionality in GSM.

The cellular network, standardized by 3GPP, is deep rooted worldwide with its broader coverage and all-time availability at almost every place. The above features of cellular network are corresponding to the seed concept of IoT which is anywhere, anytime through any device communication. The cellular network supports all levels of IoT application requirements such as device level, connectivity level, application provider level, network operator level, devices and equipment vendor level etc., The

Figure 10. Features of NB-IoT, EC-GSM and LTE-M

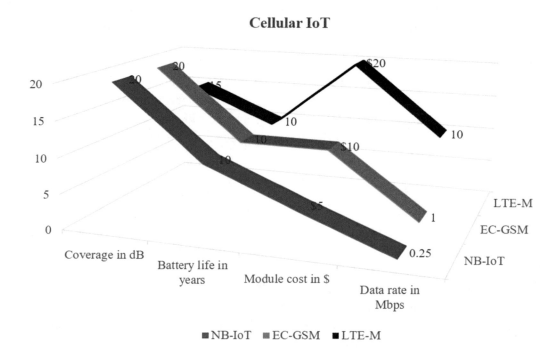

interference is also monitored and controlled since licensed spectrum is used in cellular network. The complete QoS framework is also established to support wide variety applications in all dimensions such as entertainment to time critical applications, few devices to huge device coordination, few bytes to giga bytes transmission, simple to complex network architecture and so on.

Wi-Fi (IEEE 802.11)

The Wi-Fi architecture consist of components as follows:

1. **Station (STA):** Device which supports wireless medium at physical and MAC layer interfacing
2. **Station Services(SS):** List of services that are utilized for transmission of MAC Service Data Units
3. **Base Service Set (BSS):** A unit under which several STAs are controlled with Single Coordination Function (SCF). STAs members under single BSS coverage range can communicate each other directly. Independent BSS (Adhoc Networks) can be formed instantly with direct communication between stations.
4. **Independent BSS (IBSS):** A BSS that is self-configured without any access point. One of the device initiates the coordination function and all other devices are members with the coverage is limited to the coverage ability of the coordinating wireless device. This is said to be adhoc network or infrastructure less network.
5. **Extended Service Set (ESS):** A group of BSSs interconnected using distributed system by routing all the traffic through access point as in Figure 11.

Figure 11. BSS and ESS in Wi-Fi network

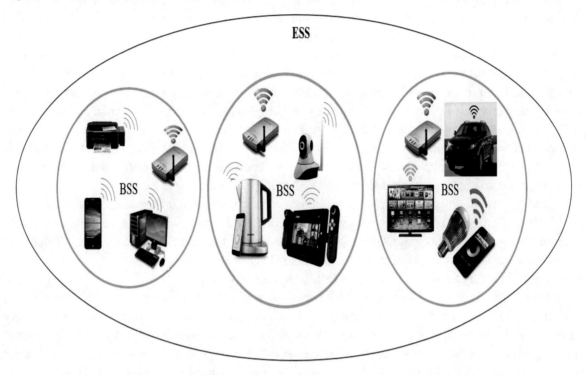

6. **Distribution System (DS):** A structure that manages the connection of BSS to form an ESS with wired or wireless, in infrastructure based Wi-Fi network

7. **Distribution System Medium (DSM):** In 802.11, the medium is divided logically based on the functionality of each component in the architecture. Hence the logical medium in which DS functions is called DSM.

8. **Distribution System Services (DSS):** Services offered within DS for MAC to establish communication among BSSs in a ESS.

9. **Access Point (AP):** Each device is associated with an access point to communicate with other devices through distribution system. The AP provides synchronization, power handling and roaming support.

10. **Basic Service Area (BSA):** The STAs in BSS are communicated in an area called Basic service area.

11. **Extended Service Area (ESA):** The BSA should be a subset of ESA. The area in which STAs of all BSS in ESS can communicate.

12. **Service Set Identifier (SSID):** Identity of a network either ESS or IBSS and the ID is of 32 bytes/256 bits long.

13. **BSS Identifier (BSSID):** ID of BSS that can be access point MAC address.it is of length 6 octets or bytes.

14. **Channel:** Channel is a predefined frequency band for transferring electromagnetic signals. Any communication should travel through channel in Wi-Fi.

A station can join a network by either passive scanning or active scanning to receive synchronization data. Passive scanning involves scanning of station from AP using beacon packet. Active scanning involves scanning of AP from station using probe request and receiving response from AP as probe response. The selection of method is based on the tradeoff between power consumption or performance. After determining the access point, authentication is initiated to ensure each other's identity to access the network. Later, the negotiation process for association between APs and STAs are carried out for knowing each other capabilities and subsequently exchange of information can take place. Carrier sense multiple access/collision avoidance (CSMA/CA) is used to transfer any kind of packet across a shared medium, between STAs and APs, between APs (IEEE 802.11 Technical Tutorial). The 802.11 MAC is using CSMA/CA which prevents the collision before it occurs unlike 802.3 MAC where only collision detection (CD) takes place after it occurs using CSMA/CD.

The MAC header types are control frames, management frames and data frames. The management frames are Beacon, Probe and Probe Response, Association Request, Association Response, Re-association Request, Re-association Response, Dis-association, Authentication, and De-authentication. The control frames are requested to send, clear to send and Acknowledgement. The data frame is MAC service data unit (MSDU) that are transferred through APs to reach the destination.

The main advantage of Wi-Fi network is its support to access locations where cables are not laid, and it is too expensive. Since it is wireless, the cost of the network also reduced, devices can move freely without loss of connection and flexible to implement. Currently, applications from almost all domains are using Wi-Fi networks such as Industrial process monitoring and control, temporary need in disaster circumstances or battlefield, surveillance networks, healthcare, educational environments and so on.

Table 1. Communication technology features mapped with application requirements

Communication Technology	Application Requirements						
	Coverage Range	Frequency	Cost	Battery life	Data rate	Scalability	Security
Wi-Fi	50m	2.4GHz	high	less	600 Mbps	yes	yes
Bluetooth(BLE)	80m	2.4GHz	low	In years	< 1Mbps	yes	yes
NFC	<0.2m	13.56 MHz	low	No power for Passive devices	106 – 424 Kbps	yes	not with RFID
ZigBee	30m/ mesh	915MHz/2.4GHz	low	In years	250 Kbps	yes	yes
Sigfox	10km – 50km	868/902Mhz	low	In years	10-1000bps	yes	yes
Lora	2-45km	Sub-GHz	low	In years	0.3-15Kbps	yes	yes
Cellular (LTE-M, NB-IoT and EC-GSM)	200km	900/1800/1900/2100 MHz	High (can use existing)	In day - years	10 kbps - 10Mbps	yes	yes
Zwave	30m/ mesh	900Mhz	low	months to years	10-100 Kbps	Limited	yes
Thread	30m/ mesh	2.4GHz	low	In years	250 Kbps	yes	yes
Weightless-N	10km	ISM/ White space	low	10-15 years	10-100 Kbps	yes	yes

Table 2. Top 10 applications searched in Google in 2016 and their suitable technologies

Application	Suitable Communication technologies	Decision Factors	IOT implementation Factors
Smart Home	ZigBee, thread, LoRa, Zwave	low cost, low power	identity, timing, chain of custody, connectivity
Wearables	Bluetooth, Wi-Fi	compact, low cost	identity
Smart City	Wi-Fi, Cellular IoT	Transmission speed, reliability	network bandwidth, timing, storage
Smart Grids	ZigBee, Wi-Fi	reliability	monitoring and control
Industrial Internet	ZigBee, Cellular IoT, Sigfox, LoRa	coverage, high performance	identity, monitoring and control, timing
Connected Cars	Wi-Fi, Cellular IoT	battery life, scalability	connectivity, Identity
Connected Health	Wi-Fi, Bluetooth	battery life, security	connectivity, Identity
Smart Retail	NFC, Wi-Fi, LoRa, Sigfox	Reliability, scalability	identity, chain of custody
Smart Supply Chain	NFC, Wi-Fi, LoRa, Sigfox	reliability, scalability	identity, chain of custody
Smart Farming	Wi-Fi, ZigBee, Cellular IoT	coverage, scalability, battery life	identity, connectivity, monitoring and control

SUMMARY

The strength of IoT is in its realization of connectivity, proactiveness, identity, monitoring & control. To efficiently implement the IoT applications, basic factors such as coverage, data rate, frequency, battery life, scalability, cost and security needs to be analysed. The basic factor values of various communication technologies and its support to scalability and security is described in Table 1. The top 10 IoT applications that are searched in google in 2016 is also listed in Table 2 with their suitable communication technologies.

REFERENCES

Z-wave Alliance. (n. d.). About Z-Wave Technology. Retrieved from http://z-wavealliance.org/about_z-wave_technology/

Agarwal, T. (2015). White Paper on Wireless Communication through ZigBee Technology. Retrieved from https://www.elprocus.com/white-papers/

Ali, M. J., Moungla, H., Younis, M., & Mehaoua, A. (2017). IoT-enabled Channel Selection Approach for WBANs. arXiv:1703.09508

Silabs. (2017). Application Development Fundamentals (Thread). Retrieved from http://www.silabs.com/documents/public/user-guides/ug103-11-appdevfundamentals-thread.pdf

Breezecom. (n. d.). IEEE 802.11 Technical Tutorial. Retrieved from http://www.breezecom.com

Coskun, V., Ozdenizci, B., & Ok, K. (2013). A survey on near field communication (NFC) technology. *Wireless Personal Communications*, *71*(3), 2259–2294. doi:10.1007/s11277-012-0935-5

Elahi, A., & Gschwender, A. (2009, December). Introduction to the ZigBee Wireless Sensor and Control Network. Retrieved from http://www.informit.com/articles/

Fernández-Garcia, R., & Gil, I. (2017). An Alternative Wearable Tracking System Based on a Low-Power Wide-Area Network. *Sensors (Basel, Switzerland)*, *17*(3), 592. doi:10.3390/s17030592 PMID:28335424

Fouad, H., & Farouk, H. (in press). Heart rate sensor node analysis for designing internet of things telemedicine embedded system. *Cogent Engineering*.

Klasman, J. (2017). Internet Access Possibilities in Bluetooth Low Energy Sensors.

Lin, J., Yu, W., Zhang, N., Yang, X., Zhang, H., & Zhao, W. (2017). *A Survey on Internet of Things: Architecture, Enabling Technologies, Security and Privacy, and Applications. IEEE Internet of Things Journal.*

Link-labs. (2016). A Comprehensive Look at Low Power, Wide Area Networks. Retrieved from https://www.link-labs.com/knowledge-center

Link-labs. (2016). Selecting a Wireless Technology for New Industrial Internet of Things Products. Retrieved from https://www.link-labs.com/knowledge-center

LoRa applications. (n. d.) LoRa Applications. *SemTech*. Retrieved from http://www.semtech.com/wireless-rf/internet-of-things/lora-applications/briefs

Mikhaylov, K., Petäjäjärvi, J., Haapola, J., & Pouttu, A. (2017). D2D Communications in LoRaWAN Low Power Wide Area Network: From Idea to Empirical Validation. arXiv:1703.01985

Naito, K. (2017). A Survey on the Internet-of-Things: Standards, Challenges and Future Prospects. *Journal of Information Processing*, *25*, 23–31. doi:10.2197/ipsjjip.25.23

ECMA International. (2005). Near Field Communication White Paper. Retrieved from http://www.ecma-international.org/activities/Communications/tc32-tg19-2005-012.pdf

Olsson, J. (2014). *6LoWPAN demystified*. Texas Instruments.

Sigmadesigns. (2016). Z-wave Overview. Retrieved from http://z-wave.sigmadesigns.com/why-z-wave/technology/

Perez-Diaz de Cerio, D., Hernández, Á., Valenzuela, J. L., & Valdovinos, A. (2017). Analytical and Experimental Performance Evaluation of BLE Neighbor Discovery Process Including Non-Idealities of Real Chipsets. *Sensors (Basel, Switzerland)*, *17*(3), 499. doi:10.3390/s17030499 PMID:28273801

Petäjäjärvi, J., Mikhaylov, K., Pettissalo, M., Janhunen, J., & Iinatti, J. (2017). Performance of a low-power wide-area network based on LoRa technology: Doppler robustness, scalability, and coverage. *International Journal of Distributed Sensor Networks*, *13*(3), 1550147717699412. doi:10.1177/1550147717699412

Pitì, A., Verticale, G., Rottondi, C., Capone, A., & Lo Schiavo, L. (2017). The Role of Smart Meters in Enabling Real-Time Energy Services for Households: The Italian Case. *Energies*, *10*(2), 199. doi:10.3390/en10020199

Poole, I. (n. d.). Weightless Wireless M2M White Space Communications. Retrieved from http://www.radio-electronics.com/info/wireless/weightless-m2m-white-space-wireless-communications/

Rohde-schwarz. (2016). White paper on Near Field Communication (NFC) Technology and Measurements. Retrieved from http://www2.rohde-schwarz.com/file_15687/1MA182_2.pdf

Sallouha, H., Chiumento, A., & Pollin, S. (2017). Localization in Long-range Ultra Narrow Band IoT Networks using RSSI. arXiv:1703.02398

Sethi, P., & Sarangi, S. R. (2017). Internet of Things: Architectures, Protocols, and Applications. *Journal of Electrical and Computer Engineering*.

Sigmadesigns.com. (2016). Why is Z-Wave the Preferred Choice for Smart Home IoT? Retrieved from http://z-wave.sigmadesigns.com/why-z-wave/

Sinha, R. S., Wei, Y., & Hwang, S. H. (2017). *A survey on LPWA technology: LoRa and NB-IoT*. ICT Express.

Solat, S. (2017). Security of Electronic Payment Systems: A Comprehensive Survey. arXiv:1701.04556

Talari, S., Shafie-khah, M., Siano, P., Loia, V., Tommasetti, A., & Catalão, J. P. (2017). A Review of Smart Cities Based on the Internet of Things Concept. *Energies*, *10*(4), 421. doi:10.3390/en10040421

Link-labs. (2016, February 8). The Complete List of Wireless IoT Network Protocols. Retrieved from https://www.link-labs.com/blog/complete-list-iot-network-protocols

Threadgroup. (2015). Thread Stack Fundamentals (Technical white paper). Retrieved from https://threadgroup.org/RESOURCES-old/White-Papers

Threadgroup. (2015). Thread Usage of 6LoWPAN (Technical white paper). Retrieved from https://threadgroup.org/RESOURCES-old/White-Papers

Townsend, K. (2014). Introduction to Bluetooth Low Energy. *Adafruit*. Retrieved from https://learn.adafruit.com/introduction-to-bluetooth-low-energy

Link-labs. (2016, March). Thread Vs. ZigBee, For IoT Engineers. Retrieved from https://www.link-labs.com/blog/thread-vs-zigbee-for-iot-engineers

Zhang, K., & Marchiori, A. (2017). Crowdsourcing Low-Power Wide-Area IoT Networks.

Compilation of References

Abdul-Manan, M., & Hyland, P. (2013). A framework for assessing ESOA Implementation Readiness. *International Journal of Intelligent Information Technologies, 9*(2), 21–37. doi:10.4018/jiit.2013040103

Abu-Jaber, M. (2007). *Readiness of the Palestinian banking sector in adopting the electronic banking system (exploratory study)*. Unpublished master's thesis, The Islamic University.

Accenture. (2009). Leadership in Customer Service: Creating Shared Responsibility for Better Outcomes Retrieved 10.07.2010 from http://www.accenture.com/Global/Research_and_Insights/Institute_For_Public_Service_Value/2008LCSROutcomes.htm

Afsar, B., Rehman, Z. U., Qureshi, J. Z., & Shahjehan, A. (2010). Determinants of customer loyalty in the bank sector: The case of Pakistan. *African Journal of Business Management, 4*(6), 1040–1047.

Agarwal, T. (2015). White Paper on Wireless Communication through ZigBee Technology. Retrieved from https://www.elprocus.com/white-papers/

Agirre, E., Ansa, O., Martinez, D., & Hovy, E. 2001. Enriching WordNet Concepts with Topic Signatures. In *Proceedings of the NAACL workshop on WordNet and other lexical resources: Applications, Extensions and Customizations*.

Agrawal, R., Imielinski, T., & Swami, A. (1993). Mining association rules between sets of items in large databases. In *Proceedings of the ACM SIGMOD Conference on Management of Data*, Washington, D.C.(*Vol. 22,* pp. 207-216). doi:10.1145/170036.170072

Ahmad, A., & Dey, L. (2007). A k-mean clustering algorithm for mixed numeric and categorical data. *Data & Knowledge Engineering, 63*(2), 503–527. doi:10.1016/j.datak.2007.03.016

Ahmadyfard, A., & Modares, H. (2008). Combining PSO and k-means to enhance data clustering. In *Proceedings of the International Symposium on Telecommunications IST '08* (pp. 688-691). IEEE. doi:10.1109/ISTEL.2008.4651388

Ahmed, M., Anjomshoaa, A., & Tjoa, A. M. (2007). User data privacy in web services context using semantic desktop - semanticLife case study. *Paper presented at the 9th International Conference on Information Integration and Web-based Applications & Services (iiWAS '07)*, Jakarta, Indonesia.

Akel, M., & Phillips, R. (2001). The internet advantage: A process for integrating electronic commerce into economic development strategy. *The Journal of Economic Development Review, 17*(3), 13–20.

Al Maghayreh, E. (2010). *Simplifying Runtime Verification of Distributed Programs: Ameliorating the State Space Explosion Problem*. Secaucus, NJ, USA: VDM Verlag.

Al Maghayreh, E. (2011). Block-based atomicity to simplify the verification of distributed applications. In *Proceedings of the 24th Canadian Conference on Electrical and Computer Engineering (CCECE)* (pp. 887–891). doi:10.1109/CCECE.2011.6030585

Al Maghayreh, E., Samarah, S., Alkhateeb, F., Doush, I. A., Alsmadi, I., & Saifan, A. (2012). A framework for monitoring the execution of distributed multi-agent programs. *International Journal of Advanced Science and Technology*, *38*(01), 53–66.

Alani, H., Kim, S., Millard, D. E., Weal, M. J., Lewis, P. H., Hall, W., & Shadbolt, N. R. 2003. Automatic Extraction of Knowledge from Web Documents. In *Proceedings of 2nd International Semantic Web Conference - Workshop on Human Language Technology for the Semantic Web and Web Services*, Sanibel Island, Florida.

Alani, H. (2006). Ontology Construction from Online Ontologies. In *Proceedings of 15th World Wide Web Conference*, Edinburgh, Scotland.

Alba, E., & Chicano, F. (2005). On the behavior of parallel genetic algorithms for optimal placement of antennae in telecommunications. *International Journal of Foundations of Computer Science*, *16*(02), 343–359. doi:10.1142/S0129054105003029

Alberti, M., Gomes, A. S., Goncalves, R., Leite, J., & Slota, M. (2011). Normative Systems Represented as Hybrid Knowledge Bases. In *Proceedings of the 12th International Conference on Computational Logic in Multi-agent Systems CLIMA'11* (pp. 330-346). doi:10.1007/978-3-642-22359-4_23

Al-Fahim, N. H. (2013). An Exploratory Study of Factors Affecting the Internet Banking Adoption: A Qualitative Study among Postgraduate Student. *Global Journal of Management and Business Research Finance*, *13*(8), 11.

Al-Fawzan, M. A. (2005). Assessing service quality in a Saudi bank. *Journal of King Saud University Engineering and Science*, *18*(1), 101–115.

AL-Hawary. S. I. S., & Hussien, A. J. A. (2017). The Impact of Electronic Banking Services on the Customers Loyalty of Commercial Banks in Jordan. *International Journal of Academic Research in Accounting, Finance and Management Sciences, 7*(1), 50 - 63.

Alhinai, Y. S. (2009). *The adoption of advanced mobile commerce services by individuals: investigating the impact of the interaction between the consumer and the mobile services provider.* Unpublished doctoral dissertation, University of Melbourne.

Ali, M. J., Moungla, H., Younis, M., & Mehaoua, A. (2017). IoT-enabled Channel Selection Approach for WBANs. arXiv:1703.09508

Ali, R., ElHelw, M., Atallah, L., Lo, B., & Yang, G. Z. (2008). Pattern Mining for Routine Behaviour Discovery in Pervasive Healthcare Environments. In *Proceedings of the 5th International Conference on Information Technology and Application in Biomedicine*, Shenzhe (pp. 241-244). doi:10.1109/ITAB.2008.4570576

Al-Mabrouk, K., & Soar, J. (2009). Delphi examination of emerging issues for successful information technology transfer in North Africa: A case of Libya. *African Journal of Business Management*, *3*(3), 107–114.

Al-Mubaid, H., & Nguyen, H. A. (2006). A cluster-based approach for semantic similarity in the biomedical domain. In *Proceedings of the 28th Annual International Conference of the IEEE* (pp. 2713-2717). doi:10.1109/IEMBS.2006.259235

Al-Sukkar, A. S. (2005). *The application of information systems in the Jordainan banking sector: A study of the acceptance of the Internet.* Unpublished doctoral dissertation, University of Wollongong.

Al-Sultan, K. S. (1995). A tabu search approach to the clustering problem. *Pattern Recognition, 28*(9), 1443–1451. doi:10.1016/0031-3203(95)00022-R

Alwadain, A., Fielt, E., Korthaus, A., & Rosemann, M. (2013). A Comparative Analysis of the Integration of SOA Elements in Widely-Used Enterprise Architecture Frameworks. *International Journal of Intelligent Information Technologies, 9*(2), 54–70. doi:10.4018/jiit.2013040105

Amatriain, X., Pujol, J. M., & Oliver, N. (2009) I like it... i like it not: Evaluating user ratings noise in recommender systems. In User Modeling, Adaptation, and Personalization (pp. 247–258). Springer.

Amin, H. (2008). Factors affecting the intentions of customers in Malaysia to use mobile phone credit cards. *Management Research News Journal, 31*(7), 493–503. doi:10.1108/01409170810876062

Amiri, E., & Mahmoudi, S. (2016). Efficient protocol for data clustering by fuzzy Cuckoo Optimization Algorithm. *Applied Soft Computing, 41*, 15–21. doi:10.1016/j.asoc.2015.12.008

Ananthi, V. P., Balasubramaniam, P., & Lim, C. P. (2014). Segmentation of gray scale image based on intuitionistic fuzzy sets constructed from several membership functions. *Pattern Recognition, 47*(12), 3870–3880. doi:10.1016/j.patcog.2014.07.003

Andrews, S., & Polovina, S. (2011). A Mapping from Conceptual Graphs to Formal Concept Analysis. In Conceptual Structures for Discovering Knowledge, the 19th International Conference on Conceptual Structures, LNCS (Vol. 6828, pp. 63–76). Springer. doi:10.1007/978-3-642-22688-5_5

Andrews, S., Orphanides, C., & Polovina, S. (2011). Visualising Computational Intelligence through Converting Data into Formal Concepts. In Next Generation Data Technologies for Collective Computational Intelligence (pp. 139–165). Springer Berlin Heidelberg, Berlin, Heidelberg. doi:10.1007/978-3-642-20344-2_6

Andrighetto, G., Conte, R., Turrini, P., & Paolucci, M. (2007). Emergence in the Loop: Simulating the two way dynamics of Norm Innovation. In *Normative Multi-agent Systems*.

Andrighetto, G., Campenni, M., Cecconi, F., & Conte, R. (2010). The complex loop of norm emergence: A simulation model. In S.-H. Chen, C. Cioffi-Revilla, N. Gilbert(Eds.), *Agent-Based Social Systems* (Vol. 7, pp. 19–35). Springer.

Armano, G., & Farmani, M. R. (2014). Clustering analysis with combination of artificial bee colony algorithm and k-means technique. *International Journal of Computer Theory and Engineering, 6*(2), 141–145. doi:10.7763/IJCTE.2014.V6.852

Arun, B., & Kumar, T. V. (2017). Materialized View Selection using Artificial Bee Colony Optimization. *International Journal of Intelligent Information Technologies, 13*(1), 26–49. doi:10.4018/IJIIT.2017010102

Askarzadeh, A. (2016). A novel metaheuristic method for solving constrained engineering optimization problems: Crow search algorithm. *Computers & Structures, 169*, 1–12. doi:10.1016/j.compstruc.2016.03.001

Asuncion, A., & Newman, D. (2007). UCI machine learning repository.

Atanassov, K. T. (2003, September). Intuitionistic fuzzy sets: past, present and future. In *Proceedings of the EUSFLAT Conf.* (pp. 12-19).

Ayo, C., Adewoye, J., & Oni, A. (2010). The state of e-banking implementation in Nigeria: A post- Consolidation review. *Journal of Emerging Trends in Economics and Management Science, 1*(1), 37–45.

Ba̎ck, T. (1995). Generalized convergence models for tournament- and (mu,lambda)-selection. In *Proceedings of the 6th International Conference on Genetic Algorithms*, San Francisco, CA (pages 2–8). Morgan Kaufmann Publishers Inc.

Baeza-Yates, R., & Ribeiro-Neto, N. 1999. Modern information retrieval. ACM Press.

Bahrami, S., & Saniee Abadeh, S. (2014). Automatic Image Annotation Using an Evolutionary Algorithm. In *Proceedings of the 7ᵗʰ International Symposium on Telecommunications* (pp. 320-325). doi:10.1109/ISTEL.2014.7000722

Baker, J. E. (1985). Adaptive selection methods for genetic algorithms. In *Proceedings of the 1st International Conference on Genetic Algorithms*, Hillsdale, NJ (pp. 101–111). L. Erlbaum Associates Inc.

Balachandran, K., & Ranathunga, S. (2016). Domain-Specific Term Extraction for Concept Identification in Ontology Construction. In *Proceedings of the 2016 IEEE/WIC/ACM International Conference on Web Intelligence* (pp. 34-41). IEEE Computer Society.

Balasubramaniam, P., & Ananthi, V. P. (2016). Segmentation of nutrient deficiency in incomplete crop images using intuitionistic fuzzy C-means clustering algorithm. *Nonlinear Dynamics, 83*(1-2), 849–866. doi:10.1007/s11071-015-2372-y

Banerjee, M. (2009). Internet banking: An interaction building channel for bank customer relationships. In Self-Service in the Internet Age (pp. 195 - 212). London Springer-Verlag. doi:10.1007/978-1-84800-207-4-10

Bashar, M. A., Li, Y., & Gao, Y. (2016, October). A Framework for Automatic Personalised Ontology Learning. In *Proceedings of the 2016 IEEE/WIC/ACM International Conference on Web Intelligence* (pp. 105-112). IEEE. doi:10.1109/WI.2016.0025

Basturk, B., & Karaboga, D. (2006). An artificial bee colony (abc) algorithm for numeric function optimization. In *Proceedings of the IEEE Swarm Intelligence Symposium 2006*, Indianapolis, Indiana, USA.

Bauernfeind, U., & Zins, A. H. (2006). The Perception of Exploratory Browsing and Trust with Recommender Websites. *Information Technology & Tourism, 8*(2), 121–136. doi:10.3727/109830506778001456

Belete, G. F., Voinov, A., & Laniak, G. F. (2017). An overview of the model integration process: From pre-integration assessment to testing. *Environmental Modelling & Software, 87*, 49–63. Retrieved from http://linkinghub.elsevier.com/retrieve/pii/S1364815216308805 doi:10.1016/j.envsoft.2016.10.013

Bellos, C. C., Papadopoulos, A., Rosso, R., & Fotiadis, D. I. (2010, November). Extraction and Analysis of features acquired by wearable sensors network. In *Proceedings of the 2010 10th IEEE International Conference on Information Technology and Applications in Biomedicine (ITAB)* (pp. 1-4). IEEE. doi:10.1109/ITAB.2010.5687761

Bellos, C., Papadopoulos, A., Rosso, R., & Fotiadis, D. I. (2012). A Support Vector Machine Approach for Categorization of Patients Suffering from Chronic Diseases. In *Wireless Mobile Communication and Healthcare* (pp. 264–267). Springer Berlin Heidelberg. doi:10.1007/978-3-642-29734-2_36

Beydoun, G., Low, G., García-Sánchez, F., Valencia-Garcia, R., & Bejar, R. M. (2014). Identification of Ontologies to Support Information Systems Development. *Information Systems Journal, 46*(November), 45–60. doi:10.1016/j.is.2014.05.002

Beydoun, G., Low, G., Tran, N., & Bogg, P. (2011). Development of a Peer-to-Peer Information Sharing System Using Ontologies. *Expert Systems with Applications, 38*(8), 9352–9364. doi:10.1016/j.eswa.2011.01.104

Beydoun, G., Xu, D., & Sugumaran, V. (2013). Service Oriented Architectures (SOA) Adoption Challenges *International Journal of Intelligent Information Technologies, 9*(2), 1–6. doi:10.4018/jiit.2013040101

Bezdek, J. C., Ehrlich, R., & Full, W. (1984). FCM: The fuzzy c-means clustering algorithm. *Computers & Geosciences, 10*(2-3), 191–203. doi:10.1016/0098-3004(84)90020-7

Bhargava, R., Tripathy, B. K., Tripathy, A., Dhull, R., Verma, E., & Swarnalatha, P. (2013, August). Rough intuitionistic fuzzy c-means algorithm and a comparative analysis. In *Proceedings of the 6th ACM India Computing Convention* (p. 23). ACM. doi:10.1145/2522548.2523140

Bianchi, F., Redmond, S. J., Narayanan, M. R., Cerutti, S., & Lovell, N. H. (2010). Barometric Pressure and Triaxial acclerometry based falls event detection. *IEEE Transactions on Neural Systems and Rehabilitation Engineering*, *18*(6), 619–627. doi:10.1109/TNSRE.2010.2070807 PMID:20805056

Bieberstein, N., Bose, S., Walker, L., & Lynch, A. (2005). Impact of service-oriented architecture on enterprise systems, organisational structures, and individuals. *IBM Systems Journal*, *44*(4), 691–708. doi:10.1147/sj.444.0691

Biffl, S., Mordinyi, R., & Moser, T. (2008), Ontology-supported quality assurance for component-based systems configuration. In *Proceedings of the 6th International Workshop on Software Quality*, Leipzig, Germany. ACM. doi:10.1145/1370099.1370113

Billsus, D., & Pazzani, M. J. (2000). User Modeling for Adaptive News Access. *User Modeling and User-Adapted Interaction*, *10*(2/3), 147–180. doi:10.1023/A:1026501525781

Binu, D. (2015). Cluster analysis using optimization algorithms with newly designed objective functions. *Expert Systems with Applications*, *42*(14), 5848–5859. doi:10.1016/j.eswa.2015.03.031

Blaschke, C., & Valencia, A. (2002). Automatic Ontology Construction from the Literature. In *Proceedings of Genome Informatics Ser Workshop Genome Informatics* (Vol. 13, pp. 201–213).

Blomqvist, E. (2006). OntoCase - Automatic ontology enrichment based on ontology design patterns. In *The Semantic Web, LNCS* (Vol. *5823*, pp. 65–80). doi:10.1007/978-3-642-04930-9_5

Blut, M., Wang, C., & Schoefer, K. (2016). Factors Influencing the Acceptance of Self-Service Technologies: A Meta-Analysis. *Journal of Service Research*, *19*(4), 396–416. doi:10.1177/1094670516662352

Boella, G., Torre, L. V. D., & Verhagen, H. (2008). Ten Challenges for Normative Multi-agent Systems. In R. Bordini et al. (Eds.), *Dagstuhl Seminar Proceedings*. Dagstuhl: SchlossDagstuhl - Leibniz-Zentrumfuer Informatik.

Boella, G., Pigozzi, G., & Torre, L. V. D. (2009). Normative Framework for Normative System Change. In *Proceedings of the 8th International Conference on Autonomous Agents and Multi-agent Systems, AAMAS'09* (pp. 169-176).

Böhm, K., Heyer, G., Quasthoff, U., & Wolff, C. (2002). Topic Map Generation Using Text Mining. *Journal of Universal Computer Science*, *8*(6), 623–633.

Bollegala, D., Matsuo, Y., & Ishizuka, M. (2009). Measuring the Similarity between Implicit Semantic Relations from the Web. In *Proceedings of the 18th International Conference on World Wide Web* (pp. 651-660). doi:10.1145/1526709.1526797

Bork, D. (2015). *Development Method for the Conceptual Design of Multi-View Modeling Tools with an Emphasis on Consistency Requirements* [Doctoral Dissertation]. University of Bamberg, Germany.

Bork, D., Buchmann, R., & Karagiannis, D. (2015). Preserving multi-view consistency in diagrammatic knowledge representation. In *Proceedings of the International Conference on Knowledge Science, Engineering and Management* (pp. 177–182). Springer.

Bose, R., & Sugumaran, V. (2006). Challenges for Deploying Web Services-Based E-Business Systems in SMEs. *International Journal of E-Business Research*, *2*(1), 1–18. doi:10.4018/jebr.2006010101

Bosse, T., Gerritsen, C., & Klein, M. C. A. (2009). Agent-Based Simulation of Social Learning in Criminology. In *Proc. of the Int. Conf. on Agents and AI, ICAART'09* (pp. 5-13).

Bougé, L. (1987). Repeated snapshots in distributed systems with synchronous communications and their implementation in CSP. *Theoretical Computer Science*, *49*(2-3), 145–169. doi:10.1016/0304-3975(87)90005-3

Bourke, A. K., OBrien, J. V., & Lyons, G. M. (2007). Evaluation of a threshold-based tri-axial accelerometer fall detection algorithm. *Gait & Posture*, *26*(2), 194–199. doi:10.1016/j.gaitpost.2006.09.012 PMID:17101272

Bray, D. (2007). *Knowledge Ecosystems: A Theoretical Lens for Organizations Confronting Hyperturbulent Environments*. In T. McMaster, D. Wastell, E. Ferneley, and J. DeGross (Eds.), Organizational Dynamics of Technology-based Innovation. doi:10.1007/978-0-387-72804-9_31

Breezecom. (n. d.). IEEE 802.11 Technical Tutorial. Retrieved from http://www.breezecom.com

Broersen, J., Dastani, M., & Torre, L. V. D. (2001). Resolving Conflicts Between Beliefs, Obligations, Intentions, and Desires. Symbolic and Quantitative Approaches to Reasoning with Uncertainty. In *Proceedings of the 6th European Conference, ECSQARU*, Toulouse, France (pp. 568-579). Springer.

Brooks, S. P., & Morgan, B. J. (1995). Optimization using simulated annealing. *The Statistician*, *44*(2), 241–257. doi:10.2307/2348448

Brusa, G., Caliusco, M. & Chiotti, O. (2008). Towards ontological engineering: a process for building domain ontology from scratch in public administration. *Journal of knowledge engineering*, 2(5), 484-503.

Burke, E. K., & Kendall, G. (2005). *Search Methodologies: Introductory Tutorials in Optimization and Decision Support Techniques*. Springer. doi:10.1007/0-387-28356-0

Cai, Y. Y., Mu, Z. C., Ren, Y. F., & Xu, G. Q. (2014). A Hybrid Hierarchical Framework for Automatic Image Annotation. In *Proceedings of the IEEE International Conference on Machine Learning and Cybernetics*, Lanzhou (pp. 30-36).

Campos, J., López-Sánchez, M., & Esteva, M. (2010). A Case-based Reasoning Approach for Norm Adaptation. In *Proceedings of the 5th International Conference on Hybrid Artificial Intelligence Systems (HAIS'10)*, Spain (pp. 168-176). Springer. doi:10.1007/978-3-642-13803-4_21

Carneiro, G., Chan, A. B., Moreno, P. J., & Vasconcelos, N. (2007). Supervised Learning of Semantic Classes for Image Annotation and Retrieval. *IEEE Transactions on Pattern Analysis and Machine Intelligence*, *29*(3), 394–410. doi:10.1109/TPAMI.2007.61 PMID:17224611

Carter, L., & Belanger, F. (2004). Citizen adoption of electronic government initiatives. *Paper presented at the 37th Hawaii International Conference on System Sciences*, Big Island, HI, USA.

Castelfranchi, C., Conte, R., & Paolucci, M. (1998). Normative Reputation and the Cost of Compliance. *Journal of Artificial Societies and Social Simulation*, *1*(3), 3.

Cavusoglu, H. (2003). *The economics of information technology investments*. Unpublished doctoral dissertation, University of Texas at Dallas.

Centeno, R., & Billhardt, H. (2012). Auto-adaptation of Open MAS through On-line Modifications of the Environment. *Proceedings of the 10th international conference on Advanced Agent Technology AAMAS'11* (pp. 426-427).

Central Intelligence Agency (CIA). (2016). *The World Factbook*. Retrieved from https://www.cia.gov/library/publications/the-world-factbook/geos/ly.html

Central Libyan Bank. (2012). *Central Libyan Bank Report*.

Chaira, T., & Anand, S. (2011). A novel intuitionistic fuzzy approach for tumour/hemorrhage detection in medical images.

Chaira, T. (2011). A novel intuitionistic fuzzy C means clustering algorithm and its application to medical images. *Applied Soft Computing*, *11*(2), 1711–1717. doi:10.1016/j.asoc.2010.05.005

Chandy, K. M., & Lamport, L. (1985). Distributed snapshots: Determining global states of distributed systems. *ACM Transactions on Computer Systems*, *3*(1), 63–75. doi:10.1145/214451.214456

Chase, C. M., & Garg, V. K. (1998). Detection of global predicates: Techniques and their limitations. *Distributed Computing*, *11*(4), 191–201. doi:10.1007/s004460050049

Chatzis, S. P. (2011). A fuzzy c-means-type algorithm for clustering of data with mixed numeric and categorical attributes employing a probabilistic dissimilarity functional. *Expert Systems with Applications*, *38*(7), 8684–8689. doi:10.1016/j.eswa.2011.01.074

Chauhan, H., Garg, V. K., Natarajan, A., & Mittal, N. (2013). A distributed abstraction algorithm for online predicate detection. In *Proceedings of the IEEE 32nd Symposium on Reliable Distributed Systems SRDS '13*, Braga, Portugal (pp. 101–110). doi:10.1109/SRDS.2013.19

Cheah, C. M., Teo, J. J., Sim, K. H., & Tan, B. T. (2011). Factors affecting Malaysian mobile banking adoption: An empirical analysis. *International Journal of Network and Mobile Technologies.*, *2*(3), 12.

Chen, C. Y., & Ye, F. (2004). Particle swarm optimization algorithm and its application to clustering analysis. In *Proceedings of the 2004 IEEE International Conference on Networking, Sensing and Control* (Vol. 2, pp. 789-794). IEEE.

Chen, H., Gong, Y., & Hong, X. (2013). Online modelling with tunable RBF network. *IEEE Transactions on Neural networks and Learning Systems*, *43*(3), 935–947.

Chen, S. Wu, Y. & Luk, B.L. (1999, September). Combined genetic algorithm optimization and regularized orthogonal least squares learning for radial basis function networks. *IEEE Transactions on Neural Networks*, *10*(5).

Chen, F. L., & Li, F. L. (2010). Comparison of the Hybrid Credit Scoring Models Based on Various Classifiers. *International Journal of Intelligent Information Technologies*, *6*(3), 56–74. doi:10.4018/jiit.2010070104

Chengzhi, Z., & Wei, S. (2008). Self-adaptive GA, quantitative semantic similarity measures and ontology-based text clustering. In *Proceedings of the 2008 IEEE International Conference on Natural Language Processing and Knowledge Engineering (NLP-KE08)*, Beijing, China (pp. 95-102).

Chen, L., Hoey, J., Nugent, C. D., Cook, D. J., & Yu, Z. (2012). Sensor-based activity recognition. *IEEE Transactions on Systems, Man and Cybernetics. Part C, Applications and Reviews*, *42*(6), 790–808. doi:10.1109/TSMCC.2012.2198883

Chen, Y. P., Yang, J. Y., Liou, S. N., Lee, G. Y., & Wang, J. S. (2008). Online classifier construction algorithm for human activity detection using a tri-axial Accelerometer. *Applied Mathematics and Computation*, *205*(2), 849–860. doi:10.1016/j.amc.2008.05.099

Chen, Z., Liu, Z., Ravn, A. P., Stolz, V., & Naijun, Z. (2009). Refinement and verification in component-based model-driven design. *Science of Computer Programming*, *74*(4), 168–196.

Chernov, S., Iofciu, T., Nejdl, W., & Zhou, X. (2006). Extracting Semantic Relationships between Wikipedia Categories. In *Proceedings of the first International Workshop on Semantic Wikis*.

Choudrie, J., Ghinea, G., & Weerakkody, V. (2004). Evaluating global e-government sites: A view using web diagnostic tools. *Electronic Journal of E-Government*, *2*(2), 105–114.

Chu, C., & Brockmeyer, M. (2008). Predicate detection modality and semantics in three partially synchronous models. In *Proceedings of the Seventh IEEE/ACIS International Conference on Computer and Information Science* (pp. 444–450). doi:10.1109/ICIS.2008.95

Chu, G., Niu, K., & Tian, B. (2014). Automatic Image Annotation Combining SVMS and KNN Algorithm. In *Proceedings of the IEEE 3rd International Conference on Cloud Computing and Intelligent Systems* (pp. 13-17).

Chu, S. C., Tsai, P. W., & Pan, J. S. (2006). Cat swarm optimization. In *Proceedings of the Pacific Rim International Conference on Artificial Intelligence* (pp. 854-858). Springer Berlin Heidelberg.

Cleveland, C. E. (2016). *A Study on How Mobile Banking Has Affected the Banking Industry: Has Mobile Banking Improved Bank Performance? (Master Degree)*. University of Mississippi.

Cobos, C., Muñoz-Collazos, H., Urbano-Muñoz, R., Mendoza, M., León, E., & Herrera-Viedma, E. (2014). Clustering of web search results based on the cuckoo search algorithm and balanced Bayesian information criterion. *Information Sciences*, *281*, 248–264. doi:10.1016/j.ins.2014.05.047

Cohen, S., & Intrator, N. (2000, June). A hybrid projection based and radial basis function architecture. In *Proceedings of the First International Workshop on Multiple Classier Systems*, Sardingia.

Coleman, J. (1998). *Foundations of social theory*. Cambridge Harvard University Press.

Cooper, R., & Marzullo, K. (1991). Consistent detection of global predicates. *SIGPLAN Not.*, *26*(12), 167–174. doi:10.1145/127695.122774

Cordeiro, J., & Filipe, J. (2004). The semiotic pentagram framework – a perspective on the use of semiotics within organisational semiotics. In *Proceedings of The 7th International Workshop on Organisational Semiotics*.

Coskun, V., Ozdenizci, B., & Ok, K. (2013). A survey on near field communication (NFC) technology. *Wireless Personal Communications*, *71*(3), 2259–2294. doi:10.1007/s11277-012-0935-5

Costello, G. I., & Tuchen, J. H. (1998). A comparative study of business to consumer electronic commerce within the Australian insurance sector. *Journal of Information Technology*, *13*(3), 153–167. doi:10.1080/026839698344800

Coyle, S., Conboy, K., & Acton, T. (2013). Group Process Losses in Agile Software Development Decision Making. *International Journal of Intelligent Information Technologies*, *9*(2), 38–53. doi:10.4018/jiit.2013040104

Cracknell, D. (2004). Electronic banking for the poor - panacea, potential and pitfalls. *MicroSave, 15*.

CSTransform. (2010). Citizen Service Transformation: A manifesto for change in the delivery of public services.

CSTransform. (2011): Interoperability A comparative analysis of 30 countries. London, UK.

Dabhi, A., & Prajapati, B. (2014). A neural network model for automatic image annotation refinement. *Journal Of Emerging Technologies And Innovative Research*, *1*(6), 561-564.

Dabholkar, P. A. (1996). Consumer evaluations of new technology-based selfservice options: An investigation of alternative models of service quality. *International Journal of Research in Marketing*, *13*(1), 29–51. doi:10.1016/0167-8116(95)00027-5

Dada, D. (2006). The failure of e-government in developing countries: A literature review. *The Electronic Journal of Information Systems in Developing Countries*, *26*.

Dahlem, N. (2011). OntoClippy: A User-Friendly Ontology Design and Creation Methodology. *International Journal of Intelligent Information Technologies*, *7*(1), 15–32. doi:10.4018/jiit.2011010102

Daqi, G., & Genxing, Y. (2002, May 12-17). Adaptive RBF neural networks for pattern classifications. In *Proceedings of the 2002 International Joint Conference on Neural Networks IJCNN '02*.

Das, A., Datar, M., Rajaram, S., & Garg, A. (2007). Google News Personalization: Scalable Online Collaborative Filtering. In *Proceedings of the 16th international conference on World Wide Web (WWW'07)* (pp. 271-280). ACM. doi:10.1145/1242572.1242610

Dautenhahn, K., Nehaniv, C. L., & Alissandrakis, A. (2003). Learning by Experience from Others—Social Learning and Imitation in Animals and Robots. In R. Kühn, R.Menzel, W. Menzelet al. (Eds.), Adaptivity and Learning: An Interdisciplinary Debate (pp. 217–421). Springer Verlag.

David, S., & Antonio, M. (2004). Creating Ontologies from Web documents. In Recent Advances in Artificial Intelligence Research and Development (pp. 11-18). IOS Press.

Davison, R., Vogel, M., Harris, A., & Jones, N. (2000). Technology Leapfrogging in Developing Countries - An Inevitable Luxury? *The Electronic Journal of Information Systems in Developing Countries*, *1*(5), 1–10.

Decker, B., Ras, E., Reck, J., & Klein, B. (2005), Self-organized Reuse of Software Engineering Knowledge supported by Semantic Wikis. In *Proceedings of the Workshop on Semantic Web Enabled Software Engineering*, Galway, Ireland.

Deljooi, H., & Amir, M. E. M. (2012). Automatic Image Annotation via the Statistical Semantic Model Based on the Relationship between the Regions. In *Proceedings of the 16th CSI International Symposium on Artificial Intelligence and Signal Processing* (pp. 101-106).

Demirkan, H., Kauffman, R., Vayghan, J., Fill, H.-G., Karagiannis, D., & Maglio, P. P. (2008). Service-oriented technology and management. *Journal of Electronic Commerce and Applications*, *7*(4), 356–376. doi:10.1016/j.elerap.2008.07.002

Deng, Z., Lu, K., Wei, J., & Zhang, J. (2010). Understanding customer satisfaction and loyalty: An empirical study of mobile instant messages in China. *International Journal of Information Management*, *30*(4), 289–300. doi:10.1016/j.ijinfomgt.2009.10.001

Dewan, S. M., Low, G., Land, L., & Dewan, A. (2009). Consumer choice model of mobile banking. *Paper presented at the 20th Australasian Conference on Information Systems*, Melbourne, Australia.

Ding, Y., & Foo, S. (2002). Ontology research and development, Part 1 – A review of ontology generation. *Journal of Information Science*, *28*(2), 123–136.

Donner, J., & Tellez, C. A. (2008). Mobile banking and economic development: Linking adoption. *impact, and use. Asian Journal of Communication*, *18*(4), 318–322. doi:10.1080/01292980802344190

Dorigo, M. (1992). Optimization, learning and natural algorithms [Ph.D thesis]. Politecnico di Milano, Italy.

Dorigo, M., Maniezzo, V., & Colorni, A. (1996). Ant system: Optimization by a colony of cooperating agents. *IEEE Transactions on Systems, Man, and Cybernetics. Part B, Cybernetics*, *26*(1), 29–41. doi:10.1109/3477.484436 PMID:18263004

Doukas, C., & Maglogiannis, I. (2011). Emergency fall incidents detection in assisted living environments utilizing motion, sound and visual perceptual components. *IEEE Transactions on Information Technology in Biomedicine*, *15*(2), 277–289. doi:10.1109/TITB.2010.2091140 PMID:21062686

Dumais, G., & Li, H. (2002). Distributed predicate detection in series-parallel systems. *IEEE Transactions on Parallel and Distributed Systems*, *13*(4), 373–387. doi:10.1109/71.995818

Dumitrescu, D. (1993). Fuzzy measures and the entropy of fuzzy partitions. *Journal of Mathematical Analysis and Applications*, *176*(2), 359–373. doi:10.1006/jmaa.1993.1220

Dunietz, J., & Gillick, D. (2014). A New Entity Salience Task with Millions of Training Examples. *Proceedings of the 14th Conference of the European Chapter of the Association for Computational Linguistics*, Gothenburg, Sweden. (Vol. 2, pp. 205–209). doi:10.3115/v1/E14-4040

Duygulu, P., Barnard, K., Freitas, J., & Forsyth, D. (2002). Object Recognition as Machine Translation Learning a Lexicon for a fixed image vocabulary. In *Proceedings of the 7th European Conference on Computer Vision* (pp. 97-112). doi:10.1007/3-540-47979-1_7

Eastridge, R., & Schmidt, C. (2008). Solving n-queens with a genetic algorithm and its usefulness in a computational intelligence course. *Journal of Computing Sciences in Colleges*, 23(4), 223–230.

Ebbers, W., Pieterson, W., & Noordman, H. (2008). Electronic government: Rethinking channel management strategies. *Government Information Quarterly*, 25(2), 181–201. doi:10.1016/j.giq.2006.11.003

Eberhart, R. C., & Kennedy, J. (1995). A new optimizer using particle swarm theory. In *Proceedings of the sixth international symposium on micro machine and human science* (Vol. 1, pp. 39-43). doi:10.1109/MHS.1995.494215

ECMA International. (2005). Near Field Communication White Paper. Retrieved from http://www.ecma-international.org/activities/Communications/tc32-tg19-2005-012.pdf

Eiben, A. E. (1997). Multi-parent recombination. In Handbook of Evolutionary Computation (p. 3). IOP Publishing Ltd. and Oxford University Press.

Elahi, A., & Gschwender, A. (2009, December). Introduction to the ZigBee Wireless Sensor and Control Network. Retrieved from http://www.informit.com/articles/

Elalagg, B. (Ed.). (2003). *Marketing in internet era*. Oman: Jourden.

Elgahwash, F., & Freeman, M. (2013). Self-Service Technology Banking Preferences: Comparing Libyans Behaviour in Developing and Developed Countries. *International Journal of Intelligent Information Technologies*, 9(2), 7–20. doi:10.4018/jiit.2013040102

Epstein, J. (2001). Learning to be thoughtless: Social norms and individual computation. *Computational Economics*, 18(1), 9–24. doi:10.1023/A:1013810410243

Erl, T. (2008). *SOA: Principles of Service Design*. Prentice Hall.

Ermolayev, V., Keberle, N., Plaksin, S., Kononenko, O., & Terziyan, V. (2004). Towards a Framework for Agent-Enabled Semantic Web Service Composition. *International Journal of Web Services Research*, 1(3), 64–87. doi:10.4018/jwsr.2004070104

European Economic and Social Committee. (2015): European passport to active citizenship. Retrieved May 15th, 2017 from http://www.eesc.europa.eu/?i=portal.en.publications.35346

Evans, N., & Sawyer, J. (2009). Internet usage in small businesses in regional South Australia: Service learning opportunities for a local university. *Education in Rural Australia*, 19(1), 15–33.

Farber, J., Myers, T., Trevathan, J., Atkinson, I., & Andersen, T. (2015). Riskr: A web 2.0 platform to monitor and share disaster information. *Int. J. of Grid and Utility Computing*, 6(2), 98–112. doi:10.1504/IJGUC.2015.068825

Farhoodi, M., Mahmoudi, M., Mohammad, A., Bidoki, Z., Yari, A. & Azadnia, M. (2009). Query Expansion Using Persian Ontology Derived from Wikipedia. *International journal of World Applied Sciences*, 7(4), 410-417.

Feng, S., Mammatha, R., & Lavrenko, V. (2004). Multiple Bernoulli Relevance Model for Image and Video Annotation. In *Proceedings of the IEEE Computer Society Conference on Computer Vision and Pattern Recognition* (pp. 1002-1009). doi:10.1109/CVPR.2004.1315274

Feng, S., & Wang, X. (2012). Research on fault diagnosis of mixed-signal circuits based on genetic algorithms. In *Proceedings of the International Conference on Computer Science and Electronics Engineering (ICCSEE)* (Vol. 3, pp. 12-15). doi:10.1109/ICCSEE.2012.60

Fernández-Garcia, R., & Gil, I. (2017). An Alternative Wearable Tracking System Based on a Low-Power Wide-Area Network. *Sensors (Basel, Switzerland)*, *17*(3), 592. doi:10.3390/s17030592 PMID:28335424

Fernandez-Lopez, M., Gomez-Perez, A., & Juristo, N. (1997). Methontology: From ontological art towards ontological science. In *Proceedings of the Spring Symposium on ontology engineering of AAAI* (pp. 37-40).

Fidge, C. (1988). Timestamps in Message-Passing Systems that Preserve the Partial Ordering. In *Proceedings of the 11th Australian Computer Science Conference* (pp. 56–66).

Flavian, C., Guinaliu, M., & Gurrea, R. (2006). The role played by perceived usability, satisfaction and consumer trust on website loyalty. *Information & Management Journal*, *43*(1), 1–14. doi:10.1016/j.im.2005.01.002

Flentge, F., Polani, D., & Uthmann, T. (2001). Modelling the Emergence of Possession Norms using Memes. *Journal of Artificial Societies and Social Simulation*, *4*(4), 3.

Floyd, R. W. (1967). Assigning Meanings to Programs. In *Mathematical Aspects of Computer Science* (Ch. 19, pp. 19–32). American Mathematical Society.

Fortuna, B., Mladenič, D., & Grobelnik, M. (2006). Semi-automatic construction of topic ontologies. In *Semantics, Web and Mining* (pp. 121-131).

Fortuna, B., Grobelnik, M., & Mladenic, D. (2005). Visualization of text document corpus. *Proceedings of the International Journal on Informatica*, *29*(4), 497–502.

Fossati, M., Giuliano, C., & Tummarello, G. (2012). Semantic Network-driven News Recommender Systems: a Celebrity Gossip Use Case. In *Proceedings of CEUR Workshop* (pp. 25-36).

Fouad, H., & Farouk, H. (in press). Heart rate sensor node analysis for designing internet of things telemedicine embedded system. *Cogent Engineering*.

Frate, F. D., Pacific, F., Schiavon, G., & Solimini, C. (2007). Use of neural networks for automatic classification from high resolution images. *IEEE Transactions on Geoscience and Remote Sensing*, *45*(4), 800–809. doi:10.1109/TGRS.2007.892009

Freiling, F. C., & Jhumka, A. (2007). Global predicate detection in distributed systems with small faults. In *Proceedings of the 9th international conference on Stabilization, safety, and security of distributed systems SSS'07* (pp. 296–310). Springer-Verlag. doi:10.1007/978-3-540-76627-8_23

Frigui, H., & Krishnapuram, R. (1999). A Robust Competitive Clustering Algorithm with Application in Computer Vision. *IEEE Transactions on Pattern Analysis and Machine Intelligence*, *21*(1), 450–465. doi:10.1109/34.765656

Galan, J. M., & Izquierdo, L. R. (2005). Appearances Can Be Deceiving: Lessons Learned Re-Implementing Axelrod's Evolutionary Approach to Norms. *Journal of Artificial Societies and Social Simulation*, *8*(3), 2.

Galliers, R. D., & Leidner, D. E. (2003). *Strategic Information Management Challenges and strategies in managing information systems.*

Gan, G., Yang, Z., & Wu, J. (2005). A genetic k-modes algorithm for clustering categorical data. In *Proceedings of the International Conference on Advanced Data Mining and Applications* (pp. 195-202). Springer Berlin Heidelberg. doi:10.1007/11527503_23

Ganapathy, G., & Sagayaraj, S. (2011). To Generate the Ontology from Java Source Code OWL Creation. *International Journal of Advanced Computer Science and Applications, 2*(2), 111–116. doi:10.14569/IJACSA.2011.020218

Gandomi, A. H., & Alavi, A. H. (2012). Krill herd: A new bio-inspired optimization algorithm. *Communications in Nonlinear Science and Numerical Simulation, 17*(12), 4831–4845. doi:10.1016/j.cnsns.2012.05.010

Gan, G., Wu, J., & Yang, Z. (2009). A genetic fuzzy k-Modes algorithm for clustering categorical data. *Expert Systems with Applications, 36*(2), 1615–1620. doi:10.1016/j.eswa.2007.11.045

Ganter, B., Stumme, G., & Wille, R. (2005). Formal Concept Analysis: Foundations and Applications. Springer.

Garg, V. K. (2002). *Elements of distributed computing.* New York, NY, USA: John Wiley & Sons, Inc.

Garg, V. K., & Mittal, N. (2001). On slicing a distributed computation. In *Proceedings of the The 21st International Conference on Distributed Computing Systems ICDCS '01* (p. 322).

Garg, V. K., & Waldecker, B. (1994). Detection of weak unstable predicates in distributed programs. *IEEE Transactions on Parallel and Distributed Systems, 5*(3), 299–307. doi:10.1109/71.277788

Garg, V. K., & Waldecker, B. (1996). Detection of strong unstable predicates in distributed programs. *IEEE Transactions on Parallel and Distributed Systems, 7*(12), 1323–1333. doi:10.1109/71.553309

Gartner. (2008). *27 Technologies in the 2008 Hype Cycle for Emerging Technologies* (Press Releases).

Gillebaart, T., Blom, D. S., van Zuijlen, A. H., & Bijl, H. (2016). Adaptive radial basis function mesh deformation using data reduction. *Journal of Computational Physics, 321*, 997–1025. doi:10.1016/j.jcp.2016.05.036

Global CCCM Cluster. (2016). The Mend Evacuation Guide, Planning Mass Evacuations in Natural Disasters. Retrieved 1/2017 from http://www.globalcccmcluster.org/system/files/publications/MEND_download.pdf

Glover, F., & Laguna, M. (1997). *Tabu search.* Boston: Kluwer Academic Publishers. doi:10.1007/978-1-4615-6089-0

Goldberg, D. (1989). *Genetic Algorithms in Search, Optimization and Machine Learning.* Addison-Wesley.

Gomm, J. B., & Yu, D. L. (2000, March). Selecting Radial Basis Function Network Centers with Recursive Orthogonal Least Squares Training. *IEEE Transactions on Neural Networks, 11*(2), 306–314. doi:10.1109/72.839002 PMID:18249762

Gong, D., Chang, J., & Wei, C. (2011, October). An Adaptive Method for Choosing Center Sets of RBF Interpolation. *Journal of Computers, 6*(10), 2112–2119. doi:10.4304/jcp.6.10.2112-2119

Gouscos, D., Laskaridis, G., Lioulias, D., Mentzas, G., & Georgiadis, P. (2002). An Approach to Offering One-Stop e-Government Services — Available Technologies and Architectural Issues. In R. Traunmüller & K. Lenk (Eds.), Electronic Government (Vol. 2456, pp. 113-131). Springer.

Green, P. E., Frank, R. E., & Robinson, P. J. (1967). Cluster analysis in test market selection. *Management Science, 13*(8), 387–400. doi:10.1287/mnsc.13.8.B387

Grobelnik, M., & Mladenic, D. (2005). Simple classification into large topic ontology of Web documents. In *Proceeding of the 27th International Conference on Information Technology Interfaces* (pp. 188-193). doi:10.1109/ITI.2005.1491120

Grossi, D., Gabbay, D., & van der Torre, L. (2010). The Norm Implementation Problem in Normative Multi-Agent Systems. In Specification and verification of multi-agent systems (pp. 195–224). Springer.

Group, T. O. (2011). 34. content metamodel. Retrieved from http://pubs.opengroup.org/architecture/togaf9-doc/arch/chap34.html

Gruber, T. R. (1995). Toward principles for the design of ontologies used for knowledge sharing? *International Journal of Human-Computer Studies, 43*(5), 907–928.

Grubic, T., & Fan, I. (2000). Supply chain ontology: Review, analysis and synthesis. *Computers in Industry, 61*(8), 776–786. doi:10.1016/j.compind.2010.05.006

Gruninger, M., & Fox, M. (1995). The role of competency questions in enterprise engineering. In *Proceedings of the IFIP WG5.7 Workshop on Benchmarking. Theory and Practice,* Troadhein, Norway. doi:10.1007/978-0-387-34847-6_3

Gulla, J. A., Auran, P. G., & Risvik, K. M. (2003). *Linguistics in large-scale web search. In Natural Language Processing and Information Systems.* Springer.

Gulla, J. A., Fidjestøl, A. D., Su, X., & Castejon, H. (2014). Implicit User Profiling in News Recommender Systems. In *Proceedings of the 10th International Conference on Web Information Systems and Technologies (WEBIST'14)* (pp. 185-192).

Gulla, J. A., Ingvaldsen, J. E., Fidjestøl, A. D., Nilsen, J. E., Haugen, K. R., & Su, X. (2013). Learning User Profiles in Mobile News Recommendation. *Journal of Print and Media Technology Research, 2,* 183–194.

Guo, H., Chen, L., Peng, L., & Chen, G. (2016, September). Wearable sensor based multimodal human activity recognition exploiting the diversity of classifier ensemble. In *Proceedings of the 2016 ACM International Joint Conference on Pervasive and Ubiquitous Computing* (pp. 1112-1123). ACM. doi:10.1145/2971648.2971708

Gurau, G. (2011). Online Self-Services: Investigating the Stages of Customer-SST Systems Interaction. In *Developing Technologies in E-Services, Self-Services, and Mobile Communication: New Concepts.* Hershey, PA: IGI Global. doi: Retrieved from www.igi-global.com/chapter/online-self-services/54958?camid=4v1 10.4018/978-1-60960-607-7.ch005

Ha, S., & Choi, S. (2016, July). Convolutional neural networks for human activity recognition using multiple accelerometer and gyroscope sensors. In *Proceedings of the 2016 International Joint Conference on Neural Networks (IJCNN)* (pp. 381-388). IEEE. doi:10.1109/IJCNN.2016.7727224

Halkidi, M., Batistakis, Y., & Vazirgiannis, M. (2002). Cluster validity methods: Part I. *SIGMOD Record, 31*(2), 40–45. doi:10.1145/565117.565124

Halstead, D., & Richards, K. (2014). From high tech to high touch: Enhancing customer service experiences via improved self-service technologies. *Innovative Marketing Journal, 10*(4), 16.

Hamed, A., Ball, D., Berger, H., & Cleary, P. (2008). The three-quarter moon: A new model for e-commerce adoption. *The Journal of Communications of the IBIMA, 4*(11), 88–96.

Han, H.-G., & Qiao, J.-F. (2012). Adaptive computation algorithm for RBF neural network. *IEEE Transactions on Neural Networks and Learning Systems, 23*(2), 342–347. doi:10.1109/TNNLS.2011.2178559 PMID:24808512

Hao, F. (2012), Semantic image understanding: from pixel to word [PhD thesis]. *University of Nottingham.*

Harrison, J. R., Lin, Z., Carroll, G. R., & Carley, K. M. (2007). Simulation modeling in organizational and management research. *Academy of Management Review, 32*(4), 1229–1245. doi:10.5465/AMR.2007.26586485

Hassanzadeh, T., & Meybodi, M. R. (2012). A new hybrid approach for data clustering using firefly algorithm and K-means. In *Proceedings of the 2012 16th CSI International Symposium on Artificial Intelligence and Signal Processing (AISP)* (pp. 007-011). IEEE.

Hatamlou, A. (2013). Black hole: A new heuristic optimization approach for data clustering. *Information Sciences*, *222*, 175–184. doi:10.1016/j.ins.2012.08.023

Hatamlou, A., Abdullah, S., & Nezamabadi-Pour, H. (2012). A combined approach for clustering based on K-means and gravitational search algorithms. *Swarm and Evolutionary Computation*, *6*, 47–52. doi:10.1016/j.swevo.2012.02.003

He, D., Zheng, Y., Pan, S., & Tang, J. (2010). Ensemble of multiple descriptors for automatic image annotation. In *Proceedings of the IEEE 3rd International Congress on Image and Signal Processing* (pp. 1642-1646).

He, Y. L., Wang, X. Z., & Huang, J. Z. (2016). Fuzzy nonlinear regression analysis using a random weight network. *Information Sciences*, *364*, 222–240.

Hearst, M. A. (1998). Automated Discovery of WordNet Relations. In C. Fellbaum (Ed.), *WordNet: An Electronic Lexical Database* (pp. 132–152). MIT Press.

Helmi, M., & AlModarresi, S. M. T. (2009). Human Activity Recognition Using a Fuzzy Inference System. In *Proceedings of IEEE International conference on fuzzy systems* (pp. 1897-1902). doi:10.1109/FUZZY.2009.5277329

Hemalatha, C. S., Vaidehi, V., & Lakshmi, R. (2015). Minimal infrequent pattern based approach for mining outliers in data streams. *Expert Systems with Applications*, *42*(4), 1998–2012. doi:10.1016/j.eswa.2014.09.053

Henderson-Sellers, B. (2012). Standards harmonization: Theory and practice. *Software & Systems Modeling*, *11*(2), 153–161. doi:10.1007/s10270-011-0213-0

Henriksson, A., Yi, Y., Frost, B., & Middleton, M. (2007). Evaluation instrument for e-government websites. *Electronic Government, an International Journal*, *4*(2), 204-226.

Hirahara, M., & Oka, N. (1993, October). A hybrid model composed of a multilayer perceptron and a radial basis function network. In *Proceedings of 1993 International Joint Conference on Neural Networks IJCNN '93*, Nagoya (Vol. 2, pp. 1353-1356).

Hlel, E., Jamoussi, S., & Hamadou, A. B. (2017). A New Method for Building Probabilistic Ontology (Prob-Ont). *International Journal of Information Technology and Web Engineering*, *12*(2), 1–25. doi:10.4018/IJITWE.2017040101

Ho, S. J., & Mallick, S. K. (2006). The impact of information technology on the banking industry: Theory and Empirics. Retrieved from http://webspace.qmul.ac.uk/pmartins/mallick.pdf

Hofacker, C. F., Goldsmith, R. E., Bridges, E., & Swilley, E. (2007). E-services: a synthesis and research agenda. *E-Services: Opportunities and Threats - Journal of Value Chain Management*, *1*(1/2), 13-44.

Hollander, C., & Wu, A. (2011). The Current State of Normative Agent-Based Systems. *Journal of Artificial Societies and Social Simulation*, *14*(2), 6. doi:10.18564/jasss.1750

Holland, J. (1975). *Adaption in Natural and Artificial Systems*. Ann Arbor, MI: University of Michigan Press.

Holsapple, C., & Joshi, K. (2002). A Collaborative approach to ontology design. *Communications of the ACM*, *45*(2), 42–47. doi:10.1145/503124.503147

Hu, Y., Koren, Y., & Volinsky, C. (2008). Collaborative filtering for implicit feedback datasets. In *Proceedings of the Eighth IEEE International Conference on Data Mining ICDM'08* (pp. 263–272). IEEE. doi:10.1109/ICDM.2008.22

Huang, , G. B., Saratchandran, P., & Sundararajan, N. (2004, December). An Efficient Sequential Learning Algorithm for Growing and Pruning RBF (GAP-RBF) Networks. *IEEE Transactions on Systems, Man, and Cybernetics. Part B, Cybernetics*, *34*(6), 2284–2292. doi:10.1109/TSMCB.2004.834428

Huang, Y., Wang, W., Wang, L., & Tan, T. (2013). Multi-Task Deep Neural Network for Multi-Label Learning. In *Proceedings of the 20th IEEE International Conference On Image Processing* (pp. 2897-2900). doi:10.1109/ICIP.2013.6738596

Huang, C. W., Lin, K. P., Wu, M. C., Hung, K. C., Liu, G. S., & Jen, C. H. (2015). Intuitionistic fuzzy c-means clustering algorithm with neighborhood attraction in segmenting medical image. *Soft Computing*, *19*(2), 459–470. doi:10.1007/s00500-014-1264-2

Huang, Z. (1997a). A Fast Clustering Algorithm to Cluster Very Large Categorical Data Sets in Data Mining. In DMKD (p. 0).

Huang, Z. (1997b). Clustering large data sets with mixed numeric and categorical values. In *Proceedings of the 1st pacific-asia conference on knowledge discovery and data mining, (PAKDD)* (pp. 21-34).

Huang, Z., & Ng, M. K. (1999). A fuzzy k-modes algorithm for clustering categorical data. *IEEE Transactions on Fuzzy Systems*, *7*(4), 446–452. doi:10.1109/91.784206

Hubert, L., & Arabie, P. (1985). Comparing partitions. *Journal of classification, 2*(1), 193-218.

Hunaiti, Z., Mansour, M., & Al-Nawafleh, A. (2009). Electronic commerce adoption barriers in small and medium-sized enterprises (SMEs) in developing countries: The case of Libya. *IBIMA Business Review Journal*, *2*(5), 37–45.

IBM. (n. d.). The Watson Ecosystem. Retrieved January 2016 from http://www-03.ibm.com/innovation/us/watson/

Ilievski, I., & Roy, S. (2013). Personalized news recommendation based on implicit feedback. In *Proceedings of the 2013 International News Recommender Systems Workshop and Challenge (NRS'13)* (pp. 10-15). ACM. doi:10.1145/2516641.2516644

Inan, D., Beydoun, G., & Opper, S. (2015). Towards knowledge sharing in disaster management: An agent oriented knowledge analysis framework. In *Proceedings of the 26th Australasian Conference on Information Systems*, Adelaide, Australia.

Inan, D., Beydoun, G., & Opper, S. (2016). Customising Agent Based Analysis Towards Analysis of Disaster Management Knowledge. In *Proceedings of the 27th Australasian Conference on Information Systems*, Wollongong, Australia.

Ingvaldsen, J. E., & Gulla, J. A. (2015). Taming News Streams with Linked Data. In *Proceedings of the IEEE 9th International Conference on Research Challenges in Information Science*, Athens.

Iváncsy, R., & Vajk, I. (2005). Automata Theory Approach for solving Frequent Pattern Discovery Problems. World Academy of Science, Engineering and technology.

Ivatury, G., & Pickens, M. (2006). *Mobile phone banking and low-income customers -evidence from South Africa: Consultative Group to Assist the Poor.*

Izakian, H., Abraham, A., & Sná, V. (2009). Clustering categorical data using a swarm-based method. In *Proceedings of the World Congress on Nature & Biologically Inspired Computing NaBIC '09* (pp. 1720-1724). IEEE. doi:10.1109/NABIC.2009.5393623

Izakian, H., & Abraham, A. (2011). Fuzzy C-means and fuzzy swarm for fuzzy clustering problem. *Expert Systems with Applications*, *38*(3), 1835–1838. doi:10.1016/j.eswa.2010.07.112

Jain, A. K., Murty, M. N., & Flynn, P. J. (1999). Data clustering: A review. [CSUR]. *ACM Computing Surveys*, *31*(3), 264–323. doi:10.1145/331499.331504

Jassim, O. A., Mahmoud, M. A., & Ahmad, M. S. (2015). A Multi-agent Framework for Research Supervision Management. In *Proceedings of the 12th International Conference on Distributed Computing and Artificial Intelligence* (pp. 129-136). Springer International Publishing. doi:10.1007/978-3-319-19638-1_15

Jegou, R., Medina, R., & Nourine, L. (1995). Linear space algorithm for on-line detection of global predicates. In *Proceedings of the International Workshop on Structures in Concurrency Theory (STRICT)*, Berlin (pp. 175–189). doi:10.1007/978-1-4471-3078-9_12

Jena. (2003). Jena – A Semantic Web Framework for Java. Retrieved from http://jena.sourceforge.ne t/documentation.pdf

JGAP. (n. d.). Retrieved 19 April, 2017 from http://jgap.sourceforge.net/

Jiang, W., & Yin, Z. (2015, October). Human activity recognition using wearable sensors by deep convolutional neural networks. In *Proceedings of the 23rd ACM international conference on Multimedia* (pp. 1307-1310). ACM. doi:10.1145/2733373.2806333

Ji, J., Bai, T., Zhou, C., Ma, C., & Wang, Z. (2013). An improved k-prototypes clustering algorithm for mixed numeric and categorical data. *Neurocomputing*, *120*, 590–596. doi:10.1016/j.neucom.2013.04.011

Ji, J., Pang, W., Zheng, Y., Wang, Z., & Ma, Z. (2015). A novel artificial bee colony based clustering algorithm for categorical data. *PLoS ONE*, *10*(5), e0127125. doi:10.1371/journal.pone.0127125 PMID:25993469

Ji, J., Pang, W., Zheng, Y., Wang, Z., Ma, Z., & Zhang, L. (2015). A novel cluster center initialization method for the k-prototypes algorithms using centrality and distance. *Applied Mathematics & Information Sciences*, *9*(6), 2933.

Ji, J., Pang, W., Zhou, C., Han, X., & Wang, Z. (2012). A fuzzy k-prototype clustering algorithm for mixed numeric and categorical data. *Knowledge-Based Systems*, *30*, 129–135. doi:10.1016/j.knosys.2012.01.006

Joachims, T. (1998). Text Categorization with Support Vector Machines: Learning with Many Relevant Feature. In *Proceedings of the 10th European Conference on Machine Learning* (pp. 137-142). doi:10.1007/BFb0026683

Jose-Garcia, A., & Gomez-Flores, W. (2016). Automatic clustering using nature-inspired metaheuristics: A survey. *Applied Soft Computing*, *41*, 192–213. doi:10.1016/j.asoc.2015.12.001

Jung, H., Yoo, H., & Chung, K. (2016). Associative context mining for ontology-driven hidden knowledge discovery. *Cluster Computing*, *19*(4), 2261–2271. doi:10.1007/s10586-016-0672-8

Kaiquan, S. J., Wang, W., Ren, J., Jin, S. Y., Liu, L., & Liao, S. (2011). Classifying Consumer Comparison Opinions to Uncover Product Strengths and Weaknesses. *International Journal of Intelligent Information Technologies*, *7*(1), 1–14. doi:10.4018/jiit.2011010101

Kaisara, G., & Pather, S. (2011). The e-Government evaluation challenge: A South African Batho Pele-aligned service quality approach. *Government Information Quarterly*, *28*(2), 211–221. doi:10.1016/j.giq.2010.07.008

Kanade, P. M., & Hall, L. O. (2007). Fuzzy ants and clustering. *IEEE Transactions on Systems, Man, and Cybernetics. Part A, Systems and Humans*, *37*(5), 758–769. doi:10.1109/TSMCA.2007.902655

Karaboga, D. (2005). *An idea based on honey bee swarm for numerical optimization* (Technical report-tr06). Erciyes University, Engineering Faculty, Computer Engineering Department.

Karaboga, D., & Ozturk, C. (2010). Fuzzy clustering with artificial bee colony algorithm. *Scientific Research and Essays*, *5*(14), 1899–1902.

Karaboga, D., & Ozturk, C. (2011). A novel clustering approach: Artificial Bee Colony (ABC) algorithm. *Applied Soft Computing*, *11*(1), 652–657. doi:10.1016/j.asoc.2009.12.025

Karantonis, D. M., Narayanan, M. R., Mathie, M., Lovell, N. H., & Celler, B. G. (2006). Implementation of a real-time human movement classifier using a triaxial accelerometer for ambulatory monitoring. *IEEE Transactions on Information Technology in Biomedicine*, *10*(1), 156–167. doi:10.1109/TITB.2005.856864 PMID:16445260

Kardaras, D., & Papathanassiou, E. (2000). The development of B2C e-commerce in Greece: Current situation and future potential. *Journal of Internet Research, 10*(4), 284–299.

Karim, A. J., & Hamdan, A. M. (2010). The impact of information technology on improving banking performance matrix: jordanian banks as case study. *Paper presented at the European, Mediterranean & Middle Eastern Conference on Information Systems (EMCIS)*, Abu Dhabi, UAE, Ahlia University, Manama, Kingdom of Bahrain.

Kaur, P., Soni, A. K., & Gosain, A. (2011, November). Robust Intuitionistic Fuzzy C-means clustering for linearly and nonlinearly separable data. In *Proceedings of the 2011 International Conference on Image Information Processing (ICIIP)* (pp. 1-6). IEEE. doi:10.1109/ICIIP.2011.6108908

Kawtrakul, A., Suktarachan, M., & Imsombut, A. (2004). Automatic Thai Ontology construction and Maintenance System. In *Proceedings of OntoLex Workshop on LREC*, Lisbon, Portugal.

Kemeny, J.G., Snell, J.L., Thompson, G.L., & Doyle, P. (1998). *Finite Mathematics, Mathematics at Dartmouth*. Retrieved from http://www.math.dartmouth.edu/~doyle/docs/finite/finite.pdf

Kennedy, J. F., Kennedy, J., Eberhart, R. C., & Shi, Y. (2001). *Swarm intelligence*. Morgan Kaufmann.

Kerr, M. K., & Churchill, G. A. (2001). Bootstrapping cluster analysis: Assessing the reliability of conclusions from microarray experiments. *Proceedings of the National Academy of the USA, 98*(16), 8961–8965. doi:10.1073/pnas.161273698 PMID:11470909

Kexing, L. A survey of agent based automated negotiation. In *Proceedings of the 2011 International Conference on Network Computing and Information Security (NCIS)* (Vol. 2, pp. 24–27). IEEE. doi:10.1109/NCIS.2011.103

Khan, A. M., Lee, Y. K., & Kim, T. S. (2010). A triaxial accelerometer based physical activity recognition via augmented signal features and a hierarchical recognizer. *IEEE Transactions on Information Technology in Biomedicine, 14*(5), 1166–1172. doi:10.1109/TITB.2010.2051955 PMID:20529753

Khatri, A., & Kurnia, K. (2011). Mobile banking adoption: In Australian rural areas. *Paper presented at the Pacific Asia Conference on Information Systems (PACIS)*, Brisbane, Australia.

Kim, J., Jin, B., & Swinney, J. L. (2009). The role of etail quality, e-satisfaction and e-trust in online loyalty development process. *Journal of Retailing and Consumer Services, 16*(4), 239–247. doi:10.1016/j.jretconser.2008.11.019

Kim, J., & Storey, V. C. (2011). Construction of Domain Ontologies: Sourcing the World Wide Web. *International Journal of Intelligent Information Technologies, 7*(2), 1–24. doi:10.4018/jiit.2011040101

Klasman, J. (2017). Internet Access Possibilities in Bluetooth Low Energy Sensors.

Klaussner, C., & Zhekova, D. (2011). Pattern-Based Ontology Construction from Selected Wikipedia Pages. In *Proceedings of the Student Research Workshop associated with The 8th International Conference on Recent Advances in Natural Language Processing* (pp. 103-108).

Kleinschmidt, S., Burkhard, B., Hess, M., Peters, C., & Leimeister, J. M. (2016a): Towards Design Principles for Aligning Human-Centered Service Systems and Corresponding Business Models. In Proceedings of the ICIS '16. Retrieved from http://aisel.aisnet.org/icis2016/ISDesign/Presentations/13

Kleinschmidt, S., Peters, C., & Leimeister, J. M. (2016b): ICT-Enabled Service Innovation in Human-Centered Service Systems: A Systematic Literature Review. In Proceedings ICIS '16. Retrieved from http://aisel.aisnet.org/icis2016/Sustainability/Presentations/3

Kohlborn, T., Weiss, S., Poeppelbuss, J., Korthaus, A., & Fielt, E. (2010). Online Service Delivery Models – An International Comparison in the Public Sector. *Paper presented at the 21st Australasian Conference on Information Systems*, Brisbane, Australia.

Kohlborn, T., Korthaus, A., Peters, C., & Fielt, E. (2013). A Comparative Study of Governmental One-Stop Portals for Public Service Delivery. *International Journal of Intelligent Information Technologies, 9*(3), 1–19. doi:10.4018/jiit.2013070101

Komarasamy, G., & Wahi, A. (2012). An optimized K-means clustering technique using bat algorithm. *European Journal of Scientific Research, 84*(2), 26–273.

Kong, H., Hwang, M., & Kim, P. (2006). Design of the Automatic Ontology Building System about the Specific Domain Knowledge. In *Proceedings of 8th International Conference on Advanced Communication Technology ICACT '06*. doi:10.1109/ICACT.2006.206235

Koontz, W. L. G., Narendra, P. M., & Fucunaga, K. (1975). A Graph Theoretic Approach to Nonparametric Cluster Analysis. *IEEE Transactions on Computers, C-25*(9), 936–944. doi:10.1109/TC.1976.1674719

Koontz, W. L. G., Narendra, P. M., & Fukunaga, K. (1975). A Branch and Bound Clustering Algorithm. *IEEE Transactions on Computers, C-24*(9), 908–915. doi:10.1109/T-C.1975.224336

Kotsiantis, S., & Kanellopoulos, D. (2006). Association Rules Mining: A Recent Overview. *International Transactions on Computer Science and Engineering, 32*(1), 71–82.

Kridan, A. B. (2006). *A knowledge management implementation framework for the Libyan banking sector.* Unpublished doctoral dissertation, University of Salford.

Krishna, K., & Murty, M. N. (1999). Genetic K-means algorithm. *IEEE Transactions on Systems, Man, and Cybernetics. Part B, Cybernetics, 29*(3), 433–439. doi:10.1109/3477.764879 PMID:18252317

Krishnamoorthy, S., Sadasivam, G. S., Rajalakshmi, M., Kowsalyaa, K., & Dhivya, M. (2017). Privacy Preserving Fuzzy Association Rule Mining in Data Clusters Using Particle Swarm Optimization. *International Journal of Intelligent Information Technologies, 13*(2), 1–20. doi:10.4018/IJIIT.2017040101

Kubicek, H., & Hagen, M. (2000). One stop government in Europe: an overview. In H. Kubicek & M. Hagen (Eds.), *One Stop Government in Europe. Results from 11 National Surveys* (Vol. 11, pp. 1–36). Bremen, Germany: University of Bremen.

Kumar, R. L., & Stylianou, A. C. (2014). A process model for analysing and managing flexibility in information systems. *European Journal of Information Systems, 23*(2), 151–184. doi:10.1057/ejis.2012.53

Kumutha, V., & Palaniammal, S. (2014). Improved Fuzzy Clustering Method Based On Intuitionistic Fuzzy Particle Swarm Optimization. *Journal of Theoretical & Applied Information Technology, 62*(1).

Lai, C. S. K., & Pires, G. (2010). Testing of a Model Evaluating e-Government Portal Acceptance and Satisfaction. *Electronic Journal Information Systems Evaluation, 13*(1), 35–46.

Lakshmi, K., Visalakshi, N. K., & Shanthi, S. (2017). Cuckoo Search based K-Prototype Clustering Algorithm. *Asian Journal of Research in Social Sciences and Humanities, 7*(2), 300–309. doi:10.5958/2249-7315.2017.00092.2

Lamche, B., Trottmann, U., & Wörndl, W. (2014). Active learning strategies for exploratory mobile recommender systems. In *Proceedings of the 4th Workshop on Context-Awareness in Retrieval and Recommendation (CARR'14)* (pp. 10-17). ACM. doi:10.1145/2601301.2601304

Lamport, L. (1978). Time, clocks, and the ordering of events in a distributed system. *Communications of the ACM, 21*(7), 558–565. doi:10.1145/359545.359563

Lamport, L. (1990). A theorem on atomicity in distributed algorithms. *Distributed Computing, 4*(2), 59–68. doi:10.1007/BF01786631

Lara, D. O., Perez, J. A., Labrador, A. M., & Posada, D. J. (2012). Centinela: A human activity recognition system based on acceleration and vital sign data. *Pervasive and Mobile Computing, 8*(5), 717–729. doi:10.1016/j.pmcj.2011.06.004

Laukkanen, T., & Pasanen, M. (2008). Mobile banking innovators and early adopters: How they differ from other online users. *Journal of Financial Services Marketing, 13*(2), 86–94. doi:10.1057/palgrave.fsm.4760077

Lavrenko, V., Mammatha, R., & Jeon, J. (2003). A Model for Learning the Semantics of Pictures. In *Proceedings of the Conference on Advance in Neural Information Processing Systems.*

Lee, J. (2006). The roles of scenario use in ontology development. *Knowledge and Process Management, 13*(4), 270–284. doi:10.1002/kpm.264

Lee, K. H., Kung, S. Y., & Verma, N. (2012). Low-energy formulations of support vector machine kernel functions for biomedical sensor applications. *Journal of Signal Processing Systems for Signal, Image, and Video Technology, 69*(3), 339–349. doi:10.1007/s11265-012-0672-8

Leek, S., Turnbull, P. W., & Naude, P. (2003). How is information technology affecting business relationships? Results from a UK survey. *Industrial Marketing Management Journal, 32*(2), 119–126. doi:10.1016/S0019-8501(02)00226-2

Leidner, D., & Kayworth, T. (2006). A Review of Culture in Information Systems Research: Toward a Theory of Information Technology Culture Conflict. *Management Information Systems Quarterly, 30*(2), 357–399.

Leung, N. K., Lau, S. K., & Tsang, N. (2012). An ontology development methodology to integrate existing ontologies in an ontology development process. *Communications of the ICISA: An International Journal, 13*(2), 31-61.

Leung, N. K. Y., Kang, S. H., Lau, S. K., & Fan, J. (2009). *Ontology matching techniques: a 3- Tier classification framework. International Journal of the computer, the Internet and Management. 17* (pp. 22.1–22.7). SPI.

Lewis, C., & Rieman, J. (1993). Task-centered user interface design.

Li, R., Zhang, Y., Lu, Z., Lu, J., & Tian, Y. (2010). Technique of Image Retrieval based on Multi-label Image Annotation. In *Proceedings of the Second International Conference on Multimedia and Information Technology.* doi:10.1109/MMIT.2010.34

Li, W., & Sun, M. (2008). Multi-model Multi-Label Semantic Indexing of Images using Un-Labeled Data. In *Proceedings of the International Conference on Advanced Language Processing and Web Information Technology* (pp. 204-209).

Liao, C., Palvia, J., & Liang, C. (2009). Information technology adoption behavior life cycle: Toward a technology continuance theory (TCT). *International Journal of Information Management, 29*(4), 309–320. doi:10.1016/j.ijinfomgt.2009.03.004

Libyan Central Bank. (2015). Libyan Central Bank.

Li, H. F., Al Maghayreh, E., & Goswami, D. (2007a). Detecting atomicity errors in message passing programs. In *Proceedings of the Eighth International Conference on Parallel and Distributed Computing, Applications and Technologies PDCAT '07* (pp. 193–200). IEEE Computer Society. doi:10.1109/PDCAT.2007.56

Li, H. F., Al Maghayreh, E., & Goswami, D. (2007b). Using atoms to simplify distributed programs checking. In *Proceedings of the Third IEEE International Symposium on Dependable, Autonomic and Secure Computing DASC '07* (pp. 75–83). doi:10.1109/DASC.2007.24

Li, H. F., & Lee, S. Y. (2009). Mining frequent itemsets over data streams using efficient window sliding techniques. *Expert Systems with Applications*, *36*(2), 1466–1477. doi:10.1016/j.eswa.2007.11.061

Li, H. F., Rilling, J., & Goswami, D. (2004). Granularity-driven dynamic predicate slicing algorithms for message passing systems. *Automated Software Engineering*, *11*(1), 63–89. doi:10.1023/B:AUSE.0000008668.12782.6c

Lim, E. P., Goh, D. H. L., Liu, Z., Ng, W. K., Khoo, C. S. G., & Higgins, S. E. (2002). G-Portal: a map-based digital library for distributed geospatial and georeferenced resources. *Paper presented at the 2nd ACM/IEEE-CS Joint Conference on Digital Libraries*. doi:10.1145/544220.544307

Lin, J., Yu, W., Zhang, N., Yang, X., Zhang, H., & Zhao, W. (2017). *A Survey on Internet of Things: Architecture, Enabling Technologies, Security and Privacy, and Applications. IEEE Internet of Things Journal.*

Lin, K. P. (2014). A novel evolutionary kernel intuitionistic fuzzy C-means clustering algorithm. *IEEE Transactions on Fuzzy Systems*, *22*(5), 1074–1087. doi:10.1109/TFUZZ.2013.2280141

Link-labs. (2016). A Comprehensive Look at Low Power, Wide Area Networks. Retrieved from https://www.link-labs.com/knowledge-center

Link-labs. (2016). Selecting a Wireless Technology for New Industrial Internet of Things Products. Retrieved from https://www.link-labs.com/knowledge-center

Link-labs. (2016, February 8). The Complete List of Wireless IoT Network Protocols. Retrieved from https://www.link-labs.com/blog/complete-list-iot-network-protocols

Link-labs. (2016, March). Thread Vs. ZigBee, For IoT Engineers. Retrieved from https://www.link-labs.com/blog/thread-vs-zigbee-for-iot-engineers

Littmann, T. (2000). An empirical classification of weather types in the Mediterranean Basin and their interrelation with rainfall. *Theoretical and Applied Climatology*, *66*(3-4), 161–171. doi:10.1007/s007040070022

Liu, B., Hsu, W., & Ma, Y. (1998). Integrating classification and association rule mining. In *Proceedings of the 4th International Conference on Knowledge Discovery and Data Mining* (pp. 80-86).

Liu, J., & Wang, B. (2007). Dual Cross-Media Relevance Model for Image Annotation. In *Proceedings of the 15th ACM international conference on Multimedia* (pp. 605-612).

Liu, Y., Liu, Y., Wang, L., & Chen, K. (2005). A hybrid tabu search based clustering algorithm. In *Proceedings of the International Conference on Knowledge-Based and Intelligent Information and Engineering Systems* (pp. 186-192). Springer Berlin Heidelberg. doi:10.1007/11552451_25

Liu, J., Dolan, P., & Pedersen, E. R. (2010). Personalized News Recommendation Based on Click Behavior. In *Proceedings of the 15th International Conference on Intelligent User Interfaces (IUI'10)* (pp. 31-40). doi:10.1145/1719970.1719976

Liu, P., Gulla, J. A., & Zhang, L. (2016). Dynamic Topic-Based Sentiment Analysis of Large-Scale Online News. In *Proceedings of the 17th International Conference on Web Information Systems Engineering (WISE)* (Part 2, pp. 3-18). doi:10.1007/978-3-319-48743-4_1

Liu, S., & George, R. (2005). *Mining Weather Data using Fuzzy Cluster Analysis*. Berlin: Springer. doi:10.1007/3-540-26886-3_5

Li, X. (2008). Inference Degradation of Active Information Fusion within Bayesian Network Models. *International Journal of Intelligent Information Technologies*, *4*(4), 1–17. doi:10.4018/jiit.2008100101

Li, X. L., & Qian, J. X. (2003). Studies on artificial fish swarm optimization algorithm based on decomposition and coordination techniques. *Journal of Circuits and Systems*, *1*, 1–6.

Li, Z. Y., Yi, J. H., & Wang, G. G. (2015). A New Swarm Intelligence Approach for Clustering Based on Krill Herd with Elitism Strategy. *Algorithms*, *8*(4), 951–964. doi:10.3390/a8040951

Lopez-Lorca, A., Beydoun, G., Valencia-Garcia, R., & Martinez-Bejar, R. (2015). Supporting agent oriented requirement analysis with ontologies. *International Journal of Human-Computer Studies*, *87*, 20–37. doi:10.1016/j.ijhcs.2015.10.007

LoRa applications. (n. d.) LoRa Applications. *SemTech*. Retrieved from http://www.semtech.com/wireless-rf/internet-of-things/lora-applications/briefs

Lu, H., Zheng, Y., Xue, X., & Zhang, Y. (2009). Content and Context-Based Multi-Label Image Annotation. In *Proceedings of the IEEE Computer Society Conference on Computer Vision and Pattern Recognition* (pp. 61-68).

Lu, J., & Hu, R. (2013). A new hybrid clustering algorithm based on K-means and ant colony algorithm. In *Proceedings of the 2nd International Conference on Computer Science and Electronics Engineering*. doi:10.2991/iccsee.2013.430

Madhuri, R., Murty, M. R., Murthy, J. V. R., Reddy, P. P., & Satapathy, S. C. (2014). Cluster Analysis on Different Data Sets Using K-Modes and K-Prototype Algorithms. In *ICT and Critical Infrastructure: Proceedings of the 48th Annual Convention of Computer Society of India-Vol II* (pp. 137-144). Springer International Publishing. doi:10.1007/978-3-319-03095-1_15

Maguitman, A. G., Cecchini, R. L., Lorenzetti, C. M., & Menczer, F. (2010). Using Topic Ontologies and Semantic Similarity Data to Evaluate Topical Search. In *Proceedings of 36th Latin American Informatics Conference*.

Mahdavi, M., Shepherd, J., & Benatallah, B. (2004). A collaborative approach for caching dynamic data in portal applications. *Paper presented at the 15th Australasian Database Conference (ADC2004) Dunedin*, New Zealand.

Mahmoud, M. A., & Ahmad, M. S. (2015c, August). A self-adaptive customer-oriented framework for intelligent strategic marketing: A multi-agent system approach to website development for learning institutions. In *Proceedings of the 2015 International Symposium on Agents, Multi-Agent Systems and Robotics (ISAMSR)* (pp. 1-5). IEEE. doi:10.1109/ISAMSR.2015.7379121

Mahmoud, M. A., & Ahmad, M. S. (2016d, August). A prototype for context identification of scientific papers via agent-based text mining. In *Proceedings of the 2016 2nd International Symposium on Agent, Multi-Agent Systems and Robotics (ISAMSR)* (pp. 40-44). IEEE.

Mahmoud, M. A., Ahmad, M. S., & Yusoff, M. Z. M. (2016b, March). A Norm Assimilation Approach for Multi-agent Systems in Heterogeneous Communities. In *Proceedings of the Asian Conference on Intelligent Information and Database Systems* (pp. 354-363). Springer Berlin Heidelberg. doi:10.1007/978-3-662-49381-6_34

Mahmoud, M. A., Ahmad, M. S., & Yusoff, M. Z. M. (2016e). A Conceptual Automated Negotiation Model for Decision Making in the Construction Domain. In *Proceedings of the 13th International Conference on Distributed Computing and Artificial Intelligence* (pp. 13-21). Springer International Publishing. doi:10.1007/978-3-319-40162-1_2

Mahmoud, M. A., Ahmad, M. S., Ahmad, A., Yusoff, M. Z. M., Mustapha, A., & Hamid, N. H. A. (2013, May). Obligation and Prohibition Norms Mining Algorithm for Normative Multi-agent Systems. In KES-AMSTA (pp. 115-124).

Mahmoud, M. A., Ahmad, M. S., Yusoff, M. Z. M., & Mustapha, A. (2014, December). Norms assimilation in heterogeneous agent community. In *Proceedings of the International Conference on Principles and Practice of Multi-Agent Systems*. Springer International Publishing.

Mahmoud, M. A., Ahmad, M. S., Ahmad, A., Mustapha, A., Yusoff, M. Z. M., & Hamid, N. H. A. (2013). Optimal environmental simulation settings to observe exceptional events in social agent societies. *Journal of Artificial Intelligence*, 6(3), 191. doi:10.3923/jai.2013.191.209

Mahmoud, M. A., Ahmad, M. S., & Yusoff, M. Z. M. (2016a). Development and implementation of a technique for norms-adaptable agents in open multi-agent communities. *Journal of Systems Science and Complexity*, 29(6), 1519–1537. doi:10.1007/s11424-016-5036-1

Maldonado, S., & Weber, R. (2010). Feature Selection for Support Vector Regression via Kernel Penalization. In *Proceedings of the 2010 International Joint Conference on Neural Networks (IJCNN)*.

Malik, N. (2009). Why the Zachman framework is not an ontology.

Mangalampalli, A., & Pudi, V. (2011, March). Fuzzy Associative Rule-based Approach for Pattern Mining and Identification and Pattern-based Classification. In *Proceedings of the 20th international conference companion on World wide web* (pp. 379-384). ACM.

Mao, K. Z. (2002, September). RBF Neural Network Center Selection Based on Fisher Ratio Class Separability Measure. *IEEE Transactions on Neural Networks*, 13(5), 1211–1217. doi:10.1109/TNN.2002.1031953 PMID:18244518

Mao, Q. (2013). Objective-Guided Image Annotation. *IEEE Transactions on Image Processing*, 22(4), 1585–1597. doi:10.1109/TIP.2012.2233490 PMID:23247859

Marshall, I., & Parulekar, A. (2009). *Research Study on The Revolution in Self-Service Channels in the Financial Services Sector*. Newcastle University and Business & Decision: Newcastle University and Business & Decision.

Martel, J. M., & Platte, R. B. (2016). Stability of Radial Basis Function Methods for Convection Problems on the Circle and Sphere. *Journal of Scientific Computing*.

Mashat, A., Ritchie, B., Lovatt, C., & Pratten, J. (2005). *The Social Role of Accounting: Views and Perceptions of the Accounting Community in Libya towards Corporate Social Responsibility and Accountability*.

Mastoori, Y. (2009). *Reasons barring customers from using Internet banking In Iran: An integrated approach based on means - end chains and segmentation*. Unpublished master's thesis, Lulea University of Technology.

Mathie, M.J., Coster, A.C.F., Lovell, N.H., & Celler, B.G. (2004). Accelerometry: providing an integrated, practical method for long-term, ambulatory monitoring of human movement. Physiological measurement, 25(2).

Mattern, F. (1989). Virtual Time and Global States of Distributed Systems. In *Proceedings of the International Workshop on Parallel and Distributed Algorithms*, Chateau de Bonas, France (pp. 215-226).

Mayall, A. and Carter, J. (2015). The essential project: Harnessing conceptual structures to expose organizational dynamics. *International Journal of Conceptual Structures and Smart Applications*, 3(2), 1–11.

McPhail, J., & Fogarty, G. (2004). *Predicting senior consumers' acceptance and use of self-service banking technologies: Test of the extended technology acceptance model*. Australia, Dunedin, New Zealand: James Cook University.

Mehmood, N., Shah, F., Azhar, M., & Rasheed, A. (2014). The Factors Effecting E-banking Usage in Pakistan. *Journal of Management Information System and E-commerce*, 1(1), 57–94.

Mei, L., & Xiang-Jun, Z. (2012). A Novel PSO k-Modes Algorithm for Clustering Categorical Data. In Computer, Informatics, Cybernetics and Applications (pp. 1395-1402). Springer Netherlands. doi:10.1007/978-94-007-1839-5_150

Mikhaylov, K., Petäjäjärvi, J., Haapola, J., & Pouttu, A. (2017). D2D Communications in LoRaWAN Low Power Wide Area Network: From Idea to Empirical Validation. arXiv:1703.01985

Miller, G. A., Beckwith, R., Fellbaum, C. D., Gross, D., & Miller, K. (1990). WordNet: An online lexical database. *Int. J. Lexicograph, 3*(4), 235–244. doi:10.1093/ijl/3.4.235

Miller, T., Lu, B., Sterling, L., Beydoun, G., & Tavetar, K. (2014). Requirements engineering using the agent paradigm: A case study of an aircraft turnaround simulator. *IEEE Transactions on Software Engineering, 40*(10), pp1007–pp1024. doi:10.1109/TSE.2014.2339827

Mittal, N., & Garg, V. K. (2001). Computation slicing: Techniques and theory. In *Proceedings of the 15th International Conference on Distributed Computing DISC '01*, London, UK (pp. 78–92). Springer-Verlag.

Mizoguchi, R. (2003). Tutorial on ontology engineering: Introduction to ontology engineering (Part 1). *New Generation Computing, 21*(4), 362–383. doi:10.1007/BF03037311

Monsen, D. E., & Romstad, P. H. (2014). *Collaborative Filtering in the News Domain with Explicit and Implicit Feedback* [MSc thesis]. Norwegian University of Science and Technology, Trondheim.

Montana, D., Brinn, M., Moore, S., & Bidwell, G. (1998). *Genetic algorithms for complex, real-time scheduling. In Proceedings of the 1998 IEEE international conference on systems, Man, and Cybernetics* (pp. 2213–2218). IEEE.

Moran, S., & Lavrenko, V. (2011). Optimal Tag Sets for Automatic Image Annotation. *BMVC, 2011*, 1–11.

Mori, Y., Takahashi, R., & Oka, R. (1999). Image-to-word Transformation Based on Dividing and Vector Quantizing Images with words. In *Proceedings of the First International Workshop on Multimedia Intelligent Storage and Retrieval Management.*

Morita, M., & Shinoda, Y. (1994). Information filtering based on user behavior analysis and best match text retrieval. In *Proceedings of the 17th annual international ACM SIGIR conference on Research and development in information retrieval* (pp. 272–281). Springer-Verlag. doi:10.1007/978-1-4471-2099-5_28

Mouelhi, R. B. A. (2009). Impact of the adoption of information and communication technologies on firm efficiency in the Tunisian manufacturing sector. *Economic Modelling, 26*(5), 961-967. doi:http://www.sciencedirect.com/science/article/pii/S0264999309000480

Mukhtar, M. (2015). Perceptions of UK Based Customers toward Internet Banking in the United Kingdom. *Journal of Internet Banking and Commerce, 20*(1). Retrieved from http://www.arraydev.com/commerce/jibc/

Naito, K. (2017). A Survey on the Internet-of-Things: Standards, Challenges and Future Prospects. *Journal of Information Processing, 25*, 23–31. doi:10.2197/ipsjjip.25.23

Najafi, B., Aminian, K., Paraschi v-Ionescu, A., Loew, F., Büla, C. J., & Robert, P. (2003). Ambulatory system for human motion analysis using a kinematic sensor: Monitoring of daily physical activity in the elderly. *IEEE Transactions on Bio-Medical Engineering, 50*(6), 711–723. doi:10.1109/TBME.2003.812189 PMID:12814238

Naser, A. M. A., & Alshattnawi, S. (2014). An Artificial Bee Colony (ABC) Algorithm for Efficient Partitioning of Social Networks. *International Journal of Intelligent Information Technologies, 10*(4), 24–39. doi:10.4018/ijiit.2014100102

Nasierding, G., & Tsoumakas, G. & Abbas Z Kouzani (2009). Clustering Based Multi-Label Classification for Image Annotation and Retrieval. In *Proceedings of the IEEE International Conference on Systems, Man and Cybernetics* (pp. 4514-4519). doi:10.1109/ICSMC.2009.5346902

Nasri, W., & Charfeddine, L. (2012). Factors affecting the adoption of Internet banking in Tunisia: An integration theory of acceptance model and theory of planned behavior. *The Journal of High Technology Management Research, 23*(1), 1–14. doi:10.1016/j.hitech.2012.03.001

National League of Cities. (2016): Trends in Smart City Development. Retrieved May 15th, 2017 from http://www.nlc. org/sites/default/files/2017-01/Trends%20in%20Smart%20City%20Development.pdf

Nazábal, A., García-Moreno, P., Artés-Rodríguez, A., & Ghahramani, Z. (2016). Human activity recognition by combining a small number of classifiers. *IEEE journal of biomedical and health informatics, 20*(5), 1342-1351.

Ng, M. K., & Wong, J. C. (2002). Clustering categorical data sets using tabu search techniques. *Pattern Recognition, 35*(12), 2783–2790. doi:10.1016/S0031-3203(02)00021-3

Nicola, G. (1998). Formal Ontology and Information Systems. In *Proceedings of the IEEE/WIC/ACM International Conference on Formal Ontology in Information Systems FOIS'98* (pp. 3-15).

Nielsen, J. (1993). *Usability engineering*. San Francisco, CA, USA: Morgan Kaufmann.

Nieman Journalism Lab. (2015). *New York Times improves its recommendations engine*. Retrieved March 28, 2015, from http://www.niemanlab.org/2013/08/new-york-times-improves-its-recommendations-engine/

Nippatlapalli, A. R. (2013). A Study On Customer Satisfaction Of Commercial Banks: Case Study On State Bank Of India. *IOSR Journal of Business and Management, 15*(1), 60 - 86. doi:www.iosrjournals.org

Noury, N., Fleury, A., Rumeau, P., Bourke, A. K., Laighin, G. O., Raille, V., & Lundy, J. E. (2007). Fall detection – principles and methods. In *Proceedings of the 29*[th] *Annual International Conference of the IEEE EMBS* (pp. 1663-1666).

Noy, N. & McGuinness, D. (2001). Ontology development 101: A guide to creating your first ontology. Stanford knowledge systems laboratory, California.

Noy, N. F., Sintek, M., Decker, St., Crubézy, M., Fergerson, R. W., & Musen, M. (2001). Creating Semantic Web Contents with Protégé-2000. *IEEE Intelligent Systems, 16*(2), 60–71. doi:10.1109/5254.920601

OASIS. (2012). Transformational Government Framework Primer Version 1.0 Retrieved 08.03.2012 from http://docs. oasis-open.org/tgf/TGF-Primer/v1.0/cn01/TGF-Primer-v1.0-cn01.pdf

OASIS. (2014): New British Smart Cities Specification Uses OASIS Transformational Government Framework. Retrieved May 15th, 2017 from https://www.oasis-open.org/news/pr/new-british-smart-cities-specification-uses-oasis-transformational-government-framework

Oberle, D. (2013). *How ontologies benefit enterprise applications*. Semantic Web Journal.

Offutt, J. (2002). Quality attributes of web software applications. *IEEE Software, 19*(2), 25–32. doi:10.1109/52.991329

Ogunde, A., Follorunso, O., Sodiiya, A., Oguntuase, J., & Ogunlleye, G. (2011). Improved cost models for agent-based association rule mining in distributed database. *SeriaInformatica., 9*(1), 231–250.

Olsson, J. (2014). *6LoWPAN demystified*. Texas Instruments.

Orr, M. (1998). Optimizing the Widths of Radial Basis Functions Optimizing the Widths of Radial Basis Functions. In *Proceedings of the Fifth Brazilian Symposium on Neural Networks* (pp. 26-29). doi:10.1109/SBRN.1998.730989

Othman, S., Beydoun, G., & Sugumaran, V. (2014). Development and validation of a Disaster Management Metamodel. *Information Processing & Management, 50*(2), 235–271. doi:10.1016/j.ipm.2013.11.001

Özgöbek, Ö., Gulla, J. A., & Erdur, R. C. (2014). A Survey on Challenges and Methods in News Recommendation. In *Proceedings of the 10th International Conference on Web Information Systems and Technologies (WEBIST'14)* (pp. 278-285).

Pandya, D., & Shah, B. (2014). Comparative Study on Automatic Image Annotation. *International Journal of Emerging Technology and Advanced Engineering.*, *4*(3), 216–222.

Parra, D., & Amatriain, X. (2011). Walk the talk: Analyzing the relation between implicit and explicit feedback for preference elicitation. In *Proceedings of the 19th International Conference on User Modeling, Adaption, and Personalization (UMAP'11)* (pp. 255–268). Springer-Verlag. doi:10.1007/978-3-642-22362-4_22

Parvathavarthini, S., Karthikeyani, N., Shanthi, S., & Mohan, J. M. (2017). Cuckoo-search based Intuitionistic Fuzzy Clustering Algorithm. *Asian Journal of Research in Social Sciences and Humanities*, *7*(2), 289–299. doi:10.5958/2249-7315.2017.00091.0

Parvathavarthini, S., & Visalakshi, N. K. & MadhanMohan J, Identification of optimal clusters by Segmenting Satellite Images. In *Proceedings of ICNICT* '11.

Patil, M. P., & Kolhe, S. R. (2014). Automatic Image Annotation Using Decision Trees And Rough Sets. *International Journal of Computer Science and Applications*, *11*(2), 38–49.

Pei, M., Nakayama, K., Hara, T., & Nishio, S. (2008). Constructing a Global Ontology by Concept Mapping Using Wikipedia Thesaurus. In *Proceedings of the 22nd International Conference on Advanced Information Networking and Applications Workshops* (pp. 1205-1210). doi:10.1109/WAINA.2008.117

Pelusi, D. (2011). Optimization of a fuzzy logic controller using genetic algorithms. In *Proceedings of the International Conference on Intelligent Human-Machine Systems and Cybernetics (IHMSC)* (Vol. 2, pp. 143 –146). doi:10.1109/IHMSC.2011.105

Perez-Diaz de Cerio, D., Hernández, Á., Valenzuela, J. L., & Valdovinos, A. (2017). Analytical and Experimental Performance Evaluation of BLE Neighbor Discovery Process Including Non-Idealities of Real Chipsets. *Sensors (Basel, Switzerland)*, *17*(3), 499. doi:10.3390/s17030499 PMID:28273801

Perreau De Pinninck, A., Sierra, C., & Schorlemmer, M. (2010). A multiagent network for peer norm enforcement. *Autonomous Agents and Multi-Agent Systems*, *21*(3), 397–424. doi:10.1007/s10458-009-9107-8

Petäjäjärvi, J., Mikhaylov, K., Pettissalo, M., Janhunen, J., & Iinatti, J. (2017). Performance of a low-power wide-area network based on LoRa technology: Doppler robustness, scalability, and coverage. *International Journal of Distributed Sensor Networks*, *13*(3), 1550147717699412. doi:10.1177/1550147717699412

Peters, C. (2015): Modularization of services [Dissertation]. Kassel University Press GmbH.

Peters, C., Kohlborn, T., Korthaus, A., Fielt, E., & Ramsden, A. (2011). Service Delivery in One-Stop Government Portals – Observations Based on a Market Research Study in Queensland. *Paper presented at the 22nd Australasian Conference on Information Systems (ACIS)*, Sydney.

Peters, C., Maglio, P., Badinelli, R., Harmon, R., Maull, R., Spohrer, J., … & Griffith, T. L. (2016). Emerging Digital Frontiers for Service Innovation. *Communications of the Association for Information Systems*, *39*(1). Retrieved from http://aisel.aisnet.org/cais/vol39/iss1/8

Peters, C., Blohm, I., & Leimeister, J. M. (2015). Anatomy of Successful Business Models for Complex Services: Insights from the Telemedicine Field. *Journal of Management Information Systems*, *32*(3), 75–104. doi:10.1080/07421222.2015.1095034

Petridou, E., Spathis, N., Glaveli, N., & Liassides, C. (2007). Bank service quality: Empirical evidence from Greek and Bulgarian retail customers. *International Journal of Quality & Reliability Management*, *24*(6), 568–585. doi:10.1108/02656710710757772

Pham, D. T., Suarez-Alvarez, M. M., & Prostov, Y. I. (2011). Random search with k-prototypes algorithm for clustering mixed datasets. In *Proceedings of the Royal Society of London A: mathematical, physical and engineering sciences* (Vol. 467, No. 2132, pp. 2387-2403). The Royal Society. doi:10.1098/rspa.2010.0594

Pierrefeu, L., Jay, J., & Barat, C. (2006). Auto-adjustable method for Gaussian width optimization on RBF neural network. Application to face authentication on a mono-chip system. In *Proceedings of the 32nd Annual Conference on IEEE Industrial Electronics IECON* (pp. 3481-3485). doi:10.1109/IECON.2006.347848

Pinto, H., & Martin, J. 2001. A Methodology for ontology integration. In *Proceedings of the 1st International conference on knowledge capture*, British Columbia (pp. 131-138).

Piskorski M.J. & Gorbatai A. (2011). Testing Coleman's Social-Norm Enforcement Mechanism: Evidence from Wikipedia. *HBS Working, 11*(055).

Pitì, A., Verticale, G., Rottondi, C., Capone, A., & Lo Schiavo, L. (2017). The Role of Smart Meters in Enabling Real-Time Energy Services for Households: The Italian Case. *Energies, 10*(2), 199. doi:10.3390/en10020199

Polovina, S. (2007). An introduction to conceptual graphs. In *Proceedings of the 15th International Conference on Conceptual Structures: Knowledge Architectures for Smart Applications ICCS '07*. Springer-Verlag.

Polovina, S., Scheruhn, H.-J., Weidner, S., & von Rosing, M. (2016a). Discovering the gaps in enterprise systems via conceptual graphs & formal concept analysis. In *Poster Proceedings, the 22nd International Conference on Conceptual Structures (ICCS)* (pp. 5–8).

Polovina, S., Scheruhn, H.-J., Weidner, S., & von Rosing, M. (2016b). Highlighting the gaps in enterprise systems models by interoperating CGS and FCA. In S. Andrews & S. Polovina (Eds.), *Proceedings of the Fifth Conceptual Structures Tools & Interoperability Workshop (CSTIW '16)* (pp. 46–54). CEUR-WS.

Poole, I. (n. d.). Weightless Wireless M2M White Space Communications. Retrieved from http://www.radio-electronics.com/info/wireless/weightless-m2m-white-space-wireless-communications/

Posner, R., & Rasmusen, E. (1999). Creating and enforcing norms, with special reference to sanctions. *International Review of Law and Economics, 19*(3), 369–382. doi:10.1016/S0144-8188(99)00013-7

Post, W. (2015). Personalized news launches on washingtonpost.com. *Washington Post*. Retrieved March 28, 2015, from http://www.washingtonpost.com/community-relations/personalized-news-launches-on-washingtonpostcom/2012/02/24/gIQAxjsXXR_story.html

Pousttchi, K., & Schurig, M. (2004). Assessment of today's mobile banking applications from the view of customer requirements. *Paper presented at the 37th Hawaii International Conference on System Sciences (HICSS)*, Big Island, Hawaii. doi:10.1109/HICSS.2004.1265440

Prabha, K. A., & Visalakshi, N. K. (2015). Particle Swarm Optimization based K-Prototype Clustering Algorithm. *Journal of Computer Engineering, 1*(17), 56–62.

Priss, U. (2006). Formal concept analysis in information science. *Annual Review of Information Science & Technology, 40*(1), 521–543. doi:10.1002/aris.1440400120

Raja, R., Roomi, S. M. M., & Kalaiyarasi, D. (2012). Semantic Modeling of Natural scenes by Local Binary Pattern. In *Proceedings of the IEEE international conference on Machine Vision and Image Processing* (pp. 169-172).

Rajabioun, R. (2011). Cuckoo optimization algorithm. *Applied Soft Computing, 11*(8), 5508–5518. doi:10.1016/j.asoc.2011.05.008

Rajagopal, & Rajagopal, A. (2007). *Emerging perspectives on self service technologies in retail banking.* Marketing Working Papers.

Rand, W. M. (1971). Objective criteria for the evaluation of clustering methods. *Journal of the American Statistical Association, 66*(336), 846–850. doi:10.1080/01621459.1971.10482356

Rani, C., & Deepa, S. N. (2011). An Intelligent Operator for Genetic Fuzzy Rule Based System. *International Journal of Intelligent Information Technologies, 7*(3), 28–40. doi:10.4018/jiit.2011070103

Rashedi, E., Nezamabadi-Pour, H., & Saryazdi, S. (2009). GSA: A gravitational search algorithm. *Information Sciences, 179*(13), 2232–2248. doi:10.1016/j.ins.2009.03.004

Rashidiniaa, J., Fasshauerb, G. E., & Khasi, M. (2016). A stable method for the evaluation of Gaussian radial basis function solutions of interpolation and collocation problems. Computers and Mathematics with Applications, 72, 178 -193.

Regis, R. G. (2014). Evolutionary programming for high-dimensional constrained expensive black-box optimization using radial basis functions. *IEEE Transactions on Evolutionary Computation, 18*(3), 326–347. doi:10.1109/TEVC.2013.2262111

Rohde-schwarz. (2016). White paper on Near Field Communication (NFC) Technology and Measurements. Retrieved from http://www2.rohde-schwarz.com/file_15687/1MA182_2.pdf

Rose, J. (2007). *Predicting mature consumers' attitudes towards use of self-service technologies in the financial services context.* Unpublished doctoral dissertation, University of Southern Queensland.

Rubin, J., & Chisnell, D. (2008). *Handbook of Usability Testing: How to plan, design and conduct effective tests* (2nd ed.). Indianapolis, IN, USA: Wiley India Pvt. Ltd.

Sadek, D., Zainal, N., Taher, M., & Yahya, A. (2010). Service quality perceptions between Cooperative and Islamic Banks of Britain. *American Journal of Economics and Business Administration, 2*(1), 1–5. doi:10.3844/ajebasp.2010.1.5

Sadri, F., Stathis, K., & Toni, F. (2006). Normative KGP agents. *Computational & Mathematical Organization Theory, 12*(2), 101–126. doi:10.1007/s10588-006-9539-5

Safeena, R., Date, H., & Kammani, A. (2011). Internet banking adoption in an emerging economy: Indian consumers' perspective. *International Arab Journal of E-Technology, 2*(1), 56–64.

Sajavičius, S. (2014). Radial basis function method for a multidimensional linear elliptic equation with nonlocal boundary conditions. *Computers & Mathematics with Applications (Oxford, England), 67*(7), 1407–1420. doi:10.1016/j.camwa.2014.01.014

Sallouha, H., Chiumento, A., & Pollin, S. (2017). Localization in Long-range Ultra Narrow Band IoT Networks using RSSI. arXiv:1703.02398

Salomann, H., Kolbe, L., & Brenner, W. (2006). Self-services in customer relationships: Balancing high-tech and high-touch today and tomorrow. *E-Service Journal, 4*(2), 65–84. doi:10.2979/ESJ.2006.4.2.65

Sandhaus, E. (2008). *The New York Times Annotated Corpus Overview.* The New York Times Company, Research and Development. New York.

Sannes, R. (2001). Self-service banking: Value creation models and information exchange. *Journal of Informing Science Special Series on Information Exchange in Electronic Markets, 4*(3), 139–149.

Santosa, B., & Ningrum, M. K. (2009). Cat swarm optimization for clustering. In *Proceedings of the International Conference of Soft Computing and Pattern Recognition SOCPAR '09* (pp. 54-59). IEEE. doi:10.1109/SoCPaR.2009.23

Sastry, K., & Goldberg, D. (2004). Let's get ready to rumble: Crossover versus mutation head to head. In Genetic and Evolutionary Computation, LNCS (Vol. 3103, pp. 126–137). Springer.

Savarimuthu, B. T. R., Cranefield, S., Purvis, M., & Purvis, M. (2010). Norm Identification in Multi-agent Societies (Discussion Paper). University of Otago.

Savita, P., Patel, D., & Sinhal, A. (2013). A Neural Network Approach to Improve the Efficiency of Image Annotation. *International Journal of Engineering Research & Technology, 2*(1), 1–5.

Scherer, A., Wünderlic, N., & Von Wangenheim, F. (2015). The Value of Self-Service: Long-Term Effects of Technology based Self- Services usage on Customer Retention. *Journal of MIS Quarterly, 39*(1), 177-200.

Scheruhn, H., Fallon, R., & Rosing, M. (2015). Information Modelling and Process Modelling. In The Complete Business Process Handbook (Vol. 1, pp. 511–550). Elsevier.

Scheruhn, H.-J., Ackermann, D., Braun, R., & Förster, U. (2013). Human-Computer Interaction. Users and Contexts of Use. In *Proceedings of the 15th International Conference, HCI International 2013* (pp. 446–455). Springer Berlin Heidelberg, Berlin, Heidelberg.

Scheruhn, H.-J., Rautenstrauch, C., Pegnetter, R., and Weidner, S. (2006). Strategische ausrichtung eines internationalen masterprogramms mit dem schwerpunkt integrationskompetenz am beispiel von mysap. *Die neue Hochschule DNH.*

Scholl, H. J. (2009). Profiling the EG Research Community and Its Core. In M. Wimmer, H. J. Scholl, M. Janssen, & R. Traunmüller (Eds.), *EGOV 2009, LNCS* (Vol. *5693*, pp. 1–12). Berlin, Heidelberg: Springer. doi:10.1007/978-3-642-03516-6_1

Schuster, Lisa, Proudfoot, Judy, & Drennan. (2015). Understanding consumer loyalty to technology-based self-services with credence qualities. *Journal of Services Marketing, 29*(6/7), 522-532. Retrieved from http://eprints.qut.edu.au/88010/1/88010.pdf

Sekine, M., Tamura, T., Togawa, T., & Fukui, Y. (2000). Classification of waist-acceleration signals in a continuous walking record. *Medical Engineering & Physics, 22*(4), 285–291. doi:10.1016/S1350-4533(00)00041-2 PMID:11018460

Selamat, Z., & Jaffar, N. (2011). Information technology acceptance: From the perspective of Malaysian bankers. *International Journal of Business and Management, 6*(1), 207–217.

Selim, S. Z., & Alsultan, K. (1991). A simulated annealing (SA) algorithm for the clustering problem. *Pattern Recognition, 24*(10), 1003–1008. doi:10.1016/0031-3203(91)90097-O

Selim, S.Z., & Ismail,, M.A. (1984). K-means-type Algorithm: Generalized Convergence Theorem andCharacterization of Local Optimality. *IEEE Transactions on Pattern Analysis and Machine Intelligence, 6*(1), 81–87.

Sen, A., & Garg, V. K. (2003). Detecting temporal logic predicates in distributed programs using computation slicing. In OPODIS (pp. 171–183).

Sen, S., & Airiau, S. (2007). Emergence of norms through social learning. *Proceedings of IJCAI '07* (pp. 1507–1512).

Sethi, P., & Sarangi, S. R. (2017). Internet of Things: Architectures, Protocols, and Applications. *Journal of Electrical and Computer Engineering.*

Shanthi, S., & Bhaskaran, V. M. (2011). Intuitionistic fuzzy C-means and decision tree approach for breast cancer detection and classification. *European Journal of Scientific Research, 66*(3), 345–351.

Shanthi, S., & Bhaskaran, V. M. (2013). A novel approach for detecting and classifying breast cancer in mammogram images. *International Journal of Intelligent Information Technologies, 9*(1), 21–39. doi:10.4018/jiit.2013010102

Shaw, D. M. (2000). *The role of information technology in the development of small firm market capabilities.* Unpublished doctoral dissertation, Kent State University.

Shelokar, P. S., Jayaraman, V. K., & Kulkarni, B. D. (2004). An ant colony approach for clustering. *Analytica Chimica Acta, 509*(2), 187–195. doi:10.1016/j.aca.2003.12.032

Shen, M., & Kshemkalyani, A. D. (2014). Hierarchical detection of strong unstable conjunctive predicates in large-scale systems. *IEEE Transactions on Parallel and Distributed Systems, 25*(11), 2899–2908. doi:10.1109/TPDS.2013.306

Shi, X. (2008). The Challenge of Semantic Web Services. *IEEE Transactions on Intelligent Systems, 23*(2), 5–5. doi:10.1109/MIS.2008.36

Siddiqui, A., Mishra, N., & Verma, J. S. (2015). A Survey on Automatic Image Annotation and Retrieval. *International Journal of Computers and Applications, 118*(20), 27–32. doi:10.5120/20863-3575

Sigmadesigns. (2016). Z-wave Overview. Retrieved from http://z-wave.sigmadesigns.com/why-z-wave/technology/

Sigmadesigns.com. (2016). Why is Z-Wave the Preferred Choice for Smart Home IoT? Retrieved from http://z-wave.sigmadesigns.com/why-z-wave/

Silabs. (2017). Application Development Fundamentals (Thread). Retrieved from http://www.silabs.com/documents/public/user-guides/ug103-11-appdevfundamentals-thread.pdf

Simon, F., & Usunier, J. C. (2007). Cognitive, demographic, and situational determinants of service customer preference for personnel-in-contact over selfservice technology. *International Journal of Research in Marketing, 24*(2), 163–173. doi:10.1016/j.ijresmar.2006.11.004

Sindwani, & Goel, M. (2016). The Relationship between Service Quality Dimensions, Customer Satisfaction and Loyalty in Technology based Self Service Banking. *International Journal of E-Services and Mobile Applications, 8*(2). doi:10.4018/IJESMA.2016040104

Singh, M.P., Chopra, A.K., & Desai, N. (2009, November). Commitment-Based SOA. *IEEE Computer.*

Sinha, R. S., Wei, Y., & Hwang, S. H. (2017). *A survey on LPWA technology: LoRa and NB-IoT.* ICT Express.

Snasel, V., Moravec, P., & Pokorny, J. (2005). WordNet ontology based model for web retrieval. In *Proceedings of the International Workshop on Challenges in Web Information Retrieval and Integration* (pp. 220-225). doi:10.1109/WIRI.2005.38

Solat, S. (2017). Security of Electronic Payment Systems: A Comprehensive Survey. arXiv:1701.04556

Sowa, J. F. (1984). *Conceptual Structures- Information Processing in Mind and Machine.* Addison-Wesley.

Sowa, J. F. (2008). Conceptual Graphs. In Handbook of Knowledge Representation, Foundations of Artificial Intelligence (Vol. 3, pp. 213–237). Amsterdam: Elsevier.

Sowa, J. F., & Zachman, J. A. (1992). Extending and formalizing the framework for information systems architecture. *IBM Systems Journal, 31*(3), 590–616. doi:10.1147/sj.313.0590

Spathis, C., & Georgakopoulou, E. (2007). The adoption of IFRS in South Eastern Europe: The case of Greece. *International Journal of Financial Services Management, 2*(1), 50–63. doi:10.1504/IJFSM.2007.011671

Spears, W. S. (2004). *The impact of bank consolidation on services quality.* Unpublished doctoral dissertation, Nova Southeastern University.

Spears, W. M. (1997). Recombination parameters. In *The Handbook of Evolutionary Computation* (pp. 1–3). University Press. doi:10.1887/0750308958/b386c73

Spezialetti, M., & Kearns, P. (1986). Efficient distributed snapshots. In ICDCS (pp. 382–388).

Spink, A., & Jansen, B.J. (2004). A Study of Web Search Trends. *Webololy, 1*(2).

Sridevi, U. K., & Nagaveni, N. (2011). An Ontology Based Model for Document Clustering. *International Journal of Intelligent Information Technologies, 7*(3), 54–69. doi:10.4018/jiit.2011070105

Stabb, R., Benjamins, V. & Fensel, D. (1998). Knowledge engineering: Principles and Methods. *Data and Knowledge engineering, 25*, 161-197.

Stan, D. & Ishwar K Sethi (2001). Mapping low-level image features to semantic concepts. In *Proceedings of the Conference on Storage and Retrieval for Media Databases* (pp. 172-179).

Subramainan, L., Mahmoud, M. A., Ahmad, M. S., & Yusoff, M. Z. M. (2016a). An Emotion-based Model for Improving Students' Engagement using Agent-based Social Simulator. *International Journal on Advanced Science, Engineering and Information Technology, 6*(6).

Subramainan, L., Mahmoud, M. A., Ahmad, M. S., & Yusoff, M. Z. M. (2016b, August). A conceptual emotion-based model to improve students' engagement in a classroom using agent-based social simulation. In *Proceedings of the 2016 4th International Conference on User Science and Engineering (i-USEr)* (pp. 149-154). IEEE. doi:10.1109/IUSER.2016.7857951

Subramaniyaswamy, V., & Chenthur Pandian, S. (2012). Effective Tag Recommendation System Based on Topic Ontology using Wikipedia and WordNet. *International Journal of Intelligent Systems, John Wiley and Sons Ltd Periodicals, 27*(12), 1034–1048. doi:10.1002/int.21560

Subramaniyaswamy, V., & Chenthur Pandian, S. (2012a). An improved Approach for Topic Ontology based Categorization of Blogs using Support Vector Machine. *J. Comput. Sci., 8*(2), 251–258. doi:10.3844/jcssp.2012.251.258

Subramaniyaswamy, V., & Chenthur Pandian, S. (2012b). A Complete Survey of Duplicate Record Detection using Data Mining Techniques. *Inform. Technol. J., 11*(8), 941–945. doi:10.3923/itj.2012.941.945

Subramaniyaswamy, V., Vijayakumar, V., & Indragandhi, V. (2013). A Review of Ontology based Tag Recommendation Approaches. *International Journal of Intelligent Systems, 28*(11), 1054–1071. doi:10.1002/int.21616

Suchanek, F. M., Kasneci, G., & Weikum, G. (2007). YAGO: A Core of Semantic Knowledge Unifying WordNet and Wikipedia. In *Proceedings of the 16th International conference on World Wide Web*. doi:10.1145/1242572.1242667

Suki, N. M. (2015). An Empirical Study of Factors Affecting the Internet Banking Adoption among Malaysian Consumers? *Journal of Internet Banking and Commerce*.

Sumathi, G., Sendhilkumar, S., & Mahalakshmi, G. S. (2015). Ranking Pages of Clustered Users using Weighted Page Rank Algorithm with User Access Period. *International Journal of Intelligent Information Technologies, 11*(4), 16–36. doi:10.4018/IJIIT.2015100102

Sun, Z. (2012). Image Annotation Based on Semantic Clustering and Relevance Feedback. In *Proceedings of the 8th International Conference on Intelligent Information Hiding and Multimedia Signal Processing* (pp. 391-394). doi:10.1109/IIH-MSP.2012.101

Sun, L. X., Xu, F., Liang, Y. Z., Xie, Y. L., & Yu, R. Q. (1994). Cluster analysis by the K-means algorithm and simulated annealing. *Chemometrics and Intelligent Laboratory Systems, 25*(1), 51–60. doi:10.1016/0169-7439(94)00049-2

Sureshchandar, G., Rajendran, C., & Anantharaman, R. (2002). The relationship between service quality and customer satisfaction–a factor specific approach. *Journal of Services Marketing, 16*(4), 363–379. doi:10.1108/08876040210433248

Sutherland, L. A., Wildemuth, B., Campbell, M. K., & Haines, P. S. (2005). Unraveling the web: An evaluation of the content quality, usability, and readability of nutrition web sites. *Journal of Nutrition Education and Behavior, 37*(6), 300–305. doi:10.1016/S1499-4046(06)60160-7 PMID:16242061

Su, X., Özgöbek, Ö., Gulla, J. A., Ingvaldsen, J. E., & Fidjestøl, A. D. (2016). Interactive mobile news recommender system: A preliminary study of usability factors. In *Proceedings of the 11th International Workshop on Semantic and Social Media Adaptation and Personalization (SMAP)* (pp. 71-76). doi:10.1109/SMAP.2016.7753387

Symeonidis, A. L., & Mitkas, P. A. (2006). Agent Intelligence Through Data Mining. In *Proceedings of the 17th European Conference on Machine Learning and the 10th European Conference on Principles and Practice of Knowledge Discovery in Databases.*

Symeonidis, A., & Mitkas, P. (2005). A Methodology for Predicting Agent Behavior by the Use of Data Mining Techniques. In Autonomous Intelligent Systems: Agents and Data Mining, LNCS (Vol. 3505, pp. 161–174). Springer. doi:10.1007/11492870_13

Syswerda, G. (1989). Uniform crossover in genetic algorithms. In *Proceedings of the 3rd International Conference on Genetic Algorithms*, San Francisco, CA (pp. 2–9). Morgan Kaufmann Publishers Inc.

Talari, S., Shafie-khah, M., Siano, P., Loia, V., Tommasetti, A., & Catalão, J. P. (2017). A Review of Smart Cities Based on the Internet of Things Concept. *Energies, 10*(4), 421. doi:10.3390/en10040421

Tanbeer, S. K., Hassan, M. M., Almogren, A., Zuair, M., & Jeong, B. S. (2016). Scalable regular pattern mining in evolving body sensor data. *Future Generation Computer Systems.*

Tang, R., Fong, S., Yang, X. S., & Deb, S. (2012). Integrating nature-inspired optimization algorithms to K-means clustering. In *Proceedings of the 2012 Seventh International Conference on Digital Information Management (ICDIM)* (pp. 116-123). IEEE.

Tang, R., Fong, S., Yang, X. S., & Deb, S. (2012). Wolf search algorithm with ephemeral memory. In *Proceedings of the 2012 Seventh International Conference on Digital Information Management (ICDIM)* (pp. 165-172). IEEE. doi:10.1109/ICDIM.2012.6360147

Tat Kei Ho, A. (2002). Reinventing Local Governments and the E Government Initiative. *Public Administration Review, 62*(4), 434–444. doi:10.1111/0033-3352.00197

Tavakolifard, M., Gulla, J. A., Almeroth, K. C., Ingvaldsn, J. E., Nygreen, G., & Berg, E. (2013). Tailored news in the palm of your hand: a multi-perspective transparent approach to news recommendation. In *Proceedings of the 22nd international conference on World Wide Web companion* (pp. 305–308). doi:10.1145/2487788.2487930

Thakker, B. (2011). Support Vector Machine.

Thangamani, M., & Thangaraj, P. (2011). Effective fuzzy ontology based distributed document using non-dominated ranked genetic algorithm. *International Journal of Intelligent Information Technologies, 7*(4), 26–46. doi:10.4018/jiit.2011100102

Thao, H. T. P., & Swierczek, F. W. (2008). Internet use, customer relationships and loyalty in the Vietnamese travel industry. *Asia Pacific Journal of Marketing and Logistics, 20*(2), 190–210. doi:10.1108/13555850810864551

The British Standards Institution (2014): The Role of Standards in Smart Cities.

The Oxford English Dictionary (2 ed.). (1989). portal (computing) Oxford University Press.

The World Bank. (2012). *Annual Report* Retrieved from http://siteresources.worldbank.org/EXTANNREP2012/Resources/8784408-1346247445238/AnnualReport2012_En.pdf

Thierens, D., & Goldberg, D. E. (1994). Convergence models of genetic algorithm selection schemes. In *Proceedings of the International Conference on Evolutionary Computation. The Third Conference on Parallel Problem Solving from Nature: Parallel Problem Solving from Nature*, London, UK (pp. 119–129). doi:10.1007/3-540-58484-6_256

Threadgroup. (2015). Thread Stack Fundamentals (Technical white paper). Retrieved from https://threadgroup.org/RESOURCES-old/White-Papers

Threadgroup. (2015). Thread Usage of 6LoWPAN (Technical white paper). Retrieved from https://threadgroup.org/RESOURCES-old/White-Papers

Thurman, N. (2011). *Making 'the daily me': Technology, economics and habit in the mainstream assimilation of personalized news. In Journalism: Theory* (pp. 395–415). Practice & Criticism.

Tiun, S., Abdullah, R., & Kong, T. E. (2001). Automatic Topic Identification Using Ontology Hierarchy. In *Proceedings of the Second International Conference on Computational Linguistics and Intelligent Text Processing* (pp. 444-453). doi:10.1007/3-540-44686-9_43

Toelle, S. (2006). *The linkages among services quality attributes, customer value, customer satisfaction, and customer loyalty in Indonesian retail banking settings* [Doctoral Degree]. Nova Southeastern University.

Townsend, K. (2014). Introduction to Bluetooth Low Energy. *Adafruit*. Retrieved from https://learn.adafruit.com/introduction-to-bluetooth-low-energy

Travica, B. (2008). Influence of information culture on adoption of a self-service system. *Journal of Information System, Information Technology and Organizations, 3*.

Tripathi, A., Gupta, P., Trivedi, A., & Kala, R. (2011). Wireless Sensor Node Placement Using Hybrid Genetic Programming and Genetic Algorithms. *International Journal of Intelligent Information Technologies, 7*(2), 63–83. doi:10.4018/jiit.2011040104

Tripathi, R. P., Gupta, M., & Bhattacharya, J. (2011). Identifying Factors of Integration for an Interoperable Government Portal: A Study in Indian Context. *International Journal of Electronic Government Research, 7*(1), 64–88. doi:10.4018/jegr.2011010105

Tripathy, B. K., Basu, A., & Govel, S. (2014), December. Image segmentation using spatial intuitionistic fuzzy C means clustering. In *Proceedings of the 2014 IEEE International Conference on Computational Intelligence and Computing Research (ICCIC)* (pp. 1-5). IEEE.

Tsai, C.-F. (2012). Bag-of-Words Representation in Image Annotation: A Review. *Artificial Intelligence*.

Twati, J. M., & Gammack, J. G. (2006). The impact of organizational culture innovation on the adoption of IS/IT: The case of Libya. *Journal of Enterprise Information Management, 19*(2), 175-191.

Twati, J.M. (2008). The influence of societal culture on the adoption of information systems: The case of Libya. *Communications of the IIMA Journal, 8*(1), 1-12. Retrieved from http://scholarworks.lib.csusb.edu/ciima/vol8/iss1/1/

UK Department for Business Innovation and Skills. (2014): Making cities smarter: Guide for city leaders.

United Nations. (2008). United Nations e-Government Survey 2008 - From e-Government to Connected Governance. Retrieved from http://unpan1.un.org/intradoc/groups/public/documents/UN/UNPAN028607.pdf

Uschold, M. (1996). Building ontologies: Towards a unified methodology. In *Proceedings of expert systems (Annual conference of the British computer society specialist group on expert systems)*, Cambridge, UK.

Uschold, M., & King, M. (1995). Towards a methodology for building ontologies. In *Proceedings of workshop on basic ontological issues in knowledge sharing (International joint conference on artificial intelligence)*, Montreal, Canada.

Vairavasundaram, S., Varadharajan, V., Vairavasundaram, I., & Ravi, L. (2015). Data mining-based tag recommendation system: An overview. *Wiley Interdisciplinary Reviews: Data Mining and Knowledge Discovery*, *5*(3), 87–112.

Van Den Bergh, F. (2001). *An Analysis of Particle Swarm Optimizers*. PSO.

Van der Merwe, D. W., & Engelbrecht, A. P. (2003). Data clustering using particle swarm optimization. In Proceedings of the 2003 Congress on Evolutionary Computation CEC'03 (Vol. 1, pp. 215-220). IEEE. doi:10.1109/CEC.2003.1299577

Van Rijsbergen, C. J. (1979). *Information retrieval*. Dept. Of Computer Science, University Of Glasgow.

Van Rijsbergen, C. J. (1979). Information retrieval. University Of Glasgow.

Várkonyi-Kóczy, A. R., Tusor, B., & Bukor, J. (2016). Data classification based on fuzzy-RBF networks. In Advances in Intelligent Systems and Computing, AISC (Vol. 357, pp. 829-840). Springer Verlag. doi:10.1007/978-3-319-18416-6_65

Vatanasombut, B., Igbaria, M., Stylianou, A. C., & Rodgers, W. (2008). Information system continuance intention of web-based applications customers: The case of online banking. *Information and Management Journal*, *45*(7), 419–428. doi:10.1016/j.im.2008.03.005

Verma, K., Sivashanmugam, K., Sheth, A., Patil, A., Oundhakar, S., & Miller, J. (2005). METEOR-S WSDI: A scalable infrastructure of registries for semantic publication and discovery of Web services. *Journal of Information Technology Management*, *6*(1), 17–39. doi:10.1007/s10799-004-7773-4

VidyaBanu, R., & Nagaveni, N. (2012). Low Dimensional Data Privacy Preservation Using Multi-Layer Artificial Neural Network. *International Journal of Intelligent Information Technologies*, *8*(3), 17–31. doi:10.4018/jiit.2012070102

Villatoro, D. (2011). Self-organization in decentralized agent societies through social norms. In *Proceedings of the 10th International Conference on Autonomous Agents and Multiagent Systems AAMAS '11* (pp. 1373-1374).

Villatoro, D., Sen, S., & Sabater-Mir, J. (2010). Of social norms and sanctioning: A game theoretical overview. *International Journal of Agent Technologies and Systems*, *2*(1), 1–15. doi:10.4018/jats.2010120101

Visalakshi, N. K., Parvathavarthini, S., & Thangavel, K. (2014). An intuitionistic fuzzy approach to fuzzy clustering of numerical dataset. In Computational Intelligence, Cyber Security and Computational Models (pp. 79-87). Springer India.

Visalakshi, N. K., Thangavel, K., & Parvathi, R. (2010). An Intuitionistic fuzzy approach to distributed fuzzy clustering. *International Journal of Computer Theory and Engineering*, *2*(2), 295–302. doi:10.7763/IJCTE.2010.V2.155

Vogel, M. A. (2005). *Leveraging information technology competencies and capabilities for a competitive advantage*. Unpublished doctoral dissertation, University of Maryland.

Voinov, A., Kolagani, N., McCall, M. K., Glynn, P. D., Kragt, M. E., Ostermann, F. O., & Ramu, P. et al. (2016). Modelling with stakeholders - Next generation. *Environmental Modelling & Software*, *77*, 196–220. doi:10.1016/j.envsoft.2015.11.016

von Rosing, M. (2016). What are artefacts & how can they be used. Retrieved from http://www.leadingpractice.com/knowledge-center/recorded-webinars/what-are-artefacts-2/

von Rosing, M., & Laurier, W. (2015). An introduction to the business ontology. *International Journal of Conceptual Structures and Smart Applications*, *3*(1), 20–41.

von Rosing, M., & von Scheel, H. (2016). Using the business ontology to develop enterprise standards. *International Journal of Conceptual Structures and Smart Applications*, 4(1), 48–70.

von Rosing, M., Urquhart, B., & Zachman, J.A. (2015). Using a business ontology for structuring artefacts: Example-northern health. *International Journal of Conceptual Structures and Smart Applications*, 3(1), 42–85.

Vu, T. H. N., Park, N., Lee, Y. K., Lee, Y., Lee, J. Y., & Ryu, K. H. (2010). Online discovery of Heart Rate Variability patterns in mobile healthcare services. *Journal of Systems and Software*, 83(10), 1930–1940. doi:10.1016/j.jss.2010.05.074

Wamalwa, T. (2006). *The impact of Internet banking on banks: A descriptive and evaluative case study of a large U.S. bank.* Unpublished doctoral dissertation, Capella University.

Wan, S. (2011). Image Annotation using the Simple Decision Tree. In *Proceedings of the IEEE International Conference on Management on e-Commerce and e-Government* (pp. 141-146).

Wang, C., Yan, S., Zhang, L., & Zhang, H.-J. (2009). Multi-Label Sparse Coding for Automatic Image Annotation. In *Proceedings of the IEEE International Conference on Computer Vision and Pattern Recognition* (pp. 1643-1650).

Wang, L., Bretschneider, S., & Gant, J. (2005). Evaluating Web-based e-government services with a citizen-centric approach. *Paper presented at the 38th Hawaii International Conference on System Sciences*, Hawaii, USA.

Wang, Z. O., & Zhu, T. (2000). An efficient learning algorithm for improving generalization performance of radial basis function neural networks. *Neural Networks*, 13(4), 545–553.

Wang, A., Chen, G., Yang, J., Zhao, S., & Chang, C. Y. (2016). A comparative study on human activity recognition using inertial sensors in a smartphone. *IEEE Sensors Journal*, 16(11), 4566–4578. doi:10.1109/JSEN.2016.2545708

Wang, H., Jiang, X., Chia, L.-T., & Tan, A.-H. (2010). Wikipedia2Onto – Building Concept Ontology Automatically, Experimenting with Web Image Retrieval. *Informatica Slovenia*, 34(3), 297–306.

Wang, Z., Wu, D., Chen, J., Ghoneim, A., & Hossain, M. A. (2016). A triaxial accelerometer-based human activity recognition via EEMD-based features and game-theory-based feature selection. *IEEE Sensors Journal*, 16(9), 3198–3207. doi:10.1109/JSEN.2016.2519679

Wei, K. (2009). Service quality index: A study on Malaysian banks. *Journal of Contemporary Management Research*, 5(2), 109–124.

Wells, J. D., Fuerst, W. L., & Choobineh, J. (1999). Managing information technology (IT) for one-to-one customer interaction. *Information and Management Journal*, 35(1), 53–62. doi:10.1016/S0378-7206(98)00076-7

Wimmer, H., Yoon, V., & Rada, R. (2014). Strategies and Methods for Ontology Alignment. *Recent Advances in Intelligent Technologies and Information Systems*, 1.

Wimmer, M., & Tambouris, E. (2002). Online one-stop government. *Paper presented at the IFIP 17th World Computer Congress-TC8 Stream on Information Systems: The e-Business Challenge*, Montréal, Québec, Canada. doi:10.1007/978-0-387-35604-4_9

Wimmer, H., Yoon, V., & Rada, R. (2012). Applying Semantic Web Technologies to Ontology Alignment. *International Journal of Intelligent Information Technologies*, 8(1), 1–9. doi:10.4018/jiit.2012010101

Wimmer, M. A. (2002). Integrated service modelling for online one-stop Government. *Electronic Markets*, 12(3), 149–156. doi:10.1080/101967802320245910

Witten, I. H., Frank, E., Hall, M. A., & Pal, C. J. (2000). *Data Mining, Practical Machine Learning Tools and Techniques* (2nd ed.). Morgan Kaufmann Publisher.

Wolff, K. E. (1993). A first course in Formal Concept Analysis. In Proceedings of StatSoft '93 (pp. 429–438). Gustav Fischer Verlag.

Wright, A. H. (1991). Genetic algorithms for real parameter optimization. In *Foundations of Genetic Algorithms* (pp. 205–218). Morgan Kaufmann.

Wu Sen, C. H., Chen Hong, C. H., & Feng Xiaodong, F. X. (2013). Clustering algorithm for incomplete data sets with mixed numeric and categorical attributes. *International Journal of Database Theory and Application*, *6*(5), 95–104. doi:10.14257/ijdta.2013.6.5.09

Xu, B., Shao, B., Lin, Z., & Shi, Y. (2009). Enterprise adoption of Internet banking in China. *Journal of Global Information Technology Management*, *12*(3), 7–28. doi:10.1080/1097198X.2009.10856495

Xu, D., Wijesooriya, C., Wang, Y., & Beydoun, G. (2011). Outbound logistics exception monitoring: A multi-perspective ontologies' approach with intelligent agents. *Expert Systems with Applications*, *38*(11), 13604–13611.

Xujuan, Z., Li, Y., Xu, Y., & Raymond, L. (2006). Relevance assessment of topic ontology. In *Proceedings of the 4th International Conference on Active Media Technology*.

Xu, Z., & Wu, J. (2010). Intuitionistic fuzzy C-means clustering algorithms. *Journal of Systems Engineering and Electronics*, *21*(4), 580–590. doi:10.3969/j.issn.1004-4132.2010.04.009

Yang, F., Shi, F., & Wang, J. (2009). An Improved GMM Based Method Or Supervised Semantic Image Annotation. In *Proceedings of the IEEE International Conference On Intelligent Computing And Intelligent Systems*.

Yang, X. S. (2010). A new metaheuristic bat-inspired algorithm. In Nature inspired cooperative strategies for optimization (NICSO 2010) (pp. 65-74). Springer Berlin Heidelberg. doi:10.1007/978-3-642-12538-6_6

Yang, X. S., & Deb, S. (2009). Cuckoo search via Lévy flights. In *Proceedings of the World Congress on Nature and Biologically Inspired Computing NaBIC '09* (pp. 210-214). IEEE.

Yang, X. S., & Deb, S. (2009, December). Cuckoo search via Lévy flights. In *Proceedings of the World Congress on Nature & Biologically Inspired Computing NaBIC '09* (pp. 210-214). IEEE.

Yang, C. C., & Hsu, Y. L. (2009). Development of a wearable motion detector for telemonitoring and real-time identification of physical activity. *Telemedicine Journal and e-Health*, *15*(1), 62–72. doi:10.1089/tmj.2008.0060 PMID:19199849

Yang, K., Hua, X.-S., Wang, M., & Zhang, H.-J. (2011). Tag Tagging: Towards More Descriptive Keywords of Image Content. *IEEE Transactions on Multimedia*, *13*(4), 662–673. doi:10.1109/TMM.2011.2147777

Yang, X. S. (2010). Firefly algorithm, Levy flights and global optimization. In *Research and development in intelligent systems XXVI* (pp. 209–218). Springer London. doi:10.1007/978-1-84882-983-1_15

Yang, X. S., & Deb, S. (2010). Engineering optimisation by cuckoo search. *International Journal of Mathematical Modelling and Numerical Optimisation*, *1*(4), 330–343. doi:10.1504/IJMMNO.2010.035430

Yang, X. S., & Hossein Gandomi, A. (2012). Bat algorithm: A novel approach for global engineering optimization. *Engineering Computations*, *29*(5), 464–483. doi:10.1108/02644401211235834

Yau, S. S., Ye, N., Sarjoughian, H. S., Huang, D., Roontiva, A., Baydogan, M., & Muqsith, M. A. (2009). Toward Development of Adaptive Service-Based Software Systems. *IEEE Transactions on Services Computing*, *2*(3), 247-260.

Yavlinsky, A., Schoeld, E., & Ruger, S. (2005). Automated Image Annotation Using Global Features and Robust Non-parametric Density Estimation. *Chapter Image and Video Retrieval. Lecture Notes in Computer Science*, *3568*, 50–517. doi:10.1007/11526346_54

Yildirim, Y., Yazici, A., & Yilmaz, T. (2013). Automatic Semantic Content Extraction in Videos Using a Fuzzy Ontology and Rule-Based Model. *IEEE Transactions on Knowledge and Data Engineering, 25*(1), 47-61.

Yin, J., & Tan, Z. (2005). Clustering mixed type attributes in large dataset. In *Parallel and Distributed Processing and Applications* (pp. 655-661).

Yingchareonthawornchai, S., Valapil, V. T., Kulkarni, S., Torng, E., & Demirbas, M. (2017). Efficient algorithms for predicate detection using hybrid logical clocks. In *Proceedings of the 18th International Conference on Distributed Computing and Networking ICDCN '17*, New York, NY. ACM. doi:10.1145/3007748.3007780

Young, H. P. (2008). Social Norms. In S. N. Durlauf & L. E. Blume (Eds.), *The New Palgrave Dictionary of Economics*. New York: Palgrave Macmillan. doi:10.1057/978-1-349-95121-5_2338-1

Yu, J., & Guo, C. (2008). An exploratory study of applying ubiquitous technology to retail banking. *Paper presented at the Allied Academies International Conference*, Tunica, USA.

Yu, T., Zhang, Y., & Lin, K.J. (2007). Efficient Algorithms for Web Services Selection with End-to-end QoS Constraints. *ACM Transactions on the Web, 1*(1).

Yu, J., Benatallah, B., Casati, F., & Daniel, F. (2008). Understanding Mashup Development. *Internet Computing, 12*(5), 44–52. doi:10.1109/MIC.2008.114

Yun, Z., Quan, Z., Caixin, S., Shaolan, L., Yuming, L., & Yangvv, S. (2008, August). RBF Neural Network and ANFIS-Based Short-Term Load Forecasting Approach in Real-Time Price Environment. *IEEE Transactions on Power Systems, 23*(3), 853–858. doi:10.1109/TPWRS.2008.922249

Zachman, J.A. (2015). John Zachman's concise definition of the Zachman Framework.

Zachman, J. A. (1987). A framework for information systems architecture. *IBM Systems Journal, 26*(3), 276–292. doi:10.1147/sj.263.0276

Zadeh, L. A. (1965). Fuzzy sets. *Information and Control, 8*(3), 338–353. doi:10.1016/S0019-9958(65)90241-X

Zammuto, R. F., & Laube, D. R. (2003). *Business-Driven Information Technology* (S. B. Books, Ed.).

Zeng, L. (2016). *Factors Influencing the Adoption of Self-Service Technologies* [Master Degree Master]. Norwegian School of Economics, Bergen.

Zhang, C., Wei, H., Xie, L., Shen, Y., & Zhang, K. (2016). Direct interval forecasting of wind speed using radial basis function neural networks in a multi-objective optimization framework. *Journal Neuro computing, 205*(C), 53-63.

Zhang, K., & Marchiori, A. (2017). Crowdsourcing Low-Power Wide-Area IoT Networks.

Zhang, Y. (2005). Bayesian graphical models for adaptive filtering. *SIGIR Forum, 39*, 57. doi:10.1145/1113343.1113358

Zhang, C., Ouyang, D., & Ning, J. (2010). An artificial bee colony approach for clustering. *Expert Systems with Applications, 37*(7), 4761–4767. doi:10.1016/j.eswa.2009.11.003

Zhao, F., Scheruhn, H.-J., & Rosing, M. (2014). Human-Computer Interaction. In *Applications and Services* (pp. 776–785). Cham: Springer International Publishing.

Zhao, L., Ren, H., & Wan, J. (2015). Automatic ontology construction based on clustering nucleus. *Wuhan University Journal of Natural Sciences, 20*(2), 129–133. doi:10.1007/s11859-015-1070-4

Zhao, X., & Lu, M. (2013). 3D Object Retrieval Based on PSO-K-Modes Method. *JSW, 8*(4), 963–970. doi:10.4304/jsw.8.4.963-970

Zheng, Z., Gong, M., Ma, J., Jiao, L., & Wu, Q. (2010). Unsupervised evolutionary clustering algorithm for mixed type data. In *Proceedings of the 2010 IEEE Congress on Evolutionary Computation (CEC)* (pp. 1-8). IEEE. doi:10.1109/CEC.2010.5586136

Zhou, P., & El-Gohary, N. (2015). Ontology-based multilabel text classification of construction regulatory documents. *Journal of Computing in Civil Engineering*, *30*(4), 04015058. doi:10.1061/(ASCE)CP.1943-5487.0000530

Zhou, P., Li, D., Wu, H., & Chen, F. (2010). A Novel OLS Algorithm for Training RBF Neural Networks with Automatic Model Selection. In *Proceedings of the International Conference on Computer Application and System Modeling (ICCASM '10)*.

Zhu, D., & Dreher, H. (2009). Discovering Semantic Aspects of Socially Constructed Knowledge Hierarchy to Boost the Relevance of Web Searching. *International Journal of Universal Computer Science*, *15*(8), 1685–1710.

Zhu, W., Cao, J., & Raynal, M. (2016). Predicate detection in asynchronous distributed systems: A probabilistic approach. *IEEE Transactions on Computers*, *65*(1), 173–186. doi:10.1109/TC.2015.2409839

Zivkovic, S., & Karagiannis, D. (2015). Towards metamodelling-in-the-large: Interface-based composition for modular metamodel development. In *International Conference on Enterprise, Business-Process and Information Systems Modeling* (pp. 413–428). Springer.

Zou, Y., Lei, G., Shao, K., Guo, Y., Zhu, J., & Chen, X. (2015, March). Hybrid Approach of Radial Basis Function and Finite Element Method for Electromagnetic Problems. *IEEE Transactions on Magnetics*, *51*(3), 1–4. doi:10.1109/TMAG.2014.2354371

Z-wave Alliance. (n. d.). About Z-Wave Technology. Retrieved from http://z-wavealliance.org/about_z-wave_technology/

About the Contributors

Vijayan Sugumaran is Professor of Management Information Systems and Chair of the Department of Decision and Information Sciences at Oakland University, Rochester, Michigan, USA. He received his Ph.D in Information Technology from George Mason University, Fairfax, USA. His research interests are in the areas of Ontologies and Semantic Web, Intelligent Agent and Multi-Agent Systems, and Component Based Software Development. He has published over 150 peer-reviewed articles in Journals, Conferences, and Books. He has edited twelve books and serves on the Editorial Board of eight journals. He has published in top-tier journals such as Information Systems Research, ACM Trans on Database Systems, IEEE Trans on Engineering Management, Communications of the ACM, and IEEE Software. He is the editor-in-chief of the International Journal of Intelligent Information Technologies. He is the Chair of the Intelligent Agent and Multi-Agent Systems mini-track for Americas Conference on Information Systems (AMCIS 1999 - 2016). He has served as the program co-chair for the International Conference on Applications of Natural Language to Information Systems (NLDB 2008, NLDB 2013, and NLDB 2016).

* * *

Mohd Sharifuddin Ahmad is currently the Head of Center for Agent Technology (CAT) at the College of Computer Science and Information Technology, Universiti Tenaga Nasional. He obtained his MSc. in Artificial Intelligence from Cranfield University, UK in 1995. He obtained his PhD. in Artificial Intelligence from Imperial College, London, UK in 2005. His research interests include Software Agents and Knowledge Management.

Eslam Al Maghayreh is an associate professor of computer science in the College of Computer and Information Sciences at King Saud University (Muzahmeah Branch). He has obtained his PhD degree in Computer Science from Concordia University (Canada) in 2008, his M.Sc. degree in Computer Science from Yarmouk University in 2003, and his B.Sc. degree in Computer Science from Yarmouk University in 2001. Before joining King Saud University, he has worked for six years in the department of Computer Science at Yarmouk University (Jordan). His research interests include: distributed systems, computational intelligence, and runtime verification of distributed programs.

Ghassan Beydoun received a degree in computer science and a PhD degree in knowledge systems from the University of New South Wales. He is currently a Professor of Information Systems at the University of Technology Sydney. He has authored more than 100 papers international journals and conferences. He is currently working on the metamodels for on project sponsored by Australian Research Council and Australian companies to investigate the endowing methodologies for distributed intelligent systems and supply chains with intelligence. His other research interests include multi agent systems applications, ontologies and their applications, and knowledge acquisition.

Fouad Omran Elgahwash Department of Information System Management, obtained his Bachelor of Management and Organisation degree (1995) from the University of Tripoli, Libya and his Master of Marketing degree (2006) from the University of Tripoli, Libya as well. and Doctorate of ICT (2013) degrees from the University of Wollongong, Australia. Dr. Elgahwash has a long record of academic and industrial experience in Administration and Customer services management teaching, research and service. Dr. El-gahwash has worked in the field of administration and services for more than 8 years. During he worked at administration as consults and gives seminars and workshops, programs for managers and Organisations' staff. Otherwise, He teach at TAFE, University of Az-Zawia and UOW- Australia many interesting courses for Undergraduate and postgraduate students, Researchers with a particular focus on strategic planning in services and managing the customer services experience and Information System Management. Dr. El-Gahwash has published several research papers in international conferences Such as ACIS in Sydney 2011; ACIS in Auckland 2014 and International Conference on Management and Information Technology at Brunei Darussalam 2016; and International Journal of Intelligent Information Technologies 2013 as well. His research interests are in the area of Customers Services, Self-Services and Information System Management. Dr. El-Gahwash is member with Computers in Human Behaviors Journal (ELSEVIER) and he received appreciated a letter as award for Journal Review Manuscript's Title: A weight and a meta-analysis on mobile banking acceptance research. Category: Literature Review (2016). Permission of the copyright holder This publication is protected by Copyright and permission should be obtained from the publisher prior to any prohibited reproduction, storage in a retrieval system, or transmission in any form or by any means, electronic, mechanical, photocopying, recording, or likewise. For information regarding permission(s), write to: Rights and Permissions Department.

Kirupa Ganapathy working as Associate Professor in department of Electronics and Communication Engineering at Saveetha School of Engineering. Pursued BE in Electronics and Communication Engineering and ME in Applied Electronics. Awarded with a Ph.D. degree for specialization in Soft Computing and Wireless Sensor Networks. Worked for various funded projects in Healthcare Applications and Surveillance Applications. Has published papers in various international and national journals with high impact factor. Areas of interest include sensor network, machine learning, artificial intelligence, image processing, network security and IoT. Guided many of the B.E and M.E. students in various domains.

Bharathi. N. Gopalsamy working as an Associate Professor in Department of Computer Science Engineering at Saveetha School of Engineering, Saveetha University. Good knowledge to work with embedded system in addition to computer science engineering concepts. Awarded with a Ph.D. degree in computer science for the research work titled "Analysis of Scheduling Configurable Computation Hardware Blocks for FPGA at Run-time" from SASTRA University, having 13 years of work experience as an academician and one and half years of industrial experience in ARM platform with ubuntu OS. M.Tech Project done at Center for High Performance Embedded System (CHiPES), Nanyang Technological University (NTU), Singapore titled "Efficient Management of Custom Instructions for Run-Time

Reconfigurable Processors" for seven months. B.E in computer science engineering was pursued in SASTRA University. Published approximately 15 research papers in reputed journals and conferences, guided many of the B.Tech. and M.Tech. students in various domains of computer science engineering and embedded systems.

Jon Atle Gulla is professor of Information Systems at the Norwegian University of Science and Technology (NTNU) in Trondheim, Norway, since 2002. He was the head of the Department of Computer and Information Science 2010—2012 and the deputy head 2009-2010 and 2012-2013. Gulla received his MSc in 1988 and his PhD in 1993, both in Information Systems at the Norwegian Institute of Technology. He also has a MSc in Linguistics from 1995 and is a Sloan Fellow from London Business School. His research interests include the Semantic Web, NLP, search technologies, and recommender systems. Gulla has published extensively in international journals and conferences and has been active in managing research projects and commercializing research results.

C. Sweetlin Hemalatha received her BE degree in Computer Science and Engineering from Sethu Institute of Technology, Kariapatti, Tamilnadu, India in 1996, ME degree in Computer Science and Engineering from Mepco Schlenk Engineering college, Sivakasi, Tamilnadu, India in 2000 and Ph.D. in Information and Communication Engineering from Madras Institute of Technology, Anna University, Chennai, India. She is currently working as Assistant Professor in Vellore Institute of Technology (VIT) University, Chennai. She has 6 years of teaching experience. Her research interest includes machine learning and data mining, especially classification and clustering problems. She has worked on mining interesting patterns from sensor observation using pattern mining algorithms and its application in health care.

K. Lakshmi received her MCA from Shrimathi Indira Gandhi College, Trichy, India in 2003 and M.Phil from Bharathiyar University, Trichy in 2004. She is a full time Research Scholar at the Department of Computer Applications, Kongu Engineering College, Perundurai, India. Her research interests include Cluster Analysis, Distributed Data Clustering, Knowledge Discovery in Databases, Cloud Computing, Optimization.

N. Karthikeyani Visalakshi is working as a Assistant Professor in Namakkal Kavignar Ramalingam Government Arts College for Women, Namakkal. She received M.C.A degree in 1992 and M.Phil degree in 1999 from Bharathiar University, Coimbatore. She completed her Ph. D. degree in the area of Distributed Data Mining in October 2010. She has got 23 years of teaching experience and 16 years of research experience. She has successfully guided for 30 M. Phil Scholars and currently guiding 3 Ph.D scholars. She has published 23 research papers in various National and International Journals. She has presented 23 papers in national and international conferences. She received Best Oral Presentation award in 4 th International Science Congress (ISC-2014) at Pacific University, Udaipur, Rajasthan, organized by International Science Congress Association during 08.12.2014 and 09.12.2014. She received Best Faculty Award at Kongu Engineering College, Perundurai during the academic year 2011-12. She organized 4 National Conferences, 11 National Seminars and 8 Research Workshops. She is a reviewer for two International Journals. Her areas of interests include Distributed Data Mining, Clustering, Image Processing, Rough sets, Fuzzy logic and Intuitionistic Fuzzy sets.

Thomas Kohlborn is a Senior Market Insights Manager at Sanofi CHC. Prior to commencing his career in the industry sector, he was a Post-Doctoral Fellow at the Woolworths Chair of Retail Innovation as part of the Business Process Management Discipline at the Queensland University of Technology (QUT) in Brisbane, Australia. His research interests are in business process management, innovation management, and IS adoption as well as in e-government. His PhD focused on service and process management in the public domain; in particular, it focused on the conceptualization of innovative methods/processes for the derivation of service bundles for governmental one-stop portals. His work has been published in peer-reviewed academic journals and presented at major international conferences.

Axel Korthaus is an Associate Professor in Information Systems at Swinburne University of Technology in Melbourne, Australia. He is currently the Acting Deputy Chair of the Department for Business Technology and Entrepreneurship and Research Director in the department. From 2010-2017, he was a Senior Lecturer at Victoria University, Melbourne, and Discipline Leader for Information Systems. He served as a Postdoctoral Research Fellow at Queensland University of Technology, Brisbane, Australia, from 2008-2010. Before that, he worked at the University of Mannheim, Germany, where he received his PhD degree in 2001. Axel's research interests include Digital Business Management, Service Systems Engineering and Management, Business Architecture, Business Process/Service Management as well as Crowdsourcing and Open Innovation. He writes and presents widely on these issues and has participated in various industry-linked projects.

Özlem Özgöbek has a PhD degree from the Computer Engineering Department at Ege University, Izmir, Turkey. Previously she worked on agent based systems and the Semantic Web. Her PhD thesis explored the use of ontologies in advanced recommender systems. She continued her research on news recommender systems as an ERCIM postdoc at NTNU. Now she continues her research with a particular focus on collaborative filtering, semantic methods and privacy concerns in news recommender systems as a postdoctoral researcher at NTNU. Özgöbek is in the organizing committee of both the Norwegian Big Data Symposium and the International Workshop on News Recommendation and Analytics.

S. Parvathavarthini is working as Assistant Professor in Kongu Engineering College, Perundurai, Tamilnadu. She received her M.Phil degree in Computer Science in 2006 and Master of Computer Applications in 2004 from Bharathiar University, Coimbatore, India. She has got 13 years of teaching experience. Her areas of interests include Data Mining, Soft computing, Image Processing, Optimization techniques and Intuitionistic fuzzy sets.

Christoph Peters is a project manager and postdoctoral researcher at the Institute of Information Management (IWI-HSG) at the University of St. Gallen in Switzerland and the Interdisciplinary Research Center for Information System Design (ITeG) at the University of Kassel in Germany. Peters studied Business Informatics at the University of Mannheim (Dipl. Wirtsch. Inf) and at the Queensland University of Technology in Australia and holds a doctoral degree from the University of Kassel (Dr. rer. pol.). He has been a visiting scholar and researcher at the iSchool / College of Information Studies at the University of Maryland, USA, the Recanati Business School of Tel Aviv University, Israel, and the Service Research Center (CTF) at Karlstad University, Sweden. He coordinates several research projects and heads a research group which focuses on 1) the systematic design and management of services and service systems, its digitization and respective business models and 2) digital work and the changing nature of work due to digital transformation, as well as the design of sustainable concepts for these new work scenarios.

Simon Polovina engages in roles that draw upon his expertise in Enterprise Architecture and Conceptual Structures (CS), which harmonises the human conceptual approach to problem solving with the formal structures that computer applications need to bring their productivity to bear. Simon is a Reader in Business Computing within the Department of Computing at Sheffield Hallam University, UK. He was a Principal Investigator for the recently completed European Commission 7th Framework Programme project CUBIST ("Combining and Unifying Business Intelligence with Semantic Technologies"), where he applied CS and co-managed the project. CUBIST centred on applying smart technologies (namely CS and the Semantic Web) to Business Intelligence. It was a €4m project funded under topic 4.3: Intelligent Information Management. Simon is the Enterprise Architect for CENTRIC (Centre of excellence in terrorism, resilience, intelligence & organised crime research). He is Co-Chairman of the Global University Alliance that partners with the LEAD (Leading Enterprise Architecture Development) practitioner community. Simon has many years of industrial experience in accounting and information and communication technologies (ICT), and has published widely with over 100 learned publications to date. His interests include the use of Smart Applications and how they can detect novel or unusual transactions that would otherwise remain as lost business opportunities or represent illicit business or criminal activity. He is editor-in-chief of the International Journal of Conceptual Structures and Smart Applications (IJCSSA) published by IGI-Global. He has expertise in Enterprise Architecture, Service Oriented Architecture, Business Process Management, SAP technologies, Web technologies, Java, Object-oriented Analysis and Design, Conceptual Modelling of organisations as Multi-agent Systems, and in Interaction Design. Simon was the General Chair for the 15th International Conference on Conceptual Structures (ICCS 2007): "Knowledge Architectures for Smart Applications", Program Chair for the 19th International Conference on Conceptual Structures (ICCS 2011): "Conceptual Structures for Discovering Knowledge", and co-chair for a number of workshops. Simon is a Steering Group Member of the Communication and Computing Research Centre (CCRC) and leads the CCRC's Conceptual Structures Research Group.

Logesh R. received the B.Tech. degree in Computer Science & Engineering and M.Tech. degree in Networking from Pondicherry University, India. Currently, he is a Junior Research Fellow and pursuing the Ph.D. degree in the School of Computing, SASTRA University, India. His research interests include Recommender Systems, Information Retrieval, and Human-Computer Interaction.

Chitrakala Sakthivel working as an Associate Professor, Department of Computer Science and Engineering, Anna University, Chennai. He has 21 years of teaching and research experience and expertise in the field of Computer Vision. He is a resource person for technical session, chairperson for International Conferences and editor for reputed journals. He has published research papers in a high reputed International Journals and also working on sponsored research projects. He is also life member of Computer Associations.

S. Shanthi received her BSc Degree in Computer Science, MCA degree in Computer Applications, Master of Philosophy in Computer Science from Bharathiar University, Coimbatore, India in the year 1993, 1996 and 2004 respectively and ME degree in Computer Science and Engineering from Anna University, Chennai, India in the year 2006. She completed her PhD degree in 2015 in Computer Science and Engineering at Anna University, Chennai, India. She is presently working as an Assistant Professor (SLG) in the Department of Computer Applications, Kongu Engineering College, Tamil Nadu, India. Her area of interest includes, Data Mining, Image Processing, Pattern Recognition and Soft Computing.

Xiaomeng Su is an associate professor at the Norwegian University of Science and Technology (NTNU) in Trondheim, Norway, since 2016. She has previously been a research scientist and a business intelligence manager at Telenor in Norway, as well as a post doc at the University of Twente in the Netherlands. After completing her Master's degree in Computer Science at Renmin University in China in 2000, she did her PhD studies in Computer Science at the Norwegian University of Science and Technology from 2000 to 2004. Her research interests include business analytics, the Semantic Web, data modelling and search technologies.

V. Vaidehi received her BE degree in Electronics and Communication Engineering from College of Engineering, Guindy, University of Madras, ME degree in Applied Electronics from Madras Institute of Technology and Ph.D in Electronics Engineering from Madras Institute of Technology, Anna University, Chennai, India in 1980 and 1998 respectively. Since 1998 she has been with Madras Institute of Technology, Anna University where she was heading various department of ICT and later as the chairman of faculty of Information and Communication Engineering and Director of AU-KBC Research Centre. Currently she is working as senior professor in School of Computing Sciences and Engineering, VIT University, Chennai. She has got more than 33 years of academic and research experience. She has received the certificate of achievement for the successful launch of ANUSAT during 2009 and faculty award by Microsoft during 2011. Her research interests include data mining, neural networks, fuzzy systems, pattern classification, wireless sensor networks, image processing and video analytics. She has done extensive research in Wireless Sensor Networks and WSN applications. She has published more than 185 technical papers in reputed international journals. She has undergone professional training in India and Abroad. She has successfully completed several funded projects from various Government Organizations, Public Limited Companies and MNCs.

Subramaniyaswamy Vairavasundaram received the B.E. degree in Computer Science & Engineering and M.Tech. degree in Information Technology from Bharathidasan University, India and Sathyabama University, India respectively. He received his Ph.D degree from Anna University, India. Currently, he is working as a Senior Assistant Professor in the School of Computing, SASTRA University, India. He has published more than 50 technical papers in reputed international journals and conferences. His research interests include Data Mining, Recommender Systems, and Big Data Analytics.

Alexey Voinov (PhD) is Professor of Spatio-Temporal Systems Modeling for Sustainability Science at ITC, University of Twente, and honorary Professor at University of Technology, Sydney, UTS. Prior to that he was coordinating the Chesapeake Research Consortium Community Modeling Program, and was also Principle Research Scientist at John's Hopkins University. He has spent one year with the AAAS Science and Technology Fellowship program working with the Army Corps of Engineers. Before that he was with the Institute for Ecological Economics, Universities of Maryland and Vermont. He has his MSc and PhD from Moscow State University, Russia. He is a keen advocate of stakeholder involvement in modeling and decision making. Dr. Voinov is Editor of Environmental Modeling and Software journal. He wrote a book on "Systems Science and Modeling for Ecological Economics" (Academic Press/Elsevier).

Index

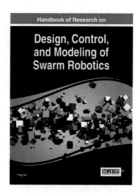

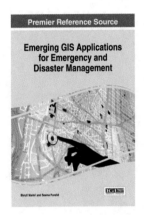 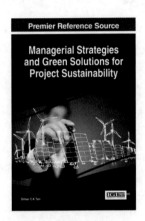  

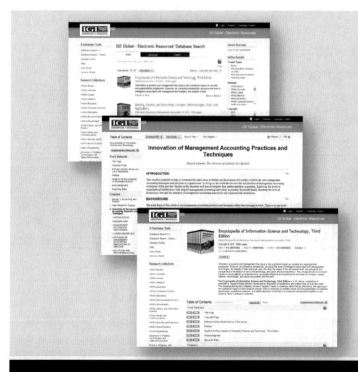